LEGAL AND ETHICAL ASPECTS OF ORGAN TRANSPLANTATION

Organ transplantation raises singularly difficult ethical and legal issues in its requirement for donated organs. Strategies to facilitate supply in the face of increasing demand must be ethically sound and subject to an appropriate and effective regulatory framework. Professor David Price reviews the ethical principles and positions underpinning such law and policies, probing for coherence, consistency and justification. The book incorporates a comprehensive analysis of existing laws and policies governing transplantation practices around the world. It examines the meaning of death, cadaver organ procurement policies, use of living donors, trading in human organs, experimental transplant procedures and xenotransplantation. Drawing upon a wide range of disciplinary and empirical materials, Price explores the balance between the interests of donors, recipients, clinicians and society, identifying the specific challenges of this subject and seeking to guide current practices and future developments in the context of cultural diversity and pluralistic societies.

DAVID PRICE is Professor of Medical Law at De Montfort University, Leicester, UK. He was Chairperson of the EUROTOLD Project Management Group funded by the European Commission and a member of the World Health Organisation Task Force on Organ Transplantation.

LEGAL AND ETHICAL ASPECTS OF ORGAN TRANSPLANTATION

DAVID PRICE

DE MONTFORT UNIVERSITY, LEICESTER

PUBLISHED BY THE PRESS SYNDICATE OF THE UNIVERSITY OF CAMBRIDGE
The Pitt Building, Trumpington Street, Cambridge, United Kingdom

CAMBRIDGE UNIVERSITY PRESS
The Edinburgh Building, Cambridge, CB2 2RU, UK
40 West 20th Street, New York, NY 10011–4211, USA
477 Williamstown Road, Port Melbourn, VIC 3207, Australia
Ruiz de Alarcón 13, 28014 Madrid, Spain
Dock House, The Waterfront, Cape Town 8001, South Africa

http://www.cambridge.org

First published 2000
Reprinted 2002

Printed in the United Kingdom at the University Press, Cambridge

Typeface 10.5pt/14pt Minion. System 3b2 [CE]

A catalogue record for this book is available from the British Library

Library of Congress Cataloguing in Publication data

Price, David P. T.
Legal and ethical aspects of organ transplantation / David Price.
p. cm.
Includes index.
ISBN 0 521 65164 6 (hardback)
1. Transplantation of organs, tissues, etc. – Law and legislation.
2. Transplantation of organs, tissues, etc. – Moral and ethical aspects.
I. Title.

K3611.T7P75 2001
174′25–dc21 00–024475

ISBN 0 521 65164 6 hardback

To Arlene, Alex and Ben

CONTENTS

PART III

GENERAL ISSUES

PREFACE

My interest in organ transplantation was kindled by an exposure to some of the depth and complexity associated with the ethics and legality of the subject and by the very potentiality of the therapy itself. I was fortunate to be part (Chairperson) of the Project Management Group of the EURO-TOLD Project, a four-year European Commission funded project supported under the BIOMED Programme (Ref. BMH1–CT92–1841), which explored the practice of living donor organ transplantation in Europe and its legal and ethical dimensions (see http://www.maths.lancs.ac.uk:2080/MedStats/EuroTold for further details). This involved interaction with transplant professionals, patients, donors, lawyers and many other interested parties across many nations. Such research sensitised me to some of the human drama of transplantation and the acute need for solutions to various ongoing dilemmas. Inevitably there are no monolithic answers to some of these complex problems, but continued evaluation of the existing procedures and possible alternatives is a crucial imperative as public policy initiatives are considered at the start of this millennium.

My heartfelt thanks are owed to Aaron Spital of the Genesee Hospital, Rochester, New York for reading and providing invaluable comments on various chapter drafts, and to John Blum of the Loyola University of Chicago for reviewing the final manuscript. Thanks also to all the staff at Cambridge University Press, and in particular to Finola O'Sullivan.

Finally, but by no means least, thanks, and apologies(!), to my wife and children for their sacrifice and support, indeed altruism!

TABLE OF LEGISLATION

Mexico: Federal Regulations of 16 August 1976 270, 310, 321, 338–9, 364
Netherlands: Law of 24 May 1996 (Stb 370) 98, 100, 162, 165, 257, 270, 277, 280, 338–9, 457
Norway: Law No. 6 of 9 February 1973 95–6, 99, 101, 247, 267, 276, 279, 338, 346
Panama: Law No. 10 of 11 July 1983 162, 212, 276, 306, 338–9, 379, 430
Paraguay: Law No. 826180 of 15 December 1980 306, 363
Peru: Law No. 23415 of 1 June 1982 272
Supreme Decree No. 014–88–SA of 19 May 1988 94
Poland: Law of 26 October 1995 94, 275–6, 279, 322, 338–9
Portugal: Law No. 12 of 22 April 1993 94, 247, 276, 321, 338–9, 430
Romania: Law Regarding the Harvesting and the Transplantation of Human Tissues and Organs 1996 54, 247, 270, 277, 339
Russian Federation: Law of 22 December 1992 270, 275–6, 297, 321, 338–9, 380, 430
Singapore: Medical (Therapy, Education and Research) Act 1972 90, 455
Human Organ Transplant Act 1987, Act No. 15 of 1987 90, 114, 455
Slovakia: Law of 24 August 1994 94, 247, 257, 270–1, 275–6, 306, 338–9
Slovenia: Law of the Transplantation of Human's Body Parts, 1996 264, 266–7, 270, 275, 321, 338
South Africa: Post Mortem Examinations and Removal of Human Tissues Act 1952 37
Human Tissue Act No. 65 of 1983 270, 338–9
Spain: Law No. 30 of 27 October 1979 54, 74, 91–2, 94, 98, 270–1, 276, 278, 297, 338–9, 379, 430
Crown Decree No. 426 of 22 February 1980 54, 74, 379
Sri Lanka: Act No. 48 of 1987 93, 270, 338–9
Sweden: Penal Code, section 11 243
Law No. 831 of 8 June 1995 98, 162, 270, 276, 279, 321, 338, 346, 352, 360
Law No. 833 of 8 June 1995 170
Switzerland: Federal Order of 22 March 1996 378
Syrian Arab Republic: Law No. 31 of 23 August 1972 83, 270–2, 338–9
Tunisia: Law No. 91–22 of 25 March 1991 87, 94, 276, 278, 338–9
Turkey: Penal Code, Article 456 243
Law No. 2238 of 29 May 1979 93, 270, 276, 338–9, 378
United Kingdom: Anatomy Act 1832 92, 100, 140
Corneal Grafting Act 1952 37

TABLE OF CASES

United Kingdom

United States

Non-UK/US cases

INTRODUCTION

This is a book exploring the legal and ethical dimensions of the modern 'miracle' (or to some 'false promise'[1]) of transplantation: a hugely complex field of human endeavour. As an evolving and pioneering field of therapeutic pursuit it can only be described as dynamic, with even more potentiality than realised actuality. Yet, it is no 'ordinary' or conventional form of therapy. Youngner describes transplantation as 'a unique way to affirm and share our humanity'.[2] Indeed, qualms themselves typically spring from the depths to which the procedure touches, as well as shares, our humanity. Its profundity is highlighted in the attention given to it in popular (science) fiction, historical, anthropological and religious writings, and folklore. To some, the lengths that it appears to take us in thwarting our natural span is deeply disconcerting. As Chadwick states, 'Technological advances, however, along with the increase in the demand for cryonics, make us confront the question of what it means to live a human life, and the extent to which we should go in trying to prolong it.'[3] Indeed, the translocation of body parts seems so largely commonplace today that one can forget its relatively very modern nature and capability, and its psychological and emotional significance for the 'players', as well as its 'incredible' intrinsic character. It has been reported for example that one domino heart transplant recipient in Britain actually raced against his

1 Fox and Swazey have long maintained that the history of transplantation bears testimony to an over-aggressive pursuit of the possible without adequate consideration for the implications and societal costs of the widespread employment of such technological capacity: see R. Fox and J. Swazey, *Courage to Fail*, University of Chicago Press, Chicago, 1974 and *Spare Parts: Organ Replacement in American Society*, Oxford University Press, New York, 1992.

2 S. Youngner, 'Psychosocial and Ethical Implications of Organ Retrieval' (1985) 313 *New England Journal of Medicine* 321 at 323.

3 R. Chadwick, 'Corpses, Recycling and Therapeutic Purposes' in R. Lee and D. Morgan (eds.), *Death Rites: Law and Ethics at the End of Life*, Routledge, London, 1994, 54 at 64.

own heart (donee) in the British Transplant Games! It has been observed though that what is truly distinctive about transplantation is not technology or cost, but ethics, emphasising the unique and (virtually) utter dependence upon the participation of the public for its continued viability as a therapeutic option at all. These two aspects are of course interrelated. The balancing of the interests of the 'giver' and 'receiver' is the great challenge for those attempting to regulate in this sphere. The 'technological imperative' to keep pushing back the barriers can place enormous strains on our legal and ethical institutions and frameworks of analysis. Yet the huge therapeutic potential requires us to embrace and confront these questions. In short, the fundamental nature of transplantation in clinical, physiological and biological terms is entirely matched by its significance in legal, ethical, theological and cultural terms. The general human rights dimensions to many transplant practices are themselves highlighted by the long-standing involvement of organisations such as the Council of Europe[4] and the World Health Organisation in this field.

'Transplanting' (that is relocating) organs from one individual human being to another is a creature of the twentieth century,[5] which has (extraordinarily) quickly developed from an experimental and unproven strategy to becoming the treatment of choice for very many diseases and conditions today.[6] In some instances it is the only available life-sustaining therapy, for example for certain types of end-stage cardiac and liver failure. Experimental transplantation (in animals) began to proceed apace in relation to vascularised organs in the early part of the twentieth century,[7] and there were even very early attempts to transplant animal

4 The recent Council of Europe Convention also contains a specific section on transplantation: see Council of Europe Convention for the Protection of Human Rights and Dignity of the Human Being with Regard to the Application of Biology and Medicine (Convention on Human Rights and Biomedicine) finalised in 1996 and signed (in Orviedo) by twenty-one Member States on 4 April 1997, Article 19(2).

5 It is reported that over 5,000 years ago skin was transplanted to replace noses destroyed by syphilis in Egyptian and Hindu societies, and teeth have been transplanted, usually from servants, in former times, for example by John Hunter the 'father of modern surgery', in Scotland in the eighteenth century.

6 It has been recently stated that 'Kidney transplantation is generally accepted as the primary therapy for chronic renal failure in most patients': see N. Lefrancois and J. Touraine, 'Living Kidney Donation: Preoperative Evaluation and Preparation for Surgery' in G. Collins, J. Dubernard, W. Land and G. Persijn (eds.), *Procurement, Preservation and Allocation of Vascularized Organs*, Kluwer, Dordrecht, 1997, 3 at 3. Kidney transplantation is also the most cost-effective therapy when compared with alternatives such as dialysis.

7 In 1902, Emerich Ullmann carried out a kidney transplant from a dog to a goat. The kidney

kidneys into humans.[8] The first human kidney allograft (between humans) was carried out in 1933 in the Ukraine by Voronoy but was unsuccessful.[9] It was not until 1954 that the first successful transplant of an organ intended as a permanent 'replacement' occurred,[10] when on the day prior to Christmas Eve, a kidney was successfully transplanted from one identical twin to another (his brother) by Dr Joseph Murray in Boston. However, limited accumulated physiological knowledge and experience, and the relative inability to control rejection,[11] conspired to make progress slow until the development of effective immunosuppressant agents (most notably cyclosporin) facilitated the rapid expansion of cadaveric transplantation in the eighties. The handful of (kidney) transplants performed in the fifties and early sixties has quickly turned into thousands each year at the advent of the new millennium. In the US alone in 1998 21,926 solid organ transplants were performed.

The first thoracic, liver and lung transplants occurred in the sixties, using cadaveric donors.[12] Most notably, the race to perform the very first human heart transplant was won by Christiaan Barnard in Cape Town, South Africa on 3 December 1967.[13] Of course, the experimental nature of these procedures made them highly contentious and attracted criticism on ethical and legal bases. Other extreme innovations included xenotransplants, such as the transplant of a baboon's heart into Baby Fae in 1984, and multi-organ transplants, such as Laura Davies's second transplant in

even passed a little urine for a short while. A number of dog-to-dog transplants were performed at the same time.

8 In 1906, Jabouley (xeno)transplanted a kidney from a pig and goat respectively into human recipients and in 1909, Unger transplanted a kidney from an ape into a young girl dying of renal failure.

9 He apparently carried out a further five such transplants. All were unsuccessful. See P. Morris, *Kidney Transplantation: Principles and Practice*, 3rd edn, W. B. Saunders Company, Philadelphia, 1988, at 5–6.

10 The first attempted cornea transplant actually occurred in 1906, although the modern era of cornea transplantation did not begin until the fifties. Today, this is the most frequent form of surgical tissue transplantation performed.

11 Which was why identical twin (syngenesious) transplants with tissue compatibility were attempted so frequently in the very early days.

12 Thomas Starzl performed the first clinical liver transplant on a human in March 1963, but this was unsuccessful. He performed the world's first successful procedure in 1967 at the University of Colorado. The first liver transplant in the UK was carried out by (now Sir) Roy Calne in May 1968. The first lung transplant took place in 1963: see J. Hardy, 'The First Lung Transplant in Man (1963) and the First Heart Transplant in Man (1964)' (1999) 31 *Transplantation Proceedings* 25.

13 In fact, an earlier, unsuccessful, transplant of a chimpanzee heart had been attempted into one Boyd Rush, in 1964 by Hardy.

Pittsburgh, and they continue to occur today accompanied by the same controversies. At the very end of the millennium, controversy surrounded the first composite tissue allograft, a hand transplant from a cadaveric donor.[14] Today, the range of transplantable body materials is mind-boggling, from hearts to intestines to corneas to brain tissue. The *sources* of such materials are also myriad, from the person's own stock, for example autologous blood or bone marrow extraction or skin patching; to the use of materials from other human beings, for example hearts, livers, kidneys, etc.; to materials of foetal origin, for example neurological tissue, islet (insulin-producing) cells;[15] to organs and tissues from other species – some already occurring, such as the use of porcine heart valves and islet cells in humans, and others likely shortly to come into widespread use, for example transgenic pig organs; to artificial organs or tissues, for example artificial hearts, knee joints, etc. This book principally addresses *organ* transplantation by which is meant *solid* organ transplantation. It is appreciated that no bright dividing line exists between such organs and other human tissues in many of the relevant legal and ethical contexts. Moreover, caution is required in so far as there is no universally accepted definition of an 'organ' and some statutory definitions, for example that in the US National Organ Transplants Act 1984, include tissues such as bone marrow within their scope.[16]

Ironically, and unfortunately, transplantation has become a victim of its own success. In the US in 1998 patients had an average survival rate after five years of 80+ per cent for kidneys, 73 per cent for livers and 69 per cent for hearts.[17] These results have in turn stimulated demand to the point where there are typically now (often woefully) insufficient numbers of donor organs for transplantation, compounded by an even wider class

[14] One reason for the controversy was that this was supposedly a procedure performed solely to improve the patient's quality of life, although of course since dialysis was introduced this might also be said about the majority of renal transplants.

[15] Their supposed advantage lies in their capacity for growth and differentiation and ability to establish necessary cellular connections in the new host as well as their lesser ability to induce rejection.

[16] See further B. Dickens, 'Donation and Transplantation of Organs and Tissues' in I. Kennedy and A. Grubb, *Principles of Medical Law*, Oxford University Press, Oxford, 1998, 787 at 789–90.

[17] See UNOS/OPTN Annual Report 1998 at http://www.unos.org/Data/anrpt98/ar98. Kidney patient survival rates will necessarily be the best as the failure of the grafted organ does not typically lead to death, due to dialysis, by contrast with most hepatic and thoracic graft failures. In the US, *graft* survival rates for kidneys at five years are 61 per cent for cadaveric kidneys and 76.6 per cent for living donor kidneys: ibid.

of individuals becoming eligible recipients, for example elderly patients, a phenomenon which could be unremittingly repeated in the future. It was recently remarked that 'a critical shortage of donor organs is the single greatest impediment facing transplant programs around the world'.[18] There are, however, developments being heralded as placing us on the verge of a panacea for the shortage. Most notably, animal-to-human transplants (xenotransplants) may soon become a customary feature of the transplant landscape, supported as they are by extremely substantial business investment.[19] Indeed, the possibility of breeding animals specifically for the purpose creates the prospect of transplanting not only those already waiting for a transplant but also those who are currently not placed on waiting lists for organs due to the shortage.[20] However, Fox and McHale have suggested that 'the legitimate boundaries of such [transplant] technology may now have been reached'.[21]

Two series of xenotransplants were performed in the sixties in the United States. In 1963–4, six patients received kidneys from chimpanzees and a further six from baboons. Patient survival times were extremely limited indeed, apart from one recipient of a chimpanzee kidney who survived for nine months.[22] Since these procedures, only a handful of xenotransplants have been performed, most notoriously the transplant of a baboon's heart into Baby Fae in 1984. Germany and Sweden still have voluntary moratoriums on xenotransplants.[23] The new era of xenotransplantation will witness not only tighter controls over the conduct of these procedures however, but also a more comprehensive regulatory framework to oversee their practice. The precise nature of this regulatory structure will vary from state to state. In the UK a new statutory authority is anticipated, and meanwhile a temporary standing body, the United

18 C. Wight *et al.*, 'Donor Action: A Systematic Approach to Organ Donation' (1998) 30 *Transplantation Proceedings* 2253 at 2253.

19 The market is estimated to be of the order of $6 billion per annum, and $100 million is estimated to have already been invested in research and development in xenotransplantation.

20 Of course, this might raise acute cost considerations, especially as, unlike human organs, animal organs would not be free at the point of delivery.

21 M. Fox and J. McHale, 'Xenotransplantation: The Ethical and Legal Ramifications' [1998] 6 *Medical Law Review* 42 at 42.

22 See A. Caplan, 'Ethical Issues raised by Research involving Xenotransplantation' (1985) 254 *Journal of the American Medical Association* 3339 at 3340.

23 In view of the risks from disease transmission, some observers have recommended a worldwide moratorium: see Fritz Bach *et al.*, 'Uncertainty in Xenotransplantation: Individual Benefit Versus Collective Risk' (1998) 4(2) *Nature Medicine* 141, and J. Hughes, 'Xenografting: Ethical Issues' (1998) 24 *Journal of Medical Ethics* 18.

Kingdom Xenotransplantation Interim Regulatory Authority, has been established to monitor moves towards initial clinical trials. The British approach to xenotransplantation during the nineties was cautious. The Nuffield[24] and Kennedy[25] Reports recommended that clinical trials not take place until further research had been conducted, that clinical trials should then take place in selected instances and that even this would not necessarily presuppose a move to a therapeutic programme. It was their view that there was limited evidence relating to transplant function, organ growth and the functioning of the recipient's immune system.[26] The UK Government has also announced that no clinical trials may proceed until it is 'fully satisfied' that the risks are acceptable.[27] In the US in 1996, the FDA joined the Centers for Disease Control and Prevention and the National Institutes of Health in drawing up a Draft Public Health Service Guideline on Infectious Disease Issues in Xenotransplantation.[28] This replaced the more ad hoc approach which previously prevailed, which relied heavily upon approval by local Institutional Review Boards (IRBs).[29] There is, however, a concern that some countries with relatively lax controls will be viewed by scientists and companies as attractive 'turf' for experimental xenotransplants. The desirability of minimum universal standards of regulation has prompted the Council of Europe to issue a Draft Recommendation on Xenotransplantation.[30] In the UK, legislation has been proposed to regulate this field. This should provide a framework for guidance for clinicians as well as public reassurance. In 1997, an Indian cardiac surgeon performed a transplant using a pig's heart and

[24] Nuffield Council on Bioethics Working Party, *Animal-to-Human Transplants*, Nuffield Council on Bioethics, London, 1995, at para. 7.7. This was also the view of the British Medical Association: see 'The Ethics of Xenotransplantation: The BMA's Views', BMA, London, May 1996.

[25] A Report of the Advisory Group on the Ethics of Xenotransplantation, *Animal Tissue Into Humans*, Department of Health, 1997, at 4.50.

[26] *Animal Tissue Into Humans*, at 4.50.

[27] J. Warden, 'Xenotransplantation Moves Ahead in UK' (1998) 317 *British Medical Journal* 365.

[28] 61 Fed. Reg. 49,920 (1996). See also J. Kress, 'Xenotransplantation: Ethics and Economics' (1998) 53(2) *Food and Drug Law Journal* 353.

[29] See F. Morgan, 'Babe the Magnificent Organ Donor: The Perils and Promises Surrounding Xenotransplantation' (1997) 14 *Journal of Contemporary Health Law and Policy* 127 at 144. In 1995 the FDA and relevant IRB approved a bone marrow transplant of baboon tissue into a patient with AIDS (baboons being resistant to the disease). The bone marrow failed to engraft, but no harm, including infection, apparently resulted from it.

[30] Draft Recommendation No. R(97) of the Committee of Ministers to Member States on Xenotransplantation.

lungs, and was arrested apparently because there was no legislation specifically authorising the procedure.[31]

There are also major initiatives in the fields of tissue engineering and cloning taking place which promise to have a major impact on transplantation in the future and may soon 'overtake' contemporary cutting edge strategies such as xenotransplantation.[32] Corneal and skin tissue have been grown in laboratory conditions as has a tissue-engineered bladder,[33] and it has been suggested that in a short time such cell cultures will be able to be used to grow organs for transplantation, although the complexities involved are much greater than with other non-vascularised grafts. Bone, cartilage and ligaments have already been grown, as has a human thumb (around a coral infrastructure), and there are presently attempts being made to grow a human ear.[34] Alternatively, cloning may be used to facilitate xenotransplants themselves, with reports being published of the first successful cloning of piglets in March 2000.[35] The history of the use of *artificial* organs, primarily hearts, has been chequered to say the least, especially with 'permanent' whole replacement organs. However, research still proceeds. Most success has been obtained with using left ventricular assist devices (LVADs), and with procedures such as the fitting of a temporary 'bridging' device, the Jarvik 2000 artificial heart, into a ten-year-old boy in 1998 in Oxford, which maintained him sufficiently to enable him to receive a human heart transplant five days later.[36] Scientists are now working on producing artificial muscles as well as an artificial pancreas, which could be implanted in the patient's abdomen releasing a steady flow of insulin as required and removing the need for daily injections. However, despite their 'promise', whether such procedures will be able to be converted into an everyday clinical reality from experimental

31 G. Mudur, 'Indian Surgeon Challenges Ban on Xenotransplantation' (1999) 318 *British Medical Journal* 79. The man died seven days after the procedure, from multiple infections. The doctor was released from arrest and is suing for damages for wrongful arrest.

32 See J. Savelescu, 'Should We Clone Human Beings? Cloning as a Source of Tissue for Transplantation' (1999) 25 *Journal of Medical Ethics* 87.

33 See J. Tanne, 'Researchers Implant Tissue Engineered Bladders' (1999) 318 *British Medical Journal* 350.

34 See 'The Child who Hopes she can Grow a Second Ear', *The Times*, 15 April 1998. A human ear was attached to the back of a mouse in an infamous televised experiment fairly recently.

35 Five female cloned piglets were born on 5 March 2000 in Virginia, US: see *The Times*, 15 March 2000.

36 See 'Boy First to be saved by New Artificial Heart', *The Times*, 17 June 1998.

procedures undertaken in the laboratory is yet to be seen, although they remain pleasing visions on the horizon.

Organ transplantation is practised in North America, in virtually all European nations, most South American and Middle Eastern nations, various Asian countries[37] and a handful of African nations. Of course, transplantation operates within the broader prevailing cultural and societal milieu in these different jurisdictions, which may lack homogeneity even within a single region. It would seem that an ethical pluralism must exist not only between sovereign states but also within them. In other words ethics are culturally relative rather than universal. Societies still differ to some degree, for instance, as to the appropriate standard for determining that a person is legally dead, with tensions which impact upon organ procurement practices. The major shift towards brain-based standards remains controversial whilst, paradoxically, transplant protocols relying (supposedly) upon traditional (cardiopulmonary) measures of determination have attracted the most criticism of late. Religious perspectives and beliefs have substantially influenced transplant laws and policies in various societies, as have the socio-economic circumstances prevailing: for instance, perceptions as to the legitimacy of commercial practices in organ procurement. The lack of access to transplantation modalities to avoid death or severely decreased quality of life through end-stage organ failure in a specific population will also create effects elsewhere. Transplantation is a *global* pursuit, and a failure to meet critical health needs in one region will drive individuals to seek alternative options elsewhere. 'Transplant tourism' is an increasing phenomenon with vendors from poorer nations in effect subsidising the health care of patients from richer countries, and patients seeking access to waiting lists of other sovereign states.

Views on many aspects of transplantation are influenced by perspectives upon the significance of 'embodiment', the concept of 'self' and how parts of the body relate to the whole (merology). These issues in turn beg questions as to whether a dualist or monist perception of the 'self' and the body is most appropriate. If the body is merely instrumental to our ends,[38] as Fletcher and Engelhardt for instance would have it, then

[37] A Report of the Asian Transplant Registry recently revealed that seventeen Asian countries have active organ transplantation programmes: see K. Ota, 'Asian Transplant Registry' (1999) 31 *Transplantation Proceedings* 205.

[38] Or as Plato put it, 'a temporary tomb' in which the soul is forced to dwell: see Plato, *Phaedo*

continued functioning of the body is morally insignificant, so that death may properly be declared despite the continued working of lower brain and various vegetative functions. Moreover, there is no reason why one should not be able to sell body parts, as with most anything else which belongs to us, that is our property. Indeed, not only does the prospect of sale of body organs assume *property*-based conceptions of parts of the human body, but maybe even 'donating' body parts implies the same. On the other hand, if the body itself forms part of the self it *is* the individual and not separate from him/her so that its continued functioning is incompatible with a declaration of death or, *prima facie* at least, with selling parts of it. Issues also arise as to the relationship that *others* enjoy with regard to one's body or parts thereof, especially one's cadaver. Whilst the corpse has traditionally been viewed as *res nullius*, property rights have sometimes been accorded to third parties in respect thereof. But can we spy some ambivalence here, arguably inherent in the judicially created concept of 'quasi-property' rights? Moreover, can individuals and institutions undertaking transplantation properly protect their possession of the cadaver for that purpose or be held to account themselves for improper use without the adoption of some notion of property rights in the human corpus?

Objections to selling body parts for transplantation are most commonly voiced independently of the issue of 'property rights', however, and instead insist that the donation of organs should be based on *altruism*. However, this partially depends upon what one means by the term 'altruism', and this itself proves to be a source of ambiguity and confusion. Some would argue that some forms of payment connected to organ procurement are not in any event incompatible with altruism. Regardless, is an act of organ transfer any less acceptable for being induced by financial reward than if it were altruistically inspired? There are both deontological and consequentialist objections to organ trading, however, albeit principally emanating from intuitiveness, which require rebutting. In the sixties, Richard Titmuss directly contrasted altruistic and paid blood donation systems on different sides of the Atlantic and stridently declared the virtues of the former model of procurement. Assuming the legitimacy of these findings though, one cannot merely presume that these

(R. Hackforth trans.), 1955, cited in T. Murray, 'On the Human Body as Property: The Meaning of Embodiment, Markets, and the Meaning of Strangers' (1987) 20 *Journal of Law Reform* 1055 at 1062 n. 27.

consequentialist concerns carry over to organ donation. It may also be that the alleged gravamen of commerce is not only relative, but also a function of whether it relates to living providers or cadaveric sources.

Difficulties of other kinds stem from the lack of clarity as to the concept of 'altruism'. Insistence on supposedly 'disinterested' motivations has led to tensions in relation to non-genetically related donors, who have sometimes been rejected on the basis of an assumption that either they were self-interested (that is were being covertly paid) or they were psychologically maladjusted. This has tended to result historically in living donation being confined almost entirely to living genetically *related* donors, a trend which has only fairly recently been broken. But this in turn poses the question whether living related donors always act entirely 'disinterestedly', and even what we mean by 'self-interestedness' in the first place. Contrariwise, objections have been raised to the insistence that 'donation' by incompetent persons (such as minors) be based on their 'best interests', which implies the need for self-interested motivations or effects. But whilst egoism is at odds with altruism, can it properly be said that acts are either altruistic or self-interested, but not both?

The removal of organs for transplantation purposes clearly involves a degree of physical damage and permanent destruction of the human body, which would constitute an 'injury', in ethical terms, if the intended use of the tissue were not ethically acceptable and appropriate. A Nuffield Council Working Party Report considered that the actual transplanting of organs was justified by the intention to avoid greater injury, and that the *removal* of tissue for therapeutic purposes was also ethically legitimate,[39] because 'It is clear that there is a close relationship between the lawfulness of the removal and the lawfulness of any subsequent use of the tissue: the propriety of the use largely determines the legality of the removal.'[40] In fact, the duty not to injure a person in a morally unacceptable way is elevated by the Nuffield Report even above the principle of autonomy, although the latter may also be a necessary feature of a morally acceptable act. But questions are then begged by how one determines the existence of injury in a context such as organ donation, where application of the concepts of non-maleficence and *primum non nocere* is itself a good deal less than obvious or straightforward. It is also left uncertain whether

[39] Nuffield Council on Bioethics Working Party, *Human Tissue: Ethical and Legal Issues*, Nuffield Council on Bioethics, London, 1995, at paras. 6.5 and 13.34.

[40] Ibid., at 65.

non-autonomous beings possess the necessary human dignity which is the touchstone of whether an activity constitutes an 'injury'. Indeed, a broad and uncritical application of such 'principles' to *living* organ donation would appear to endorse a sweeping utilitarian perspective upon transfers of body parts.

On the other hand, the notions of *primum non nocere* and of non-maleficence are guiding forces in medicine generally, and whilst they would tend broadly to favour *cadaveric* organ donations, they would contrastingly appear *prima facie* to enjoin donation even by a competent and consenting living donor who, of necessity, has no pre-existing ailment that it is the intention to cure. Moreover, there is the potential for living but insentient individuals, for example permanently insensate individuals such as anencephalics and patients in a permanent vegetative state, to be harmed by utilitarian measures intended primarily to benefit others and in the absence of consent. But many argue that such individuals cannot be *harmed* (or at least only 'symbolically') on account of lacking any interests at that point in time. Whilst it is often asserted that one should not use another individual solely as a means to the ends of others, there is disagreement as to the classes of beings protected by such a tenet, and a tension between perspectives upon *personhood* which might even transcend the importance of the dead/alive distinction.

Risk/benefit determinations are a dominant feature in contemporary medico-ethical decision-making, and relate to both donors and recipients. Even where there are few or no harms attaching to the donor, there are generally perceived to be limits in terms of the extent to which it is legitimate to carry out highly experimental transplantation procedures, even with the full consent of the patient. Assuming such consent is freely given (problematic some would allege where the recipient might inevitably succumb without such an intervention) and with full knowledge of the known and unknown risks and consequences, there is an anticipated 'threshold of benefit' which must accompany the procedure.[41] For many this was not the case with regard to certain highly experimental and risky transplantation procedures which have been performed, where the patient's consent alone should not have been sufficient. However, to

41 The Nuffield Working Party considered that xenotransplants should only commence when there was a 'reasonable chance of success': see Nuffield Council, *Animal-to-Human Transplants*, at para. 7.7. This was also the view of the British Medical Association: see 'The Ethics of Xenotransplantation: The BMA's Views', BMA, London, May 1996.

others, the expectation of benefit needed only to be slim to justify the attempt, in view of the absence of alternatives. But how does one ascertain the appropriate *threshold* weighed against the potential for harm? Bach *et al.* have observed that 'The history of medical innovation has shown us unwilling to resist tangible benefit even in the face of unknown risks.'[42] Fox and McHale note however that, 'Interestingly, xenotransplantation is being classified as an experimental clinical procedure to be subject to clinical trials, rather than an innovative surgical treatment under development.'[43] In the light of many of the premature and ultimately 'hopelessly cavalier'[44] previous attempts at xenotransplantation this might seem wholly appropriate and is perhaps an approach to be recommended in the context of all significant transplant innovations. However, in determining the likely efficacy of xenotransplants for recipients one must identify the probable source animal.[45] Both the Nuffield and Kennedy Committees regarded the use of pig organs for transplantation as acceptable in principle.[46] Species closest to humans, so-called concordant (closely related) species, such as non-human primates, offer the best means for reducing rejection as they do not induce a potentially devastating phenomenon – hyperacute rejection in the host, unlike so-called discordant (distantly related) species, such as pigs. Thus, if pigs were to be used they would have to be genetically modified (creating so-called *transgenic* pigs) in order to avoid the overwhelming problems of rejection, and such research and production has been undertaken in Britain for many years by Imutran, a subsidiary of Novartis. Of course such genetic modification raises its own ethical

[42] Bach *et al.*, 'Uncertainty in Xenotransplantation', at 144. This is borne out by the continued use of foetal tissue in transplantation, despite McCullagh's assertion, having previously reviewed the empirical evidence, that 'the history of foetal tissue transplantation fails to justify the extension of foetal tissue transplantation': see P. McCullagh, *The Foetus as Transplant Donor: Scientific, Social and Ethical Perspectives*, John Wiley, Chichester, 1987, at 94.

[43] Fox and McHale, 'Xenotransplantation', at 54. The Kennedy Report stated that clinical xenotransplantation trials should be 'considered to be medical research', *Animal Tissue Into Humans*, at xx.

[44] Editorial, 'Guidance on Xenotransplantation Sought' (1997) 3(9) *Nature Medicine* 935.

[45] In the US, attention has been primarily focused on non-human primates, whereas in the UK only pigs have been seriously considered, although some discussion has taken place with respect to ruminants and even kangaroos.

[46] By contrast, the US Institute of Medicine endorsed the use of primates as *source* animals as well as experimental recipients: see Committee on Xenograft Transplantation: Ethical Issues and Public Policy, *Xenotransplantation: Science, Ethics, and Public Policy*, Institute of Medicine, National Academy Press, Washington D.C., 1996.

questions.[47] Assuming that the transplanted organs will function physiologically in the human host the primary clinical obstacle then is the possibility of disease transmission from the source (zoonoses). Indeed, in the early stages at least, recipients would receive very high levels of immunosuppression in order to counter rejection, and this would render them very susceptible to infections. These include bacteria, fungi, viruses and prions.[48] Ironically now the closer 'genetic distance' of non-human to human primates may facilitate such transmission.[49] Vascularised rather than non-vascularised organs or tissues are a greater concern here,[50] so although pig insulin and heart valves have been used in humans without misadventure, there are much smaller risks involved.[51]

It is also necessary to weigh in the balance the actual or potential harm(s) to the relevant sources/donors. This may be easily satisfied in respect of now-dead beings (assuming consent has been given) but less easily so with regard to still-living beings. There are limits imposed to the 'altruism' of even seemingly fully competent living adults in all jurisdictions, thus mandating that the removal of (whole) vital organs be confined to cadaveric sources (the dead donor rule). Moreover, assuming certain animals, intended for either therapeutic transplantation procedures or pre-clinical experimentation, do have relevant interests and are capable of being harmed, how do we weigh those interests against those of human individuals and society?[52] It is not appropriate here to debate the merits or otherwise (the 'acceptability') of using animals as organ sources for humans – this is a project requiring more scope and space. However, to

47 The transgenic pigs contain the human complement regulating protein DAF, and promising results have been obtained in transplants into primates: see D. White, 'Xenotransplantation – Scientific Aspects' (1997) 29 *Transplantation Proceedings* 2727.

48 Prions are infectious agents thought to cause diseases such as bovine spongiform encephalopathy (BSE) and human Creutzfeldt–Jakob disease (CJD). There is evidence that prion-related diseases can pass between species but they are unlikely to pass into the wider community due to the fact that transmission generally only results from either transplantation or eating infected material.

49 Pigs are easily bred in large numbers as compared with primates, and by approximately four months old their organs are large enough for transplantation into humans. By contrast, chimpanzees are an endangered species.

50 Sheep intestines have been used for surgical sutures, and cow tendons and bones to replace human ones, but these are also non-vascularised tissues.

51 A recent large study of 160 patients exposed to pig tissue, for example skin grafts, heart valves and insulin, or who had experienced extra-corporeal perfusion through pig spleens, livers or kidneys, found no evidence of infection: see J. Hopkins Tanne, 'Study Gives Reassurance on Safety of Xenotransplantation' (1999) 319 *British Medical Journal* 533.

52 See R. Downie, 'Xenotransplantation' (1997) 23 *Journal of Medical Ethics* 205.

assert that it is permissible to use animals in this way because they *are* animals is argued by many commentators to be speciesist and should be rejected. If, on the other hand, we look for morally relevant features, such as awareness, sentience, etc., then whilst some animals may not 'score' highly others will do so,[53] and may even possess more in terms of these qualities than some human beings, for example the permanently vegetative or comatose, anencephalics, etc.[54] James Walters for instance would accord the highest moral status to those animals possessing the most qualities similar to humans and argues that it may be more justifiable to use anencephalic infants than chimpanzees.[55] The Nuffield Report stated that 'Whether the argument is framed in terms of the interests or rights of animals, the crucial point is the extent to which animals share the features supposed to be important to human interests and rights. The feature to which most importance has generally been attached is that of self-awareness.'[56] It went on to state that 'the saving of human life or significantly enhancing its quality may justify a certain amount of animal suffering, provided this is kept to a minimum'.[57] Obviously where there is a potential harm to one living being weighed against a benefit to another the wishes of the parties themselves (if ascertainable) will carry great sway, but there is also a societal dimension where there is a risk of disease transmission from known and unknown agents into the population as a whole.[58] For instance, endogenous retroviruses in particular can become inserted into the genetic make-up of the host and be passed on to offspring.[59] These issues raise the question of what the appropriate harm–benefit threshold for xenotransplantation is. Until this has been ascer-

53 See W. Cartwright, 'The Pig, the Surgeon and the Nuffield Council' [1996] 4 *Medical Law Review* 250 at 263.

54 Frey argues that we must be consistent and therefore should permit experimentation to take place upon certain humans: see R. Frey, 'Medicine, Animal Experimentation, and the Moral Problem of Unfortunate Humans' (1996) 13 *Social Philosophy and Policy* 181.

55 J. Walters, Presentation to the IOM Conference on Xenograft Transplantation: Science, Ethics, and Public Policy, 25–27 June 1995

56 Nuffield Council, *Animal-to-Human Transplants*, at para. 10.7. It expressed the view that pigs share fewer capacities with humans than primates although 'unquestionably intelligent and sociable animals', ibid., at para. 4.42.

57 Ibid., at para. 4.6.

58 Concerns on this score have led to the initiation of a policy that any trial recipient must agree permanently to forgo having children: see L. Rogers, 'Transplant Pioneer Plans to Offer Pig Hearts in Britain', *Sunday Times*, 31 October 1999.

59 In 1997 researchers discovered that the PERV-PK virus could infect human cells under laboratory conditions and replicate: see J. Wise, 'Pig Virus Transfer Threatens Xenotransplantation' (1997) 314 *British Medical Journal* 623.

tained all policy-makers are stumbling around in the dark to some degree.[60] In view of the wider risks to society, however, Bach *et al.* observe: 'Where the risks are collective, the public must not only be educated about the risk but must also be involved in decision-making.'[61]

The official policy underpinning almost all transplant regimes is that of organ *donation*. However, although we typically conceive of the 'gift' being made by the 'donor', the decision to permit removal is not always made by the individual from whom the organs are removed, for example where next of kin give permission for the organs of a dead relative to be used for transplantation purposes or organs are removed from living, but decisionally incapacitated, individuals. The term 'donor' will be used across the board though for convenience to refer to the (human) organ source. Autonomous donation is nonetheless a broad cornerstone of transplant policy. With regard to living donors, the requirement of donor consent is self-evident, although even here it might sometimes be permissible for individuals lacking capacity through immature years or otherwise to provide organs where this would be for their own benefit. Societies across the world, formally at least, eschew also the 'taking' of organs from cadavers, so-called routine procurement, without at least some form of (alleged) 'consent' to the removal. It is also generally accepted that it is primarily for the individual whose organs will be used to direct the use of his/her body parts even after death. But whilst we generally see no objection to a (now-deceased) person having the prerogative to dictate or forbid the uses to which his/her cadaver may be put, from what source does the right of a relative to consent to the use of the cadaver or to object to any specific use emanate?

The importance of autonomy in medical practice is now self-evident and deeply entrenched, being manifested here by means of consent. Consent assumes a central place in legal and ethical analysis of transplantation practices, notably with regard to living donors, but also vis-à-vis cadaveric donors, even if this is dressed up in legal parlance as, for example, a 'request'. In the latter connection there is an ongoing debate as to whether express or presumed consent regimes are the preferred legal response, the premiss being that the latter will result in a greater volume of organs for transplant. However, assuming for a moment that that is

60 See H. Vanderpool, 'Critical Ethical Issues in Clinical Trials with Xenotransplants' (1998) 351 *Lancet* 1347 at 1348.

61 Bach *et al.*, 'Uncertainty in Xenotransplantation', at 142.

indeed true, one needs to assess the true ethical character of such a legal regime. Whilst this genus of regime is described as being a 'presumed consent' regime, many would deny that that is truly what it is, and allege that it constitutes no more than a routine taking under another guise and implies public ownership of the cadaver. Proponents on the other hand assert that a tacit consent is just as much a consent as one explicitly declared.

As regards living organ donation the central importance of consent is conceded by all. But the fraught and intimate family circumstances surrounding most living related donation decisions and the typically instinctive nature of the decision-making has called into question the suitability of existing legal and ethical frameworks for determining the validity of a particular consent. These proceed from an individualistic standpoint and assume the feasibility of autonomous independent decision-making. It is suggested by some that the complex relationships and circumstances should themselves form part of the legal and ethical evaluatory process, an 'ethic of care' framework. But, assuming a valid consent is given for organ removal, should this not be sufficient *per se* to justify organ removal where it is intended for a therapeutic purpose such as transplantation?

Foetal tissue for transplantation is potentially advantageous in terms of efficacy for the recipient by virtue of its ability to differentiate, implant and proliferate, and, in some circumstances, to avoid a significant immune response from the host. In particular, foetal islet cells have been used for treating diabetics, and foetal neurological cells for treating Parkinson's disease. However, where the use of organs and tissues from dead foetuses is concerned there is an additional concern for some, that the process is 'inextricably linked to abortion'.[62] Mason and McCall Smith comment that 'morally speaking, those who are opposed to abortion can accept foetal brain implantation only on the basis that it is desirable to extract some good from an intrinsically bad action if it is possible to do so'.[63] This has led to calls from some quarters for the confining of the use of human foetal tissue to materials derived from ectopic pregnancies or spontaneous, as opposed to induced, abortions.[64] As Botros notes, 'A

62 See J. Mason and A. McCall Smith, *Law and Medical Ethics*, 4th edn, Butterworths, London, 1994, at 311.

63 Ibid.

64 See, for instance, K. Nolan, '*Genug ist Genug*: A Fetus is not a Monkey' (1988) 18 *Hastings*

criterion will be required, however, to distinguish between salvaging good from evil and actually condoning evil'.[65] But even if this 'retrospective' view of abortions which have already occurred is rejected, there is concern in some quarters that abortions will be encouraged, and will increase in volume, as a consequence. Caplan, however, notes that 'Aborted foetuses, with few exceptions, cannot serve as the donors of organs. Abortion is usually conducted early on in pregnancy at a time when the major organs have not developed.'[66] Essentially the foetal *organs* which have been used for transplantation thus far are the thymus, pancreas and liver.[67] Although these have often been transplants of parts or cells rather than whole organs this has not been so in every instance. As regards foetal liver, it seems that foetuses with an age range of from four to twenty-two weeks have been used for such purposes.[68]

Where transplantation is a central public health policy goal, decisions as to whether to seek to maintain a high rate of transplantation, as opposed to offering other therapies such as dialysis instead, or maybe not even accepting some patients for organ replacement therapy at all, have led to different policies in different countries relating to kidney transplantation in particular, partly because of differing risk/benefit assessments. Where the cadaveric donor rate is insufficient to meet demand, decisions as to whether to promote living organ donation have varied dramatically between nations. In Norway for instance the view that 'medical personnel have a duty towards society in providing the best possible medical treatment to as many as possible at the lowest possible price'[69] led them to

Center Reports 13. A study in the US, however, concluded that foetal materials for transplantation obtained from these sources would be 'quite limited': see D. Ware Branch *et al.*, 'Suitability of Fetal Tissues from Spontaneous Abortions and from Ectopic Pregnancies for Transplantation' (1995) 273 *Journal of the American Medical Association* 66. There is generally a high incidence of genetic abnormality in foetuses that have spontaneously aborted.

65 See S. Botros, 'Abortion, Embryo Research and Fetal Transplantation: Their Moral Interrelationships' in P. Byrne (ed.), *Medicine, Medical Ethics and the Value of Life*, John Wiley, Chichester, 1990, 47 at 73.

66 A. Caplan, 'Should Foetuses or Infants be Utilised as Organ Donors?' (1987) 1 *Bioethics* 119 at 124.

67 See Council on Scientific Affairs and Council on Ethical and Judicial Affairs, 'Medical Applications of Fetal Tissue Transplantation' (1990) 263 *Journal of the American Medical Association* 565.

68 See McCullagh, *The Foetus as Transplant Donor*, at 86.

69 See A. Jakobsen, 'Living Donor Practices and Processes in Europe' in D. Price and J. Akveld (eds.), *Living Organ Donation in the Nineties: European Medico-Legal Perspectives*, EUROTOLD, 1996, 1 at 3. Between 1969 and 1995 3,262 renal transplants were performed in Norway, with 1,992 being living donor transplants.

a decision to maintain a high living donor transplant rate in order to achieve a high overall rate of transplantation (measures taken to improve significantly the rate of cadaveric organ donation having met little success). This has not been the response in many continental European nations though, for example France. This is probably due to many factors, but differing assessments of the risk/benefit balance in living organ donation would seem to be among them. Indeed, despite their widespread use around the globe, certain centres refuse to use living donors on ethical grounds.

The preceding analysis has been predominantly focused on the procurement side of the organ transplantation equation. However, no less significant in ethical terms is the process of allocation and distribution of organs. Although concentrating solely upon recipients here, there are also tensions between a utilitarian approach and one more sensitive to the demands of justice. Whilst there is relative unanimity that where access to an organ transplantation is not governed by the ability to pay, that distribution should be based upon medical factors, this does not serve to end the debate as to who is eligible to receive, and who should actually receive, a particular organ donated for transplantation. There is also a symbiotic relationship between organ procurement and organ distribution. Perceptions as to the fairness of organ distribution processes affect donation as do perceptions as to the area in which the donation is used. The degree to which one may exercise autonomy over the fate of a donated organ may conflict with perceptions of organs being donated to society generally for the latter to distribute in accordance with its own publicly endorsed principles. Should we permit the provider to designate the recipient of a donated organ for instance?

The law has played a very prominent part in transplantation practices since the beginning. Transplantation has not been viewed as an appropriate therapy and medical domain for purely private decision-making between patient and physician, primarily because of the interposition of the donor into the relationship. Moreover, from early on medical professionals have sought the clarification, guidance and protection of legislation for their actions. This is unsurprising when one considers the legal and ethical minefield in which they were treading, especially in the early days. Today, virtually all nations with a transplantation programme have transplant legislation of one degree of comprehensiveness or another. This is probably the first area of medicine to become comprehensively regulated. Of course, legislation is not necessarily the most flexible and responsive mechanism to the sensitive problems arising in this field. But arguably only legislation is appropriate to deal with many fundamental concerns, such as the proper meaning of death. Attempts to deal with this issue through judge-made law have proved inadequate and piecemeal. Legislation is a more overt expression and democratic endorsement of societal policy even if, of necessity, it will often have to deal with issues in broad terms. In addition, legislation needs to be enacted against a backdrop of internationally accepted principles and policies, from organisations such as the European Community, the Council of Europe, the World Health Organisation and the United Nations, which direct a minimum human rights content of such legislation.

There are many factors which conspire to limit the pool of potential donors, and various strategies which might be employed to expand the donor pool. Many of these have ethical and legal dimensions. The major objective of this book is to assess the ethical and legal character of existing transplantation practices and legal regimes and proposals mooted to increase the supply of organs. In so far as it is ethically and legally acceptable to do so, initiatives which will improve the supply of donor organs should be supported. However, expediency cannot be the sole guide here. As the King's Fund Report stated, 'Until medical science learns to replicate human tissue or replace organs with those from animals, the problem will remain: how can we maximise the supply of these organs by organisational or legal reforms without offending ethical principles?'[70] The balancing of the rights and interests of the various participants, but most notably the donor and the potential recipient, however conspire to render this an enormously complex affair and one which may even swing as clinical needs fluctuate. Respect for the rights and interests of the donor must be safeguarded in the face of proper clinician striving to maximise the availability of this overly subscribed-to therapy. It has been suggested that the history of transplantation until recently displayed a utilitarian, recipient-oriented character, but whether this is actually so is for the reader to judge. Moreover, one must not forget the insights offered by Chadwick,[71] who notes the culturally specific value of organ transplants themselves. She remarks that most of the debates seem to assume that the

[70] King's Fund Institute, *A Question of Give and Take*, Research Report 18, King's Fund Institute, London, 1994.

[71] R. Chadwick, 'Corpses, Recycling', at 63–4.

issue is simply one of increasing the number of donated organs, but she states that views on the symbolic importance of the corpse and the questioning of our lack of acceptance of death are of 'crucial importance when looking at the imperatives which drive us towards ever more demands for more bodily parts'.[72] Other values may easily be sacrificed if too single-minded and aggressive a strategy is adopted towards any such life-saving treatment.

72 Ibid.

PART I

Cadaveric organ donor transplantation

Introduction to cadaveric organ transplantation

Cadaveric organ (homo)transplantation (CDT) was, as a clinical therapeutic alternative, essentially an innovation of the sixties.[1] This decade witnessed the first human liver transplant[2] and the first lung transplant in 1963, and the first human heart transplants, including Christiaan Barnard's momentous first cardiac transplant performed in Cape Town in 1967, all procedures which are now commonplace at the start of the new millennium. In addition, heart/lung, pancreas, intestine and various tissue transplants such as bone, corneas and heart valves are widely performed using cadaveric donors. CDT is the dominant form of transplantation for all forms of organ transplantation in most developed transplant nations,[3] and is practised on a truly massive scale. In 1997 alone 11,831 renal, 4,207 liver and 3,257 thoracic cadaveric transplants were carried out in Europe and 8,613 renal, 4,159 liver and 3,348 thoracic in the United States.[4]

Since the beginning though, CDT has generated a plethora of challenging legal and ethical issues, as well as clinical and organisational obstacles

1 The first cadaveric organ transplant actually took place in Boston in 1947, when a kidney was stitched on to the arm of an acutely uraemic patient, but this was only intended as a 'stop gap' measure to allow the patient's own kidney to recover, which it did. Cornea transplantation essentially began in the fifties although there were isolated procedures performed substantially earlier. In 1906 Edward Zirm successfully transplanted the cornea of a boy who had been injured by a foreign body into a man who was blind following lime burns: see E. Zirm, 'Eine Erfolgreich Totale Keratoplastic' (1906) 64 *Archives of Opthalmology* 580.

2 Although the first successful cadaveric liver transplant was performed by Starzl in 1967 at the University of Colorado.

3 The first composite cadaveric *and* living bone transplant occurred in the United States in 1999. The first composite tissue hand transplant was carried out in 1998. It has been predicted that we are on the threshold of the first face transplant from a cadaveric source to a person whose own face has become disfigured through an accident or suchlike. See 'Arm Transplant Patient doing well in Hospital', *The Times*, 25 September 1998, and 'Surgeon Predicts Face Transplant "Within Months"', *Daily Telegraph*, 1 October 1998.

4 ITCS World Transplant Statistics 1997.

to be overcome. Further, despite a general 'surge' in transplant activity during the eighties,[5] the rising tide of demand for organ replacement therapy has ensured that almost everywhere there is a shortage of organs for transplant. In the United States waiting lists and times for transplants continue to rise despite an increase in the number of cadaveric kidney transplants from 7,782 in 1990 to 8,938 in 1998.[6] However, the problem has been exacerbated in some regions by the fall, or 'plateauing out', of cadaveric donor organ procurement and transplantation rates in the early nineties and beyond. In the United Kingdom, 842 kidney transplants were performed in 1979, rising to 1,730 in 1990, but falling to 1,534 in 1997 and 1,373 in 1998.[7] Within the Eurotransplant region 3,171 cadaveric kidney transplants were performed in 1990, dropping to 3,064 in 1995. Heart, lung and liver transplants show a slightly different pattern with typically less stability in trends.

Clinical matters

The success of any specific cadaveric transplant depends primarily on the following clinical factors: (a) blood and tissue compatibility between donor and recipient; (b) effective immunosuppression; and (c) limited ischaemia (both warm (where blood supply is maintained) and cold (where the organ is cooled)) time. Tissue matching is of major importance to outcomes of renal and pancreatic transplants, whereas organ size[8] has generally been a more significant factor in liver and heart transplantation.[9] Until the introduction of cyclosporin in the eighties, available immunosuppression was only moderately effective to prevent rejection, and

[5] The King's Fund Report revealed that between 1985 and 1992 there were percentage increases in renal transplantation activity in Belgium (55), France (52), the Netherlands (48) and West Germany (46), but that there were decreases in Canada (5), Switzerland (8), Sweden (13) and Denmark (21): see King's Fund Institute, *A Question of Give and Take*, Research Report 18, King's Fund Institute, London, 1994, at 20 (Fig. 8).

[6] See UNOS/OPTN Annual Report 1998 at http://www.unos.org/Data/anrpt98/ar98-data.

[7] In France, 1,897 cadaveric kidney transplants were performed in 1990 but only 1,391 in 1995. Exceptions are Spain and Portugal which have seen substantial increases over the same period. In Spain, 1,224 renal transplants were performed in 1990 compared with 1,765 in 1995, and in Portugal the figure for the same period rose from 256 to 368.

[8] Total lung capacity and ABO blood group compatibility are the primary clinical factors for lung transplantation.

[9] Organ size matching difficulties account for the high volume of deaths of paediatric patients whilst awaiting a transplant and the growth of split liver procedures. Basic (ABO) blood matching is routinely carried out in relation to all contemporary organ transplants.

consequently patient and graft survival outcomes were modest. Up to that time results from living renal donation were substantially superior to CDT across the board. The differences have been less marked subsequently, and during the eighties this generated a substantial swing in favour of cadaveric transplantation.[10] Ischaemia time is also a vital factor affecting results. Organs such as lungs can survive only very limited periods of cold ischaemia time before permanent damage is done to the organ, rendering it unfit for transplantation.[11] Kidneys, on the other hand, can be preserved in crushed ice for up to thirty-six hours.[12] As yet, banking of organs for later transplantation is not a feasible option, although it is for tissues such as corneas, bone, skin, heart valves, etc.[13] Organs must therefore be retrieved immediately after circulatory arrest (or at least cooled and perfused immediately thereafter), or preferably whilst still being perfused with oxygenated blood. The first cadaveric renal donors were asystolic (non-heart-beating) donors (NHBDs), but as Rapaport states, 'The incidence of organ failure after transplantation in these studies, and the concurrent growing acceptance of brain death criteria, caused a progressive loss of interest in this option',[14] except in one or two countries such as Poland and Japan where brain death was not initially accepted within society. There has however been a resurgence of interest in asystolic donors in recent years. These donors fall into four categories (the so-called 'Maastricht' categories): (1) patients declared dead outside the hospital; (2) patients unable to be resuscitated in the emergency room; (3) terminally ill patients who wish to forgo further treatment; and (4) presumed brain-dead patients who suffer a cardiopulmonary arrest prior to the determination of death or the procurement of organs.

10 The difference is still fairly pronounced though. The 1998 Annual Report of the UNOS/OPTN shows graft survival rates for cadaveric kidneys post-transplant to be 87.5 per cent at one year and 61 per cent at five years compared with 93.5 per cent at one year and 76.6 per cent at five years for living donor kidneys.

11 Hearts, heart/lungs and lungs for transplant can generally be preserved for up to four hours, and pancreases and livers for between eight and ten hours: see P. Hauptman *et al.*, 'Procurement and Allocation of Solid Organs for Transplantation' (1997) 336 *New England Journal of Medicine* 422 at 428.

12 Greater preservation times facilitate matching procedures for these organs and conversely militate against their performance in respect of other organs.

13 Corneas can generally be removed up to forty-eight hours after circulatory arrest, and eye banks can store corneas for up to thirty days.

14 F. Rapaport, 'Alternative Sources of Clinically Transplantable Vital Organs' (1993) 25 *Transplantation Proceedings* 42 at 42. Of course, immunosuppression was fairly crude at that stage. NHBDs have been used throughout at the University of Wisconsin at Madison.

NHBD protocols provide either for organ retrieval or for organ perfusion and cooling *in situ* after death has been determined on the basis of irreversible cardiorespiratory failure. In the US, twenty-nine out of the sixty-three Organ Procurement Organisations have NHBD protocols, the majority of which concern 'controlled' donors, that is category 3 patients (above),[15] the most famous being the University of Pittsburgh protocol where donors are individuals for whom a decision has been made to forgo further life-sustaining treatment and in respect of whom permission exists for organ donation. Uncontrolled donor protocols are most common in Europe,[16] that is applying primarily to category 2 patients, and employ cooling and perfusion techniques. Such protocols are in operation at nine centres in Britain covering fifty donor hospitals, and elsewhere in Europe, the most extensive being at the University Hospital Maastricht.[17] Youngner and Arnold state that 'Recent estimates suggest that use of NHBCs could increase the number of potential organ donors by at least 50 per cent.'[18]

Most organ donors are artificially ventilated however and therefore typically die in hospital, generally in the intensive care unit (ICU) environment. The use of artificial ventilation raises an outstandingly critical question: 'When is a person dead?' The traditional cardiopulmonary standard of death is inappropriate where respiration and circulation are still functioning, albeit supported by artificial means. CDT is very largely (wholly in respect of heart transplantation) dependent on the notion of 'heart-beating' donors and acceptance of death based upon brain death.[19] The King's Fund Report notes that 'The concept and diagnosis of brain stem death is central to cadaveric donation, and to intensive care in general; but it is one which is often difficult for the

[15] Institute of Medicine Report, *Non-Heart-Beating Organ Transplantation: Medical and Ethical Issues in Procurement*, Institute of Medicine, National Academy Press, Washington D.C., 1997. Twenty-four of the twenty-nine protocols apply only to controlled donors, whilst the remaining five apply to both controlled and uncontrolled donors.

[16] Although 'retrieval' protocols have been implemented at the King's College Hospital in Dulwich and at the University of Zurich.

[17] Similar protocols are in operation at the Hachioji Medical Centre of Tokyo Medical College and at the Hospital Universitario San Carlos in Madrid and some US centres. There have also been 'whole body' cooling techniques utilised at the Hospital Henri-Mondo Creteil in France.

[18] S. Youngner and R. Arnold, 'Non-Heart-Beating Cadavers: The Beat Goes On' in B. Spielman (ed.), *Organ and Tissue Donation: Ethical, Legal and Policy Issues*, Southern Illinois University Press, Carbondale, 1997, 69 at 70.

[19] Where brain death was not accepted within the society, overall transplant rates have generally been (comparatively) either fairly or very low, for instance in Japan.

general public to understand, although it is no longer controversial among the medical profession.'[20] Lack of public comprehension or support fosters anxiety as to the possibility of being declared dead prematurely and reflects itself in the reluctance of some to assent to the removal of organs, as it did following the controversial BBC *Panorama* programme in Britain in 1980 and in Denmark after extensive public debate on the issue around the turn of the previous decade. In fact, despite the widespread acceptance of brain death, opposition if anything intensified at the end of the millennium, although most notably in Germany.

The donor pool

The King's Fund Report noted in the mid-nineties that 'The plateau in donor rates indicated by the kidney transplantation data is a cause of some concern. The reasons are likely to be manifold, but particularly significant may be the reduction in the size of the potential pool of donors – those who die in ways which lead to brain stem death and artificial ventilation.'[21] Cadaveric organ donors die predominantly either from head injuries caused by accidents, generally road traffic accidents, or from intracranial haemorrhage. Deaths from both sources have generally declined in recent years. In the UK road traffic accident fatalities dropped from 7,883 in 1970 to 3,679 in 1995, one of the lowest rates in Europe.[22] Data from across fourteen of the major transplanting nations shows that road deaths declined by almost 30 per cent between 1970 and 1990.[23] When such suitable donors die, they must also be *accessible* to the medical services. The King's Fund Report found that population densities of less than 20 per square kilometre have a significant impact on a country's ability to procure cadaveric kidneys, such as in Finland, Sweden, Norway, Australia and Canada.[24] The fact that there is typically a need for ICU

20 King's Fund, *A Question of Give and Take*, at 9.

21 Ibid., at 14.

22 The King's Fund Report found a correlation between road traffic death rates and organ procurement rates across nations in Europe. The top four countries in terms of organ procurement were also the top four countries in terms of road traffic deaths per million population (Austria, Belgium, France and New Zealand). In England and Wales the volume of deaths from subarachnoid and intracerebral haemorrhage also declined, by 70 per cent between 1970 and 1990: ibid., at 14–15.

23 Ibid. The volume fell from 124,000 to 88,000.

24 Ibid., at 28.

facilities to be made available to support the donor's organs until retrieval, and for appropriate staff (and sometimes also equipment, e.g. EEG machines) to be on hand to diagnose brain death, means that the availability of intensive care staff and beds, and of operating theatre time, undoubtedly all impact on donor rates. In 1996 the British Transplantation Society Working Party noted[25] the depressing effect upon donor rates of the low level of intensive care provision in the UK as compared with many other European nations.[26] Where such resources are wholly lacking, no CDT programme typically exists at all.

Organisational factors

There are a variety of other factors affecting the likelihood of an individual becoming an organ donor.[27] First, an individual has to be *identified* as a potential organ donor, which will depend on the training of involved staff and probably the existence of appropriate protocols. In 1987, the Hoffenberg Report found that in the UK 'Knowledge of the criteria for brain stem death, of the arrangements for transplantation and of the benefit of transplantation is not universal' and suggested a reluctance to certify brain (stem) death.[28] There is an overlap between the identification of potential donors and the absence of medical contraindications though. The King's Fund Report stated: 'The first possibility – suggested by the findings of the national audit – is to increase the numbers of individuals who undergo brain stem death tests when they "possibly satisfy" brain stem death criteria.'[29] However, later research has shown that in most of these

25 The British Transplantation Society Report showed a tendency for the patients with the poorest prognoses to be increasingly unlikely to be transferred to ICU facilities, aided by the increasing capacity to diagnose the clinical course of a condition through sophisticated imaging techniques, etc.: see *British Transplantation Society Working Party Report on Organ Donation*, BTS, 1996, at 33.

26 The Hoffenberg Report had earlier noted that it was not possible to transfer all potential organ donors to ICUs in Britain: see Conference of Medical Royal Colleges and their Faculties in the UK, *Report of the Working Party on the Supply of Donor Organs for Transplantation* (Hoffenberg Report), 1987, at 4.

27 King's Fund, *A Question of Give and Take*, listed various factors which impact upon the supply of donor organs, at 26.

28 It noted that doctors then generally had little experience of brain (stem) death and requesting organ donation. See Hoffenberg Report, at 2.

29 King's Fund, *A Question of Give and Take*, at 47. See S. Gore, D. Cable and A. Holland, 'Organ Donation from Intensive Care Units in England and Wales: Two Year Confidential Audit of Deaths in Intensive Care' (1992) 304 *British Medical Journal* 349.

instances there were medical contraindications to donation anyhow, and that it was reassuring that 'so few transplantable organs were being missed'.[30] There are also other logistical difficulties which can sometimes lead to viable organs not being used, principally non-renal organs.[31] The motivation of staff towards organ transplantation will be influential (including the existence and number of transplant co-ordinators) as well as the organisational arrangements and relationships between donor hospitals and transplant centres. Hoffenberg recognised the time involved in contacting transplant co-ordinators and relatives, etc. The existence of adequate reimbursement to donor hospitals may also be important.[32] In some instances donor hospitals are not reimbursed for their costs at all, or only at a modest rate (UK hospitals presently receive £1,000),[33] whereas in some countries (for example in the United States) full cost recovery is permitted and in others even more (for example in Spain).

Many of the above factors are beyond direct legal regulation or influence and are primarily dependent on good management systems, educational programmes and information dissemination. However, in procurement terms legal provisions may impact upon other aspects of the 'process'. These primarily pertain to the requirements for establishing and confirming the existence of death, and satisfaction of the stipulated criteria relating to consent to organ removal. The legal framework governing organ retrieval for transplantation, in particular the degree of required involvement of relatives, is frequently identified as a major determinant of levels of organ donation. However, in certain relevant jurisdictions, it is alleged that relatives are often not consulted in the first place, whether through reluctance on the part of health care professionals to intrude upon their grief or because a refusal is anticipated in any case.[34]

[30] S. Gore *et al.*, 'Consensus on General Medical Contraindications to Organ Donation' (1992) 305 *British Medical Journal* 406 at 409. This follow-up to the earlier national audit of intensive care unit deaths in the UK found that in only 6 per cent of instances where brain stem tests were not performed were the kidneys actually transplantable and only 1 per cent of livers and no hearts or lungs. See also G. Smith *et al.*, 'Organ Donation from Intensive Care Units' (1992) 304 *British Medical Journal* 916.

[31] See King's Fund, *A Question of Give and Take*, at 48.

[32] This was identified in the British Transplantation Society Working Party Report for instance.

[33] The Report of the Royal College of Surgeons Working Party to Review Organ Transplantation recommended this be increased to £2,500: see Royal College of Surgeons of England, *The Report of the Working Party to Review Organ Transplantation*, Royal College of Surgeons of England, London, 1999, at para. 138.

[34] Canadian federal and provincial task forces have also identified the reluctance to approach relatives as a 'major, significant' barrier to increased donation: see for instance Task Force on

A large study in the early eighties by the US Center for Disease Control concluded that the 'small number of transplantable cadaveric kidneys retrieved was not attributable to the lack of suitable organs but rather the failure to identify suitable donors, obtain consent, and retrieve kidneys'. A perception grew in the eighties that clinicians themselves were the primary barrier to higher donation rates. As a response to the recommendations of the United States Task Force on Organ Transplantation,[35] the Joint Commission for the Accreditation of Healthcare Organisations (JCAHO) included a requirement for formal organ donation policies which identified potential donors and provided next of kin with opportunities for donation, as part of their annual acute care hospital reviews. Moreover, the Budget Reconciliation Act 1986 required hospitals to establish written protocols for identifying eligible organ donors and notifying procurement agencies of them and informing families of their option to donate, as a condition for eligibility for Medicaid and Medicare. Section 5 of the revised Uniform Anatomical Gift Act (UAGA) in 1987 also incorporated 'required request' provisions for the first time. Over forty-four US jurisdictions have adopted such laws since the first statutes were enacted in 1985. In the United Kingdom the Hoffenberg Report also recognised that some doctors do not initiate discussions with relatives about organ donation, but rejected similar legislation to that in the US, preferring instead to establish procedures for referral coupled with an effective audit of practices by every authority. Indeed, an audit of intensive care deaths in the UK found that relatives were approached in 94 per cent of instances and concluded that 'required request legislation is unnecessary for the United Kingdom'.[36] A Department of Health Circular has subsequently required all health authorities to ensure that relevant hospitals have explicit procedures for the identification of potential organ donors, for

Organ Donation, *Organ Donation in the Eighties: The Minister's Task Force on Kidney Donation*, The Task Force, Toronto, 1985.

35 The United States Task Force on Organ Transplantation stated that 'a major problem with the current voluntary system of organ donation is that families often are not informed of their option to donate organs and tissues after brain death is determined': see *Organ Transplantation: Issues and Recommendations*, US Department of Health and Human Services, Washington D.C., 1986, at 31. In 1985 a special Hastings Center Report also found that 'the failure to ask about donation, the failure to recognise the key role played by family members' was critical: see *Ethical, Legal and Policy Issues Pertaining to Solid Organ Procurement*, The Hastings Center, Hastings-on-Hudson, N.Y., 1985, at 15.

36 Gore *et al.*, 'Organ Donation from Intensive Care Units', at 353.

notifying the appropriate transplant unit or co-ordinator, and for assigning responsibility for approaching relatives.[37]

Family refusals are a major factor impacting on rates of organ procurement where permission for removal is sought. Matas and Veith reported a rate of refusal in excess of 50 per cent at their centre in the US.[38] A more extensive and recent study by Siminoff *et al.* in twenty-three acute-care general hospitals in two US metropolitan areas revealed that only 46.5 per cent of families approached agreed to donate organs.[39] In Great Britain, Gore *et al.*'s audit of intensive care deaths found the refusal rate by relatives was approximately 30 per cent.[40] This was confirmed by a study carried out by the UK Transplant Co-ordinators' Association and the British Association of Critical Care Nurses between July 1992 and June 1994, which found a rate of relatives' refusal of 26 per cent. In Europe generally, substantial rates of refusal by relatives have also been reported, for instance a 26 per cent refusal rate in a 1992 study in France.

Despite the above, surveys in virtually all jurisdictions show a majority of members of the public prepared to donate organs for transplantation purposes upon their death. A 1993 survey of the US public by Gallup showed 69 per cent of the public willing to donate organs after death.[41] Yet, in systems which rely primarily on donor cards and declarations upon driving licences as the means of expressing willingness to donate, only a fairly small proportion of such potential donors are found to be carrying such a card or licence with them at the point of their death. In

[37] HC(88)63.

[38] A. Matas and F. Veith, 'Presumed Consent for Organ Retrieval' (1984) 5 *Theoretical Medicine* 155 at 157. A sample of the US public questioned in 1984 found that 53 per cent of relatives would have given permission: see J. Prottas and H. Batten, 'The Willingness to Give: The Public and the Supply of Transplantable Organs' (1991) 16(1) *Journal of Health Politics, Policy and Law* 121.

[39] L. Simonoff, R. Arnold, A. Caplan, B. Virnig and D. Seltzer, 'Public Policy Governing Organ and Tissue Procurement in the United States' (1995) 123 *Annals of Internal Medicine* 10. Moreover, 22 per cent of families that did agree placed conditions upon the donation. Chatterjee has stated that family refusals constitute the most important brake on organ donation in the US: see S. Chatterjee, 'Difficulties in Obtaining Kidneys from Potential Postmortem Donors' (1975) 232 *Journal of the American Medical Association* 822.

[40] The King's Fund Institute's own survey reported that 23 per cent of respondents stated that they would refuse to give permission for the organs of a relative to be removed where the deceased had no donor card in his possession. Moreover, a Dutch study found that 56 per cent of relatives would have given permission in a similar scenario. See King's Fund, *A Question of Give and Take*, at 42.

[41] Council on Ethical and Judicial Affairs of the American Medical Association, 'Strategies for Cadaveric Organ Procurement: Mandated Choice and Presumed Consent' (1994) 272 *Journal of the American Medical Association* 809 at 811.

the UK in 1992, approximately 27 per cent of persons had donor cards, but only one in five persons actually carried one.[42] This compares with a figure of 25 per cent of persons found in 1987 to be carrying such cards/authorisations at any one time in the US.[43]

An ethical preface

There are myriad potential uses of the cadaver, set out more than a quarter of a century ago by Willard Gaylin,[44] ranging from direct therapeutic uses to research, scientific and commercial applications and (medical) training (for instance, practising intubation and resuscitation procedures[45]), and although society generally harbours an aversion to procedures performed upon the corpse, it tolerates, permits, and even encourages, many such activities. Indeed, many are authorised by legislation, notably removal of organs for transplantation, forensic post-mortems, autopsies, and research and medical educational uses.[46] The Nuffield Council considered that the removal of tissue from a corpse may constitute degradation, and therefore an 'injury', in ethical terms, unless either governed by a therapeutic intention or part of accepted funerary rites.[47] This would clearly embrace transplantation procedures. Indeed, in view of the substantial potential benefits achievable, as Chadwick observes: 'From a consequentialist point of view it might seem to be clear that it is desirable, if not a moral requirement, to use recyclable corpses to prolong the lives of those who are desperately ill and in need of organs.'[48] This is presumptive though, in so far as it appears to assume that no, or at least little, harm can accrue from organ explantation for such purposes. If this

[42] See King's Fund, *A Question of Give and Take*, at 66.

[43] See R. Evans and D. Manninen, 'US Public Opinion Concerning the Procurement and Distribution of Donor Organs' (1988) 20 *Transplantation Proceedings* 781.

[44] W. Gaylin, 'Harvesting the Dead' (1974) 249 *Harpers* 23.

[45] Such as central venous line and chest tube thoracostomy techniques.

[46] In Britain, educational, therapeutic and research uses are governed by the Human Tissue Act 1961 (1962 Act in Northern Ireland), anatomical examinations by the Anatomy Act 1984 and forensic post-mortems by the Coroners Act 1988. There are nevertheless a range of other procedures not governed by legal provisions, for example archiving of human tissue, collection of tissue in tissue banks, removal of tissue during non-forensic post-mortems, etc.: see Nuffield Council on Bioethics Working Party, *Human Tissue: Ethical and Legal Issues*, Nuffield Council on Bioethics, London, 1995, at para. 7.14.

[47] Ibid., at para. 6.29.

[48] R. Chadwick, 'Corpses, Recycling and Therapeutic Purposes' in R. Lee and D. Morgan (eds.), *Death Rites: Law and Ethics at the End of Life*, Routledge, London, 1994, 54 at 57.

is indeed the case, there is the potential to reconcile both utilitarian and deontological perspectives here, as although Kantian doctrine requires that individuals must not be used solely as means to the ends of others, if the dead have no rights, and are incapable of being harmed, then no conflict seemingly arises. Partridge[49] maintains that the dead have no interests and are consequently beyond harm or benefit, and Harris goes even further and argues that respect is owed only to *persons*, that is those individuals who have the capacity to value their existence (which would also of course exclude many living human beings).[50] This debate is especially pertinent to the liberal perspective which typically only permits criminal sanctions where these are necessary to prevent, deter or punish 'harms' caused to individuals.[51] The employment of the criminal law in the context of other kinds of 'wrongful' behaviour, even causing 'offence to others', is substantially more contentious.

Chadwick argues that we can only have duties *regarding* rather than *towards* the dead, so that the interests of the living would inevitably assume precedence, favouring the potential recipients of such (recycled) organs. But could the 'duties to the living' also embrace the once living (ante-mortem) person's wishes as regards his or her corpse? Courts have in general denied that property rights exist in a corpse even in favour of third parties, let alone the (now) deceased. Magnusson opines however that 'To hold that human tissue cannot be the subject of proprietary rights suggests that, in the absence of specific empowering legislation, such tissue could not be gifted, bought or sold, stolen or converted, bailed or patented.'[52]

The proper and decent treatment of the cadaver is nonetheless viewed as a serious matter across all jurisdictions and is in general a potential criminal matter.[53] The Law Reform Commission (LRC) of Canada

49 E. Partridge, 'Posthumous Interests and Posthumous Respect' (1981) 91 *Ethics* 243 at 243–4. See also B. Levenbook, 'Harming Someone After His Death' (1984) 94 *Ethics* 407. Joan Callahan argues that interests can survive a person's death but can only be carried on by *living* interest-bearers: see 'On Harming the Dead' (1987) 97 *Ethics* 341.

50 J. Harris, *The Value of Life*, Routledge, London, 1985, at 242.

51 What Feinberg terms the 'harm principle': see J. Feinberg, *The Moral Limits of the Criminal Law. Vol. I: Harm to Others*, Oxford University Press, Oxford, 1984.

52 R. Magnusson, 'Proprietary Rights in Human Tissue' in N. Palmer and E. McKendrick (eds.), *Interests in Goods*, Lloyd's of London Press, London, 1993, 237 at 237.

53 In the UK, there are common law offences of 'outraging public decency', 'offering indignities or indecencies to the dead', 'unlawfully and indecently mutilating a corpse' and 'unlawfully preventing burial': see S. White, 'An End to D-I-Y Cremation?' (1993) 33 *Medicine, Science and the Law* 151.

remarked[54] that the offence in the Canadian Criminal Code of offering indignities to, or indecently interfering with, the dead 'expresses the long-held view that the dead human body is entitled to respect. Furthermore, it expresses respect for the emotional and religious sentiments of the next of kin and the moral tranquillity of society at large. In practical terms, the provision aims at preventing physical abuse of the dead body, protecting the public health and minimising public nuisances.'[55] Transplant legislation itself commonly contains provisions proscribing the unnecessary mutilation of the cadaver in the context of organ removal,[56] and sometimes even makes explicit its rationale. Austrian law states that the organ removal may not result in 'disfigurement of the cadaver that is incompatible with the dignity of the deceased'.[57]

However, concepts of 'disrespectful' or 'degrading' treatment are highly malleable as regards a corpse and are intimately wedded to perceptions of the interconnection between the body and the 'self'. The LRC Report states that, 'under one view, persons are seen as inseparable from their bodies. Consequently, the dignity of the human body is inseparable from the dignity of the person. This nexus survives death, because the body symbolises the person who once lived.'[58] Kass has drawn attention to the ambiguity of our reactions towards a corpse. He observes that it is more than it seems, in that it is not just a piece of matter, having been associated with a human personality.[59] This link has indeed often been reinforced by public action. The manner of treatment after death has

54 Law Reform Commission of Canada, *Procurement and Transfer of Human Tissues and Organs*, Working Paper 66, Minister of Supply and Services, Ottawa, 1992, at 109. This offence is contained in section 182.6 of the Canadian Criminal Code.

55 There are criminal offences proscribing the mistreatment of the dead in most US states. For instance, in California it is an offence to mutilate a corpse: see California Health and Safety Code, s. 7052 (West 1988 Supp.), and in Pennsylvania it is an offence to abuse a corpse: see Pennsylvania Consolidated Statutes Annotated, vol. 18, s. 5510 (Purdon 1990 Supp.).

56 For instance in Argentina, Italy, the Philippines and Singapore.

57 Federal Law of 1 June 1982, section 62a(1). Belgian law states that 'The removal of organs . . . shall be carried out in such a way as to respect the remains of the deceased and spare the feelings of the family': see Law of 13 June 1986, section 12.

58 Law Reform Commission of Canada, *Procurement and Transfer*, at 40 and 54. It notes that those who deny this connection will typically view the body in instrumentalist terms, and not as having inherent value in its own right. Of course, this 'separatist' perception feeds off a dualist notion of mind and body.

59 Leon Kass describes our instinctive responses to the cadaver graphically in L. Kass, 'Thinking About the Body' (1985) 15 *Hastings Center Reports* 20, which suggests our instinctive response (which he considers sound) is to treat the mortal remains of the deceased person with respect. William May has also commented that the complete identification of person with body 'does not terminate abruptly with death': see W. May, 'Attitudes Toward the

historically been regarded as at least partially reflective of the respect, or lack of it, accorded to the once living individual. In the nineteenth century, for instance, public dissection of the judicially executed cadaver was viewed as an ingredient of the punishment itself.[60] However, as Chadwick observes 'Even those world-views which do not regard the corpse as the shell of a now departed person, still treat the body with respect.'[61]

Conceptions of respect and decency are infused and intertwined with cultural beliefs which in turn are fashioned by religious standpoints.[62] Dickens, Fluss and King note that 'How dead bodies may be treated often reflects religious convictions regarding afterlife and resurrection, which may be common to a country or legally protected according to individual personal or family beliefs.'[63] The LRC observed that 'Embedded in these notions of potential moral wrongs is a premise that dead bodies deserve moral protection by virtue of their symbolic function. This view is especially prevalent in religions that demand respect for the dead body in the belief that both living and dead human beings are created in the image of God.'[64] In *Kohn* v. *United States*, the federal US court stated that 'Most religions in the world hold that the remains of a deceased must be treated with honor and respect. Judaism believes in the principle that body and soul are sacred because both are the handiworks of God and hence are entitled to reverence.'[65] Nonetheless, very few religions proscribe organ transplantation generally as opposed to certain specific forms (or ancillary aspects) of transplantation, for example selling organs. The US Task Force on Organ Transplantation commented that 'No major religious group in the United States opposes organ donation as a matter of formal doctrine',[66] a remark applicable to most Western societies. Although

Newly Dead' (1973) 1 *Hastings Center Studies* 3 at 3. Chadwick has remarked that 'In part the newly dead corpse remains a symbol of the person': 'Corpses, Recycling', at 62.

60 As in the public dissection of William Burke who was convicted and executed for murdering individuals whose bodies he sold to Scottish anatomists.

61 Chadwick, 'Corpses, Recycling', at 63.

62 See T. Grey, *The Legal Enforcement of Morality*, Alfred Knopf, New York, 1983, at 105.

63 B. Dickens, S. Fluss and A. King, 'Legislation on Organ and Tissue Donation' in J. Chapman, M. Deierhoi and C. Wight (eds.), *Organ and Tissue Donation for Transplantation*, Arnold, London, 1997, 95 at 100.

64 Law Reform Commission of Canada, *Procurement and Transfer*, at 46.

65 591 F. Supp. 568 at 572–3 (1984).

66 US Task Force on Organ Transplantation, at 38. Trivedi maintains that 'There is nothing in the Hindu religion indicating that parts of humans, dead or alive, cannot be used to alleviate the suffering of other humans': see H. Trivedi, 'Hindu Religious Views in Context of

Christian Scientists, North American Indians and Aborigines generally reject organ transplantation, and Jehovah's Witnesses only permit transplantation in the absence of a blood transfusion, it is typically left as a personal decision. Muslim scholars have agreed that it is permissible to use the organs of one human, alive or dead, to treat another, to achieve real benefit, and this view was endorsed in 1988 in Jedda at the Fourth Session of the Islamic Law Academy.[67] Moreover, there are thriving cadaveric organ transplant programmes in Saudi Arabia and Singapore, both with very substantial Muslim populations. However, there are some individuals, scholars, lawyers and clerics who adhere to views contrary to organ transplantation, outside the mainstream. Further, Shintoism, by its very nature, has constituted an obstacle to the development of cadaveric organ transplantation in Japan by virtue of the respect for the integrity of the corpse (and the itai) at the heart of that religion, although even there changing religious patterns and plurality are producing a substantially more liberal contemporary attitude to organ transplantation. Daar has concluded that 'More often than not . . . religious constraints are more imagined than real.'[68] In any event, Quay rightly reinforces the fact that the sacredness of human remains is not linked just to any one religion or to religion generally, it is also a secular notion and one with particular significance for relatives.

Regulatory structures

The Third Report of the Conference of European Health Ministers held in Paris in November 1987 stated that

Transplantation of Organs from Cadavers' (1990) 22 *Transplantation Proceedings* 942 at 942. See generally, W. May, 'Religious Obstacles and Warrants for the Donation of Body Parts' (1988) 20 (Supp. 1) *Transplantation Proceedings* 1079.

67 Article 5 of the Unified Draft Arab Law on Human Organ Transplantation (A.40/INF.DOC/6–30 April 1987) states that 'Organ transplants may be performed from a dead body, provided that consent is obtained from the next of kin, under the following conditions . . . Death has been definitely established . . . The deceased, while alive, did not object to the removal of any organ from his body.' In 1990, Daar remarked that 'It would appear that, on the whole, there are no legal, ethical, or religious obstacles to post mortem organ donation in the Islamic world': see A. Daar, 'Current Practice and the Legal, Ethical and Religious Status of Post Mortem Organ Donation in the Islamic World' in W. Land and J. Dossetor (eds.), *Organ Replacement Therapy: Ethics, Justice, Commerce*, Springer-Verlag, Berlin, 1991, 291 at 298.

68 A. Daar, 'A Survey of Religious Attitudes towards Organ Donation and Transplantation' in G. Collins, J. Dubernard, W. Land and G. Persijn (eds.), *Procurement, Preservation and Allocation of Vascularized Organs*, Kluwer, Dordrecht, 1997, 333 at 333.

> in all civilisations the body of a dead person, though devoid of life, inspires the respect due to what has been the outer material image of a living personality. Hence the reservations, particularly on the part of the family of the deceased, about mutilating the body. On the other hand, the dead body is destined to decomposition and many countries consider it a waste that life-saving organs are left to rot. These considerations give rise to two issues concerning the consent of the deceased: ascertaining the consent for donation; determining to what extent the family of the deceased is entitled to object to the decision of the deceased or to take a decision in his place.[69]

This statement however begs additional questions as to the appropriate form that a consent should take, that is, express or presumed? To a large degree this depends upon how the interests of sick individuals are weighed as against the importance attached to self-determination.

In the following sections, different legal organ procurement regimes will be reviewed leading to their reappraisal. The intended thoroughgoing analysis will facilitate a proper evaluation of the impact of different legal provisions on rates of organ donation and the extent to which regimes take proper account of minimum ethical considerations. Transplant regimes have historically been skewed towards the needs of recipients, and cadaver donor frameworks inevitably place greater emphasis than live donor frameworks on encouraging donation and less upon respect for the donor. But as Dunstan states as regards even different cadaveric procurement regimes, 'Utility alone cannot determine the ethics of choice between them, even though it must be weighed in the political process of legislation.'[70]

Many of the earliest laws governing cadaveric donation covered only corneal grafting, for instance the Law of 7 July 1949 in France and the Corneal Grafting Act 1952 in the United Kingdom. The first piece of legislation applicable to cadaveric *organ* donation was the Post Mortem Examinations and Removal of Human Tissues Act 1952 in South Africa. In the UK, the 1952 legislation was replaced in 1961 by the Human Tissue Act governing cadaveric organ and tissue donation for transplantation more generally. The pace of legislative change stepped up in the sixties across the board, with similar legislation being passed in Ontario in 1963 (and amended in 1967), in Nova Scotia and New Brunswick in 1964, and

69 Conference of European Health Ministers, November 1987, *Third Report: Legislative Measures in Relation to Organ Transplantation and to European Co-operation*, Strasbourg, 1987, at 6.

70 G. Dunstan, 'The Ethics of Organ Donation' (1997) 53(4) *British Medical Bulletin* 921 at 922.

in Denmark in 1967.[71] Moreover, many US states[72] had passed organ bequest laws in the sixties, prior to the formulation of the Uniform Anatomical Gift Act (Mark 1) in 1968, which Model Law was enacted in all the states by 1973. At present almost all legal regimes are statutory in nature and only a smattering of jurisdictions still lack such legislation, prominent exceptions being China, some of the Swiss cantons, the Republic of Ireland and New Zealand.

Whilst nearly all present statutory transplant regimes prioritise the aspirations of the deceased over those of relatives and others, such legislative provisions were required in many jurisdictions because no binding testamentary direction could be given and no guarantee existed that his/her wishes would be respected.[73] Meyers has stated that 'at common law the living had little encouragement that what they wished to authorise would be honoured after their death',[74] and that 'the Anglo-American common law, in the absence of statutory provisions, requires permission for the removal of organs from the corpse to be obtained from the person who possesses the right to burial'.[75] By contrast, under Roman–Dutch law the heirs or executors were required to carry out the terms of the deceased's will regarding burial, as faithfully as possible.[76] Whilst the wishes of the now-deceased person as regards the disposal of the body have always been accorded weight, more so in the United States than in Britain, these have rarely been decisive.[77] In various instances, US

[71] See World Health Organisation, *Use of Human Tissues and Organs for Therapeutic Purposes: A Survey of Existing Legislation*, WHO, Geneva, 1969, at 6.

[72] Up to thirty-nine states and the District of Columbia had donation statutes of various hues: see the Prefatory Note of the National Commissioners of Universal State Laws to the Uniform Anatomical Gift Act 1968.

[73] Indeed, under Regulation 7, Cremation Regulations 1965 SI 1965 No. 1146 amending Regulation 4, Cremation Regulations 1930 SRO 1930 No. 1016, it is still permissible to cremate a deceased person even contrary to his/her express wishes.

[74] D. Meyers, *The Human Body and the Law*, 2nd edn, Edinburgh University Press, Edinburgh, 1990, at 189.

[75] Ibid., at 188. Vestal *et al.*'s view expressed in 1955 that 'It would seem fair to conclude that a person at the present time in the United States probably has the right to control the disposition of his body after death so long as no public policy is contravened, and it seems to follow that an individual, in his lifetime, can give permission for the taking of tissue from his body after death', would appear to be rather too sweeping and partially aspirational: see Vestal *et al.*, 'Medico-Legal Aspects of Tissue Homotransplantation' (1955) 18 *University of Detroit Law Journal* 283 at 287.

[76] Ibid., at 187.

[77] An exceptional case was *O'Dea v. Mitchell* 213 N.E. 2d 870 (1966) where the Supreme Judicial Court of Massachusetts declared that 'The absence of contrary directions by the decedent must be alleged by the next of kin in order to establish their standing to sue.' The case was

courts have accorded precedence to the views of relatives over those of the deceased,[78] although they have often attempted to accommodate the views of both and reach a socially acceptable solution.[79] Thus, although the wishes of the deceased have generally been significant, as Grey states, even there,

> As a result of the scarcity of judicial declarations dealing specifically with donations, the existence of any common-law right of an individual to donate his own organs or tissue for use after his death may only be derived by analogy from a closely related situation – where a decedent has directed his manner or place of burial. Unfortunately, an examination of these cases proves similarly inconclusive.[80]

brought by the decedent's next of kin for alleged misconduct in handling the corpse and improper burial by an undertaker, who had followed the deceased's instructions.

78 For instance in *Holland* v. *Metalious* 198 A. 2d 654 (N.H. 1964) in a dispute between the executors of the deceased's will and the family. The court found in favour of the family and allowed funeral services to be performed despite the fact that the deceased had expressly requested that there be no such service. The deceased had willed her remains to a university for medical research, but the university had declined to accept it.

79 For instance, in *Yome* v. *Gorman* 242 N.Y. 395 (N.Y. Ct of Apps. 1926) where there was a difference of opinion regarding the resting place of the, already buried, deceased, the New York Court of Appeals stated that the deceased's wishes 'must be ascertained and the intensity of his feelings measured, [and] must be compared with the sentiments and wishes of wife and kin surviving'. The court stated that 'Only some rare emergency could move a court of equity to take a body from its grave in consecrated ground and put it in ground unhallowed if there was good reason to suppose that the conscience of the deceased, were he alive, would be outraged by the change': at 402–3.

80 Grey, *The Legal Enforcement of Morality*, at 120–1.

1

Why and when is a potential donor a cadaver?

'What is so intricate, so entangled as death?'
John Donne, 1628

Few other issues pertaining to transplantation have generated as many quandaries and as much attention as the 'Gordian knot' of death, whose essence is of crucial importance to the very existence and success of cadaveric transplantation programmes. Moreover, the character of applicable regulatory regimes hinges directly upon the dichotomy between cadaveric and living donation created by it. The so-called 'dead donor' rule requires that vital organs be removed only from *cadaveric* donors. Duties to respect the autonomy and to avoid maleficent treatment of the donor take on a very different hue and import in the event of the individual's death. It has been alleged that certain classes of donors have generally been located in the wrong 'camp' (for example anencephalics and non-heart-beating donors) resulting in the application of inappropriate principles for procurement.[1] Whilst the dead donor rule has itself recently become a subject of re-appraisal, debated in a following chapter, its contemporary significance is indisputable and pivotal.

There are dilemmas here attaching to both 'heart-beating' donors and, the increasingly popular, 'non-heart-beating' (asystolic) donors. The former depend upon the relatively modern notion of *brain death* as marking the end of life of the individual human being, the practical effect of which can be illustrated by comparing volumes of transplants between nations. In Japan, which until recently shied away from the notion of brain death, the mean annual volume of cadaver kidney transplants was

[1] See D. Vawters, 'Ethical Frameworks for Live and Cadaveric Organ Donation' in B. Spielman (ed.), *Organ and Tissue Donation: Ethical, Legal and Policy Issues*, Southern Illinois University Press, Carbondale, 1997, at 53.

approximately 200, contrasted with, for instance, 1,600 in the United Kingdom and 8,000 in the United States. Moreover, multi-organ transplantation, and thoracic organ transplantation in particular, is practically ruled out in its absence.[2] Whilst most nations of the world now endorse brain death as the death of the individual, some societies have been slow to accept it (for instance Denmark, Poland and Japan) and some societies still either wholly or partially reject it (for example, China, Iran, Israel and Korea). Despite what has been described as a 'remarkable consensus' having generally developed supporting brain death, Miles observes that 'It is ironic that so soon after the medical and legal legitimisation of the concept of brain death, whole-brain criteria for death seem to be disintegrating – neurologically, clinically, and socially.'[3] Whilst this is undoubtedly an overstatement, brain death indeed continues to generate significant controversy, both conceptually and pragmatically.

Paradoxically, whilst brain death has attracted criticism and scrutiny because of its supposed *departure* from traditional notions of death, non-heart-beating donor (NHBD) protocols have attracted at least as much criticism for their supposed reliance upon orthodox cardiopulmonary determinants of death. Whilst not a thesis on the meaning and determination of death in general terms, this chapter will debate the validity of brain death and cardiopulmonary standards of death due to their centrality to transplantation practices, and will additionally consider proposals to extend neurological formulations of death to the realms of *higher brain* death, because of the greater inclusiveness of certain classes of potential organ donors resulting therefrom. It then remains to consider the most appropriate form of legal regulation of these matters.

A convenient fiction?

Although in 'pre-technological' days, traditional cardiorespiratory/cardiopulmonary perceptions of death were employed, as Gervais states,

> Until we developed the power to maintain cardiac and respiratory functions mechanically, there was really no need to scrutinise the

2 For instance, up until 1990, when Denmark passed legislation adopting brain death, many patients were sent abroad to receive heart and lung transplants.

3 S. Miles, 'Death in a Technological and Pluralistic Culture' in S. Youngner, R. Arnold and R. Schapiro (eds.), *The Definition of Death: Contemporary Controversies*, Johns Hopkins University Press, Baltimore, 1999, 310.

> conceptual underpinnings of our decision to declare a person dead when his heart and lungs ceased functioning: heart and lung failure brought on the failure of all the other major organ systems almost immediately. Hence the whole individual appeared to die at once.[4]

Thus, different notions of death tended to coalesce. But whilst kidneys and corneas might still be viable for transplantation for a short time after circulation had ceased, organs such as hearts and lungs, more vulnerable to hypoxia, essentially required a still-beating heart at explantation in order to function properly post-transplant. However, the application of the technology to facilitate such a (heart-beating) state then begged the question about the continued legal status of the individual whose respiration and circulation had been maintained. Indeed, because of such uncertainty, until well into the latter half of the twentieth century the integrity of the dead body was typically preserved until the point in time when *all* critical functions of the body had necessarily ceased.[5] The Australian Law Reform Commission (ALRC) once commented that 'the practice of transplantation forces the close attention of the community to the subject of death and in many cases greater accuracy and care to be brought to bear in determining that death has occurred'.[6] Evans, however, notes that 'Of the [other] kinds of death-behaviour, there is only one where haste [of this kind] is usual – for the successful procurement of transplantable organs, time is of the essence.'[7] Moreover, it is alleged by some that the global movement towards endorsement of brain death has been entirely driven, even manipulated, by the necessities of transplantation. Indeed, Evans and Hill have accused that 'There is, of course, no need for a so-called "brain death" criterion of death except for the purposes of organ transplantation, specifically the provision of hearts, livers and lungs.'[8] Singer has pronounced brain death a 'convenient

[4] See K. Gervais, *Redefining Death*, Yale University Press, New Haven, 1986, at 2.

[5] The practices of anatomists and medical schools with regard to cadavers typically require no 'living' tissue and thus no urgency as regards the timing of death.

[6] Australian Law Reform Commission, *Human Tissue Transplants*, Report No. 7, Canberra, 1977, para. 127, at 59.

[7] M. Evans, 'Against Brain-stem Death' in R. Gillon (ed.), *Principles of Health Care Ethics*, John Wiley, Chichester, 1994, 1041 at 1044.

[8] See D. Evans and D. Hill, 'The Brain Stems of Organ Donors are Not Dead' (1989) (August) *Catholic Medical Quarterly* 113 at 114. Seifert states even more trenchantly that 'The only cogent pragmatic motive for introducing the criterion of brain death is its purpose of allowing organ-transplantations without the need to commit active euthanasia or manslaughter by killing persons who are still alive': see J. Seifert, 'Is "Brain Death" Actually Death?' (1993) 76 *Monist* 175 at 178.

fiction'[9] and Taylor describes it as a 'social construct' created for wholly utilitarian (that is transplantation) purposes.[10] These are potent charges requiring that any definition of death operative in this sphere be independently supportable on sound ethical and public policy grounds. Expediency cannot be a total justification in itself, but as Birnbacher observes, 'the practical usefulness of a criterion is no reason to doubt its adequacy'.[11]

The evolution of brain death

In the fifties, when transplantation considerations were not directly implicated,[12] the (ventilator) technology was already developing to allow patients whose brains were totally dead[13] to have their breathing and heartbeat maintained for a substantial period of time, coinciding with a rapid increase in acquired knowledge of the physiology of the brain,[14] out of which the notion of brain death evolved.[15] Clinicians began at this time to doubt the traditional criteria for establishing death and the value of ventilating all such patients to asystole (cardiac standstill). Acceptance of the clinical notion of brain death did not necessarily imply any normative proposition as to whether an *individual* whose brain had died was dead however.[16] This further deductive step was not long in being forthcoming

[9] P. Singer, *Rethinking Life and Death*, Oxford University Press, Oxford, 1994, at 35.

[10] R. Taylor, 'Reexamining the Definition and Criteria of Death' (1997) 17(3) *Seminars in Neurology* 265.

[11] D. Birnbacher, 'Philosophical Arguments for Accepting the Brain Death Criterion' in G. Collins, J. Dubernard, W. Land and G. Persijn (eds.), *Procurement, Preservation and Allocation of Vascularized Organs*, Kluwer, Dordrecht, 1997, 339 at 341.

[12] Jennett notes that a further ten years were to elapse from the identification of the concept of 'coma dépassé' before the UK transplant rate exceeded even one per week: B. Jennett, 'Brain Death' (1981) 53 *British Journal of Anaesthesiology* 1111.

[13] As autopsy frequently undeniably substantiated.

[14] In 1959, a group of neurophysiologists and neurosurgeons in Lyons first described a condition termed 'death of the central nervous system': see M. Jouvet, 'Diagnostic electro-souscorticographique de la mort du système nerveux central au cours de certains comas' (1959) II *Electroencephalography and Clinical Neurophysiology* 805.

[15] Two Parisian neurologists dubbed the condition 'coma dépassé' (beyond coma) later that same year: see P. Mollaret and M. Goulon, 'Le coma dépassé (mémoire préliminaire)' (1959) 101 *Review of Neurology* 3.

[16] The Danish Council of Ethics developed a perspective of a 'death process' which began when, *inter alia*, the brain had died, but which only ended when all three functions, circulatory, respiratory and brain, had all definitely ceased. However, in order not to impede organ transplantation, it would nevertheless be permissible to prolong the death process to that end and to remove organs for transplantation after brain death had occurred: see Danish Council of Ethics Report, *The Criteria of Death*, Copenhagen, December 1988.

though. In 1968, an Ad Hoc Committee of the Harvard Medical School Report argued, although without any supporting rationale, that an individual whose brain had irreversibly ceased to function should be considered dead.[17] A brain death formulation was also adopted in August of the same year by the World Medical Association as part of the Declaration of Sydney.[18] In the UK in January 1976, the Conference of Medical Royal Colleges published a memorandum on 'The Diagnosis of Brain Death', identifying with the concept of brain death, with the ostensible principal purpose of establishing criteria justifying the removal of a patient from a ventilator.[19] A further memorandum from the Medical Royal Colleges in January 1979 took the further step of equating the death of the brain with the death of the individual.[20] Evans and Hill have argued that transplantation concerns were the *sole* reason for the attempt by the Medical Royal Colleges in Britain to enforce acceptance of its version of brain death, and state: 'Contrary to what some have claimed, it was never necessary to certify death prior to discontinuing futile and unkind life-support measures.'[21] Although neither memorandum specifically alluded to transplantation, these perceptions were fostered when the memoranda were incorporated into *Cadaveric Organs for Transplantation (A Code of Practice including the Diagnosis of Brain Death)* issued in 1983.[22] The Code of Practice issued by the Department of Health in 1998 softens this association slightly by reversing the emphasis, being entitled *A Code of Practice for the Diagnosis of Brain Stem Death: Including Guidelines for the Identification and Management of Potential Organ and Tissue*

[17] 'A Definition of Irreversible Coma', Report of the Ad Hoc Committee of the Harvard Medical School to Examine the Definition of Brain Death (1968) 205 *Journal of the American Medical Association* 337.

[18] 22nd World Medical Assembly, adopted 9 August 1968.

[19] (1976)(ii) *British Medical Journal* 1187 and (1976)(ii) *Lancet* 1069. These recommendations were very similar to the Minnesota Code for Brain Death formulated by Mohandas and Chou in 1971.

[20] Conference of Medical Royal Colleges and their Faculties in the United Kingdom, 'Memorandum on the Diagnosis of Death' (1979)(i) *British Medical Journal* 332; Conference of Medical Royal Colleges and their Faculties in the United Kingdom, 'Diagnosis of Death' (1979)(i) *Lancet* 261.

[21] Evans and Hill, 'The Brain Stems of Organ Donors are Not Dead', at 114.

[22] *Cadaveric Organs for Transplantation (A Code of Practice including the Diagnosis of Brain Death)*, Health Departments of Great Britain and Northern Ireland, 1983. Julius Korein previously accused the British Code of linking the diagnosis of brain death 'irretrievably with transplantation': see J. Korein, 'Diagnosis of Brain Death' (1980) 281 *British Medical Journal* 1424.

Donors![23] It is indeed very likely that transplantation concerns were at least in the background of the policy-makers' minds at this time, if not in the forefront. In the US, the evolution of the notion of brain death was explicitly motivated in part by transplantation considerations, although the Harvard Committee in particular attempted to play down such a connection.[24] McCullagh is nonetheless right to assert that the notion of brain death was not, in the first instance, a contrivance to facilitate the identification of subjects who would be suitable donors of transplantable organs, as considerable doubt did exist at that time as regarded the legality of such withdrawal of life-supporting measures.[25] But it was nevertheless a factor, as such legal doubt resulted in the removal of organs from brain-dead donors typically taking place only once asystole had occurred – with consequent potential organ damage.[26] This historical excursus, however, tells us little about the legitimacy of a determination of death founded upon brain death.

Concepts, standards, criteria and tests

The rationale for the adoption of (that is the concept underpinning) any particular standard(s) of death has typically remained unarticulated, but as Gervais rightly observes, 'behind the use of any criterion for declaring death there lies what I shall call a decision of significance, that is, a decision that there is a certain feature (or cluster of features) whose permanent absence constitutes the death of the person'.[27] Thus, there is an *a priori* issue as to what death *means*, posed by Veatch in terms of: 'What is so essential to our concept of human life such that when it is lost

[23] *A Code of Practice for the Diagnosis of Brain Stem Death: Including Guidelines for the Identification and Management of Potential Organ and Tissue Donors*, Department of Health, March 1998.

[24] See discussion by Singer in *Rethinking Life and Death*, at 24–7. Fost describes the Harvard Committee deliberations as 'an explicitly utilitarian exercise': see N. Fost, 'The Unimportance of Death' in Youngner *et al.*, *The Definition of Death*, 161 at 165.

[25] See P. McCullagh, *Brain Dead, Brain Absent, Brain Donors*, John Wiley & Sons, Chichester, 1993, at 8. See also J. Bleich, 'Moral Debate and Semantic Sleight of Hand' (1993) 27 *Suffolk University Law Review* 1171 at 1175.

[26] Whatever the legal doubts, as early as 1957, Pope Pius XII removed (Catholic) religious impediments to such a practice, at an international gathering of physicians, surgeons and scientists. He suggested that the soul might have left the body despite the continued functioning of certain organs.

[27] Gervais, *Redefining Death*, at 2.

we should treat the individual as dead?'[28] The expression *concept* of death is preferred here to describe this abstraction, as the alternative phrase 'definition of death' is frequently used also as a label for legislative formulations based upon a second-level enquiry as to the physiological state representing (this concept of) death.[29] This general physiological state will be designated the *standard(s)* of death here. For instance, Bernat *et al.*[30] support the permanent cessation of functioning of the entire brain as the standard of death, underpinned by a concept of death based upon the permanent cessation of the functioning of the organism as a whole. I adopt the term 'criteria' to refer to the *operational diagnostic criteria* required to be satisfied in order to ensure that the physiological standard(s) equating with death exist(s).[31] Finally, there are the actual 'tests' or procedures employed for determining that the criteria for death exist in the individual instance. This lexicography and ordering is crucial and is succinctly and elegantly summed up by Engelhardt in the statement: 'To give a coherent account of how one should determine death, one must know what it is no longer to be alive, both in terms of knowing what life is so that it can be gone, as well as where that life is necessarily embodied so that one can know what tests to cluster under what genre of general criteria.'[32] This fourfold taxonomy is preferred for its flexibility and clarity to the more straightforward threefold taxonomies employed by various commentators, which display a tendency to conflate different categories of assessment.[33] In most instances though, there is little to choose between them as where commentators innocuously use the expression 'criteria' to additionally include testing procedures for determining death. As

[28] R. Veatch, 'The Definition of Death: Ethical, Philosophical, and Policy Confusion' in N. Abrams and M. Buchner (eds.), *Medical Ethics*, MIT, Cambridge Mass., 1983, 30 at 30. Hans Jonas poses the primary question more pithily in terms of 'What counts for life?': see H. Jonas, 'Against the Stream: Comments on the Definition of Death and Redefinition of Death' in *Philosophical Essays: From Ancient Creed to Technological Man*, Prentice-Hall, Englewood Cliffs N.J., 1974, 132.

[29] For this reason, I have not simply adopted Bernat *et al.*'s threefold classification, that is 'definition', 'criteria' and 'tests' of death: see J. Bernat, C. Culver and B. Gert, 'On the Definition and Criterion of Death' (1981) 94 *Annals of Internal Medicine* 389.

[30] Although they term this the 'criterion' of death: ibid.

[31] The President's Commission referred to them as 'operational criteria': see President's Commission for the Study of Ethical Problems in Medicine, *Defining Death: A Report on the Medical, Legal and Ethical Issues in the Determination of Death*, US Government Printing Office, Washington D.C., 1981.

[32] H. Engelhardt, 'Redefining Death' in Youngner *et al.*, *The Definition of Death*, 319 at 325.

[33] The President's Commission also employed this fourfold classification in preference to the more typical scheme.

Engelhardt notes, 'Operational concerns, it should be noted, bring together both criteria for death and tests for death. Criteria for death function as chapter headings for tests, indicating what genre should be employed as dictated by a definition of death, which gives an account of what it is to be alive and to be embodied.'[34]

But is death a biological matter, a philosophical matter (that is, a 'truth' to be discovered, an *ontological* investigation into the essence of human life) or merely an issue of social engineering? This is a subject which continues to generate confusion between combatants. Lord Kilbrandon, at a symposium in the sixties, declared that 'the question of what is death . . . is a technical, professional medical matter'.[35] Indeed, historically the meaning of death was frequently left inexplicit in terms of the law, and left to the medical profession to decide. The notion of death as a biological phenomenon is still one obstinately clung to by many analysts. Taylor for instance has criticised the notion of brain death as being merely a 'legal construct' rather than, as he considers it should properly be regarded, a biological phenomenon. By contrast, the President's Commission,[36] Bernat *et al.* and Veatch all view the determination of the proper concept of death as 'primarily a philosophical task'. However, this enquiry is not susceptible to a straightforward response, and it is necessary to have regard to the taxonomy above to assist us. It hinges on whether we are considering the meaning of death itself, the physiological state manifesting it or the criteria and/or tests utilised to establish such a state.

The concept of death is clearly a primarily philosophical question. As Veatch remarks, 'No amount of neurological study could possibly determine whether those with dead brains should be considered dead people. This is a religious, philosophical, ethical, or public policy question, not one of neurological science.'[37] Singer maintains that 'If we choose to mark death at any moment before the body goes stiff and cold (or to be

34 Engelhardt, 'Redefining Death', at 327.

35 Lord Kilbrandon, 'Closing Remarks' in G. Wolstenholme and M. O'Connor (eds.), *Ethics in Medical Progress: With Special Reference to Transplantation*, CIBA Foundation Symposium, J. & A. Churchill, London, 1966, at 213.

36 See the President's Commission Report, *Defining Death*, at 55.

37 R. Veatch, 'The Conscience Clause' in Youngner *et al.*, *The Definition of Death*, 137 at 140. In similar vein, Rabbi Bleich states that 'Newly formulated criteria of death are no more and no less than determinations of who shall be accorded, or better, who shall be denied, standing as a member of the human community with its attendant rights, entitlements, and claims. Such a determination is a moral, philosophical, religious, and legal issue. Most emphatically, it is not a scientific issue': see Bleich, 'Moral Debate and Semantic Sleight of Hand', at 1175.

really on the safe side, before it begins to rot) we are making an ethical judgment.'[38] But even this assertion incorporates an *a priori* assumption that death is in reality *cellular death* not some other sort of death. Yet, as the ALRC noted, 'there is, and has always been, a great difference between the questions "Is he dead?" and "Is life extinct in every part of his body?"', that is between somatic (cellular) death and the death of the *individual.*[39] In some cultures and societies, theological perspectives dictate responses to this question. Although mainstream religious thought in the great majority of jurisdictions has not obstructed acceptance of brain death, in Japan for instance reform has only recently been forthcoming due partially to reticence rooted in Confucian ideals, and Shinto and Buddhist thought, which see death as an evolving process. In addition, many orthodox Jews, Aborigines and Native Americans place great significance upon the continued functioning of the heart even today.[40]

In 1988, the Danish Council of Ethics, in a Report on Death, drew attention to a perceived divide between 'scientific' (unseen) and 'ordinary' (seen) views of death. It stated that 'The concept of death must relate to the everyday experience', according to which 'the identity of the person relates no less to the body than to the mind', and recommended that the standard of death should be cessation of respiration and cardiac activity.[41] This raises questions as to the extent to which policies should reflect 'ordinary' emotional reactions as opposed to rational thought. Martyn Evans contends that our reactions may be morally significant, even decisive, here and states: 'I don't believe we would display, embalm, bury or cremate someone until her heart had stopped beating – because we would not until then *see her* as dead', and observes that this obstacle seems only not to apply in the sphere of transplantation.[42] It is suggested however that our intuitions should act as a 'check' on our intellectual

38 See Singer, *Rethinking Life and Death*, at 32.

39 See the Australian Law Reform Commission, *Human Tissue Transplants*, at para. 118.

40 In the 1970s, Frank Veith asserted that brain death was a concept compatible with all three major Western religions, and apart from small factions, this still holds good today: see F. Veith *et al.*, 'New Developments in the Use and Recognition of Brain Death in the United States and other Countries' (1981) 13 *Transplantation Proceedings* 689 at 691.

41 Danish Council of Ethics Report, *The Criteria of Death.*

42 Evans, 'Against Brain-stem Death', at 1044. See also M. Evans, 'A Plea for the Heart' (1990) 4 *Bioethics* 227.

inclinations, but should not be wholly controlling or sufficient moral guides, even assuming that there is a consensus here.[43]

To some extent, the concept of death to which we subscribe is a function of whether we hold a 'mentalist' or a 'physicalist' viewpoint and, to a lesser degree, 'dualist' or 'monist' views regarding the human mind. Some supporters of mentalist, personhood perspectives on the nature of human life regard the mind as being the critical entity, distinct from matter, the human body. Others take a similar view but regard the mind as either located within the body or dependent upon the body. On the other hand, those who regard the biological functioning of the body as being the primary matter of importance might also regard the mind as being distinct from the body or as a part of it. The former in either camp display a (Cartesian) dualist perspective, the latter a monist view, and we can therefore see that a mentalist or physicalist perspective does not in itself commit one to any particular standard of death. Devettere notes that even the neocortical criterion of human death is consistent with some non-dualistic conceptions of human beings which focus on the human body.[44] We can see in this discussion the process of *translation* of abstract conceptual notions into a physiological basis for empirical determination and the variety of variables which might impact on this process. Similar difficulties arise in the translation of religious doctrine or teachings in some instances. For example, Rosner illustrates how the two sides in the brain death debate in Israel under Jewish law line up in polarised fashion based upon differing interpretations of the pivotal talmudic and other classic Jewish sources as regards whether cessation of cardiac as well as respiratory activity is a prerequisite for death.[45] Thus, whilst the concept of death may be a wholly philosophical enquiry, there are biological and medical determinants to all the remaining levels of enquiry, although as

[43] Angstwurm has stated that 'it can prove difficult to understand the permanent and complete loss of brain function as a definitive sign of death. Unlike rigor mortis, livor mortis, and signs of decay and putrefaction, brain death can only be determined and distinguished from the death-like state of an intensively treated individual by means of specific tests': see H. Angstwurm, 'Brain Death' in Collins *et al.*, *Procurement, Preservation and Allocation*, 331 at 332.

[44] In particular he cites the work of Alfred North Whitehead and Maurice Merleau-Ponty: see R. Devettere, 'Neocortical Death and Human Death' (1990) 18(1–2) *Law, Medicine and Health Care* 96 at 98–100.

[45] See F. Rosner, 'The Definition of Death in Jewish Law' in Youngner *et al.*, *The Definition of Death*, at 270.

one can see from the above discussion, philosophical perspectives intrude to some degree on outcomes at nearly every stage.[46]

Process or event?

In biological terms death is a process not an event. As Miles puts it, 'Biological processes and organ systems shut down over time in individualised sequences.'[47] Indeed, even the brain itself dies in stages. But if one focuses instead on the *individual* rather than specific parts of the organism it is easier to conceive of death being an event rather than a process. Indeed, Bernat contends that 'Because all organisms must be either alive or dead, death is an inherently discontinuous and instantaneous event.'[48] However, the Danish Council of Ethics argued that whilst total destruction of brain function meant the 'death process' had *begun* and was irreversible, it did not signify that the death process was *complete*, although it might still be ethically and legally defensible to remove organs for transplantation at that point.[49] Bernat *et al.*'s convincing retort is that

> a definition of death stipulating that it occurs at a more or less definite time is preferable to a definition that makes death a process. If we regard death as a process, then either the process starts when the person is still living, which confuses the 'process of death' with the process of dying, for we all regard someone who is dying as not yet dead, or the 'process of death' starts when the person is no longer alive, which confuses death with the process of disintegration.[50]

Indeed, if the individual was not yet 'dead' when such organs were removed, he/she must presumably still have been alive and the removal

[46] Bearing in mind the differences in terminology (see note 29), Bernat *et al.* state that 'providing a definition of death is a philosophical task; the choice of criterion is primarily medical; and the choice of tests . . . is solely a medical matter': see Bernat *et al.*, 'On the Definition and Criterion of Death', at 389.

[47] Miles, 'Death in a Technological and Pluralistic Society', at 313.

[48] J. Bernat, 'A Defense of the Whole-Brain Concept of Death' (1998) 28 *Hastings Center Report* 14 at 16. Engelhardt's suggestion of the notion of different deaths for different purposes would be extremely difficult to translate into (legal) reality. See also D. Smith, 'Legal Recognition of Neocortical Death' (1986) 71 *Cornell Law Review* 879, and S. Brennan and R. Delgado, 'Death: Multiple Definitions or a Single Standard?' (1981) 54 *Southern California Law Review* 1323.

[49] B. Rix, 'Danish Ethics Council Rejects Brain Death as the Criterion of Death' (1990) 16 *Journal of Medical Ethics* 5.

[50] See Bernat *et al.*, 'On the Definition and Criterion of Death', at 389.

would thus have contravened the dead donor rule.[51] It is also necessary for legal purposes to be able to isolate a moment of death, as the person's legal status then radically alters and with it attendant rights, claims and entitlements.

Legal complications

Whilst the medical community gradually accepted the phenomenon of brain death during the sixties and early seventies, laws and policy statements at that time pretty universally omitted to engage with it, thus leaving substantial uncertainty as to the legal status of the brain-dead patient. This incertitude coincided with various pathbreaking transplantation ventures, notably the series of first heart transplants performed in the late sixties. Indeed, in the first such attempted cardiac transplant on 3 December 1967 in Cape Town, Christiaan Barnard implicitly relied on brain death in order to facilitate it.

However, whilst legislative statements on (brain) death are almost exclusively a feature of the seventies or later, the question of what constituted death arose indirectly in a smattering of early judicial decisions. These cases were often concerned with matters relating to insurance claims or the criminal liability of third party assailants. An early example of the latter, which also incidentally implicated the removal of organs for transplantation, was the British case of *R* v. *Potter* in 1963.[52] Fourteen hours after being admitted to hospital following a head injury sustained in a fight, the patient stopped breathing and was connected to an artificial respirator. Twenty-four hours later a kidney was removed (with his wife's consent) and transplanted into another man. The respirator was then disconnected and it was found that there was no spontaneous respiration or circulation. Although at the subsequent coroner's inquest it was decided that the removal of the kidney had not contributed to the death, and the assailant was committed for trial, a medical witness had testified that the man had 'virtually died' at the time when he was put on the respirator although it would be 'legally correct' to

[51] For this, logical, reason clinicians in Denmark refused to remove organs from brain-dead, but not actually 'dead', individuals, for fear of legal repercussions, despite the expressly stated permissibility of so doing: see B. Rix, 'Brain Death, Ethics, and Politics in Denmark' in Youngner *et al.*, *The Definition of Death*, 227 at 233.

[52] *The Times*, 26 July 1963; (1963) 31 *Medical Legal Journal* 195.

say that death did not occur until twenty-four hours later, when breathing and heartbeat had ceased, thus suggesting he was not dead when the removal occurred. At the eventual trial the accused was found guilty only of common assault, although charged with manslaughter, suggesting that the patient was indeed not legally dead until the respirator was removed, so that the removal of the kidney must presumably have been a criminal battery. Amongst other things, this case illustrates the ambivalence and uncertainty of judicial decision-making on this issue at that time and in general.[53]

The inherent dangers for surgeons at this time were even more vividly illustrated by the *Wada* case in Japan in 1968. A man was pulled from a frozen lake unconscious and declared dead on the basis of brain death criteria despite the fact that no law or policy then sanctioned the determination of death on brain-related criteria. The following day his heart was transplanted by Dr Wada into an eighteen-year-old with chronic heart disease who survived for eighty-three days.[54] Dr Wada was charged with murder, although the prosecution was ultimately aborted due to lack of material evidence. This was the only heart transplant performed in Japan and undoubtedly impeded acceptance of brain death by Japanese society.[55] In the United States though, such decisions were more liberal and less equivocal from the outset. In *Tucker* v. *Lower*[56] in 1972, the judge directed a jury in Virginia that they could either apply the traditional cardiorespiratory standard of death *or* the brain death standard

[53] Quite a diversity of judicial response resulted however. In the United States, in *Commonwealth* v. *Golston* 366 N.E. 2d 744 (Mass. 1977), a person sustained brain death following an assault. The judge, relying on a brain-death standard, decided that the discontinuance of treatment by doctors following such a diagnosis did not break the chain of causation between the original assault and the victim's death. In Scotland, in the High Court of Justice, by contrast, in a case decided on similar facts at around the same time, the court declined to adopt a brain-stem standard of death, and held that the person died only after the artificial ventilation was terminated, in *Finlayson* v. *H.M. Advocate* [1978] SLT (Notes) 60. In *R* v. *Malcharek; R* v. *Steel* [1981] 1 WLR 691 (CA) the English court adopted the same view as in *Golston* as regarded causation, but did not conclude as regarded any legal standard(s) of death. See also *R* v. *Kitching and Adams* [1976] 6 WWR 697 (Manitoba) and *R* v. *Kinash* [1982] Qld R 648 (Qld).

[54] There was significant doubt whether the patient even really needed a transplant: see Provisional Commission for the Study on Brain Death and Organ Transplantation, *Important Considerations with Respect to Brain Death and Organ Transplants*, Japan, 1992.

[55] See K. Hoshino, 'Legal Status of Brain Death in Japan' (1993) 7 *Bioethics* 234, and K. Bai, 'The Definition of Death: The Japanese Attitude and Experience' (1990) 22 *Transplantation Proceedings* 991.

[56] VA No. 2831, May 1972. Brain death was first accepted judicially in the US in *United Trust Co.* v. *Pyke* 427 P. 2d 67 (Cal. 1967).

in the context of a case where a person's heart was removed for transplantation purposes immediately after ventilation was stopped, the patient having been assaulted. The doctors were found not to be liable for causing the death. Moreover, in a criminal context in California, in *People v. Lyons*,[57] it was held that a shooting victim was legally dead prior to being used as a transplant donor, despite the continuance of artificial respiration. In spite of the general legal void, clinicians therefore repeatedly took matters into their own hands, forcing the hand of policy-makers. As in Japan, this sometimes backfired, but in most instances it prompted positive action to facilitate transplantation based on brain death and a protective framework for clinicians.[58] Of course, in the US the medical profession had embraced the notion of brain death very early on by contrast with many other nations, but even there, as Capron notes, the greatest pressure for legislation came from physicians concerned about the potential civil or criminal ramifications of cadaveric organ donation practices.[59]

Legislative responses

In many jurisdictions, the relevant transplant legislation merely refers to the definition of death established through other legal sources. For instance, the UK Human Tissue Act 1961 merely states that a registered medical practitioner removing parts of a body must have satisfied himself by personal examination of the body that 'life is extinct' (in addition to the physician who certified the death initially).[60] When life is 'extinct' cannot be determined from the statute itself and, due to the absence of a statutory definition elsewhere, case law and medical guidelines would need to be turned to for assistance. The Uniform Anatomical Gift Act in the United States refers to a 'determination of death' and to the 'decedent',

[57] Sup. Ct No. 56072, Alameda Co. (Cal. 1974).

[58] Contrast the extrajudicial remark made by the then Dame Elizabeth Butler-Sloss that 'The idea that either Parliament or indeed lawyers should be allowed to get their hands on this particular delicate matter fills me with horror, as one of those who might end up trying it'! See C. Pallis, 'Brain Stem Death: The Evolution of a Concept' (1987) 55 *Medico-Legal Journal* 84 at 106 (Discussion).

[59] A. Capron, 'The Bifurcated Legal Standard for Determining Death: Does it Work?' in Youngner *et al.*, *The Definition of Death*, 117 at 119. He notes that thirty-six US jurisdictions have today adopted the Uniform Determination of Death Act incorporating dual standards of death, including the brain-death standard.

[60] In section 4.

but the drafters properly decided not to include any further definition in that (model) law by way of further elaboration.[61] Virtually all US states however have independent statutes establishing standards of death. Other jurisdictions by contrast have incorporated the concept of brain death into their transplant statutes rather than including it in a discrete piece of legislation. In fact, three US state laws passed in the seventies actually had a specific standard of death which applied *only* in the context of organ transplantation, that is West Virginia (1975), Illinois (1975)[62] and Connecticut (1979). Another example is the 1979 Spanish transplant Law which stipulates[63] that organs may be removed from deceased persons 'After death has been determined on the basis of irreversible brain damage that is incompatible with life'.[64] Likewise, the 1996 Romanian transplant statute states that 'Harvesting of tissue and organs from dead persons is allowed only if the brain death has been medically confirmed',[65] and is supplemented in an Annex by specific criteria for the diagnosis and confirmation of brain death.[66] The danger is that the perception will be generated that organ donors are to be handled in different fashion to other patients. Even aspects of testing can be productive of such an impression. In 1984 a Report produced by the Swedish Government endorsed destruction of the brain as the standard of death. This was to be ascertained by clinical examination alone unless organ transplantation was anticipated, in which case radiological examination of blood flow cessation was required. McCullagh rightly observes that this suggests that one needs to be more certain about death in some (that is transplant) settings than others.[67]

[61] See Comment to section 1. It was supposed that implicit reference was made to the definition contained in the Uniform Determination of Death Act anyhow.

[62] Illinois still has the American Bar Association model brain-death law in effect in its version of the Uniform Anatomical Gift Act.

[63] Spanish Law of 27 October 1979 on the Removal and Transplantation of Organs, Article 5(1).

[64] Crown Decree of 22 February 1980, Article 10 implementing the above Law states that 'Organs which are required to be viable for transplantation purposes may be removed from the cadaver of the deceased person only following determination of brain death, based on simultaneous observation for at least 30 minutes and persistence for six hours after onset of coma of the following signs: (1) absence of cerebral response, with absolute loss of consciousness; (2) absence of spontaneous respiration; (3) absence of brain reflexes, with muscular hypotonia and mydriasis; and (4) a "flat" electroencephalogram, indicating lack of bioelectrical activity in the brain.'

[65] Law Regarding the Harvesting and the Transplantation of Human Tissues and Organs, Article 6(1).

[66] Article 7(1).

[67] McCullagh, *Brain Dead, Brain Absent, Brain Donors*, at 25.

A high percentage of jurisdictions now have legislation incorporating brain death, although this has only occurred recently in one or two, for example Denmark[68] in 1990 and Japan in 1997.[69] In 1994, Pallis and Harley listed twenty-eight countries[70] and most US states[71] as having legislation explicitly recognising brain death as the death of the individual.[72] The first legislative initiatives were in Italy in 1967, in the state of Kansas in 1970 and in Finland in 1971. These statutory provisions are either unitary brain death statutes or contain bifurcated, alternative standards of death, as was the case under the early Kansas statute.[73] The US Uniform Determination of Death Act (UDDA)[74] states that 'An individual who has sustained either [1] irreversible cessation of circulatory and respiratory functions, or [2] irreversible cessation of all functions of the entire brain, including the brain stem, is dead. A determination of death must be made in accordance with accepted medical standards.'[75] Bernat *et al.* have criticised the UDDA for creating two separate standards of death rather than two sets of criteria supporting one unitary standard.[76] This issue of sole versus dual standards of death is a constantly recurring one. Transplant protocols and legislative provisions display a tendency to conflate the distinctions between different levels of enquiry, and perpetuate ambiguities. Problems arise in the context of both heart-beating and

[68] Law of 13 June 1990.

[69] See E. Feldman, 'Culture, Conflict and Cost: Perspectives on Brain Death in Japan' (1994) 10(3) *International Journal of Technology Assessment in Health Care* 447. Up until relatively recently, the concept was not accepted in Latvia either.

[70] See C. Pallis and D. Harley, *ABC of Brain-stem Death*, 2nd edn, BMJ Publishing Group, London, 1995, at 40–3. Germany, India and Japan should now be added to that list.

[71] All US states now recognise brain death. Twelve states had already done so by 1977 and twenty-five had done so by 1981: see D. Jones, 'Retrospective on the Future: Brain Death and Evolving Legal Regimes for Tissue Replacement Technology' (1992–3) 38 *McGill Law Journal* 394.

[72] See C. Pallis, *ABC of Brain Stem Death*, BMJ Publications, London, 1983, at 26–7. See also A. Walker, *Cerebral Death*, 2nd edn, Urban & Schwartzenberg, Baltimore, 1981.

[73] Kan. Stat. Ann. @77–202.

[74] It superseded the Uniform Determination of Death Act 1978. This 1980 model law is similar to that proposed by the Law Reform Commission of Australia: see *Human Tissue Transplants*. The omitted reference to cessation of spontaneous respiratory function is relatively insignificant in view of the fact that such cessation usually precedes circulatory failure.

[75] This at least ameliorated the position whereby there were seven different death formulations across the country, so that one could be actually 'raised from the dead' in driving over a pertinent state line in order to reach the nearest hospital! The Law resembles the Kansas statute but contains no reference to mechanical means of support or transplantation.

[76] Although rather inexplicably Bernat himself described this as a 'theoretical quibble'! See J. Bernat, 'A Defense of the Whole-Brain Concept of Death' (1998) 28 *Hastings Center Report* 14 at 21.

non-heart-beating donors. Typically, doubts are generated by the adoption of the irreversible cessation of cardiopulmonary function as a relevant feature in the determination of death. Judicial decisions can however create the same, if not greater, ambivalence and doubt, as British case law illustrates.

In three recent cases, none of which were cases involving transplantation, the courts in England and Wales have unequivocally declared that a brain-stem-dead patient is dead for legal as well as medical purposes. In *Mail Newspapers* v. *Express Newspapers*[77] and *Re A (A Minor)*[78] the High Court held simply that the brain-stem-dead patients concerned were dead despite the fact that the patients were on ventilatory support at the relevant time.[79] In *Airedale NHS Trust* v. *Bland*[80] by comparison, the House of Lords decided that Tony Bland, who was *not* ventilator dependent, was *not* dead – as his brain stem was still functioning – despite his permanent vegetative state (PVS) condition. Their Lordships however made a number of broad remarks concerning legal and medical definitions of death. Although Lord Keith explicitly stated that 'In the eyes of the medical world and of the law a person is not clinically dead so long as the brain stem retains its function'[81] (a view of clinical perceptions not borne out by many of the NHBD protocols discussed below!), this was not a central facet of the decision and thus amounted to no more than an *obiter dictum*. Tony Bland could not, in the circumstances of that case, have been adjudged dead according to traditional criteria, as his heartbeat and respiration continued to function spontaneously. This ambiguity was not resolved, indeed it was seemingly compounded, by the initial UK Code of Practice issued in 1983 which stated that 'There is no legal definition of death. Death has traditionally been diagnosed by the irreversible cessation of respiration and heart-beat. This Working Party accepts the view held by the Conference of Royal Colleges that death can *also* be diagnosed by

77 [1987] Fleet Street Reports 90.

78 [1992] 3 Medical Law Reports 303.

79 It was fairly recently established as constituting death in Northern Ireland, by the High Court of Justice in *Re T.C. (A Minor)* [1994] 2 *Medical Law Review* 376, so that it was permissible to detach the newborn child from the ventilator.

80 [1993] 1 All ER 821 (HL).

81 [1993] 1 All ER 821 at 859C. See also the remarks made by Lord Goff at 865F. Lord Browne-Wilkinson gave an equally clear vision of death in medicine, stating: 'In medicine, the cessation of breathing or of heartbeat is no longer death . . . This has led the medical profession to redefine death in terms of brain-stem death, i.e. the death of that part of the brain without which the body cannot function at all without assistance': at 878C–E.

the irreversible cessation of brain-stem function – "brain death"' (my emphasis).[82] This suggests *alternative* standards of death. The 1998 Code, on the other hand, states that 'brain stem death equates with the death of the individual'.[83] Thus, although the common law in Britain would appear to favour a unitary standard of (brain) death, the status of persons sustaining irreversible cardiopulmonary failure is still uncertain. The NHBD protocols discussed below drive a wedge between these two approaches and illustrate that it is far from a purely 'academic' matter.

A conservative revision?

It may be argued that the traditional cardiorespiratory standard of death was largely self-serving based on the irreversible loss of flow of essential body fluids, and not rooted in any underpinning *concept* of death that such loss represented. However, many have argued that we had always, maybe only subconsciously and implicitly, alluded to a concept of death based on the loss of functioning of the brain. Birnbacher asserts that 'That is why accepting the brain death criterion does not mean "redefining" death but only recognising one further criterion for the same fact that is traditionally indicated by the criteria of irreversible heart and respiration failure.'[84] As the President's Commission put it, 'breathing and heartbeat are not life itself. They are simply used as signs – as one window for viewing a deeper and more complex reality: a triangle of interrelated systems with the brain at its apex.'[85] Indeed, even in Japan the traditional criteria were based on not just these two but *three* 'symptoms' and included also the dilation of the pupils, indicating that we were always essentially searching for windows into the mind/brain/soul.[86] McCullagh on the other hand has remarked: 'I am not convinced that cessation of cardiac function, for example, has been traditionally regarded as signifying death because of its consequences for brain function, rather than on account of its intrinsic importance.'[87] There is some force in this, notably

[82] Code of Practice, *Cadaveric Organs for Transplantation*, at para. 28.

[83] Code of Practice, *Diagnosis of Brain Stem Death*, at 4.

[84] Birnbacher, 'Philosophical Arguments', at 341.

[85] President's Commission Report, *Defining Death*, Chapter 3, at 33.

[86] Observing dilation of the pupils would seem to have been the *practice* everywhere (that is absence of pupillary light response), although not accorded a precise status in official statements: see Bernat *et al.*, 'On the Definition and Criterion of Death', at 392.

[87] McCullagh, *Brain Dead, Brain Absent, Brain Donors*, at 20.

in so far as religious perceptions of death typically focus upon the separation of the soul from the body, with differences of view as to where the locus of the soul can be found. In orthodox Jewish thought, for instance, reference is made to Genesis,[88] where it is written: 'In whose nostrils was the breath of the spirit of life'.

Cold Lazarus

The traditional cardiorespiratory *standard* cannot, it seems, continue to be supported though, except based upon certain religious beliefs where arational rather than rational factors predispose one to conclusions. However, irreversible cardiopulmonary cessation should rightly continue to be supported as a proper *criterion* for the determination that the brain death standard has been satisfied. However, as we have seen, some commentators regard death in purely cellular terms as a wholly biological phenomenon. Taylor for instance argues that death occurs at the point when the overall process of bodily disintegration begins, which he takes to be the point at which the cessation of the circulation of vital fluids occurs. Veatch counters though that if the critical function here is the circulation of fluids, this is not only simplistic but *biologically reductionist* and makes no distinction between the human and the human body. He adds: 'It can at least be said for the defenders of the idea that death occurs when the soul departs from the body, that they recognised that a human is more than his body and some of its lesser functions.'[89] The isolated functioning of individual parts of the human body does not signify life in the 'individual' as opposed to life in that individual part. As Birnbacher observes, 'The physical aspect of death is the disintegration of the *organism* rather than the cessation of all life and growth processes in its parts and subsystems' (my emphasis).[90]

Commentators such as Bernat and Lamb contend that brain death is the appropriate standard of death because individuals die when they cease to be both conscious and working as an integrated functioning unit as a whole.[91] The President's Commission contended that 'what is missing in the dead is a cluster of attributes, all of which form part of an

[88] Chapter 7, verse 22.
[89] Veatch, 'The Definition of Death', at 32.
[90] Birnbacher, 'Philosophical Arguments', at 341.
[91] D. Lamb, *Organ Transplants and Ethics*, Routledge, London, 1990, at 36–7.

organism's responsiveness to its internal and external environment', that is either the triangular organ functions of the body (lungs, heart and brain) have ceased to work as a functional integrated unit, or the brain, as the primary organ of the body, has ceased to be able to regulate the functioning of the body.[92] In Britain, the Royal College of Physicians (RCP) recently advanced a definition of death based upon 'The irreversible loss of the capacity for consciousness combined with irreversible loss of the capacity to breathe'.[93] Pallis and Harley proffer the same view.[94] These formulations concededly amount typically to no more than an *ex post facto* rationalisation of the prior adoption in practice of brain death. This is so as regards the RCP in Britain, in much the same way that Bernat *et al.*'s formulation rationalised the whole-brain formulation of death developed by the Harvard Committee in the US. In Britain they have underpinned a brain-*stem* death standard and elsewhere a *whole*-brain death standard.

Brain death therefore ordinarily rests on two separate but connected justifications, that is loss of mental life (cognitive capacity/awareness) *and* loss of biological functioning. Birnbacher comments that

> The human individual is not only body, but a unity of both physical and mental aspects. To be dead or living is not a property of the human body but of the full human individual. It is the human individual as a complex whole that is born, grows old, and finally dies . . . Life and death are, accordingly, distinguished by the functioning and non-functioning of two systems: of consciousness and of the physical organism.[95]

Thus, the notion of brain death does not entirely depend upon physicalism or a mind/body duality. Where higher brain activity controlling consciousness continued to function but the body had otherwise ceased

92 President's Commission Report, *Defining Death*, at 36. Engelhardt states though that 'This has been the difficulty with the strategic ambiguity built into the understanding of the meaning of death forwarded by the President's Commission, which incorporated both a "primary organ view – [which] would be satisfied with a statute that contained only a single standard – the irreversible cessation of all functions of the entire brain" and an "integrated functions view [that] would lead one to a definition of death recognising that collapse of the organism as a whole can be diagnosed through the loss of brain functions as well as through loss of cardiopulmonary functions" ': see Engelhardt, 'Redefining Death', at 325.

93 Review by a Working Group convened by the Royal College of Physicians, 'Criteria for the Diagnosis of Brain Stem Death' (1995) 29(5) *Journal of the Royal College of Physicians of London* 381.

94 Pallis and Harley, *ABC of Brain-stem Death*, at 3.

95 Birnbacher, 'Philosophical Arguments', at 340.

to, death would not have occurred, and similarly vice versa.[96] Skegg properly suggests that 'If the head of a human being who had been born alive was maintained in this state, and still had cognitive function, the human being should certainly not be regarded as dead for legal purposes.'[97]

Psychological decapitation

Evans finds the ignoring of the still spontaneously functioning heart puzzling though.[98] McCullagh argues that support for brain death is often based upon the widely held view that functions such as circulation will inevitably cease imminently thereafter.[99] Indeed, the 1998 UK Code of Practice on Brain Stem Death states that 'Even if ventilation is continued both adults and children will suffer cessation of heart beat within a few days, very occasionally a few weeks, of the diagnosis of brain stem death.'[100] However, even if this is true (and it is seemingly not, as some studies show that the bodily functions of brain-dead patients can be maintained for periods as long as 201 days),[101] it is Evans and McCullagh's contention that we are treating dying patients as if they were already dead, and thereby confusing a prognosis with a diagnosis. But in so far as the heart and circulation are being supported by artificial respiratory measures, the circulation in the brain-dead patient is not really sponta-

[96] Birnbacher states: 'Even the irreversible loss of the capacity (possessed by the brain) to integrate the various bodily functions into the unity of the organism would not be sufficient to call a man dead if the process of consciousness continued, for example, if (contrary to fact) consciousness depended on the activity of the heart. Even in this hypothetical case only one of the two necessary conditions of death would have been fulfilled': ibid., at 341.

[97] P. Skegg, *Law, Ethics and Medicine*, Clarendon Press, Oxford, 1988, at 207 n. 98. So far it has not been possible to connect nerves and other tissues to a 'new body', but this may soon be feasible according to the pioneer in the field, Dr Joseph White. Heads have in fact been removed from dogs and kept functioning for varying periods of time. This subject raises issues of personal identity. Is the 'new' body the individual or the 'new' head? Presumably it is the latter, and that is why such procedures would properly be seen as 'whole body transplants' not 'brain' transplants, for example in quadriplegic patients. See G. Northoff, 'Do Brain Tissue Transplants Alter Personal Identity? Inadequacies of Some "Standard" Arguments' (1997) 22 *Journal of Medical Ethics* 174.

[98] See Evans, 'Against Brain-stem Death', at 1046. He queries why the capacity for spontaneous respiration is such an important contraindication to death, when the logical corollary of brain death is that one should have no objection to cremating a beating-heart 'cadaver'.

[99] McCullagh, *Brain Dead, Brain Absent, Brain Donors*, at 14. The causes of acute cardiac failure essentially lie in the heart itself, although the brain stem retains some large degree of control over blood pressure.

[100] Para. 3.4.

[101] See Singer, *Rethinking Life and Death*, at 3.

neously functioning at all, being wholly dependent on artificially supported respiratory function. The Australian Law Reform Commission observed that 'It is scientifically possible, after the guillotine has beheaded a man, to keep the heart and lungs going for days. Nobody, in such a case, could claim that the victim was alive, or not dead.'[102] Many in fact equate brain death with *psychological decapitation*, indeed it is on this basis that whole-brain death is supported, when it is, in Jewish circles.

Higher brain death

Certain commentators maintain that it is not the brain's role as the facilitator of biological functioning which underpins the notion of brain death but rather its association with consciousness and personality. Veatch asserts that the integrated functioning perspective on brain death also endorses a biologically reductionist view of life and death, whereas notions of higher brain death instead focus on capacities for consciousness, social interaction, etc.[103] There are consistent attempts by supporters such as Veatch, Harris and Singer to promote a higher brain oriented notion of death,[104] which generally emphasise the death of the *person* rather than the death of the organism. Such a development would potentially facilitate transplantation. In respect of adults the spotlight has tended to fall on individuals in a permanent vegetative state,[105] and in respect of minors upon anencephalic newborns, primarily because of the particular shortage of small infant donor organs for transplant.[106] Up to

102 ALRC, *Human Tissue Transplants*, at para. 117.

103 Veatch, 'The Definition of Death', at 34. Cranford and Smith, for instance, maintain that consciousness is the most important moral standard for human personhood: see R. Cranford and D. Smith, 'Consciousness: The Most Critical Moral (Constitutional) Standard for Human Personhood' (1987) 13 *American Journal of Law and Medicine* 233.

104 Such proposals have not been entirely confined to philosophical circles though. In 1975, Sir Michael Woodruff, in a Report of the British Transplantation Society, endorsed the notion of cerebral death as a standard of death, as a means of increasing the supply of transplantable organs: see L. Brent, 'The Shortage of Organs for Clinical Transplantation: Document for Discussion' (1975) (i) *British Medical Journal* 251.

105 PVS patients have a clinical condition resulting in complete unawareness of the self and their environment, accompanied by sleep/wake cycles with either complete or partial preservation of hypothalamic and brain-stem autonomic functions. The vegetative state may be either transient or permanent and can result from either traumatic injuries to the brain (for example cardiac arrest, suffocation, near drowning), progressive degenerative or metabolic neurologic diseases or from developmental malformations of the nervous system.

106 See W. Holzgreve *et al.*, 'Kidney Transplantation from Anencephalic Donors' (1987) 316 *New England Journal of Medicine* 1069.

1990, forty-one anencephalics had been used as a source of organs for transplant purposes worldwide.[107]

Whilst PVS patients are not comatose, they irretrievably and entirely lack consciousness and awareness, although they may survive, with nutritional and hydrational assistance, for very many years. Anencephalic newborns[108] are born with an absence (either total or substantial) of skull, scalp and forebrain (cerebral hemispheres) due to a congenital disorder.[109] It is an invariably fatal condition, usually within seventy-two hours of birth.[110] That such different clinical conditions are spoken about in similar terms is unsurprising. An American Multi-Society Task Force on PVS recently stated that PVS and anencephaly are two of the four major forms of *permanent unconsciousness*. Because of the relative state of preservation of the brain stem (and maybe certain hypothalamic functions), many functions are typically retained, such as the capacity for spontaneous respiration[111] and cardiovascular function, but such individuals lack consciousness, experience and the ability to communicate. The advantages in terms of transplantation of viewing such classes of individuals as being (already) dead are self-evident. There would be no need to provide artificial ventilation in order to maintain organ viability as, although dead, such persons would maintain spontaneous respiration

[107] See the US Medical Task Force on Anencephaly, 'The Infant with Anencephaly' (1990) 322 *New England Journal of Medicine* 669 at 673. See also R. Cranford, 'Anencephalic Infants as Organ Donors' (1992) 24 *Transplantation Proceedings* 2218. Anencephalic organ recovery programmes have been established at one time or another in Belgium, Canada, Germany, Japan, the Netherlands, the UK and the USA.

[108] The term 'anencephaly' literally means 'no brain' and is therefore a misnomer. Friedman describes it as a 'lethal congenital malformation in which the cerebrum (often called the forebrain or "higher brain") and the cerebellum are absent, while the midbrain and the pons (which comprise the brain-stem or "lower brain") are usually present': see J. Friedman, 'Taking the Camel by the Nose: The Anencephalic as a Source for Pediatric Organ Transplants' (1990) 90 *Columbia Law Review* 917 at 921 n. 19.

[109] Alan Shewmon notes that no operational definition of anencephaly has been agreed, because of the absence of clear uniqueness of the condition as a form of congenital brain malformation in all cases: see A. Shewmon, 'Anencephaly: Selected Medical Aspects' (1988) 18 *Hastings Center Reports* 11.

[110] Eighty per cent die in this period and, apart from in exceptional instances, the remainder die within the first two weeks.

[111] See Multi-Society Task Force on PVS, 'Medical Aspects of the Persistent Vegetative State' (1994) 330 *New England Journal of Medicine* 1499 (Part 1) and 1572 (Part 2). When Karen Quinlan, who was diagnosed as being PVS, was disconnected from the respirator in the expectation that this would end her life, she unexpectedly breathed spontaneously and survived for many more years.

and circulation, and organs could be removed at any time.[112] However, no jurisdiction has yet adopted a higher brain definition of death, although in 1986 in California Senator Milton Marks proposed an amendment to the legislation which stated that 'An individual born with the condition of anencephaly is dead.'[113] Such individuals are clearly not dead according to generally prevailing standards, due to the presence of lower brain functioning. In *Re TACP*,[114] the Supreme Court of Florida declined to accede to the request of the parents that an 'extended' common law concept of death be elucidated, for the purpose of allowing an anencephalic child to become an organ donor. It is submitted that the court was right to be so reticent. Even leaving aside the difficulties inherent in accurately diagnosing a '*permanent* vegetative state' or 'anencephaly',[115] there are substantial obstacles in the way of accepting a revised formulation of death based on loss of higher brain functions, discussed further below. Thus, we should reject the view that anencephalic infants should be subject to less exacting criteria for determining death (and thus become eligible as organ donors) than other living human beings.[116]

With regard to anencephalics in particular, some allege that such beings are not even 'live born' in law in the first place. For instance, Professor Fritz Beller, who carried out kidney transplants in 1987 from anencephalics to both children and adults at the University Hospital Münster, is quoted as saying: 'The anencephalic child is being developed, not born, for he does not live.'[117] They are sometimes described as 'brain absent'. However, the capacity to breathe and to maintain an independent existence for whatever length of time would militate against such a view. Moreover, although historically the common law recognised a category of 'non-human beings' who would not be 'reasonable creatures in being' for

112 It is the view of the British Medical Association that such individuals should not currently be considered as potential organ donors: see *BMA Guidelines on Treatment Decisions for Patients in Persistent Vegetative State*, BMA, London, 1994, at 4.

113 Cal. S. 2018 (1986) to amend sections 7180–3 of the California Health and Safety Code.

114 609 So. 2d 588 (Fla. 1992).

115 Recovery after a prolonged period in a vegetative state is by no means uncommon, although the length of time in such a state is a strong indication as to likely outcome: see K. Andrews, 'Recovery of Patients after Four Months or More in the Persistent Vegetative State' (1993) 306 *British Medical Journal* 1597.

116 See A. Caplan, 'Ethical Issues in the Use of Anencephalic Infants as a Source of Organs and Tissues for Transplantation' (1988) 20(Supp. 5) *Transplantation Proceedings* 42.

117 See Seifert, 'Is "Brain Death" Actually Death?', at 175. It appears that, at the time, such anencephalics were not viewed as having been 'born alive' anyhow in law, in the Federal Republic of Germany.

the purposes of the law of homicide, this ('monstrous beings') argument is no longer tenable today.[118] Thus, they would currently be viewed as born alive, probably in all jurisdictions. The only judicial decision to consider the issue confirms this analysis. In *Re TACP*,[119] the anencephalic who in fact was still breathing nine days after birth was held to be 'alive' according to conventional standards in the state of Florida. The dead donor rule cannot therefore be evaded so easily, and the 'inapplicability' argument fails.[120] The alleged parallelism often advocated between 'brain death' and 'brain birth' fails to appreciate that just as brain stem function is enough to avoid a determination of death, so it would be enough to signify that life has begun, albeit that higher brain functioning no longer exists or could never exist.

Personhood

Gervais states: 'Underlying these different analytical approaches is a fundamental difference in focus – either on the human as organism or on the human as person.[121] This choice of perspective must be justified.'[122] Bernat *et al.* state: 'We must not confuse the death of an organism which was a person, with an organism's ceasing to be a person',[123] and add: 'The concept "person" is not biological but rather a concept defined in terms of certain kinds of abilities and qualities of awareness. It is inherently vague. Death is a biological concept. Thus in a literal sense, death can be applied directly only to biological organisms and not to persons.'[124] Such ontological or personhood formulations of death raise extremely contentious issues as to the extent to which the 'self' is identifiable with the body – at present the public perception appears to recognise a very strong

[118] See D. Brahams, 'Transplantation, the Fetus and the Law' (1988) 138 *New Law Journal* 91 at 91–2, and B. Dickens, 'The Infant as Donor: Legal Issues' (1988) 20 (Supp. 5) *Transplantation Proceedings* 50.

[119] 609 So. 2d 588 (Fla. 1992).

[120] The tag given to it by Sharon Sytsma: see S. Sytsma, 'Anencephalics as Organ Sources' (1996) 17 *Theoretical Medicine* 19.

[121] Schrader remarks that 'I for one wish to say . . . "I am not simply a person; I am also a biological organism" ': see D. Schrader, 'On Dying More than One Death' (1986) 16 *Hastings Center Report* 12 at 13.

[122] See Gervais, *Redefining Death*, at 20.

[123] Bernat *et al.*, 'On the Definition and Criterion of Death', at 391.

[124] Ibid., at 390. See also T. Kushner, 'Having a Life Versus Being Alive' (1984) 10 *Journal of Medical Ethics* 5.

identity between the two, even persisting after death, and rejects exclusive reliance on absence of *mental* and psychosocial functioning. Truog,[125] probably correctly, considers that the greatest objections to the higher brain formulation emerge from the implications of treating breathing patients as if they were dead, in other words that, certification of death or not, such a being would continue to breathe spontaneously and that, in order to cause respiration to cease, deliberate affirmative measures to terminate respiration would have to take place, measures which would currently be taken to 'kill' the patient and contravene the dead donor rule. Lamb argues that personal identity is a *quality* of a living thing not a reference to an individual's physical state or structure, quite apart from considering that personhood formulations lack a sufficient level of diagnostic accuracy.[126] Furthermore, there are many perspectives offered on the constituent qualities and nature of 'personhood' in the literature.[127] Indeed, many higher-brain death campaigners currently adopt a *via media* and support a whole-brain,[128] or brain-stem death, standard as a pragmatic holding position.[129]

Free fall

Bernat states that 'applying the higher-brain formulation creates a serious slippery slope problem in which the criterion for death becomes indistinct. If patients in persistent vegetative states were considered dead, perhaps so should severely demented patients because they too lack experiential and social integrating functions.'[130] Anencephaly is a condition analogous to others, quite apart from the fact that there are

125 R. Truog, 'Is it Time to Abandon Brain Death?' (1997) 27 *Hastings Center Report* 29 at 32.

126 See Lamb, *Organ Transplants and Ethics*, at 43. Such doubts are echoed by some critics of brain-death standards of any kind. For instance, it has been stated that 'in the present state of scientific knowledge . . . permanent loss of the capacity for consciousness is essentially untestable': see Evans and Hill, 'The Brain Stems of Organ Donors are Not Dead', at 119.

127 As Veatch states, 'Among defenders of the higher-brain concept, there are countless variations on what counts as "higher": everything above the brain-stem, the cerebrum, the cerebral cortex, the neocortex, the sensory cortex, and so forth': see Veatch, 'The Conscience Clause', at 142.

128 Wikler, for instance, describes such a standard as 'not very practical' in view of the present inability to diagnose loss of consciousness with any certainty: see D. Wikler, 'Brain-Related Criteria for the Beginning and End of Life' (1990) 22 *Transplantation Proceedings* 989 at 990.

129 For instance B. Schone-Seifert, 'Defining Death in Germany' in Youngner *et al.*, *The Definition of Death*, 262.

130 Bernat, 'A Defense of the Whole-Brain Concept', at 17.

various other, much less severe, conditions in neonates where 'personhood' (in the sense of awareness of self and environment) is very probably absent. Once an 'extended' definition came into currency, what other analogous states would fall within its compass?[131] Would the definition apply outside as well as within the transplant context? If not, the dangerous impression that the definition of death is being manipulated in the context of transplantation would be generated. There is no reason why such catastrophically handicapped newborns should have their lives *extended* by medical treatment, but that is a different issue linked to their own interests. Shewmon argues that 'Manipulating the definition of death – by including anencephalic infants, whose spontaneous breathing, sucking, crying, and the like separate them from the dead bodies that society is usually willing to label cadavers and bury – may undermine the public's already tenuous confidence in brain-based determinations of death.'[132]

Caplan's support for allowing the removal of organs from anencephalics even though brain death has not been established is partially based on the fact that brain death is especially difficult to apply to very immature infants.[133] A US Task Force for the Determination of Brain Death in Children published guidelines in 1987 which stated that clinical criteria for determining brain death were inapplicable to infants under seven days of age.[134] Because of these difficulties, a Working Party Report of the Conference of Royal Medical Colleges on Organ Transplantation in Neonates in Britain[135] stated that brain-stem death criteria cannot be used

[131] Shewmon emphasises that anencephaly is not an entirely discrete clinical entity and overlaps with many other conditions: see Shewmon, 'Anencephaly: Selected Medical Aspects', at 11–12. Arras and Shinnar state that 'if the theory is carried out to its logical conclusion, other infants with conditions such as holoprosencephaly, hydranencephaly, and certain trisomies as well as adults in permanent vegetative states should be considered as potential organ donors': see J. Arras and S. Shinnar, 'Anencephalic Newborns as Organ Donors: A Critique' (1988) 259 *Journal of the American Medical Association* 2284 at 2284.

[132] A. Shewmon *et al.*, 'The Use of Anencephalic Infants as Organ Sources – A Critique' (1989) 261 *Journal of the American Medical Association* 1773 at 1778.

[133] The British Paediatric Association Working Party Report stated that it was rarely possible confidently to diagnose brain death in children between thirty-seven weeks' gestation and two months of age: see *Working Party Report on the Diagnosis of Brain Stem Death in Infants and Children*, BPS, November 1991.

[134] 'Guidelines for the Determination of Brain Death in Children: Report of the Task Force' (1987) 80 *Pediatrics* 298.

[135] *Report of the Working Party of the Conference of Royal Medical Colleges and their Faculties in the United Kingdom on Organ Transplantation in Neonates*, 1988, at para. 5.3.

to justify the removal of organs from neonates (that is anencephalics) with beating hearts for transplantation, and that organs may only be removed when spontaneous respiration has ceased. The Working Party felt that by (a supposed) analogy with adults, the absence of the forebrain in these infants plus loss of spontaneous respiration should similarly be recognised as death. Of course many otherwise viable organs would be lost during the 'wait', but the volume would be modest. Only a relatively small number of anencephalics are born annually and the number is dwindling.[136] Only a small percentage of these are suitable as organ donors, estimated at around twenty per annum in the United Kingdom.[137]

Raising the standard

It is essential that whatever standard of death is adopted adequately supports the underlying concept of death subscribed to, and that criteria and tests utilised do indeed establish that the standard(s) of death exist(s).[138] Brain death standards have come under increasing scrutiny and challenge in recent years on both grounds. Brody asserts that 'The proponents of the standard criterion of [whole] brain death . . . encounter difficulties in reconciling it with the definition (irreversible loss of integrative functioning) and the clinical tests (no stem reflexes, no respiratory efforts, no responsiveness) normally associated with that criterion.'[139] Similarly, Truog states that 'the whole-brain concept is plagued by internal inconsistencies in both the tests-criterion and the criterion-definition relationships, and these problems cannot be easily solved'.[140] In particular, whole-brain death is criticised on the basis that currently there is no necessity to establish that all functioning of the brain be found to have irreversibly ceased, thereby casting doubt on whether the integrated functioning, or other concept of death, is truly satisfied.

[136] The annual rate of decline of live anencephalic births is about 2.7 per cent: see J. Botkin, 'Anencephalic Infants as Organ Donors' (1988) 82 *Pediatrics* 250 at 251.

[137] It is estimated that approximately 100 such infants are born in the United States annually: see US Medical Task Force on Anencephaly, 1990.

[138] See generally D. Lamb, *Death, Brain Death and Ethics*, State University of New York Press, Albany, 1985.

[139] B. Brody, 'How Much of the Brain Must be Dead?' in Youngner *et al.*, *The Definition of Death*, 71.

[140] Truog, 'Is it Time to Abandon Brain Death?', at 31. He is using the term 'criteria' to describe 'standards' in the terminology adopted here.

Integrated circuits?

Supporters of the 'integrated functions' view are therefore being attacked on their own terms. Taylor observes that

> Persons who meet the whole-brain criteria of death, if mechanically ventilated, typically remain normothermic, continue to grow hair and fingernails, often retain spinal reflexes, maintain cardiac and circulatory function, digest and absorb food, filter blood through both liver and kidneys, urinate and defecate, heal wounds, and may even gestate fetuses. A mechanically ventilated person who meets whole-brain criteria for death is not biologically dead. The persistence of circulation, even though artificially supported, permits continued cellular and organ system function, preventing the onset of the process of disintegration, and thereby maintains the life of the organism.[141]

Truog states that 'many of these individuals retain clear evidence of integrated brain function at the level of the brain-stem and mid-brain, and may have evidence of cortical functioning'.[142]

Truog, Halevy and Brody identify various areas of tension based upon evidence of continuing activity typically attributed to brain functioning, in terms of neurohormonal regulation, temperature homeostasis, blood pressure control, cortical functioning as shown by significant nonisoelectric electroencephalograms, brain-stem functioning as shown by evoked potentials and continuing cerebral circulation. Research exists which shows that the brain (hypothalamus) continues to secrete antidiuretic hormone (ADH) even after brain death, and this is why brain-dead patients typically have no signs of diabetes insipidus.[143] The neurologically regulated secretion of other hormones is also apparently quite common. Of this, Brody states[144] that 'this regulation is just as much and as important an example of the integrative functioning of the brain as the brain's control of respiration or of responsive movements'.

141 Taylor, 'Reexamining the Definition and Criteria of Death', at 268. Indeed, Singer enquires how, without integrated functioning, a pregnant brain-dead woman could be maintained sufficiently to allow the delivery of a viable foetus at some later (maybe three months later) point. See Singer, *Rethinking Life and Death*, at 31.

142 Truog, 'Is it Time to Abandon Brain Death?', at 29.

143 A. Halevy and B. Brody, 'Brain Death: Reconciling Definitions, Criteria and Tests' (1993) 119(6) *Annals of Internal Medicine* 519 at 520. See also R. Wetzel *et al.*, 'Hemodynamic Responses in Brain Dead Organ Donor Patients' (1985) 64 *Anesthésie, Analgésie, Réanimation* 125.

144 Brody, 'How Much of the Brain Must be Dead?', at 72.

There is also evidence that such patients (20 per cent in one study) continue to show residual electrical activity in their brains on an electro-encephalogram (EEG),[145] but Bernat describes these as 'isolated nests of neurons' not contributing to the overall integrated functioning of the organism as a whole.[146] There is also some proof of a paradoxical absence of hypothermia in the majority of brain-dead individuals, indicating the continuance of neurologically mediated temperature homeostasis, in that hypothermia is a *contraindication* to a diagnosis of brain death.[147] However, even Brody concedes that the neurohormonal regulation is the most important example of continued brain activity and that evidence in support of other features is less consistent and more dubious. As regards brain-stem evoked potentials and positive EEG readings, Brody himself states that 'while they constitute brain functions, it is not clear that either integrates the functioning of the entire organism', and adds: 'I would today put less emphasis on them.'[148] Nonetheless, on the basis of such findings, Bleich concludes that '"Brain death" represents neither the destruction nor dysfunction of the brain in its entirety. Currently accepted neurological criteria of death, singly or in combination, demonstrate only that specific neurological activities have ceased',[149] and asserts that past and present reliance on a whole-brain legal standard of death is misplaced, as such individuals cannot be shown to have lost the 'entire functions of the brain' and therefore are not truly dead.

Semantic sleights of hand?

Truog states that, 'Faced with these facts, even supporters of the current statutes acknowledge that the criterion of "whole-brain" death is only an

145 See Halevy and Brody, 'Brain Death: Reconciling Definitions, Criteria, and Tests', at 521. An EEG test is not used in the UK, although it is in the US and many other jurisdictions, as one of the battery of tests for determining brain death. This has been said to be a function of many things, but may be primarily because the UK criteria relate to brain-*stem* death rather than *whole-brain* death.

146 Bernat, 'A Defense of the Whole-Brain Concept', at 18. There is also some research showing electrical responses to acoustic stimuli in the brain-dead patient demonstrating brain-stem evoked potentials, but this is limited and seriously doubted by other commentators.

147 There is also some evidence of raised heart rate and blood pressure upon surgical incision linked to organ removal: see Wetzel *et al.*, 'Hemodynamic Responses', and F. Conci *et al.*, 'Viscero, Somatic and Viscero-visceral Reflexes in Brain Death' (1986) 49 *Journal of Neurology and Psychiatry* 495.

148 See Brody, 'How Much of the Brain Must be Dead?', at 72–3.

149 Bleich, 'Moral Debate and Semantic Sleight of Hand', at 1176.

"approximation".'[150] Indeed, Bernat has long maintained that that is so.[151] He argues that it is only necessary that a *critical* number of neurons permanently cease functioning. Pallis considers it 'naive' to believe that we can ascertain the total and irreversible loss of all brain functioning. Whilst it has been observed that even the President's Commission said that the expression 'functions of the entire brain' referred only to those functions that could be *clinically assessed*, there is obviously still a danger of the tail (existing tests) wagging the dog (death). A shift in the debate has therefore occurred here, from total loss of functioning of the entire brain to the loss of functioning of the 'critical functions' of the organism. Indeed, Bernat regards continued secretion of ADH as a continued 'function' but not a 'critical function' of the organism, as individuals without such secretion can survive.[152] Halevy and Brody by contrast assert that such hormone is 'certainly essential to the functioning of the whole organism and not "mere activity"'. Bernat retorts that 'Awareness, breathing, and circulatory control are more critical to life than is the secretion of ADH.'[153] Nevertheless, the debate continues as to how far continued brain functioning contributes to the 'critical' (integrated or otherwise) functioning of the organism as a whole. Indeed, in so far as this must inevitably be a matter of *degree* there is endless room for debate as to the point at which one can state with assuredness that the 'disintegration of the organism' has occurred. It has been argued that another shift has occurred,[154] from a concentration on the destruction of the brain to the loss of *functioning* of the brain. However, it has been contended that 'From the start, the criterion for whole-brain death was functional rather than anatomic.

150 Truog, 'Is it Time to Abandon Brain Death?', at 30. Veatch also considers that 'No one really believes that every last function of the entire brain must be irreversibly lost for a brain to be dead. That would include all electrical functions, all neurohumoral functions, and cellular functions': see Veatch, 'The Conscience Clause', at 143.

151 J. Bernat, 'How Much of the Brain Must Die in Brain Death?' (1992) 3(1) *Journal of Clinical Ethics* 21 at 25.

152 Bernat, 'A Defense of the Whole-Brain Concept', at 17.

153 He regards the vital functions of spontaneous breathing and autonomic control of circulation, the integrating functioning of maintaining homeostasis of the organism, and consciousness, as the primary elements of functioning: see J. Bernat, 'Refinements in the Definition and Criterion of Death' in Youngner *et al.*, *The Definition of Death*, 82 at 86.

154 This shift is observable in the President's Commission Report. McCullagh contends that one should be attempting to ascertain an underlying structural change and not just loss of functioning prior to a diagnosis of death: see McCullagh, *Brain Dead, Brain Absent, Brain Donors*, at 22.

What mattered was the loss of identified functions of the brain, not activity in individual cells or clusters of cells.'[155]

The body's internal milieu[156]

Pallis and Bernat both confess that in the usual clinical context of brain death it cannot be ascertained that major areas of the brain such as the cerebellum, the basal ganglia or the thalami have irreversibly ceased to function.[157] However, Bernat contends that there is a good reason for this based on the pathophysiology of the brain, that is damage to the *brain stem* assures that damage has also occurred to these other neurological structures.[158] Pallis dismisses the relevance of this on the (only slightly) different basis that in Britain the emphasis is on brain-*stem* death rather than whole-brain death and that some of these functions are not brain-stem functions anyhow. For instance, ADH is produced by the hypothalamus. Now this would seem at first glance to be a semantic sleight of hand, but is justified, it is alleged, on the basis that in Britain the *concept* of death underpinning brain-stem death is irreversible loss of consciousness and of spontaneous respiration, rather than the loss of integrated functions of the organism, critical or not.[159] If brain-stem death is reliable evidence of both of these elements then any criticism should be aimed at the concept and not the standard. Loss of the capacity for consciousness is a crucial ingredient of all formulations so that the key issue is whether the loss of capacity for spontaneous respiratory functioning is itself sufficient loss of biological capacity. Certainly the idea of the 'breath of life' is a

155 See 'The Interface Between Philosophy and the Clinic' in Youngner *et al.*, *The Definition of Death*, at 67. See also D. Lamb, 'What is Death?' in R. Gillon (ed.), *Principles of Health Care Ethics*, John Wiley & Sons, Chichester, 1994, 1027 at 1034.

156 The term coined by Claude Bernard in 1865. See F. Plum, 'Clinical Standards and Technological Confirmatory Tests in Diagnosing Brain Death' in Youngner *et al.*, *The Definition of Death*, 34 at 53.

157 Indeed, the usual bedside determination of whole-brain death in any event focuses essentially on an assessment of *brain-stem* functions.

158 He notes that it is this feature that underpins the reliance in Britain upon brain-*stem* death.

159 Evans and Hill argue that current brain-stem death tests do not establish that the brain stem is dead either. They state that vasomotor centre activity should be ruled out but no testing for persisting barareceptor reflex or vagal motor nucleus function is included in the prescribed tests, nor testing of oesophageal motility centres, despite evidence published in 1987 of persisting muscular activity in the lower part of the oesophagus which is usually attributed to brain-stem function: see Evans and Hill, 'The Brain Stems of Organ Donors are Not Dead', at 116–18.

pervasive one pivotal to all other cellular or organic functions. Maybe it is perceived as 'integrating' all the others. Brain-stem death also rests on clinical beliefs about consciousness where the brain stem has been destroyed but the higher brain remains undamaged, for example in rare cases of isolated brain-stem cellular necrosis when the cerebral hemispheres remain intact.[160] But Miles states: 'Neuroscience is finding that consciousness is not, as had been thought, anatomically grounded exclusively in the neocortex. Consciousness requires neocortical activation by lower brain structures, although there is no clear understanding of the status of consciousness when the activation of the neocortex is destroyed but neocortical activity remains, as evidenced by neurophysiological studies.'[161]

These are profound matters which are partially unresolvable. The contention that there remains some integrated functioning even after the individual has satisfied the brain-death standard may nevertheless at least suggest the need for more extensive brain testing.[162]

Double standards?

Moving from heart-beating to non-heart-beating donors we run into some obverse arguments, that is that it is *not* appropriate to rely on cardiorespiratory cessation to establish death under such organ procurement protocols. Some contend that there is only a unitary (brain death) standard of death and not binary standards. Indeed, it is where binary standards do exist that brain death is typically perceived as a 'different' form of death, reserved primarily for organ donors.[163] The protocols currently in place focus our attention very precisely upon the actual time of death, as well as the proper meaning of the concept of 'irreversibility' in this context.

160 See I. Pearson, 'Brain Death' in J. Chapman, M. Deierhoi and C. Wight (eds.), *Organ and Tissue Donation for Transplantation*, Arnold, London, 1997, 69 at 79.

161 See Miles, 'Death in a Technological and Pluralistic Culture', at 312.

162 Although McCullagh states that 'I believe that this change in attitude carries more substantial implications for brain death as a *concept* than it acknowledges in terms of the practicability of brain death *criteria*': see McCullagh, *Brain Dead, Brain Absent, Brain Donors*, at 29.

163 See King's Fund Institute, *A Question of Give and Take*, Research Report 18, King's Fund Institute, London, 1994, at 9.

Non-heart-beating donor protocols

NHBD protocols involve either the procurement of organs or the use of cooling and perfusion techniques immediately following death, which is determined according to cardiorespiratory benchmarks. However, many of the NHBD protocols set out in the literature are vague as to exactly how death is to be determined and the point at which removal or preservation procedures are initiated. At both Barcelona and Tokyo procedures are simply said to be initiated after cardiac arrest.[164] Other published protocols are by contrast extremely explicit on such matters, for example at the Universitario San Carlos in Madrid.[165] Similarly detailed is the University of Pittsburgh protocol regarding patients with neurological damage who are gradually removed from ventilatory support (with either the patient's or relatives' consent, or both) and whose organs are removed after death is pronounced, after being shown to be apnoeaic and unresponsive for two minutes to one of three electrocardiographic criteria, that is ventricular fibrillation, electric asystole or electromechanical dissociation.[166] A recent Institute of Medicine Report in the US stated that regarding controlled donors, 'Existing NHBD protocols either are unclear or specify organ removal from immediately to 5 minutes after heart stoppage.'[167] Where a period of 'delay' was specified, it ranged from sixty seconds to five minutes.

There is an inherent tension in such protocols between cardiopulmonary cessation employed as an independent (physiological) *standard* of death and cardiopulmonary *criteria* used instead as indicia of (brain)

164 In Barcelona, 'after cessation of cardiac activity' precisely: see A. Castelao *et al.*, 'Update of our Experience in Long-term Renal Function of Kidneys Transplanted from Non-Heart-Beating Cadaver Donors' (1993) 25 *Transplantation Proceedings* 1513 at 1513; in Tokyo, 'immediately after cardiac arrest': see M. Kozaki *et al.*, 'Procurement of Kidney Grafts from Non-Heart-Beating Donors' (1991) 23 *Transplantation Proceedings* 2575 at 2575.

165 Under this protocol, death is determined by '1. Cardiac arrest unresponsive to prolonged cardiopulmonary resuscitation (CPR) for at least 30 minutes 2. Absence of any electrocardiographic activity after 10 minutes of CPR cessation 3. Absence of any neurological activity after 15 minutes of normothermic CPB.'

166 S. Youngner *et al.*, 'Ethical, Psychosocial, and Public Policy Implications of Procuring Organs from Non-Heart-Beating Cadaver Donors' (1993) 269 *Journal of the American Medical Association* 2769.

167 Institute of Medicine Report, *Non-Heart-Beating Organ Transplantation: Medical and Ethical Issues in Procurement*, Institute of Medicine, National Academy Press, Washington D.C., 1997, at 5 and 40–1. Several protocols merely declare death and begin organ procurement 'immediately after determination of cardiac arrest'.

death. According to the former view, irreversible loss of cardiopulmonary function *is* itself death, whilst according to the alternative view, in Pallis's words: 'A person is not dead unless his brain is dead. Arrest of the heart and circulation indicate death only when they persist long enough for the brain to die,'[168] that is they are a *cause* of death and form part of the testing procedure for brain death. The tension between these perspectives is evident from an exchange which took place at a pivotal symposium on non-heart-beating donors held in Maastricht in the Netherlands. During one interchange, a speaker asked: 'When we test for brain death we test for brain stem reflexes. Does anybody know that the patients you are perfusing have no brain stem reflexes left? Do you test for brain stem reflexes?' To which another participant replied 'Well of course not, they are dead.'[169] The legal implications of this debate are brought out in another paper presented at the symposium, by a Spanish team considering whether their NHBD protocol was consistent with the Spanish legislation passed in 1979/1980.[170] They stated: 'In the case of brain death, the law specifies the conditions for the diagnosis and the requirements for the death certificate. As the classic cardiac death is not considered in the law, it presumes that the diagnosis and certification will be performed in the standard way.'[171] It seems that a different *standard* of death is being alluded to here because, as we saw earlier, Spanish law explicitly sets out the criteria needing to be established to diagnose *brain* death.

It appears therefore that in general under NHBD protocols irreversible loss of cardiopulmonary function is relied upon as the *standard* of death, as opposed to being a diagnostic criterion for the existence of brain death.[172] In many jurisdictions, such as Denmark and most of the US

[168] C. Pallis, 'Reappraising Death' (1982) 285 *British Medical Journal* 1409 at 1410. Mason and McCall Smith have expressed the same thing in a different way. They state: 'If we are to accept the concept of "brain death" as argued below, we should treat the person in irreversible cardiorespiratory failure as dying rather than dead – for the true agonal period in natural death is that which lies between cardiac arrest and cerebral failure': see J. Mason and A. McCall Smith, *Law and Medical Ethics*, 4th edn, Butterworths, London, 1994, at 281.

[169] R. Valero *et al.*, 'Organ Procurement from Non-Heart-Beating Donors Through in situ Perfusion or Total Body Cooling' (1995) 27 *Transplantation Proceedings* 2899 at 2900.

[170] It has been seen above that the Spanish Law does not 'dictate' that all organ donors must have been declared brain dead, although the mandatory terms of the Crown Decree appear to be somewhat at odds on this matter with the very Law it is intending to implement (unless something has got lost in the translation of course!).

[171] J. Alvarez-Rodriguez *et al.*, 'Legal Aspects of Non-Heart-Beating Donors: The Madrid Solution' (1995) 27 *Transplantation Proceedings* 2933 at 2933.

[172] As is highlighted by the response to the questioner at Maastricht, above.

states, there are dual standards of death in law anyhow, but in others death is explicitly stated in legislation to be only brain death. Is it the case though, as the Madrid team argue, that in any event it always operates against the *backdrop* of a traditional legal cardiorespiratory standard of death?[173] Such uncertainty is partially, but not wholly, a function of the 'dabbling' by transplant legislation in these jurisdictions. But it is also relevant to Britain, in the absence of a complete judicial picture and a statutory definition of death. Where there is a dual (statutory) definition of death (as in most US states) therefore, it might seem as if many of the legal problems associated with NHBD protocols are alleviated, but in fact there are still major difficulties, as discussed below.[174]

Either he's dead or my watch has stopped

It is submitted that the death of the brain is an essential prerequisite to a finding that death has occurred in law. It is illuminating to discover that under many NHBD protocols, after a certain period of cardiopulmonary 'silence', artificial ventilation and/or cardiac massage is applied to maintain the condition of the organs as far as possible. But if the heart and lungs are restarted, how can they be 'non-heart-beating' donors? How can there be an *irreversible* loss of cardiorespiratory functioning? If sole reliance is placed upon cardiorespiratory *standards* we appear to have a problem here. I would argue, however, that there is no dichotomy between heart-beating and non-heart-beating donors. Cessation of cardiopulmonary function is merely evidence, a *criterion* for establishing, that brain death has occurred.

Loss of cardiopulmonary function does not in and of itself produce brain-stem (*a fortiori* whole-brain) death. It is acknowledged that brain function will be caused to cease irreversibly only after a certain period of time elapses. There would appear to be a fairly widespread consensus that this period is longer than, for instance, the two minutes stipulated by the Pittsburgh protocol. Indeed, a ten-minute time period was broadly agreed upon at the NHBD symposium in Maastricht in 1994,[175] which accords

173 As mentioned above, such an argument could not prosper directly in a jurisdiction such as Romania where the relevant statute explicitly states that *only* brain death can be used to determine that death has occurred, although it is argued further on that there may be no conflict at the level of 'standards' as opposed to the performance of specific prescribed tests.

174 Relating to the notion of 'irreversibility'.

175 See (1995) 27 *Transplantation Proceedings* 2891–939.

with the period of time recommended by the Consultants to the President's Commission attached to its Report *Defining Death*: at least ten minutes of proven lack of circulation to the brain.[176] The US Institute of Medicine Report recommended more loosely that, with regard to controlled NHBDs, 'not less than a 5-minute interval, determined accurately by electronic and arterial pulse monitoring, be required to determine donor death'.[177] The dilemma, of course, is that adherence to strict guidelines before certifying death may prevent many organs, certainly non-renal organs, from being viably procured from NHBDs. But would such lapse of time be avoided if we *could* instead rely on loss of cardiopulmonary function as a *standard* of death?

Even where it is a separate and unequivocally legitimate independent standard of death, cessation of spontaneous breathing and circulation does not occasion death *per se*. It is universally agreed that *irreversibility* of cessation of functions is an essential constituent of any ethically and legally acceptable standard of death. It is a uniform feature of (model) laws and ethical formulations and codes. Tomlinson has, however, suggested that 'irreversibility' is not an empirical idea but one based on what is 'ethically significant'.[178] However, this dangerously conflates whether someone 'is dead' with whether someone 'will die'. In other words, whether we *should* have reversed it as opposed to whether we *could* have reversed it. Irreversibility is partially linked to time and culture but is not a variable phenomenon between individuals in the same culture and at the same relevant time. It is an empirical concept which can generally be determined only with the benefit of some degree of hindsight, that is after some period of time has elapsed. There is a danger that the implementation of certain NHBD protocols may preclude the application

[176] President's Commission for the Study of Ethical Problems in Medicine and Biomedical and Behavioral Research, *Guidelines for the Determination of Death*, US Government Printing Office, Washington D.C., 1981. The *Guidelines on the Termination of Life-Sustaining Treatment and the Care of the Dying* published by the Hastings Center in 1987 also stated: 'Complete cessation of circulation to the normothermic adult brain for more than ten minutes is incompatible with survival of brain tissue.'

[177] Institute of Medicine, *Non-Heart-Beating Organ Transplantation*, at 5.

[178] T. Tomlinson, 'The Irreversibility of Death: Reply to Cole' (1993) 3 *Kennedy Institute of Ethics Journal* 157. As Brock states, 'There is relativity within the notion of the irreversibility of death, but it is relativity dependent on whether it is possible to restore life functions here and now, not on whether we choose to do so': see D. Brock, 'The Role of the Public in Public Policy on the Definition of Death' in Youngner *et al.*, *The Definition of Death*, 299.

of hindsight in order to preserve the optimum condition of organs for transplantation.

Cole has asserted that the notion of irreversibility is superfluous because it is out of line with the 'ordinary concept' of death, based on the loss of a *natural* capacity to resume cardiopulmonary function, and that consequently such a notion should not form any part of a legal definition of death.[179] However, people's lives are frequently supported by all manner of 'artificial' means yet such persons are unequivocally alive, for example individuals with life-sustaining heart pacemakers or even artificial (temporary or permanent) hearts. But, why should reversibility not itself be an integral aspect of natural functioning? A patient preserved by artificial means after a heart attack who makes a full recovery (or a patient with brain injuries kept on a ventilator to assist recovery) has reversible cardiopulmonary function. But is a patient alive (that is is his condition reversible) right up to the point where technology cannot precipitate gas exchange and the circulation of blood to any degree?[180] If so, there is no such entity as a 'beating heart' cadaver.[181]

The engine's running but there's no one behind the wheel

There is a clear distinction between a machine permanently and entirely 'taking over' the central functions of the human body and a machine facilitating certain capabilities of the body. Such technology is not *assisting the whole organism* to function in the first scenario, only isolated organs or tissues.[182] As Birnbacher states,

> It is essential, furthermore, that these activities of control and integration are exercised by the organism itself. If computers should be developed one

179 D. Cole, 'The Reversibility of Death' (1992) 18 *Journal of Medical Ethics* 26.

180 See further D. Price, 'Organ Transplant Initiatives: The Twilight Zone' (1997) 23 *Journal of Medical Ethics* 170 at 172–4.

181 It might appear as if a cardiopulmonary standard of death is relied upon under Elective Ventilation (EV) protocols (considered in chapter 5) where patients are moved to ICU so that artificial ventilation can be commenced immediately respiratory arrest occurs. However, supporters of the Exeter EV protocol maintain that the patient is already brain dead at the time he is ventilated. Whilst the previous Code of Practice lends some support to this contention (see *A Code of Practice including the Diagnosis of Brain Death* (Memorandum on the Diagnosis of Death, 1979, para. 6)), this is somewhat dubious. See discussion in Price, 'The Twilight Zone', at 172–4.

182 For example, whilst the heart can be used as a kind of inert bag and the pumping mechanism maintained by rhythmical compression, and gas exchange facilitated by the ventilator, the body's functions are essentially being replaced or 'taken over', not being 'assisted'.

> day with the capacity of exercising these integrative functions even after complete loss of brain function (thus making a dead man act as a living one) this would in no way falsify the proposition that the man is dead.[183]

Once brain death has occurred, however, irreversibility is established. Referring to the practice associated with NHBD protocols of ventilating and applying cardiac massage (for up to two hours in some cases) on patients previously declared dead according to cardiopulmonary standards, in another debate at the Maastricht NHBD symposium, a speaker tendered 'I think we have to make a clear distinction between resuscitating the patient and trying to maintain the organs in optimal condition.'[184] This is true, but if breathing and circulation are restored, the patient *is* resuscitated according to cardiopulmonary benchmarks! It is submitted, however, that the proper interpretation of events here is that the patient is already dead at the time that artificial ventilation and cardiac massage are applied because the *brain* has certainly died during the period when unsuccessful resuscitation was employed, that is it is brain death that is implicitly and properly being alluded to. This is why the concept of 'reanimation', whereby donors (to date lambs and baboons) are left undisturbed for between twenty and thirty minutes following cardiac arrest before organ (including heart) retrieval takes place with transplantation in prospect, is ethically unproblematic from this perspective.[185] Brain death has indisputably intervened in the 'fallow' period of time. Proposals have been put forward for similar protocols to be applied to humans.

Law reform

The advantages of a clear definition of death were said by the Law Reform Commission of Canada to be that it reduces uncertainty and confusion over when a person is legally dead. 'It gives families a contemporary societal standard for making difficult decisions concerning treatment and non-treatment; it clarifies professional duties, patient rights and the limits of criminal liability. A clear definition of death thus facilitates organ

[183] Birnbacher, 'Philosophical Arguments', at 341.

[184] E. Heineman, 'Non-Heart-Beating Donors: Methods and Techniques' (1995) 27 *Transplantation Proceedings* 2895 at 2897.

[185] See R. Orr, S. Gundry and L. Bailey, 'Reanimation: Overcoming Objections and Obstacles to Organ Retrieval from Non-Heart-Beating Cadaver Donors' (1997) 23 *Journal of Medical Ethics* 7.

procurement and transplantation.'[186] This would preferably be a *statutory* definition. As Capron and Kass state, 'Reliance on judge-made law would, however, neither actively involve the public in the decision-making process nor lead to a prompt, clear, and general "definition" ',[187] a view which can be seen to contain substance through observation of the picture in Britain. Capron also adds that in any event the judiciary may be too narrowly based for the task and too constrained by the setting of the dispute and the evidence available to it. He cogently maintains that 'judge-made law has been most successful in factual settings embedded in well-defined social and economic practices, with the guidance of past decisions and commentary'.[188]

The most appropriate level of determination for adoption in a legislative definition is the chosen standard(s) of death rather than the more abstract concept of death buttressing it.[189] The two basic legislative strategies can be illustrated by comparing the *unitary* standard Model Law of the Canadian Law Reform Commission with the *binary* approach in the UDDA adopted across most of the US. By contrast with the UDDA the Canadian statute provides

> (1) A person is dead when an irreversible cessation of all that person's brain functions has occurred (2) The irreversible cessation of brain functions can be determined by the prolonged absence of spontaneous circulatory and respiratory functions (3) When the determination of the prolonged absence of spontaneous circulatory and respiratory functions is made impossible by the use of artificial means of support, the irreversible cessation of brain functions can be determined by any means recognised by ordinary standards of current medical practice.

It is submitted that, all things being equal, a unitary (brain death) law expressed in terms similar to the Canadian Model Law is to be preferred.

186 Law Reform Commission of Canada, *Procurement and Transfer of Human Tissues and Organs*, Working Paper 66, Minister of Supply and Services, Ottawa, 1992, at 99. One of the primary reasons for the Australian Law Reform Commission recommending a statutory definition of death in its Report in 1977 was the lack of certainty surrounding the issue in its absence.

187 A. Capron and L. Kass, 'A Statutory Definition of the Standards for Determining Human Death: An Appraisal and a Proposal' (1972) 121 *University of Pennsylvania Law Review* 87 at 96.

188 A. Capron, 'The Bifurcated Legal Standard for Determining Death' in Youngner *et al.*, *The Definition of Death*, at 126.

189 The President's Commission explicitly chose to adopt this determinative tier as the basis for its model law.

Lynn and Cranford state that 'At present, the major statutes and discussions construe the situation as if there are two separate ways to know that death has occurred and make no particular connection between the two. This gives rise to the troubling conception that one might be dead by one set of criteria and not dead by the other.'[190] As Skegg states, 'The Canadian proposal avoids giving the impression that there are two definitions of death, and shows how the traditional tests can be linked to the new approach',[191] that is in ordinary circumstances the *criteria* for determining that death has occurred are the traditional ones, albeit that it is brain death that is *the standard of death* itself.[192] Brain function tests to support a finding that death has occurred are only necessary where artificial means of support preclude reliance on tests showing an absence of spontaneous circulatory and respiratory functions. Any statutory definition would of course require 'fleshing out' with clinical guidelines or codes drawn up by the medical profession. The ALRC in its Report stated: 'It was also said that in modern times, medical technology is advancing and changing with such rapidity that scientific criteria embedded in a statute may well become outmoded or obsolete and yet remain legally compulsory.'[193]

A superficial and fragile consensus?

In reality, as has been shown above, adoption of one standard rather than another should make no substantive difference, but perceptions and simplicity are vital features especially in organ donation contexts where what would otherwise appear as 'undue haste' might arise. Moreover, an all-purpose unitary legislative standard of death would enable us to

[190] J. Lynn and R. Cranford, 'The Persisting Perplexities in the Determination of Death' in Youngner, *et al.*, *The Definition of Death*, at 112.

[191] Skegg, *Law, Ethics and Medicine*, at 226.

[192] From the beginning the dual standards in the early Kansas statute, which alluded specifically to the use of artificial means of determination and potential transplantation procedures, drew criticism: see Kan. Stat. Ann. @77–202. Kennedy stated that it created the perception that the law was being 're-written in favour of the potential recipient and against the interests of the moribund donor': see I. Kennedy, 'The Kansas Statute on Death – An Appraisal' (1971) 285 *New England Journal of Medicine* 946.

[193] ALRC, *Human Tissue Transplants*, at para. 130. This was a particular concern of the English Criminal Law Revision Committee in its Fourteenth Report in 1980. However, legislative *standards* will not require constant amendment, whereas *tests* may do and should consequently be excluded from legislation. Indeed, many statutes defer to the standard of death being 'determined according to accepted medical criteria and means'.

dispense with the epithet 'brain' death altogether. The potential effects of uncertainty and doubt for organ donation are all too vividly illustrated by the effects of the BBC's *Panorama* programme in 1980,[194] and by the recent declining donor rates in Germany. Rates of organ donation are said to suffer because of a concern that individuals will be prematurely declared to be dead, in the interests of transplantation. Pearson *et al.* certainly revealed a link between reluctance to donate organs by family members, and a lack of knowledge about brain death.[195] There is also evidence that many clinicians have difficulty coming to terms with it.[196] A 1984 study of 200 neurosurgeons and 100 neurologists in the US found substantial diversity in the criteria used to declare brain death and in attitudes towards it.[197] In another study of US physicians and nurses it was discovered that only 35 per cent could correctly identify the legal and medical criteria for determining brain death.[198] It is frequently suggested that this is because brain death constitutes a departure from traditional views and takes us into terrain that we are emotionally still unprepared for. It would seem to be a notion more easily accepted as a social policy than as a diagnosis in an individual instance. Truog argues that brain death is counter-intuitive to transplantation and actually serves to *restrict* the potential donor pool. He contends that 'Only by abandoning the concept of brain death is it possible to adopt a definition of death that is valid for all purposes, while separating questions of organ donation from dependence upon the life/death dichotomy.'[199] This suggestion needs to be taken seriously but is in fact a recommendation for the abolition of the dead donor rule itself, and is considered in chapter 5. Fost also asserts that adoption of brain death has led to conceptual confusion which is itself counterproductive for organ transplantation. This prompted a different suggestion: to adopt different types of death for different purposes, for example for treatment withdrawal, organ explantation, burial/cremation,

194 'Transplants – Are the Donors really Dead?', BBC, 13 October 1980.

195 I. Pearson, P. Bazeley, T. Spencer-Plane, J. Chapman and P. Robertson, 'A Survey of Families of Brain-dead Patients: Their Experiences and Attitudes to Organ Donation and Transplantation' (1995) 23 *Anaesthesia and Intensive Care* 88.

196 See, for example, Editorial, 'Appropriate Confusion Over "Brain Death"' (1989) 261 *Journal of the American Medical Association* 2246.

197 P. Black and N. Zervas, 'Declaration of Brain Death in Neurosurgical and Neurological Practice' (1984) 15 *Neurosurgery* 170.

198 S. Youngner, M. Allen and E. Bartlett, 'Psychological and Ethical Implications of Organ Retrieval' (1985) 313 *New England Journal of Medicine* 321.

199 Truog, 'Is it Time to Abandon Brain Death?', at 35.

insurance, etc. Whilst superficially attractive this is an appeal to a different type of death. We are not here merely considering appropriate societal attitudes or responses to certain states, but the end of the existence of the *organism*. Whilst notions of 'personal' death may coincide with the point we generally accept for treatment withdrawal, and 'brain' death equate with the proper stage for organ removal, the justifications underpinning these policies are wholly different, a factor masked by such proposals.

2

Organ procurement systems

The survival lottery

All jurisdictions currently explicitly require either the express or presumed 'consent' of the deceased, or sometimes alternatively the express consent of a relative, in order to legitimate organ removal from a cadaver for transplantation purposes. Although there have frequently been proposals for the introduction of a mandatory procurement policy (that is permitting organ removal in every case regardless of the wishes of either relatives or the deceased[1]), this has yet to be converted into any official policy,[2] although in certain jurisdictions, most notably China,[3] organs are allegedly removed from executed prisoners. The Chinese authorities have occasionally asserted that the consent of the prisoner was previously obtained, although Rothman contends that 'no one should take such a

[1] See, for example, J. Harris, 'The Survival Lottery' (1975) 50 *Philosophy* 81. In the late sixties a 'proposal for routine salvaging of cadaver organs' was put forward by Dukeminier and Sanders, but the 'routinisation' was intended to refer to the normal course of events, not to mean that the deceased or next of kin would be unable to object to donation: see J. Dukeminier and D. Sanders, 'Organ Transplantation: A Proposal for Routine Salvaging of Cadaver Organs' (1968) 279 *New England Journal of Medicine* 413.

[2] There is some doubt as to whether organ procurement in Switzerland is lawful, whether or not consent is given, through the doctrine of necessity: see E. Bernat, 'Opting-in, Opting-out, and Necessity: The Law of Organ Transplantation in Germany, Austria and Switzerland' (1994) 5(2) *International Journal of Bioethics* 101, but the matter is governed in some instances by cantonal law, for example in Vaud (where the deceased may object), and in any event it is unlikely that the courts would deem it permissible to override the express objection of a deceased person.

[3] For instance, the law of the Syrian Arab Republic permits the removal of organs for transplantation from persons 'whose death is the result of capital punishment', without there being any reference to the need for consent or to any discretion to object to such removal: see section 3, Law of 23 August 1972. There are reports of executed prisoners serving as sources of organs also in Taiwan and Egypt.

claim seriously'.[4] A scheme of 'compulsory taking' is married to the notion that cadavers belong to the state, to be used for valid therapeutic purposes. Blasszauer states that 'While Western nations typically legislate stringent consent requirements governing the use of the dead body, in post-Communist countries and countries with developing democracies or no democracy at all, the dead body is generally considered the property of the state, with the medical establishment acting as trustee.'[5] This has sometimes been termed 'escheatage', but it begs the question whether the property originally belonged to another, that is is it a form of *confiscation* or *forfeiture*?

Such a compulsory policy would in effect render organ donation after death a moral and legal duty owed by individuals. The failure of societies to adopt such a policy would appear to be primarily because of a universally held perception that an individual has a right to exercise control over the use of his/her cadaver, and/or maybe next of kin's. However, some commentators regard the true character of so-called 'presumed consent' laws as being in essence compulsory recycling anyhow. Kevorkian has even described it as tantamount to 'theft' of organs by the state.[6] Ruth Richardson has commented that

> In the present day, from time to time, suggestions are raised, particularly in the medical press, that we should extend the law covering organ transplantation in line with a policy referred to as *presumed consent*. This is one of the many misnomers with which the language of transplantation is peppered. Here, lip service is paid to the *need* for consent, but in practice its existence is irrelevant, because it is *assumed* to exist. *Presumed consent* is public-relations-speak for the denial of a need even to *seek* consent.[7]

More recently, Erin and Harris have described presumed consent as a 'fiction' and asserted that 'Without the *actual* consent of the individual,

[4] It is reported that in 1989 1,000 kidneys were removed from executed prisoners in China for transplantation purposes: see D. Rothman, 'Bodily Integrity and the Socially Disadvantaged: The Traffic in Organs for Transplantation' in B. Spielman (ed.), *Organ and Tissue Donation: Ethical, Legal and Policy Issues*, Southern Illinois University Press, Carbondale, 1997, 35 at 39.

[5] B. Blasszauer, 'Autopsy' in H. Ten Have, J. Welie and S. Spicker (eds.), *Ownership of the Human Body*, Kluwer, Dordrecht, 1998, 19 at 19.

[6] J. Kevorkian, 'A Controlled Auction Market is a Practical Solution to the Shortage of Transplantable Organs' (1992) 11 *Medicine and Law* 47 at 48.

[7] R. Richardson, 'Fearful Symmetry' in S. Youngner, R. Fox and L. O'Connell (eds.), *Organ Transplantation: Meanings and Realities*, University of Wisconsin Press, Madison, 1996, 66 at 78. See also R. Richardson, *Death, Dissection and the Destitute*, Penguin, London, 1989.

there is *no* consent.'[8] The riposte of supporters is however that under all regimes, the deceased (and possibly also relatives) may object to this taking, so that it is nonetheless still a *consensual* removal, not a 'taking'. We shall explore these competing perceptions below. Certainly Engelhardt's observation that the more one presumes that organs are not societal property the more difficult it is to justify shifting the burden to individuals to show that they do not want their organs used[9] is wholly apposite.

The dichotomy between express consent (EC) and presumed consent (PC) (or 'opting-in' versus 'opting-out', or 'contracting-in' versus 'contracting-out')[10] schemes is intended to reflect the fact that under the former regimes organ donation is a result of a *positive expression of willingness* of the deceased or maybe of a relative, whereas in the others organ donation is permitted in the *absence of any objection* of the deceased, or in some instances also of the deceased's relatives. Somerville has stated that the fundamental difference between the two prevailing types of system is the initial presumption which governs: is it 'No . . . unless' or 'Yes . . . but'?[11] However, the process of labelling can itself sometimes be counterproductive, because observers categorise regimes inconsistently, and frequently inappropriately, thus undermining the very integrity of the classifications themselves and rendering discussions of implications flowing from different regimes at best valueless and at worst misleading. Nonetheless, they are convenient and do embody an important conceptual distinction. Such regimes are frequently further sub-divided into 'strong' or 'weak' (express or presumed consent) systems. Under strong systems, the positive wish of the deceased (express consent systems) or the lack of an objection from the deceased (presumed consent systems) is itself sufficient authorisation for organ donation to proceed. In weak systems, the deceased's actual or supposed will is insufficient, and the agreement of

8 C. Erin and J. Harris, 'Presumed Consent or Contracting Out' (1999) 25 *Journal of Medical Ethics* 365 at 365.

9 See H. Engelhardt, 'Allocating Scarce Medical Resources and the Availability of Organ Transplantation' (1984) 311 *New England Journal of Medicine* 66 at 70.

10 Nothing of significance hangs on these terms in themselves or terminology which is adopted. I employ the express/presumed consent vocabulary, as the term 'presumed consent' is typically used to describe their own schemes of this type.

11 M. Somerville, '"Procurement" vs "Donation" – Access to Tissues and Organs for Transplantation: Should "Contracting Out" Legislation be Adopted?' (1985) 17 *Transplantation Proceedings* 53 at 58.

relatives or the lack of an objection from relatives (in the respective systems) is also a prerequisite. Somerville states:

> In a weak contracting in system, a relative of the deceased must authorise organ donation although the deceased consented before death. In a weak contracting out system, relatives can object to donation despite the fact that the deceased, during life, did not contract out. A strong contracting in system mandates that the deceased's decision is final; and a strong contracting out system would not allow any objections by relatives to impede the procurement of organs.[12]

However, even this sub-division does not truly reflect the plurality and diversity of such systems, where subtle nuances can radically affect their character and impact.

Most of the early laws passed were of the express consent variety. That picture soon changed. In 1981 Stuart *et al.* reported that thirteen out of the twenty-eight countries outside the US surveyed had some form of presumed consent regime,[13] and a Council of Europe survey in 1987 found that twenty-one Member States and Finland had presumed consent regimes in Europe at that time. There is a geographical factor here.[14] Whereas most jurisdictions in North America have express consent systems for organ donation, many if not most nations in continental Europe have presumed consent regimes.[15] The position in South America is very varied whilst in Asia only Singapore currently has a presumed

12 Ibid.

13 See F. Stuart, F. Veith and R. Cranford, 'Brain Death Laws and Patterns of Consent to Remove Organs for Transplantation from Cadavers in the United States and 28 other Countries' (1981) 31 *Transplantation* 238.

14 Lee *et al.*, albeit rather simplistically, state that 'The available laws can be grouped along a spectrum based on the level of consent needed. At one end of the spectrum, reflecting a universal custom and heritage, the surviving family has controlling authority to donate a loved one's organs and tissues. At the other, unless an objection is registered prior to death, organs and tissues are routinely removed as needed. Geographically, culturally and philosophically, Asian and Latin American countries are overwhelmingly concentrated in the former group whilst continental European nations constitute most of the presumed consent. Countries with a strong English or American legal heritage tend to a more middle course': see P. Lee *et al.*, 'Worldwide Legal Requirements for Obtaining Corneas' (1992) 11 *Cornea* 102 at 105.

15 A survey in 1992 in Europe by Wolfslast detected a trend towards express consent within Europe at that time, but the picture across the whole of the nineties was much more heterogeneous: see G. Wolfslast, 'Legal Aspects of Organ Transplantation' (1992) 11 *Journal of Heart and Lung Transplantation* 160. Poland and Portugal passed presumed consent laws during this period, whilst Romania, Germany and the Netherlands enacted express consent laws.

consent law[16] (applicable to the majority of its population only), and in Africa just Tunisia.[17] Presumed consent laws are more common in respect of tissue than of organ donation though.[18] For instance, many US states have presumed consent laws applicable to cornea removals only.

The terrible imbalance

We should initially examine the tenability of the premiss that PC systems generate more organs for transplantation as this is the predominant rationale underpinning PC systems.[19] Although there is a general *perception* that they enhance donation rates, the conclusions of analysts vary. Land and Cohen commented in 1992 that 'there is no obvious correlation between high post mortem rates and the existence of presumed consent laws'.[20] On the other hand, Roels has gone so far as to say, based on the Belgian experience, that the 'data presented show that, at least in Europe, the problem of chronic organ shortage can adequately be solved in the setting of an opting-out legislation'.[21] It is by no means easy though to evaluate this proposition in view of the infinite variables which might impact upon donor rates. Moreover, in many jurisdictions, the donation system is not *operated* in a manner consistent with the legal framework, or at least not in every case.[22] As a consequence, all conclusions must necessarily be tentative. The primary European jurisdictions with PC

16 Although it will be argued that the Human Tissue Act 1961 in Britain is in essence a presumed consent law, and therefore Act No. 130 of 1974 in Malaysia is to be viewed likewise as it is precisely modelled upon it.

17 Law of 25 March 1991, section 3.

18 Many US states have such laws applicable only to cornea removal, as shall be seen below.

19 For instance, in the UK the recent change of policy by the BMA was founded on the prevailing cadaveric organ shortage there. Whilst supporters contend that PC systems are more respectful of the autonomy of the (now) deceased, this appears to be a secondary consideration for most, and merely a factor tending to produce higher donor rates.

20 W. Land and B. Cohen, 'Postmortem Living Organ Donation in Europe' (1992) 24 *Transplantation Proceedings* 2165 at 2167. In complete contrast, Michielsen has declared that 'Taken together these data suggest that at least in Europe and among countries with active transplantation programmes, there is a correlation between the existence of a presumed consent law and a higher organ retrieval': see P. Michielsen, 'Informed or Presumed Consent Legislative Models' in J. Chapman, M. Deierhoi and C. Wight, *Organ and Tissue Donation for Transplantation*, Arnold, London, 1997, 344 at 354.

21 See M. Mehlman, 'Presumed Consent to Organ Donation: A Reevaluation' (1991) 31 *Health Matrix* 31 at 40.

22 In France, Spain and Poland strong PC laws are not in fact operated in this fashion by clinicians anyhow.

regimes providing fruitful data and experience for comparative purposes are Austria and Belgium, whilst outside Europe Singapore's experience is also instructive as are, to some degree, some state laws in the US relating principally to corneal donation.

In Austria, the fifteen kidney donors per million population (pmp) in 1985 doubled to thirty in 1990, the highest donor rate in Europe, after which it levelled off.[23] Nonetheless, in 1991 51.2 pmp kidney transplants were performed compared with 28.2 pmp in the UK. Many have attributed such high procurement rates to the existence of a strong PC law under which relatives have no right to object to organ removal.[24] There was, however, a substantial downturn in donors at the start of the nineties. In 1990 there were 146 donors in Vienna, which dropped to 115 in 1991 and fell further in 1992. A survey conducted by Gotzinger *et al.* concluded that 'The downwards trend of donor rates in our area clearly shows that it takes more than a stable legal situation to ensure the necessary amount of donor organs; even a very successful transplant center has to work hard to maintain a certain standard of knowledge, information and motivation amongst the staff of the peripheral hospitals.'[25] Moreover, the rise in the number of donors started only in 1985 despite the presumed consent law having been passed in 1982. Wamser *et al.* have drawn attention to the massive public relations campaign instituted in 1986.[26] In addition, certain centres (Vienna and Linz) gradually introduced a 'decentralised' model of organ procurement as from 1984 and it appears that it was in these centres that the very large increases in organ donation and transplantation occurred.[27] The figures for Graz and Innsbruck, with centralised models, remained fairly static. Nevertheless, despite the reduction in the early nineties, comparatively high transplantation levels have generally

23 The King's Fund Report found there to have been a 33 per cent increase in the kidney donor rate as between 1985 and 1992: see King's Fund Institute, *A Question of Give and Take*, Research Report 18, King's Fund Institute, London, 1994, at 20 (Fig. 8).

24 There is no duty to inform relatives of the death and the intended organ procurement, although apparently 34.8 per cent of staff generally, and 1.7 per cent always, do so inform, leading to a refusal rate of somewhere around 5 per cent: see *Eurotransplant Newsletter*, June 1994, at 6.

25 Ibid.

26 P. Wamser *et al.*, 'Discontinuing of a Permanent Information and Education Program Among Donor ICUs Leads to a 50% Decrease of Organ Donor Rates' (1993) 25 *Transplantation Proceedings* 2988.

27 In Vienna, the number of donors rose from 40 in 1985 to 146 in 1990.

been maintained. In 1997, 42.9 pmp kidney transplants were carried out, a figure exceeded in that year in Europe only by Spain.[28]

Belgium is frequently held up as an 'advert' for presumed consent, in terms of its success in increasing organ donation/transplantation rates. Before the passing of the (weak) PC law in 1986, there was substantial uncertainty as to the legal position governing organ procurement. Following its passing, the number of kidneys available for transplantation increased by 114 per cent between 1985 and 1989, from 18.9 pmp to 41.3 pmp. Due to the increased number of donors, the number of persons on the transplant waiting list remained stable despite unlimited admission to that list by non-residents,[29] and the dialysis rate also remained static despite the very high rate of dialysis in Belgium.[30] It is also noteworthy that during this same period other countries in a similar geographical region but without PC laws, for example the Netherlands and Germany, did not experience similar increases.[31] Although, like Austria, Belgium has a high rate of road traffic deaths, Roels states that 'As less than half of the donors reported in 1989 were road traffic casualties, it is unlikely that this increased supply of donor organs could be attributed to a high number of fatal traffic accidents in Belgium, as suggested elsewhere.'[32] However, as the King's Fund Report noted, there was a good deal of publicity accompanying the implementation of the 1986 Law as well as a significant increase in the number of transplant co-ordinators, and a new system was introduced for the formal reimbursement of donating hospitals.[33]

[28] Only twenty-four of these were from living donors: see ITCS transplant statistics, 1997 at http://www.kuleuven.ac.be/Facdep/medicine/itcs/Home.html.

[29] Primarily from Italy. There is also, as in Austria, a very high rate of acceptance for renal replacement therapy in Belgium, illustrating that it is too simplistic to compare procurement regimes with effects on waiting list sizes in isolation from other factors.

[30] Indeed, Belgium was able to export organs in 1987, 1988 and 1989 to other nations within Eurotransplant, prompting the remark that 'The existence of different organ procurement policies among countries collaborating within the same organ exchange organisation leads to a permanent imbalance in organ availability, which could ultimately jeopardise the survival of these institutions': see L. Roels *et al.*, 'Effect of a Presumed Consent Law on Organ Retrieval in Belgium' (1990) 22 *Transplantation Proceedings* 2078 at 2079.

[31] The discrepancies between rates in Austria and those in the Netherlands and Germany are also fairly stark, trends which have continued subsequently. Between 1993 and 1995, the mean kidney procurement rate was 46 pmp in Austria, 39.9 pmp in Belgium, 27.9 pmp in the Netherlands and 24.2 pmp in Germany.

[32] L. Roels *et al.*, 'Three Years of Experience with a "Presumed Consent" Legislation in Belgium: Its Impact on Multi-Organ Donation in Comparison with other European Countries' (1991) 23 *Transplantation Proceedings* 903 at 904.

[33] King's Fund, *A Question of Give and Take*, at 58.

Further, Michielsen also notes how the decentralised model of organ procurement has flourished in many regions of Belgium since the passing of the 1986 legislation. On the other side of the coin though, data from the different Belgian centres after the enactment of the 1986 Law show substantial variations in organ donation rates between centres, such as Leuven, which adopted presumed consent and those, such as Brussels and Antwerp, which continued to seek relatives' permission despite the provisions of the new law. There was a sharp increase in the former but a fairly static picture in the latter. Moreover, the high rate of transplantation has been maintained, and in 1997 Belgium performed 419 kidney transplants, constituting 41.2 pmp.[34]

In Singapore, donation rates rose sharply after the passing of the new presumed consent law in 1987, the Human Organ Transplant Act. Between 1972 and 1982, when the Medical Therapy Act 1972 express consent law alone was in force, only thirty cadaveric kidneys were transplanted in total.[35] With the passing of the 1987 Act the number of kidneys donated annually rose from an average of 4.7 between 1972 and 1987 to 31.3 between 1988 and 1990. Interestingly though, the publicity surrounding the introduction of the 1987 presumed consent law had the incidental effect of also increasing the number of those giving express consent under the pre-existing 1972 Act (from 4.7 per year to 13). Within the United States many states have passed laws since 1975 permitting forensic pathologists to procure corneas either after efforts have been made to contact next of kin but no objections have been revealed or simply where no objections are known. This has resulted in a substantial increase in corneal donation and transplantation in those states.[36] The Georgia statute was passed in 1978. Prior to its enactment, approximately twenty-five cornea transplants were performed annually, whereas in 1984 for instance more than 1,000 cornea transplants were performed.[37] As a brief aside, it might also be added that Denmark, prior to the introduction

[34] Only eighteen of these were from living donors: see ITCS transplant statistics. The figures also include those transplants performed in Luxembourg but these are very modest in volume.

[35] King's Fund, *A Question of Give and Take*, at 58. But note that between 1982 and 1987 an attempt was made to increase the transplantation rate through the use of 'imported' kidneys.

[36] Farge *et al.* have stated that such statutes have 'led to a substantial increase in our eye banking activities': E. Farge *et al.*, 'The Impact of State Legislation on Eye Banking' (1994) 112 *Archives of Opthalmology* 180 at 183.

[37] See *Georgia Lions Eye Bank* v. *Lavant* 335 S.E. 2d 127 (Sup. Ct Ga. 1985) at 128. This picture is replicated in other states. In Florida, in 1976, 500 cornea transplants were performed, but after the passing of such a statute in 1976, this rose to 3,000 in 1985.

of an express consent law in 1986, had one of the highest cadaveric procurement rates in Europe under its PC regime, since when donation rates have fallen by a half.[38]

That presumed consent systems will yield more organs is logical. In PC systems (now) deceased persons have rarely objected to donation. In Belgium, a centralised Registry was established to record objections, but only 1.8 per cent of Belgians have in fact recorded such an objection. By contrast, in systems primarily relying on express statements of intention from the deceased, the evidence reveals that such express statements are available to procurement staff in a much smaller percentage of instances than reflect the true size of the potential donor pool (as gauged by public opinion surveys).[39] Thus, the deceased's express wish to donate may be defeated in many instances, because the views of relatives are the determining feature of most organ procurement scenarios. The influence of relatives typically reduces levels of organ procurement substantially. As noted earlier, where asked to supply it, relatives refuse *permission* in a sizeable percentage of cases. But where relatives are merely accorded a power to veto donation, their objections are generally at a fairly modest level. In Belgium, it appears that very few currently object to organ removals from deceased relatives, although the evidence for this is mainly anecdotal.[40]

Based on the above data, there would appear to be substantial *prima facie* evidence that presumed consent laws *are* a major factor in increasing organ donation. However, that is not to say that other factors may not be important, possibly more important. For instance, in Spain, despite the *de jure* strong presumed consent law, the family are invariably involved in decision-making and clinical staff usually defer to their wishes (that is it is a *de facto* express consent law). Ironically, both Gerson and Sipes refer to the 'failure' of the Spanish presumed consent law to generate adequate

[38] See B. Rix, 'Brain Death, Ethics, and Politics in Denmark' in S. Youngner, R. Arnold and R. Schapiro (eds.), *The Definition of Death: Contemporary Controversies*, Johns Hopkins University Press, Baltimore, 1999, 227 at 235. Refusal rates increased: see S. Birkeland *et al.*, 'Organ Donation: Number of Brain Deaths, Refusal Rate, Actual Donation, and Multiorgan Transplantation 1990–1994 in a Danish Population of 1 Million Compared to the Whole of Denmark' (1995) 27 *Transplantation Proceedings* 3521 at 3522–3.

[39] There are often practical difficulties such as statements on driving licences being separated from casualties by emergency personnel at the scene of road traffic accidents, in addition to eligibility to drive, etc.

[40] The figure is reported to be less than 10 per cent: see I. Kennedy *et al.*, 'The Case for "Presumed Consent" in Organ Donation' (1998) 351 *Lancet* 1650 at 1651.

numbers of organs by virtue of this fact.[41] Yet Spain now has the highest rate of organ donation in Europe! In 1997, Spain performed 1,861 kidney transplants (46.9 pmp), more than any other European nation.[42] Moreover, Matesanz *et al.* have also shown that any association between high road traffic death rates and high procurement rates is modest.[43] It appears that a highly organised and well-resourced system, employing large numbers of transplant co-ordinators in a decentralised system, can itself have a major impact on donor rates. The organisational and resource-related changes to the system seem to have created a 'success' even without there being, in practice, a presumed consent system. Thus, presumed consent would appear to be one mechanism for helping to facilitate the supply or organs but it is by no means a necessary or sufficient condition for success.[44]

An analysis of existing ('consent') legislation

Practically all jurisdictions with so-called express consent laws have enacted 'strong' versions.[45] There are very few jurisdictions with the 'weak' variant whereby relatives are permitted to veto the deceased's explicit request to donate.[46] One exception is that of Japan, where the 1997 Law states:

> In cases where a deceased person had, during his lifetime, expressed his intention in writing to donate his organs for the purposes of transplantation, the physician may remove organs from the body of his person (in whom brain death has been established) in order to carry out a

[41] W. Gerson, 'Refining the Law of Organ Donation: Lessons from the French Law of Presumed Consent' (1987) 19 *New York University Journal of International Law and Policy* 1013 at 1029 n. 88; D. Sipes, 'Does it Matter whether there is a Public Policy for Presumed Consent in Organ Transplantation?' (1991) 12 *Whittier Law Review* 505 at 516 n. 57.

[42] Only twenty were from living donors: see ITCS transplant statistics.

[43] They note that a new road traffic law was passed in Spain in June 1992 following which there was a 21 per cent decrease in the volume of road traffic fatalities. However, there was also an 11.3 per cent increase in organ donations over the same period: see R. Matesanz *et al.*, 'Organ Procurement in Spain: The National Organisation of Transplants' in J. Touraine *et al.* (eds.), *Organ Shortage: The Solutions*, Kluwer, Dordrecht, 1995, 167 at 171.

[44] See also Michielsen, 'Informed or Presumed', at 354.

[45] For instance in Argentina, Australia, Belarus, Canada, Denmark, Norway, the Philippines, Romania, Slovenia, the United Kingdom, Venezuela, Zimbabwe and almost all states in the US.

[46] Although this was the position in England and Wales as regards anatomical examination and dissection under the provisions of the Anatomy Act 1832.

transplantation in accordance with this Law if the family of the deceased, having knowledge of this intention, are not opposed to such removal, or if the deceased does not have a family.[47]

Another is Lebanon where organ removal is only permissible where both the deceased *and* members of the family, in a priority order, have given their consent.[48] Nevertheless, in many jurisdictions, whilst the law does not confer a right to override the express wishes/request of the deceased, in practice this discretion is accorded to relatives by medical staff. This is the prevailing situation across the United Kingdom, Australia and the United States.

However, whilst almost all EC regimes are 'strong' versions this is only part of the story. They invariably also allow relatives to give consent to donation where the deceased did not (formally) express a wish to donate, unless there is any evidence that the deceased would have objected. For instance, in the US, under the 1987 Uniform Anatomical Gift Act (UAGA), a member of a specified class of persons, in the order of priority stipulated, may make an anatomical gift of all or part of the decedent's body unless the decedent at the time of death has made an unrevoked refusal to make that anatomical gift.[49] The 1997 Law enacted in Germany similarly stipulates that organ donation is permissible where the organ donor has consented to organ removal *or* where there is neither written evidence of consent by the deceased nor written evidence of objection by the deceased, when a decision to allow organ donation is made by the next of kin in a list containing an order of priority. Similar legislative schemes exist around the world; they are not confined to Europe and North America.[50]

Jurisdictions with strong *presumed* consent systems include Austria,

[47] Law of 16 July 1997, section 6(1).

[48] Decree of 16 September 1983, section 2. This would also appear to be the legal position in Kyrgyzstan, although there is a lack of clarity as to whether relatives actually possess a right of veto or merely a right to challenge in court whether the consent of the deceased truly reflected his/her will.

[49] Section 3. The 1987 UAGA largely replicates the 1968 UAGA on this, although Sullivan rightly notes that, generally speaking, the 1987 version is 'not a mere update of the 1968 Act. It is a comprehensive revision, a replacement': see G. Sullivan, 'The Uniform Anatomical Gift Act' in Spielman, *Organ and Tissue Donation*, 19 at 25. All US states have enacted one or other variant of the UAGA.

[50] For instance, section 2 of the 1994 Resolution implementing the 1992 Law in Venezuela has almost identical provisions. Other examples can be given from such diverse locations as Algeria, Sri Lanka and Turkey.

France, Luxembourg, Poland, Portugal, the Slovak Republic and Spain. Under section 62a of the Austrian Federal Law, organ removal is permissible unless the deceased person expressly declared an objection to organ donation. Similarly, under Article 4 of the 1995 Law passed in Poland, organ removal from a cadaver is permissible unless the person indicated a refusal to permit such a procedure during his or her lifetime.[51] Although such laws are primarily to be found in Europe, this is not exclusively the case. Section 23 of the Supreme Decree in Peru, for instance, states that organ removal for transplantation is permissible where the deceased did not expressly object to this during his or her lifetime. Brazil has a similar legal regime, as has Singapore.

Jurisdictions which have 'weak' presumed consent laws include Belgium, where organ removal is permissible unless the deceased expressed an objection *or* if a close relative has communicated an objection to the physician.[52] Similarly, Finnish law specifies that a deceased person's organs may be removed for transplantation purposes provided that the deceased did not object during his or her lifetime and that there is no reason to believe that the next of kin or guardian *would* object to the procedure. The italics in this last sentence highlight an important distinction between the Belgian and Finnish regimes and raise an issue which will be picked up again later concerning the extent to which the onus is on the health professionals involved to *seek* out or anticipate possible objections.

There is a substantial degree of misclassification of different systems, however, which impedes clarity of analysis and the integrity of evaluations of systems and their effects.

Miscasting?

Under the Human Tissue Act 1961 in England, Scotland and Wales,[53] organ removal may be authorised if the deceased had requested to donate prior to death or if, 'having made such reasonable enquiry as may be practicable', the person concerned has no reason to believe that the

[51] Law of 26 October 1995, Article 4. A further example is the 1994 Law of the Slovak Republic which provides in section 47 that organs may be harvested from cadavers for transplantation unless the deceased made a written statement or otherwise demonstrable proclamation of his/her objection.

[52] Tunisia also has a weak PC statute: see Law of 25 March 1991, section 3.

[53] The relevant Act in Northern Ireland is the Human Tissue Act (Northern Ireland) 1962.

deceased had expressed an objection or that any surviving spouse or relative objects thereto.[54] This is frequently held out as being the classic exemplar of an express consent system[55] and is regularly contrasted with other, supposedly presumed consent, regimes such as in Norway. Under Norwegian law organs may be removed from a deceased person if he/she had made a written or oral instruction prior to death or, in the absence of such an instruction, if neither the deceased nor the nearest relative has expressed an objection thereto, and there are no grounds for assuming that the procedure would be contrary to the fundamental convictions of the deceased or the nearest relative.[56] Sweden has a very similar law.[57] There is no difference in substance between these laws and that in Britain however. Whilst under all of them an express consent of the deceased suffices to justify removal, so that it would seemingly qualify as an express consent regime, they also permit organ removal for transplantation *without any express consent* from either the deceased or relatives, in the absence of any objection from either, consistent with allegedly *presumed* consent schemes.

So, whilst essentially the same, which type of system are they? Some analysts conceive certain legislative regimes as creating *first tier* 'express' and *second tier* 'presumed' consent regimes.[58] However, it is submitted that it is these very 'second tier' provisions which fundamentally encapsulate the nature of the scheme, that is one can only evaluate a scheme *as a whole*. Under none of the above schemes is it a precondition that a consent to removal has been obtained, from either the deceased or a relative. They do not fit into a 'No . . . but' framework and are consequently (weak) presumed consent systems all. It is therefore some-

[54] See 1961 Act, section 1(2).

[55] The King's Fund Report stated that 'The UK, along with Germany, the Netherlands, Italy, Canada, Australia and New Zealand, have what might be termed "opting-in" legal systems': see King's Fund, *A Question of Give and Take*, at 56. See also the Law Reform Commission of Canada, *Procurement and Transfer of Human Tissues and Organs*, Working Paper 66, Minister of Supply and Services, Ottawa, 1992, describing British law as an 'express consent approach', at 145.

[56] Law of 9 February 1973, section 2. It is obligatory that the relatives be informed, as far as possible, of the death prior to any removal procedure.

[57] And also, I shall suggest, those in Belgium, Finland and Tunisia, etc., despite the differences in legislative style between the relevant statutory provisions.

[58] This analysis has been offered by both Kennedy and Skegg, for instance, with respect to the Human Tissue Act: see I. Kennedy, 'The Donation and Transplantation of Kidneys: Should the Law be Changed?' (1979) 5 *Journal of Medical Ethics* 13 at 15, and P. Skegg, *Law, Ethics and Medicine*, Clarendon Press, Oxford, 1988, at 242–4.

what ironic that in the UK the notion of presumed consent has generally been shunned as being insufficiently 'PC'! The paradox is heightened by a resolution of the British Medical Association at its 1999 annual representative meeting to agitate for legal reform and a move *to* a presumed consent law (which could therefore of course juristically mean no more than a change from a weak to a 'strong' PC law, which would exclude the significance of the views of relatives entirely; an extremely improbable development).[59] Whilst in practice the *consent* of relatives is invariably sought in the UK, even in fact in cases where the deceased *had* expressed a positive wish to donate, the law does not require this. Thus, it is *practices* that may arguably need to change, not the law. This analytical reappraisal is especially important in so far as many Commonwealth jurisdictions have laws modelled on the British statute, including many of the territories and states of Australia.[60] The result is that there may be many more presumed consent systems in existence and more basic similarities between regimes than formerly supposed.

Misconceptions appear to flow either from confusion between *de facto* and *de jure* systems or between matters of form as opposed to substance.

Form or substance?

Certainly, orthodox express consent regimes generally kick off with the pronouncement that organ removal for transplantation is permitted if the deceased made a written (sometimes, alternatively, an oral) statement of the request or wish to donate organ(s). However, a significant number of stereotypical presumed consent laws contain a similar provision, albeit not usually so prominently.[61] Moreover, many of these jurisdictions (for example Belgium and Finland) have provisions stipulating that where the express request of the deceased exists, no objection of relatives may override such a wish. These are, of course, a mirror image of provisions in

[59] The United Kingdom Government rejected the BMA's proposal: see Erin and Harris, 'Presumed Consent', at 365.

[60] For example, in South Australia: see the Transplantation and Anatomy Act 1983, section 21. However, other jurisdictions have subtly different regimes; for instance in Queensland, under the Transplantation and Anatomy Act 1979, the senior next of kin must *consent* where the deceased has not explicitly requested to donate: see section 22. Jurisdictions such as those in Malaysia and India have laws closely fashioned on the British statute also.

[61] Although, as seen above, Norwegian law, which is indeed a presumed consent law, leads off with such a provision in its section on cadaveric donation: see 1973 Law, section 2.

most unequivocally express consent jurisdictions.[62] Thus, most laws start from a common base. But in the absence of an express request/consent, what then?

In strong PC jurisdictions the absence of an objection from the deceased is itself sufficient to condone organ removal, regardless of relatives' views. By contrast, in EC jurisdictions, in the absence of any expressed view of the deceased, the views of relatives, where ascertainable, are almost *always* relevant and influential. But this is true also in weak presumed consent jurisdictions, so that the primary distinction is between strong PC systems and EC systems generally. However, under weak PC laws there is no necessity to procure a 'consent' from relatives or anyone else, where the deceased made no explicit request but is not known to have objected. Organs can be removed simply where there is no *objection* communicated by a relative. As Crothers and Uglem state, a law is a PC law where it 'allows organ procurement without specific consent by the donor or the donor's next-of-kin'.[63]

One might wish to argue though that the difference between jurisdictions such as in Britain and undoubted PC jurisdictions such as in Belgium, Finland and Tunisia lies in the fact that in the latter the silence of the deceased is itself an authorising factor, that is a presumed 'consent', whereas in EC systems no such consent/authorisation can be 'read into' the deceased's silence. It is submitted however that silence (that is a failure to object) is not in truth a species of 'consent' and that there is a confusion between form and substance at play here. The structure and character of these legislative provisions are virtually identical. In Britain removal may take place if the deceased did not object (nor did a contacted relative), as well as where a positive request is made, as in say Belgium and Finland. Skegg has commented of the legislation in Britain that 'it differs from the "opting out" schemes which have sometimes been proposed in that there is no provision for a register in which objections could be recorded, and which would have to be consulted before authorisation is given',[64] but these are pragmatic (although no less (ethically) important for that) concerns and not matters affecting how one *classifies* the relevant system.

[62] For instance in Denmark and Germany and those US states with laws modelled upon the 1968 UAGA.

[63] D. Crothers and C. Uglem, 'A Proposal for a Presumed Consent Organ Donation Policy in North Dakota' (1992) 68 *North Dakota Law Review* 637 at 646.

[64] Skegg, *Law, Ethics and Medicine*, at 244.

Admittedly in some jurisdictions it is very much easier to record or register an objection. But why should the deceased's 'silence', that is failure to object, be interpreted differently in terms of legal status between the respective jurisdictions merely on that account? It might be desirable to 'publicly construe' silence in such a fashion (that is a tacit consent) but that cannot alter the crux of it, which is that the deceased merely has not exercised his/her power of veto. Arguably then, 'presumed consent' is a misnomer.

Whatever the colour of the system there is no means of expressing either positive or negative wishes regarding organ donation peculiar or discrete to a particular type of system. Some EC systems have organ donation registries as do nearly all PC systems (for example Austria, Belgium, France and Portugal). Some registries allow persons to express either positive wishes *or* objections, for example in Belgium, Denmark, the Netherlands, Spain and Sweden, whereas others allow only express willingness (for example in the UK) or only objections (for example in Portugal) to be registered. Most nations with EC systems have some form of donor card system, but some PC systems also have a (non-)donor card system in place. In many PC jurisdictions there may be no obvious or official means of expressing or registering a *positive* request (although in Belgium and Sweden a positive wish may be recorded on the centralised computer system), but in the same way there is generally no formal mechanism for recording *objections* in many EC jurisdictions. However, it will become clear that such mechanisms are not merely formal aspects of such systems but also affect one's ethical appraisal of the relevant system in place. Akveld and De Charro properly emphasise that

> Preference for a certain decision system does not necessarily follow from the concept of respecting the right of self-determination. The extent to which self-determination is respected and done justice to does not depend on the system as such, it depends more on the organisation of the system and on the way in which assistance functions within a given system.[65]

Hybrids

In almost all express consent jurisdictions properly so called, in the absence of the deceased's explicit request, a relative (usually in a defined

[65] J. Akveld and F. de Charro, 'Organ Donation and Regulation' in F. de Charro, D. Hessing and J. Akveld (eds.), *Systems of Donor Recruitment*, Kluwer, Deventer, 1992, 113 at 116.

sequence) must provide consent. However, some do not *require* any direct approach to be made to relatives at all, only a reasonable search to be made. Whilst in the US the 1968 UAGA necessitates a consent to be given by either the deceased or relatives in every instance, the 1987 version of the UAGA stipulates that either the *medical examiner (coroner) or the local public health officer* may release and permit removal of any part of the dead body for transplantation *where a reasonable effort has been made* to locate and examine the decedent's medical records and inform the relatives listed of their option to make or object to making an anatomical gift.[66] In other words, a search must be made to locate next of kin and to obtain their consent but, if the search for relatives is unsuccessful, organs may be removed in any event in the absence of any explicit consent, unless there is evidence that the decedent did not want to donate.[67] The Comment to the 1987 UAGA described this provision as a 'residuary authorisation for transplant or therapeutic purposes only'. Nonetheless, this provision of the Model Law has been adopted in various states, usually only in relation to corneas but in some instances in connection with organs in general.[68] In Louisiana, the law, which is applicable to organs and tissue generally, permits explantation where there has been a 'good faith effort to locate the decedent's next of kin'.[69] In Arizona, as regards only corneas, a 'diligent effort' is required, which is stated to mean that it lasts not less than four hours nor more than five, and the medical examiner is obliged to attempt to notify the decedent's next of kin at fifteen-minute intervals on the telephone, or contact him/her in person if they have no telephone.[70] Some commentators have observed that such

66 Section 4. It is also made clear that what is a 'reasonable effort' is conditioned upon taking into account 'the useful life of the part'. The implication is the same under section 2 of the 1973 Norwegian Law.

67 Under the 1968 UAGA there was a provision in section 2(b)(6) allowing for a final category of person to authorise removal, namely 'any other person authorised or under an obligation to dispose of the body'. This provision was deleted in the 1987 amendments and replaced by its more limited provisions. It would seem that that provision in the 1968 version was ignored in practice in any event.

68 I.e. in California (Cal. Gov't. Code s. 27491.45 (Deering Supp. 1991)), Louisiana (La. Rev. Stat. Ann. s. 2354.3 (West Supp. 1989)) and s. 2354.2 (West Supp. 1982), Maryland (Md. Est. & Trusts Code Ann. s. 4–509 (Supp. 1989)), Mississippi (Miss. Code Ann. s. 41–61–71 (Supp. 1989)), Texas (Tex. Rev. Civ. Stat. Ann. Art. 4590–6 (Vernon Supp. 1989)) and Utah (Utah Code Ann. s. 26–4–23 (Supp. 1989)).

69 La. Rev. Stat. Ann. s. 2354.3 (West 1982).

70 In Mississippi, with regard to 'tissues' in general (including organs), a 'reasonable attempt' must be made to contact next of kin. In relation to corneas only, in Illinois, a 'reasonable and good faith effort' is necessitated.

laws based upon the 1987 UAGA in fact contradict the original 1968 version of the UAGA,[71] which was premised on the need for an express consent to donation. Indeed, as Sipes rightly observes, 'Of course, the quasi-presumed consent statutes that allow for the bypass of the search if the viability of the organs or tissues is in question translate in result into pure presumed consent, since no search takes place.'[72] They are indeed hybrid, quasi-presumed consent laws. By contrast, in 'true' express consent regimes such as in Denmark and the Netherlands, no removal is permissible in the absence of such a consent being procured. In Denmark the 1990 Law explicitly states that 'In the event that the deceased person leaves no close relative, the intervention may not be performed.'

Unclaimed bodies

Many presumed consent laws have their origins in the unclaimed body statutes passed in the nineteenth century to facilitate the supply of corpses to medical schools for anatomical dissection (for example the Anatomy Act 1832), which permitted authorisation to be given for their use where no relatives had come forward to claim the body of the deceased.[73] They required no 'consent' to be obtained. Despite remarks made by the US Task Force on Organ Transplantation in 1986 that 'present efforts should focus on enhancing the current voluntary system rather than on reducing the role of actual consent',[74] there are at least thirteen US states[75] which have enacted laws of this ilk, currently only applicable to corneal tissue and only to corpses in the custody of the coroner,[76] many of which have already been judicially upheld as being constitutional.[77] The typical statute requires *no search* and allows for the removal of corneas without the family's consent, as long as there is *no known objection.* These laws

[71] See D. Sipes, 'Does it Matter Whether there is a Public Policy for Presumed Consent in Organ Transplantation?' (1991) 12 *Whittier Law Review* 505 at 528.

[72] Ibid., at 526 n. 89.

[73] See Richardson, *Death, Dissection and the Destitute.*

[74] Report of the Task Force on Organ Transplantation, *Organ Transplantation: Issues and Recommendations*, US Department of Health and Human Services, Washington D.C., 1986, at 31.

[75] See Sipes, 'Does it Matter?', at 525. The states are California, Connecticut, Delaware, Florida, Georgia, Kentucky, Maryland, Michigan, North Carolina, Ohio, Tennessee, Texas and West Virginia.

[76] There are various other similar statutes applicable to pituitary glands, but these are removed for scientific rather than therapeutic purposes.

[77] For instance in Florida, Georgia and Michigan: see below.

have been properly dubbed 'pure' PC laws – there is no need to secure any consent whatever prior to organ removal. For this reason, the Human Tissue Act 1961 and its progeny are of the same genus; the search is for potential *objections* to removal, not in order to solicit a consent or permission for removal.

Wherever objections to donation will defeat a proposed removal, a further distinguishing feature resides in the locus and extent of the onus of discovering or communicating objections. This is especially pertinent where the objections of relatives are influential. In Britain the person lawfully in possession of the body *must* make 'such reasonable enquiry as may be practicable' to ascertain that neither the deceased nor any relatives object to the removal.[78] In Norway, it is obligatory that the nearest relative be informed of the death, as far as is possible, prior to any removal procedure. By contrast, in Finland the removal may proceed as long as the physician had 'no reason to consider' that such an objection existed, and in Belgium it may be carried out unless such an objection has *been communicated to* the physician. In the latter instances the degree of responsibility placed on physicians is vague, and may even be non-existent. Indeed, Matas *et al.* have argued that the likelihood of any relatives objecting under many presumed consent jurisdictions is minimised simply by virtue of the absence of any responsibility placed on doctors to inform relatives of the practice and to give them an opportunity to lodge a protest.[79]

Assuming for the present that a consent may be either express or presumed, the principal distinctions between different systems therefore reside in whether, where there is a 'consent' given by the (now) deceased, this can be overridden by the objection of a relative, whether, if the deceased has not 'consented' to donation, the views of surviving relatives are of any relevance and, if they are, whether there is a duty to obtain an explicit consent from a relative or merely to determine whether any objection(s) exist(s). But it is submitted that there *is* nevertheless a real difference between these two supposed species of 'consent' and that, in the absence of a need for an express consent, there must be an *a priori*

[78] See further discussion of the meaning of this expression in G. Dworkin, 'The Law relating to Organ Transplantation in England' (1970) 33 *Modern Law Review* 353 at 364–5, and P. Skegg, 'Human Tissue Act 1961' (1976) 16 *Medicine, Science and the Law* 193 at 197.

[79] A. Matas *et al.*, 'A Proposal for Cadaver Organ Procurement: Routine Removal with Right of Informed Refusal' (1985) 10(2) *Journal of Health Politics, Policy and Law* 231 at 237.

justification for organ removal, that is '*Yes* . . . unless'. One can override this initial presumption under a presumed consent system, but from where does it originally emanate? Dickens, Fluss and King contend that 'Presumed consent legislation treats cadaveric materials as a public asset, but permits individuals who object to their own or deceased family members' materials being removed to prohibit recovery.'[80] By contrast, Childress asserts that presumed consent 'does not presuppose that bodily parts belong to the state. The individual and/or family still controls the disposition of those bodily parts; the only difference is the shift in presumption about the individual's wishes.'[81]

Required request/routine enquiry

In most jurisdictions, where an express consent is preconditional to organ removal, legal provisions do not necessitate that an approach actually be made to patients or relatives for permission for organ removal, despite the fact that organs may sometimes be lost if not. Legislation to ensure this takes place has been shunned to date in the United Kingdom,[82] although an audit has subsequently been implemented. However, as we have already noted, legislation has been enacted in the US and in certain Canadian provinces to address this issue. Virnig and Caplan have classified such legislation into either 'strong' or 'weak' laws. Strong laws require documentation on the death certificate of a request and its outcome, whilst weak types require simply that hospitals develop policies or protocols to ensure that families are asked to donate. These have, alternatively, and more typically, been dubbed 'required request' and 'routine enquiry' laws respectively. By 1990 twenty-six US states and the District of Columbia had enacted required request laws and a further eighteen states had enacted routine enquiry laws.[83]

[80] B. Dickens, S. Fluss and A. King, 'Legislation on Organ and Tissue Donation' in Chapman *et al.*, *Organ and Tissue Donation for Transplantation*, 95 at 101.

[81] J. Childress, 'Some Moral Connections between Organ Procurement and Organ Distribution' (1987) 3 *Journal of Contemporary Health Law and Policy* 85 at 94.

[82] A private member's bill, the Transplant Notification Bill, introduced in 1988 by Cardiff North MP Mr Gwilym Jones, which would have required health authorities to establish effective systems for identifying donors and notifying relevant procurement organisations, was ordered to be read a second time on 15 April but got no further. See *Hansard*, House of Commons, 3 February 1988, at 1005 (Bill 92).

[83] A. Gaber, G. Hall and L. Britt, 'An Assessment of the Impact of Required Request Legislation

The first required request law was passed in Oregon in 1985.[84] Under that statute, where no anatomical gift has been made in respect of a death occurring in hospital, the hospital administrator is obliged to request the person listed in priority order to consent to donation, when persons in prior classes are not available at the time of death. New York's Law[85] is to very similar effect and there are equivalent laws in Alabama, Indiana and West Virginia, amongst other states. Arizona, California, Connecticut, Georgia, Kentucky, New Hampshire, Pennsylvania, Rhode Island and Tennessee have state laws requiring hospitals to develop protocols which require that families be informed of the option to donate organs. California passed a law in 1985 which stated that

> Each general acute care hospital shall develop a protocol for identifying potential organ and tissue donors. The protocol shall require that any deceased individual's next of kin or other individual at or near the time of notification of death be asked whether the deceased was an organ donor or if the family is a donor family. If not, the family shall be informed of the option to donate organs and tissues.[86]

Robertson *et al.* assert that 'Required Request legislation did not produce the desired results and, in fact, it is estimated that as many as one third of families of medically suitable potential donors are never approached about donation options by hospital staff.'[87] There are indeed high levels of physician non-compliance (50+ per cent in some states),[88] and even Caplan, the initial designer of such policies, admits that such laws have had only a 'small positive impact on the supply of organs available for transplantation',[89] and that they have had a far greater impact in indirect (routinisation) than direct terms. This appears to be the case even where

on the Availability of Cadaveric Organs for Transplantation' (1990) 22 *Transplantation Proceedings* 318.

84 Chapter 379, Laws 1985, House Bill No. 2902, An Act Relating to Organ Transplants, approved 3 July 1985. An exception was created where the organ would not be of any use for transplantation.

85 Chapter 801, Laws 1985, Senate Int. No. 4925–C.

86 Chapter 779, Assembly Bill No. 631. It added that 'The protocol shall encourage reasonable discretion and sensitivity to the family circumstances in all discussions regarding donations of tissue and organs.'

87 V. Robertson, G. George, P. Gedrich, R. Hasz, R. Kochlik and H. Nathan, 'Concentrated Professional Education to Implement Routine Referral Legislation Increases Organ Donation' (1998) 30 *Transplantation Proceedings* 214.

88 Only in Kentucky is there any sanction for non-compliance.

89 A. Caplan, 'Professional Arrogance and Public Misunderstanding' (1988) 18 *Hastings Center Report* 34 at 35.

compliance is high. A fairly recent survey across twenty-three US hospitals in two metropolitan areas found that relatives were approached for consent to donate in 86.6 per cent of cases of prospective organ donation, but only consented in 46.5 per cent of instances. The authors ultimately conclude that 'Required Request legislation has not, however, resulted in the expected increase in the number of procured organs, tissues, or corneas. Studies in several states have shown that although there was a small immediate increase in procurement after the passage of Required Request laws, these increases were modest and levelled off after the first 2 years.'[90] There is evidence of increased referrals and donations immediately post-legislation in some states. For example in Arizona there was a three- to fivefold increase, which may be contrasted with the situation in Nevada, where no such legislation was passed and no increase in donor organs occurred during the same period. Similar increases occurred in New York and Oregon, especially donations of corneas,[91] but in most states these increases tailed off again shortly afterwards. An analysis of all referrals made in Tennessee between 1985 and 1988 showed that the total of donor referrals increased in the year of implementation (1987) but levelled off to pre-legislation levels over the next year,[92] as did the total number of donors.

Some clinicians object to the bureaucratic intrusion on clinical discretion here. The King's Fund Report stated that, whilst recognising that such policies have the potential to reduce tensions on health care professionals and families at a time of great (di)stress,

> There is also a danger that respect for donors may be eroded in the constant search for organs and this may have long term implications for public confidence in the medical team and the organ donation process. In general it seems clear that required request's prescriptive nature, and the associated problems of enforceability, mean that it is ethically unsustainable. There is also little evidence that it would be effective in improving the supply.[93]

[90] L. Siminoff, R. Arnold, A. Caplan, B. Virnig and D. Seltzer, 'Public Policy Governing Organ and Tissue Procurement in the United States' (1995) 123 *Annals of Internal Medicine* 10 at 11.

[91] See S. Tolle *et al.*, 'Responsibilities of Primary Physicians in Organ Donation' (1987) 106 *Annals of Internal Medicine* 740.

[92] There were forty-six referrals in 1985, sixty-four in 1986, eighty-five in 1987 and fifty-six in 1988.

[93] King's Fund, *A Question of Give and Take*, at 63.

This may be rather sweeping, but it is certainly no independent or magical panacea. However, there are many variants of such laws and some may be more successful than others in increasing procurement. The experience under a 1994 statute passed in Pennsylvania which required notification of all patient deaths to the relevant Organ Procurement Organisation has shown, under the Delaware Valley Transplant Program, a 24 per cent increase in the number of organ donors between 1994 and 1996.[94] Indeed, there is evidence that higher rates of family consent are obtained when a transplant co-ordinator or other party (for example a clergyman or social worker) rather than hospital staff approaches relatives.[95] In the United Kingdom, the involvement of chaplains has been shown to lower refusal rates.

Required request policies reinforce the underlying character of the scheme being operated however. As in most express consent systems the relatives have a pivotal role in practice, such laws will tend to embed this feature, even when public policy is supposedly in favour of maximising the wishes of the deceased rather than those of relatives. Moreover, without extensive support mechanisms, such as bereavement care strategies, they are also unlikely to witness much of an improvement in procurement rates. Sullivan comments that 'The new required request laws, when implemented, were criticised as imposing too great a burden on physicians and families. Moreover, they too failed to increase donations.'[96]

A 'systems analysis' and critique

Give or take?

There is a preponderant view that consent in one form or another should be required for organ donation. Both the World Health Organisation Guiding Principles (Principle 1) and the Council of Europe Resolution in 1978 recognised the different forms that a 'consent' might take. The latter in fact gave explicit endorsement to presumed consent, permitting organ

94 Robertson *et al.*, 'Concentrated Professional Education', at 215.

95 See Letter, 'Public Policy Governing Organ and Tissue Procurement' (1996) 124 *Annals of Internal Medicine* 374.

96 R. Sullivan, 'The Uniform Anatomical Gift Act' in Spielman, *Organ and Tissue Donation*, at 24.

removal where the deceased had not objected to it or 'would not have been expected to have objected to it'.[97] The Conference of European Health Ministers declared that 'Legislation and practice in all Member States in fact acknowledge the right of a person to consent during his lifetime to donate an organ after death for transplant purposes . . . and . . . envisage two ways of ascertaining consent . . . express consent and presumed consent.'[98]

Advocates of presumed consent contend that it is just as much a form of 'consent' as any other. Indeed, it has been asserted that presumed consent is a legal and moral doctrine already employed in medicine, for instance with regard to the treatment of unconscious or incompetent patients in emergencies.[99] However, this analogy is false. Carrying out treatment necessary to preserve life or health where the person is unable to consent in such circumstances is typically justified on the basis of the (objectively assessed) best interests of the patient or on the basis of a substituted judgement by a third party. It is true that in both instances one is attempting to decide on the basis of what the individual *would have* decided, in the former instance based upon what persons typically would decide to do (because this would generally further their interests) and in the latter based upon knowledge of the person's attitudes, beliefs and values, but this is not a (presumed) *consent* (even where virtually everybody would have consented had they been competent to do so) although it attempts to give effect to the supposed *wishes* of that person. In any event, why is organ donation so unequivocally either 'beneficial' or something one would generally want? (Empirical evidence of existing rates of organ donation certainly would not bear this out.)

Silence is not generally regarded as consent *per se* either in most legal contexts or in everyday life. However, Beauchamp and Childress assert that it is perfectly plausible to view presumed consent as a form of 'tacit' consent, assuming certain preconditions are satisfied. They offer the example of a hospital patient who is informed that an HIV antibody test will be performed unless he/she objects. They state that 'If a patient is silent when told the test will be performed unless he or she objects, silence

[97] Article 10, Council of Europe Resolution (78) 29.

[98] Third Report of the Conference of European Health Ministers (Paris, 16–17 November 1987), *Organ Transplantation: Legislative Measures in Relation to Organ Transplantation and to European Co-operation*, Council of Europe, Strasbourg, 1987, at 6.

[99] See R. Veatch, 'Routine Enquiry about Organ Donation – An Alternative to Presumed Consent' (1991) 325 *New England Journal of Medicine* 1245 at 1247.

constitutes valid tacit consent as long as understanding and voluntariness are present.'[100] Childress stipulates that: (a) the potential refuser/consenter must be aware of the system and the implications of action or inaction; (b) they must have a reasonable time period in which to object; and (c) the potential effects of refusing must not be 'extremely detrimental'.[101] We shall gloss over the latter point here as it relates primarily to situations where the allocation of organs is potentially linked to a willingness to donate.[102] It is submitted though that whilst these commentators' views have great force, a presumed consent is not a true consent. There is no 'No . . . but' inference at work. One can only surmise that a *decision* to permit donation was made by the person whilst still alive no matter how easy it was for the individual to register an objection, whereas an express consent is definite evidence of such a decision and wish. They describe tacit consent as tending towards an 'implied' consent, but one would generally ascribe wishes to much less equivocal accompanying conduct.

Although in (weak) PC jurisdictions organ removal may not take place where, although the deceased has expressed no objection (but is 'presumed' to have consented), relatives object, in many of those same jurisdictions it is explicitly stipulated that if the deceased had expressed a *positive wish to donate* then relatives have no right to override those wishes (for example in Belgium and Finland). This suggests that presumed and express consents are not on a par. It at least recognises the obvious fact that an express request is *substantially better* evidence of a person's wishes than a tacit acceptance. This is emphasised in the remarks made at the Conference of European Health Ministers that

> The role of the family in deciding on organ removal is much more important in cases of presumed consent than in those of express consent. In the latter case, the sentimental objections of the family have to be weighed against the legal rights of the deceased who has willed organ

[100] T. Beauchamp and J. Childress, *Principles of Biomedical Ethics*, 4th edn, Oxford University Press, Oxford, 1994, at 129.

[101] J. Childress, 'Ethical Criteria for Procuring and Distributing Organs for Transplantation' in D. Mathieu (ed.), *Organ Substitution Technology: Ethical, Legal, and Public Policy Issues*, Westview Press, Boulder, Colo., 1988, 87 at 96.

[102] An example of which derives from the 1987 legislation in Singapore considered in the final chapter.

donation. In the case of presumed consent, the family's express objection weighs more heavily against the presumed consent of the deceased.[103]

But many would argue that in any case it is the right to control one's cadaver that is in issue, that is the right to avoid certain uses of it, not the right to give, which requires protection, so that it is the right to *object* which is critical, not the fact of whether a positive request was made. Consent is one (albeit the best) indicator of a lack of objection but need not be the only evidence. Moreover, in the face of a genuine societal need for organs to save lives, and improve the quality of lives, it may also be acceptable to lower the threshold in terms of the reliability of the evidence of willingness required. It may be appropriate to put more onus on to the potential organ source. The issue then re-emerges as to whether the opportunity to object was sufficient in the circumstances.

A Report of the Council on Ethical and Judicial Affairs of the American Medical Association[104] (AMA Report) stated that 'When individuals and families are not told that they can object or how to object to organ donation, presumed consent becomes in effect a strategy for avoiding consent entirely.' Childress takes the view that in the United States, because of the lack of knowledge of the corneal tissue (presumed consent) laws operative in some states, such policies may be ethically dubious. He suggests that in some instances 'the policy is actually one of expropriation masquerading as presumed consent'.[105] If no easy, accessible and confidential means were provided to record objections this view would have a good deal of potency, but most jurisdictions with presumed consent systems have established a centralised registry to 'house' such views which may well satisfy the prerequisites set out by Childress above.[106] On the other side of the coin, we should also not forget the substantial deficiencies in many of the (actual or supposedly) express consent jurisdictions in determining the deceased's wishes, discussed more fully below.

103 Conference of European Health Ministers, at 8.

104 Council on Ethical and Judicial Affairs of the American Medical Association, 'Strategies for Cadaveric Organ Procurement: Mandated Choice and Presumed Consent' (1994) 272 *Journal of the American Medical Association* 809 at 811.

105 Childress, 'Ethical Criteria', at 98. This is Blasszauer's view of the operation of the autopsy laws in Hungary: see 'Autopsy', at 9. The absence of a reliable recording mechanism for deceaseds' wishes was the reason behind clinicians consulting relatives in France.

106 In Austria, in the absence until 1996 of a registry to house objections, a debate developed as to whether clinicians had any obligation to enquire whether the deceased harboured objections or whether there was a minimum duty to search the deceased's possessions at the time of death for any evidence, where this could be done without undue delay.

Promoting autonomy

In Britain, the Hoffenberg Report in 1987 identified the primary danger under a presumed consent regime as being that 'There would be a risk that organs might be removed when this had not been the wish of the person or their relatives.'[107] Express consent systems typically attract the opposite criticism, that the organs will frequently *not* be used where the deceased *would* in fact have wished that they had been. Interestingly, the above assessments of the impact of such systems may be rather incomplete and misconceived. Whilst a *presumed* consent is not in truth an individual 'consent' to donate, the ultimate goal is to give effect to the individual's wishes. Supporters of PC argue that an absence of objection is just as much an expression of autonomy as an explicit consent and that such laws *enhance* the self-determination of the deceased, by according a *higher* priority to the deceased's wishes than do alternative regimes, where the opinion of the family is often the decisive factor. The experience in the US would appear to bear them out to some degree although ironically official policy there is to give primacy to the wishes of the deceased over those of relatives.[108]

Indeed, any appraisal of presumed consent regimes must incorporate an evaluation of their character and operation *in toto*, that is at a societal or 'systems' level, and by comparison with alternative regimes. Cohen states that there is no moral difference between positive and negative acts and that 'We may presume one way, or presume the other, but presume we must.'[109] He argues that

> If persons do in reality object to the use of their organs (but never register that objection) a system that requires express consent will protect his autonomy more surely than the revised system here defended. But with the presumption reversed, the very same point can be made in reverse: if one

107 Conference of Medical Royal Colleges and their Faculties in the UK, *Report of the Working Party on the Supply of Donor Organs for Transplantation* (Hoffenberg Report), 1987, at 6. Wolfslast has also commented that the apparent motive behind the trend towards express consent at the outset of the nineties was the desire, warranted or not, to increase donor protection and enhance the donor's right to self-determination: see Wolfslast, 'Legal Aspects of Organ Transplantation', at 160.

108 With respect to the UK, Kennedy has also noted that the 1961 Act was intended to accord priority to the deceased's views: see Kennedy, 'The Donation and Transplantation of Kidneys', at 15–16. The UAGA was intended to reverse the effect of the pre-existing common law under which control of the cadaver was generally accorded to the next of kin.

109 C. Cohen, 'The Case for Presumed Consent to Transplant Human Organs After Death' (1992) 24 *Transplantation Proceedings* 2168.

> does in reality consent to the use of one's organs (as most of us do, although never registering that consent) a system which presumes consent will protect his autonomy more surely than the present system can.[110]

In fact, in view of the role of relatives under express consent systems, even the former point may be dubious. Somerville has remarked:

> This raises an interesting point, specifically, that under a contracting in system, which is usually regarded as promoting individual liberties more than any other system, persons can do little before their deaths to ensure that their organs will not be donated by their relatives after death, despite their strong objections. Somewhat paradoxically, under a contracting out system, such persons would be better able to control this situation because there would be formal mechanisms established to record objections and these would have to be respected.[111]

On this view, the likelihood of organs being 'falsely' removed (that is where the deceased would not have wished this) is *minimised* in practice under the typical presumed consent regime because there would normally be reliable recording mechanisms for objections, and because relatives are provided with no power to 'donate' organs in their own right. These remarks highlight the importance of the mechanism(s) available for recording requests or objections.

The proposition that PC systems are *more*, not less, respectful of donor autonomy because they permit most people to donate organs is dependent on the assumption that the majority of persons do wish to donate, that is that 'errors' (vis-à-vis true wishes) are *reduced* by such means. The majority of opinion polls do appear to support this. Cohen asserts that such systems are not just expedient but are just and good, and that we should adopt presumptions which are consistent with what we know people really want.[112] In express consent systems, organ procurement levels are generally well below the levels of polled willingness of individuals to donate their organs after their death. The AMA Report, however, stated that 'a plebiscite is an unsatisfactory answer to the ethical problems raised by presumed consent. Even if the plebiscite passed and presumed consent was adopted, individuals who did not want to donate organs still deserve to have their wishes respected. An individual's desire not to donate should

[110] Cohen, 'The Case for Presumed Consent', at 2172.
[111] Somerville, '"Procurement" vs "Donation"', at 62.
[112] Cohen, 'The Case for Presumed Consent', at 2172.

not be overridden by majority vote.'[113] Prottas considers that this argument fails in the light of the 'fallacy of division', that is that there is a logical fallacy that because something is true of a class considered collectively, therefore it is true of each member of that class – a micro decision from a macro fact.[114] If on the other hand though it is the will of the majority which is being appealed to here, then this is instead a recognition of different interests having priority, and the justification, if there is one, is founded instead upon the prioritisation of certain (communitarian) interests above (individualistic) others. Because errors are endemic across the board, arguments that presumed consent will result in errors as regards the deceased's true wishes are inconclusive in themselves. However, many would argue that to avoid organ removal in cases of doubt is the 'right side' to err upon, whereas others say that there is no 'right side' or that, contrariwise, errors resulting in organ donation are the 'right side' in view of the compelling need universally for organs.[115] Cohen has remarked that 'while the lifesaving use of organs that ought not to have been used cannot be right; it is at least a wrong more tolerable than the wrong of not using organs that should have been used'.[116] The Report of the Conference of European Health Ministers stated that 'when the right to life and health of the diseased person awaiting transplantation comes into conflict with the supposed "right" of a cadaver which is no longer a person, the right of the living recipient is certainly predominant over that of the dead donor. The interest of the community prevails over that of the individual dead body.'[117] Presumed consent is a reflection of such a perception, and notions of *a priori* rights which can only be repealed by an individually expressed objection.

The sounds of silence

We should examine the implications of the *silence* either of the deceased or of relatives under the varying regimes. In presumed consent jurisdic-

113 AMA, 'Strategies for Cadaveric Organ Procurement', at 811.

114 J. Prottas, 'The Rules for Asking and Answering: The Role of Law in Organ Donation' (1985) 63 *University of Detroit Law Review* 183 at 187.

115 See B. Hoffmaster, 'Freedom to Choose and Freedom to Lose: The Procurement of Cadaver Organs for Transplantation' (1985) 17 (Supp. 4) *Transplantation Proceedings* 24.

116 Cohen, 'The Case for Presumed Consent', at 2171.

117 Conference of European Health Ministers, at 7. Bernat states that this was the approach taken by the Swiss Supreme Court in a decision in 1972 decided according to ordinary civil law principles: see Bernat, 'Opting-in, Opting-out', at 105–6.

tions the silence of the deceased person as regards his/her wishes is itself taken to be an expression of a willingness to donate and arguably an authorisation for organ donation to proceed. But what about express consent systems where the basic inference is 'No . . . unless'?

Some would assume that just as under a PC system silence constitutes a presumed *willingness to donate*, so under an express consent system silence should constitute a *presumed objection*. However, if this were so, no organ removal would generally be permissible at all, as statutory regimes universally preclude removal where the deceased has objected to it. Moreover, in some jurisdictions even *anticipated* objections have to be respected; for example under German law the next of kin must 'respect the *presumed wishes* of the potential donor' (my emphasis), and similarly in Norway. But if silence constituted an objection *per se* such provisions would be superfluous and incompatible with the right of relatives to consent to removal in these same jurisdictions. Mehlman has said that 'Currently in the United States . . . ours is a system of "presumed nonconsent".'[118] On this more cogent view, silence is best perceived as no more than a neutral feature and no indication either way of the deceased's wishes as to organ removal.[119]

Mehlman suggests that in an express consent system, where consent may be given instead by relatives, silence might indicate a delegation of the matter to relatives or at least no lack of willingness (for them) to donate. Whilst this may be the practical effect of silence in most instances, to impute such a wish to the (now) deceased is probably to read overly much in. The deceased may even have failed to consider organ donation at all during his or her lifetime. Moreover, in so far as there are often inadequate mechanisms for recording objections other than by means of communicating with relatives, this may be an unjustifiable assumption. If this is the deceased's wish, it would be very much preferable for him or her to be able to declare this expressly, and indeed the new Dutch and German laws specifically cater for such a possibility to leave it to the family. Moreover, Californian law provides for the appointment of an attorney under a durable power of attorney, given express authorisation to make an organ donation decision, who then ranks highest in the order

[118] M. Mehlman, 'Presumed Consent to Organ Donation', at 31.

[119] This interpretation finds support in section 2(j) of the 1987 UAGA which stipulates that an anatomical gift of part(s) of a body should not be taken to constitute a refusal to donate other parts. Yet many would consider that that was exactly what it was.

of those entitled to give a gift of the decedent's organs at death.[120] It would seem that whatever the system the silence of the deceased is equivocal, although more equivocal in some than in others. This is primarily dependent on the *mechanisms* available for expressing one's views either way.

A hint of coercion?

There is a distinct possibility of organs being removed under a (PC) regime where the deceased has remained silent, despite the deceased possessing an objection to organ donation, if for no other reason than the tendency for people, especially young people, to fail to consider their own mortality and to confront the issue squarely, and because of inertia generally, for example a reluctance to register. The AMA Report stated that

> the claim that presumed consent enhances individual autonomy is dubious. In many cases it is incorrect to assume that an individual who does not clearly express a preference would in fact be willing to serve as an organ donor. If 69% of the population would be willing to donate their own organs, then the presumption of consent would be incorrect up to 31% of the time.[121]

It went so far as to say that 'More organs may be procured under presumed consent, but only because such a system takes advantage of the public's general reluctance to dissent and ignorance or temporary confusion of those who do not wish to donate but do not register their objection.'[122]

Nonetheless, as we have seen, organs may be removed under virtually all systems where the wishes of deceased persons are not expressly known. Indeed, *objections* as well as requests are inadequately recorded in many systems, both presumed consent and express consent. Those systems with inadequate means of recording objections may be inferior to others, *no matter what formal classification is given to the system.* For that reason, many PC systems are superior simply by virtue of their tendency to have a register for soliciting and housing objections. PC regimes necessarily

120 See section 7151(a)(1).

121 AMA, 'Strategies for Cadaveric Organ Procurement', at 811.

122 Ibid.

throw the onus on to the now deceased individual to communicate his objection prior to death in order to avoid organ removal though. Dickens, Fluss and King state that 'The right to withhold permission preserves personal autonomy, but it may require individuals who object to recovery of material to identify themselves to health or other public authorities, to place their personal religious or other convictions on record, and to declare that they decline to contribute an asset to the public.'[123] Dickens infers that the burden placed on individuals who do not wish to donate organs to 'opt out' by recording their wishes on a register or otherwise is illegitimate.[124] This latter point may have even more force in jurisdictions where there are substantial percentages of individuals holding beliefs, whether based on religion or otherwise, opposing organ donation. Mehlman states that a presumed consent law in the US might have to cater for special religious objections,[125] as the Tennessee presumed consent law for cornea removal does for Christian Scientists.[126] Indeed, this feeling probably underpins the thinking behind the Singapore presumed consent legislation in 1987 which presumes agreement, subject to an opt-out, for the whole population apart from Muslims. The AMA Report stated that 'Systems of presumed consent that fail to verify the absence of objections – for instance, by excluding families from the decision-making process – are ethically problematic because they may fail to respect individual preferences.'[127] Interestingly, in France, despite the strong presumed consent law, relatives were approached historically for precisely that reason. However, to fail to appreciate that express consent systems generate similar tensions even though relatives *are* involved seems somewhat blinkered.[128]

The availability of a 'reasonable opportunity to object' would seem to be the minimum ethical requirement for decedents under all regimes. In EC systems where the means of objecting is primarily via relatives, this would seem to be less than adequate in this regard. Dickens *et al.*

[123] Dickens, Fluss and King, 'Legislation on Organ and Tissue Donation', at 101.

[124] B. Dickens, 'Legal and Judicial Aspects of Post Mortem Organ Donation' in G. Collins *et al.* (eds.), *Procurement, Preservation and Allocation of Vascularized Organs*, Kluwer, Dordrecht, 1997, 343 at 346.

[125] Mehlman, 'Presumed Consent to Organ Donation', at 50–2.

[126] See Sipes, 'Does it Matter?', at 530.

[127] Ibid.

[128] Indeed, it need not necessarily even be a close relative in all cases who provides the necessary 'consent'.

themselves note that an express consent regime 'also requires people who do not want their organs to be removed after death on consent of their family members to demonstrate their refusal in a way that reasonably anticipates the usually unforeseeable circumstances of their death'.[129] Quay states, even more graphically,

> In sum, the UAGA wrongfully presumes that another may speak for the decedent unless the latter *both* disallows such a gift *and* has effectively communicated his refusal to some of his next of kin *and* that one of these is at home and available to respond to a single phone-call at the time of death, *and* that he actually remembers the decedent's refusal and makes it known in appropriately formal language despite the overpowering emotional nature of the situation.[130]

There is rarely a permanent and reliable record available to medical staff at the time of death. Allowing registration of objections would also ease the burden upon relatives, who will it seems only rarely veto a removal where there is evidence that the deceased person did not object to the removal.

The views of the AMA appear to perceive a need for an explicit consent to donation in every case, either from the deceased or from relatives. It is this consent which provides the authorisation for the organ explantation and subsequent use for transplantation. Moreover, it considers that the family are necessarily involved in order to avoid false imputations of wishes and to convey the true wishes of the deceased. However, where relatives are involved there is the distinct possibility under any system that it will be the *relatives'* wishes that are given effect to, and not those of the deceased, a potential increased where there is no reliable recording mechanism provided, as historically in France.

In 1976 the Caillavet Law eventually formally embodied (strong) presumed consent in French law.[131] The Law was however accompanied by a Circular from the Ministry of Health and Social Security which stated that

[129] Dickens, Fluss and King, 'Legislation on Organ and Tissue Donation', at 101.

[130] P. Quay, 'Utilizing the Bodies of the Dead' (1984) 28 *Saint Louis University Law Journal* 889 at 894.

[131] See W. Gerson, 'Refining the Law of Organ Donation: Lessons from the French Law of Presumed Consent' (1987) 19 *International Law and Politics* 1013. A Decree was issued to similar effect in 1947. A decision of the Conseil d'Etat in 1983 confirmed that family members could not prevent organ removal when the deceased did not object. Objections could be registered by anyone admitted to hospital, with that hospital.

> Under the law, only the wishes expressed by the person before his or her death should be considered, not those of the family. However, the family is still most often the privileged depositary of these wishes, whether the deceased has confided them to relatives, or whether relatives are in possession of documents or other evidence of the deceased's refusal or consent to the procurement. Where the family is not the direct depositary of the deceased's last wishes, it is often in the best position to know or discover the deceased's motivations and communicate them to the medical professional or institution.[132]

As a consequence of this guidance many doctors still routinely sought the permission of the family, despite the intention behind the 1976 Law to eliminate this practice.[133] Although France has now established a new centralised computerised Registry to record objections administered by the Government-controlled Etablissement Français des Greffes, the 1994 Law appears to perpetuate the same confusion and conflation of views. It states that organs may be removed provided the deceased did not object, but adds that 'If the physician has no direct knowledge of the wishes of the deceased, he must endeavour to obtain the testimony of his family.'[134]

The AMA Report states that

> Some proponents argue that presumed consent could be effective even if the family is routinely contacted. In this version, families would not be asked to consent to donation but only to verify they do not object. This would 'allow physicians to broach the issue [of donation] as a matter of hospital and societal routine, while merely requiring the inaction of informed next-of-kin'. Some commentators doubt that this approach could be effective; the same families that object to donation under the current system of required request would still object under presumed consent if given the opportunity. Thus, though this version of presumed consent does incorporate an adequate opting-out mechanism and therefore is ethically acceptable, it is unlikely to be much more effective in procuring organs than the present system.[135]

[132] Circular of 3 April 1978.

[133] The absence of a national register undoubtedly contributed to the 'uncertainty' as to the deceased's wishes and the consequent reluctance to proceed without family endorsement.

[134] The primary reason for the continuing ambivalence may well be the public outcry generated in 1991 when a boy's corneas were accidentally removed for transplantation without parental permission in Amiens. Between 1991 and 1994 the donation rate fell from 70 to 60 per cent of potential donors: see I. Durand-Zaleski, 'Nonprocurement of Transplantable Organs in a Tertiary Care Hospital' (1996) 62 *Transplantation* 1224.

[135] AMA, 'Strategies for Cadaveric Organ Procurement', at 809.

There is certainly a tendency for PC systems to be operated in the same way as under an EC system, and the *consent* of relatives sought in each case, and not just objections. In the eighties, Caplan suggested a modified form of presumed consent in the United States under which there would be a duty upon medical staff to find out if the donor or his/her family objected to organ removal. Matas argues that such a proposal occupies a middle ground between 'encouraged voluntarism' and presumed consent. However, although this proposal creates a duty to discover if there were any *objections* to removal rather than seek a *consent* to removal, in all likelihood the two would conflate in practice. This has proved to be the case in the United Kingdom, where only reasonable enquiries need to be made to ascertain the existence of objections by relatives, but in practice *consent* is always sought from them. This is an issue of some importance. In Belgium, despite the lack of any legal obligation, the 11 April 1987 advice of the Order of Physicians states that physicians must inform the close relatives of the intention to remove the organs. This apparently creates pressure for some physicians to seek explicit *consent* from relatives to removal. In many centres relatives are not asked at all if they object, whereas in others relatives are still asked for explicit permission for donation.[136]

Such views, however, gloss over the extremely important *conceptual* shift that would occur under such a scheme. The empirical observations are partially persuasive, but there is some evidence to suggest (including from, for example, Belgium) that if relatives are not asked to *decide* they will not take positive steps to intervene and veto removal. Nevertheless, it must be conceded that any degree of involvement of relatives will lead to a diminution in procurement levels. This would appear to be inevitable in the light of the devastating emotional impact of the death on the family and the speed with which 'decisions' typically have to be made. Indeed, it is these factors which cause physicians and other health care professionals to be reluctant to approach grieving relatives at this time. Such a subtle change of emphasis (from consent to non-objection) would though seem to reflect more faithfully existing conceptions of the role accorded to the family in Western societies. Respect accorded by physicians to the family's wishes would equally be afforded where relatives were informed of the

[136] See H. Nys, 'Belgium' in *International Encyclopaedia of Medical Laws*, Kluwer Law International, The Hague, 1997, at paras. 394–5. In Norway there is a statutory duty, where possible, to inform relatives of the individual's death.

right to object to donation but were left to come forward with such an objection on their own initiative. Where the family have to give consent, this would seem largely to flow from views regarding rights to possession of the corpse, which may in turn flow from cultural values, for example in Japan, where Shinto beliefs vest rights of disposal of the cadaver squarely in the hands of the family; indeed even the very idea of the 'person' in Japanese culture has a communal nature. In Western societies, including Anglo-American and Anglo-Australian cultures, the family's role appears to stem from the right to dispose of the body and the lack of an alternative medium for reliably recording an objection to organ removal (and maybe even positive wishes). It is this lacuna which is at the heart of the dilemma in many jurisdictions. However, where an adequate mechanism does exist for recording objections, for example a centralised registry, there is arguably no sufficient rationale for allowing relatives to object to (that is to veto) organ removal. The wishes of the deceased should take precedence. It is interesting then that weak presumed consent systems are not seen as a *contradiction*, that is the deceased has conveyed (through silence) a wish to donate, but relatives are still legally permitted to override such a wish. In express consent regimes, relatives are not officially accorded such a privilege. Does this cast doubt on the deceased's wishes even where a registry exists to record objections? If so, this says much about the ambivalence inherent in PC regimes.

In jurisdictions such as the UK, Norway, Sweden, etc., in the absence of a positive expression of willingness to donate by the now deceased, there is only a legal duty to take steps to discover if the deceased or any surviving spouse harbour(ed) any *objection* to donation. This appears not to create any right to use or authorise the use of the corpse, merely to object to its use for certain specific purposes conferred by statute. But Chadwick asks, 'If it is simply to spare their feelings, why should they take priority over the feelings of the relatives of people waiting for organs?'[137] One can, however, offer a different and more convincing rationale for allowing relatives a power of *veto*, based upon the *profound offence* caused by interfering with the corpse of the deceased in certain ways. Such distress is predictable and substantial, and is itself compensable in various circumstances across the US. (Whilst arguably such a cause of action

[137] R. Chadwick, 'Corpses, Recycling and Therapeutic Purposes' in R. Lee and D. Morgan (eds.), *Death Rites: Law and Ethics at the End of Life*, Routledge, London, 1994, 54 at 61.

exists in the UK, it would be extremely difficult to succeed in such a claim.) Although Feinberg asserts that 'Repugnance alone will not outweigh the humanitarian benefits Gaylin describes',[138] this is not 'mere repugnance' or offended sentiment. In terms of ethical principles, societal needs should bend exceptionally to the duty of non-maleficence owed to relatives in extreme cases.

The analogous issue also arises as to what one should assume from the silence of relatives where they are accorded a power of veto. This will depend upon whether relatives are directly approached at all, and what information they possess at the time. If they are aware of the death and their power of veto, but remain silent, one can assume a lack of objection, but the practicalities of the situation and informational inadequacies may dilute or obliterate such a real power. They have only a small 'window of opportunity' immediately after the death, and their accessibility itself is partially a matter of chance. Moreover, their own grief and emotional trauma may act as 'interference on the line'.[139] Those laws which allow organ removal where there are no known objections already in existence may give insufficient scope for objections by relatives in cases where the deceased's wish is unknown. Some corneal removal laws in the United States have adopted such a 'pure' presumed consent model.[140] Although most have passed constitutional muster,[141] one or two federal decisions have found an infringement of the relatives' constitutional rights in such circumstances, suggesting a need for a fuller 'pre-deprivation' process in order to satisfy due process rights typically connected to property rights in the deceased's cadaver.

The Law Reform Commission of Canada advanced three rationales underpinning the 'gift ethic' in Canadian transplantation: 'These are that altruistic tissue transfers nurture community bonds and generosity, accord respect that is due the dead human body and avoid the perceived ills and risks of routine procurement policies.'[142] Hoffmaster, however,

138 J. Feinberg, 'The Mistreatment of Dead Bodies' (1985) 15 *Hastings Center Report* 31 at 33.

139 Sproat highlights the general failure of 'bereavement care' here: see G. Sproat, 'Incorporating Required Request in Acute Bereavement Care: Protocols and Incentives' in Spielman, *Organ and Tissue Donation*, 135.

140 In some respects this is surprising in so far as surveys show the greatest reticence in donating corneal tissue of all tissues and organs which might be donated.

141 In these decisions the courts have generally found that tort remedies suffice here.

142 Law Reform Commission of Canada, *Procurement and Transfer*, at 39.

contends that there is no *a priori* ethical necessity for a policy that gives overriding effect to individual consent.[143] He states that

> Ramsey's preference for consensual community and fostering the virtue of generosity over the routine prolonging of lives simply cannot be accepted . . . As Ramsey has pointed out, we can begin with the judgment that neither the giving nor the taking of cadaver organs is intrinsically wrong. The moral conflict is between the interests of potential recipients and the freedom of potential donors.[144]

He also says:

> The determination of a policy for organ acquisition is largely a function of a society's underlying social and political philosophy, and different policies assign different degrees of importance to the value of individual freedom . . . A communitarian society takes seriously the notion of obligations to determinate others, even if these obligations are not voluntarily incurred.[145]

Moreover, cultural and historical influences crucially shape policies here, including the role of the family (which is especially decisive in Asian countries) and beliefs relating to rebirth and reincarnation.[146] These phenomena are *evolutionary* in nature even within specific cultures. In many regions individual autonomy over one's body has substantially increased in importance in recent years, although less so in Asia than in Europe and North America. Hoffmaster remarks that 'It is no accident that in North America, where a philosophy of liberal individualism reigns supreme, autonomy and freedom are the paramount values and an opt-in policy for organ donation exists.'[147] The need to involve relatives appears to be less keenly felt in certain parts of continental Europe than in the UK and North America though, especially those governed by the former Austro-Hungarian empire with a heritage of autopsies performed without consent.

143 Hoffmaster, 'Freedom to Choose', at 24.

144 Ibid., at 27.

145 Ibid., at 24.

146 For instance, Feldman says of the situation in Japan, that Shinto beliefs 'reflect a commitment to the idea that the family should have the ultimate say in what happens to the corpse after death': see E. Feldman, 'Defining Death: Organ Transplants, Tradition and Technology in Japan' (1988) 27 *Social Sciences and Medicine* 339 at 342.

147 Hoffmaster, 'Freedom to Choose', at 25.

3

Interests in the corpse

Having analysed the essential character of different legislative regimes, we should now examine and prioritise the values and interests implicated by the process of organ explantation and transplantation, and consequently the proper roles of the various actors. We may then move tentatively towards a legislative model for organ procurement meeting appropriate ethical standards as well as (it is to be expected) generating an adequate volume of organs for transplantation.

The United States National Conference of Commissioners on Uniform State Laws stated[1] that the principal competing interests in the disposal of the dead body are: (1) the wishes of the deceased during his lifetime concerning the disposition of his body; (2) the desires of the surviving spouse or next of kin; (3) the interest of the state in determining, by autopsy, the cause of death in cases involving crime or violence; (4) the need of autopsy to determine the cause of death when private legal rights are dependent upon such cause; and (5) the need of society for bodies, tissues and organs for medical education, research, therapy and transplantation. In some instances these pull in the same direction, whilst in others they are competing. Where no executors have been named in the will, the legal locus of the duty of disposal devolves initially to the surviving spouse or relatives in the US and Canada, and in the UK to the individual(s) appointed as administrator(s) of the estate, who may or may not be surviving relatives of the deceased. Relatives in the UK and Australia would seem to have no right to possession for such purposes *qua* relatives *per se*.[2] Powers of control over the disposition of the human corpse, or parts thereof, stem from rights or duties either *regarding* or *to*

[1] Prefatory Note to the Uniform Anatomical Gift Act 1968. See National Conference of Commissioners on Uniform State Laws, *Handbook on Uniform State Laws*, 1968.

[2] See *Dobson* v. *North Tyneside Health Authority* [1996] 4 All ER 474 below. Note that relatives

the cadaver. One potential source of rights in or over the deceased are property rights.

Property interests

Property rights confer (sometimes exclusive) rights of control and prevention of interference by others, as well as rights of use and alienation, that is *negative* and *positive* rights.[3] Part of the reason for the uncertainty and inconsistency attaching to the import of property rights in this context lies in the inherent ambiguity in the term 'property' itself. In law, this typically refers to the 'bundle of rights in an object' as opposed to the nature of the item itself. Even then, 'property' in an item is frequently viewed as synonymous with *proprietary* rights in it, especially in Roman-law-based systems, whereas there are a broader range of types of 'property' recognised by law in many other legal systems, that is *possessory* rather than *proprietary* entitlements.[4] In *Meek* v. *State* the Supreme Court of Indiana stated that

> There is much conflict in the authorities as to whether there may be a property right in a dead body. Some of the confusion arises upon a failure to distinguish between the thing in which a property right is held and the right itself. It has been urged that there is no property right since the body may not be sold or bartered away. But this is not conclusive, since the same argument may apply to many things in which there may be an unquestioned right of property. Property rights are more limited in some objects than in others, but, if there is any right of control over or interests in an inanimate material thing, it would seem to be a property right.[5]

may, as those most entitled to become administrators of the estate, be entitled to possession on that basis.

3 In this enquiry we are concerned only with unburied/uncremated bodies, as transplantation concerns arise solely in that context. Where the body has already been disposed of, there are laws in every jurisdiction prohibiting disturbance of, or interference with, the corpse. In *R* v. *Lynn* 100 English Reports 394 (1788), the English courts declared it to be a crime and *contra bonos mores* to desecrate a grave in order to remove a corpse, which could not be redeemed by the fact that it was to be used for anatomical dissection.

4 Under Roman law, a person exercised 'dominium' over an item to which they were entitled – possession was essentially only a matter of fact – whereas under common law systems possessory rights were independent property rights in many instances: see L. Griggs, 'The Ownership of Excised Body Parts: Does an Individual have the Right to Sell?' (1994) 1 *Journal of Law and Medicine* 223, and G. Bouckaert, 'What is Property?' (1990) 13(3) *Harvard Journal of Law and Public Policy* 775.

5 *Meek* v. *State* 185 N.E. 899 at 901 (1933).

However, the ambivalent jurisprudential status of the corpse is evidenced by the pervasive references to *quasi*-property rights attaching to the corpse in US case law, and by the 'no property' in a corpse doctrine prevalent in Anglo-Australian authority.

Both the common and the civil law adopted the general rule that there is no property in a corpse and it remains pervasive today.[6] However, as Magnusson states, a survey of Anglo-Australian authorities reveals 'First, judicial support for the "no property" rule can be confined to *obiter dicta*. Secondly, the no property rule itself arose from inadequate reporting and misreading of early cases. Thirdly, the relevant authorities are old and for this reason ought to invite reconsideration.'[7] It will be suggested here that whilst the rule, properly interpreted, may continue to have some limited force its continued endorsement in sweeping terms is unwarranted and indeed anachronistic. In 1977 the Australian Law Reform Commission stated that 'there is no reason to endow such tissue with the attributes of property'.[8] It is submitted here that contrariwise there *is* indeed a need for a property-based legal framework, more protective of the interests of the participants in the transplantation enterprise, and for ensuring adequate quality and safety standards.

The earliest case to consider the issue of property rights in respect of corpses was *Haynes's Case* in 1614,[9] in which William Haynes was indicted for the larceny of four winding-sheets used for the purpose of the burial of four corpses. Despite the fact that the judges merely opined that *the corpse itself* was incapable of owning the sheets, the opinions were taken instead to mean that no one was capable of *owning the corpse*,[10] and such influential commentators as Blackstone[11] and (in particular) Sir Edward Coke perpetuated the view that there was 'no property in a corpse'. The latter asserted that burial matters were within the domain of the Church

6 Regarding the civil law perspective, see R. Dierkens, *Les droits sur le corps et le cadavre de l'homme*, Masson, Paris, 1966, 157–8.

7 R. Magnusson, 'Proprietary Rights in Human Tissue' in N. Palmer and E. McKendrick, *Interests in Goods*, Lloyd's of London Press Ltd, London, 1993, 237 at 242.

8 Australian Law Reform Commission, *Human Tissue Transplants*, Report No. 7, Canberra, 1977, at 7.

9 77 English Reports 1389.

10 For instance, both East and Sir James Stephen relied upon this authority for the proposition that 'the dead body of a human being is not capable of being stolen'. See Matthews for a full elucidation of the authorities and their interpretation by writers: P. Matthews, 'Whose Body? People as Property' (1983) 36 *Current Legal Problems* 193.

11 2 William Blackstone, *Commentaries*, 1766, at 429.

and that the burial of cadavers was *nullius in bonis* (among the goods of no one).[12] In *Doctor Handyside's Case* in 1749, an action for trover was brought against the doctor in respect of two unburied deceased children that grew together as a consequence of a birth defect. However, although East states that 'Lord CJ Willes held that the action would not lie, as no person had any property in corpses', it has been shown that the case was compromised and not decided at all.[13] Nevertheless, this alleged 'no property' rule was asserted (albeit *obiter*) in various other (early nineteenth-century) cases.[14] It was applied also in the more modern-day authority of *Williams* v. *Williams*[15] in 1882. W, a woman friend of the deceased, disposed of the deceased's body by cremation in accordance with a request in the deceased's will and expressed also in private conversations, and then sued the estate for expenses incurred in connection therewith. The court declared 'it is quite clearly the law of this country that there can be no property in the dead body of a human being', and dismissed her suit on the basis that it could not therefore form part of his estate.[16]

However, the 'no property' concept has not always been viewed as absolute. An extremely influential Australian authority was the case of *Doodeward* v. *Spence*[17] which concerned a two-headed stillborn child that had been kept preserved in a bottle of spirits as a curiosity, and bought by Doodeward's father at auction and then passed to Doodeward, but which was seized under warrant. Doodeward commenced civil proceedings for conversion and detinue of the corpse. In the High Court all three judges accepted that immediately after death a corpse is not the subject of

[12] 3 Co. Institutes 203 (1644). He referred to the corpse as *cara data vermibus* ('flesh given to worms'). Although his rationale could apply only to buried corpses, his opinions were expressed much more broadly.

[13] *Exelby* v. *Handyside* (1749) 2 East P.C. 652.

[14] In *R* v. *Sharpe* (1857) 169 English Reports 959, the rule was applied in the context of a disinterment of a buried corpse. See also *R* v. *Price* (1884) 12 QBD 247. Of course, it is much less contentious that no one has a right to possession of a *buried* corpse.

[15] *Williams* v. *Williams* (1882) Ch. 659. Greater rights generally exist in the US for a deceased to direct the manner and place of his burial and one or two other matters: see A. Sadler and B. Sadler, 'Transplantation and the Law: The Need for Organised Sensitivity' (1968–69) 57 *Georgetown Law Journal* 5.

[16] The court held that as the corpse could not be disposed of by will, she had no right to claim against the estate for doing what the decedent had no right legally to order. However, Matthews regards the primary objection as being to the transmission of property rights by means of one's will, and thus views statements concerning the 'no-property' status of the corpse as being *obiter dicta*: see Matthews, 'Whose Body?', at 212.

[17] (1908) 6 Commonwealth Law Reports 406.

property, but the plaintiff nonetheless succeeded in his claim, by a majority. The dissenting judge, Higgins J, stated that 'no one can have, under British law, property in another human being – alive or dead'.[18] Griffith CJ, however, decided that if some work was carried out on the body, for example to preserve it, which changed its nature, then it could acquire the characteristics of property and be subject to property rights. It was held that the foetus had been so changed by the lawful exercise of human skill that it was no longer a mere corpse awaiting burial and that the plaintiff therefore had a right to possession of the corpse as against any person entitled to possession for the purposes of burial.[19]

Whatever the dubious origins of the rule there is no doubting its vitality and continuing impact today.[20] In Britain, the general rule was recently affirmed by both the Civil and Criminal Divisions of the Court of Appeal in *Dobson* v. *North Tyneside Health Authority*[21] and *R* v. *Kelly*[22] respectively. In the former case, the deceased's body had been subject to an autopsy and her brain removed and preserved in paraffin before being ultimately disposed of. An action was brought by her mother for conversion and breach of the obligations of a bailee as a potential preliminary to a medical negligence action. She alleged that she had a right to possession of the deceased's brain as administratrix and next of kin. Whilst the Court endorsed the general 'no property' rule, it recognised two exceptions to it, that is where there was a right of possession for the purposes of the disposal of the body and where there had been an application or process of skill such as stuffing or embalming. On the facts of the case it decided that neither of the exceptions were applicable and her (property-based) claim therefore failed. She had no right to possession for disposal of the body merely due to her relationship to the deceased and had not at the relevant time actually been appointed as administratrix of the estate. Moreover, the preservation of the brain was not itself a process akin to stuffing or embalming. In *R* v. *Kelly*,[23] the defendant was charged with the theft of thirty-five to forty parts of corpses which had been originally in the possession of the Royal College of Surgeons as anatomical specimens. The Court of Appeal, whilst accepting the existence

[18] Ibid., at 419.

[19] In fact, Barton J merely decided that the foetus was property in view of its being stillborn. If the child had been born and subsequently died he would have joined Higgins J.

[20] Although in Scotland a different approach has been taken for many years: discussed further below.

[21] [1996] 4 All ER 474 (CA).

[22] [1998] 3 All ER 741 (CA).

[23] Ibid.

of the general 'no property in a corpse' rule, nevertheless found him guilty of the offences, thereby becoming the first English authority to decide that parts of dead bodies could constitute 'property' in law. It held that the body parts constituted 'property' within section 4 of the Theft Act 1968, as they had acquired different attributes by virtue of the application of skills such as dissection and preservation techniques, for exhibition or teaching purposes. The College was also found to have sufficient possession under section 5(1) of the Theft Act so that the body parts 'belonged to them' for the purposes of that offence.

A transatlantic (good old British!) compromise?

In very early times, the primary concern as regards the corpse was its decent interment. Such matters were dealt with initially in Britain by the ecclesiastical courts before jurisdiction was gradually transferred to the common law courts. However, in America, as the Georgia court in *Georgia Lions Eye Bank* v. *Lavant* noted, 'because there were no ecclesiastical courts in this country to resolve matters relating to corpses, the courts conceived the notion of "quasi-property right" when referring to the interest of relatives in the bodies of their next-of-kin'.[24] This has tended to spawn an at least superficially distinctive approach in the US with the courts more routinely accepting the applicability of notions of property vis-à-vis cadavers.[25] Such a property-based approach tends to emphasise the role of relatives. Nonetheless, US courts have not generally employed a 'full' property rights analysis in this context, and indeed some courts have paid at least lip service to the 'no property' notion.[26] The picture varies as between the states, reflecting a deep conceptual issue incapable of easy and straightforward resolution.

The predominant approach however is, as in *Georgia Lions*, one founded on the idea of 'quasi-property' rights in a corpse. The US Congress Office of Technology Assessment, however, stated in its Report on the *Ownership of Human Tissues and Cells* (OTA Report) that

[24] 335 S.E. 2d 127 at 128 (Ga. 1985).

[25] As early as 1860, a US court declared, in *Bogert* v. *City of Indianapolis* 13 Ind. 134 at 138 (1860), 'We lay down the proposition, that the bodies of the dead belong to the surviving relatives, in the order of inheritance, as property, and that they have the right to dispose of them as such, within restrictions analogous to those by which the disposition of other property may be regulated.'

[26] In the United States a deceased cannot leave his corpse as part of his estate either: see, for example, *Enos* v. *Snyder* 63 P. 170 at 171 (1900), and *Smart* v. *Moyer* 577 P. 2d 108 (1978).

> Judicial references to property rights in corpses were misleading, however. While common law property rights generally include the right to possession and use, to transfer by sale or gift, and to exclude others from possession, few of these rights were applied to bodies: the theft of a cadaver was not larceny, the sale of a cadaver was a common law crime, the heirs had no right to repossess a body wrongfully taken from them, and a cadaver could not be the subject of a lien.[27]

It added, 'Recognizing the limited applicability of property law to corpses, 20th century courts retreated from the broad pronouncement of bodies as property and began referring to more limited "quasi-property rights" vested in the next of kin and arising out of their legal duty to bury the dead.'[28]

The ambivalent status of 'quasi-property' interests is transparent here. In certain cases courts have held that 'quasi-' property rights *were* 'true' property rights, whilst various commentators have argued that courts dubbed such rights 'quasi-property' rights specifically *in order to avoid* treating them as property rights! Dean Prosser, for instance, alleges that 'It seems reasonably obvious that such "property" is something evolved out of thin air to meet the occasion, and that in reality the personal feelings of the survivors are being protected, under a fiction likely to deceive no one but a lawyer.'[29] O'Carroll observes that 'In adopting this standard, American courts had reached a comfortable balance between the two competing interests by refusing to fully recognise a property right in a dead body, while at the same time ensuring proper respect for the dead.'[30]

Of course, in the US, the very constitutionality of a statute may be contested on the basis that property rights have been infringed. In *Georgia Lions*, a Georgia statute which permitted the removal of the decedent's corneas where there was no objection from either the deceased or from the next of kin was alleged to be violative of due process in that it deprived relatives of a property right in the corpse of their next of kin. The appeal court, however, held that there were no constitutionally protected

[27] US Congress, Office of Technology Assessment, *New Developments in Biotechnology: Ownership of Human Tissues and Cells – Special Report*, US Government Printing Office, Washington D.C., 1987, at 72.

[28] Ibid.

[29] W. Prosser and D. Keeton, *The Law of Torts*, 2nd edn, West Publishing Co., St Paul, Minn., 1955, at 43–4.

[30] T. O'Carroll, 'Over my Dead Body: Recognising Property Rights in Corpses' (1996) 29(4) *Journal of Health and Hospital Law* 238.

property rights in a decedent's body.[31] A similar claim arose for resolution before the Supreme Court of Florida in *State of Florida* v. *Powell*.[32] The Court upheld the constitutionality of the statute and determined that the appellees had no protectable liberty or property interest in the remains of their decedent. The appellees were not denied due process as rights of action existed in tort to remedy unlawful infringements of their interests. Thus, in these early cases, clear presumed consent statutes applicable to corneas in Michigan, Georgia and Florida were held to be constitutional. As can be seen in the next section though, this has not been the universal judicial response.

Catch-22?

Although the above authorities represent the characteristic judicial attitude of the state courts, vacillation and differences of opinion are evident in some of the more recent decisions of the federal Circuit Court of Appeals. In *Brotherton* v. *Cleveland*[33] in the Sixth Circuit, the Court reviewed an Ohio statute which permitted a coroner to remove corneas from a deceased provided he 'did not know of any objection by the decedent, the decedent's spouse, or the person authorised to dispose of the body'. In this case the spouse had objected to such removal, but the hospital had not communicated this to the coroner, who removed the deceased's corneas. It was decided that this removal constituted a deprivation of the constitutionally protected due process rights of the spouse under the US Constitution in so far as she had a 'legitimate claim of entitlement' in the decedent's body. This was followed by another decision of the Sixth Circuit Court of Appeals in *Whaley* v. *County of Tuscola* on similar facts to *Brotherton*, although on this occasion reviewing Michigan law. It was held that Michigan law provides the next of kin with a constitutionally protected property interest in a deceased relative's body, including the eyes. As under Ohio law, the Court stated that the relatives had a right to dispose of the body and to prevent others from damaging it. It was stated that such rights in an object 'are the heart and soul of the

[31] Similarly in *Tillman* v. *Detroit Receiving Hospital* 360 N.W. 2d 275 (1984). A Michigan statute permitted a medical examiner to remove corneas for transplantation in the absence of any knowledge of any objections to removal. A complaint by a mother that her daughter's eyes had been removed without permission was dismissed by the appeals court.

[32] *State of Florida* v. *Powell* 497 So. 2d 1188 (Fla. Sup. Ct 1986).

[33] *Brotherton* v. *Cleveland* 923 F. 2d 477 (6th Cir. 1990).

common law understanding of "property" '.[34] The Court held that the section 1983 action for damages against the county was successful as no consent had been obtained from the next of kin. The Sixth Circuit is currently 'out of sync' with the other circuits and state courts on this issue but the effect of these decisions is that the 'pure' presumed consent statutes applicable to corneal tissue in various states are unconstitutional (certainly in those states within the jurisdiction of the Sixth Circuit) and that the consent of the next of kin would need to be obtained before a legitimate removal could take place, as part of the 'predeprivation process'. Moreover, the question arises as to whether the next of kin have a constitutionally protected property interest in the deceased's body requiring compensation to be paid under the 'Takings Clause' in the Fifth Amendment for the 'taking' of private property for public use, that is the tissues of the deceased. Ironically though, by virtue of federal law, such direct payments to relatives (possibly as opposed to more 'indirect' compensation through, for example, burial expenses assistance) would be illegal!

As a result of these decisions, questions must also be asked as to the constitutional status of statutes which require a 'reasonable effort' to be made to trace relatives and to inform them of their right to make an anatomical gift or to object thereto, based upon the 1987 UAGA. As we have seen, although many such state statutes apply only to cornea removal, others apply also to other organs and tissues for transplantation.[35] Yet the UAGA was specifically amended so as to allow for the possibility of removals of organs without explicit authorisation in certain circumscribed circumstances, in the expectation that this might facilitate an increased flow of organs for transplantation. To require permission to be obtained, or an opportunity for an objection to be vented, in every case, would defeat the objective behind the amendments to the UAGA themselves.

It is submitted that surviving next of kin cannot be viewed as possessing proprietary property rights in the corpse of a dead relative but that it is entirely appropriate to view relatives as possessing 'property' rights of

[34] *Whaley* v. *County of Tuscola* 58 F. 3d 1111 at 1115 (6th Cir. 1995), *cert. denied* 116 S. Ct. 476 (1995).

[35] For example, in California, Louisiana, Maryland, Mississippi, Texas and Utah: see D. Sipes, 'Does it Matter Whether there is a Public Policy for Presumed Consent in Organ Transplantation?' (1991) 12 *Whittier Law Review* 505 at 525 n. 86.

some sort arising out of the right to possess the body for the purposes of disposal. However, by virtue of the limited nature of this property right, the removal of organs would not typically infringe that right, so there would be no constitutional requirement to acquire the consent of next of kin, nor to pay compensation under the Fifth Amendment. Similar perspectives might be applied to other jurisdictions, although the right to possession of the body for disposal will vest in relatives less frequently in certain other jurisdictions.

Critique

Although we have already noted that the term 'property' usually alludes to the bundle of rights attaching to the item(s) in question, this is only part of the story as if the item is not 'property' in itself then it generally cannot become the subject of certain legal causes of action at all. If it is not 'goods' then no action in tort for either trespass to goods or conversion will lie.[36] If it is not a 'product' then strict statutory products liability, such as the provisions of the Consumer Protection Act 1978, could not apply so as to provide a remedy, in the absence of fault, for a 'defective' product. There is, therefore, a preliminary question in most instances of whether the dead body, or parts thereof, can be 'property' or 'goods'. In *R* v. *Kelly* the Court of Appeal provided an affirmative answer to this question on the facts of that case, by virtue of the degree of application of work and skill applied to the body parts in question which had altered their character. Had it not been property, then the offence of theft would not have been able to have been committed. In *Dobson* the Court appeared also to accept that in principle the brain of the deceased could constitute 'goods' for the purposes of a conversion claim. Moreover, in the US decisions in *Pierce* and *Hecht* considered below, the courts accepted probate jurisdiction with regard to the body parts or tissues in question, although ambivalence as regarded other aspects of the 'property' analogy was apparent.

As the LRC of Canada observed, reticence in viewing a human corpse as property stems originally from the sacrosanct nature of the cadaver in religious custom. However, this view today seems to have possessed more

[36] In Britain such an action would be brought under the Torts (Interference With Goods) Act 1977.

credence in the past and with respect to cadavers as a whole rather than merely parts of cadavers. In *In re Estate of Johnson*[37] Surrogate Delehanty stated that

> there is thus expressed by Coke a conception of the human body which was most congenial to the human mind in the 17th century. The body was the temple of the Holy Ghost from which at his death a man was temporarily to be separated. That this sacred object should be property was unthinkable to Lord Coke and his contemporaries. A man had a right to the decent interment of his own body in expectation of the day of resurrection.

It has been asserted that our perceptions have now changed and that emphasis upon respect for the body emanates instead from respect for the person whom the corpse still represents and for personhood in general.[38] Moreover, once severed from their body of origin, body parts take on many more of the characteristics of 'things' distinct from the person of whose body they once formed a part.[39] Not only did treating the body parts in *Kelly* as property fail to threaten respect for the bodies from whence they came, but such an approach ensured a proper dealing with those parts and their use for their intended purposes. There seems no objection to viewing the corpse and the parts of a corpse prior to burial or cremation as 'property' or 'goods' as such. One is not thereby implying any specific rights 'over' the body, which is the especially contentious issue. Without acceptance of this, there would be nobody at all able to maintain an action to enforce possession of the cadaver or parts thereof and it would be incapable of being stolen or its use subverted by anyone.

Ownership of the cadaver

Chadwick observes that, 'In the case of the corpse, it might be argued that since a person owns her body when alive, she has the right to dispose of it

[37] 7 N.Y.S. 2d 81 (Sur. Ct. 1938).

[38] W. Boulier, 'Sperms, Spleens, and other Valuables: The Need to Recognise Property Rights in Human Body Parts' (1995) 23 *Hofstra Law Review* 693 at 718.

[39] Counsel for the prosecution in *Kelly* asserted that 'Parts of a corpse have all the properties of a thing' and the court did not demur from this, deciding the issue on the basis of statutory interpretation: [1998] 3 All ER 741 at 749.

as she wishes after death.'[40] But the notion of self-ownership is unconvincing and largely rhetorical. In any event, Chadwick goes on to state that

> it might be objected that the arguments against viewing the body as property during the life of the person, for example, that my body is not 'mine' but 'me', do not apply when the person is dead. The body of the deceased is much more similar to other material objects such as personal effects. Other arguments, however, might be appealed to: The circumstances which make it similar to other material objects are just those which make understandable the claim that it no longer (in so far as it is true to say it ever did) has an owner, for the 'owner' is dead.[41]

A deceased person cannot own his (now dead) body and, whilst alive, he *was* his body. The legal position that one cannot pass title to one's body or its parts after death by will seemingly reflects these perceptions.[42] But if we accept that the ante-mortem (now-deceased) person may possess *personal* rights with respect to the uses of his/her corpse (for example authorising the use of organs for transplantation), discussed further below, why not property rights? It might in fact seem that the right to consent to the use of body parts for transplantation itself presupposes (inchoate) property rights. Of course, we must be envisaging 'future property' here as there is no property in existence until death, possibly till the severance of body parts thereafter. Moreover, one would have to dismiss the necessity for *scintilla temporis* here, as at the moment property is created the owner of it must inevitably have ceased to exist![43] If this postulating fails to convince then it must be seriously questioned how a scheme of payments for 'futures' involving contractual obligations upon the organ procurer and provider could be legally workable, assuming for a minute that it otherwise would be.[44]

In the present legal climate, however, at least in Britain, there is little mileage in the notion of an individual whilst alive owning yet non-existent

40 R. Chadwick, 'Corpses, Recycling and Therapeutic Purposes' in R. Lee and D. Morgan (eds.), *Death Rites: Law and Ethics at the End of Life*, Routledge, London, 1994, 54 at 61.

41 Ibid.

42 In *Hecht* v. *Superior Court of the County of Los Angeles and W. E. Kane* 20 Cal. Rptr. 2d 275 (Cal. Ct App. 1993), the court declined to regard the stored sperm of the deceased as part of the deceased's estate whilst at the same time viewing it as a 'unique form of property' nonetheless.

43 However, in *Abbey National Building Society* v. *Cann* [1990] 1 All ER 1085, Lord Oliver stated that 'The *scintilla temporis* is no more than a legal artifice': at 1099–100.

44 This particular issue is discussed at some length in chapter 9.

property in his own cadaver or the parts thereof. Thus, in property terms, the 'crunch issue' is the extent to which those *other than the deceased* have rights 'over' the corpse in terms of controlling or authorising its use. In the lower California decision in *Moore* v. *Regents of the University of California*, the court asserted that 'There is, however, a dramatic difference between having property rights in one's own body and being the property of another.'[45] Nevertheless, both the Supreme Court of California in *Moore* and the Nuffield Council Working Party were seemingly comfortable with the idea of third parties possessing property rights in human body parts, although not the source. To have property in a thing is to have certain rights, powers, duties and liabilities in relation to it. The primary objection to the use of property concepts here is the fear that body parts will become objects of commerce. This need not necessarily flow, however, even if proprietary rights in the cadaver or parts thereof are conceded (discussed further in subsequent chapters). But to many, proprietary rights of any kind over the cadaver of another (once-living) person is anathema. Ownership of the corpse is viewed as contrary to human dignity. In *Pierce* v. *Proprietors of Swan Point Cemetery*, the court stated:

> Although as we have said, the body is not property in the usually recognised sense of the word, yet we may consider it as a sort of *quasi* property, to which persons may have rights, as they have duties to perform towards it arising out of our common humanity. But the person having charge of it cannot be considered as the owner of it in any sense whatever; he holds it only as a sacred trust for the benefit of all who may from family or friendship have an interest in it.[46]

Moreover, in *Hecht* v. *Superior Court of the County of Los Angeles*,[47] the California Court of Appeal held, in a case concerned with the disposition of sperm left in the deceased's will to his girlfriend, that stored sperm could be viewed as a 'unique' type of property. However, the court avoided adopting a *full* property analogy which would have involved applying the law of personal gifts/property in straightforward fashion.[48]

[45] 249 Cal. Rptr. 494 at 504. See Law Reform Commission of Canada, *Procurement and Transfer of Human Tissues and Organs*, Working Paper 66, Minister of Supply and Services, Ottawa, 1992, at 73.

[46] 10 R.I. 227 (1872).

[47] 20 Cal. Rptr. 2d. 275 (Cal. Ct App. 1993).

[48] This may of course have been because of the unique nature of reproductive materials.

Nine-tenths of the law?

Quite clearly though, laws grant possessory rights to next of kin, executors/administrators and coroners, for various purposes, although they are reluctant to confer general powers of use vis-à-vis the cadaver. The Law Reform Commission of Canada remarked that 'These rights and duties highlight a conspicuous ambivalence in the law. Technically, possession is a legal property interest that includes the basic rights of dominion and control. On the one hand, the traditional rule maintains that there is no property in the corpse; on the other hand, the law recognises formal possessory or property interests in the dead.'[49] Those with the duty to dispose of the corpse have an enforceable right to possession for burial purposes in the United Kingdom and elsewhere. In *R* v. *Fox* a peremptory mandamus was awarded where a gaoler refused to give up the body of a prisoner to the prisoner's executors until he was paid a sum of money owed to him.[50] Even coroners carrying out a statutory inquest are entitled to take legal action to enforce their right to possession of the body until the inquest is satisfactorily concluded.[51] In the United States withholding the body for an unreasonable time whilst determining organ donor status has been held to give rise to an action for damages in favour of relatives entitled to the body for disposal.[52]

Removal of organs for transplantation, even if unauthorised, may not always itself constitute an infringement of the right to possession for burial purposes though,[53] as a proper burial of the corpse may still be feasible. In some instances in the United States the right to possession for disposal has been held to include the right to be delivered of the corpse in the same state as it was in at death.[54] An unauthorised removal of organs might possibly therefore infringe such rights. For instance, in *Whitehair* v. *Highland Memory Gardens Inc.*,[55] the Supreme Court of Appeals of West Virginia stated that 'The quasi-property rights of the survivors include the right to custody of the body; to receive it in the condition in which it was

[49] Law Reform Commission of Canada, *Procurement and Transfer*, at 69.

[50] *R* v. *Fox* (1841) 2 QB 246.

[51] See *R.* v. *Bristol Coroner ex parte Kerr* [1974] 1 QB 652.

[52] See *Strachan* v. *John F. Kennedy Memorial Hospital* 538 A. 2d 346 (N.J. 1988).

[53] In *Dobson*, for instance, the basis of the action was not that burial or disposal of the body was infringed by the keeping of the deceased's brain, and this must have undermined the claim.

[54] See Law Reform Commission of Canada, *Procurement and Transfer*, at 67.

[55] 327 S.E. 2d 438 at 441 (W. Va. 1985).

left without mutilation; to have the body treated with decent respect, without outrage or indignity thereto; and to bury or otherwise dispose of the body without interference.' Next of kin have also been held to be entitled to sue for 'wrongful interference' with the cadaver of a deceased relative resulting from, for example, mutilation of the corpse from an unauthorised autopsy.[56] The OTA Report quotes from the American Law Institute's *Restatement of Torts* which states that 'one who intentionally, recklessly or negligently removes, withholds, mutilates or operates on the body of a dead person or who prevents the proper interment or cremation is subject to tort liability to a member of the family who is entitled to disposition of the body'. This cause of action was, however, said to be a *personal* rather than a property-based right of the survivor, since the courts are not primarily concerned with the extent of the physical mishandling or injury to the body *per se*, but rather with the effect of such improper activities on the emotions of the surviving kin.[57]

A lacuna?

Dworkin and Kennedy state with regard to British law and the Human Tissue and Human Organ Transplants Acts, that 'Whatever view is taken on problems of supply, these Acts provide little support for the existence of property rights in the cadaver, or parts of it: references are to persons "lawfully in possession" of the body and the emphasis is centred far more on the issue of donor consent.'[58] Skegg contends that English, although not Scots,[59] law is inadequate in the limited protection it extends to corpses or parts of corpses prior to burial or cremation, and states that

> This inadequacy could be overcome by the courts taking the view that, until such time as a corpse or part thereof is buried, cremated, or otherwise disposed of, it is the subject of property. Unburied corpses, and anatomical specimens and transplant material removed from corpses, would then be

56 As they are also in Scotland and Canada, amongst other jurisdictions.

57 OTA, *Ownership of Human Tissues and Cells*, at 73. It noted that recovery is only permitted if distress actually occurs, and not just where it could be anticipated.

58 G. Dworkin and I. Kennedy, 'Human Tissue: Rights in the Body and its Parts' [1993] 1 *Medical Law Review* 291 at 298.

59 Under Scots law, primarily deriving from *dicta* in *Dewar* v. *HM Advocate* (1945) JC 5 (Court of Justiciary), a corpse is the subject of property and can therefore be stolen or converted until such time as it is buried or cremated. In fact the case is not so authoritative in so far as it concerned the theft of six coffins and 600 coffin lids, rather than corpses *per se*.

protected by, amongst other things, the crime of theft and the tort of trespass to goods.[60]

But are the existing exceptions sufficient anyhow?

Sweat/equity

It might be argued that the other existing exception to the 'no property' rule under Anglo-Australian law (apart from the right of possession for disposal) provides adequate protection in respect of *parts* of corpses. Indeed, a conviction for theft of body parts was upheld in *Kelly*. However, in *Kelly* there was evidence that 'the preparation of the specimens by prosecution . . . would have involved many hours, sometimes weeks, of skilled work'[61] and thus the body parts were property in the possession of the Royal College. This suggests that anatomical specimens would typically be viewed as property under the exception to the general rule based on the application of human skill. But this would by no means always be the case with body parts or organs destined for transplantation, *a fortiori* with unburied corpses generally. Such an exception might be justified by reference to the 'earning' of property through the investiture and mixing of the 'thing' with one's own labour, consistent with the philosophy espoused by John Locke. However, if so, the assumption implicit in *Dobson*, that where such work was carried out the brain would have become the property of those entitled to the body for the purposes of burial, seems misguided. It could not have been the mother's before the work was carried out and the doctrine of *specificatio* would vest the rights of property in the *doer* of the work instead.[62]

Moreover, it is interesting to note the different perspectives as to what constitutes 'an application of human skill' sufficient to render the item 'no longer merely a corpse awaiting burial'. Skegg once stated, somewhat prophetically it transpires, that

> One drawback of Griffith CJ's principle is the difficulty of its application. If the principle were adopted in England, it would no doubt apply to

[60] P. Skegg, 'Human Corpses, Medical Specimens and the Law of Property' (1975) 4 *Anglo-American Law Review* 412 at 420.

[61] [1998] 3 All ER 741 at 743.

[62] John Locke's rationale would support this view: see J. Locke, *Two Treatises of Government*, 1690, as would the Roman doctrine of *occupation* of things *res nullius*: see A. Grubb, 'Property Rights and Body Parts' [1997] 5 *Medical Law Review* 110 at 113.

> Egyptian mummies in museum collections and probably also shrunken heads, or heads which had been tattooed after death. But much more difficult would be the question of whether it would apply to anatomical specimens, and tissues and organs awaiting transplantation. If the English courts were prepared to apply the principle in the same way as the majority of the High Court of Australia in *Doodeward* v. *Spence* these objects might very often be considered the subject of property. However, when dealing with an object on which no more labour or skill had been expended than was on the corpse in *Doodeward* v. *Spence*, which had simply been placed in spirits, an English court might favour the approach of the dissenting judge in *Doodeward* v. *Spence*. He said that 'No skill or labour has been exercised on it; and there has been no change in its character'.[63]

Indeed, in *Doodeward* itself the 'mere preservation' of the two-headed foetus was sufficient to constitute such an application, yet in *Dobson* Peter Gibson LJ stated that the exception did not apply in that case because the preservation of the brain was not comparable to the 'stuffing or embalming a corpse or preserving an anatomical or pathological specimen for a scientific collection or with preserving a freak such as a double-headed foetus that had some value for exhibition purposes'.[64] Amongst other things, this suggests that this 'exception' is more appropriately applied to *whole corpses* rather than parts of corpses, as the exception based on 'change of character' is to the normal subject of burial or cremation. The Nuffield Report stridently declared that 'It cannot plausibly be argued that University College London does not own Bentham's skeleton',[65] a persuasive view in so far as there has been a fundamental change in the character of that particular dead body.[66]

Grubb has opined that what is required is an additional intention to create a novel item with a use of its own, and that this was the difference between the two (*Dobson* and *Kelly*) cases. However, this might create its own potential for differences of view and consequent uncertainty, as well as ignoring the *inherent* use and value of these parts. The 'exception' approach to parts of corpses does not fit the bill. Grubb rightly observes[67]

63 Skegg, 'Human Corpses', at 419.

64 [1996] 4 All ER 474 at 479G.

65 Nuffield Council on Bioethics Working Party Report, *Human Tissue: Ethical and Legal Issues*, Nuffield Council on Bioethics, London, 1995, at para. 10.6.

66 Just as Lenin's body has been preserved for more than seventy years in Red Square and other museum skeletal remains are preserved and retained.

67 A. Grubb, 'Theft of Body Parts: Property and Dead Bodies' [1998] 6 *Medical Law Review* 247 at 250.

that to view body parts *per se* as property would be to rewrite the 'no property' rule so that it became: 'There is "no property" in corpses (excluding excised body parts).' But this seems entirely proper and would close a lacuna in the context of organs and tissues removed for transplantation in the possession of medical professionals or institutions. In fact, in *Kelly*, Rose LJ stated that in the future property rights might well be held to attach to body parts that 'have a use or significance beyond their mere existence', quite apart from the application of the *Doodeward* exception, and he specifically identified parts for use in organ transplantation (as well as DNA for use in, for example, a future court case) as examples of such materials. The Nuffield Report asserted that 'Common sense as well as the common law require that the user of tissue acquires at least possessory rights and probably a right of ownership once tissue is removed.'[68] The Nuffield Council thought that this would apply *mutatis mutandis* to a hospital which has tissue in its possession, for example for transplant, which would have such property rights over the tissue to be able to exclude any claim of another, as does a coroner or pathologist who has carried out a post-mortem and retains body parts for examination.[69] This was not made dependent upon work having been done upon it and the Council's approach was thus more consistent with a (trust) *res nullius* rationale.

The 'no property' rule is an anomaly because individuals do have the right to possession of dead bodies (that is property rights) enforceable by reference to property-based concepts or causes of action in law in all jurisdictions – albeit limited to certain uses and subject to substantial constraints. These are typically rights emanating from *duties* to deal with the corpse in certain ways, for example the right to implement a decent burial or to carry out a post-mortem. In Britain, the law also endorses the notion that a person or institution (for instance a hospital) has a protectable right to property in a deceased person where it is lawfully in possession of the body, even where there is another person in existence able to assert a greater right to possession, for burial or cremation purposes, at least where that right has yet to be exercised. Under the Human Tissue Act 1961 the party entitled to authorise the use of the body for transplantation is expressly stated to be the person who is 'lawfully in possession of the body'. It would seem that a party, such as a hospital,

[68] Nuffield Council, *Human Tissue*, at para. 10.6. [69] Ibid.

need not be the individual with the primary duty to dispose of the body in order to be lawfully in possession of it, despite the contentions of a minority of commentators[70] that it is next of kin who are lawfully in possession of the corpse under English law.[71] Lanham expresses the correct contemporary legal position in Britain:

> The strongest case is one in which the person who dies in hospital dies intestate and without a spouse or relatives. In such a case there is no one at the time of death with a better right to possession than the hospital and it cannot be doubted that the hospital is lawfully in possession of the body. But even if there is someone with a better right to possession than the hospital, it does not follow that he is in possession as soon as the patient dies. Suppose the patient has made a will naming executors. The executors will have a better right to possession than the hospital, but at the time of the patient's death they may not even know that there is a body over which they have a right to possession. Without knowledge they cannot have the intention to possess and so one of the elements normally required for the acquisition of possession is missing . . . At the very least until the executors or relatives know about the death, the hospital must be regarded as lawfully in possession of the body. In other cases there is more room for argument. Presumably the mere fact that the executors or relatives know about the death is not enough to vest possession in them. There must be an intention to possess. Furthermore, that intention must presumably be communicated to the hospital, since intention by itself does not constitute possession.[72]

This view appears to reflect the intention of Parliament when passing the 1961 Act, which incorporates an implicit recognition that more than one party might potentially have lawful possession of the body.[73] There nevertheless remains a small degree of uncertainty regarding the concept of the 'person lawfully in possession of the body' under English law. If this is not the person with the primary responsibility for burial, why are rights

[70] Such as, for example, J. Finch, *Health Care Law*, Sweet and Maxwell, London, 1981, at 258.

[71] Moreover, under English law it would seem that where there is no executor or administrator at that time, the duties of disposal may vest first of all in the occupier of the property either where the person died or where his body lies: see P. Skegg, 'The Interpretation of the Human Tissue Act 1961' (1976) 16 *Medicine, Science and the Law* 193 at 193–4.

[72] D. Lanham, 'Transplants and the Human Tissue Act' (1971) 11 *Medicine, Science and the Law* 16 at 20.

[73] The then Government resisted an amendment put forward at the Committee stage in the House of Commons that an explicit provision be added that the hospital in which the body lay was to be seen as being in 'lawful possession' of it, on the basis that this might imply that the hospital had a right to possession enforceable against executors: see HC Deb., vol. 643, col. 836.

to authorise the use of body parts for transplantation, research, etc., afforded to him? However, it may be that a pragmatic interpretation was intended, an extension from the use of the same concept under the Anatomy Act 1832, whereby possession and control *per se* were the key elements, allowing bailment of the body for certain purposes assuming that rightful possession was not previously revoked and subject to the satisfying of the preconditions stipulated in the statute to their use. But even the supposed *golden rule*, that under English law whole corpses cannot be stolen (it could not have formerly constituted larceny),[74] which was endorsed in *Kelly* and said in that case to be only able now to be changed by Parliament, seems dubious in the light of recent cases. If individuals with a right to dispose of the body can bring an action for conversion (which according to *Dobson* they can), then why not also for theft? And if so, then why could not a party in possession of the corpse, such as a hospital, bring an action likewise against a third party 'appropriator' in certain circumstances? This would not have to be founded upon proprietary, only possessory, rights in the corpse.

In *Kelly* it was also asserted that it might even be immaterial whether the possession is 'lawful' or not with regard to whether, assuming the body parts constitute 'property', they are to be viewed as 'belonging to another',[75] that is, that actual possession is itself a protected interest.[76] This would presumably imply that the hospital would have an enforceable right to possession of the body apart from where it did not respond in a reasonable time to a demand for possession of the body from someone with a better right to possession for the purpose of burial. It surely cannot mean that a person with a lesser right to possession would be entitled to enforce possession even against a party with a better right to it. Rights to possession, as Matthews notes, are typically premised at common law upon there being no one with a *better* right to possession at the relevant time.[77]

[74] See A. Smith, 'Stealing the Body and its Parts' [1976] *Criminal Law Review* 622.

[75] The primary case relied upon, *R* v. *Turner (No. 2)* [1971] 2 All ER 441 (CA), has been widely criticised in Britain as having been based upon fallacious reasoning.

[76] This assertion has been challenged, and it has been observed that even in *Doodeward* the court spoke of the work being done by someone in 'lawful possession' of the corpse: see (1908) 6 Commonwealth Law Reports 406 at 414.

[77] Matthews, 'Whose Body?', at 215–18. On the other hand, in the United States the OTA Report stated that 'To successfully bring a claim of conversion a plaintiff must be entitled to immediate possession', which raises questions as regards a hospital's rights to sue for

Where parts have already been removed, for example for transplant, although no one would necessarily have a better right to possession of them, they would seemingly not presently constitute 'property' anyhow, unless work has been expended upon them to alter their nature! Thus, under English law as it currently stands, *parts* of bodies may not necessarily be protected to the same degree as whole corpses, and Skegg's previous identification of a 'lacuna' remains telling. Skegg argues though that

> most of the remaining effects of the no property rule could be avoided without the courts discarding or qualifying that rule. If the courts were prepared to take the view that there can be 'special property' in an object even though it is not the subject of property at common law, the torts of trespass to goods, conversion and detinue [the latter is now defunct] would apply to corpses, and parts thereof. Logical though the contrary rule undoubtedly is, it is undesirable that it should limit the scope of torts which are supposed to protect possessory rather than property rights.[78]

If so, hospitals could, for instance, maintain an action for trespass to goods under the Torts (Interference with Goods) Act 1977 without asserting proprietary rights.

It would certainly appear as if at present proprietary rights do not exist in either the whole corpse or parts of corpses (including tissues and cells) intended for transference to the same or another human corpus. The Human Tissue Act 1961 appears to presuppose such a legal framework and a 'bailment' of human tissues for transplantation which have been 'donated'.[79] The hospital(s) or other institution(s) carrying out the explantation and transplantation would be obliged to act within the terms of the bailment and could be held liable for breach thereof.[80] Another way of perceiving this would be, as Swain and Marusyk describe it: 'for the purpose of transplantation, the legal system could deem those in possession of the excised tissue – physicians, nurses, or tissue transporters – as being possessors "in trust" of the tissue until the transplant was complete.

dispossession by a third party not entitled to possession of the body for burial purposes: see OTA, *Ownership of Human Tissues and Cells*, at 80.

78 Skegg, 'Human Corpses', at 420–1.

79 In the same way that presumably the body is bailed to an undertaker for the purposes of burial or cremation: see N. Palmer, *Palmer on Bailment*, 2nd edn, Sweet and Maxwell, London, 1991, at 881 n. 4. See also D. Brahams, 'Bailment and Donation of Parts of the Human Body' (1989) 139 *New Law Journal* 803.

80 See Brahams, 'Bailment and Donation', at 803.

During this period, the tissue would be classified as *trust res nullius*; a thing owned by nobody but held in trust for the recipient.'[81] Such possession would be legally enforceable. One objection here, however, is that *possessory* (special property) rights cannot exist in isolation from, or despite the lack of, *proprietary* rights existing in the item(s), but it is submitted that the views of Matthews are to be preferred in so far as the 'rights' of the parties involved here are to possess for specific ends, not to confer an entitlement to (authorise the) use (of) the body; they stem wholly from duties.

It may be that the desire for protection of the body against misuse *by hospitals and hospital staff* is the motivation behind the greater support for proprietary rights pertaining to the corpse in the United States (vesting typically in surviving relatives). Magnusson states that 'Although criminal law sanctions interference with a corpse after burial, there do not appear to be any authorities prohibiting the mutilation or indecent treatment of a body part, which has not and will not be buried, and which does not also interfere with an executor's rights over the body.'[82] Whilst a little too sweeping, in so far as there are offences such as outraging public decency which might apply, there is an important truth in this remark. There are general common law offences of mistreatment of the corpse which could potentially be invoked, but are very unlikely to be in the absence of flagrantly gross misconduct. Ironically, there would appear to be a lacuna under English law in so far as the Human Tissue Act 1961 creates no specific offence pertaining to non-compliance with its provisions and it is extremely unlikely that a court would entertain a prosecution for disobedience to the statute today.[83] Moreover, an action for breach of statutory duty would be equally unlikely to succeed. This was clearly an oversight. An action for negligence might lie if the general conditions for such an action were satisfied and some physical harm was suffered, but there are enormous difficulties in the way of a successful action based solely upon emotional or mental distress to relatives.[84] However, of

[81] M. Swain and R. Marusyk, 'An Alternative to Property Rights in Human Tissue' (1990) 20 *Hastings Center Report* 12 at 13.

[82] Magnusson, 'Proprietary Rights', at 249.

[83] Although it previously did in the case of *R* v. *Lennox-Wright* [1973] *Criminal Law Review* 529. But see now *R* v. *Horseferry Road Justices ex parte Independent Broadcasting Authorities* [1987] QB 54.

[84] The legal panorama on this subject in the US is highly variable, with some jurisdictions, for example Florida, insisting upon physical impact/injury in order for a claim for negligent

course, in very many of these potential instances, relatives would not even have any possessory rights to rely upon, at least in their capacity *qua* relative, as opposed to as executor or administrator of the estate (as *Dobson* illustrates).[85] In this sense, there are few mechanisms available for 'policing' the application of the law. In very many nations with transplant legislation in this sphere a specific offence is created for infraction of its provisions. For instance, in Germany, the 1997 Act stipulates a maximum sentence of three years' imprisonment or a fine for violation of the terms relating to organ procurement from cadavers. In some instances, breach of the legislative provisions is deemed to be an administrative offence.

In the United States also, state laws applying the UAGA create no sanctions in themselves and enforcement is primarily delegated to the family. As Jaffe notes, 'the UAGA (1968) did not explicitly address when people *would* be liable, it was enacted as a permissive statute against a background of laws restricting unauthorised dissection of the human body'.[86] These are the 'quasi-property' rights discussed earlier. Generally, these give rights to recover for emotional distress, but in those jurisdictions where it has been held that the relatives have constitutional due process rights, they would appear to have exclusive rights (in the absence of the decedent's intent being manifest) to be involved in decisions as to the use of the corpse. This might at first sight appear wholly appropriate. But in so far as they can already recover for mental/emotional distress, that is physical or psychological harm, it would seem anomalous to allow recovery based upon their rights *per se* to control the uses of the corpse. If it is in their discretion, then as one commentator has observed, they would also have a discretion to 'waive' these rights and to permit any particular use.[87]

Magnusson argues that executors' rights should be regarded as being

infliction of mental distress arising from the mishandling of a dead body to succeed: see, for example, *Gonzalez* v. *Metro Dade City Health Trust* 651 So. 2d 673 (1995). See also Andrew Grubb, 'Psychiatric Injury and Mishandling of a Corpse' [1996] 4 *Medical Law Review* 216.

85 In *Holtham* v. *Arnold* (1986) 2 BMLR 123 (Ch. D), it was held that the deceased's wife, being entitled to letters of administration of her husband's estate, was also entitled to his corpse in order to dispose of it.

86 E. Jaffe, '"She's Got Bette Davis['s] Eyes": Assessing the Nonconsensual Removal of Cadaver Organs under the Takings and Due Process Clauses' (1990) 90 *Columbia Law Review* 528 at 533 n. 28. He cites as an example the New York Public Health Law section 4210–a which creates the misdemeanour of unlawful dissection.

87 R. Veatch, 'The Newly Dead: Mortal Remains or Organ Bank?' in R. Veatch (ed.), *Death, Dying and the Biological Revolution*, Yale University Press, New Haven, 1989, 197 at 220.

proprietary in nature across the board and considers that the UAGA indeed vests ownership of donated tissue in the donee, but states that 'The position in England and Australia is less clear.'[88] It is undoubtedly much easier to argue that the structure of the North American legislative provisions actually invests proprietary rights in the relatives of the deceased, presumably emanating from the fact that they frequently have primary responsibility for the disposal of the corpse.[89] There are authorities where relatives have been awarded damages for interference with the corpse *per se*, and even where this does not compromise the burial of the cadaver. Remarks have been made judicially that there is a right to receive the cadaver for disposal in the same state it was in at the moment of death. Moreover, the UAGA talks of an 'anatomical gift' and of gifts to 'donees', which might be easily perceived as a transfer of proprietary rights to one's designated organs and tissues. Dickens analyses the powers of control in terms of there being a bailment to the physician or hospital wherever the gift is to a specified recipient (the 'donee') but of there being a *trust* wherever the hospital or physician is it/himself stipulated to be the donee.[90] In the latter scenario, the hospital or physician would enjoy legal ownership of the property albeit subject to the terms of the (purpose) trust, with the powers of ownership having been conferred by either the deceased or the relatives of the deceased.

Non-property interests

Apart from property interests there are other rights, duties or interests pertaining to the corpse. But to whom are these owed and to whom do they belong? Chadwick contends that the only duties here are owed *to* the living, and states:

> Duties regarding the dead could be seen as indirectly duties towards living persons, who certainly do have preferences about how the dead should be treated. The preferences of living persons include both those of the loved

88 Magnusson, 'Proprietary Rights', at 247.

89 In *Cohen* v. *Groman Mortuary* 41 Cal. Rptr. 481 at 483–4 (1964) the court stated that 'The duty to bury a corpse and to preserve its remains is a legal right which courts of law will recognise and protect; such right, in the absence of any testamentary disposition, belongs exclusively to the next of kin.'

90 B. Dickens, 'Who Legally Owns and Controls Human Organs after Procurement?' in W. Land and J. Dossetor (eds.), *Organ Replacement Therapy: Ethics, Justice, Commerce*, Springer-Verlag, Berlin, 1991, 385 at 391.

> ones of a dead person who cannot bear to think of their friend or relative being disfigured in an organ transplant operation, and the preferences of persons currently alive who do not like the thought of such procedures being carried out on their own bodies after death.[91]

Indeed, in this context various US courts have determined that the (personal and property) rights of the deceased do not survive death. In *Powell* v. *State of Florida* for instance, the Supreme Court of Florida declared that 'In addressing the issue of the statute's constitutionality, we begin with the premise that a person's constitutional rights terminate at death. If any rights exist, they belong to the decedent's next of kin.'[92] These perceptions seemingly deny that the dead can themselves be harmed by procedures such as organ removal.[93] But even if the dead are themselves beyond harm, what of the *ante-mortem person* who is now deceased? Can they possess rights and interests which survive death? If not, then on what basis do we permit individuals to leave property by will and authorise the use of their corpse (for example for transplantation) after death?[94] Indeed, many such (autonomous) wishes are only capable of being respected after that person's death. The Law Reform Commission of Canada stated that 'Strictly speaking, the functions of personal autonomy are no longer relevant to the cadaver, then, because the dead have no moral authority' but that

> Since interests are products of subjective states of mind, such as desires, it does make some sense to talk about our desires or interests being fulfilled after death. The knowledge that our wishes will be respected after death may well give us a fuller sense of personal autonomy. It would also seem to impart a greater sense of peace in the preparation for and contemplation of

91 Chadwick, 'Corpses, Recycling', at 58.

92 497 So. 2d 1188 at 1190 (1986). In the case of *Tillman* v. *Detroit Receiving Hospital* 360 N.W. 2d 275 at 277 (Mich. 1984) the Court of Appeals of Michigan similarly stated that 'The privacy right encompasses the right to make decisions concerning the integrity of one's body. This right is, however, a personal one. It ends with the death of the person to whom it is of value.' The court also made it clear that if the relatives have rights these are *their own* rights, as it stated that the (now-dead) individual's personal rights cannot 'be claimed by his estate or his next of kin': ibid.

93 Russell Scott states that 'Certainly the dead must be respected . . . but the dead body is utterly different from the living body. The idea of applying the notion of personal autonomy to a corpse is absurd; at most personal autonomy is only artificially extended beyond death': see R. Scott, *The Body as Property*, Viking Press, New York, 1981, at 260.

94 Adopting the views of Raymond Belliotti in 'Do Dead Human Beings Have Rights?' (1979) 60 *The Personalist* 201, Feinberg asserts that the dead are harmed whenever their interests are 'set back' in any way.

> death. Thus, the utter disregard of one's burial wishes, or the failure to honour one's express wishes on the post-mortem use of one's body, lend credence to the claim people have interests that survive their deaths and that they may be harmed when their interests are violated.[95]

Desires, wants and aims are crucial to the concept of interests, which may be projected forward. Their later contravention casts doubt on whether that person truly possessed autonomy at that earlier time. Feinberg states that 'Events after death do not retroactively produce effects at an earlier time, . . . but their occurrence can lead us to revise our estimates of an earlier person's well-being, and correct the record before closing the book on his life.'[96]

Feinberg suggests that this paradoxical conclusion requires us to think of interests as fulfilled only by the coming into existence of that which is desired, and not simply as 'satisfaction of desire' in the sense of contentment in the mind of the desirer when he believes that his desire has been fulfilled.[97] Both Feinberg and Steinbock draw a distinction between 'hurt' and 'harm'. The latter maintains that 'The common saying that the dead are beyond harming refers, I think, to the fact that the dead cannot be hurt, angered or distressed. But, their surviving interests can be defeated, and when this happens, the subject of posthumous harm is the antemortem person, for it is the antemortem person who cared about what would happen after he died.'[98] A person's interests may therefore be infringed even though there can be no subjective experience of the person him/herself, something which has been judicially recognised. In the Court of Appeal in *Airedale NHS Trust* v. *Bland*, Lord Justice Hoffman stated:

> At least a part of the reason why we honour the wishes of the dead about the distribution of their property is that we think it would wrong them not to do so, despite the fact that we believe that they will never know that their will has been ignored. Most people would like an honourable and

95 Law Reform Commission of Canada, *Procurement and Transfer*, at 44–5.

96 J. Feinberg, *Moral Limits of the Criminal Law. Vol. I: Harm to Others*, Oxford University Press, Oxford, 1984, at 93.

97 Ibid. Belliotti also believes that only if the object of our interests and desires *is* realised, not simply believed to be realised, can it properly be said that they are fulfilled: see 'Do Dead Human Beings', at 203.

98 B. Steinbock, *Life Before Birth: The Moral and Legal Status of Embryos and Fetuses*, Oxford University Press, New York, 1992, at 26. These views parallel those of George Pitcher, who states that 'if we allow our unfettered intuition to operate on certain examples, it becomes abundantly clear that we think the dead can indeed be wronged': see G. Pitcher, 'The Misfortunes of the Dead' (1984) 21 *American Philosophical Quarterly* 183.

> dignified death and we think it wrong to dishonour their deaths, even when they are unconscious that this is happening. We pay respect to their dead bodies and to their memory because we think it an offence against the dead themselves if we do not.[99]

A (now) deceased person could therefore be 'harmed' by, for instance, an organ removal to which he objected, or possibly even by the ignoring of a positive wish to donate.[100] As Hardwig observes, 'Each of us can imagine things that we would not want done to our bodies after we are dead, and as a matter of practice, we do continue to respect the autonomy of dead persons.'[101]

Organs are transplanted into people not society

We can therefore ascribe interests to the formerly alive, now-dead person. These include our wishes as regard the use and disposal of our corpses and our universal interest in the dignified treatment of our human remains. Giving precise content to the notion of 'dignified treatment' is rather more problematic though. Orlowski *et al.*, for instance, claim that in the context of intubating newly dead bodies, such respect is limited to avoiding disfigurement or ridicule of the cadaver.[102] The Nuffield Council on Bioethics, however, observed that although persons from different cultures may have varying opinions as to what would constitute *degrading* ways of treating dead bodies, it nevertheless considered that such variation does not entitle us to disregard bodily degradation or to regard it as any less than a serious form of injury.[103] Many argue that misgivings must give way to the needs of the living though. Harris argues that if having respect for the dead requires us to tolerate harm to the living, we should

[99] [1993] 1 All ER 821 at 853. He contrasted these types of wrongs with those associated with 'animal feelings of pleasure and pain', mirroring the harm/hurt dichotomy: ibid.

[100] The Law Reform Commission of Canada supported the notion that the dead can be harmed but opined that 'What remains refractory is providing a coherent philosophical explanation of this intuition': see *Procurement and Transfer*, at 45. However, Feinberg states that 'Posthumous harm too can occur, when a "surviving interest" of the deceased is thwarted after his death': *Harmless Wrongdoing*, Oxford University Press, Oxford, 1988, at xi.

[101] J. Hardwig, 'Treating the Brain Dead for the Benefit of the Family' (1991) 2(1) *Journal of Clinical Ethics* 53 at 55.

[102] J. Orlowski, G. Kanoti and M. Mehlman, 'The Ethical Dilemma of Permitting the Teaching and Perfecting of Resuscitation Techniques on Recently Expired Patients' (1990) 1(3) *Journal of Clinical Ethics* 201 at 203.

[103] See Nuffield Council, *Human Tissue*, at paras. 6.7–6.9. Moreover, we have already noted that all jurisdictions have criminal offences relating to the indecent treatment of the cadaver.

not abandon our notions of respect for the dead, but instead modify our conception of what such respect involves.[104] Feinberg, adopting a utilitarian approach (where the pre-deceased did not object thereto), states that

> a newly dead human body is a sacred symbol of a real person, but to respect the symbol by banning autopsies and research on cadavers is to deprive living human beings of the benefits of medical knowledge and condemn unknown thousands to illnesses and deaths that might have been prevented. That is a poor sort of 'respect' to show a sacred symbol.[105]

The notion of 'symbolic harm'[106] is more than mere sentiment here though as regards the right to control the uses of one's cadaver and to be protected from its merely instrumental usage. Klepper and Truog state that

> A person may have interests that survive loss of personhood or death. For example, a person has an interest in the disposition of his estate and his mortal remains after his death. A person may thus, as Aristotle argued, be harmed after his death, but there need be nothing metaphysically mysterious about this. These interests are grounded in desires held by the person while alive . . . When those desires are frustrated, the person is harmed.[107]

You can't take it with you

Harris advocates routine organ removal regardless of the deceased's or relatives' wishes, turning the discussion upon its head by saying that the deceased would not wish to be perceived as having been mean, and that to assume as much would be a mark of *dis*respect.[108] He notes that most countries already legally permit, indeed require, the performance of forensic autopsies to determine the cause of death regardless of the wishes

104 J. Harris, *The Value of Life*, Routledge, London, 1985, at 220.

105 J. Feinberg, 'The Mistreatment of the Dead' (1985) 15 *Hastings Center Report* 31 at 35. He adds: 'May speaks dismissively of those who let mere "social needs" override all other considerations, as if a desperate patient's need for an organ transplant were a mere social need like a city's call for an additional public library or improved public transportation': ibid.

106 May, however, emphasises the importance of symbols in organising communities, beyond a mere matter of internal feelings: see W. May, 'Religious Justifications for Donating Body Parts' (1985) 15 *Hastings Center Report* 38 at 38.

107 H. Klepper and R. Truog, 'Treating the Patient for the Benefit of Others' (1997) 6 *Cambridge Quarterly of Healthcare Ethics* 306 at 309.

108 Harris, *The Value of Life*, at 221–2.

of the deceased or the next of kin,[109] and asks, if societal needs relating to criminal justice justify such a policy, why not an enterprise devoted to saving lives? Those who reject the notion of harm occurring to the ante-mortem person through undignified dealing with his/her cadaver, and who regard the corpse as a purely symbolic entity, would tend to support such a utilitarian-based organ procurement regime.

Easy rescue

Menzel advances the view that there is a moral duty to donate organs at death, based on the notion of easy rescue. He emphasises the great value of organ donation to living people who are suffering, the ease with which donation may be accomplished without any harm being suffered by the donor, and the special relationship we hold to the person to whom we owe a duty.[110] Another supporter of such a communitarian philosophy, Perry, draws analogies with duties of non-wastage of essential commodities such as food in times of great shortage.[111] On this approach, although there is no duty to 'give' there *is* a duty not to allow the wasting of valuable products where no sacrifice is implicated. Such a policy might be additionally supported on the basis that we all may require such assistance at some stage, a view which would also attract support from Rawls's perceptions of justice based on decision-making 'behind a veil of ignorance'. Menzel asserts that

> We thus mistakenly assume that the use of a moral duty of easy rescue to shape organ procurement policy amounts to making altruism into some sort of requirement. Duties to rescue, however, can be based on tacit agreements of mutual self-interest, not altruism: if we are talking about easy rescues of great benefit, it would seem to be in everybody's mutual interest to at least morally bind themselves to a universal practice of easy rescue.[112]

109 Indeed, autopsies of all kinds have been carried out in this fashion in some jurisdictions, for example Hungary: see B. Blasszauer, 'Autopsy' in H. Ten Have, J. Welie and S. Spicker (eds.), *Ownership of the Human Body*, Kluwer, Dordrecht, 1998, at 19, as also in Austria and Belgium.

110 P. Menzel, 'The Moral Duty to Contribute and its Implications for Organ Procurement Policy' (1992) 24 *Transplantation Proceedings* 2175.

111 C. Perry, 'The Right not to Donate Transplantable Organs' in B. Spielman (ed.), *Organ and Tissue Donation: Ethical, Legal and Policy Issues*, Southern Illinois University Press, Carbondale, 1997, 123 at 128.

112 Menzel, 'The Moral Duty to Contribute', at 2176. Indeed, the Law Reform Commission of

However, as a meeting of European Health Ministers in 1987 observed, 'It is an accepted rule of law that the wishes of the deceased person should be executed – a rule which is equally applicable to organ donations.'[113] Audi comments that 'There is, I think, a moral presumption that one's relation to one's body is so intimate that the body should not be invaded, even after one's death, without at least one's prior tacit consent or at worst the consent of relatives or friends who can be assumed to speak authoritatively for one's interests (prior to death)'.[114] Orthodoxy therefore maintains that in the absence of consent society does not have a right to the organs of the deceased, nor any specific individual. Indeed, even Menzel would permit potential organ sources to 'opt out' if they objected to organ removal. In effect, this caveat converts such a proposal into one of 'presumed consent'. Perry, however, argues that the differences between presumed consent and communitarian organ procurement policies lie in the rationale underpinning the scheme rather than in the rules of operation. Beauchamp and Childress have described one perception of a presumed consent system as a form of 'well-defined community project'.[115] However, if this is so, then it is not based upon any kind of individualised consent at all. The rationale is instead that the individual's will must submit to the collective need. But if this is so, why should one be allowed to opt out at all? Why should there be any 'free riders'?

The Report of the AMA Council on Ethical and Judicial Affairs (AMA Report) considered that 'Though some would argue that requiring express consent for invasions of the body should apply only to the living, the Council feels that control over the disposition of the dead should remain governed by individual and familial values rather than by a communitarian ethic.'[116] It noted that although we generally all concede a duty not

Canada even opined that rational, self-interested persons might choose a societal procurement policy that maximised their probability of receiving a transplant if one was required, at the risk of having their tissues taken posthumously: see *Procurement and Transfer*, at 52.

113 Third Report of the Conference of European Health Ministers, (Paris, 16–17 November 1987), *Organ Transplantation: Legislative Measures in Relation to Organ Transplantation and to European Co-operation*, Council of Europe, Strasbourg, 1987, at 6.

114 R. Audi, 'The Morality and Utility of Organ Transplantation' (1996) 8(2) *Utilitas* 141 at 147.

115 T. Beauchamp and J. Childress, *Principles of Biomedical Ethics*, 4th edn, Oxford University Press, Oxford, 1994, at 82.

116 Council on Ethical and Judicial Affairs of the American Medical Association, 'Strategies for Cadaveric Organ Procurement: Mandated Choice and Presumed Consent' (1994) 272 *Journal of the American Medical Association* 809 at 812.

to harm one another, we are far more ambivalent as regards a universal duty to benefit others, and that where we do impose a duty to benefit third parties we would not require any invasion of bodily privacy relating thereto. The communitarian-based obligation of easy rescue assumes *a priori* that any sacrifice is 'easy', which has already been questioned above.

Feinberg notes that 'writers have objected that since a person's body is essential to his identity while alive, it becomes a "sacred possession" whose fate after death he must actively control, and that these facts are properly recognised only by a system that renders a body's transfer to others into a freely given *gift*'.[117] Indeed, there is an almost universal policy consensus not only that organ removal should not take place where an individual (now-deceased) person objects to this, but also that donation is permissible where the deceased has explicitly requested this, without more. These features emphasise the rights of autonomy of the ante-mortem individual which would be crucially compromised by the routine recycling of corpses.[118] However, in some societies there is more than a little resistance to such a straightforward approach in practice. In both the UK and the US, for instance, relatives are typically asked for permission to take organs from the deceased even where the deceased had provided an explicit request to donate, as also happens in certain jurisdictions with strong presumed consent laws, such as Spain and France. As regards allowing relatives to overrule a loved one's wishes on a donor card, Chadwick nevertheless maintains that 'Morally, it is difficult to find an argument for it.'[119] Roels *et al.* argue that this is equally the case in a presumed consent jurisdiction. They state that 'asking the relatives for consent is equal to ignoring the deceased's right to dispose of his body after death'.[120] The deceased's wishes should assume primacy here, in so far as the organs concerned formed a part of his persona and identity prior to death and remain a reflection of it immediately thereafter. Even in PC jurisdictions such as Belgium and Finland, where non-objection (silence) can be sufficient authorisation for organ donation, relatives are not permitted by law to object where there is a *positive* expression of a desire to donate rather than a 'presumed' consent. Although the relatives

117 Feinberg, 'Mistreatment', at 32.

118 Chadwick in particular emphasises this aspect.

119 Chadwick, 'Corpses, Recycling', at 62.

120 L. Roels *et al.*, 'Three Years of Experience with a "Presumed Consent" Legislation in Belgium: Its Impact on Multi-Organ Donation in Comparison with Other European Countries' (1991) 23 *Transplantation Proceedings* 903 at 904.

of the deceased may potentially be distressed by an organ explantation, it would be unwarranted to compromise the pre-deceased's autonomy. In any event, surveys suggest that relatives rarely attempt to override such a positive wish.

Family matters

But what of situations where the deceased has not expressed a willingness to donate? Do relatives have any authority to consent to organ removal in that instance? With reference to jurisdictions where relatives may consent (usually in a priority order) to organ removal where the deceased has not objected thereto, Quay asserts, as regards the US legal position, 'The UAGA is, then, bad law not only because it implies that the survivors own the corpse and may have it used within broad limits as they choose but, more importantly, because it presumes that the state may make what provisions it wishes in this domain without regard to the rights of the deceased.'[121] The rights of relatives are personal and not property-based as regards organ explantation, and extend only to the avoidance of 'offence', discussed further below. Moreover, next of kin are likely to be functioning in a spontaneous and irrational manner due to shock or grief, and their consent, or lack of it, may not be consistent with their more reflective wishes.[122]

Naylor argues that several social values necessitate family involvement in organ removal decisions though, namely protection of the donor from over-zealous organ procurers, respecting individual autonomy, promoting a sense of community through acts of generosity, showing respect for the decedent, avoiding exacerbated grief amongst family members, and respecting religious rights or preferences.[123] He says the family consequently should be viewed as important in its own right.[124] The duty to ensure that the corpse is dealt with properly falls initially upon the family

[121] P. Quay, 'Utilising the Bodies of the Dead' (1984) 28 *Saint Louis University Law Review* 889 at 907.

[122] Martyn *et al.* argue that asking next of kin sets the stage for potential undue influence or psychological coercion in view of the suddenness of the death and the grief-stricken situation of the relatives: see S. Martyn *et al.*, 'Required Request for Organ Donation: Moral, Clinical, and Legal Problems' (1988) 18 *Hastings Center Report* 27 at 29.

[123] C. Naylor, 'The Role of the Family in Cadaveric Organ Procurement' (1989) 65 *Indiana Law Journal* 167.

[124] Quay argues that the family's concerns relate only to the need for a decent burial, to the public health and to the obligations owed to the deceased: see 'Utilising the Bodies', at 901ff.

in most jurisdictions because it is the basic social group and the one containing those with whom the deceased had the closest natural bonds.[125] They may themselves be legally accountable under the criminal law for the failure to ensure a decent burial.[126] However, although in view of this relatives typically have been approached for *permission* for organ removal, this does not in itself imply that there *is* a proper power of authorisation in their hands.

It is clear that reliance on the next of kin has been the primary means whereby a person can ensure that after death his wishes are given effect. Relatives are of course typically best placed to know these, and to give effect to them. However, this is referring to *proxy consent* or *substituted judgement* and not to relatives expressing *their own* wishes. However, Quay argues that the giving of legislative power to relatives to consent to organ removal (based on the 1968 version of the UAGA) exceeds the legitimate powers of the state, and that

> The state has shifted from a fundamental presumption that the citizen has a right to provide effectively through his next-of-kin for the disposition of his body in accordance with his own religious convictions and piety (save when such provisions might threaten grave harm to the common good) to a presumption that the state has plenary rights over the cadavers of its citizens.[127]

Ironically, the UAGA was partially designed to reduce the influence of relatives in the organ donation process in order to increase the volume of organs for transplant.

In *Kohn* v. *United States*, the federal court stated, in awarding damages against the hospital concerned for the unauthorised retention and cremation of organs,

> The applicable law thus requires those who deal with the body to do so with due regard to the feelings and beliefs of the next of kin. In other words the next of kin have an interest in the respectful treatment of the corpse, and in the case of those holding the views such as the plaintiff's, an interest akin to that protected by the First Amendment [Constitutional protection of religious freedom].[128]

[125] Because of the need to protect the public health, he notes that the obligation to dispose of the corpse 'vests in progressively higher-level social structures': ibid.
[126] See, for instance, *State* v. *Bradbury* 9 A. 2d 657 (Maine Sup. Ct. 1939).
[127] Quay, 'Utilising the Bodies', at 894.
[128] 591 F. Supp. 568 at 572–3 (1984).

Indeed, the LRC of Canada Report commented that 'The unauthorised autopsy cases suggest that the law protects the bodily integrity of the deceased as it relates to the *emotional and religious interests* of his or her spouse or next of kin' (my emphasis).[129] However, various US decisions have at least inferred that the rights of relatives extend beyond their own emotional well-being. Although it has frequently been asserted in the US courts that the relatives' right to possession of the body is a right to have the body 'in the condition found when life became extinct',[130] in *Kirker* the court declared: 'The courts are not primarily concerned with the extent of the mishandling or injury to the body, *per se*, but rather with the effect of the same on the feelings and emotions of the surviving relatives, who have the right to burial.'[131] In other words, the *interest* to be protected is *personal* as opposed to property-based. Indeed, as Quay observes, the family do not own the cadaver and only hold it on trust, 'none of which creates any independent basis for giving or donating the cadaver, still less for utilising it or selling it'.[132] Indeed, it makes no sense to talk of the next of kin having an independent right to protect the corpse from violation as it would imply that such protection would be offered merely at the survivor's discretion, whereas any so-called 'rights' here are in reality 'duties'.[133] Such a perspective suggests that relatives have no independent powers to authorise uses of the cadaver, apart from those incidental to the duty to dispose of the corpse. Meyers observes that 'In other words, the basic interests in the surviving spouse, children or next of kin of the deceased are emotional interests connected with the dignity of the disposition of the body and their own peace of mind.'[134] He adds that the right of action of relatives is not to recover damages for harming the corpse but rather is a solatium for the injured feelings of the affected relative.[135]

Post(humous) reflections

The principal goal of an organ procurement policy must be to ascertain the actual wishes of the deceased. It is necessary for such wishes to be

[129] Law Reform Commission of Canada, *Procurement and Transfer*, at 69.

[130] For instance *obiter* in *Kirker* v. *Orange County* 519 So. 2d 682 (Fla. App. 5 Dist. 1988).

[131] Ibid., at 684.

[132] Quay, 'Utilising the Bodies', at 906.

[133] See Veatch, 'The Newly Dead', at 220.

[134] D. Meyers, *The Human Body*, 2nd edn, Edinburgh University Press, Edinburgh, 1990, at 184.

[135] Indeed, in *Kirker* the successful action was brought on the basis of the intentional infliction of emotional distress, and in many other instances for the tort of outrage.

made available at the time of death in a much higher percentage of instances than at present. It may be that the existence of a register is the only proper way to ensure this. Michielsen alleges that without one under any system individual autonomy is no more than a 'polite fiction' and is given mere lip-service.[136] This is because procurement personnel will otherwise feel obliged to turn to relatives for a decision. If one wishes to leave the decision to relatives this ought to have been expressed as one's wish, that is an express delegation of decision-making authority. In Germany, for instance, there is a legislative provision allowing the deceased expressly to delegate the decision to a specified person, who need not be a relative, who may give a consent.

However, the dilemma is how to cause individuals to express their opinion on this issue in sufficient volume to remove the inherent deficiencies of the current systems. To require individuals to make a decision (or to confirm their existing supposed wishes), would for some be too intrusive.[137] Nonetheless, the AMA Report stated that 'Requiring individuals to make a choice about organ donation may be considered by some to be coercive or an invasion of privacy. However, this objection holds little weight when the costs of mandated choice are compared with the social benefits of such a policy.'[138] Moreover, it added that 'Mandated choice is in no way coercive with regard to the particular choices individuals make; individuals who do not want to serve as organ donors are free to say no.'[139] It should also be remembered that choices will be made *for* such persons in any event, in the absence of such expressed wishes. If families are still permitted to object, there is much less likelihood where such evidence exists. As the AMA Report states, 'Clear knowledge of the decedent's preferences may make it easier for families who might be opposed to accept the decision to donate. One recent survey indicated that 93% of respondents would honor the expressed wishes of their family member regarding organ donation if those wishes were known.'[140] There is

[136] See P. Michielsen, 'Informed or Presumed Consent Legislative Models' in J. Chapman, M. Deierhoi and C. Wight, *Organ and Tissue Donation for Transplantation*, Arnold, London, 1997, 344 at 345.

[137] See G. Pennings, 'Ethics of Organ Retrieval' in Y. Englert (ed.), *Organ and Tissue Transplantation in the European Union*, Martinus Nijhoff, Dordrecht, 1995, 166.

[138] AMA, 'Strategies for Cadaveric Organ Procurement', at 809.

[139] Ibid., at 810. See also A. Spital, 'Mandated Choice: A Plan to Increase Public Commitment to Organ Donation' (1995) 273 *Journal of the American Medical Association* 504.

[140] AMA, 'Strategies for Cadaveric Organ Procurement', at 810.

similar evidence in the United Kingdom. As with presumed consent, the idea of *mandated choice* is founded on the belief that this would increase procurement rates because a greater percentage of those expressing a positive opinion in favour of donation would result as compared with those currently expressing a positive wish by means of donor cards, registration, etc. There is some reason to accept this presupposition based on the percentage of respondents who express a willingness to donate their own organs after death in public opinion polls. Although a scheme of this sort in Texas seemingly failed to live up to expectations, Spital notes that this was not truly a mandated choice scheme as it was open to people 'not to answer or to respond 'don't know'.[141] Michielsen, an ardent supporter of presumed consent, argues that 'Mandated choice, however, conflicts . . . with the deeply rooted human attitude of denial of one's own death . . . Coercing into an explicit choice does not seem to be the best way to preserve the individual autonomy.'[142] But if people fail to think about organ donation due to denial of mortality then this undercuts the view that a consent can be gleaned from passivity under a presumed consent system!

Such mandated choice would in effect constitute a form of 'required request'. There are two quite different types of required request policies. The above would focus upon ascertaining the wishes of the person about how they wish their cadaver to be treated after their death, whereas most prevailing required request policies in North America currently target the *relatives* of deceased persons. Of these latter policies, Veatch states that

> Postmortem familial requests nevertheless raise a serious problem . . . [F]amilial request, as originally incorporated into the Uniform Anatomical Gift Act, was clearly meant to be a backup in those cases where the autonomously expressed will of the individual could not be determined . . . Now, however, postmortem familial request is becoming the centerpiece of procurement policy. What was clearly a second-best, decision-making mechanism has become the dominant one.[143]

Even more forcefully, it has been asserted that 'Congress failed to realise

[141] A. Spital, 'Public Policy Governing Organ and Tissue Procurement' (Letter) (1996) 124 *Annals of Internal Medicine* 374. All renewers of driving licences in the state are asked whether they wish their organs to be used after their death for transplantation or not. However, there is no obligation to answer and all those who either respond 'Don't know' or who do not respond at all are defaulted to 'No'.

[142] Michielsen, 'Informed or Presumed', at 355.

[143] Veatch, 'The Newly Dead', at 215.

that a system of routine enquiry contradicts the basic premise of the UAGA – that the individual, not the family, should determine the post-mortem disposition of the individual's body.'[144] Indeed, it has been questioned above what authority there is for relatives to 'donate' the organs of others at all. Of course, such remarks do not touch upon proper decision-making by parents on behalf of their deceased children.

If people voluntarily and of their own initiative expressed their wish to donate or not to donate their organs in sufficient volume there would be no need for any policy of mandated choice at all. Maybe there are simply insufficient *opportunities* to consider the subject and to record wishes at that point. We could increase these opportunities, but would these also be viewed as 'coercive'? All patients attending hospital could be asked their opinion but this might seem inappropriate especially if the patient is suffering from a serious condition at the time. Such a policy is contained in section 5 of the 1987 UAGA and adopted in some US states. However, to ask general practitioners to raise this subject routinely at appropriate visits would seem to be entirely acceptable, as part of a broader understanding of individuals' wishes in a health care setting and in building a deeper relationship with the patient from an early age. If such information were then fed directly into a centralised computerised database, the volume of information would surely increase enormously. But it would be essential that individuals' *objections* as well as positive wishes were able to be recorded by these means.[145]

Under any scheme which permits organ removal without the explicit consent of the pre-deceased, there must be an adequate means for objections to be recorded. The critical issue would then be where the burden of action lies. Again the guiding light must be the autonomous wishes of the now deceased. If he/she has not objected at death then arguably the individual has consented to organ removal anyhow. But Veatch responds to this view by stating that 'It is simply wrong to claim that consent can be presumed in the face of data showing that a significant number of people disapprove.'[146] Erin and Harris, along with Veatch,

[144] 'Developments in the Law – Medical Technology and the Law' (1990) 103 *Harvard Law Review* 1614 at 1621.

[145] The European Parliament adopted a Resolution on 17 April 1996 in favour of a European health card carried by all citizens, which would include, *inter alia*, information about willingness to be an organ donor: see (1996) 47(4) *International Digest of Health Legislation* 550 at 551.

[146] Veatch, 'The Newly Dead', at 213.

allege that in adopting the language of 'consent' we are disguising what we are doing and that there are no truly 'presumed consent' laws in force in reality. In fact the former commentators argue that by presuming *consent* we are being disrespectful of individual autonomy.[147] They contend, again with Veatch, that such laws are in reality policies for permitting procurement without consent. However, unlike Veatch, they support such a policy based on societal need, whereas Veatch asserts that 'If the body is essential to the individual's identity, in a society that values personal integrity and freedom, it must be the individual's first of all to control, not only over a lifetime, but within reasonable limits after that life is gone as well',[148] and adds that 'If the state can assume that human bodies are its for the taking . . . , what will be the implication for less ultimate, less-sacred possessions?'.[149]

147 C. Erin and J. Harris, 'Presumed Consent or Contracting Out' (1999) 25 *Journal of Medical Ethics* 365 at 365.

148 Veatch, 'The Newly Dead', at 213.

149 Ibid.

4

The maintenance and preservation of the cadaver

Issues pertaining to the maintenance and preservation of the cadaver with a view to subsequent organ removal for transplantation have arisen only rarely, but have surfaced recently in connection with the cooling and perfusion of organs of (generally uncontrolled) non-heart-beating donors (NHBDs). Youngner and Arnold state:

> The moral questions raised by the postmortem infusion without family consent are more substantial than its advocates contend. For instance, if the controversy about practising intubation on dead patients is any indication, there is little consensus about the moral acceptability of performing invasive procedures on dead patients to benefit others. Critics believe that these procedures are unethical because they are disrespectful of the dead, disregard families' wishes, and foster undesirable attitudes in health care professionals. The practice is also legally ambiguous.[1]

Typically,[2] an incision is made in the groin and a catheter inserted into the femoral artery and perfusion and cooling initiated using cold preservation solution and cannulation.[3] These are often temporary measures

1 S. Youngner and R. Arnold, 'Ethical, Psychosocial, and Public Policy Implications of Procuring Organs from Non-Heart-Beating Cadaver Donors' (1993) 269 *Journal of the American Medical Association* 2769 at 2770.

2 Such potential donors are those who have come off by-pass during cardio-thoracic surgery, intra-operative neurosurgical deaths, rapidly deteriorating intracerebral bleeds and subarachnoid haemorrhages, failed resuscitations in coronary care units, cardiac arrests on hospital wards, deaths in accident and emergency departments or deaths from primary brain tumours in a hospice environment.

3 Youngner and Arnold have described the normal procedure as follows: 'This approach involves the following two steps: (1) A double – or triple – lumen catheter is inserted with one or two balloons via the femoral artery into the abdominal aorta, and an occluding balloon is inflated above the renal arteries (and in some techniques a second balloon is inflated below the renal arteries) (2) the kidneys are then cooled by infusion of a cold preservation solution and insertion of two cannulas percutaneously through the abdominal wall for continuous

designed to minimise organ deterioration during the time required for acquisition of authorisation for organ donation to be obtained. It is not the 'purpose' of the procedures which is ethically or legally problematic here, as the objectives are, either directly or indirectly, therapeutic in character. What emerges is 'disagreement over the necessity for consent as a means of balancing the concerns'.[4]

Non-heart-beating donors

Techniques of preserving organs by means of post-mortem perfusion had already been developed by the early 1970s but were rarely used thereafter when the preference for heart-beating donors became widespread.[5] However, the popularity of NHBDs generally, and cooling and perfusion specifically, has increased of late; nine British centres now have such protocols covering fifty donor hospitals.[6] Moreover, at Maastricht in the Netherlands, one of the pioneering centres, it has been reported[7] that there is 'no significant difference in long-term graft survival between the

intraperitoneal infusion': see Youngner and Arnold, 'Ethical, Psychosocial, and Public Policy Implications', at 2770.

4 Law Reform Commission of Canada, *Procurement and Transfer of Human Tissues and Organs*, Working Paper 66, Minister of Supply and Services, Ottawa, 1992, at 114. The Report also asserted, with respect to analogous procedures: 'Minimally invasive experimentation or medical education techniques may not disfigure or mutilate the newly dead or otherwise violate their bodily integrity. However, even marginally invasive techniques such as intubation might be considered an indignity or mistreatment, if consent is not obtained from a family that considers such techniques offensive, outrageous or violative of religious beliefs': ibid. at 114–15.

5 Studies in the 1970s, by Starzl, Turcotte, Schweizer, Bankowski, Garcia-Rinaldi and Johnson and others established the feasibility of preserving and using organs from NHBDs: see F. Rapaport, 'Alternative Sources of Clinically Transplantable Vital Organs' (1993) 25 *Transplantation Proceedings* 42. Further research into these forms of preservation was typically held in abeyance as interest in asystolic donors waned generally.

6 The British Transplantation Society Working Party Report on Organ Donation, BTS, London, 1996, found that 87 per cent of centres without an asystolic donor protocol at that time had considered setting one up. Five Organ Procurement Organisations have such protocols up and running in the US at present: see Institute of Medicine Report, *Non-Heart-Beating Organ Transplantation: Medical and Ethical Issues in Procurement*, Institute of Medicine, National Academy Press, Washington D.C., 1997, at 43.

7 This was based on a ten-year period. Albeit based on a shorter period of time, the Leicester centre which has led the way in England reports six- to eighteen-month graft survival of 87 per cent as contrasted with 92 per cent for heart-beating donor transplants: see K. Varty *et al.*, 'Kidney Retrieval from Asystolic Donors: A Valuable and Viable Source of Additional Organs' (1994) 81 *British Journal of Surgery* 1459.

two groups', that is non-heart-beating and heart-beating renal donors.[8] At present NHBDs are almost exclusively kidney donors, although there is some evidence that such donors may also produce good results in respect of livers.[9] The use of NHBDs holds a great deal of potential[10] for increasing organ procurement rates.[11] Although in the US such donors accounted for only 1 per cent of all cadaver donors in the years 1993–6, over ten years at Maastricht[12] 20 per cent more kidneys were retrieved by such means.[13] In the United States, Professor Potts, the principal investigator for the recent Institute of Medicine study on NHBDs, estimated that such donors could represent an increase of at least 1,000 organ donors annually.[14]

Legal and ethical quandaries

The major legal and ethical dilemmas attaching to such cooling and perfusion protocols arise out of the fact that consent will sometimes not have been provided before the initiation of the relevant procedures.[15] To be effective such procedures need to be instituted as soon as possible

[8] M. Booster *et al.*, 'In Situ Preservation of Kidneys from Non-Heart-Beating Donors – A Proposal for a Standardised Protocol' (1993) 56 *Transplantation* 613. A broader survey of fifty-seven transplants from twenty-one centres in the Eurotransplant region revealed a higher rate of delayed graft function in the non-heart-beating donor group as contrasted with the heart-beating group, but after five years graft survival was very similar, 54 per cent as against 55 per cent: see R. Wijnen *et al.*, 'Outcome of Transplantation of Non-Heart-Beating Donor Kidneys' (1995) 345 *Lancet* 1067.

[9] M. Gomez *et al.*, 'Liver Transplantation with Organs from Non-Heart-Beating Donors' (1997) 29 *Transplantation Proceedings* 3478.

[10] M. Nicholson *et al.*, 'Work-load Generated by the Establishment of a Non-Heart-Beating Kidney Transplant Programme' (1996) 9 *Transplant International* 603.

[11] Significant factors in the adoption of such protocols are resources and motivation. They are labour-intensive and require a committed staff who are at a greater 'level of readiness' than usual.

[12] G. Koostra *et al.*, 'Twenty Percent More Kidneys Through a Non-Heart-Beating Program' (1991) 23 *Transplantation Proceedings* 910.

[13] At Leicester, the organ procurement rate was up 38 per cent during the first year of its programme. The six units in the UK in 1993 which used asystolic donors reported that these accounted for 6.5 per cent of all the cadaveric renal organs procured in that year, and in two units the proportion was 20 per cent: see BTS Report, 1996.

[14] Nathan had previously estimated a potential 20–25 per cent increase in the US: see H. Nathan *et al.*, 'Estimation and Characterization of the Potential Renal Organ Donor Pool in Pennsylvania' (1991) 51 *Transplantation* 142.

[15] This will often depend on the location of the individual at the time of death and how death occurred.

following cardiopulmonary arrest,[16] but clinicians have reported on the 'major logistical problems of obtaining consent within the few minutes available immediately after death', which made it 'impossible to retrieve organs in this fashion'.[17] In certain jurisdictions, prior consent is, or has been, an *explicit* legal requirement. Until 1998, Dutch law stipulated that relatives' consent was required prior to the performance of any procedures upon the body of the cadaver, even where the deceased had explicitly requested to donate organs. In most jurisdictions though, its legal status is unclear and there are no such explicit legal provisions.

The general legislative framework governing organ removal for transplantation is itself extremely influential here. If the deceased expressed a positive wish that his/her organs be used for transplantation purposes, then the preservation techniques are simply ancillary to the main procedure and will be impliedly authorised even in jurisdictions where the permission of relatives is routinely solicited anyhow for organ removal. A handful of jurisdictions even have legislation expressly adopting such a legal posture. Panama's 1983 Law, for example, states that 'The donation of an organ of the human body or any anatomical part shall include, without the need for any other declaration, authority to perform any procedures and examinations deemed necessary for the appropriate use of the organ or anatomical part.'[18] Similar reasoning applies to the silence of the now deceased in (strong) presumed consent jurisdictions. Bos states: 'Under an opting-out system, the in situ preservation procedure can be used for every deceased person immediately following death when it has been established that he or she did not object to organ donation. One does not have to wait for the family to be present to decide about inserting the preservation catheter.'[19] Indeed, such a rationale would also justify such procedures in a *weak* presumed consent jurisdiction, such as in Finland or Sweden, where the relatives as well as the deceased may object to organ removal. The 'presumed consent' (implicit authority) of the deceased would enable the preservation procedures to go ahead until the relatives

[16] Youngner and Arnold, 'Ethical, Psychosocial, and Public Policy Implications', at 2770.

[17] For instance, R. Orr *et al.*, 'Reanimation: Overcoming Objections and Obstacles to Organ Retrieval from Non-Heart-Beating Cadaver Donors' (1997) 23 *Journal of Medical Ethics* 7 at 8.

[18] Law of 11 July 1983, section 11. Such a broadly framed provision could conceivably even legitimise organ preservation measures implemented prior to death.

[19] M. Bos, 'Legal Issues Concerning the Use of Non-Heart-Beating Donors' (1995) 27 *Transplantation Proceedings* 2929 at 2930.

could be contacted and given an opportunity to object to such preservation and/or organ removal procedures (assuming there is no other evidence that the deceased objected).

Further, under statutes such as the Human Tissue Act 1961, organ removal may take place if no objections are actually or constructively known to the 'person lawfully in possession of the body'.[20] Relatives are often the primary conduit through which such objections (of the deceased or relatives) may be communicated, and if they are not contacted these objections will be simply disregarded. Moreover, under certain legislative formulations, attempted contact with relatives is obligatory in order to ensure a lack of such objections. For instance, under the 1961 Act there must be 'such reasonable enquiries as may be practicable' to ascertain the existence of such objections. Under such legislation the issue arises as to whether the period of viability of the organ for transplantation itself influences the scope of the expected enquiries.[21] This debate continues in Britain although US state statutes modelled on the 1987 UAGA put this issue to bed by declaring that what constitutes a 'reasonable effort' is to be determined taking into account the useful life of the part. If not, then it would seem that if preservation methods were not permissible prior to contact then all such organs would inevitably be wasted. But if this *is* a relevant consideration and *in situ* preservation is not permissible then the life of the part is negligible and the organ may be removed with only minimal efforts to contact relatives beforehand. This would appear to constitute a denial of the right to *refuse* to donate organs. Such scant regard to the need to ascertain the existence of objections prior to removal cannot have been the objective of the legislature and this applies *a fortiori* where objections would already have to have been 'in the system', as under many of the 'pure' (generally corneal removal) PC laws in the US.[22]

The problems really begin though where the deceased has provided no explicit assent to organ removal in a system requiring explicit consent either from the deceased or from relatives, such as in Germany, Denmark and those US states adopting the 1968 version of the UAGA. In such jurisdictions, if the deceased's wishes are not known, then contactable

[20] Section 1(2).

[21] The better view, expressed by, for instance, Lanham, is that it does: see D. Lanham, 'Transplants and the Human Tissue Act 1961' (1971) 11 *Medicine, Science and the Law* 16 at 18.

[22] And maybe also in jurisdictions such as Belgium.

relatives generally have the right to decide whether the deceased's organs should be used for transplantation purposes. However, if cooling/perfusion is not initiated in many instances *before* relatives can be contacted, the organs will cease to be viable and the issue will become academic. The relatives will therefore be unable to make a decision *for* the deceased (that is a form of substituted decision-making) nor will they be able to exercise any independent right of donation. Thus, where laws confer such powers upon relatives, preservation methods serve to promote the autonomy and wishes of deceased persons,[23] and of relatives as a class, albeit at the expense of such procedures offending some relatives.

Veatch, however, contends that such arguments are wide of the mark. He alleges:

> Some people might mistakenly claim that inserting a catheter prior to consent preserves the family's option to donate until informed consent can be exercised, and therefore is more respectful of patient autonomy or informed consent. This claim, however, shows a misunderstanding of the notions of consent and autonomy . . . Autonomy in no way gives one the right to be a subject of a medical procedure, an experiment, or organ procurement . . . The only relevance of autonomy to perfusion is that any perfusion prior to consent violates the individual's autonomy rights. This is true not only for the half of the population that would refuse to consent to donation if asked, but also of the group who would consent if asked but who would object to invasion of the body without being asked.[24]

There is force in these remarks, but of course such preservation procedures take place in the broader organ procurement context rather than in isolation (as discussed above). Their use would also appear to further the intention of the relevant legislatures. Where a now-deceased person did not donate in an express consent system such as applies to organs across most of the US, one can very reasonably interpret the policy as one whereby the choice is left to close relatives. Silence is not evidence of an objection to organ removal (let alone organ preservation procedures), it is simply a 'non-consent'. Moreover, there is no formal

[23] Admittedly, in so far as in most express consent systems there are public mechanisms for stipulating a *positive* wish to donate, for example by donor card, this medium will often be more important as a source of information concerning potential *objections*.

[24] R. Veatch, 'Consent for Perfusion and other Dilemmas with Organ Procurement from Non-Heart-Beating Cadavers' in R. Arnold, S. Youngner, R. Schapiro and C. Mason Spicer (eds.), *Procuring Organs by Transplant: The Debate Over Non-Heart-Beating Cadaver Protocols*, Johns Hopkins University Press, Baltimore, 1995, 195 at 201.

mechanism for recording a positive wish for *organ preservation methods* to be implemented to facilitate such delegated decision-making.

The King's Fund Report, contrasting organ removal and organ preservation procedures, considered that 'Ultimately, the ethical issues revolve around consent in both cases, and not the nature of the act to which consent is, or is not, presumed',[25] and counselled against inconsistency of approach. In the absence of explicit authorisation, it regarded the issues to be very similar to those raised by the more general presumed consent debate. However, it noted that although both procedures involve cutting into a corpse without consent, it is a 'less significant' presumption in the context of organ preservation procedures, that is that the individual and/or the family would not object to minimally invasive procedures. The Regional Organ Bank of Illinois (ROBI) in fact specifically relied upon the presumed consent rationale to support its NHBD protocol.[26] It seems entirely reasonable to apply such a rationale to organ cooling and perfusion. Nevertheless, the preferred legal framework would be to have a mechanism for expressly leaving this matter to relatives, leaving no room for inferences. Indeed, the recent Dutch Law[27] has such a provision and additionally provides that

> In the absence of any declaration of intent by the person, as referred to in Section 9 or 10, or if use has been made of the possibility mentioned in the second sentence of subsection 2 of Section 9 [that is delegation to a family member], the necessary measures to maintain the organ in a suitable condition for transplantation may be taken after death, so long as the procedure for obtaining the necessary consent to removal in accordance with this Law has not been completed.

This is an interesting, innovative and useful provision. As Bos states, 'The rationale for this is that through in situ preservation organs may be preserved for transplantation as long as the consent procedure for procurement has yet to be completed.'[28] The Dutch Law enables such measures to be used whenever the deceased has expressly left the issue of

[25] King's Fund Institute, *A Question of Give and Take*, Research Report 18, King's Fund Institute, London, 1994 at 66.

[26] Although it did so apparently because it had been refused permission on thirty-five consecutive occasions on which it had been sought prospectively: see Youngner and Arnold, 'Ethical, Psychosocial, and Public Policy Implications', at 2770.

[27] Law of 24 May 1996 on Organ Donation.

[28] Bos, 'Legal Issues', at 2931.

authorisation for organ removal to relatives, or the deceased (having not expressly left the decision to relatives) has not expressed any decision whilst alive either for or against organ donation. This will have the effect of preserving not only the organs but the right of decision-making for relatives, and in this way furthers the autonomy of both relatives and the deceased.

In addition, cadavers are typically 'maintained' on artificial ventilation and organs preserved with the use of certain drugs, when there sometimes has been no express request for donation by the deceased and relatives have yet to be contacted, or at least to give consent to it. These are 'heart-beating' donors.

Heart-beating donors

Because, once asystole occurs, organs 'die' and cease to be viable for transplantation, it is now usual to maintain a (brain-)dead patient by ventilatory means and to use organ-maintaining drugs where organ donation is in prospect. In Britain at least, public policy statements appear to both recognise and endorse such procedures. The former United Kingdom Code of Practice *Cadaveric Organs for Transplantation*[29] published in 1983 stated that 'After a person is dead there is no legal objection to administering any drugs necessary to maintain the condition of the organs or to conducting the necessary diagnostic tests.' It is added that 'Before removal of the organs all practicable measures should be taken to ensure that their condition is optimal . . . Drugs to maintain renal function should be given. Antibiotics may be required and fluid intake should be maintained.'[30] Moreover, the revised 1998 Code states that relatives, unless they raise it themselves, should not be approached regarding organ donation until after brain-stem death has been formally diagnosed, and maybe even after death is pronounced.[31] Thus, official endorsement is given to such procedures even where no consent has previously been obtained from either the (now) deceased or relatives, and

[29] *Cadaveric Organs for Transplantation*, Health Departments of Britain and Northern Ireland, 1983, at paras. 24, 32 and 34.

[30] Ibid., at paras. 24, 31 and 32.

[31] The 1998 Code seems to be ambivalent on this, there being inconsistency between the wording, on page 16, and the diagram, on page 19: see *A Code of Practice for the Diagnosis of Brain Stem Death (Including Guidelines for the Identification and Management of Potential Organ and Tissue Donors)*, Department of Health, London, 1998.

in practice the corpse is maintained quite routinely for at least some limited period whilst the consent, or lack of objection, of relatives is sought.[32]

Again, where the deceased had expressly 'willed' his organs for transplant no legal or ethical difficulties materialise, although laws typically fail to deal explicitly with this matter. In Britain, the Human Tissue Act 1961, in section 1(8), merely states that 'Nothing in this section shall be construed as rendering unlawful any dealing with, or with any part of, the body of a deceased person which is lawful apart from this Act.'[33] Skegg states that the prior request of the deceased *or* the consent of those entitled to possession of the body could authorise what would otherwise be an unlawful interference with the corpse, although he does not consider that all 'interferences' with the cadaver which were not authorised would automatically be unlawful or unethical.[34] Paradoxically, artificial ventilatory techniques employed both before and after death and in the absence of prior consent have been tolerated without controversy for a very long period, and are analogous to cooling procedures, being no less invasive and lengthy (although there is generally no need for any surgical incision). Indeed, one can imagine, ironically, that in many situations, if preservation through cooling was not permissible, many such potential donors would be simply ventilated instead, with increasing pressure on ICU facilities.

The English judiciary clearly recognises notions of respect and dignity with regard to the dead human form. Where no legitimate purpose is furthered by continued (cellular) 'existence' after death, it should not be artificially extended. In the High Court in *Re A*,[35] Johnson J said that it would be contrary to the interests of A, a brain-stem dead child of nineteen months, and unfair to the nursing and medical staff at the hospital, for his body to be subjected to the 'continuing indignity' to which it was subject, that is continued ventilation, hydration and nutrition. It was, therefore, somewhat surprising to find that the court's order permitted the physicians a *discretion* as to such withdrawal. The Northern Ireland High Court of Justice in *Re TC (A Minor)* viewed

32 Because of the lapse of time whilst brain death is confirmed there is often less of a dilemma as a greater period of time has been permitted for contact with relatives to be made.

33 In fact the Act seems to permit the use only of *parts* of the cadaver anyhow, not of the whole body.

34 P. Skegg, *Law, Ethics and Medicine*, Clarendon Press, Oxford, 1988, at 254.

35 [1992] 3 Medical Law Reports 303.

likewise in similar circumstances, prompting Professor Kennedy to comment that 'If the child was dead there seems no basis in law for continuing to ventilate it until the medical staff decided otherwise, save, perhaps in the unlikely event that organs were to be used for transplant.'[36] The courts do therefore appear to recognise common law rights to 'maintain' the cadaver over and above specific legislative empowerments.

Skegg states that

> there are no well-established common law offences that will apply to most unauthorised uses of corpses for medical education or research, although there are some offences which could sometimes be applicable. There is also a possibility that some judges would adopt the view that the unauthorised use of corpses for medical education or research amounts to a common law offence of unlawful interference with a corpse.[37]

However, he had already expressed the view that 'Judges would therefore have no difficulty in holding that the unauthorised use of a corpse for medical education and research did not amount to any common law offence which prohibits certain unauthorised interferences with a corpse prior to burial or cremation.'[38] Concepts such as 'indignity', 'mistreatment' and 'mutilation', which are common to offences designed to protect the integrity of the cadaver, are problematic in terms of their scope though. They are context and culture specific and linked to the purposes for which the intervention was intended.[39] There are of course many significant 'intrusions' upon the cadaver routinely carried out and which attract no opprobrium, such as various funereal practices,[40] procedures which are designed to *promote* not compromise the dignity of

[36] [1994] 2 Medical Law Review 376. He argues that to continue to ventilate a corpse otherwise would be an unjustifiable waste of resources unless possibly done to allow parents and close relatives to be at the child's bedside when artificial support was withdrawn.

[37] P. Skegg, 'Criminal Liability for the Unauthorised Use of Corpses for Medical Education and Research' (1992) 32 *Medicine, Science and the Law* 51 at 54.

[38] Ibid.

[39] See earlier views expressed in the Nuffield Council on Bioethics Working Party, *Human Tissue: Ethical and Legal Issues*, Nuffield Council on Bioethics, London, 1995, at paras. 6.7–6.9.

[40] As Dukeminier notes, 'Many violations occur, for example, in preparing the body for burial; arteries are cut, blood is removed, and formaldehyde is pumped into the blood vessels. Similarly, eyelids may be sewn closed, and faces may be restored. Practices such as these are accepted largely because people do not think about them; they are routinely performed behind the closed doors of the undertaking establishment': see J. Dukeminier, 'Supplying Organs for Transplantation' (1970) 68 *Michigan Law Review* 811 at 824.

the deceased.[41] The King's Fund Report took the view that in Britain, in the light of the fact that society sanctions coroners performing autopsies as well as the embalming process, it is unlikely that the minimally invasive incision associated with NHBD cooling procedures would be viewed as unreasonable and unethical mutilation of the cadaver.[42] It has also been held in the United States that making a small incision in the groin to determine the extent of an abscess was not a mutilation of the corpse, nor was an unauthorised embalming.[43] In the US there are cases though which highlight that relatives, in the light of their right to possession of the body for burial purposes, have a right to the body in the state it was in at the time of death. This might consequently give rise to a potential civil action by relatives for emotional distress, although in some states this might have to have been inflicted intentionally or recklessly, and not just negligently. Such a cause of action seems unlikely to be successful though, and in Britain it is highly debatable. Moreover, preservation measures employed over an excessive period of time might theoretically constitute an offence of preventing the disposal of the body. A refusal to make the body available within a reasonable time to a person with a right to possession of the body who had requested it might give rise to damages in a civil action as for example in *Strachan* v. *John F. Kennedy Memorial Hospital* where there was prolonged ventilation for the purpose of ascertaining organ donor status.[44]

Thus, just because transplantation legislation such as the Human Tissue Act 1961 does not explicitly provide for or authorise such maintenance procedures on the cadaver, it does not mean they are necessarily unlawful, even in the absence of consent. Indeed, the Nuffield Council Report noted that it is open to the courts to permit certain dealings with the corpse outside the existing statutes, under the common law, where there was perceived to be a 'good reason' for them.[45] This

[41] Which Nuffield viewed, together with therapeutic procedures, as constituting ethically acceptable conduct.

[42] See King's Fund, *A Question of Give and Take*, at 66. Such procedures are not disfiguring and may not even result in any apparent change in the physical appearance of the corpse.

[43] See D. Anaise *et al.*, 'An Approach to Organ Salvage from Non-Heartbeating Cadaver Donors under Existing Legal and Ethical Requirements for Transplantation' (1990) 49 *Transplantation* 290 at 293. See also *People* v. *Bullington* 80 P. 2d 1030 (Cal. 1938).

[44] 538 A. 2d 346 (N.J. 1988). See also *Edmonds* v. *Armstrong Funeral Home* [1931] 1 DLR 676 (Alta. S.C.).

[45] Nuffield Council, *Human Tissue*, at para. 6.14.

might, indeed should, apply to such preservation methods.[46] Presently such procedures may become judicially sanctioned if the need arises, but this is an inadequate substitute for statutory guidance. Express legislative provision is the preferred strategy with respect to organ preservation measures, for both public and clinician reassurance and guidance, as has occurred in Sweden and the Netherlands. These remarks have application to various other procedures performed upon the cadaver. The Swedish legislation states:

> Once it has been established that death has occurred, measures may be taken, if appropriate, in order to preserve organs or other biological material pending transplantation or, in the case of a pregnant woman carrying a viable fetus, in order to save the life of the unborn child. Unless there are special circumstances, such measures should not continue beyond 24 hours.[47]

This model has much to recommend itself in the transplant context and also more broadly. Such reform should ride on the back of a general societal consensus following widespread public education and debate.[48] Democratic endorsement through legislation is consequently appropriate. However, there is seemingly less than widespread acceptance in the United States, as was discovered in the Institute of Medicine study, whose Report[49] states that there is a prevailing sense that the public is likely to disapprove of non-consensual cannulation and cooling and that strong opposition was expressed in surveys conducted in three cities.[50] This may depend upon the jurisdiction though. There have been statutes passed in the states of Virginia and Florida and in the District of Columbia permitting such cooling and perfusion procedures to be carried out even

[46] Ibid., at para. 13.23, stating that 'removal of tissue from the dead for purposes which are acceptable in that they contribute directly or indirectly to medical treatment, but may not be expressly provided for by statute should, if appropriate consent has been obtained, be regarded as lawful'. The same view would presumably apply to invasive procedures not involving the removal of tissue.

[47] Law of 8 June 1995, section 2(a).

[48] In Britain the Leicester NHBD protocol was introduced only after local publicity in newspapers, and appeared to be uncontroversial: see *Leicester Mercury*, 14 February 1992. The Institute of Medicine Report recommended that all NHBD protocols be available for public scrutiny. Like the Institute Report, the British Transplantation Society has stated that such protocols should be consistent and accord with national guidelines.

[49] Institute of Medicine, *Non-Heart-Beating Organ Transplantation*, at 54.

[50] See R. Arnold, Testimony at Public Workshop on the Medical and Ethical Issues of Maintaining the Viability of Organs for Transplantation, Washington D.C., 30 July 1997.

without consent.[51] There will be an increasing number of situations involving the potential use of procedures upon a cadaver to benefit others in instances where the deceased has not previously provided a formal consent or authorisation for the procedure. A mechanism for respecting the person's wishes should be facilitated if the procedure cannot be justified generally on the basis of statutory authority. It has even been suggested that it is also appropriate to 'maintain' a cadaver for a limited period to assist the psychological adjustment of relatives to the death.[52]

[51] Although only the District of Columbia has actually initiated a practice of *non-consensual* cooling/perfusion in accordance with the statute: see Institute of Medicine, *Non-Heart-Beating Organ Transplantation*, at 26. It may be that adverse publicity surrounding NHBDs generally in the US has coloured attitudes towards cooling and perfusion procedures.

[52] See F. Miedema, 'Medical Treatment after Brain Death: A Case Report and Ethical Analysis' (1991) 2(1) *Journal of Clinical Ethics* 50.

5

The treatment of potential donors prior to death

There are a wide variety of issues canvassed in this chapter, all drawn together by the thread that the sole, or principal, purpose of the intervention is the facilitation of transplantation through the preservation of viable organs, rather than potential benefit to the patient. Such individuals, although alive at the relevant time, are frequently in moribund condition and consequently typically lack capacity to give consent to such interventions. Such interventions appear to transgress the broad proposition set out in the former Code of Practice of the Medical Royal Colleges in Britain[1] that 'Any tests or treatment carried out on a patient before he dies must be for his benefit and not solely to preserve his organs.'[2] Moreover, in some instances they would also appear *prima facie* to contravene the so-called 'dead donor' rule, which comprises the notion that patients must not be killed either *for* or *by* organ retrieval.[3] Similar controversies arise outside the transplant context. Comatose pregnant women have been maintained for a sufficient time to facilitate the delivery of viable babies, and it has even been prophesied that in the future medical experiments will be routinely carried out on long-term coma

[1] *Cadaveric Organs for Transplantation: A Code of Practice Including the Diagnosis of Brain Death*, Health Departments of Great Britain and Northern Ireland, 1983, at para. 22.

[2] Knight puts it in terms of not doing anything which would not have been done anyway in the furtherance of treatment: see B. Knight, *Legal Aspects of Medical Practice*, 5th edn, Churchill Livingstone, Edinburgh, 1992, at 54. He gives an example of transferring a patient to a different hospital, which has resonances for the practice of EV discussed below. However, he sees nothing objectionable about taking an enhanced blood sample to allow tissue typing tests to be carried out: ibid. The 1983 Code of Practice explicitly permitted such tests to be carried out where blood was already being taken for the patient's own care: *Cadaveric Organs for Transplantation*, at para. 22.

[3] Certain practices may infringe one aspect of the rule but not the other: for example if a patient was killed for the purposes of an organ transplant the first element of the rule would be contravened, but not the latter, as the patient would be dead when organ retrieval took place.

victims.[4] The discussion here raises a host of issues, such as the essence of the concept of 'harm' in ethical and legal terms in relation to insentient beings and the relevance of the moral notion of personhood, the doctrine of double effect and problems pertaining to conflicts of interest in the transplant context. It crucially implicates the question whether deontological concerns are raised by procedures intended only to benefit others. If not, then utilitarian considerations appear to pull in the direction of their employment.

Clinical protocols considered

Tensions arise in relation to all manner of different transplant protocols and practices, but typically involve ventilation, cooling and perfusion, and drug administration procedures, or strategies for facilitating a 'controlled' death to expedite a successful transplantation. In order to ensure viable organs for transplant, it may be necessary to 'manage' the death process more directly than normal. Where death occurs 'naturally' through cardiorespiratory cessation, organs will often not be usable unless organ retrieval (or cooling) begins very soon thereafter, and this has led to the growth of (controlled and uncontrolled[5]) non-heart-beating donor (NHBD) protocols. The primary alternative is to ensure that at the point of death the organs are being maintained by artificial ventilation, and maybe also by drug administrations, that is heart-beating donation.

Such (actual or proposed) protocols often attach to particular *classes* of patients such as anencephalics and permanent vegetative state (PVS) patients. Attention has focused upon anencephalic neonates as a source of organs for transplantation into children.[6] The most famous case was that of Baby Gabrielle[7] born in 1987, whose heart was transplanted into Paul

4 By Professor David Morton: see 'Coma Victims to replace Animals in Experiments' *The Times*, 8 April 1996. In addition, a recent controversy flared in Britain with regard to the taking of sperm from the husband of a woman who wished to become pregnant through the posthumous use of it, whilst he lay in a terminal coma – the Diane Blood affair.

5 See chapter 4 on 'The Maintenance and Preservation of the Cadaver'.

6 Between 1988 and 1991, 239 articles on the subject appeared in the medical literature. It has been estimated that in the US between 40 and 70 per cent of children on the waiting list die whilst awaiting a suitable organ: see J. Friedman, 'Taking the Camel by the Nose: The Anencephalic as a Source for Pediatric Organ Transplants' (1990) 90 *Columbia Law Review* 917 at 920. Organ size is a particularly important factor in outcomes of cardiac transplantation: see J. Botkin, 'Anencephalic Infants as Organ Sources' (1988) 82 *Pediatrics* 250.

7 See T. Frewin *et al.*, 'Clinical Summary: Baby Gabrielle' (1988) 20 (Supp. 5) *Transplantation Proceedings* 81.

Holc, a newborn with hypoplastic left-heart syndrome.[8] Anencephalics are generally given 'comfort care' during their short lifespan but even though parents frequently give permission for organ donation, once cardiac arrest intervenes the organs invariably cease to be viable, especially the heart and liver. PVS patients are not generally reliant on medical technology for continued survival, apart from the (artificial) administration of nutrition and hydration by means of a nasogastric tube or similar device, nor are they generally destined to die imminently. Decisions are often taken to cease to continue to provide such nutrition and hydration though, and if so death typically occurs ten to twelve days later following cardiorespiratory failure. However, again the organs are by this stage unsuitable for transplantation (because of dehydration or electrolytic instability).[9] They are not presently used for transplant purposes. Other 'classes' of patients include those dependent upon (continued) life-sustaining medical care, and the profoundly neurologically impaired.

The main protocols of this type will be briefly outlined and then the implications in terms of both law and ethics will be considered.

The cause of death

Because of problems of organ viability, there have been occasional suggestions to allow the removal of organs from anencephalics before death occurs in the normal way.[10] Indeed, it is reported that kidneys were

[8] The first kidney transplant from an anencephalic child took place at the University of California in Los Angeles in 1961: see W. Goodwin *et al.*, 'Human Renal Transplantation, I: Clinical Experiences with Six Cases of Renal Homotransplantation' (1963) 89 *Journal of Urology* 13. The transplant lasted a mere three months. The University of Ohio has reported a 50 per cent success rate with kidneys procured from anencephalics, including one transplant that functioned for twenty-two years: see K. Iitaka *et al.*, 'Transplantation of Cadaver Kidneys from Anencephalic Donors' (1978) 93 *Journal of Pediatrics* 216.

[9] According to the US Multi-Society Task Force on PVS, there were approximately 10,000–25,000 adult and 4,000–10,000 child PVS patients in the US in 1994: see Multi-Society Task Force on PVS, 'Medical Aspects of the Persistent Vegetative State' (1994) 330 *New England Journal of Medicine* 1499 (Part One) and 1572 (Part Two). Andrews has estimated that in Britain there are probably less than 1,000 PVS patients. See also J. Downie, 'The Biology of the Persistent Vegetative State: Legal, Ethical, and Philosophical Implications for Transplantation' (1990) 22 *Transplantation Proceedings* 995.

[10] A protocol of this type was apparently developed by Vacanti and Epstein at the Boston Children's Hospital in 1986, although it was not implemented because of legal constraints: see W. Holzgreve *et al.*, 'Kidney Transplantation from Anencephalic Donors' (1987) 316 *New England Journal of Medicine* 1069.

transplanted from anencephalic newborns to both adults and children at the University Hospital Münster in 1987 in this fashion, with parental permission.[11] It has also been argued by some commentators that donors under the Pittsburgh, and certain other, controlled NHBD protocols are not certainly dead at the point of organ retrieval, that is that too much haste has been employed. This has been debated earlier and, if the argument can be sustained, would have the same impact as the above proposals/protocols in terms of infringing the dead donor rule, that is death would be caused *by* organ removal. Moreover, the International Forum on Transplant Ethics (IFTE) recently proposed that once a decision to allow a PVS patient to die has been made, they should be given a lethal injection thereby preserving the viability of the organs for transplantation (a request having been made for organ donation),[12] although there appears to be no prospect whatever of official endorsement of such a policy at present. Although the removal of organs would not occur until after death here, death might be viewed as having been caused *for* organ retrieval.

Hastening death

Organ/body cooling and perfusion generally takes place after death has occurred, but in respect of anencephalics Fletcher, Harrison and Robertson articulated a proposal under which such newborns would be gradually 'cooled' in order to avoid warm ischaemia time through decreased organ perfusion. The authors appreciated that this procedure would have the effect of hastening the newborn's death due to cerebral swelling but contended that such procedures were justified, a contention evaluated below.[13] Where death is hastened by such organ preservation

[11] Ibid. Two kidneys were removed from one newborn anencephalic forty-five minutes after delivery. It was stated that the courts in the Federal Republic of Germany did not at that time consider such a neonate to have ever been born alive.

[12] See K. Hoffenberg, M. Lock, M. Tilney *et al.*, 'Should Organs from Patients in Permanent Vegetative State be used in Transplantation?' (1997) 350 *Lancet* 1320, and see Letters at (1998) 351 *Lancet* 211–12. The British Medical Association has previously stated that 'Patients in persistent vegetative state should not at present be considered as potential organ or tissue donors': see *BMA Guidelines on Treatment Decisions for Patients in Persistent Vegetative State*, BMA, London, 1996, at para. 9, and 'BMA Slams Lethal Injection Donor Idea', BBC Ceefax, 31 October 1997, at 121.

[13] J. Fletcher, M. Harrison and J. Robertson, 'Primates and Anencephalics as Sources for Pediatric Organ Transplants: Medical, Legal and Ethical Issues' (1986) 1 *Fetal Therapy* 150.

measures the dead donor rule is contravened however and thus they are *prima facie* illegitimate.

The patients subject to controlled NHBD protocols in the United States are either competent with intolerable quality of life or incompetent, but not brain dead, due to severe, generally neurological, illness or injury with an extremely poor prognosis as to survival or meaningful functional status. They are maintained on artificial ventilation or circulatory assistance and will suffer irreversible cardiorespiratory cessation very shortly after withdrawal of support.[14] Under the University of Pittsburgh protocol, the still-living patient is 'heparinized, prepped, and draped for the subsequent organ procurement'.[15] Indeed, a 1996 survey in the US by the Institute of Medicine (IOM Report) found that fifteen of the twenty-nine existing NHBD protocols specified using heparin (an anticoagulant) or a combination of heparin and phentolamine (a vasodilator) at some point during the death and donation process. Five specifically permitted the use of heparin before withdrawal of life supports, and another after withdrawal but before the declaration of death. A further protocol permitted the use of both heparin and phentolamine after withdrawal but before death. Because of their potential to hasten death, the IOM recommended that a 'case-by-case' assessment be made and that they should never be used in instances of ongoing intracranial bleeding or other deficiencies in blood volume.[16]

The process of death

Of course, even where death is not hastened, many such procedures are still intended to benefit the patient. Alluding to the use of drugs such as heparin to maintain organ integrity and speaking in respect of the Pittsburgh NHBD protocol, Lynn has commented that 'the current understanding that all interventions prior to a determination of death

[14] Institute of Medicine Report, *Non-Heart-Beating Organ Transplantation: Medical and Ethical Issues in Procurement*, National Academy Press, Washington D.C., 1997, at 1.

[15] M. De Vita *et al.*, 'Procuring Organs from a Non-Heart-Beating Cadaver: A Case Report' (1993) 3 *Kennedy Institute of Ethics Journal* 371 at 380.

[16] Institute of Medicine, *Non-Heart-Beating Organ Transplantation*, at 52–3 and 439–40. Half of the protocols also permitted the insertion of femoral arterial cannulas prior to the withdrawal of life support, for *in situ* flushing and preservation after death, although most explicitly required consent to their placement. Because perfusion (although not cannulation *per se*) might hasten death the Report stated that perfusion should not take place until after death: ibid., at 38 and 53.

must be justified on the basis of the patient's welfare is challenged by the new protocol because it opens the possibility of implementing interventions to preserve organs during the time needed to confirm death, and possibly before death has occurred'.[17] Drugs are in fact routinely used to maintain organ quality and viability under all forms of transplant protocols and especially in relation to heart-beating donors. As noted above, however, the 1983 Code of Practice in Britain made it abundantly clear that the administration of drugs to preserve organ function could not be justified until the patient was dead as it would not be for the patient's benefit.[18] Whilst such drugs may not hasten death or cause injury to the patient in the conventional sense, they are nonetheless administered wholly in the interests of others. Skegg comments that

> it is often desirable to administer drugs to maintain the condition of the organs, and also to carry out various tests. The potential donor will rarely have consented to these, and only some of them can be regarded as being in any sense for his benefit. Where they are not, they will be illegal, unless the potential donor is already dead.[19]

In order to avoid organ damage resulting from cardiorespiratory collapse, protocols have also been implemented to employ the use of resuscitation and ventilatory techniques in anencephalics from either birth or cardiac arrest, either until death or a pre-set period of time has elapsed. The Loma Linda University Medical Center issued a (revised) protocol in December 1987 under which anencephalics would be attached to mechanical ventilation immediately after birth and for a maximum period of one week, during which it was anticipated brain death would occur and organ procurement could take place.[20] Similar problems of organ viability arise in respect of adult patients who sustain profound intracranial haemorrhage and will quickly succumb to brain death but who are on general medical wards where, if they suffer respiratory arrest,

[17] J. Lynn, 'Are the Patients Who Become Organ Donors under the Pittsburgh Protocol for "Non-Heart-Beating Donors" Really Dead?' (1993) 3 *Kennedy Institute of Ethics Journal* 167 at 168.

[18] Paragraph 24 stated: 'After a patient is dead there is no legal objection to administering any drugs necessary to maintain condition of the organs': see *Cadaveric Organs for Transplantation*.

[19] P. Skegg, *Law, Ethics and Medicine*, Clarendon Press, Oxford, 1988, at 201.

[20] Centres in Münster and in Rome (the Bambino Gesu Hospital) have adopted a similar protocol, although with very limited success: see A. Abbattista *et al.*, 'Anencephalic Neonates and Diagnosis of Death' (1997) 29 *Transplantation Proceedings* 3634.

their organs will not generally be viable for transplantation. However, the immediate provision of artificial ventilation might ensure a different outcome. In the UK, Elective (Interventional) Ventilation[21] (EV) protocols, as they became known, were designed to address this dilemma, through the moving of such patients to the ICU, with the consent of relatives, so that ventilation could be initiated immediately respiratory arrest occurred.[22] The first hospital in Britain to initiate such a protocol was the Royal Devon and Exeter Hospital in May 1988. By 1994, when such protocols were abandoned following a governmental directive, eight centres had implemented them. The pool of potential additional (EV) donors is a sizeable one. It was estimated that at the Royal Devon the donor rate from the ICU averaged thirty donors pmp, just over twice the national average.[23]

Apparently EV is a uniquely British phenomenon and is not practised *overtly* elsewhere. This is partly because of resource matters. It has been remarked that 'To many outside Britain, the idea that seriously ill, comatose patients are not routinely admitted to an intensive care unit seems extraordinary.'[24] However, as Walters and Ashwal note, the standard practice everywhere is 'to give optimal care to the patient while viable life can be sustained, but to shift emphasis from prolongation of life to maintenance of organ vitality at an appropriate point in the organ

[21] The epithet 'elective' seems to have attained broader usage than 'interventional', but both are employed here interchangeably.

[22] The criteria for identification of patients with intracranial vascular accidents as potential organ donors were: characteristic mode of onset; sudden with rapid development of coma; progressive decline in consciousness level; deep coma; lack of withdrawal response to painful stimuli: and exclusion of reversible causes of coma: see T. Feest *et al.*, 'Protocol for Increasing Organ Donation after Cerebrovascular Deaths in a District General Hospital' (1990) 335 *Lancet* 1133.

[23] The King's Fund estimated that an additional 900 kidneys could be achieved per annum if each of the 277 ICUs produced an extra ten donors pmp by such means: see King's Fund Institute Report, *A Question of Give and Take*, Research Report 18, King's Fund Institute, London, 1994, at 55–6. See also M. Salih *et al.*, 'Potential Availability of Cadaver Organs for Transplantation' (1991) 302 *British Medical Journal* 1053.

[24] C. Wight and B. Cohen, 'Shortage of Organs for Transplantation' (1996) 312 *British Medical Journal* 990 at 991. As Sells states, '[elective ventilation] would never have been a necessary extreme if there had been sufficient numbers of staffed beds in intensive care units in the United Kingdom to offer routine resuscitation to the great majority of stroke patients, as is commonly done in other, better funded Western health services': see R. Sells, 'Practical Implications' (1995) 310 *British Medical Journal* 717 at 717. It is additionally a function of an increasing ability to diagnose severe neurological conditions accurately and predict prognoses accurately.

donor's dying process'.[25] It may be extremely crucial though, from an ethical and legal perspective, whether this 'change of tack' (from care of the 'patient' to maintenance of the potential 'donor') occurs whilst the person is dying or when he/she is already dead. Martyn *et al.* allude to the temptation of 'switching loyalties' further and further back from the time of a brain death diagnosis.[26] Thus, EV protocols may only explicitly formalise a ('switch') practice occurring everywhere in the course of ICU procedures, although less transparently.

The perception in Britain that EV was ethically defensible was reinforced by the statement in Paragraph 26 of the previous Code of Practice that 'Very occasionally it will be considered certain that death will inevitably occur shortly (in the case, for example, of gross trauma and progressive cerebral tumour) . . . [I]n these cases doctors should seek the agreement of relatives for the initiation of artificial ventilation to preserve organ function before death has been diagnosed.'[27] This should be contrasted with Paragraph 25, which addressed patients thought to have irreversible brain damage who require ventilation, but in respect of whom it *cannot* be said with certainty that brain death will occur. In such cases ventilation can be justified before death on the basis of potential benefit to the patient.[28] Apparently, artificial ventilation was sometimes perceived to be justified prior to death even where no benefit could accrue, for the sole purpose of a potential organ transplant, and with *or* without the consent of relatives.[29] The ambiguity of domestic policy here was commented upon by the Exeter clinicians themselves, who stated: 'The dilemma we face now is the fact that we have an official government document which

[25] J. Walters and S. Ashwal, 'Organ Prolongation in Anencephalic Infants: Ethical and Medical Issues' (1988) 18 *Hastings Center Report* 19 at 23.

[26] S. Martyn *et al.*, 'Required Request for Organ Donation: Moral, Clinical and Legal Problems' (1988) 18 *Hastings Center Report* 27 at 27. The need for 'fluid management' as early as possible to preserve organs is another important issue.

[27] *Cadaveric Organs for Transplantation*, para. 26.

[28] Interestingly, paragraph 25 is repeated verbatim in the National Health and Medical Research Council of Australia's Code of Practice on Cadaveric Transplantation, but there is no equivalent of paragraph 26 in that Code, thereby producing the completely opposite effect, that is artificial ventilation can *only* be justified where it is for the benefit of the patient, so that EV would be illegitimate: see NHMRC, *Code of Practice for Transplantation of Cadaveric Organs and Tissues*, The Council, Canberra, 1989.

[29] Paragraph 26 went on to say that 'If it is not possible to obtain the relatives' views before the situation arises, doctors should exercise their judgment in the light of the circumstances of the individual case whether or not to initiate artificial ventilation, so as to enable enquiries to be made about the views of the deceased and the relatives about the removal of organs after death has been diagnosed': see *Cadaveric Organs for Transplantation.*

approves elective ventilation but which may not be legally binding. Can we be criticised and found to be acting illegally when we follow clear departmental guidelines?'[30]

In so far as such 'ethical' perceptions are shared, they drive a wedge between legal and ethical perspectives of such procedures. Sells has remarked:

> To many transplanters, the elective ventilation protocol was a welcome initiative, and the plan to resuscitate stroke patients for organ donation was perceived as altruistic, imaginative, useful, and safe. The Exeter team quickly showed that a considerable increase in donation was possible given a flexible use of beds in intensive care units, cooperation by relatives, and the alertness of medical and nursing staff.[31]

However, despite its use over a period of six years, the growing interest in it from many quarters and the explicit support given to the practice from professional bodies such as the British Medical Association (BMA), the Royal College of Physicians in London, the Royal College of Nursing and the British Transplantation Society,[32] the practice was suspended in October 1994 following the issuance of a Department of Health Guideline[33] advising that it was unlawful.[34] This followed immediately on the heels of the King's Fund Institute Report[35] which asserted that the practice of ventilating in such circumstances constituted an unlawful battery (although not necessarily being unethical) because the patient could not consent to it,[36] and because the procedure was not in the best interests of that individual.

The dead donor rules OK?

Practices which contravene the dead donor rule are universally illegal (typically murder), even with the full consent of the patient, and are

[30] H. Riad and A. Nicholls, 'Elective Ventilation of Potential Organ Donors' (1995) 310 *British Medical Journal* 714 at 715.

[31] Sells, 'Practical Implications', at 717.

[32] Although not from the Intensive Care Society nor from many anaesthetists: see, for example, (1994) 28(1) *Journal of the Royal College of Physicians of London* 85.

[33] Acute Services Policy Unit, *Identification of Potential Donors of Organs for Transplantation*, NHS Executive HSG (94) 41, 1994.

[34] This was the view of the Law Commission in its Report on *Mental Incapacity*, Law Comm. No. 231, HMSO, London, 1995, at 85.

[35] King's Fund, *A Question of Give and Take*, at 63–4.

[36] And, of course, would rarely have given any prospective authorisation for such a procedure prior to having lost decision-making capacity.

condemned by the overwhelming majority of transplant professionals and medical societies across the board. It would not matter that the transplanted organs could save the lives of even a handful of individuals or more.[37] The killing is viewed as 'wrong' from a 'rights-based' perspective and would infringe the sanctity of life doctrine. Nevertheless, some believe that whatever the legal position, it is morally acceptable to carry out such actions. Fletcher *et al.* have asserted in the context of organ removal from (not yet dead) anencephalics that 'We think it is unreasonable to construe legal and ethical doctrines against direct, active killing so broadly as to prohibit organ preservation in such cases and believe that reasonable people would agree with such a conclusion.'[38] Indeed, a survey of eighty-three clinicians and bioethicists conducted in 1990 in North America found that the majority of respondents favoured allowing anencephalics to be used as organ sources even *before* the brain stem had irreversibly ceased to function.[39] Moreover, in 1995 a Report from the American Medical Association's Council on Ethical and Judicial Affairs (AMA Report) in fact endorsed such a practice and urged a change in the law to facilitate this (although the policy was later reversed).[40] Some proponents of organ removal from anencephalic neonates have campaigned for a change in the law so as to view such individuals as *already being dead* to facilitate organ removal thereby.[41] A New Jersey legislative initiative which attempted instead to alter the state's version of the Uniform Anatomical Gift Act (not its death statute) failed, but would have created an exception to the dead donor rule specifically for such a class of beings.[42] It will be argued here that not only should the dead donor rule be retained, but moreover there can be no warrant for creating an exception for any specific class of individuals.

[37] Indeed, the organs from one donor could potentially save the lives of nine patients or more.

[38] See Fletcher, Harrison and Robertson, 'Primates and Anencephalics', at 150.

[39] J. Walters, 'Anencephalic Infants as Organ Sources. Report from North America' (1991) 5 *Bioethics* 326 at 334–5. This proposition was supported by 52 per cent of MDs and 70 per cent of PhDs.

[40] AMA Council on Ethical and Judicial Affairs, 'The Use of Anencephalic Neonates as Organ Donors' (1995) 273 *Journal of the American Medical Association* 1614, policy reversed at (1996) 275 *Journal of the American Medical Association* 443.

[41] In Walters's survey 49 per cent of MDs and 32 per cent of PhDs preferred that this be facilitated by making anencephalics a 'one-off' exception to brain-dead standards of death rather than by expanding the definition of death across the board.

[42] N.J. Stat. Ann. (West 1987 & Supp. 1989). Assembly Bill No. 33677.

Abandon the dead donor rule?

More fundamentally, there have been various proposals for the wholesale abandonment of the rule here and its replacement by other guiding ethical principles, that is autonomy and non-maleficence. Such a change of emphasis would divorce the ethical acceptability of an organ removal procedure from the status of the patient as either dead or alive. Truog states:

> For example, policies could be changed such that organ procurement would be permitted only with the consent of the donor or appropriate surrogate and only when doing so would not harm the donor. Individuals who could not be harmed by the procedure would include those who are permanently and irreversibly unconscious (patients in a persistent vegetative state or newborns with anencephaly) and those who are imminently and irreversibly dying . . . This alternative approach to organ procurement would require substantial changes in the law. The process of organ procurement would have to be legitimated as a form of justified killing, rather than just as a dissection of a corpse.[43]

Arnold and Youngner have similar leanings and state that, 'From a patient's perspective, the consequences of organ procurement (death) may not be that different except that organ procurement may help others.'[44] Arguments for abandonment, however, hinge upon spurious and dangerous assertions relating to classes of individuals (or 'non-persons') being 'beyond harm' and possessing no relevant moral interests. Fost, for instance, advocates a 'violates no interests' maxim in place of the dead donor rule here.[45] However, even supporters recognise the serious ethical and legal problems that such an abandonment may precipitate.[46]

[43] R. Truog, 'Is it Time to Abandon the Dead Donor Rule?' (1997) 27 *Hastings Center Report* 29 at 34.

[44] R. Arnold and S. Youngner, 'The Dead Donor Rule: Should we Stretch it, Bend it, or Abandon it?' (1993) 3 *Kennedy Institute of Ethics Journal* 263 at 270.

[45] N. Fost, 'Organs from Anencephalic Infants: An Idea whose Time has not yet Come' (1988) 18 *Hastings Center Report* 5 at 9.

[46] See R. Taylor, 'Reexamining the Definition and Criteria of Death' (1997) 17(3) *Seminars in Neurology* 265. Bernat contends that irreparable damage to the public's confidence in transplantation would be generated by the abandonment of the rule: see J. Bernat, 'A Defense of the Whole-Brain Concept of Death' (1998) 28 *Hastings Center Report* 14 at 22.

Where the action is

The gravamen in many of the scenarios discussed above is the *active* means used to procure death. Where ventilation is withdrawn from a competent patient who refuses further treatment or from a moribund patient in the context of a controlled NHBD protocol,[47] or comfort measures only are applied to anencephalics, or further nutrition/hydration is withheld from a PVS patient, with the effect that life is foreshortened as a result, this is potentially legitimate even though active measures to terminate life would not be. Whether it is in fact legitimate will depend upon whether the patient who refuses is competent and whether, in respect of a patient lacking competence, further treatment is in the best interests of that individual or (in some jurisdictions) is supported by a substituted judgement.

Laws are dogmatic in reinforcing the acts/omissions division regardless of the potential benefits to others. This dichotomy has however been condemned by a variety of commentators. Indeed, in the House of Lords in the *Bland* case (considered below), Lord Mustill offered the opinion that 'however much the terminologies may differ the ethical status of the two courses of action is for all relevant purposes indistinguishable'.[48] The IFTE advocated a rethink here in respect of PVS patients whose organs will go to waste if active measures to terminate life are not implemented (and a similar argument could be made in respect of permanently comatose individuals and anencephalics). The contention is that the decision to end the individual's life has already been made, and that the means of implementing that decision are not morally important. The decision not to provide any further life-sustaining treatment (including nutrition and hydration), and to bring about death, is based solely on the interests of the patient, although the means of death would be tailored to the transplantation enterprise but without any harmful implications for the patient.[49] A somewhat similar suggestion has appeared in the academic legal literature in the US by virtue of which PVS patients, or otherwise incompetent patients whose lives may lawfully be ended, may

[47] Assuming, of course, that such patients are indeed dead when organ retrieval occurs.

[48] *Airedale NHS Trust* v. *Bland* [1993] 1 All ER 821 at 885J.

[49] Active means of killing, for instance of animals, are often specifically advocated, in order to minimise suffering, but the consensus is that PVS patients and anencephalics are unable to experience pain or suffering even from the withholding of further nutrition and hydration.

be allowed to die by organ removal or in a fashion which facilitates organ retrieval.[50] Assuming that one could be assured of adequate separation of decision-making (see discussion below), the views of the IFTE have much to commend them. Morally there would indeed seem to be little difference between such a scenario and the situation under controlled NHBD protocols where the 'process of death' is designed to facilitate the procurement of transplantable organs but is nonetheless in itself morally unobjectionable. Indeed, the very 'haste' created under NHBD protocols results from the need to act swiftly where death results from a withdrawal of treatment. However, such arguments are unlikely to sway policy-makers in the immediate future. We may have to wait for a change in the legal climate relating to active euthanasia generally before such a proposal would command sufficient support. Were such a change to be forthcoming however, there have also been proposals to allow a *competent* adult to elect to die by the removal of an organ or in a manner consistent with, rather than inconsistent with, organ retrieval, that is where the law permits aid-in-dying based on the individual's medical condition.[51]

Fletcher, Harrison and Robertson's proposal for the cooling of the organs of newborn anencephalics to avoid warm ischaemia time through decreased organ perfusion would, as the authors appreciated, have the effect of hastening death due to cerebral swelling.[52] At present such procedures would constitute homicide as they hasten death by active measures. However, supporters argue that the procedure is justified partly by virtue of the doctrine of double effect (DDE) under which an unintended, merely foreseen, evil consequence is permitted if overall the procedure can be justified according to the totality of the circumstances, whereas intended bad actions (either by virtue of bad means or bad ends) are always morally wrong. Similar arguments have been put forward in support of the Pittsburgh protocol and some of the ancillary procedures employed there which are not intended for the benefit of the patient.

[50] Report, 'Living Organ Donor Act' (1993) *Journal of Corporate Law* 583 at 591.

[51] Ibid., at 590. This would be permitted where the individual had not previously objected, and either he/she had executed a health care power of attorney whilst competent, or the procedure was authorised by the 'Organ Transplant Board'.

[52] See Walters and Ashwal, 'Organ Prolongation', at 20.

Who do you think you are kidding?

I have argued strenuously elsewhere as to the unacceptable nature of DDE in both law and ethics.[53] As a matter of law, liability often entirely turns upon whether conduct was intended or not. If not, no further justification for it is required. Where there *is* such a justification (as with proportionate life-shortening pain-relieving measures employed *for the benefit of the patient*), then no harm may be done by such a finding. But the upshot in these transplantation contexts would be that there would be no requirement for any justification to be shown whatever. Yet surely it is the supposed outweighing benefits to others that are viewed as justifying the procedures, not simply that the clinician merely had the interests of others in mind rather than the hastening of the donor's death. Furthermore, in law the concept of 'intention' usually *includes* situations where the actor foresaw the (virtually) inevitable consequences ensuing. Foresight of *certain* consequences equates with intention, or at least is evidence of intention, in most jurisdictions (at least in relation to homicide).[54] DDE does nothing to address the real issues here. It is little more than linguistic subterfuge and should be summarily discounted. Weisbard maintains that in the Pittsburgh NHBD context, 'The principle operates here, it seems to me, principally to obscure the actor's moral responsibility and to provide a layer of protection from potential legal liability, not to provide persuasive moral justification.'[55] All consequences of one's actions should be weighed in determining the moral permissibility of a medical intervention. In any event, if such effects are viewed as unintended, DDE merely throws us back to the question whether the action can be justified in all the circumstances anyhow!

On benefits

As we have already seen, even if death is not hastened nor the means of death tailored to the needs of transplant recipients, tensions arise wherever

[53] See D. Price, 'Euthanasia, Pain Relief and Double Effect' (1997) 17(2) *Legal Studies* 323, and D. Price, 'Assisted Suicide and Refusing Medical Treatment: Linguistics, Morals and Legal Contortions' [1996] 4 *Medical Law Review* 270.

[54] In Australia this *is* intention. In England and Wales foresight of a virtually certain consequence is either intention or at least evidence from which intention can be inferred: see *R* v. Woollin [1999] AC 82 (HL).

[55] A. Weisbard, 'A Polemic on Principles: Reflections on the Pittsburgh Protocol' (1993) 3 *Kennedy Institute of Ethics Journal* 217 at 223.

procedures are intended to benefit an ultimate recipient, but which can, to put things at their blandest, have no potential beneficial effects for the 'donor'. Arguably, in some instances such procedures will constitute not only a legal wrong but also, in ethical terms, a 'harm' to that individual. In some circumstances, such action will inevitably alter the *nature of the dying process* by extending the life of the individual through the use of artificial ventilation. This might impact adversely upon the dignity of, and the respect owed to, the individual.[56] With regard to EV procedures, one of the ethical concerns that was repeatedly expressed was that patients subject to the protocol might be induced into a PVS state as a result of the intervention. A PIVOT study to determine the likelihood of this occurring was never ultimately conducted in Britain although publicly mooted. It appears to be accepted that such ventilatory procedures may prolong the lifespan of anencephalics. At Loma Linda in April 1988 a statement was made that evaluation of their protocol had highlighted the fact that such full intensive care from birth altered both the natural course of dying and resulted in the prolongation of life of some of these newborns.[57] In many instances cardiac arrest occurred prior to the determination of brain death and the organs consequently deteriorated. As a consequence of the lack of efficacy of such ventilation procedures, ventilation was subsequently only to be instituted at Loma Linda once cardiorespiratory failure occurred, and such support maintained for no more than twenty-four hours, after which, if brain death had not occurred, ventilation would cease.

[56] Commentators such as Ivan Illich have linked the lack of dignity in contemporary notions of death and dying to the 'medicalisation' of death and the invasion of life by technology: see I. Illich, *Limits to Medicine. Medical Nemesis: The Exploration of Health*, Penguin Books, London, 1990.

[57] Although not the invariable scenario (Baby Gabrielle succumbed to brain death after forty-eight hours of ventilator support), this was also the experience at the Bambino Gesu Hospital in Rome: see R. Cecchi and S. Del Vecchio, 'Diagnosis of Brain Death in Anencephalic Infants: Medicolegal and Ethical Aspects' (1995) 14 *Medicine and Law* 3. Further, Winkler observes that 'It is unclear, on theoretical grounds, why an anencephalic infant, born with an intact brain stem should become brain dead if cardiopulmonary support is maintained': see E. Winkler, 'Consideration of Anencephalic Newborns as Organ Donors: Ethical Problems Related to the Determination of Death' in C. Machado (ed.), *Brain Death*, Elsevier Science, Amsterdam, 1995, 207 at 209.

Insentient beings: playing the symbols

Despite the lack of potential benefits, it has been argued that many of these interventions upon permanently insentient beings constitute no ethical 'harm'. Robertson asserts that 'reservations about the ability of the Pittsburgh protocol to observe punctiliously the dead donor rule amount more to a symbolic than a substantive concern because the nearly dead patient no longer has substantive interests to be protected. (If this assumption is not true, then the Pittsburgh protocol raises much more serious concerns and will be difficult to justify.)'[58] As regards anencephalics, Robertson remarks, in similar vein, 'intentionally and directly causing the death of an anencephalic infant, who has no chance of living even with maximal treatment and no consciousness, cannot be said to harm his interests or injure him in any way'.[59] Indeed, the initial AMA Report argued that the dead donor rule should not guide us in this context and stated that the rule is designed to ensure that one person's life is not sacrificed for the benefit of another person, even to save his/her life, but that anencephalics have no interest in staying alive because of their permanent lack of consciousness. Moreover, the reassurance provided by the rule for potential organ donors generally cannot be eroded because such individuals contemplating donation can never become anencephalic.[60]

The idea of 'symbolic harm' and its supposedly lesser injurious status than *substantive* harm trades in this analysis upon the idea that such patients lack interests. If they or their interests cannot be harmed there is very much less objection to such procedures. This notion of 'symbolic harm' can also be found in the statements of various other influential bodies. For instance, on the subject of EV, the British Medical Association concedes that 'The possibility of causing symbolic harm by accepting relatives' views, as if the dying patient were already legally dead, is recognised. Nevertheless, EV and the intensive nursing accompanying it, although not undertaken with the purpose of benefiting a potential donor, are not clinically deleterious to the patient.'[61] But does the epithet

[58] J. Robertson, 'Policy Issues in a Non-Heart-Beating Donor Protocol' (1993) 3 *Kennedy Institute of Ethics Journal* 241 at 249.

[59] Ibid.

[60] AMA, 'The Use of Anencephalic Neonates', at 1615.

[61] BMA, *Medical Ethics Today: Its Practice and Philosophy*, BMA, London, 1993, at 28.

'symbolic' act so as to minimise the significance of the infringement implicated here? What constitutes a 'harm' to an insentient being will however be significantly influenced by perceptions of autonomy, interests, *personhood* and the mind/body interface. These issues will be considered below.

Juristic matters

If a patient possesses decision-making capacity at the time of the proposal to initiate organ preservation measures, he/she has a right in law to authorise them, at least where they will not hasten the death of the patient or produce severe injury, and even though they will not be of any benefit whatever to the patient. It is unlikely that a court would declare them to be unlawful as there are extremely good policy reasons for endorsing practices which could not harm others and which might facilitate the supply of organs for transplantation.[62] However, many protocols have been designed to be employed at a point in time when the individual manifestly lacks decision-making capacity. Generally, in such circumstances the law looks for authorisation from prior statements from a formerly competent person, from consent given by parents in respect of minors, and/or to what is in the best interests of the person concerned (and in certain jurisdictions, to the substituted judgement of the patient's 'proxy').[63]

Certain procedures will have been administered solely as a preliminary to a potential transplant, whereas others such as artificial ventilation will frequently have initially been instituted for therapeutic purposes (for example to supplement attempts at ensuring the survival of the individual). In the latter circumstances no legal or ethical obstacles will arise unless and until they are continued beyond the point where they continue to afford any potential beneficial effects for that individual – a line which will often be blurred, especially where the patient was already in the ICU. In *Bland*, Lord Goff stated that

[62] This is the conclusion reached by all commentators, but is discussed most fully by Sheila McLean: see S. McLean, 'Transplantation and the "Nearly Dead": The Case of Elective Ventilation' in S. McLean (ed.), *Contemporary Issues in Law, Medicine and Ethics*, Dartmouth Press, Aldershot, 1996, at 151–5.

[63] In very exceptional cases the law will sanction procedures not in the patient's interests on the basis of benefit to society, even in the absence of consent, for example quarantine or mandatory treatment laws, but usually these will only be imposed in emergency circumstances.

> where, for example, a patient is brought into hospital in such a condition that, without the benefit of a life support system, he will not continue to live, the decision has to be made whether or not to give him that benefit, if available . . . No doubt, his best interests will ordinarily require that he should be placed on a life support system as soon as necessary, if only to make an accurate assessment of his condition and a prognosis for the future. But, if he neither recovers sufficiently to be taken off it nor dies, the question will ultimately arise whether he should be kept on it indefinitely. As I see it, that question (assuming the continued availability of the system) can only be answered by reference to the best interests of the patient himself, having regard to established medical practice.[64]

Because of this change of emphasis, the argument of the formulators of the Exeter EV protocol that 'The patients admitted to ICU differed from the others only in that respiratory arrest occurred immediately before or on arrival at hospital'[65] is wide of the mark. In the latter instance the prognosis of the patient was uncertain and was under investigation with the assistance of such ventilatory support, whereas in the former the prognosis was clear and hopeless.

In the EV context, the BMA has remarked that 'Patient autonomy could be preserved if patients were able to express their views on this practice in advance, either through some form of advance directive or re-worded donor card, but public knowledge about this practice is not yet widespread.'[66] There has been no revised donor card though and, despite the fact that such advance statements (which may be positive as well as negative) now have legal effect in Britain and the US,[67] relatively few patients make any such advance statement about their future health care generally, let alone about ancillary procedures to organ donation for transplantation.[68] McHale comments 'whether the courts would uphold a

[64] [1993] 1 All ER 821 at 869.

[65] Feest, 'Protocol for Increasing Organ Donation', at 1134.

[66] BMA, *Medical Ethics Today*, at 28.

[67] See *Re T (Refusal of Treatment)* [1992] 4 All ER 649 (CA), and the BMA Code of Practice, *Advance Statements about Medical Treatment*, BMJ Publishing Group, London, 1995. McHale expresses some doubt as to whether a court would uphold an advance directive authorising elective ventilation should the patient become incapacitated and lapse into a hopeless condition: see J. McHale, 'Elective Ventilation – Pragmatic Solution or Ethical Minefield?' (1995) 11(1) *Professional Negligence* 23 at 24.

[68] Buchanan states: 'Instead of being seen simply as devices for protecting the patient or for exercising autonomy for its own sake, they might in addition become vehicles for new forms of altruism, new ways of exercising the virtue of charity. For example, instead of specifying that if one comes to be in a persistent vegetative state all means of life support are to be

direction which requested that elective ventilation be given is unclear. Nevertheless, a court might be influenced by the fact that in giving effect to the wishes of the deceased their life would not be prolonged unduly – patients are ventilated for no more than 48 hours.'[69] However, it would seem unlikely that the significant and uncertain risks of inducing a PVS state would have generally been communicated to such persons, thereby casting doubt on the validity of any 'DIY' advance statement at least.[70] Express consent in this context will consequently invariably be either absent or insufficient.

The Royal College of Nursing (RCN) has argued that *implied* consent exists though, whenever an organ donor card has been completed. The College urges 'prior to brain death, the normal rules about consent to treatment apply. A competent patient can give express consent to organ donation. By implication, the patient thereby gives consent to all procedures necessary to keep the organs viable for transplantation, including elective ventilation prior to brain death.'[71] However, such procedures are carried out *prior to*, rather than after, death. As a consequence, it is unlikely that such procedures would have been even partially in the contemplation of the individual signing the donor card. Indeed, as the BMA has explicitly noted above, widespread public knowledge about such procedures is scant. Arguably, whilst there is a kernel of truth to the RCN's submission, it is too sweeping as it stands. It cannot impliedly authorise such extensive procedures performed prior to death (especially where there is a risk of significant detrimental consequences flowing from it, for example a PVS), although it might justify procedures such as blood sampling for tissue typing to ascertain organ donation potentiality and compatibility, which are a routine, minor and necessary prerequisite to organ donation anyhow.

withdrawn, a person with a strong sense of social obligation might instead request to be sustained in such a condition until his organs and other transplantable tissues are needed to save or enhance the lives of others': see A. Buchanan, 'Advance Directives and the Personal Identity Problem' (1988) 17 *Philosophy and Public Affairs* 277 at 278.

69 McHale, 'Elective Ventilation', at 24. Shaw rightly suggests that there is no reason in principle why a court should not uphold such an advance statement of consent to EV procedures: see A. Shaw, 'Non-therapeutic (Elective) Ventilation of Potential Organ Donors: The Ethical Basis for Changing the Law' (1996) 22 *Journal of Medical Ethics* 72.

70 The Law Commission has stated that even if an advance statement has been made, consideration should still be given to the best interests of the patient: see Law Commission, *Mental Incapacity*, at 68–9. If a PVS might ensue, this might be difficult to substantiate.

71 Royal College of Nursing, *Review of the Legal, Ethical and Nursing Issues of Harvesting of Organs*, RCN, London, 1993.

Although patient consent would not exist in the overwhelming majority of cases, EV protocols primarily rely on the consent of relatives rather than the comatose individual anyhow and many US protocols do likewise with regard to controlled non-heart-beating donors. However, British law and the laws of many other jurisdictions are clear on the point that relatives have no legal power to give proxy consent on behalf of incapacitated individuals, with the exception of parents on behalf of their minor children.[72] Thus, reliance on relatives' consent in the case of adult patients is entirely inappropriate and provides no valid authorisation for EV procedures. By contrast, in North America, many jurisdictions permit decision-making on the basis of the 'substituted judgement' of the incompetent person, usually by relatives.[73] Where a *substituted judgement* approach is applicable a decision would be made as to what the person *would have decided* had he or she retained capacity and been able to make that decision for him- or herself, but where the person made no specific advance statement of his/her wishes beforehand. It would appear that reliance is placed on this doctrine in the context of NHBD protocols in the US. This *might* extend also to such procedures as EV. On the other hand, dependence upon the authorisation of relatives under legislation modelled upon the 1968 Uniform Anatomical Gift Act (or analogous statutory provisions) would be inappropriate in view of the fact that the legislation accords powers to relatives with respect only to the use of the *deceased's* body.[74] A substituted judgement approach would be more faithful to the individual's values and wishes, especially where organ donation was a very fervent wish and would otherwise be precluded. Indeed, Article 9 of the Council of Europe Convention states that the previously expressed wishes of individuals who are now unable to make such decisions for themselves 'shall be taken into account'. It is, however, a particularly difficult concept to apply to a very specific procedure such as elective ventilation.

Moreover, it could seemingly have no application in cases where the person concerned never formerly possessed any decision-making

72 See, for example, *Re T (Refusal of Treatment)* [1992] 4 All ER 649.

73 See, for example, *Superintendent of Belchertown* v. *Saikewicz* 370 N.E. 2d 417 (Mass. Sup. Jud. Ct 1977).

74 This is also the view expressed in J. Mason and A. McCall Smith, *Law and Medical Ethics*, 4th edn, Butterworths, London, 1994, at 305.

capacity.[75] By virtue of this, the US and UK authorities which have applied the doctrine in cases of *living* organ donation have in reality sought potential benefit to the incapacitated individual.[76] In other words, a best interests approach was applied in substance.[77] In *Little* v. *Little* the court stated:

> It is clear in transplant cases that courts, whether they use the term 'substituted judgment' or not, will consider the benefits to the donor as a basis for permitting an incompetent to donate an organ. Although in *Strunk* the Kentucky Court discussed the substituted judgment doctrine in some detail, the conclusion of the majority there was based on the benefits that the incompetent donor would derive, rather than on the theory that the incompetent would have consented to the transplant if he were competent. We adopt this approach.[78]

Regarding minors, parents are able to make general health care decisions on behalf of their offspring. In most instances, such procedures are intended to benefit that child. More difficult issues arise when they are not. Of course, anencephalic newborns can obtain no benefit themselves from artificial ventilation designed to preserve organ viability for transplantation, so it would seem that if the parents were only permitted to authorise procedures on their children that were in *their* best interests, then artificial ventilation for such purposes would not be within their powers, let alone cooling procedures. However, in Britain, in the context of procedures performed primarily in the interests of others, the 'not against the interests of the minor' test has sometimes been utilised, notably in regard to blood testing for paternity purposes.[79] Indeed, the Nuffield Council considered that the 'not against the interests of' test might apply in the context of the removal of tissue from a minor, and that

[75] In *Cruzan* v. *Director, Missouri Health Department* 111 L. Ed 2d 224 (1990), the United States Supreme Court held that an intermediate standard of proof, that of 'clear and convincing evidence', may be mandated by the due process clause of the Fourteenth Amendment to the US Constitution when the individual interests at stake in a state proceeding are both particularly important and more substantial than mere loss of money.

[76] For example, *Strunk* v. *Strunk* 445 S.W. 2d 145 (Ky. 1969) and *Hart* v. *Brown* 289 A. 2d 386 (Sup. Ct Conn. 1972). See chapter 8 for further detail.

[77] That is not to say that the person's past and present wishes are not relevant to the determination of what is in his/her best interests. The English Law Commission would make this formally part of the assessment in its newly formulated best interests test: see Law Commission, *Mental Incapacity*, at 44.

[78] 576 S.W. 2d 493 at 498 (Tex. Civ. Ct 1979).

[79] *S* v. *S, W* v. *Official Solicitor (or W)* [1972] AC 24 (HL).

the test would be satisfied where it posed no more than a negligible risk and minimal burden to the minor and such tissue could not equally well be taken from an adult.[80] Could this same stance and approach be adopted for EV procedures performed on minors? In the ventilation context, however, the minor could obtain no benefit whatever to 'balance out' any potential harms, whereas in these other scenarios this was a factor present. In any event, it is generally accepted that only minimal harms should be implicated. However, the precise scope and degree of any 'harms' occurring in these contexts simply beg difficult questions addressed further on, although seemingly the risks of inducing a PVS condition cannot be dismissed as negligible. This test has no application to mentally incapacitated *adults* anyway, as there is no one comparable to a parent of a minor to make the decision and to be held accountable for it.[81]

In the absence of consent, the notion of best interests ordinarily applies to decision-making in respect of mentally incapacitated adults and children in many jurisdictions,[82] and would seemingly do so here.[83] In Britain, this was confirmed by the House of Lords[84] in *Airedale NHS Trust* v. *Bland*[85] where it was held that further provision of nutrition and hydration to a patient in a PVS condition would not be in his best interests and so could not be legally justified.[86] Lord Keith stated that it was lawful to cease to treat, 'considering that to do so involves invasive manipulation of the patient's body to which he has not consented *and which confers no benefit upon him*' (my emphasis).[87] It is not clear what benefits *could* accrue to a comatose individual from such procedures –

80 Nuffield Council on Bioethics, *Human Tissue: Ethical and Legal Issues*, National Council on Bioethics, London, 1995, at para. 7.8. Note that this was made in the context of organ removal procedures.

81 Ibid., at para. 7.9.

82 A view endorsed by the King's Fund Report, *A Question of Give and Take*, as well as the Law Commission Report, *Mental Incapacity*, at paras. 6.24–6.26.

83 In the United States, whether a substituted judgement standard is recognised varies from state to state, but in many states the best interests test applies across the board.

84 Although itself relying heavily upon the decision of the House in *Re F (Mental Patient: Sterilisation)* [1990] 2 AC 1 (HL). Sheila McLean has described the British courts, by contrast with various other jurisdictions, as being 'in thrall' to the best interests test when making decisions for (incompetent) others: see McLean, 'Transplantation and the "Nearly Dead"', at 156.

85 [1993] 1 All ER 821 (HL).

86 In *Bland*, Lord Mustill stated that Tony Bland 'has no best interests of any kind': [1993] 1 All ER 821 at 894F.

87 Ibid., at 861.

such persons are even denied the psychological benefits of altruism.[88] For that reason, the view of (two of the Exeter clinicians) Riad and Nicholls that 'Respecting the right of a dying patient to donate organs is in any case acting in their best interests'[89] is patently spurious and self-serving. Moreover, even if such individuals do have subsisting interests it is undoubtedly difficult, if not impossible, to *weigh* the interests of such individuals. Walters and Ashwal consider that in the case of anencephaly the best interests standard really just begs the question of the proper grounds for decision-making.[90]

Nevertheless, the dilemmas here arise from the fact that the procedures are patently *not* in the individual's best interests on any conventional view. There could consequently be no obligation to carry out such procedures.[91] But that of course is not the crucial question here, which is instead whether, if such procedures *were* applied, they would be unlawful (or unethical). The advice of the Department of Health that EV procedures would be unlawful appears correct in view of the statements made by three of the five Law Lords in *Bland*, the effect of which was that not only do such procedures not need to be applied, but they *must* not be.[92] Lord Lowry stated: 'if it is not in the interests of an insentient patient to continue the life-supporting care and treatment, the doctor would be acting unlawfully if he continued the care and treatment and would

[88] Indeed, the very impossibility of assessing the best interests of such individuals in such a context, and incidentally also with regard to decisions relating to the withdrawal of life-supporting treatment from adults in PVS, led the Law Commission, in its Report *Mental Incapacity*, to recommend a different legal framework in such contexts as opposed to a best interests test. A statutory framework was proposed for EV and similar procedures, should such procedures prove acceptable to society at large: at para. 6.24.

[89] Riad and Nicholls, 'Elective Ventilation of Potential Organ Donors', at 715.

[90] Walters and Ashwal, 'Organ Prolongation', at 21.

[91] As Gillon has stated, 'The primary moral purpose of medicine is to try to benefit people in health-related ways and this is incorporated into a doctor's moral and legal duty of care. Where an intervention is highly unlikely to provide such benefit to the person there is no medico-moral or legal obligation to provide it and withholding or withdrawing it does not infringe the doctor's duty of care': see R. Gillon, 'Persistent Vegetative State, Withdrawal of Artificial Nutrition and Hydration, and the Patient's "Best Interests"' (1998) 24 *Journal of Medical Ethics* 75 at 75.

[92] Lord Browne-Wilkinson, by contrast with the other two Law Lords, appeared to confer a discretion upon doctors here, but added that 'Unless the doctor has reached an affirmative conclusion that it is in the patient's best interests to continue the invasive care, such care must cease': at [1993] 1 All ER 821 at 883. His basic approach is less convincing than his brethren's though, unless intended to do no more than confer a good faith immunity in some instances. The patient's best interests must light one path only here. Moreover, Lord Mustill cast doubt on the application of the *Bolam* principle in this context.

perform no guilty act by discontinuing'.[93] Lord Goff commented that such treatment *should* be discontinued where its continuance is no longer in the patient's best interests.[94]

Taking an interest

The essence of the approach of the House in *Bland* was on the surface a narrowly legalistic one, namely that any touching without consent constitutes a battery unless a justification exists for it. The continuation, not the withdrawal, of treatment therefore had to be justified. Lord Goff stated: 'This is because the question is not whether it is in the best interests of the patient that he should die. The question is whether it is in the best interests of the patient that his life should be prolonged by the continuance of this form of medical treatment or care.'[95] Thus, the House took the view that to say that such treatment does not serve his best interests is not at the same time to declare that such procedures were *contrary* to his best interests – the House explicitly declined to declare that death was better than life.[96] Such reasoning, however, elides important implicit value-laden judgements in the decision. To concentrate upon the supposed futility of the *treatment* concealed inherent 'quality of life' judgements including the impact of that continuing treatment. Differences in approach here partly stem however from whether one adopts a 'duty-based' or 'rights-led' approach, that is is the nature of the doctor's duty dictated by the patient's rights or instead by the perceived value of the treatment? The House of Lords apparently favoured the latter approach but, in the Court of Appeal, Lord Justice Hoffmann in particular developed a patient's rights-based approach and spoke of the patient's right of 'dying with dignity'.

The House seemingly based its decision upon the perception that he

93 [1993] 1 All ER 821 at 877.

94 Ibid., at 869.

95 Ibid., at 869G. See also the comments of Lord Mustill at 894G. Gillon comments that 'this conclusion does not entail that LPT [life-prolonging treatment] would be against the person's interests – merely that it would not be in that person's best interests': see Gillon, 'Persistent Vegetative State', at 75.

96 Lord Mustill also asserted that 'although the termination of his life is not in the best interests of Anthony Bland, his best interests in being kept alive have also disappeared': [1993] 1 All ER 821 at 894J.

possessed no remaining interests whatever, and so could obtain no conceivable benefit from any medical treatment. Lord Keith stated that

> In the case of a permanently insensate being, who if continuing to live would never experience the slightest actual discomfort, it is difficult, if not impossible, to make any relevant comparison between continued existence and the absence of it. It is, however, perhaps permissible to say that to an individual with no cognitive capacity whatever and no prospect of ever recovering any such capacity in this world, it must be a matter of complete indifference whether he lives or dies.[97]

Lord Mustill stated that 'the distressing truth which must not be shirked is that the proposed conduct is not in the best interests of Anthony Bland, for he has no best interests of any kind'.[98] However, to say that this patient had *no* interests requires one immediately to *discount* certain potential interests, including (and many would say not least!) an interest in continuing to live *per se*. After *Bland*, *Cruzan*,[99] *Auckland Health Board*[100] and *Dieu*,[101] amongst other cases, it would seem that it is indeed no longer possible to assert that continued existence is in itself a benefit however.

There's no substitute for experience

The legal requirement that procedures which would otherwise constitute a battery must, in the absence of consent, be in the person's best interests implies that an individual is 'harmed' by procedures constituting a battery. On this view there is a dissonance between legal and (most) ethical evaluations of such procedures. However, the House's reliance upon Tony Bland's lack of interests suggests that he could *not* in fact be harmed by continued treatment (that is there would be no infringement of the duty of non-maleficence), even though a battery would be committed. Lord Keith's references to his inability to experience discomfort and his supposed indifference as to whether he lived or died are indicative of such a view. This is from whence the notion of 'symbolic harm' emanates, that is no 'real' harm to interests,[102] a concept which, as

[97] Ibid., at 861. [98] Ibid., at 894E–F.

[99] *Cruzan* v. *Director, Missouri Health Department* 111 L. Ed 2d 224 (1990).

[100] *Auckland Health Board* v. *Attorney-General* [1993] 1 New Zealand Law Reports 235.

[101] *Nancy B* v. *Hotel-Dieu de Québec* (1992) 86 DLR (4th) 385 (Que. Sup. Ct).

[102] See D. Price, 'Contemporary Transplantation Initiatives: Where's the Harm in Them?' (1996) 24(2) *Journal of Law, Medicine and Ethics* 139.

we have seen, has been applied to EV procedures as well as to organ removals from non-heart-beating donors and anencephalics. As regards the latter for instance, Caplan states: 'It is difficult to see how children born with anencephaly could be harmed or injured in any way by allowing them to serve as organ donors.'[103] Certainly, although a battery might be committed by procedures designed only to preserve organ viability, the individual cannot *experience* or achieve any state of awareness of them. This is what persuades many to argue that such a person is consequently not really 'harmed' thereby, that is any 'battery' is simply a 'technical' one, the product of an overly narrow and legalistic analysis. The BMA partially endorsed EV ethically on the basis that the procedures are 'not clinically deleterious',[104] and the King's Fund Report did so on the ground that 'Even though the patient is placed on a ventilator when this is not for their own benefit, the procedure does not cause distress.'[105]

The suggestion here appears to be that the ethical duty owed is simply one of non-maleficence, and that maleficence is concerned wholly with associated *physical* and *psychological* phenomena.[106] But it is nonetheless arguable that actual ethical harm may result from such procedures in the sense that rights owed to the individual have been infringed. Klepper and Truog have observed the distinction drawn between 'hurt' and 'harm'.[107] They note that a person cannot be hurt by what he is unaware of, but his interests may nevertheless be harmed thereby, and vice versa where he

103 A. Caplan, 'Ethical Issues in the Use of Anencephalic Infants as a Source of Organs and Tissues for Transplantation' (1988) 20 (Supp. 5) *Transplantation Proceedings* 42 at 47. Fost similarly remarks that 'Removal of organs would not seem to violate any interests of the anencephalic infant, whose imminent death is certain and who presumably is incapable of experiencing pain or discomfort': see Fost, 'Organs from Anencephalic Infants', at 5. Caplan draws parallels with a heart-beating patient maintained on ventilator support and asks why, in view of the lack of self-awareness and consciousness and the inability to experience pain, discomfort or disfigurement, one should have to wait for brain death before permitting organ retrieval: 'Ethical Issues in the Use of Anencephalic Infants', at 47.

104 As we saw earlier, the BMA also viewed EV procedures as causing only symbolic harm: see BMA, *Medical Ethics Today*, at 28.

105 King's Fund, *A Question of Give and Take*, at 65.

106 BMA, *Medical Ethics Today*, at 28. The BMA also stated that 'In other cases the risk of symbolic harm to some apparently may be outweighed by some very desirable benefits for others. An example may be seen . . . of the ventilation of moribund patients for organ donation. We recognise the risk of appearing to undervalue, and thus symbolically harm the status of dying patients, but believe that the important and tangible benefits to others may justify the action': ibid., at 323.

107 H. Klepper and R. Truog, 'Treating the Patient to Benefit Others' (1997) 6 *Cambridge Quarterly of Healthcare Ethics* 306. Feinberg talks in terms of a person's interests being 'set back': see J. Feinberg, *Social Philosophy*, Prentice Hall, Englewood Cliffs, N.J., 1973, at 26–8.

possesses such awareness.[108] Indeed, Lord Justice Hoffmann in *Bland* stated:

> I think that the fallacy in this argument is that it assumes that we have no interests except in those things of which we have conscious experience. But this does not accord with most people's intuitive feelings about their lives and deaths. At least a part of the reason why we honour the wishes of the dead about the distribution of their property is that we think it would wrong them not to do so, despite the fact that we believe that they will never know that their will has been ignored. Most people would like an honourable and dignified death and we think it wrong to dishonour their deaths, even when they are unconscious that this is happening . . . Once again I am not concerned to analyse the rationality of these feelings. It is enough that they are deeply rooted in our ways of thinking and that the law cannot possibly ignore them . . . It is demeaning to the human spirit to say that, being unconscious, he [Tony Bland] can have no interest in his personal privacy and dignity, in how he lives or dies.[109]

This supports the idea of undignified treatment of the insentient, moribund individual which we will probe more deeply below.

Surviving interests

Certain interests may therefore survive loss of consciousness. Fenwick contends that 'These "subsisting interests" include religious beliefs, former opinions as to his present situation, feelings towards his family, and perhaps even beneficence towards others (for example, strong personal belief in organ donation).'[110] Steinbock asserts that

> it should not be assumed that keeping someone alive in a persistent vegetative state does not harm his (antevegetative) interests. Most people do not regard the prospect of living in a vegetative state with equanimity. The idea of existing as a permanently unconscious body fills many people with distress and horror . . . We have as much reason to respect this sort of surviving interest as any other.[111]

108 Klepper and Truog, 'Treating the Patient to Benefit Others', at 307.

109 [1993] 1 All ER 821 at 853.

110 A. Fenwick, 'Applying Best Interests to Persistent Vegetative State – A Principled Distortion' (1998) 24 *Journal of Medical Ethics* 86 at 91.

111 B. Steinbock, *Life Before Birth: The Moral and Legal Status of Embryos and Fetuses*, Oxford University Press, New York, 1992, at 30.

Similar remarks emanated from the dissenting judgments of the United States Supreme Court in *Cruzan*. Lord Justice Hoffmann's remarks in *Bland* convey his view that both autonomy and dignity interests survive loss of consciousness.[112] The symbiosis between dignity and autonomy and loss of control in dying has been commented upon by Madan:

> those who still see some virtue in these ideas [dignity and freedom] will find it remarkable how across many cultures (and not only in Christian, Hindu and Jain cultural traditions) loss of autonomy, and loss of control over oneself in the context of death, are seen to result in undignified death, that is death which lacks nobility, distinction and illustriousness.[113]

The right to respectful and dignified treatment implies a right to control one's personal integrity and the 'uses' to which one's body may be put.[114] In *Bland*,[115] Lord Justice Butler-Sloss said that Tony Bland

> has the right to avoid unnecessary humiliation and degrading invasion of his body for no good purpose . . . I cannot believe that a patient in the situation of Mr Bland should be subjected to therapeutically useless treatment contrary to good medical practice and medical ethics which would not be inflicted upon those able to choose. It is an affront to the right to be respected.[116]

Certain dignitary interests therefore survive loss of consciousness and capacity. Even the judges in the House of Lords at times alluded to such interests, and suggested that continuing to be sustained and to live in such a state threatened these very dignitary interests. Lord Goff referred to the treatment being in medical terms 'useless' and 'futile', but he added that, furthermore, it was burdensome to Tony Bland by reason of the

[112] Indeed, the High Court of New Zealand in *Auckland Health Board* v. *Attorney-General* [1993] 1 New Zealand Law Reports 235 at 245 stated that the values of human dignity and personal privacy belong to everyone, whether living or dying, and are central to our concept of life.

[113] T. Madan, 'Dying With Dignity' (1992) 35(4) *Social Science and Medicine* 425 at 431.

[114] Where such interests are later infringed they constitute a revised reflection of the interests possessed by such an individual at an earlier time. Norman Cantor has stated that 'It is useful for every citizen to know that, in the event he or she is incompetent during the dying process, human dignity will be respected': see N. Cantor, 'Conroy, Best Interests, and the Handling of Dying Patients' (1985) 37 *Rutgers Law Review* 543 at 570.

[115] In *Frenchay NHS Trust* v. *S* [1994] 2 All ER 403, the Court of Appeal also alluded to the importance of dignity, and the indignity attached to being maintained in a living death.

[116] [1993] 1 All ER 821 at 848C (CA).

'invasiveness of the treatment and of [its] indignity'.[117] Finnis argues that Tony Bland did retain interests and could be harmed, and Keown graphically asks the rhetorical question 'Would it not have been contrary to his interests to use him as, for example, a sideboard?'[118]

Thus, the concept of dignity and respect has independent and discrete content. The Nuffield Council on Bioethics Report on Human Tissue observed that across all societies *degrading* treatment of the human body is a serious form of ethical injury.[119] In the Court of Appeal in *Bland*, Lord Justice Hoffmann said: 'Another principle (in addition to self-determination) closely connected, is respect for the dignity of the individual human being: our belief that quite irrespective of what the person concerned may think about it, it is wrong for someone to be humiliated or treated without respect for his value as a person.'[120] This perception of dignity as a free-standing interest *of the individual* is especially relevant to those patients who have not previously formulated desires or wishes, especially individuals who lack consciousness. But we must ask how we can impute interests to individuals who have never exercised the prescience to imagine themselves in such a condition or who lack the ability so to do. Can they have an interest in dignified treatment nonetheless? Although it is difficult to assign content to this interest in the absence of any pre-formed wishes, this is not a reason to deny its existence. If one can really only have interests when it matters what is done to one, what of individuals who, due to learning difficulties, are unable to conceptualise 'indignities to themselves'? Dignity is surely an interest *inhering* in all living human beings, not merely the formerly competent. Klepper and Truog note that it is a pervasive interest in all cultures and consider that there may be grounds for *imputing* interests to individuals in specific instances, either where the overwhelming majority of persons subscribe to such a position or view, or where there are grounds for believing that any reasonable person would hold such an interest, absent evidence to the contrary.[121] Nonetheless, what constitutes

[117] Ibid., at 870F.

[118] J. Finnis, '*Bland*: Crossing the Rubicon?' (1993) 109 *Law Quarterly Review* 329 at 336; J. Keown, 'Restoring Moral and Intellectual Shape to the Law After *Bland*' (1997) 113 *Law Quarterly Review* 481 at 494.

[119] Nuffield Council, *Human Tissue*, at paras. 6.7–6.9. It viewed all bodily damage, destruction or degradation not having a therapeutic intention as constituting an 'injury'.

[120] Hoffmann LJ, [1993] 1 All ER 821 at 851.

[121] Indeed, this is seemingly the proper philosophical basis of the necessity defence in law.

lack of respect will vary between cultures. Further, dignity is an evolving concept,[122] highlighted in the statement in the King's Fund Report:

> But we should remind ourselves that acceptable modes of dying whilst attached to various forms of machinery would no doubt have seemed undignified to some. As the rationales for new practices are understood, new contexts for dying become acceptable. It may not be long before actively managing death to save other lives is as 'good' and dignified a form of dying as any other.[123]

Reification

If a mental life *is* a necessary, as well as sufficient, condition for the possession of interests then prohibitions based on undignified treatment would have to be based on moralistic presuppositions rather than on libertarian concerns attaching to the 'harm' principle. But intuitively we do view such individuals, and not just society generally, as having been 'harmed' by undignified treatment. Infringement of dignity wrongs as well as harms such individuals in addition to whatever injurious *symbolic ramifications there are for society in general.* One would imagine that at the very least, in the absence of consent, insentient beings should not be treated wholly as a means to the needs of others, *à la* Kant. To 'reify' an individual by treating a still-living being as an object or resource for organ recycling is not mere symbolism. The notion of symbolic harm simply relates to the fact that we hold generalised notions of how people should be treated in different contexts even though the individual himself may be unaware of this harm.

To be or not to be?

Certain philosophers, however, contend that beings lacking awareness and conscious experience are not 'persons' in the moral world, that is they are

[122] Rights of dignity have been attached to the 'manner of dying' even in competent patients in recent times. Such rights have been asserted in the context of decisions concerning the legality of physician-assisted death in the US in particular. It has been said that the interest in one's dignity extends beyond the physical integrity of the body itself to the values an individual holds, and that this dictates *inter alia* that individuals should have a right to control their excised body parts: see S. Perley, 'From Control over One's Body to Control over One's Body Parts: Extending the Doctrine of Informed Consent' (1992) 67 *New York University Law Review* 335 at 349.

[123] King's Fund, *A Question of Give and Take*, at 65.

not individuals towards whom one can owe moral obligations, because of their inability to value and experience their lives. As a consequence, duties to respect autonomy and to avoid non-maleficent actions towards them no longer apply. The interests of others therefore 'trump' any significance attaching to continued existence, albeit in a living being. Harris argues with reference to living 'non-persons' that 'where its organs or tissues can be used to save the lives of other people who have not lost personhood but who may be in danger of losing their personhood through death or some other cause, then we have a motive for keeping alive the body of the former person so that the tissues and organs remain alive and usable'.[124] Such allegedly 'non-persons' would include individuals in a permanently comatose or vegetative state or those suffering other devastating neurological impairment (for example very many of those subject to EV and NHBD protocols). On such a view, brain-dead individuals are merely part of a broader class of beings possessing no interests. Such perspectives often underpin proposals for the law to treat anencephalics as *sui generis* for organ removal purposes and as a class for whom special rules and laws should apply.[125] As regards the latter, Harris asserts that 'The use of their organs seems to me to be entirely analogous to the use of "cadaver" organs, that is organs from bodies kept alive on life support machinery although they have permanently lost all that makes life worth having, all that makes them a person.'[126] However, Keown properly notes that 'The law does not deny personhood, and the rights it attracts, because the person has lost the ability to think', even if it is true to say that what constitutes the necessary legal 'respect' varies from one context to another.[127] The initial AMA Report opined that it is not clear that respect

124 J. Harris, *The Value of Life*, Routledge, London, 1985, at 242.

125 Ethical and Social Impact Committee Transplant Policy Center, 'Anencephalic Infants as Sources of Transplantable Organs' (1988) 18 *Hastings Center Report* 28. Caplan has also suggested that organs (including vital organs) should be able to be removed from individuals who are either dead or anencephalic, that is they should become a special class of eligible donor where their parents consent thereto: see Caplan, 'Ethical Issues in the Use of Anencephalic Infants', at 49.

126 Harris, *The Value of Life*, at 104. Serafini asserts that 'because anencephalics are not persons, there are no reasons – based on questions of personhood – why anencephalics cannot be killed, and, it is hoped, be used as sources of organs': see A. Serafini, 'Is Coma Morally Equivalent to Anencephalia?' (1993) 3(2) *Ethics and Behavior* 187 at 196.

127 Keown, 'Restoring Moral and Intellectual Shape', at 493. See John Porter, 'Reason, Law and Medicine: Anencephalics as Organ Donors' in McLean, *Contemporary Issues in Law, Medicine and Ethics*, 163 at 177–8. He states that Tony Bland was entitled to full legal protection despite his condition.

for the essential worth of an anencephalic requires the preservation of his/her life, because the anencephalic has no interest in remaining alive, and asserted that 'society should show its respect for the anencephalic neonate by treating the neonate as it does persons whose organs are removed for transplantation after their death. In short, permitting parental donation of organs from anencephalic neonates is consistent with the social value of respect for life.'[128] In other words this tack creates an easy utilitarian equation.[129] Thomasma argues that respect for the lives of anencephalics 'takes the form of utilitarian concern, of benefiting others through transplant of tissues and organs'.[130]

Notions of 'personhood' are themselves contingent though upon perspectives of the centrality of the body to the 'self'. The Law Reform Commission of Canada observed that[131]

> Paralleling the ethical debate over harms to the dead, proponents and detractors of the special-category or non-person approach to anencephalic newborn organ procurement seem to differ fundamentally in their views on the relation between the body and self. Proponents tend to reduce persons to their sentient or cognitive capacities, by equating persons with their rational selves. The body tends to become morally irrelevant. Those reluctant about taking organs from anencephalic infants seem more inclined to view persons as embodied selves, wherein moral respect is owed to the body as well as to its sentient, rational attributes. A conception of persons as embodied selves may not be amenable to rational justifications, because the respect it accords the body likely derives from fundamental sentiments that transcend rational argument.

These perceptions are generalisable and not just applicable to anencephalics. The notion of our 'selves' as embodied is deeply felt and not able to be dismissed on the ground of mere sentiment.[132]

128 On this view there would be no breach of the dead donor rule either: see AMA, 'The Use of Anencephalic Neonates', at 1616.

129 See also J. Arras and S. Shinnar, 'Anencephalic Newborns as Organ Donors: A Critique' (1988) 259 *Journal of the American Medical Association* 2284 at 2284. They state that 'Admirable goals should not be advanced by improper means': at 2285.

130 D. Thomasma, 'Anencephalics as Organ Donors' (1989) *Biomedical Ethical Reviews* 25 at 43.

131 Law Reform Commission of Canada, *Procurement and Transfer of Human Tissues and Organs*, Working Paper 66, Minister of Supply and Services, Ottawa, 1992, at 105.

132 Meilander, a Protestant theologian, opposes the use of such procedures upon anencephalics, and states: 'We can know human beings whatever their cognitive capacities, only in their bodies': see G. Meilander, 'Commentary' upon 'The Anencephalic Newborn as Organ Donor' in (1986) 16 *Hastings Center Report* 22 at 22.

The above personhood arguments can be challenged on both deontological and utilitarian grounds. Kant argued that all human beings have intrinsic and not merely instrumental worth. Such procedures would consequently transgress the second form of Kant's categorical imperative, 'Act so that you treat humanity, whether in your own person or in that of another, always as an end and never as a means only.'[133] Some allege that Kant did not intend this notion to apply to individuals incapable of autonomy. As Sytsma states, 'Some argue that the Kantian dictum does not apply to anencephalics because only beings who have "ends" in the sense of "goals" are beings who must be treated as "ends", that is, beings worthy of respect.'[134] She argues though that this view conflates 'having ends' with 'being an end' and asserts that Kant intended to include non-sentient beings in the category of human beings having intrinsic worth. But *should* the prescription apply to insentient beings? Caplan argues that 'The prohibition against using human beings solely as a means to advance the interests or desires of others is based on a conception of humanness that is connected to a desire to respect the capacity for autonomy and choice rather than mere humanness.'[135] But it has been argued above that dignitary interests are in fact much more pervasive. Utilitarian assessments necessitate consideration of harms and their effects, and thus in themselves incorporate deontological evaluations. Moreover, one cannot ignore slippery slope concerns here.

Absolutely unique?

The initial AMA Report stated that 'Anencephalic neonates are unique among persons because they have no history of consciousness and no possibility of ever being conscious.'[136] However, 'anencephaly' is not an entirely discrete and separate diagnostic category.[137] If a different

[133] I. Kant, *Fundamental Principles of the Metaphysics of Morals* (trans. T. Abbott), Bobbs Merrill Co. Inc., Indianapolis, 1946, at 46.

[134] See S. Sytsma, 'Anencephalics as Organ Sources' (1996) 17 *Theoretical Medicine* 19 at 21. James Walters falls into this category for instance. He asserts that Kant's thesis was only intended to apply to 'rational' beings.

[135] Caplan, 'Ethical Issues in the Use of Anencephalic Infants', at 48.

[136] AMA, 'The Use of Anencephalic Neonates', at 1616.

[137] Shewmon notes that anencephaly is classically divided into two forms: holo-anencephaly (complete absence of forebrain and cranium) and mero-anencephaly (where forebrain and cranium exist in rudimentary form), moreover that there are other closely related conditions such as hydroencephaly, microencephaly and amniotic band syndrome: see D. Shewmon, 'Anencephaly: Selected Medical Aspects' (1988) 18 *Hastings Center Report* 11.

approach were to be adopted towards such a class of beings, one would have to wonder what other individuals would fail or cease to be members of the moral community, and one could anticipate the very worst form of slippery slope.

One or two commentators have however sought to draw a distinction between those permanently insensient beings that once possessed awareness and autonomy and those that are doomed never to be able to acquire these. Thomasma for instance rejects the idea that formerly sentient beings may lose personhood, because they have a 'value history', but contends that anencephalics without any potentiality for autonomy should be viewed in a different light and, whilst deserving of 'respect', this involves no more than that such beings be used to benefit others, the decision lying in the hands of the parents. The initial AMA Report also commented that 'While patients who are in a persistent vegetative state no longer are conscious, they once were conscious and have therefore previously established an identity and a set of interests', that is they are 'former persons', and that 'Because they have never experienced consciousness and will never experience consciousness, anencephalic neonates cannot have interests of any kind.'[138] Sytsma on the other hand maintains that our obligations to neonates and children may not be based wholly upon their potentiality for autonomy. Duties of respect and dignified treatment are owed even to anencephalics and require support for the stance of the European Parliament which has called for a code of practice banning the removal of organs from live anencephalics.[139]

It cannot be said that any particular procedure applied to an insentient person either is or is not an affront to dignity by virtue of the procedure itself. It is instead a function of the purpose and effect of such a procedure. Most medical procedures are intended to be therapeutically beneficial to the subject of them, and it is this that justifies them, even if it is a 'totally artificial and technologically supported existence'.

[138] AMA, 'The Use of Anencephalic Neonates', at 1616.

[139] Resolution on Prohibiting Trade in Transplant Organs, adopted by the European Parliament on 14 September 1993, at para. Q.5(e). Not to provide minimum comfort care might also infringe disability legislation in the United States: see L. Hanger, 'The Legal, Ethical, and Medical Objections to Procuring Organs from Anencephalic Infants' (1995) 5 *Health Matrix* 347 at 361.

Prolonging dying

Whilst acts hastening death are typically illegitimate whether performed in the interests of that individual or entirely for the benefit of others, what is the relevance of procedures intended solely for the benefit of others which have the effect of *prolonging life*?

Some commentators[140] would argue, generally from a theological standpoint, that deliberately *prolonging the dying process* is itself a moral wrong,[141] but there are substantial difficulties in determining when a person is *dying* (how imminent must death be?).[142] On a secular level, on the other hand, the King's Fund Report stated: 'Even if the moment of brain stem death can be shown to have been postponed for a short period in the electively ventilated patient, this does not automatically indicate that the patient's interests have been abused.'[143] Klepper and Truog note that whilst there is a general interest in a dignified death, there is no consensus as regards whether such death should be 'speedy' or not, and that it is very controversial because some regard the prolongation of any life to be an intrinsic good.[144] However, there must be some adequate justification offered for extending life through the continued application of medical procedures. A competent patient's right to self-determination has been elevated above the sanctity of life in terms of priority with regard to decisions about life-prolonging treatment.[145] With regard to patients who lack capacity to make such decisions, Lord Goff in *Bland* stated: 'But for my part I cannot see that medical treatment is appropriate or requisite simply to prolong a patient's life when such treatment has no therapeutic purpose of any kind, as where it is futile because the patient is unconscious and there is no prospect of any improvement in his condition.'[146] Some autonomy- or beneficence-based justification would appear to be neces-

140 For example G. Park *et al.*, 'Organ Donation' (letter) (1993) 306 *British Medical Journal* 145, in a response to reports of EV practices. This view is usually founded upon the theistic notion that God is calling his servant home and should not be prevented from so doing.

141 P. Ramsey, *The Patient as a Person*, Yale University Press, New Haven, 1970, at 210.

142 See, for example, H. Kuhse and P. Singer, 'Prolonging Dying is the Same as Prolonging Living – One More Response to Long' (1991) 17 *Journal of Medical Ethics* 205. Is a person with end-stage renal disease on dialysis having his life or his death prolonged?

143 King's Fund, *A Question of Give and Take*, at 65.

144 Klepper and Truog, 'Treating the Patient to Benefit Others', at 309.

145 See, for example, *Secretary of State for the Home Department* v. *Robb* [1995] 1 All ER 677. Lord Goff expressed similar views in *Bland*.

146 [1993] 1 All ER 821 at 870.

sary. The law fails to embrace naked utilitarian ideals in the absence of either an expression of consent (autonomy) or potential benefit to the individual (beneficence). Artificial ventilation is therefore morally neutral as a procedure whether it prolongs life or otherwise. It is the intended use which matters and the existence, or otherwise, of consent to its use.

De minimis?

Despite the general analysis above, some commentators have suggested that some procedures ancillary to transplantation and performed prior to death may nevertheless be lawful as well as ethically acceptable because they do not infringe the incapacitated person's right to respect or dignity since they are *de minimis*. Lynn, for instance, asserts: 'The clearly living patient who will become a donor must not be harmed, wronged or killed. However, the placement of aortic lines in an insentient patient or a consenting patient near death, for example, would probably be acceptable. The risks are so small and the patient or family consents.'[147] But it is the legitimacy of the purpose and the general consent here that matters, not the extent of the infringement. The argument that many such individuals are extremely near to death is also sometimes invoked to justify procedures done wholly in the interests of others. However, not only is that an insufficient reason to withhold the normal moral and legal entitlements of such individuals but it is fraught with empirical and prognostic difficulties. Whilst most anencephalics die within seventy-two hours of birth, one child lived for two and a half years, and one 43-year-old woman in a coma lived for thirty-seven years![148]

Chinese walls

The notion that conflicts of interest should be removed, as far as possible, from decisions having a bearing on transplantation is established and

[147] Lynn, 'Are the Patients?', at 176.

[148] Rothenberg records a wide disparity in recorded duration of survival of anencephalics: see L. Rothenberg, 'The Anencephalic Neonate and Brain Death: An International Review of Medical, Ethical and Legal Issues' (1990) 22 *Transplantation Proceedings* 1037 at 1037. A Californian study conducted between 1978 and 1982 found that nearly 8 per cent of higher birth weight anencephalic babies survived for between one week and one month and 1 per cent survived for approximately three months: ibid. See also B. McGillivray, 'Anencephaly – The Potential for Survival' (1988) 20 (Supp. 5) *Transplantation Proceedings* 9.

accepted. Most nations have laws requiring that the clinicians certifying the death of a potential donor should be separate from the transplant team in order to ensure that the individual's (the potential donor's) interests are properly protected. In some instances this is to protect the integrity of decision-making by the 'patient' and in others that of the clinician. There are guidelines or laws relating to foetal tissue transplantation (for example in Britain the Code of Practice drawn up by the Polkinghorne Committee Report) in many jurisdictions insisting that decisions by a woman relating to abortion be kept entirely separate from decisions relating to subsequent use of tissue, for instance for transplantation.[149] For some it may also be necessary to separate the *practice* of abortion from that of transplantation.[150] Polkinghorne recommended that an intermediary organisation should exist separating contact between the personnel involved in the different processes, for example the Medical Research Council foetal tissue bank.[151] This would avoid what was once described as the 'sinister relationship' potentially existing between, for example, the neurosurgeon transplanting foetal neural tissue into patients with Parkinson's and those performing the abortion.

In some of the scenarios considered earlier the patients would be competent individuals able to make their own decisions and would be the primary decision-makers. Some of the protocols discussed above, however, concern individuals patently and gravely lacking such capacity, for example anencephalics, PVS and other neurologically impaired patients. As the decisions in such cases about patient care are made principally by physicians (albeit in conjunction with the family), or by the family itself, the reality and perception of influence are heightened. Decisions not to prolong, or actively to end, a life similarly ought not to be influenced by organ donation in such instances. Under the University of Pittsburgh protocol, the decision to terminate life support is seemingly a joint one between medical staff and the patient and/or family. However, the difficulties of separation are clearly apparent and indeed this is a dilemma in relation to controlled NHBD protocols across the board. The

149 *Review of the Guidance on the Research Use of Fetuses and Fetal Materials (Polkinghorne Report)*, Cmd 762, HMSO, 1989. See also Council on Scientific Affairs and Council on Ethical and Judicial Affairs, 'Medical Applications of Fetal Tissue Transplantation' (1990) 263 *Journal of the American Medical Association* 565 at 568.

150 See generally J. Robertson, 'Abortion to Obtain Fetal Tissue for Transplant' (1993) 27 *Suffolk University Law Review* 1359 at 1361.

151 Institute of Medicine, *Non-Heart-Beating Organ Transplantation*, at paras. 5.1–5.10.

IOM Report related that its survey of US NHBD protocols showed that the policy of drawing a strict line between patient and donor was present in every case and that most OPOs are contacted only after the decision to withdraw support has been made and before the option of donation is presented and discussed with families. It noted, however, that 'the protocol for implementing and safeguarding this policy varies greatly among OPOs'.[152] The Report states that not only should the different decisions be kept separate, but safeguards should include 'scrupulous separation of patient care personnel from procurement and transplant personnel'.[153] Proponents of the proposals relating to PVS patients also assert the need for a division between the medical team that is involved in the decision to abbreviate life and the personnel concerned with the transplantation of the dead person's organs. Martyn *et al.*, however, argue that 'moving the wall' separating patient care teams and transplant teams is not enough here.[154] It would certainly be probable, if not inevitable, that the medical caring team, especially if situated in the same medical facility as the transplant unit, would indeed be influenced by the potential benefits to be achieved in terms of prestige, research support, patient care reimbursement and staff recruitment through a thriving transplantation programme. Of course, if an independent decision to allow such a person to die were made, for instance by a judicial body, then even if active means of producing death were permissible there would presumably be no objection to the transplantation of that individual's organs post mortem, provided there was also a valid request or consent for organ removal in the case. In such instances the patient's life would not have been terminated *for* organ procurement, and so the dead donor rule would not have been transgressed. But this would be a rigid and cumbersome process which would be difficult to employ across the board. The IOM Report considered that no matter what safeguards were employed it would be impossible to eradicate such 'institutional bias' or conflicts generally, but it did not consider that this cast doubt on the

[152] The Report states that 'Four OPOs begin evaluating and testing the donor for suitability (including clinical evaluation, medical history review, and laboratory tests) before the decision to withdraw life support has been made, and about half of the OPOs begin clinical evaluation before obtaining consent for donation. A few protocols describe discussion among attending physicians and transplant surgeons before the decision to withdraw life support, and a large majority before decisions to donate': ibid., at 36.

[153] Ibid., at 55.

[154] Martyn *et al.*, 'Required Request', at 28.

legitimacy of such protocols. Nevertheless, *perceptions* that transplantation factors were influencing decisions to terminate or help terminate a person's life prematurely could be as damaging as the reality. However, if the protocols themselves were transparent and ethically and legally sound, the damage from such 'perceptions' would simply have to be weighed against the potential overall net impact of the protocol in terms of procurement.[155] There is no crucial ethical dimension there though.

There is no means of preventing a competent person committing suicide unassisted in order to become an organ donor, even if that were desirable, although he/she would of course have no command over the ultimate use or otherwise of his/her organs after death. However, where the suicide has been assisted by physicians one needs to be more cautious in view of the potential influence of the physician upon the individual's decision to die, especially where the individual's request to have their organs removed was made in the very end stages of their life. There is proper concern here for a *separation* to exist between the decision to die and the decision to donate organs, which should be respected even if physician-assisted suicide were to be legal in any particular jurisdiction.[156] However, where the decision to donate organs, and the decision to request assistance to die are unconnected, the use of such organs would be acceptable.[157] In 1998 Dr Jack Kevorkian offered for transplantation purposes the organs of a quadriplegic man whom he had assisted to commit suicide, the dead man allegedly having donated his organs prior to death.[158] The difficulty here stems partially from the possible lack of separation of *personnel* in that a prime mover might easily be manipulating the situation to the ends of transplantation. This is of course ironically *more* likely in an unregulated environment, where negative perceptions are inescapable.

Concluding remarks

There is an undeniable tension under many transplant protocols between the patient's rights to autonomy and dignity and the interests of the

[155] This is Robertson's assertion: see 'Policy Issues', at 247.
[156] Currently it is only legal in certain jurisdictions, for example Oregon.
[157] See further Report, 'Living Organ Donor Act', at 592.
[158] See (1997) 315 *British Medical Journal* 1116, and 'Suicide's Kidney Offered', *The Times*, 9 June 1998.

transplantation enterprise.[159] Without much greater general awareness of various procedures it must be for the still living to specifically authorise procedures compromising physical integrity where the procedures implicated have no potential benefit for them. However, where an individual has requested that his/her organs be used for transplantation after death, it seems correct to infer that permission is granted for procedures which form part of the routine preliminaries to transplantation without seriously compromising the patient in any way, for example tissue typing procedures carried out on blood taken from the patient, in the laboratory.

Where relatives' rather than the specific patient's consent is relied upon to justify such (non-therapeutic) procedures, unless weight can legitimately be placed on the doctrine of substituted judgement there is room for concern. The personal rights of relatives are generally reserved for intrusions upon the individual *after* death only and even then only in certain jurisdictions. Substituted judgement *would* appear to be an appropriate basis for decision-making though, where the patient has already requested to donate organs, but only where there is 'clear and convincing evidence' of the wishes of that individual and where there are no substantial deleterious sequelae attaching to them. The US Institute of Medicine recently concluded that decisions as to the use of drugs such as heparin and phentolamine, and pre-mortem cannulation (with family consent), in still-living patients should be made on a 'case-by-case' basis.[160] A substituted judgement basis for such a decision might be appropriate there for instance. But even then, many would see such a profound decision as necessitating an explicit consent from the individual. Such procedures should not be employed except in relation to competent or 'formerly competent' individuals.

It is suggested that practical changes to everyday procedures could solve many of the dilemmas in this sphere. Donor cards or registry applications might be amended to include a provision which might be deleted by an unwilling individual, or alternatively a separate but related 'donor' card authorising EV in a particular case could be created.[161] Either way, the potential subject of the procedure would need to be given full

[159] Arras and Shinnar, 'Anencephalic Newborns as Organ Donors', at 2284.

[160] Of course, if the family gave consent on the basis of a substituted judgement standard this would satisfy legal requirements.

[161] The latter strategy is favoured by Jean McHale: see McHale, 'Elective Ventilation', at 25. In Great Britain a new central computerised registry was set up in 1995 which might feasibly also record individuals' wishes regarding EV.

information about the procedure and its risks, including the possibility of a PVS being induced thereby. Greater public awareness is required all round. It may even be preferable for certain acceptable protocols to be expressly supported by legislation.[162] There is a danger that common law principles might have unexpected and broader applications and ramifications. At present only a handful of jurisdictions have laws explicitly providing for such procedures or which are sufficiently broadly drafted that they might be taken to extend to them. One exception of the latter kind is in Panama, where the 1983 Law permits, without more, 'any procedures and examinations deemed necessary for the appropriate use of the organ or anatomical part'.[163] If EV were to be deemed to be acceptable, there should be necessary safeguards, including a requirement for a medical assessment of a hopeless prognosis and imminent death, confirmed independently by a non-involved party. For procedures designed only to benefit others to be permissible in the absence of consent, societal and democratic approval in a general form is required. The English Law Commission recommended that 'the Secretary of State may make an order providing for the carrying out of a procedure in relation to a person without capacity to consent if the procedure, although not carried out for the benefit of that person, will not cause him or her significant harm and will be of significant benefit to others'.[164] This facilitatory measure would become operational should legislative support be forthcoming. It might be argued though that, in view of the importance of such a measure, primary rather than subordinate legislation would be more appropriate in that event.

Walters notes that we *do* sometimes permit procedures to be done to individuals lacking capacity in the interests only of others. He cites the examples of pregnant women in a coma kept artificially supported until a viable child can be delivered. One has to be rather cautious here though. The treatment of the pregnant woman can be supported on the ground that this *is* in the best interests of the individual because this would generally be the implicit wish of the pregnant woman herself and not just a flight of altruism.[165] However, one should be wary of over-generalisation

[162] As the King's Fund noted in its Report, *A Question of Give and Take*, at 64.

[163] Law No. 10 of 11 July 1983, section 11.

[164] See Draft Bill, Clause 10(4), Law Commission Report on *Mental Incapacity*.

[165] Dworkin's distinction between *critical* and *experiential* interests may be especially pertinent here.

about individuals' wishes, and this is an obvious situation where some mechanism for the operation of the substituted judgement principle is required.

The effect of many of the above submissions would be to preclude such measures and frustrate organ procurement efforts in some instances. This might be significant in terms of procurement volumes in some contexts, such as EV, but it is unlikely that populations of insentient donors, such as anencephalics and PVS patients would be so significant.

PART II

Living donor organ transplantation

Introduction to living donor organ transplantation

As we have seen, much of the pioneering clinical work in connection with transplantation, including the first successful solid organ (kidney) transplants, involved living donors.[1] Good results were achieved with many of these early grafts, largely due to the use of genetically related, generally (frequently minor, and even sometimes mentally incapacitated adult) sibling donors, with good tissue compatibility between donor and recipient.[2] In the first kidney transplant in 1954, the operation was so successful that the patient completely recovered and went on to marry one of the nurses who had cared for him.[3] Although the results of cadaveric transplantation considerably improved in the eighties, results of living donor transplantation (LDT) of kidneys are still consistently better than with cadaveric transplantation.[4] Cecka and Terasaki's analysis of the UNOS renal data from 1987 to 1995 showed that the one- and five-year graft survival figures for wholly incompatible (HLA antigen mismatched) living related and unrelated kidney donors were comparable to the figures for *identically* matched cadaveric transplants, and much superior to cases where the cadaver donors were mismatched to any degree.[5] Alfani *et al.* state that 'According to international evidence, long-term results of living

[1] Many forms of *tissue* donation also rely heavily or entirely upon living donors, for example bone marrow donation.

[2] This offset the fact that in the early days immunosuppression was fairly crude and often relatively ineffective.

[3] At this time, of course, end-stage renal failure was a fatal condition, prior to the advent of kidney dialysis developed by Wilhelm Kolff in the Netherlands.

[4] Centre as well as meta-studies continue to bear this out, for example 20 per cent higher graft survival at ten years: see N. Lefrancois and J. Touraine, 'Living Kidney Donation: Preoperative Evaluation and Preparation for Surgery' in G. Collins, J. Dubernard, W. Land and G. Persijn (eds.), *Procurement, Preservation and Allocation of Vascularized Organs*, Kluwer, Dordrecht, 1997, 3 at 3.

[5] J. Cecka and P. Terasaki, 'Living Donor Kidney Transplants: Superior Success Rates Despite Histoincompatibilities', (1997) 29 *Transplantation Proceedings* 203.

kidney transplantation, both related and unrelated, are better than those observed after cadaver transplantation except those with 0MM [zero mismatched], which can only infrequently be performed'.[6] In the sixties kidneys were not infrequently transplanted from genetically unrelated donors (so-called allogeneic transplants). The first transplant using a genetically unrelated donor took place in 1960 from a brother-in-law, performed by René Kuss. However, results were generally disappointing and such transplants typically fell into disfavour outside nations unable to accommodate the brain death concept. Graft survival results have improved significantly though and the use of unrelated kidney donors has recently increased substantially, most notably in the US (discussed in detail further on).

Living kidney donors play a major role in the transplant strategy of very many centres and nations around the world. However, their use is extremely variable between continents, nations and even centres within nations. They are more prevalent in North and South America and in Asia than in continental Europe.[7] In 1997 in Europe 1,196 living kidney donor transplants were performed as contrasted with 3,579 in the United States (2.7 transplants per million population (pmp) compared with 13.7 pmp).[8] At a European national level there is also considerable diversity. In 1995, Norway had an LDT rate of 15.7 pmp compared with 9.4 in Sweden, 5.8 in Switzerland, 2.1 in the UK and Eire, 1 in Germany, 0.4 in Finland and 0.2 in Portugal.[9] The King's Fund Institute estimated that between 1985 and 1992 there was a substantial increase across the board in LDTs

[6] D. Alfani *et al.*, 'Issues in Organ Donation: Living Unrelated Kidney Transplantation' (1998) 30 *Transplantation Proceedings* 2255 at 2256. In Norway, 25 per cent of cadaveric kidneys are zero mismatched: see A. Jakobsen, 'Living Donor Practices and Processes in Europe' in D. Price and J. Akveld (eds.), *Living Organ Donation in the Nineties: European Medico-Legal Perspectives*, EUROTOLD, 1996, 1 at 9. It is reported that the half life (that is the time from transplantation until only half of the number of such transplants will still function) of a cadaver kidney is eight years compared with twelve years for a half-matched and twenty-six years for a wholly matched kidney from a living donor: see M. Nicholson and A. Bradley, 'Renal Transplantation from Living Donors' (1999) 318 *British Medical Journal* 409.

[7] Within Asia the majority of transplants are still from living donors. Between 1993 and 1997, 32,645 kidney transplants were performed, 18,579 (56.9 per cent) of which were from living donors: see K. Ota, 'Asian Transplant Registry' (1999) 31 *Transplantation Proceedings* 205 at 206.

[8] ITCS World Transplant Statistics, 1997: http://www.kuleuven.ac.be/facdep/medicine/itcs/Home.html.

[9] See R. Allen, S. Lynch and R. Strong, 'The Living Organ Donor' in J. Chapman, M. Deierhoi and C. Wight, *Organ and Tissue Donation for Transplantation*, Arnold, London, 1997, 162 at 164.

performed,[10] and based on data from thirteen of the leading European transplanting nations, the EUROTOLD Project revealed an increase of 35.7 per cent by volume between 1990 and 1995.[11] Increases in LDTs frequently coincide with shortages in cadaveric donations and this rise is probably partly explained by the general reduction or plateauing out of overall cadaveric donor rates at the end of the eighties and into the nineties.[12]

The probable reasons why results are generally superior using living donors can be identified. Tissue compatibility is ordinarily closer and ischaemia time, during which damage occurs to the functioning organ, is minimised. Moreover the procedures can be synchronised to the best effect, for example carried out when the patient is in optimum condition and even pre-dialysis.[13] There is also a reduced need for immunosuppression, thereby minimising risks to the recipient from infections and malignancies.[14] Of course, the organs of living donors are generally in better condition than those from cadaveric donors.[15]

Living donation is also advantageous in various respects apart from clinical ones. Not only is transplantation the most cost-effective treatment for end-stage organ failure, living organ donation is the least expensive option of all even taking into account possible post-operative complica-

[10] Based on data from eighteen of the world's leading transplant nations, it recorded an annual increase in LDTs from 2,500 in 1985 to 3,200 in 1992, and a rise from 13 per cent to 15 per cent between 1988 and 1992 in the proportion of LDTs in total transplants performed annually: see King's Fund Institute, *A Question of Give and Take*, Research Report 18, King's Fund Institute, London, 1994, at 13.

[11] EUROTOLD Project Report to the European Commission of the European Communities (ed. P. Donnelly and D. Price), *Questioning Attitudes to Living Donor Transplantation*, EUROTOLD, 1997, at 18–23. In Germany, the Netherlands, Spain and Switzerland this represented an increase of more than 50 per cent, albeit in Germany and Spain from an initially very low base.

[12] Within the UK there was a 38 per cent increase in the volume of living donor kidney transplants between 1997 and 1998.

[13] Ischaemic damage is a particular problem for non-renal organs where preservation times are shorter. Recent data, however, suggests that shorter ischaemia time may not be as influential a factor in enhanced outcomes as was generally thought.

[14] This is especially important for living intestinal transplantation because the intestine is not a sterile organ and rejection episodes can often prove catastrophic.

[15] There are stricter selection criteria for living donors. For instance, living kidney donors generally have a normal glomerular filtration rate and are free from conditions that may compromise renal function. Moreover, they are not subject to the detrimental cardiovascular, metabolic and hormonal disturbances present in brain-dead donors: see J. Pratschke *et al.*, 'Brain Death and its Influence on Donor Organ Quality and Outcome after Transplantation' (1999) 67 *Transplantation* 343.

tions and additional hospitalisation for the donor, by virtue of the lesser need for immunosuppression and the reduced hospitalisation of the recipient consequent upon episodes of rejection.[16] Cadaveric transplantation is extremely resource and personnel intensive and requires a high level of organisation and co-ordination between hospitals and personnel. This can be extremely problematic even in the so-called 'developed' transplant nations (for example, there is an acute shortage of ICU beds in the UK), let alone in developing nations (even assuming that brain death has been accepted in culture and society). These realities mean that countries embarking on a (kidney) transplantation programme will typically commence with a substantial reliance upon living rather than cadaveric donors.

There are inevitably short-term risks of both mortality and morbidity attaching to all organ removal procedures. A survey of 19,368 kidney removal (nephrectomy) procedures performed in the US between 1980 and 1991 revealed five donor deaths (0.026 per cent or 1 in 3,874),[17] and a survey of all US UNOS centres (75 per cent response) revealed three deaths between 1987 and 1992 (0.03 per cent or 1 in 3,231).[18] There is now a substantial volume of data relating to the morbidity risks to the donor from nephrectomy, both short and long term. Lefrancois and Touraine, however, state that 'The short and long term risks to the donor are minimal in any evaluation.'[19] Initially though, there was much speculation and concern relating to the long-term risks to the donor from living with only a single kidney.[20] Studies over a long period have failed to reveal any increased risk of renal failure following nephrectomy though. Indeed, in some instances renal insufficiency was found to be lower than in the general population. A recent meta-study of nephrectomy in 3,124 patients and 1,703 controls by Kasiske *et al.* found that 'there is little long-

[16] This is by virtue of the reduced need for immunosuppression and hospital time for the recipient. See F. De Charro and A. De Wit, 'An Appraisal of Living Donor Kidney Transplantation' (1996) 28 *Transplantation Proceedings* 3559 at 3660.

[17] J. Najarian *et al.*, '20 Years or more of Follow Up of Living Kidney Donors' (1992) 340 *Lancet* 807. Most deaths resulted from pulmonary embolism.

[18] M. Bir, E. Ramos and G. Danovich, 'Evaluation of Living Renal Donors – A Current Practice of UNOS Transplant Centers' (1995) 60 *Transplantation* 322. Very many centres with extremely extensive experience of LDT report no donor deaths, for example from nearly 3,300 nephrectomies at the University of Oslo, and at the University of Minnesota.

[19] Lefrancois and Touraine, 'Living Kidney Donation', at 7.

[20] Studies in rats had shown that the compensatory hyperfiltration in the remaining kidney produced glomerulosclerosis after severe reduction in renal mass.

term risk associated with organ donation. Potential donors can be told that the chances of developing end-stage renal disease as a result of successful organ donation appear to be remote.'[21] Narkun-Burgess *et al.* reached the same conclusion after forty-five years, with regard to sixty-two American soldiers who lost a kidney during World War II (contrasted with 620 controls).[22] There are, however, significant short-term risks relating to the surgery. Major early complications[23] are typically reported to be of the order of 1–2 per cent.[24] Minor complications apparently arise in between 10 and 20 per cent of instances.[25] Much of the morbidity is related to the wound,[26] but modern methods have dramatically improved post-operative recovery and pain and there have been recent developments in surgical techniques, including laparoscopic harvesting techniques, which involve a shorter stay in hospital and a faster return to work.[27] There were also early studies reporting psychosocial complications, including post-donation depression.[28] However, the evidence is inconclusive, especially bearing in mind the substantial evidence that most donors show improved self-esteem and well-being post-donation, over both the short and the long term. A recent survey of 524 living kidney

[21] B. Kasiske *et al.*, 'Long-Term Effects of Reduced Renal Mass in Humans' (1995) 48 *Kidney International* 814.

[22] D. Narkun-Burgess, C. Nolan and J. Norman, 'Forty-Five Year Follow-Up after Uninephrectomy' (1993) 43 *Kidney International* 1110. Indeed, a 1986–7 survey of US insurance companies found that all companies would insure such donors and only one company out of fifty-four would raise premiums, although several companies would postpone a decision until three months after the operation or until full recovery had taken place: see A. Spital, 'Life Insurance for Kidney Donors – An Update' (1988) 45 *Transplantation* 819.

[23] These potential complications include deep wound infection, local haemorrhage, myocardial infarction, thrombophlebitis, and damage to the spleen or adrenal glands. One *beneficial* side-effect of living donation may be the discovery of previously unknown health problems: see J. Jones *et al.*, 'Unrecognised Health Problems Diagnosed During Living Donor Evaluation: A Potential Benefit' (1993) 25 *Transplantation Proceedings* 3083.

[24] See, for instance, M. Waples *et al.*, 'Living Donor Nephrectomy: A 20 Year Experience' (1995) 45(2) *Urology* 207, and W. Bay and L. Hebert, 'The Living Donor in Kidney Transplantation' (1987) 106 *Annals of Internal Medicine* 719. See more generally the EUROTOLD Project Report, *Questioning Attitudes*, at 61–4.

[25] See Allen *et al.*, 'The Living Organ Donor', at 183. These include urinary infections, superficial wound infections, atelectasis and pneumothorax, etc.

[26] The donor kidney is usually removed through a large loin incision, often accompanied by the removal of the twelfth rib.

[27] See L. Ratner *et al.*, 'Laparoscopic Assisted Live Donor Nephrectomy – A Comparison with the Open Approach' (1997) 63 *Transplantation* 229.

[28] P. Morris *et al.*, 'Psychosocial Complications in Living Related Kidney Donors: An Australian Experience' (1987) 19 *Transplantation Proceedings* 2840. Complications were reported in one-third of all donors in this study.

donors at the University of Minnesota between 1984 and 1996 revealed that the vast majority reported themselves as having an excellent quality of life, scoring higher than the national norm. However, 4 per cent were dissatisfied and regretted having donated, but in a significant percentage of these cases the recipient had died within one year post-transplant.[29]

Living donor pancreas transplants have been performed for some while – the pancreas was the first extra-renal organ to be transplanted using living donors. Their advantage over cadaver pancreas transplants is the long-term graft survival (insulin-independency) results and the reduced need for immunosuppression. However, because of technical complexities and the fact that there is no severe shortage of cadaveric pancreases, their use has been limited outside one or two main centres.[30] Their main application today is in simultaneous pancreas and kidney transplants (SPKs) where uraemic patients wish to avoid the potentially long wait for a cadaveric SPK, or where they would otherwise have bypassed a living donor kidney transplant in order to wait for a combined cadaveric graft, so as to avoid two operations. Reviews of twenty-three recently performed SPKs at the University of Minnesota revealed that although some donors had surgical complications (about 10–15 per cent),[31] all were alive and insulin-independent, leading the authors to contend that such a procedure was safe for both donors and recipients.[32]

Until fairly recently though, solid organ transplantation from living donors was almost exclusively confined to kidneys, but this picture is dramatically changing. The first living-related (segmental) liver transplant (LRLT) was performed in 1988 at São Paulo Medical College Hospital in Brazil from a mother to her four-year-old child. This was soon followed in July 1989 in Brisbane, Australia, by a 29-year-old mother who donated to her seventeen-month-old son, and another such transplant at the University of Chicago in November 1989.[33] Up to 1998, more than 700 LRLTs

[29] See E. Johnson *et al.*, 'Long-Term Follow-Up of Living Kidney Donors: Quality of Life After Donation' (1999) 67 *Transplantation* 717.

[30] Up to 1998, only 1 per cent of pancreas transplants reported to the International Registry used living donors: see D. Sutherland, J. Najarian and R. Gruessner, 'Living Versus Cadaver Donor Pancreas Transplants' (1998) 30 *Transplantation Proceedings* 2264.

[31] Four donors required splenectomy, three a percutaneous fluid drainage and one had gastritis. There were no donor deaths amongst the eighty-two living donors used up to 1994.

[32] R. Gruessner, J. Leone and D. Sutherland, 'Combined Kidney and Pancreas Transplants from Living Donors' (1998) 30 *Transplantation Proceedings* 282.

[33] A 29-year-old mother, Teresa A. Smith, donated to her 21-month-old daughter Alyssa.

had been performed worldwide at about fifty centres.[34] The overwhelming majority of recipients were paediatric patients who were expected to die imminently, due to the extremely limited volume of suitable cadaveric organs available for transplantation into children.[35] The graft and patient survival rates using LRLT are better than those from using cadaver donors, especially in paediatric recipients.[36] Data relating to morbidity and mortality from living-related liver transplantation are obviously more limited at present than as regards kidneys.[37] One death has so far been reported, as a result of pulmonary embolus, and Allen *et al.* report 'Sporadic instances of major biliary injury, splenic trauma, median nerve injury, subphrenic abscess, peptic ulcer, incisional hernia and minor wound complications'.[38] Long-term risks should be minimal in view of the fact that the reduced-size liver will return to its normal size in due course in the donor.

The first living donor lobar lung transplantation was performed in October 1990 at the Stanford University Medical Center. Versell Johnson donated one-third of her right lung to her twelve-year-old daughter who was terminally ill suffering from bronchopulmonary dysplasia. There are now programmes around the world, including in the UK and Denmark. Between 1990 and 1998, at the University of Southern California at Los Angeles, sixty such procedures were performed on patients who otherwise would have died, generally from cystic fibrosis (lobes of lung are usually removed from two separate donors and transplanted into the patient). The one-year patient survival rate was 71.7 per cent, infection being the primary cause of mortality. Barr *et al.* state that 'Survival of our patients has been comparable to results in cadaveric lung transplantation despite

[34] Including centres in the UK, Belgium, Germany, Japan, Israel, the Netherlands, Spain and Turkey. See M. Malago, X. Rogers and C. Broelsch, 'Liver Splitting and Living Donor Techniques' (1997) 53 (No. 4) *British Medical Bulletin* 860 at 862–3.

[35] Although reduction hepatectomy (the cutting down of a larger cadaveric liver) reduced mortality rates significantly.

[36] The largest programme is in Kyota where more than 400 children have received such grafts. Five-year graft survival in Japan and the US is reported to be in the range of 80–90 per cent: see Allen *et al.*, 'The Living Organ Donor', at 186.

[37] Data from the analogous procedure of liver section in elective patients with non-cirrhotic livers indicates a mortality rate of 0–4 per cent and a morbidity rate of between 10 and 20 per cent. Mortality for LRLT has consequently been predicted at a rate of between 1 and 2 per cent: see R. Busuttil, 'Living-Related Liver Donation: CON' (1991) 23 *Transplantation Proceedings* 43.

[38] 'The Living Organ Donor', at 192.

the urgency involved and the severity of the underlying illness.'[39] Of the 120 living lobar lung donors evaluated post-operatively, four required surgical re-exploration but none had any long-term complications.[40] There were no deaths and all returned to normal, unrestricted lifestyles.[41] Dark has stated that 'The risks of donor lobectomy probably lie midway between live donor nephrectomy, with a mortality rate estimated at 0.03%, and live donor liver transplantation where a donor death has been recorded relatively early in the experience.'[42] As yet, the long-term effects from reduced pulmonary reserve are unknown. Apart from in relation to kidneys, the use of unrelated donors is extremely rare, although four living lobar lung transplants have been performed in the US using non-family members, and in the UK a non-genetically related adult donor has also been used.

The first successful living intestinal transplant was performed by Deltz in Kiel in 1988, and the second in Leeds, England, in 1995. Results have been promising, but it is still too early to draw any firm conclusions as to long-term success and safety.[43] Although of course living donors do not donate hearts in the ordinary course of events, they not infrequently 'become' such donors when they receive a transplanted heart and lungs themselves. Where a patient requires a lung transplant, for instance because of cystic fibrosis, it is regarded as clinically preferable to transplant the heart as well *en bloc*, leaving the recipient's heart 'spare' and able itself to be used for transplantation – known as a 'domino heart transplant'.[44]

[39] M. Barr *et al.*, 'Recipient and Donor Outcomes in Living Related and Unrelated Lobar Transplantation' (1998) 30 *Transplantation Proceedings* 2261 at 2262.

[40] They state that 'Despite the constant concerns regarding the risk to living donors, our results have demonstrated the safety of the procedure with resulting organ availability that has been life saving in severely ill patients who will either die or become unsuitable recipients before a cadaveric organ becomes available': ibid., at 2263. In the UK some centres are experiencing nearly 50 per cent mortality amongst those patients awaiting a transplant.

[41] Extrapolating from the results of lobectomy in lung cancer patients, it has been estimated that the likely mortality risk is less than 1 per cent (1.3 per cent of cancer patients died but their general health at the time of operation was necessarily seriously impaired): see L. Shaw *et al.*, 'Ethics of Lung Transplantation with Live Donors' (1991) 338 *Lancet* 678 at 679.

[42] J. Dark, 'Lung: Living Related Transplantation' (1997) 53 (No. 4) *British Medical Bulletin* 892 at 901. The risks have also been equated with living liver segment donation by other commentators: see, for example, Allen *et al.*, 'The Living Organ Donor', at 193.

[43] Although a number of unsuccessful attempts were made in the sixties. The risks to the donor are from deep vein thrombosis, pulmonary embolus, chest infection, wound infection and specific risks attaching to the surgery. See S. Pollard, 'Intestinal Transplantation: Living Related' (1997) 53 (No. 4) *British Medical Bulletin* 868.

[44] The first such operation was carried out in the US in 1987. Corneas also are extremely rarely used in 'domino' fashion.

Developments proceed apace. In October 1998, at the Albert Einstein Hospital in São Paulo, Brazil, a 26-year-old son donated a kidney *and* part of a liver to his 53-year-old father who would have died without it, in the first case of its kind.[45]

An ethical overview

A consequentialist perspective would tend to favour living organ donation, especially renal donation where outcomes are extremely good, outweighing the modest risks posed to donors. This perspective is also consistent with a beneficence-based approach to medicine, the central Hippocratic ideal. A procedure performed without an ethically acceptable objective would be unethical and unlawful, even where a consent was given, but the ethical acceptability of LDT in general terms is accepted. Consent has never been a defence to the ancient (but still possibly subsisting) common law offence of maim or mayhem[46] committed where a person deliberately injured another person for an 'antisocial' purpose, but this would seem to be wholly inapplicable to this context.[47] The Nuffield Council considered that there was no 'injury' (in ethical terms) arising from an organ removal which had an intended therapeutic use, that is a proposed transplantation. Indeed, the Council of Europe Convention stipulates the need for a 'therapeutic use' for an organ removed from a living human being.[48] This is too restrictive a view though, owing to the involvement of a third party, the donor, who is not the intended (treatment) beneficiary. As Gillon states, 'if overall maximisation of welfare is the supreme moral objective the individual seems to be in permanent jeopardy before the overriding

[45] 'Son's Transplanted Organs save Father', *The Times*, 20 February 1999.

[46] Dukeminier once remarked that 'Under modern law, it is possible to contend that surgically removing an internal organ from a person constitutes a mayhem': see J. Dukeminier, 'Supplying Organs for Transplantation' (1970) 68 *Michigan Law Review* 811. This is no longer plausible today. Moreover, in *R* v. *Brown* Lord Mustill observed that the rationale of maiming as a distinct offence is now outdated: see [1993] 2 All ER 75 at 106.

[47] The offence was originally committed only where the conduct was designed to disable a person from fighting for his country or defending himself, or from annoying an adversary. Despite its desuetude, the offence has never been formally abolished in Britain, although in *R* v. *Brown* Lord Mustill described the offence as 'obsolete': [1993] 2 All ER 75 at 106. See also *R* v. *Owen* [1976] 1 WLR 840.

[48] Council of Europe Convention for the Protection of Human Rights and Dignity of the Human Being with Regard to the Application of Biology and Medicine, Directorate of Legal Affairs, Council of Europe, Strasbourg, November 1996.

interests of society'.[49] Such an approach would appear to render donation obligatory rather than elective despite a consensus to the contrary. Deontological, rights-based, perspectives, on the other hand, emphasise the right of the individual to dictate the uses of his/her body, no matter what the likely benefit to be derived by, or denied to, another from donation. Notably, Kant counselled that individuals should not be used solely as a means to the ends of others.

Clinicians are constrained by ethical obligations of non-maleficence owed to the subjects of all medical procedures. In this context, the principle is a problematic one as all organ removals are potentially harmful. Lamb reminds us though that 'The principle of non-maleficence is not absolute. When intended benefits accrue to others, public interest objections to self-harm can be overruled.'[50] But if we *can* take into account the potential benefit to the recipient and weigh this up against the harms to the donor, are we not back where we started, with a utilitarian weighing process which favours the interest of the recipient? This raises the unique character of risk/benefit assessments when applied to two-party situations as opposed to just a single patient. How gains to others are to be weighed against risks to donors is not self-evident. Caplan contrasts 'absolutists' and 'proportionalists' in this domain, the latter requiring a clear balance in favour of benefits over risks.

The doctrine of double effect (whereby all intended bad means/ends are morally wrong, but foreseen side effects of actions may be justified with regard to all the circumstances) is sometimes advanced as a mechanism whereby one can conclude that LDT involves no 'harm' anyhow.[51] Lamb states that 'kidney donation is acceptable because, despite potential risk to the donor, potential loss of function is not part of one's chosen means but only an acceptable side effect. Thus, according to the doctrine of double effect, the degree of mutilation that is ethically permissible will depend on perceptions regarding acceptable risks.'[52] However, surely it is more plausible to assert that the removal of the kidney, which must inevitably constitute a loss, is in fact *the very means chosen* in order to achieve the benefit to the other individual? In that case,

[49] R. Gillon, *Philosophical Medical Ethics*, John Wiley, Chichester, 1986, at 25.

[50] D. Lamb, 'Ethical Aspects of Different Types of Living Organ Donation', in Price and Akveld, *Living Organ Donation in the Nineties*, at 45.

[51] See chapter 5 on the 'Treatment of Potential Donors Prior to Death' for further detail relating to the principle in this context.

[52] Lamb, 'Ethical Aspects', at 45.

the doctrine would force the conclusion that every case of living organ (and even tissue) donation was morally impermissible, itself a morally unacceptable conclusion. It is necessary to *accept* that harms are indeed intentionally inflicted and that it is the willingness of the individual to consent to that harm and the potential benefits accruing to others (and also donors) which ultimately justify any particular procedure. In any event, the upshot of a finding that no harm is intended is, as Lamb highlights, only to allow the procedure to be justified in the light of all the factors, which begs the question anyhow whether any specific intervention should be permissible.

The concept of autonomy and the individual's right to self-determination is the central legitimating feature of LDT together with beneficence, although limits are universally imposed on the ambit of autonomous supererogatory conduct. John Stuart Mill, however, classically asserted that the only justification for placing prohibitions upon the conduct of individuals would be the protection of others – termed the 'harm' principle. Feinberg asserts that

> The harm principle will not justify the prohibition of consensual activities even when they are likely to harm the interests of the consenting parties; its aim is to prevent only those harms that are wrongs . . . It follows from these premises that no one can rightly intervene to prevent a responsible adult from voluntarily doing something that will harm only himself (for such a harm is not a 'wrong') and also that one person cannot properly be prevented from doing something that will harm another when the latter has voluntarily assumed the risk of harm himself through his free and informed consent.[53]

On this view, where there is consent no breach of the principle of non-maleficence can have occurred. Although some attempts have been made to reconcile such perspectives with limits on permitted conduct, they would appear to contravene libertarian principles. Such constraints may instead be generated by paternalistic and moralist concerns, but the appropriateness of interventions on such bases is itself controversial. Finally, one must not forget the other actor in this stage play, the medical professional, who has his/her own interests and views to reconcile and apply, which may place limits on the scope of permitted donation.

[53] J. Feinberg, *The Moral Limits of the Criminal Law. Vol. I: Harm to Others*, Oxford University Press, Oxford, 1984, at 116.

The unique character of LDT creates a challenge for orthodox analysis and development of an adequate regulatory infrastructure. The *prima facie* clash between interests of the potential donor and those of the intended recipient requires accommodation and resolution. Societies and cultures may balance these interests in different ways. For instance, Evans has asserted that the European approach is more *donor*, and non-maleficence, orientated and the United States approach more *recipient*, and utilitarian, orientated.[54] There is certainly a clear tension between those who perceive the autonomous wishes of the person (that is the donor) to be the cardinal factor in LDT and those who advocate an evaluation which places decision-making more centrally in the hands of medical practitioners. Individualistic communities will tend towards the former model. It may then be that societies with a supposed 'recipient bias' are simply more 'autonomy biased'. Nonetheless, autonomy of donors, as well as recipients, is a crucial justificatory criterion in all systems and is embedded in all laws and ethical codes.[55] Whether this emanates from a personal or property-based perspective on the human body will be examined below.[56] However, in view of the potential harms to living donors, not only have all systems imposed limits on permissible donation of body parts, but public policies often express a preference for cadaveric transplantation. The pervasive shortage of cadaveric organs, however, means that a straightforward choice between these alternatives is not always available.

Clinician perspectives upon living organ donor transplantation vary markedly, including over time and space. A survey of European transplant centres in the early eighties revealed that 22 per cent considered the use of living organ donors 'ethically unacceptable'.[57] No such large minority view has prevailed in most other parts of the world, and even within

[54] M. Evans, 'Organ Donations should not be Restricted to Relatives' (1989) 15 *Journal of Medical Ethics* 17 at 18.

[55] The Nuffield Council on Bioethics stated that 'In general, action that is clearly guided by a therapeutic intention must also be consented to by the particular patient or volunteer if it is to be ethically permissible': see *Human Tissue: Ethical and Legal Issues*, Nuffield Council on Bioethics, London, 1995, at paras. 6.6 and 6.18.

[56] In *Wright's Case* in 1603, 1 Coke on Littleton, para. 194 at 126.6, a 'strong and lustie rogue' directed his companion to cut off his left hand so that he could avoid work and beg more effectively. Both the rogue and his companion were convicted of mayhem despite the consent to the act. Similarly, in the more recent US case of *State* v. *Bass* 130 S.E. 2d 481 (1961), a physician who cut off a man's fingers to enable him to collect insurance monies was convicted as an accessory to mayhem.

[57] Editorial, 'Living Related Kidney Donors' (1982) (ii) *Lancet* 696.

Europe the great preponderance of countries have a living organ donor programme.[58] Attitudes are seemingly partly a function of the adequacy of cadaveric procurement within European nations, although attitudes to dialysis may also be germane.[59]

[58] See EUROTOLD Project Report, *Questioning Attitudes*, at 87–9.

[59] This might include the financial rewards from private dialysis use: see reference to research by Lorentzen and Paterson in A. Garwood-Gowers, *Living Donor Organ Transplantation: Key Legal and Ethical Issues*, Ashgate, Aldershot, 1999, at 35 n. 135.

6

The rationale and limits of living donor organ transplantation

The inherently controversial nature of living donor transplantation (LDT) and the vagueness of application of general legal principles (in view of its non-therapeutic character for the donor) led to pressure for legislation to provide guidance, clarity and, not least, protection for the practitioners involved. Indeed, the absence of such legislation stifled or slowed the growth of LDT in various nations. Some jurisdictions have had legislation relating to LDT for some while though. Czechoslovakia, as it then was, passed legislation in 1966, followed by Denmark and Italy in 1967, Hungary in 1972 and Bulgaria in 1973.[1] The very first legislative intervention in fact occurred in 1932 when the Italian Civil Code was specifically amended to prohibit LDT, after the revelation that a young Neapolitan man had sold a testis for transplantation into a wealthy Italian, a procedure which was seemingly otherwise lawful at that time.[2] Today, most countries with a transplant programme have such legislation.[3] These are all essentially permissive statutes although the additional role of law in proscribing unethical practices (generally commercial trading in human organs) has been the spur to legislation in some nations, for example in the United Kingdom and the United States.[4] Such statutory provisions are also

[1] There are some examples of fairly early legislation in other parts of the world also, for example the Law of 20 August 1974 in Costa Rica and the Law of 21 March 1977 in Argentina.

[2] Testis transplants were fairly common in the 1920s, the principal pioneer being Sergei Voronoff. In England a surgeon, Kenneth Walker, also carried out a number of such procedures.

[3] Exceptions being Austria, Israel, Liechtenstein, Malta, New Zealand, the Republic of Ireland and certain Swiss cantons and US states.

[4] In 1987 the Council of Europe remarked that 'Most countries have therefore shown a greater concern to legislate on deceased donors, mostly because the overwhelming majority of organs used come from deceased donors. Strict guidelines concerning living donors seem important nonetheless in view of the fact that there is a greater temptation towards commercialism of organs among living donors': see Third Report of the Conference of European Health Ministers (Paris, 16–17 November 1987), *Organ Transplantation: Legislative Measures in*

important as a means of safeguarding the interests of vulnerable individuals and as a medium for the democratic endorsement of, and expression of the basic moral and ethical principles underpinning, LDT.[5]

Much of the legislation deals with LDT in fairly comprehensive terms, but where it is more piecemeal in nature, as under the Human Organ Transplants Act 1989 in the UK, detailed regulation has been devolved to the application of general legal principles. However, in the UK, until the passing of the 1989 Act, the judicial and legislative hiatus generated substantial doubt as to whether LDT was legal at all,[6] despite its fairly liberal practice from the early sixties.[7] Brazier, however, observes that 'In the very early days of transplantation it is conceivable that the courts might have hesitated to approve of the removal of a healthy organ; and it might have been held that consent to such procedures was not permitted . . . But we have proceeded too far along the transplantation road for that argument to be of any avail today.'[8] The 1989 Act tacitly accepts its general legality, and the English Law Commission recently opined that 'Whatever the true legal analysis, there can be no doubt that, once a valid consent has been forthcoming, English law now treats as lawful operative procedures designed to remove regenerative tissue, and also non-regenerative tissue that is not essential for life.'[9]

By comparison with the UK, there was overwhelming judicial evidence

Relation to Organ Transplantation and to European Co-operation, Council of Europe, Strasbourg, 1987, at 4.

[5] See D. Price, 'The Texture and Content of Living Donor Transplant Laws' (1996) 28 *Transplantation Proceedings* 378; D. Price, 'The Scope and Function of Living Organ Donor Transplant Laws' (1996) 28 *Transplantation Proceedings* 3601; and T. Iyer, 'The Function of Legislation in Transplant Programs' (1992) 24 *Transplantation Proceedings* 2120.

[6] The nearest one came to authority was the extra-judicial remark of Lord Justice Edmund Davies that 'He would be surprised if in Britain any liability, civil or criminal, attached to a surgeon who performed a transplant operation on a competent donor who freely consented to the operation, provided that it did not present an unreasonable risk to the donor's life or health': see Edmund Davies, 'A Legal Look at Transplants' (1969) 62 *Proceedings of the Royal Society of Medicine* 633 at 634.

[7] Dworkin stated that 'In legal theory then, the transplantation of kidneys or other organs from live, healthy donors could be attacked as being unlawful operations although the question is not free from doubt. Medical practice has, by and large, progressed in this field without too much attention to the niceties of the law': see G. Dworkin, 'The Law Relating to Organ Transplantation in England' (1970) *Modern Law Review* 353 at 362. This issue was hardly academic in view of the potential liability for manslaughter of a donor who died following an unlawful organ removal procedure.

[8] M. Brazier, *Medicine, Patients and the Law*, 2nd edn, Penguin Books, London, 1992, at 396.

[9] Law Commission Consultation Paper, *Consent in the Criminal Law*, Consultation Paper No. 139, HMSO, 1995, at para. 8.32.

from an early stage that in North America living kidney donation was potentially lawful despite the legislative vacuum at state level. In 1941, in *Bonner* v. *Moran*,[10] a federal court decided that a skin graft taken from a 15-year-old boy for grafting to his cousin was illegal in the absence of the consent of the parents, implying that had such consent been given the tissue removal procedure would have been lawful. Whilst this was not a case concerning *organ* donation, courts in Alabama, Connecticut, Kentucky, Massachusetts, Minnesota and Texas explicitly endorsed the legality of living kidney donation from the fifties to the seventies. In 1957 in the three *Harrison* cases in Massachusetts the courts sanctioned donation by twin minors.[11] In 1969, a Kentucky court, in *Strunk* v. *Strunk*,[12] permitted the donation of a kidney from a mentally incapacitated adult to his brother. And in 1972, a Connecticut court allowed a seven-year-old to donate a kidney to her twin sister, in *Hart* v. *Brown*.[13] If living kidney donations were legal in such instances involving (sometimes very young) minors and mentally incapacitated adults, then *a fortiori* they were legal from a competent adult donor who had given an informed consent. This conclusion was endorsed by the outcome in certain 'rescue' cases where a relative donated a kidney in circumstances where, due to negligence, an individual had no remaining functioning kidney because, for instance, medical staff had inadvertently removed his/her one and only kidney. In *Sirianni* v. *Anna*,[14] for example, the New York court at no time suggested or remarked that the procedure was itself unlawful, nor was this a contention on behalf of the plaintiff.[15] Similarly in 1978 in Canada, the judge in the Manitoba Queen's Bench in *Urbanski* v. *Patel* described the decision of the father to donate a kidney as 'not surprising'.[16]

[10] 126 F. 2d 121 (1941).

[11] Aged nineteen, fourteen and fourteen respectively. See *Masden* v. *Harrison* No. 68651, *Hushey* v. *Harrison* No. 68666, *Foster* v. *Harrison*, No. 68674 (Mass. Sup. Jud. Ct 1957)

[12] 445 S.W. 2d 145 (Ky. 1969).

[13] 289 A. 2d 386 (Conn. 1972).

[14] 285 N.Y.S. 2d 709 (Supreme Court of New York, Niagara County, 1967).

[15] Although damages were refused to the plaintiff (mother) on other grounds. See also *Moore* v. *Shah* 458 N.Y.S. 2d 33 (Sup. Ct App. Div. 1982) where the son was refused damages in similar circumstances having donated a kidney to his father.

[16] (1978) 84 DLR (3d) 650 at 672 (Manitoba Queen's Bench). See also J. Spencer, 'Tissue Donors: Are they really Rescuers, or merely Volunteers?' [1979] 38 *Cambridge Law Journal* 45, and G. Robertson, 'A New Application of the Rescue Principle' (1980) 96 *Law Quarterly Review* 19.

Conscription of body parts?

Having observed that LDT is generally legitimate, we should enquire whether it can ever be, morally or legally, obligatory. In the only case to address this issue directly, a US court in *McFall* v. *Shimp* declined to order a man, who had undergone initial tests to determine tissue compatibility but then refused to go through further tests to establish genetic suitability, to donate compatible bone marrow to his cousin in order to save his life.[17] The court took the view that 'to compel the defendant to submit to an intrusion of his body would change every concept and principle upon which our society is founded. To do so would defeat the sanctity of the individual and would impose a rule which would know no limits and one could not imagine where the line would be drawn.'[18] The Nuffield Report considered that *McFall* probably represented the position in English law also, *a fortiori* where a solid organ was implicated, commenting that 'The fact that there may be urgent need for certain tissue cannot legally justify its being taken without consent; the law's commitment to the absolute right to "bodily security" of one person cannot be abandoned in order to save the life of another person.'[19]

The decision in *McFall* implicitly rejects the notion that others have rights of property in the body of another living person.[20] If our bodies *were* the property either of the state or of a sick individual we *would* seemingly be obligated to donate at least some body parts or tissues. Calabresi considers that the decision in *McFall* was probably correct in so far as American society is based on an 'autonomistic, rather libertarian

[17] No. 78–17711. 10 Pa. D & C 3d 90 (Pa. 1978). See also F. Huffman, 'Coerced Donation of Body Tissues: Can we Live with *McFall* v. *Shimp*?' (1979) 40 *Ohio State Law Journal* 409.

[18] No. 78–17711 at 2. The patient actually died forgiving his cousin. The judge added that 'For a society, which represents the rights of *one* individual, to sink its teeth into the jugular vein or neck of one of its members is revolting to our hard-wrought concepts of jurisprudence. Forcible extraction of living body tissue causes revulsion to the judicial mind': at 2–3.

[19] Nuffield Council on Bioethics Working Party Report, *Human Tissue: Ethical and Legal Issues*, Nuffield Council on Bioethics, London, 1995, at para. 7.6.

[20] Article 3 of the United Nations Universal Declaration of Human Rights, for instance, states that 'Everyone has the right to life, liberty and property', a statement echoed in Article 2 of the European Convention on Human Rights, which Scott declares to be a metaphor for the proposition that 'the human person (and the human body) should be considered inviolable and inalienable': see R. Scott, 'The Human Body: Belonging and Control' (1990) 22 *Transplantation Proceedings* 1002 at 1002. Indeed, the idea of property rights in another's living body smacks of slavery, which is internationally defined as arising in relation to 'a person over whom any or all of the powers attaching to the right of ownership are exercised': ibid. at 1003.

philosophy, and this individualistic point of view remains at the root of much of our law'.[21] He observes that whilst in common law systems there are relatively few Good Samaritan-type duties, many other jurisdictions, generally continental European systems, do have laws incorporating more communitarian, collectivist values requiring individuals to take steps to assist a person in danger or distress.[22] However, he adds: 'But as far as I know no one goes as far as Marx, who said: "From each according to his ability, to each according to his utility functions." In Marx's terms, it is not what you possess that counts because you do not own that. Rather, it belongs to the state, or if the state determines, to someone else in need.'[23] He cites examples of laws that do essentially treat persons as if they were the property of others (that is the state) though, for example conscription into military service, where people are required to give of their bodies for the common good.

The reluctance to create legal duties to rescue in many jurisdictions is a reflection of a will to preserve freedom and liberty of action to the maximum extent. Yet even those laws which mandate affirmative action in certain scenarios do not require that the 'rescuer' place himself in any significant danger.[24] It is difficult to see how such laws could apply even by analogy to living organ donation. The requirement of autonomy with respect to control of bodily integrity would appear to be too deep-seated in most nations' jurisprudence to contemplate the proposition, even ignoring the attendant physical risks attached to the procedures.

Love thy neighbour

Whilst the court in *McFall* viewed the man's refusal to donate bone marrow as legally irreproachable, it also described it (albeit on a seemingly intuitive basis) as '*morally* indefensible' (my emphasis).[25] However, in legal terms the decision seemingly reinforces the Kantian

[21] G. Calabresi, 'Do we Own our Own Bodies?' (1991) 1(5) *Health Matrix* 5 at 6. He states that 'If we own our own body parts, as we think we do, we tend to push society's values in an individualistic direction. If, instead, we say that body parts belong to those who need them, we focus on society and on its values in a communitarian way': at 15.

[22] For instance, Belgium, France, Germany, Norway and the Russian Federation.

[23] Calabresi, 'Do we Own our Own Bodies?', at 6.

[24] In Vermont, reasonable assistance to a person exposed to grave physical harm is required where that can be provided 'without danger or peril to himself or without interference with important duties owed to others': see 12 Vt. Stat. Ann., s. 519.

[25] No. 78–17711 at 2.

ideal of respect for persons, that is that a person should not be used solely as a means to the ends of others, and rejects an entirely consequentialist approach to transfers of body parts.[26] However, Peter Singer has proposed an ethical obligation of beneficence which embraces a duty to prevent evil where this can be accomplished without sacrificing *anything of comparable moral importance*, that is up to the point where we would cause more suffering to ourselves than we would relieve through giving.[27] Beauchamp and Childress describe such a nakedly utilitarian strategy as 'overly demanding'.[28] They nevertheless consider that the *McFall* case was a 'borderline case' viewed against their ethical framework which requires action where a person at substantial risk of harm can achieve a high probability of avoiding that harm through the actions of another, which do not present significant risks, costs or burdens to that other, and where the anticipated benefit outweighs any risks, costs or burdens implicated by it.[29] They imply that had the probability of saving Robert McFall's life by the bone marrow transplant been high, this might have tipped it into the realms of obligation. However, it would seem that living *organ* donation would always present 'significant risks, costs and burdens' so that the penultimate condition would never be satisfied. Thus, much is influenced by the type of tissue solicited. The prevailing consensus is that solid organ donation is a supererogatory act not a morally obligatory one, regardless of the morally virtuous nature, or otherwise, of the individual (non-)donor, that is donation displays *moral goodness* but not a *moral duty*.[30] There are relatively few ethical or legal duties of beneficence as compared with duties of non-maleficence, that is positive as opposed to negative duties.[31] The notion of transferring body parts is therefore universally perceived to be an act of *giving* or *donation*.

[26] However, from a Rawlsian perspective, if placed 'behind a veil of ignorance' not knowing our ultimate lot in life, the answer may be less self-evident in view of the possibility of our being one of the potentially needy recipients.

[27] P. Singer, 'Famine, Affluence, and Morality' (1972) 1 *Philosophy and Public Affairs* 229.

[28] T. Beauchamp and J. Childress, *Principles of Biomedical Ethics*, 4th edn, Oxford University Press, Oxford, 1994, at 265.

[29] Ibid., at 266–7.

[30] See the discussion of 'character' or 'virtue' ethics, ibid., at 62–9.

[31] Comments in *Urbanski* such as 'what father would not donate' merely serve to bolster the application of the rescue principle, not to imply any obligation to donate: see Robertson, 'A New Application of the Rescue Principle', at 19.

Whose kidney is it anyway?

Prior to any alienation or severance, the issue of property rights or ownership of our own bodies would appear to be a sterile one adding, as Harris alleges, nothing of substance and designed only to 'shore up' our existing *personal* rights.[32] Nevertheless, although the crucial issue is the right of control of the body, which undoubtedly vests in the individual, this is still an important issue not least because, on Locke's thesis, 'Only because people have physical ownership of their bodies do they have ownership of their body products.'[33] Some commentators, such as Lori Andrews, advocate rights of property in one's own body because it is perceived that this would increase the autonomy one was able to exercise over one's body and be more protective of the individual.[34] However, not only do we generally perceive ourselves *as* our bodies but we tend to view items of property as things over which 'we' (including our bodies) exercise dominion and control. The Law Reform Commission (LRC) of Canada stated:

> Why, then, should bodies not be regarded as ordinary property? An important answer may be that notions of bodily property do violence to our concepts of personal autonomy and human dignity. Property is traditionally associated with things, not with the human body. To equate the body with a thing is to dehumanise human existence; in the extreme, it suggests the repulsive notion that human beings may be owned. This answer hinges in a thing–person dualism, and an inference that human bodily parts are reflective of our notion of self.[35]

Parts of our intact bodies are then consequently part of our personal rather than property interests and are principally protected through rights of self-determination and respect.[36] However, whilst we should reject

[32] J. Harris, 'Who Owns My Body?' (1996) 16(1) *Oxford Journal of Legal Studies* 55 at 65.

[33] See M. Bray, 'Personalising Personalty: Toward a Property Right in Human Bodies' (1990) 69 *Texas Law Review* 209 at 212.

[34] See L. Andrews, 'My Body, My Property' (1986) 16 *Hastings Center Report* 16, and 'The Body as Property: Some Philosophical Reflections – A Response to J. F. Childress' (1992) 24 *Transplantation Proceedings* 2149.

[35] Law Reform Commission of Canada, *Procurement and Transfer of Human Tissues and Organs*, Working Paper 66, Minister of Supply and Services, Ottawa, 1992, at 57.

[36] Resnik states that 'The body is not like a coat that we can wear or a tool that we can use. Although it is possible to distinguish between the person and the body, these two entities are intimately connected in human beings . . . Only those who maintain a rigid mind/body dualism will not concede that there is an intimate relationship between the mind and the

Lockean notions of self-ownership and the idea that the whole living body should be perceived as property, there is no similar reason why severed body parts should not be so viewed.[37]

Kant argued that the 'body is part of the self; in its togetherness with the self it constitutes the person' and that this also applied to parts severed from the body.[38] Of course it is only after severance (of body parts) that this issue generally has any real import, as only then do such items acquire utility and scarcity, the essential hallmarks of 'property'. Freeman, however, identifies a fallacy and *non sequitur* in Kant's reasoning that because persons cannot have property rights in themselves (assuming this to be true) they cannot have property rights in parts of their bodies.[39] As Audi states, 'We may assume, however, that the body as a *whole* is not our property and still maintain that parts of it are, at least so long as we do not hold that one owns *all* the parts, since presumably to own all the parts of something implies owning *it*.'[40] Indeed, the LRC has observed that a view of there being no property rights in human body parts makes it difficult to explain how we can then *donate* organs.[41]

The Nuffield Council Report, however,[42] considered that English law, although generally silent on this issue, endorsed the notion that property rights do not usually attach to the tissue 'source', and opined that any claim should 'proceed on the basis of the consent given to the removal rather than any claim in property'. As far as English legal precedent is concerned though, Dworkin and Kennedy, reversing the emphasis, state that 'apart from prohibited acts, there appears to be nothing at common law, apart from vague arguments as to immorality and public policy, which would prevent courts from regarding parts of the body, or at least

body': see D. Resnik, 'The Commodification of Human Reproductive Materials' (1998) 24 *Journal of Medical Ethics* 388 at 389.

37 Radin states that 'We have an intuition that property necessarily refers to something in the outside world, separate from oneself, so that it would seem appropriate to call parts of the body property only after they have been removed from the system': see M. Radin, 'Property and Personhood' (1982) 34 *Stanford Law Review* 957 at 966. See also M. Radin, 'Market-Inalienability' (1987) 100(8) *Harvard Law Review* 1849 at 1881.

38 I. Kant, *Lectures on Ethics* (trans. L. Infield), Harper and Row, New York, 1963, at 124.

39 See M. Freeman, 'Taking the Body Seriously' in K. Stern and P. Walsh (eds.), *Property Rights in the Human Body*, Occasional Papers Series No. 2, King's College, London, 1997, 13. Of course implications of slavery have much less (if any) significance for body parts than for whole bodies.

40 R. Audi, 'The Morality and Utility of Organ Transplantation' (1996) 8(2) *Utilitas* 141 at 143.

41 Law Reform Commission of Canada, *Procurement and Transfer*, at 56–7.

42 Nuffield Council, *Human Tissue*, at 67.

most parts of the body, in the same way as other forms of personal property, once the parts have been removed from the body'.[43] Existing legislation would appear to be equivocal on the issue, for example in the Human Organ Transplants Act 1989, the Human Fertilisation and Embryology Act 1990, etc.[44] For many, as seemingly also for the Nuffield Council Working Party, it is the potential linking of tissue procurement to commercial arrangements which is the primary impediment to adopting a broad property rights analysis. However, the existence of property rights does not preclude the potential outlawing of (specific or all) commercial transactions, and so this objection falls away. The Report took the (for many paradoxical) view that its stance as regards the tissue provider did not preclude *users* having such property rights, asserting that 'common sense as well as the common law require that the user of tissue acquires at least possessory rights and probably a right of ownership over tissue once removed'.[45] This approach was clearly driven by the perceived need to facilitate research upon, and exploitation of, products using material derived from human beings. The decision in *Moore* v. *Regents of the University of California*, in which the California Supreme Court rejected John Moore's claim to property rights in his spleen, which had been removed for therapeutic purposes, can be seen in the same light.[46] In terms of legal precedents, the contention that parties other than the tissue provider can have property rights in human body materials is admittedly on firmer ground.[47] But these cases merely

[43] G. Dworkin and I. Kennedy, 'Human Tissue: Rights in the Body and its Parts' [1993] 1 *Medical Law Review* 291 at 302.

[44] Although the Nuffield Working Party stated that under these statutes the implication is that tissue removed is given free of all claims as an unconditional gift, it offered as a supporting rationale only that the statutes adopted a system of consents: see Nuffield Council, *Human Tissue*, at para. 9.2. However, the 1989 Act incorporates no such framework except as a subsidiary issue concerning *unrelated* living donors. Moreover, Nuffield's view implies that the concepts of consent and proprietary/property rights are necessarily mutually exclusive.

[45] Nuffield Council, *Human Tissue*, at para. 10.6.

[46] The Court stated: 'The theory of liability that Moore urges us to endorse threatens to destroy the economic incentive to conduct important medical research', *Moore* v. *Regents of the University of California* 271 Cal. Rptr. 146 at 162 (Sup. Ct Cal. 1990). The California Court of Appeals had in fact previously upheld his claim for conversion of the tissues resulting from their subsequent exploitation for commercial purposes. Moreover, Justice Broussard, dissenting in the Supreme Court, stated that 'it is clear under California law that a patient has the right, prior to the removal of an organ, to control the use to which the organ will be put after removal. It is also clear, under traditional common law principles, that this right of a patient to control the future use of his organ is protected by the law of conversion', 793 P. 2d at 502.

[47] In *R* v. *Welsh* [1974] Road Traffic Reports 478 and *R* v. *Rothery* [1976] Road Traffic Reports

emphasise the disparity with the position of the tissue provider. Why should the parts/tissues not also be able to be stolen or converted from him/her? One of the principal characteristics of the property approach is to confer upon individuals the freedom to bring claims, which may be especially important from the point of view of properly protecting one's interests in severed body materials. Indeed, in November 1993, the German Federal Court created a property rights framework in respect of parts removed from the human body. It considered that where a part is removed and is intended to be transferred to another individual it becomes 'property' at the point of severance, as it no longer forms a functional unity with the body of the donor, and that it is the person *of whose body it was once part* who has property rights in the severed part.[48]

The Nuffield Council's view was that 'where tissue is removed in the course of treatment, consent to the treatment will entail the abandonment of any claim to the tissue. Where tissue is voluntarily donated any claim will be based on the terms of the donation.'[49] It stated that 'The word donation clearly indicates that what is involved is a gift.'[50] In support of the concept of abandonment, the Report drew for authority upon a sole US case decided in a wholly different context,[51] and the perceived approach adopted by the California Supreme Court in the *Moore* case. Matthews observes of this approach though that 'if the court had found abandonment, it would logically entail the prior existence of property rights to abandon. But the Supreme Court held that Moore never had any. Abandonment was hence irrelevant.'[52] However, body parts are typically donated specifically for *transplantation*, rather than simply being removed in circumstances forming part of ongoing medical treatment.[53] Dickens states that 'When tissues are clearly designated to an identified recipient

550 the actual providers of the urine and blood samples (given for testing alcohol levels in a driver) were found guilty of stealing them from the police who were in possession of them.

48 *Bundesgerichtshof*, Urteil 9 November 1993, Aktenzeichen VI ZR 62/93. See F. Heubel, 'Defining the Functional Body and its Parts: A Review of German Law' in H. Ten Have, J. Welie and S. Spicker (eds.), *Ownership of the Human Body*, Kluwer, Dordrecht, 1998, 27.

49 Nuffield Council, *Human Tissue*, at 67.

50 Ibid., at para. 9.4. In fact the word 'donation' is not one that is used in the relevant statutory provisions anyhow.

51 *Venner* v. *State of Maryland* 354 A. 2d 483 (Md. 1976).

52 P. Matthews, 'The Man of Property' [1995] 3 *Medical Law Review* 251 at 268.

53 A possible exception being heart donation in the context of a domino heart transplant procedure.

or type of recipient . . . the presumption [of abandonment] is displaced.'[54] Matthews also queries why the removing surgeon should not be regarded as the agent of the patient here rather than an independent operative.[55] The approach of the Nuffield Report ironically appears to assume *a priori* property rights, and a divestment of such rights by donation or through abandonment. What else has he/she abandoned? Moreover, as Dworkin and Kennedy state, 'legal title to property cannot be transferred until it comes into existence; at the most, a purported transfer of future property may take effect as a contract to transfer the title once the property is created. Thus, the title must vest, in the first instance albeit momentarily, in the patient. Gift, sale, consumer liability, patent rights follow.'[56]

The Nuffield Working Party offered a further alternative analysis based upon *res nullius*, and observed that this would reflect the traditional 'no property in the body' approach, adding that on this view 'It would also mean that a person could not prospectively donate "his" tissue, once removed from his body. All he could do would be to consent to the removal.'[57] On this approach, such body parts would belong to no one at the time of removal, but once brought under the dominion of the first person to obtain possession, property would vest in that individual. However, Matthews notes that 'there is no English authority for treating human tissue as "*res nullius*", as if it were some sort of wild animal or plant'.[58] Swain and Marusyk argue that removed tissues could be treated as *res nullius* but nonetheless be perceived in law as being a *trust res nullius*, that is a thing owned by nobody but held in trust for the recipient.[59] They contend that the benefit of such an approach is that it would preserve the altruistic spirit of the donation and remove it from the commercial sphere.

[54] B. Dickens, 'Excised Organs Prior to Implantation: Belonging and Control' (1990) 22 *Transplantation Proceedings* 1000 at 1000.

[55] Matthews, 'The Man of Property', at 265–6.

[56] Dworkin and Kennedy, 'Human Tissue: Rights in the Body', at 302–3.

[57] Nuffield Council, *Human Tissue*, at para. 9.11.

[58] Matthews, 'The Man of Property', at 263.

[59] M. Swain and R. Marusyk, 'An Alternative to Property Rights in Human Tissue' (1990) 20 *Hastings Center Report* 12 at 13. These writers would adopt a different approach to tissues intended to be *permanently* removed from the body, that is never to be reintegrated into the body of a human, for example cells for biotechnological research.

Dismemberment

Under either of these latter strategies the possessor of an organ for transplantation would acquire a right to it. The Nuffield Working Party would confer powers of possession and use over the item concerned, although subject to the original terms of the gift. The Report states that 'it is probable that the user of tissue acquires at least the right to possess, and probably a right of ownership over, the tissue'.[60] By contrast, Swain and Marusyk contend that the orthodox *res nullius* stance should be adapted here to confer merely rights of possession, and not rights of ownership. As far as the rights of *users* are concerned, the Nuffield Report relied most heavily upon the Australian authority of *Doodeward* v. *Spence*[61] and the idea that where work was expended on the part or tissues then it could acquire the characteristics of property and be subject to property rights, based upon John Locke's labour theory of property (although in fact only Griffiths CJ in *Doodeward* can unequivocally be said to endorse such an idea with respect to human body parts). This 'work' rationale was employed also in the Court of Appeal in the recent prosecution in *R* v. *Kelly*.[62] However, the Report regards the user as having possessory rights, and maybe even ownership rights, even where no work is expended on it, which is more consistent with the *res nullius* approach outlined above.[63] Moreover, the Report offers no answers as to why the individual should not be viewed as owning his/her own body so that he/she thus owns the fruits of his/her own body instead, based on the same Lockean labour theory. Nozick, for instance, has developed the idea of 'self-ownership' which would lead towards such an opposite result.[64] Who is the 'creator' here? It is a cogent view that property rights should not be dependent upon such work or effort, but in that case, again, why do such body parts not initially belong to the original source?

The notion that property in severed body parts vests, despite donation, in the person from whom the materials are removed, at least momentarily

60 Nuffield Council, *Human Tissue*, at 77.
61 (1908) 6 Commonwealth Law Reports 406.
62 *R* v. *Kelly* [1998] 3 All ER 741.
63 In *Dobson* v. *North Tyneside HA* [1996] 4 All ER 474, with respect to parts of a cadaver, the Court of Appeal suggested, rather puzzlingly, that where such work had been expended on the relevant part, the right to possession of it would have vested in the next of kin, although they had not themselves carried out such work.
64 See R. Nozick, *Anarchy, State and Utopia*, Blackwell, Oxford, 1974.

after severance, is entirely persuasive as regards living organ donation.[65] In fact there is no reason why such proprietary rights should not be viewed as vesting in the donor until 'corporeal reintegration' occurs in the recipient. This is consistent with the approach of the German Federal Court above.[66] It requires no dubious assertion that a person owns his or her body prior to severance. Dickens considers that when tissue is donated to a designated recipient, the donor retains legal control in the form of a property right until implantation. He adds:

> A physician or hospital obtaining physical possession of the tissue will accordingly not enjoy legal ownership, but will only be a bailee of the property, bound by a duty to take reasonable care of it. Their proprietary duty is owed to the donor, not to the designated donee or recipient. Deliberate destruction or misuse, such as transplantation to another, may constitute theft, and negligent misuse may be unlawful conversion.[67]

On this approach, enforceable rights of possession would vest in the bailee (for example a hospital) if the bailee is acting within the terms of the bailment. This is a plausible and convincing proposition. However, even if such proprietary rights no longer remain vested in the 'donor', this is no reason to view the possessor of body parts *per se* as having proprietary rights. As Harris states, 'Stored bodily parts may be the subject of trespassory rules, together with role-duties imposed on particular officials, without either ownership or quasi-ownership being reserved to any person or institution.'[68]

General legal perspectives

In jurisdictions with a general Criminal Code there is often a specific provision catering directly for the legitimacy of medical or surgical procedures either within the Code itself or in separate legislative provisions. Whilst they would apply to transplantation procedures, whether they would apply to organ *removal* procedures is more problematic, as these provisions often apply only where the procedure is done 'for the

[65] Indeed, the Nuffield Report explicitly recognised that many see the 'logical essentiality' of such perspectives: see *Human Tissue* at para. 9.7.
[66] If this is the case, then abandonment could only occur after property rights *had* already vested in the donor source.
[67] Dickens, 'Excised Organs', at 1001.
[68] Harris, 'Who Owns My Body?', at 76.

patient's benefit'.[69] Section 61A of the New Zealand Criminal Code, on the other hand, is more broadly framed and seemingly applicable also to non-therapeutic procedures. It states: 'Everyone is protected from criminal responsibility for performing with reasonable care and skill any surgical operation upon any person if the operation is performed with the consent of that person, or of any person lawfully entitled to consent to the operation, and for a lawful purpose.'[70] Where legislation has been passed governing and legitimating LDT, it is often stated to constitute an exception to the general provisions of the Criminal Code, as in Spain,[71] thus obviating certain potential difficulties and conflict. However, such provisions still do not provide clear-cut answers to the legality of certain medical procedures, notably here non-therapeutic procedures. Under most European penal codes, no public prosecution may be brought for less serious assaults in the absence of a complaint by the aggrieved person. As the Law Commission noted, these codes recognise that it is the wishes of the victim alone which determine whether or not a prosecution is appropriate in such cases.[72]

In common law jurisdictions, medical treatment ordinarily, and organ donation in particular, is governed by the general legal infrastructure, and is typically perceived as being *prima facie illegal*. Courts and legislatures have fashioned a *quantitative harm threshold* for the purpose of analysing the legality of such actions, and in England and Wales all actions are required to be justified where *actual bodily harm* is either intended or caused, even where there is consent.[73] Where no actual harm is intended and/or caused, there are no public interests implicated and consent therefore suffices to legitimate the conduct.[74] The position in the

69 See Canadian Criminal Code, section 45 and (New Zealand) Crimes Act 1961, section 61.

70 Crimes Act 1961, section 61.

71 See C. Casabona, 'The Living Donor in Spanish Law', paper lodged with the EUROTOLD Project.

72 See Law Commission, *Consent in the Criminal Law*, at 214. In Finland, no prosecution for assault or petty assault may occur in the absence of a complaint from the injured party. Turkey and Italy have similar provisions: see Article 456 of the Turkish Penal Code and Article 581 of the Italian Penal Code. In Sweden, unless the victim reports the incident, no prosecution for an assault which is not 'grave' is permitted: see Swedish Penal Code, section 11.

73 Skegg has argued that transplantation procedures should not, in view of the objective being to benefit the patient, be perceived as a 'harm' at all, but even he concedes the point as regards living *donors*, as they are not intended for his/her benefit: see P. Skegg, *Law, Ethics and Medicine*, Clarendon Press, Oxford, 1988, at 30–2.

74 In Greece, bodily injury is justified where the victim consented unless it is *contra bonos mores*:

common law states and territories of Australia is not wholly clear, but may be the same as in England and Wales.[75] In fact, the position in (even civil law) jurisdictions with criminal codes may be little different from the position in common law jurisdictions. In Tasmania it would appear as though the law under the Criminal Code is the same as in England and Wales,[76] and regarding New Zealand the English Law Commission commented that 'It may therefore be that the limitations on consent, in the sense of the degree of harm to which it is possible to give a valid consent and the types of conduct to which consent may be given, are the same in England and New Zealand.'[77] In most European jurisdictions it is outside the discretion of the parties themselves whether a prosecution should be initiated where the harm exceeds a certain level or other features are present.

Thus, very typically above the level of actual bodily harm, some further legitimating feature is required, apart from consent, to justify acts by third parties infringing upon the physical integrity of the body, including medical procedures. The English Law Commission has suggested that this threshold be raised so that consent would be a sufficient justificatory factor up to the point where 'seriously disabling injury' was caused.[78] Although under the US Model Penal Code consent is stated to be a defence to any offence involving 'bodily injury' which is not 'serious',[79]

see Article 308(2) of the Greek Penal Code. Germany has similar provisions: see section 226a of the German Criminal Code.

75 Although consent precludes liability for a common assault, whether it is sufficient in itself to preclude liability for greater assaults/injuries is uncertain. The Law Commission noted that although the Court in *Pallente* v. *Stadiums Pty Ltd (No. 1)* [1976] Victorian Reports 331, spoke of the 'boundary' at 'grievous' bodily harm, a leading textbook writer has asserted that the Court in fact meant to fix the boundary at 'actual' bodily harm: see Law Commission, *Consent in the Criminal Law*, at 219.

76 See the decision of the Tasmanian Supreme Court in *R* v. *Holmes* (1993) 2 Tasmanian Reports 232. In Queensland, the Criminal Code Review Committee has proposed that consent should preclude liability for harms up to the level of serious bodily harm/ disfigurement: see *Final Report of the Queensland Criminal Code Review Committee*, 1992, at 199–200.

77 Law Commission commenting on the decision of the New Zealand Court of Appeal's decision in *R* v. *Nasif* [1987] 2 New Zealand Law Reports 122: see *Consent in the Criminal Law*, at 227.

78 Law Commission, *Consent in the Criminal Law*, at paras. 4.16–17. Lord Slynn in *Brown* would similarly have drawn the threshold line at serious bodily harm: see [1993] 2 All ER 75 at 118. Stephen wrote in the nineteenth century that 'Everyone has the right to consent to the infliction upon himself of bodily harm not amounting to a maim': see Sir J. Stephen, *Digest of the Criminal Law*, 3rd edn, 1883, at 141–2, Article 206.

79 American Law Institute, *Model Penal Code, Official Draft and Explanatory Notes*, 1985, at

the US courts have in fact taken a restrictive view of the degree of harm to which consent can provide a valid defence.[80] Inevitably, all organ removal procedures cause actual bodily harm, as conventionally perceived. However, in any event, with the possible (but unlikely) exception of the removal of a kidney, it is very probable that all other forms of living organ donation would be viewed as constituting serious disabling injury, and it would remain necessary to justify such interventions in appropriate instances.

The centrality of consent is a major part of the common law tradition.[81] The English Law Commission nevertheless commented in an earlier consultation paper that 'While doctors are undoubtedly exempt from criminal liability for acts done in the course of lawful medical or surgical treatment that would otherwise be serious assaults, for instance the amputation of a limb, the consent of the patient to the injury may usually be a necessary, but it is certainly not a sufficient, condition of that exception.'[82] The Nuffield Council Report also asserted that the consent of the donor is important in justifying procedures involving the removal of body tissues, but that it is not the primary consideration,[83] and in the specific context of living organ donation, the Law Reform Commission of Canada recently asserted that 'Consent alone . . . does not ensure the moral acceptability of the medical intervention.'[84] In England and Wales, in the *Attorney-General's Reference (No. 6 of 1980)*, Lord Lane stated broadly that nothing in the law denies the legitimacy of, *inter alia*,

section 2.11(1) and (2). Under the Texas Penal Code it is provided that the consent of the victim will constitute a defence to an assault but that this will only be so where 'the conduct did not threaten or inflict serious bodily injury': see Texas Penal Code, s. 22.06.

80 See, for instance, *R* v. *Gray* 36 Cal. Rptr. 263 (1964) and *R* v. *Samuels* 58 Cal. Rptr. 439 (1967).

81 Although Skegg observed in the early sixties that dilemmas in analysis of the legality of medical treatment generally spring 'largely from a too easy assumption that consent is the vital factor in establishing the legality of a surgical operation. If it were recognised that consent is no more than one important aspect of public policy in such cases, admittedly crucial in most cases but not necessarily in all, then some of the difficulty might disappear': see P. Skegg, 'Two Views on Consent in the Criminal Law' (1963) 26 *Modern Law Review* 233 at 236.

82 Law Commission Consultation Paper, *Consent and Offences Against the Person*, Consultation Paper No. 134, HMSO, 1994, at para. 2.4.

83 Nuffield Council, *Human Tissue*, at para. 6.6.

84 Law Reform Commission of Canada, *Procurement and Transfer*, at 47. Gerald Dworkin has also previously stated that 'one person does not have a licence to mutilate or cause bodily harm to another for any purpose merely because that person has consented': see Dworkin, 'The Law Relating to Organ Transplantation', at 355.

'reasonable surgical interference' which is demanded by the public interest.[85] The public interest is an omnipresent feature here both in the approach of the common law and in the general Criminal Codes. The flexibility inherent in the application of public policy is necessary to keep up with medical progress, in the absence of specific legislation catering for specific forms of activity.[86] It creates considerable doubt though in relation to procedures such as living organ donation.

The legality of medical procedures consequently depends not only on the purpose of the procedure and the consent of the subject of it, but the extent of the harm(s) implicated by it. However, whilst the law will accept the deliberate infliction of, or the running of (sometimes very) substantial risks of causing, very serious harms, where the overriding objective is the therapeutic benefit of the individual, the issue is much more problematic where the individual (the donor) is not intended to receive any direct benefit from the procedure, that is the procedure is *non-therapeutic*. In the therapeutic context the harms and risks are outweighed by the anticipated gain to that patient, that is the risk/benefit balance is advantageous. In the non-therapeutic context it is less easy to see what should be weighed against the potential harms from the donor's point of view and to find a proper justification for it.[87] The English Law Commission recognised the particular challenge in this context and asserted that although the living donor procedure has been an established therapeutic procedure for decades, 'What is more difficult is to identify the principles on which English law sanctions these operations, since they do not confer any therapeutic benefit on the donors.'[88]

When viewed from the general standpoint of the 'public interest' it also seems *prima facie* to be easier to subscribe to a *maximum* level of permitted harm here. Giesen has proclaimed that 'It is an established

[85] [1981] QB 715 at 719E.

[86] This is Dworkin and Kennedy's view: see 'Human Tissue: Rights in the Body', at 299.

[87] Dworkin's preconditions to legitimate medical interventions highlight the limitations of conventional analyses in requiring, in addition to consent being obtained and the procedure being performed by a properly qualified professional, that the operation be therapeutic (that is for the patient's benefit) *and* that there be a lawful justification for it: see Dworkin, 'The Law Relating to Organ Transplantation', at 356–7. But the typical rationale for supporting LDT relies on the latter condition *at the expense of* the penultimate one, that is one would need to read them disjunctively not conjunctively. Indeed, if all conditions had to be satisfied, all forms of tissue and organ donation would be automatically forbidden. However, it seems that Dworkin may have intended these conditions to be *alternatives*: see Law Commission, *Consent in the Criminal Law*, at 106 n. 20.

[88] Law Commission, *Consent in the Criminal Law*, at para. 8.32.

principle both at Common Law and in Civil Law countries, that a person cannot consent to his being killed, self-mutilated or seriously injured.'[89] It is as yet unclear what rationale such limits are founded upon though.

The law and living organ donation generally

Legislation frequently imposes a ceiling on permissible living organ and tissue donation, although in many instances such provisions are either too broad or too vague to be helpful, or are distinctly unrealistic. Some laws, for example in Romania, state that LDT may be performed provided that there is no threat to the donor's life, whilst others place a limit on risks of serious *effects* on the donor's health. In Portugal there must not be a 'strong probability' of serious *and permanent* impairment of the physical integrity and health of the donor.[90] In Germany, the donor must not be 'likely to suffer any serious damage to health (other than the direct results of the organ removal)'.[91] These provisions allude to serious effects on health but vary in the degree of probability implicated. Other laws require that there must be no *serious risk* to health although not necessarily no *serious damage* to health. For example, in Greece there must not be 'any manifest serious risk to the life *or health* of the donor' (emphasis mine).[92] The Council of Europe's Draft Protocol stipulates that there must be 'no serious risk to the life or health of the donor'.[93] However, whilst there is little risk of serious harm to health from living kidney donation, it cannot be said that there is *no* risk of some serious damage to health, *a fortiori* no risk to health whatever. Indeed, it might be said that there is even a *serious* (in the usual sense of being 'significant') risk of direct or immediate damage to health (albeit generally short-term) from surgical complications from renal donation, *a fortiori* living non-renal donation. Consequently, if many of the above laws were applied literally and stringently

89 D. Giesen, *International Medical Malpractice Law*, Martinus Nijhoff, Dordrecht, 1988, at 609.

90 Law of 22 April 1993, section 6(4).

91 Law of 5 November 1997, section 8(1). This presumably means only organ removal *per se* not the potential consequences of surgery, for example infection.

92 Law of 2 August 1983, section 5. In the Slovak Republic the procedure must not 'seriously jeopardise the donor's state of health': Law of 24 August 1994, section 46(2). In Norway, there must be no 'direct danger' to the donor's life or health (Law of 9 February 1973, section 1), and in Denmark no 'immediate danger' to health (Law of 13 June 1990, section 13(4)).

93 Article 10, Draft Additional Protocol to the Convention on Human Rights and Biomedicine, on Transplantation of Organs and Tissues of Human Origin, 9 March 1999, Council of Europe.

then even living kidney donation from an entirely fit and healthy donor would be precluded.[94] Such laws are in practice interpreted and applied with a degree of latitude, but provide little in the way of guidance as to the actual permitted upper limit of risk taking. This is particularly unsatisfactory in the light of the evolution of various forms of *non-renal* donation where greater risks are posed than with conventional living donation procedures.

Thresholds and ceilings

The 'criminal – but' (that is *prima facie* unlawfulness) approach evolves out of the *quantification of harm* scheme developed by the respective courts and legislatures. However, liberalists typically assert that interventions by the criminal law which have the effect of negating autonomy are only permissible where wrongful actions cause 'harm' to the interests of another or, maybe also, 'offence' (hurt/distress). Indeed, many support restrictions founded on the former basis alone. Roberts condemns the prevailing approach as authoritarian and argues that it is inconsistent with liberal principles to criminalise self-injury, even where it is against the individual's own interests or well-being. He states that this would apply equally where the harm was inflicted by a third party with the consent of that person, that is it would not be 'wrongful' in that event.[95] Thus, legal restrictions on living organ donation by a person with capacity who has given a free and informed consent *prima facie* are repudiated by liberalists, who also impliedly reject a 'quantification of harm' (plus exceptions) approach.[96] Indeed, Alldridge contends that 'We do not need a medical exception, because we do not need the rule to which it would provide an exception.'[97] Nevertheless, as we have already seen, the preponderance of

[94] Various laws also require that the donor's pre-operative health be satisfactory and that this be directly tested and ascertained.

[95] P. Roberts, 'The Philosophical Foundations of Consent in the Criminal Law' (1997) 17(3) *Oxford Journal of Legal Studies* 389 at 404. The alternative approach is to deem consented-to conduct lawful subject to there being categories of cases where it would be criminal, for certain reasons.

[96] See also J. Feinberg, *The Moral Limits of the Criminal Law. Vol. I: Harm to Others*, Oxford University Press, Oxford, 1984.

[97] Alldridge supports a wider defence of consent which 'genuinely honours autonomy' and rejects a threshold approach or any ceiling on permissible risk taking: see P. Alldridge, 'Consent to Medical and Surgical Treatment – The Law Commission's Recommendations' [1996] 4 *Medical Law Review* 129 at 143.

legal systems adopt one threshold or another tied to the extent of harm in order to 'trigger' public interest considerations.

It is sometimes maintained, however, that when harm rises above a certain level a person is either incapable, or *prima facie* incapable, of giving an autonomous consent to such a procedure. This argument was considered meritorious by the English Law Commission which recommended the drawing of a general threshold at the level of seriously disabling injury on account of the fact that 'if seriously disabling injury results, we will take the view that a person who consents to it has made a mistake and that to be really disabled is against his or her interests'.[98] It stated that, in such circumstances, 'we cannot be sure that the consent will be entirely voluntary'. If this view is persuasive, it should enlist even the support of liberalists who rest autonomous wishes and actions on the ability to give a voluntary and informed consent. It is not, however, able to be supported in such a sweeping form even with regard to non-therapeutic procedures. There is no convincing reason to believe that all potential organ donors running risks of serious injury act involuntarily. Just because many, or even most, people would decide to act differently does not support the view that any one individual cannot give an autonomous and voluntary consent. Indeed, in certain specific instances, we can clearly understand and relate to cases of attempted and extreme altruism, as in the remarkable case involving Mr Prendergast Senior who, in his mid-sixties, wished to donate his remaining kidney to his son who had been dependent on dialysis for many years, having given his first kidney to his other son at an earlier time (no surgeon was prepared to carry out the procedure, and ultimately the mother donated a kidney instead). The Law Commission's approach is either paternalistic or moralistic, but not liberal. But placing limits on actions under either of these alternative philosophies is also problematic. Just as under the liberal approach there is no obvious reason to place any limits on permissible autonomous action where no harm is caused to others, so why not intervene to prevent *any and all* potentially harmful procedures in the name of paternalism/moralism? However, the recognition of a 'medical exception' even where the harm exceeds the relevant threshold impliedly acknowledges that a valid and voluntary consent *may* be given to medical procedures exceeding the relevant harm threshold.

[98] Law Commission, *Consent in the Criminal Law*, at 20.

Ultimately, the Commission proposed a medical exemption which permitted any degree of seriousness of injury caused in the context of 'proper medical treatment or care' administered with the consent of that person. However, the nature of the problem with regard to non-therapeutic procedures such as living organ donation is highlighted by the fact that this was deemed to fall outside the compass of the phrase 'normal medical treatment' and a specific 'exception' or 'extended ambit' was necessitated to cater specifically for it,[99] that is 'any treatment or procedure to facilitate the donation of regenerative tissue, or the donation of non-regenerative tissue not essential for life'. The Commission ultimately justified this and all other 'exceptions' on the basis that they are activities 'very widely regarded as beneficial and for which the state is satisfied that the risks are properly controllable and containable',[100] even where serious disabling injury would or might occur. It would appear then that the law does, and will continue to, accord substantial deference with regard to living organ donation procedures. In endorsing these procedures it seemingly adopts a conservative moralist approach, based on endorsement of the (accepted medical practice) status quo, as *a*, if not *the*, principal legitimising factor. This is less than convincing. As Alldridge comments 'Unfortunately, the Commission does not advance particularly good justifications for the state of the law which it favours. It simply uses current medical practice as the test of acceptability, rather than producing a justifying account.'[101]

It is not clear whether there is any additional justifying feature being advanced here, over and above the scope of current accepted practice. Alldridge points to difficulties with regard to LDT in this connection because

> The Commission seems, however, already to have decided that the mere fact of satisfying a desire will not suffice, and is left without the tools to justify the exceptions in these cases . . . The standard liberal proposition is, by contrast, that the desire of the person upon whom the surgery or treatment is carried out, expressed as a consent by a person of full capacity should always, without more, suffice to render the conduct lawful.[102]

The current position creates uncertainty as to the 'ceiling' of permissible

[99] Ibid., at 117. [100] Ibid.

[101] Alldridge, 'Consent to Medical and Surgical Treatment', at 139.

[102] Ibid. He notes that the rationale underpinning the crime of maim is now redundant, but nonetheless this was an offence targeted at a specific evil of a particular type of conduct.

living organ donation. Is this to be governed purely by evolving medical consensus? Is living lobar lung transplantation permissible purely by virtue of its being practised around the world without substantial criticism from within the medical community? This surely will not do. It amounts to abdicating responsibility to the medical community but at the same time requires practitioners to work in an atmosphere of uncertainty. Probably legislatures ought to address specific forms of therapy individually.

Maybe though, despite the conflation in liberal opinion between self-harm and consented-to harms inflicted by others, the prevailing approach is based on a distinction between one-party and two-party situations.[103] Clinicians share moral responsibility for any organ removal and therefore must decide if they are morally justified in so doing. The surgeon has been described as an *accomplice* in the transaction.

Saints and heroes

It has been argued that the application of liberalist perspectives to two-party situations threatens an opposite, even more potent, danger of an excessive swing towards reliance on donor autonomy, in view of the fact that the procedure is not ordinarily intended to serve the individual's welfare. Carl Elliott asserts: 'In a moral framework shaped by respect for patient autonomy, whether or not to undergo risk or harm can come to seem a matter solely for patients to decide,'[104] but he contends that most physicians feel some duty not to expose a person to the risk of harm and entertain an intuition that they should not respect this person's sincere wish to undergo the procedure in question. He asserts that

> A more important reason for our divided intuitions about this case is the fact that, morally, self-sacrifice is a double-edged sword. On the one hand, it is an aspect of actions which we generally judge to be morally admirable. Placing one's own interests above those of others is often the reason that we call an action morally wrong, and sacrificing one's interests for others is often a reason for calling an action morally praiseworthy. On the other hand, a sacrifice is still a sacrifice; that is, in making it a person has caused

[103] The continued prohibition on assisting suicide in most jurisdictions which have also decriminalised attempted suicide probably trades on this distinction.

[104] C. Elliott, 'Doing Harm: Living Organ Donors, Clinical Research and *The Tenth Man*' (1995) 21 *Journal of Medical Ethics* 91 at 91–2.

> some harm to himself, and harm is certainly something that we want to minimise.[105]

A great deal of his argument hangs on the distinction between obligatory and supererogatory actions. He states:

> That is, we might well say that in general a person is at least morally justified, and perhaps obliged, to help a person who is trying to do his duty. It is a morally good thing for me to help a person provide food or medical care to his children, to help him keep his promises, tell the truth, and so on. But it does not follow that, in general, I am justified in helping him to go beyond his duty – to be a saint or hero.[106]

These views are more thought-provoking than persuasive. They rest on the notion that supererogatory actions are 'self-sacrificial' and involve 'placing another's interests above one's own'. If, say, a parent of a dying child decides that, taking the situation overall, it would be better to attempt to save the child's life by donating a segment of liver, for instance, this is not a purely other-regarding decision but one with a net potential benefit to him/her and with ramifications also for the family unit as a whole. Whilst the mother may not be capable of placing moral or legal *obligations* upon a surgeon in such circumstances, this does not suggest that a surgeon who is prepared to remove her kidney for transplantation into a son or daughter is in any way involved in a morally dubious act, where autonomous informed consent has been provided.

At times though, Elliott is less dogmatic and suggests the need for a *weighing* of the respective interests involved. He states:

> Thus, we might imagine problematic cases involving a person who has sacrificed his own interests for those of others, an aspect which we consider morally praiseworthy, but who has also caused more harm to himself than he has prevented – for instance, if he has undergone tremendous self-sacrifice in return for relatively trivial benefit to another.[107]

He adds:

> The donor, we think, should be praised for valuing his own interests less than those of the transplant recipient; at a minimum, he is justified in valuing his interests less. But not so for the physician: we usually think that

[105] C. Elliott, 'Constraints and Heroes' (1992) 6 *Bioethics* 1 at 8–9.
[106] Ibid., at 10. [107] Ibid., at 9.

> he ought to value the interests of his patients equally . . . By performing the transplant, he is endorsing the donor's sacrifice, and thereby valuing the interests of the recipient more than those of the donor.[108]

This suggests the need for a risk/benefit evaluation by the physician or surgeon concerned, a criterion which is widely adopted in this sphere anyhow, albeit one complicated by the existence of a donor and a patient.

Criteria for permissible living organ donation

The Law Reform Commission of Canada Report on *Human Tissue* proposed that 'three conditions emerge for the permissibility of using organs from the living: (1) the donor must consent freely and knowledgeably; (2) there must be some reasonably expected benefit to the donor; and (3) likely benefits to the recipient must considerably outweigh likely harms to the donor'.[109] These conditions attempt to reconcile the three key operational ethical principles here: (donor) autonomy, non-maleficence (to the donor) and beneficence (for the recipient). The notion of consent is developed more fully in the following chapter but the notions of 'benefit' and 'risk' are examined below.[110]

Risk/benefit equation

The imperative on physicians to act *non-maleficently* is pervasive and applies synonymously with the ethical dictum *primum non nocere*, that is (above all, or first) do no harm.[111] The import of this seemingly simple maxim is more problematic though than is generally supposed. Siegler has stated that

> From the outset, some surgeons and ethicists took an absolute position and said '"Do no harm" means that healthy volunteers could not be

[108] Ibid.

[109] Law Reform Commission of Canada, *Procurement and Transfer*, at 48.

[110] See further D. Price and H. Akveld, 'Living Donor Organ Transplantation in Europe: Re-Evaluating its Role' (1998) 5 *European Journal of Health Law* 19 at 22–7.

[111] This ethical maxim is widely believed to have emanated from the Hippocratic Oath, when in fact it is to be found in the Hippocratic corpus rather than the Oath itself. Moreover, as Beauchamp and Childress note, the maxim has become confused with another imperative to be found in that corpus: 'At least, do no harm' (see Beauchamp and Childress, *Principles of Biomedical Ethics*, at 189). Nevertheless, the Oath itself does contain duties of both beneficence and non-maleficence generally.

> operated on to save others'. Others took a less extreme position and suggested that 'do no harm' often represents and requires a risk/benefit assessment. In this view 'do no harm' really means to benefit the patient as much as possible while doing as little harm as possible to others.[112]

Applied rigidly, therefore, this maxim would preclude participation in non-therapeutic medical research and even blood donation, let alone the donation of a solid organ for transplantation. However, as Burgio observes,

> In our age, organ transplants from living donors have occasionally given a strong impulse towards reconsidering the ancient doctrine of 'do no harm', since living organ donation is considered acceptable and is tolerated. However, it must be evaluated with a particularly careful and critical assessment of the risk (or cost)/benefit balance. Yet there are some European countries and even some American transplant centers, including Pittsburgh, which tend not to perform living donor operations precisely for fear of violating the 'do no harm' rule.[113]

Caplan notes that individuals are typically either 'absolutists' or 'proportionists' with regard to risk taking for others, with the latter undeniably in the ascendancy.[114] The test has generally been reformulated today as a duty to balance the risks and benefits.[115] In other words, the principle of non-maleficence is not absolute and requires to be weighed against the duty of beneficence and respect for autonomy. But how exactly does such balancing occur and what exactly is being balanced? Jonsen has suggested four possible interpretations of the maxim, the last of which, the 'benefit–detriment' equation, is most suited to the living donation context, that is 'do no harm unless that harm is necessarily associated with a compensating benefit'.[116] But Jonsen explicitly appreciates that the most difficult

[112] M. Siegler, 'Liver Transplantation Using Living Donors' (1992) 24 *Transplantation Proceedings* 2223 at 2223.

[113] G. Burgio, '"Primum Non Nocere" ("Above all, do no Harm"), Today' in G. Burgio and J. Lantos (eds.), *Primum Non Nocere Today*, Elsevier Science BV, Amsterdam, 1994, at 4.

[114] A. Caplan, 'Am I My Brother's Keeper?' (1993) 27 *Suffolk University Law Review* 1195 at 1198–9.

[115] R. Gillon, '"Primum Non Nocere" and the Principle of Non-Maleficence' (1985) 291 *British Medical Journal* 130 at 131.

[116] A. Jonsen, 'Do No Harm' (1978) 88(6) *Annals of Internal Medicine* 827. This category is most appropriate because these are not merely cases where one *risks* harm in search of benefit where the straightforward 'risk/benefit' evaluation is applicable, but instances where a detriment is necessarily caused to this same end, as for instance where a patient consents to the amputation of a gangrenous leg.

cases to fit into this 'felicific calculus' are cases in which the benefit accrues to one party and the detriment to another.[117] Although some generalisations might be appropriate, such as with regard to the type of organ to be donated or the tissue match/compatibility between classes of donors and recipients,[118] the assessment must of necessity be an individualistic one based on the circumstances of each specific case. For example, some donors are at specific risk, that is additional risks over and above the norm, for example because of age, elevated blood pressure, etc.

It might be suggested though that all one need do is weigh the potential benefits to the recipient against the potential and actual harms to the (living) donor. However, as we have already seen, most reject a simple utilitarian 'weighing process' because of the undue jeopardy placed on donors. Public policy does not tolerate the taking of risks beyond a certain threshold no matter what the anticipated benefit to the recipient. Nonetheless, one cannot realistically sever the detrimental impact upon the donor from the expected benefit to the recipient, and there is indeed the nucleus of a utilitarian appraisal in the contemporary consensus that the benefits to the recipient should outweigh, if not easily outweigh, the likelihood of harms to the donor, that is the proportionalist philosophy.[119] The Ethical Committee of UNOS remarked during the nineties that 'Transplantation of a lung or liver segment to a paediatric recipient from a living-related donor is likely to be lifesaving. In that sense the donation *justifies an increased risk to the donor*'(my emphasis).[120] On this view, if a procedure is anticipated to be life-saving then greater risks may be taken. In so far as kidney transplantation is rarely life-saving today, as opposed to leading to an improved quality of life, then it is justified because the general risks to donors as a whole are only modest. Although living liver segment donation is more risky than renal donation it is very frequently life-saving, in particular for paediatric recipients. The Council of Europe Recommendation on Living Related Liver Transplantation

[117] Ibid.

[118] But see section on unrelated donors in chapter 8.

[119] The Law Reform Commission of Canada preferred the latter, that is that 'likely benefits to the recipient must *considerably outweigh* the likely harms to the donor' (my emphasis): *Procurement and Transfer*, at 48. Caplan describes the proportionist stance as being that the benefits must be so certain and of a kind that *manifestly outweigh* the risks of harm: see Caplan, 'Am I My Brother's Keeper?', at 1199.

[120] 'Ethics of Organ Transplantation from Living Donors' (1992) 24 *Transplantation Proceedings* 2236 at 2236.

states that at present such a procedure should be considered only for children.[121] This would appear to be because the risks to donors donating to other adults, owing to the quantity (at least half) of liver having to be removed, cannot justify the risks no matter what the plight of the patient.[122] Living lung lobe donation is rather more problematic because not only are the risks to donors substantial and not fully known, but there are generally *two* donors involved, not just one. In fact, it has been remarked that it is the only procedure potentially having a 300 per cent mortality rate! However, Mason and McCall Smith highlight the fact that, due to the increasing technological capacities of medicine, this 'equation' is constantly changing with regard to all organ donation procedures.[123] Amongst other things, this assessment highlights the fact that any clear division between non-regenerative donation and regenerative donation is too bright and unreliable. As Kennedy and Grubb note, the distinction is intended to reflect the fact that non-regenerative organ donation typically poses greater potential risks to the donor.[124] However, segmental liver donation is a widely used procedure these days although it creates significant risks for donors – yet it is regenerative tissue and a more hazardous procedure than removal of a single, non-regenerative kidney.

A *de facto* line would seem to have arisen in practice in most jurisdictions, permitting living renal (single kidney) donation, and possibly also liver segment or even lung lobe transplants to relatives, but rejecting, for example, living cornea donation (unless removal occurred for therapeutic reasons) and whole liver/heart donation. This accords with the view expressed by the Law Commission that where consent existed, 'English law now treats as lawful operative procedures designed to remove

[121] Council of Europe Recommendation No. R(97) 16 of the Committee of Ministers to Member States on Liver Transplantation from Living Related Donors, at (i).

[122] Although in fact one or two procedures have been carried out involving adults, in Britain and Japan, with no detrimental consequences: see 'A Daughter's Gift to her Mother', *Daily Telegraph*, 15 December 1998, describing a procedure carried out at the King's College Hospital in London involving a twenty-year-old daughter donating to her 43-year-old mother.

[123] J. Mason and A. McCall Smith, *Law and Medical Ethics*, 4th edn, Butterworths, London, 1994, at 294. They comment that 'the starting-point must be the principle that no person is to be deemed capable of consenting to his being killed or seriously injured. The living donation of a heart is thereby precluded. This, of course, is the extreme case and, beyond it, legality would depend upon the presumed risk–benefit ratio involved in the procedure': ibid.

[124] I. Kennedy and A. Grubb, *Medical Law: Text with Materials*, 2nd edn, Butterworths, London, 1994, at 1085.

regenerative tissue, and also non-regenerative tissue that is not essential for life.'[125] This statement would, if taken literally, in actual fact cover not only both liver segmental (regenerative tissue) and lobar lung procedures, but even corneal (not essential for life) donation, although not of course whole liver or lung or heart donation.

Crossing the threshold

Although, as we have seen, legislative measures frequently stipulate a maximum limit upon donor risk taking, they are typically silent on the degree of anticipated *benefit* to the recipient required. In Colombia though, one of paired organs may only be donated whilst the donor is alive where the 'purpose is a transplantation that is indispensable from the therapeutic standpoint',[126] which might be taken to mean that otherwise the recipient would die. Another exception is Belgian law, which stipulates with respect to non-regenerable organs or tissues that the recipient's life must be endangered before LDT is permitted.[127] Pitching the expected benefit so high would repeatedly jeopardise living *renal* transplantation today though, due to the availability of dialysis.

Risk/benefit balancing is even more infrequently alluded to explicitly in legislation, although any provisions specifying a threshold anticipated benefit need to be read in conjunction with the maximum extent of permissible risk taking by donors. However, Dutch law states that if it may reasonably be supposed that organ removal will have lasting effects on the health of the donor over his lifetime, the removal may not be performed unless the future recipient of the removed organ is 'in danger of losing his life and if this danger may not be as readily averted in any other way'.[128] The effect of this provision would seem to be that whilst living renal, and living liver segment (because of the liver's regenerative properties), donation would be permissible even where the patient's life was not immediately at risk, living lung segment donation would not be because of the permanent loss of pulmonary reserve.

[125] Law Commission, *Consent in the Criminal Law*, at para. 8.32.

[126] Decree of 6 June 1989, Section 24.

[127] Law of 13 June 1986, Section 6.

[128] Law of 24 May 1996, Article 3(3). Slovakian law requires that a special advisory committee determine that the benefits to the recipient outweigh any detriment to the donor: see Law of 24 August 1994, Section 46.

Benefit for the donor

The LRC would require that some (reasonably expected) benefit attach *to the donor* as well as to the recipient. It asserted that 'Commonly accepted biomedical principles [also] suggest that the donor should gain from the sacrifice, through the prevention of foreseeable harm or the acquisition of benefit.'[129] But is such a benefit really an independent ethical and legal *precondition*? Whilst benefit must be intended, this is to the recipient rather than to the donor – (psychological/emotional) benefit to the donor is seemingly an incidental feature, in the same way that, during evaluation and work-up, factors affecting the donor's health may incidentally be exposed.

It is suggested that benefit to the donor is not a separate requirement for competent adult donors, although it should be for minors or mentally incapacitated adults, discussed more fully in a subsequent chapter. It is subsumed within the requirement of informed consent. The competent potential donor can protect his own bodily integrity. An insistence on a benefit accruing would invoke value judgements about what constitutes an appropriate 'benefit' here. Kennedy and Grubb also doubt a requirement of benefit to the donor and suggest that what is really required is that there be no serious risk to the donor's health or life, rather than any positive benefit.[130] But this is subsumed within the risk/benefit weighing process discussed above.

Of course, such psychological fulfilment will often be an important, if not pivotal, motivational force for the donor. Moreover, none of this is to deny the attainment of benefit by donors *in fact*. As the King's Fund Report states,

> However, although doctors' reluctance can be appreciated, can we be sure that there is no benefit at all to the donor? Recent conceptualisations of health include many more dimensions than simply the absence of symptoms, or the adequate functioning of limbs and organs. Psychological health is also important and there is evidence that health as measured on these less objective grounds is improved by the act of donation. Indeed, it would be surprising, and worrying, if this were not the case for it would imply that the donors were not doing what they really wanted. If they are,

[129] Law Reform Commission of Canada, *Procurement and Transfer*, at 47.
[130] Kennedy and Grubb, *Medical Law: Text with Materials*, at 1085.

> then it seems that the original principle [*primum non nocere*], though stretched a little more, is still intact.[131]

What the suggestion of required donor benefit does do though is highlight the fact that the perceptions and feelings of the donor are themselves factors which form part of the assessment of risk versus benefit in the donor's decision to consent or otherwise. Whilst stipulations attaching to the required relationship between the parties may also attempt to reflect this anticipated level of benefit, this is too crude and generalised an indicator.

Autonomy versus paternalism

Whilst the surgeon must be convinced that the proposed procedure satisfies the risk/benefit assessment, a substantial degree of latitude needs to be afforded to the prospective donors. An initial risk/benefit assessment can only ensure that the procedure falls within the broad parameters of permissible intervention. This is merely the first stage in the assessment process. Spital alleges that 'Since the earliest days of living kidney donation, transplant centers have generally acted paternalistically, deciding whether or not the chance of benefiting the recipient is worth the risk to the donor.'[132] In theory there is a danger that if one allows clinicians to balance up the risks/harms against the expected benefits it will become a crude utilitarian exercise where the interests of the donor typically become subjugated to those of the recipient. In reality, the greater likelihood is that clinicians will tend towards an opposite, and unduly conservative/cautious, posture. Yet, as we have seen, the weighing of risks and benefits can be properly evaluated only by the individual who is affected by the outcome, the donor. It is not an *objective* matter. As a consequence, notions of 'proportionality' have a rather hollow ring. As Caplan rightly observes, 'No universal magic number or ratio exists such that the proportionality of risk to benefit can be shown to be satisfied.'[133] Moreover, he argues that the extent to which the potential psychological

131 King's Fund Institute Report, *A Question of Give and Take*, Research Report 18, King's Fund Institute, London, 1994, at 67.

132 A. Spital, 'The Ethics of Unconventional Living Organ Donation' (1991) 5 *Clinical Transplantation* 322 at 323.

133 Caplan, 'Am I My Brother's Keeper?', at 1202. He adds that 'Proportionality cannot be assessed without some attention to the responsibilities and duties which adhere to the relationships and bonds that tie prospective donors and recipients together': ibid., at 1203.

rewards are 'worth it' must be for the *donor* to weigh in deciding whether to donate. It is a private, personal and subjective assessment, involving emotional and psychological characteristics including the relationship and ties with the recipient, not amenable to evaluation by clinicians. Spital states:

> Thus, living organ donation has always posed the difficult question of how to determine whether the benefit to the recipient is worth the risk to the donor. This determination has traditionally been made by physicians, occasionally with the help of ethicists. I believe that this approach is misguided. Balancing the risks and benefits of a proposed living donor transplant is a burdensome responsibility for physicians that should not be delegated to them alone.
>
> Indeed, the critical question is not how we decide, but rather who should decide.[134]

Living organ donation presents the difficulty that, whilst it is appropriate for risk/benefit balancing to be carried out for the transplant *recipient*, involving fairly standard features of clinical decision-making, the position of the donor is not analogous because the donor's decision is inevitably intertwined with the recipient's position and with factors unrelated to the medical condition or health of the donor him/herself. To refuse donor X involves a potential denial of treatment to individual Y and may itself also cause (emotional) harm to donor X. The United States Task Force on Organ Transplantation stated that 'Refusing to use a kidney from a competent living donor is unduly paternalistic where a donor is well informed, understands, and is willing to accept the risks of kidney donation.'[135] Spital has stated:

> When, because of the risk involved, we physicians reject competent, altruistic donors whose desire to donate is strong, whom are we really protecting? I suggest that under these circumstances, although well-intentioned, we are primarily protecting ourselves – we are defending and imposing our own values rather than empathising with those of the donor. Yet it is the donor who is most affected by the decision and the one who will live with the outcome.[136]

[134] A. Spital, 'Living Organ Donation: Shifting Responsibility' (1991) 151 *Archives of Internal Medicine* 234 at 234.

[135] *Report of the Task Force on Organ Transplantation: Issues and Recommendations*, US Dept of Health and Human Services, Washington D.C., 1986, at 37.

[136] Spital, 'Shifting Responsibility', at 234.

Potential living donors typically come forward only in circumstances of extreme need and clear commitment. They should be entitled to be involved in the process of decision-making. This is not to deny the physician or surgeon a decision-making role of his or her own, merely to be respectful of a potential donor's wishes.

In view of the non-therapeutic character of the procedure, one would not deny the right of an individual clinician to 'object out' of LDT. Moreover, to suggest that donors' autonomy should be given greater application does not imply that there is a legal 'right to donate'. There is no person with any correlative duty (applying Hohfeldian theories of rights creating reciprocal duties) to remove an organ (even assuming the clinician is competent to perform such a procedure) nor any duty upon a recipient to accept an organ from any particular donor. Childress states that 'the physician has no moral duty to satisfy the patient's desires if he finds them incompatible with acceptable medical practice'.[137] Spital contends that if, despite these considerations, the centre still feels unable to accept the individual, it has an obligation to give reasons and to tell him/her that not all centres share the same views, and to offer the donor a referral to another centre for a second opinion.[138]

Subsidiarity

If sufficient cadaveric organs were available for transplantation and LDT failed to offer at least equally good prospective results, LDT would fail to satisfy the ethical principle of *equipoise*.[139] To offer an inferior therapy to a patient is ethically indefensible and breaches the legal duty of care owed by the doctor to the patient; an action would lie for negligence/malpractice. It might also result in legal liability to the *donor* who has made a sacrifice which was either unnecessary or unacceptable. McK Norrie states:

> If a donation is taken from the body of a living person, then it is probably the case that the surgeon doing so has a duty to ensure that there is a real need for the donation and that the transplantation has a real and acceptable

137 J. Childress, *Who Should Decide? Paternalism in Health Care*, Oxford University Press, New York, 1982, at 3.

138 Spital, 'The Ethics of Unconventional', at 324.

139 A principle applied widely in the field of research ethics: see for example P. Singer *et al.*, 'Equipoise and the Ethics of Segmental Liver Transplantation' (1988) 36 *Clinical Research* 539.

> chance of success. Thus, the surgeon owes a duty to the donor as much as to the recipient to try all other methods of cure before attempting transplantation and to ensure that the donation itself is suitable enough to provide an acceptable chance of success, and, if the donor is thereby substantially injured for what turns out to be no justifiable reason, then he may claim damages.[140]

Similarly, in view of the application of the ethical principle of *primum non nocere* here, if cadaveric sources of organs are available and would produce *equally efficacious results*, they should be preferred to those from living donors because of the duty of non-maleficence owed to the latter.

In this sense then, LDT may be perceived as an acceptable *supplement* to cadaver donation where certain conditions are met,[141] that is an *ultimum remedium*.[142] In other words, all things being equal one should utilise a deceased rather than a living donor. Belgian law stipulates, for instance, that LDT may be performed only 'if the transplantation of organs or tissues from a deceased person could not produce an equally satisfactory result'.[143] The Third WHO Guiding Principle appears to express this same stance in the statement that 'Organs for transplantation should be removed preferably from the bodies of deceased persons.' Similarly, the Council of Europe Convention states that 'Removal of organs or tissue from a living person for transplantation purposes may be carried out solely for the therapeutic benefit of the recipient *and where there is no suitable organ or tissue available from a deceased person and no other alternative method of comparable effectiveness*' (my emphasis).[144] Thus, if a cadaveric organ were available and LDT offered similar *but no better* prospects, there would be no ethical justification for proceeding with the use of a living donor. However, things are in fact very rarely equal. Although there is an imperative for an individual assessment in each case, in view of the importance of tissue compatibility, in fact LDT

[140] See K. McK Norrie, 'Human Tissue Transplants: Legal Liability in Different Jurisdictions' (1985) 34 *International and Comparative Legal Quarterly* 442 at 444.

[141] This is sometimes expressed as the *subsidiarity* principle: see C. Casabona, 'Legal Issues Concerning the Living Donor and Some Criteria for Harmonised European Legislation' in D. Price and J. Akveld (eds.), *Living Organ Donation in the Nineties: European Medico-Legal Perspectives*, EUROTOLD, 1996, 139 at 146.

[142] This finds expression in the statements in the WHO Guiding Principles and the Council of Europe Convention that the use of cadaver donors is 'preferable' to the use of living donors.

[143] Law of 1986, section 6.

[144] Council of Europe Convention on Human Rights and Biomedicine, Article 19.

results are invariably superior to cadaver transplantation across the board at the present time.

The situation is different where LDT *is* the best therapeutic alternative for the recipient. Although views differ, even where sufficient cadaver organs are available to satisfy demand without a significant waiting time, there is a substantial minority view amongst clinicians that living renal donation should still continue in exceptional cases where outstanding results are anticipated. Koene, for example, asserts that 'even if there were no organ shortage at all, it would still be justifiable to transplant kidneys from completely HLA-identical family donors, because the results in this specific group are so outstanding'.[145] This would be both ethically, and usually legally,[146] acceptable. The patient is being offered the optimum therapy in the circumstances. The necessity for such an enhanced anticipated outcome is embedded in certain legislative provisions relating to LDT. Slovenian law declares that LDT *must* assure 'much better possibilities of medical treatment as another form of substitute medical treatment for the final failure of kidneys or liver'. The commentary to the Draft Council of Europe Protocol says that the intention behind the provision in the Convention (and reiterated in the Protocol) is that organs and tissues should be removed from deceased rather than living donors whenever possible, that is where an appropriate cadaver organ is available, and that living donation should remain an 'exceptional procedure'.[147] It adds though that if the results of transplantation from a living donor are expected to be *significantly better* than from a cadaver donor then living donation is the preferred therapeutic option in the circumstances. These provisions emphasise the need for a *clear advantage* to justify LDT.

Of course the above discussion has revolved essentially around living *renal* donors where the risks to donors are modest. There are many who would adapt this ethical assessment in the context of *non-renal* donation where the risks to donors are higher. Some would insist that the possibility of a cadaveric transplant had been completely ruled out. The Council of

145 R. Koene, 'Long Term Clinical and Ethical Issues in Living Organ Donation' in Price and Akveld, *Living Organ Donation in the Nineties*, 33 at 35.

146 One or two policy directives and laws mandate that 'substantially better' outcomes be likely to ensue before LDT is permissible: for example, 'far more advantageous' in Guideline 8 of 1979 Council of Europe Recommendation No. R(79) and 'much better possibilities' in Article 8 of the 1996 Law in Slovenia.

147 Draft Additional Protocol to the Convention, commentary to Article 9, at para. 54.

Europe Living Related Liver Transplantation Recommendation states that 'LRLT should be considered only when there is a shortage of cadaver organs, that is when alternatives that do not carry the risks incurred by a living donor have been exhausted.'[148] In other words, regardless of the comparative results from living as opposed to cadaveric liver donation, wherever a cadaver liver exists it should be used in preference to the living donor organ segment in view of the significant risks attached to its removal. The Recommendation states that other alternatives must have been exhausted before living donation is considered and the patient should remain on the cadaver waiting list in case a cadaveric liver becomes available. A similar approach might be adopted vis-à-vis lobar lung donation. Mason and McCall Smith, for instance, contend that because of the relative risks and benefits of living lung donation it should probably be used only as a supplement to cadaveric donation, by which they probably mean where a cadaveric transplant is not a feasible option.[149] But if significantly improved outcomes *are* anticipated from the use of a living donor, some would argue that a potential donor should be permitted to accept such a risk. Indeed, the Slovenian law set out above clearly contemplates this as regards liver segment donation. Any cadaveric organ could then be employed elsewhere and potentially save another life.

The justifications for LDT are the very good results typically achieved and/or the shortage of cadaveric, and other sources of, organs. Skegg commented (in the British context) in the eighties that 'as there is a shortage of kidneys for transplantation, and as transplants from living donors are at least as successful as those from cadavers, the courts may be expected to accept that there is a "just cause or excuse" or "good reasons" for such operations'.[150] Thus, one needs to 'factor in' the time scale of the availability of other therapeutic options, that is of a cadaveric organ becoming available. There will be an anticipated waiting period for a cadaveric organ in most regions due to the existing waiting list for transplantation. This is itself a significant burden to be weighed together with the eventual cadaveric transplant and affects how one contrasts the therapeutic benefits to be anticipated from the respective forms of transplantation. Skegg stated that in Britain 'A court is not likely to inquire closely into whether there are good reasons for a particular intervention.

[148] Liver Transplantation from Living Related Donors, Recommendation No. R(97) 16 at (i).
[149] Mason and McCall Smith, *Law and Medical Ethics*, at 294.
[150] Skegg, *Law, Ethics and Medicine*, at 43.

There is no danger of a court attempting to decide whether there were good reasons for removing a kidney from a living donor, instead of keeping the patient on dialysis in the hope that a suitable cadaver kidney would become available.'[151] The patient will suffer a decreased quality of life during the wait, even when on kidney dialysis, and the wait may even compromise, wholly or partially, any ultimate transplantation. Thus, as well as almost universally poorer results from cadaveric organs, there are other increased costs associated with a cadaveric transplant.

By contrast with living renal donation, other than for patients with an extremely labile diabetes leading to unavoidable severe hypoglycaemic attacks, pancreatic grafting is not obviously the optimum procedure and is not life-saving either. Although better graft survival rates are achieved using living rather than cadaveric donors, there is a high technical failure rate with the procedure (higher than using a cadaveric donor) and inevitably significant risks to living pancreatic donors. In the light of the fact that there is no shortage of cadaver pancreas donors in most parts of the world, many take the view that the use of living pancreatic donors is not presently ethically acceptable.

Availability

The exercise of comparing expected outcomes from various therapies therefore also implicates the issue of the 'availability' of alternative therapies when comparing anticipated outcomes from differing therapies. This is in fact a more delicate and complicated issue than would at first appear, one often lacking transparency. Laws implicitly raise this issue of *availability* of a cadaver organ transplant but it is generally unclear whether the provisions refer to a general theoretical comparison of outcomes using cadaveric as opposed to living donors (*in abstracto*), or to a comparison between the expected outcome from a living donor presently offering to donate and any cadaveric donor organ that is *currently* available (*in concreto*).[152] There are also both spatial and temporal issues implicated here. Nys enquires over what radius we should be assessing availability in this context. Locally? Globally?[153] One should

[151] Ibid., at 36.

[152] This problem arises directly under the 1986 Law in Belgium for instance.

[153] See H. Nys, 'Desirable Characteristics of Living Donation Transplant Legislation' in Price and Akveld, *Living Organ Donation in the Nineties*, 127 at 134.

presumably consider normal distribution patterns and policies which may sometimes be multinational, for example within Eurotransplant.

The Council of Europe Convention refers to there being 'no suitable organ or tissue available from a deceased person' for the purposes of comparison. This would appear to focus attention on the intended time of the organ removal and transplantation. The recently enacted German transplant law makes this explicit, stipulating that living organ donation is permissible only where a suitable organ from a cadaver organ 'is not available at the time when the organ removal takes place'. Where this is the approach adopted then a definite (*in concreto*) comparison of anticipated outcomes may be carried out. However, a cadaver organ is rarely *immediately* available even in a region where overall there is no shortage of cadaver organs to meet the demand, and even taking into account the period of work-up time required for a living donation. This is due not only to waiting list sizes but also to organ distribution practices and the partial precedence given to patients with the longest waiting time.[154] Consequently, if availability is interpreted narrowly (to mean *immediately* available), the removal from a living donor would presumably and necessarily satisfy this condition even where enough cadaver organs existed generally to meet demand. However, even if a broader view were taken, and where there was a general sufficiency of cadaveric organs in the region concerned, a transplant would sometimes be immediately required and a living donor source would *have* to be used due to the absence of a cadaveric organ there and then, for instance for an end-stage renal patient who can no longer tolerate dialysis, or for a patient who is suffering terminal hepatic failure where a transplant is essential to safeguard life.

It may be generally preferable though to have regard to the anticipated length of waiting time, especially as it is the absence of the additional burden of waiting which gives living donors the edge where results are not significantly superior (where they are superior this is irrelevant, as regards kidneys). Waiting time is dependent upon the size of the waiting list as well as other factors specific to the individual, for example the patient's blood group or tissue type.[155] For this reason, LDT decisions are always *individual* decisions, not blanket policy initiatives. Slovenian law states

[154] See chapter 10 on allocation issues for further discussion of such factors.

[155] In Norway, for instance, waiting time overall for transplant in 1995 was eight months. However, for patients with blood group A it was less than four months whilst for patients

that LDT is permissible only 'where it is not possible to get a cadaver within a reasonable time'.[156] The 'reasonable time' here should be a function not just of length of time but of the medical need and quality of life of the patient. The *burden* of waiting times differs from patient to patient and from area to area also; for example, in Norway the burden is especially heavy in view of the distance to travel for dialysis treatment because of the drastic effect on normal lifestyle and quality of life. Some patients also tolerate dialysis better than others. Thus, 'availability' will often consist of an amalgam of hypothetical (*in abstracto*), but *feasible*, comparable outcomes, that is a prediction.

Least restrictive alternative

In practice, most renal transplant centres will consider LDT only after the patient has had a period on dialysis and after a period of time has elapsed on the cadaver transplant waiting list without success. EUROTOLD discovered that such time periods vary markedly from centre to centre.[157] In practice, the decision is often made to refuse to allow a donor to donate where the waiting time is not perceived as 'unacceptable'. However, waiting time is not only a factor influencing clinical judgement, it is also a factor to be 'weighed' by the potential donor in deciding whether to donate and by the recipient in formulating treatment preferences.

Linked to the above, the generally accepted criterion that the therapy (LDT) be the 'least drastic alternative' in the circumstances is often inappropriately married with the idea that it is acceptable only once all other therapies have been attempted, that is as a 'last resort'. Giesen states: 'It would seem that both donor and recipient have the right to expect that the surgeon has made sure that the transplant is absolutely necessary and is only performed after all other methods of treatment have failed.'[158] In Argentina it is stated that LDT is to be used only 'where other means have

with blood group O it was ten months. See A. Jakobsen, 'Living Donor Practices and Processes in Europe' in Price and Akveld, *Living Organ Donation in the Nineties*, 1 at 7.

[156] 1996 Law, Article 8. The Dutch Health Council states that LDT is permissible if no cadaveric organ appears likely to become available 'in the near future': see Gezondheidsraad, *General Transplantation Problems*, The Hague, 1988, at 125.

[157] EUROTOLD Project Management Group Report to the European Commission of the European Communities (ed. P. Donnelly and D. Price), *Questioning Attitudes to Living Donor Transplantation*, EUROTOLD, 1997, at 128–9.

[158] Giesen, *International Medical Malpractice Law*, at 608.

been exhausted or are insufficient, or if they do not constitute an appropriate therapeutic solution for a particular patient'.[159] But would one have to wait indefinitely for a cadaver organ before it could be said that that therapy has 'failed' or 'been exhausted'? To require the transplant to be absolutely necessary would often be to let the patient deteriorate to the point where the condition has become imminently life threatening and where the transplant can be expected to produce significantly less potential gain (indeed a futile transplant would be both unethical and illegal). This is implicitly conceded in the Living Related Liver Transplantation Recommendation which permits a living donor to be used where 'it is unlikely that a suitable cadaveric liver will become available within the required timescale'. LDT may therefore be obviously the 'best' available therapy and 'necessary' despite the fact that all other therapies have not been attempted.[160] A discussion has arisen in the context of living lobar lung donation, which has traditionally been confined to extremely sick patients with an imminently terminal prognosis, as to whether it should also be offered to less sick patients whose outcome with such a transplant can be expected to be even more beneficial and successful.[161]

[159] Law of 24 March 1993, section 2. The last part of the section may, however, provide a 'release valve' from such a dilemma.

[160] Moreover, pre-dialysis LDT has even been described as the 'gold standard' for transplantation as it is so effective: see P. Donnelly *et al.*, 'Pre-Dialysis Living Donor Transplantation: Is it still the "Gold Standard" for Cost, Convenience and Graft Survival?' (1995) 27 *Transplantation Proceedings* 1444.

[161] See V. Starnes *et al.*, 'Living-Donor Lobar Lung Transplantation Experience: Intermediate Results' (1996) 112(5) *Journal of Thoracic and Cardiovascular Surgery* 1284 at 1289.

7

Informed consent to living organ donation

Assuming no public interest exists condemning the particular form of living organ donation concerned, the primary ethical issue relates to the autonomous nature of the consent given by the donor.[1] Gutmann and Gerok have commented that 'The main concern of international legislation in living organ donation is to ensure that informed consent to the removal is voluntarily given by the potential donor.'[2] Both these items (informedness and voluntariness) evoke especially problematic issues in the context of living donor transplantation (LDT). It has been observed that 'Psychoanalytic theory suggests that when confronted with inescapable conflictual situations of great stress, people revert to earlier modes of thinking and feeling, and become less intellectually autonomous, less reasonable and more vulnerable to coercion.'[3] There is no doubting that the patent suffering of a relative or other 'cared-for' individual in particular generates an enormously stressful decision-making environment. Even the 'search' for a related donor has itself been shown frequently to generate significant stress in the family as a whole.[4] Even more fundamentally, the nature of most decision-making in this sphere challenges the legal and ethical framework itself, based on an individualistic, rational model of decision-making. Majeske, Parker and Frader allege that

[1] The *capacity* of the donor to make the decision here will be assumed. The position of donors lacking decision-making capacity is considered in the following chapter.

[2] T. Gutmann and B. Gerok, 'International Legislation in Living Organ Donation' in G. Collins, J. Dubernard, W. Land and G. Persijn (eds.), *Procurement, Preservation and Allocation of Vascularized Organs*, Kluwer, Dordrecht, 1997, 317 at 317.

[3] B. Zeichner, 'The Role of Unconscious Conflict in Informed Consent' (1985) 13(3) *Bulletin of the American Academy of Psychiatry and Law* 283 at 286.

[4] R. Simmons *et al.*, 'Family Tension in the Search for a Kidney Donor' (1971) 215 *Journal of the American Medical Association* 909.

> The traditional requirements of informed consent do not appear well suited to evaluations of living related donors' decision making, however, with its frequent emphasis on feelings of relatedness, interconnectedness, and obligation – a sharp contrast to the unpressured, rational decision making typically said to underlie informed consent . . . The traditional model of informed consent is based on an impartialist understanding of the requirements of autonomy that de-emphasises personal relationships so that each decision maker is conceived as being free to pursue autonomous goals.[5]

Indeed, observational studies have led to allegations that informed consent in this context is no more than a 'myth'. Various alternative ethical frameworks have been advanced, including an 'ethic of care' approach.

There are issues of both form and substance here, relating not only to the subject-matter of information disclosure, but also to the manner in which consent was given and to how the initial decision to donate was arrived at in the first place.[6] The Council of Europe Convention prescribes that an express consent to LDT must have been given either in written form or before an official body,[7] and most jurisdictions have written consent requirements in legislation[8] and some have additional requirements relating to witnesses[9] or for consent to be given before an official such as a notary.[10] French law for instance requires that the donor must express consent before the Presiding Judge (or other designated judge) of

[5] R. Majeske, L. Parker and J. Frader, 'In Search of an Ethical Framework for Consideration of Decisions Regarding Live Donation' in B. Spielman (ed.), *Organ and Tissue Donation: Ethical, Legal and Policy Issues*, Southern Illinois University Press, Carbondale, 1997, 89 at 95.

[6] Some laws require that at least twenty-four hours have elapsed between the obtaining of the consent and the removal of the organ, for example in Spain and most of the states and territories of Australia.

[7] Council of Europe Convention for the Protection of Human Rights and Dignity of the Human Being with Regard to the Application of Biology and Medicine (Convention on Human Rights and Biomedicine), 1996, Article 19(2).

[8] There is legislation to this effect in Algeria, Belgium, Bolivia, Bulgaria, Costa Rica, Cyprus, Denmark, Finland, Germany, Greece, Hungary, Italy, Lebanon, Luxembourg, Mexico, the Netherlands, Norway, Panama, the Philippines, Poland, Queensland, Romania, the Russian Federation, the Slovak Republic, Slovenia, South Africa, South Australia, Spain, Sri Lanka, Sweden, the Syrian Arab Republic, Tasmania, Turkey, Venezuela, Vietnam, Western Australia and Zimbabwe. Even in the absence of legislation, an *express* consent would undoubtedly be legally required: see R. Adams, 'Live Organ Donors and Informed Consent: A Difficult Minuet' (1987) 8(4) *Journal of Legal Medicine* 555 at 564.

[9] There is legislation on this subject in Belgium (one witness), Algeria, Costa Rica, Mexico, the Philippines, Romania and Venezuela (two witnesses).

[10] In Bolivia, Ecuador (or alternatively a judge), Hungary and Venezuela.

the *tribunal de grande instance*.[11] In a minority of jurisdictions, the approval of an independent body must be obtained.[12] Such formalities attempt not only to ensure the genuineness of the decision, but also to emphasise its importance and the need for prior deliberation.

Informedness

The difficulties attendant upon the notion of 'informed' consent in this context mesh issues relating to the content, manner, timing and sources of information disclosure to potential living donors and their actual understanding of such information.

General principles of law relating to therapeutic procedures across all jurisdictions insist that a certain degree of knowledge be disclosed by health care professionals in order to avoid civil, and possibly also criminal, proceedings. Generally, patients must be informed, in broad terms, concerning the *nature* of the intended procedure in order to avoid an action for battery in common law, or delict in civil law, jurisdictions. Further, a failure to disclose information about risks, alternative treatments, the prognosis in the absence of any treatment, etc., may also give rise to a potential action for negligence/malpractice or delict. The application of general legal principles of law to LDT is not straightforward though, by virtue of the fact that the prospective donor is a 'volunteer' engaging in procedures whose primary purpose is to benefit another rather than him- or herself.[13] However, most states have legislation which incorporates specific information disclosure requirements for living donors and often contains sanctions for failure to adhere to its provisions,[14] although in some instances such legislation merely stipulates that consent must be obtained, leaving the issue of the content of information

[11] Law of 29 July 1994, Article L.671–3. In Greece, the declaration of willingness must be made in notarial form or on a form upon which the police authority has verified the authenticity of the signature, or orally, the declaration being recorded in a special register kept by the treatment establishment. In Spain, consent must be given in the presence of a magistrate, and all interested parties must sign.

[12] In Finland approval must be given by the National Board of Health, in the Slovak Republic by a special advisory committee and in Syria by a commission consisting of three independent clinicians.

[13] Peter Morris has described it as being 'unique' amongst major surgical procedures: see P. Morris, *Kidney Transplantation: Principles and Practice*, W. B. Saunders, Philadelphia, 1988, at 96.

[14] In many instances these are penal sanctions.

disclosure to be determined by the general law.[15] Where the legislation is explicit though, it varies markedly in terms of the depth and breadth of information required. One or two jurisdictions only have such statutory obligations for 'unrelated donors'.[16] The World Health Organisation Guiding Principles state that 'The donor should be sufficiently informed to be able to understand and weigh the risks, benefits and consequences of consent.'[17] The Council of Europe Draft Protocol reiterates the general provisions of the Convention in this context, namely that the donor should be given appropriate information as to the purpose and nature of any medical intervention as well as on its consequences and risks.[18]

General legal requirements

The organ removal procedure would be viewed, from an ethical and legal perspective, as *non-therapeutic*, and consequently disclosure requirements applicable to therapeutic interventions may not be wholly applicable to this context. McK Norrie has commented

> With the donor it is, however, arguable that a *far stricter* requirement of disclosure is necessary than for the recipient . . . [B]ecause of this, it may be suggested that the information which must be given to the donor should be of the fullest degree possible, rather in the way that the law would demand that medical research volunteers be given the fullest information about the experiments performed upon them, because such activities are not usually undertaken for the direct therapeutic benefit of the volunteer [my emphasis].[19]

In the absence of legislative guidance, the actual depth and breadth of disclosure required in many jurisdictions is less than transparent though.

[15] This would appear to be the case in Ecuador, Peru, the Syrian Arab Republic, Uruguay, Vietnam and Zimbabwe.

[16] For instance, India and the United Kingdom.

[17] World Health Organisation Guiding Principles on Organ Transplantation, 1991, Principle 3.

[18] Draft Additional Protocol to the Convention on Human Rights and Biomedicine, on Transplantation of Organs and Tissues of Human Origin, 9 March 1999, Council of Europe, Article 11. This reiterates Article 19 of the Convention which in turn refers back to Article 5.

[19] K. McK Norrie, 'Human Tissue Transplants: Legal Liability in Different Jurisdictions' (1985) 34 *International and Comparative Law Quarterly* 442 at 452. Giesen states in like vein that 'extensive and detailed information must be required since no therapeutic treatment of him is intended, and thus he will not therapeutically benefit from the operation': D. Giesen, *International Medical Malpractice Law*, Martinus Nijhoff, Dordrecht, 1988, at 609.

Moreover, in common law jurisdictions the question arises whether a battery or a negligence/malpractice action is appropriate for such failures of communication. Giesen opines that 'Failure to disclose all pertinent facts will make the physician liable for breach of duty of care and, as has been shown, for battery in common law jurisdictions.'[20] Although case law relating to non-therapeutic procedures is extremely limited, the Canadian case of *Halushka* v. *University of Saskatchewan*[21] in the analogous context of a non-therapeutic research protocol is instructive. In that case the failure to disclose all material risks led to a successful claim for battery. Despite the judicial antipathy to battery as a cause of action in the medical context, there is much to be said for the view that in the context of non-therapeutic measures the wrong lies in the non-disclosure of information *per se*, rather than in its potentiality for resulting physical harm.[22] The Nuffield Council appeared to share such a view, stating:

> We recommend that those involved in the removal of tissue from donors should ensure that the explanation given to the donor is explicit about the range of intended uses of the tissue and about any risks the donor may incur either in having the tissue removed or as a consequence of its removal. Only on these conditions can the consent of the donor, and hence the procedure itself, be valid.[23]

This nevertheless still begs questions as to the appropriate *standard* of disclosure. In *Halushka* Hall JA stated:

> There can be no exceptions to the ordinary requirements of disclosure in the case of research as there may well be in ordinary medical practice. The researcher does not have to balance the probable lack of treatment against the risk involved in the treatment itself . . . The subject of medical

[20] D. Giesen, 'Civil Liability of Physicians for New Methods of Treatment and Experimentation: A Comparative Examination' [1995] 3 *Medical Law Review* 22 at 46.

[21] (1965) 52 WWR 608.

[22] Battery is of course actionable without proof of any (further) harm, that is *per se*. Indeed, causation would be a major stumbling block if liability was always located in negligence.

[23] Nuffield Council on Bioethics Working Party Report on *Human Tissue: Ethical and Legal Issues*, Nuffield Council on Bioethics, London, 1995, at para. 13.16. It considered that the duty should be equivalent to that stipulated by statute for genetically unrelated donors under the HOTA Regulations. Whilst in *Gold* v. *Haringey Health Authority* [1987] 2 All ER 888 the Court of Appeal applied a negligence analysis to a (contraceptive) procedure dubbed by the trial judge as 'non-therapeutic', the procedure, although 'elective', was intended to benefit only her and her spouse and so did have a therapeutic intention. Similarly, in *Zimmer* v. *Ringrose* considered further on, the Canadian court distinguished *Halushka* (and the battery analysis adopted there) and applied negligence principles to a very similar (contraceptive) context.

> experimentation is entitled to a full and frank disclosure of all the facts, probabilities and options which a reasonable man might be expected to consider before giving his consent.[24]

The implications of such remarks are twofold. First, they suggest that, in this and all other analogous contexts, information should be *full and frank* as regards risks, consequences and alternatives.[25] Secondly, any room for any notion of withholding information based on accepted practice[26] (or even 'therapeutic privilege'[27] or waiver[28]) would appear to be vanishingly small here.[29] The Nuffield Report considered that 'Where the procedure is non-therapeutic, there are not two levels of consent and thus there is no room for medical discretion. Consent must be explicit and all the relevant information must be provided.'[30] Accordingly, the standard for disclosure should be generated by the needs of donors rather than the needs of recipients or the practices or views of clinicians.

In *Halushka* the learned judge adopted a reasonable patient standard to

[24] (1965) 52 WWR 608 at 616.

[25] Giesen states that 'Since research experiments are inherently dangerous and are carried out for the benefit of others, disclosure to the test subject must be "perfect" or "fuller than full" ': see 'Civil Liability of Physicians', at 46. Indeed, most codes addressing non-therapeutic research require full disclosure of information to the subject: see Adams, 'Live Organ Donors and Informed Consent', at 561.

[26] That is, the notion that a doctor cannot be held liable if he adhered to a practice accepted as proper by a responsible body of medical opinion: see *Bolam* v. *Friern Hospital Management Committee* [1957] 1 WLR 582.

[27] Giesen has argued that therapeutic privilege can have no application to purely research procedures: see 'Civil Liability of Physicians', at 50, and this would seem equally pertinent to LDT.

[28] Lord Justice Edmund Davies has stated, extra-judicially, that 'however eager the donor is to play out his self-sacrificial role, the surgeon is under a legal duty to make clear to him the risks involved. He may not want the truth, but in this case the truth must be forced upon him': see Edmund Davies, 'The Patient's Right to Know the Truth' (1973) *Proceedings of the Royal Society of Medicine* 533 at 535.

[29] Skegg has remarked that 'If a doctor involved in renal transplantation failed to disclose the risk of nephrectomy to a potential living donor, before obtaining his consent to the removal of one of his kidneys, a judge would be virtually certain to hold that the doctor was in breach of his duty of care to the donor, even if (which is not the case) the doctor could adduce evidence that his conduct was in accord with a common and professionally approved practice': see P. Skegg, *Law, Ethics and Medicine*, Clarendon Press, Oxford, 1988, at 85.

[30] Nuffield Council, *Human Tissue*, at para. 7.7. The Report cited the example of a volunteer in a research project. The primary objections to providing adequate disclosure to facilitate an informed consent – that patients do not want to know the risks, that they do not properly understand or retain the information, that it may harm the patient physically and psychologically and thus jeopardise medical outcomes, and that it may impair medical decision-making – are all inapplicable to this specific context even assuming they have validity in general.

guide him. Arguably though, as both Picard and Giesen maintain,[31] a *subjective* patient standard would be more appropriate and respecting of patient autonomy in this context, that is what does *this* patient wish to know? Indeed, Kennedy and Grubb state that they have no doubt that in the non-therapeutic context British courts *would* adopt a subjective patient test of materiality as regards the risks of the procedure.[32] This is the test which is pervasive in general across the major civil law jurisdictions and in Australia.[33] For instance, in *Castell* v. *De Greef* (1994)[34] the Supreme Court of South Africa employed the reasonable patient to set an initial standard which was then modified by a subjective patient standard, that is, what additional informational needs of the patient were or should reasonably have been known by the doctor?

In addition to information about uses of the removed tissue and the risks of the procedure, Dickens has opined that donors are entitled to be informed in all instances of the anticipated recovery and rehabilitation process and the expected level of restoration of functional capacity.[35]

Legislative sources

Legislative provisions concerning *depth* rather than breadth of information vary greatly. Whilst some require that donors merely 'be informed' about the prescribed matters, others require that the donor be 'fully informed'[36] or given 'complete information',[37] whilst in still others (as well as under the Council of Europe Convention) 'appropriate' information must be given, for example in Slovenia.[38]

Some statutory provisions merely require information to be trans-

[31] E. Picard, *Legal Liability of Doctors and Hospitals in Canada*, 2nd edn, Carswell, 1984, at 118; Giesen, 'Civil Liability of Physicians', at 34–5.

[32] I. Kennedy and A. Grubb, *Medical Law: Text with Materials*, 2nd edn, Butterworths, London, 1994, at 1057. They rely heavily upon the Canadian case of *Weiss* v. *Soloman* (1989) 48 CCLT 280 (Qu. Sup. Ct) where the highest standards of disclosure were insisted upon. See also B. Freedman and K. Glass, '*Weiss* v. *Soloman*: A Case Study in Institutional Responsibility for Clinical Research' (1990) 18(4) *Law, Medicine and Health Care* 395.

[33] This was the approach adopted by the High Court of Australia in *Rogers* v. *Whitaker* [1993] 4 Medical Law Reports 78.

[34] (1994) (4) SA 408.

[35] See B. Dickens, 'Donation and Transplantation of Organs and Tissues' in I. Kennedy and A. Grubb (eds.), *Principles of Medical Law*, Oxford University Press, Oxford, 1998, at para. 15.50.

[36] E.g. under Slovakian and Bolivian law.

[37] For instance under section 12 of the 1992 Law of the Russian Federation and section 9 of the 1986 Law in Belgium. In Poland the information must be provided 'in detail'.

[38] 1996 Law, Article 10.

mitted as regards the nature of the procedure and its consequences. For instance, Kuwaiti law states that the donor must be informed about the effects on his health that may result from organ removal.[39] Whilst these would probably be taken to include the risks of the procedure, this is made explicit in most jurisdictions.[40] For instance, Polish law states that 'A candidate for a donor must be informed in detail about the intervention, the risk connected with it and any possible typical consequences for his health condition.'[41]

Certain jurisdictions go further than merely requiring *medical* information to be given, and stipulate a broader range of matters requiring communication to the donor.[42] Belgium's Law of 13 June 1986 states, in line with the provisions of the 1978 Council of Europe Resolution,[43] that 'He [the physician who intends to carry out the removal procedure] shall provide clear and complete information to the donor and any persons whose consent is required, on the physical, mental, family, and social effects of the withdrawal.'[44] In Spain,[45] the donor must have been

[39] Decree of 20 December 1987, section 4. In like vein, Cypriot law requires that the donor be informed of the 'medical consequences of removal', 1987 Law, section 7(3).

[40] In one or two other instances though, it is not wholly clear from the provisions themselves whether the 'consequences' are only health-related ones. For instance, Portuguese law states that 'The physician shall inform the donor and recipient in an honest, appropriate and comprehensible manner of the possible risks, the consequences of donation and treatment, and any untoward effects, as well as the precautions to be observed subsequently': see 1993 Law, section 7.

[41] Law of 26 October 1995, Article 9(1)(5). Denmark's transplant legislation mandates that the donor be told of the 'nature of the intervention, its consequences, and the risks', 1990 Law, section 13(3). There are similar provisions in legislation in Bolivia, Costa Rica, Finland, Greece, Hungary, Norway, Panama, the Russian Federation, the Slovak Republic and Sweden.

[42] Outside Europe, Colombian law mandates that the 'donor must have been given prior information on the consequences of his decision to the extent that they are foreseeable from the somatic, mental, and psychological standpoint, and on the possible repercussions that the donation may have for his personal, family, and professional life, as well as on the anticipated benefits of the transplantation for the recipient': Decree of 6 June 1989, section 35(e). Tunisian law is in similar terms: see 1991 Law, section 7; likewise Turkey's 1979 Law.

[43] Resolution (78) 29 on the harmonisation of legislations of Member States to removal, grafting and transplantation of human substances, Article 2. This was itself reiterated in Council of Europe Recommendation No. R(79).

[44] Law of 13 June 1986, section 9. Luxembourg law contains similar provisions. Whilst French law (1994 Law, Article L 671–3) merely stipulates that the donor must be informed of the 'risks to which he is exposed and the possible consequences of removal', Decree No. 96–375 of 29 April 1996 elaborates upon this and states that this information shall include 'all the foreseeable consequences of the removal of a physical and psychological nature, and also the potential repercussions of such removal on the donor's personal, family, and professional life. It shall also concern the anticipated results of the transplant for the recipient.'

[45] Law of 27 October 1979, section 4(b).

informed of 'the foreseeable physical, mental, and psychological consequences, the possible effects of the donation on the donor's personal, family, and professional life, and the benefits which it is hoped the recipient will derive from the transplantation'.[46]

Proper disclosure matters

The voluntary and non-therapeutic character of the procedure justifies the extension of information about consequences to effects both upon non-medical aspects of one's life and upon others. Arguably, it should extend also to *financial* implications, again despite the general lack of such an obligation in respect of medical treatment in general.[47] There should be an obligation to disclose generalised information about likely time off work and costs to be incurred in the clinical and psychological evaluation, in-patient and recuperative stages. Where assistance with costs or expenses is obtainable from medical or social security sources this should also be the subject of mandatory disclosure. Indeed, Dutch law requires that the donor 'has been informed of the provisions of this Law *concerning the reimbursement of expenses*' (emphasis added).[48]

Because of the fairly unique and special *interconnection* between donor and recipient in this context, information relating to the prospects of success of the transplant for the recipient, and other options available to him/her, should also be required by law, to enable the person to make a

[46] The Law of 5 November 1997 enacted in Germany requires that the donor shall be informed 'about the type of intervention, its scope and the possible, also indirect, repercussions and delayed sequelae of the intended organ removal for his or her health, the organ transplant's chances of succeeding as well as other facts which are evidently of importance to him or her with respect to the organ donation': see section 8(2). Romanian law states that the donor must be fully informed about the 'possible physical, psychical, family and professional risks and consequences following the act of harvesting': see Law of 1996, Article 4(2).

[47] The Supreme Court of California in *Arato* v. *Avedon* 858 P. 2d 598 (1993) held that a clinician was not liable in negligence to a patient dying of pancreatic cancer for failing to disclose information material to the patient's non-medical interests where the doctor did not have a conflict of interest. In *Sidaway* v. *Board of Governors of the Royal Bethlem Hospital* [1985] 1 All ER 643 (HL), Lord Scarman expressed concerns that clinicians would generally be unaware of the individual's family, business or social activities or responsibilities: at 652.

[48] In certain nations it is made explicit that organ donation is a legitimate 'illness' justifying receipt of sick pay, for example in Austria. See E. Bernat, 'Marketing of Human Organs?' (1995) 14 *Medicine and Law* 181 at 186. See also A. Garwood-Gowers, 'To Pay or not to Pay; That is the Question. The Economic Rights of the Living Donor' in D. Price and J. Akveld (eds.), *Living Organ Donation in the Nineties: European Medico-Legal Perspectives*, EUROTOLD, 1996, 179.

rational decision as to whether to donate.[49] Such a requirement is already a feature of various laws (for example in Colombia, Germany, Spain and Tunisia).[50] This has even greater import in connection with living lung lobe donation where two donors are usually implicated. Although each should be treated individually, each donor should be aware of the risks incurred by the other donor as well the potential impact upon the recipient.[51]

Source(s) of the disclosure

Most laws are either silent as to the source(s) of the required information or simply state that 'the' or 'a' physician should be the source, which would typically be the clinician carrying out the organ removal procedure and which might even be the same person doing the transplantation procedure. Consequently, there may be no necessity for any independent source of information for donors. This would not seem to be sufficient. The clinicians involved will typically strongly endorse the transplantation decision and may therefore present the information, whether wittingly or unwittingly, in an overly positive light.[52] The Council of Europe's Draft Protocol states that donors shall be 'informed of the right to have access to independent advice about such risks by a health professional having appropriate experience and who is not involved in the organ or tissue removal or subsequent transplantation procedures'.[53] The Council of Europe Recommendation on Living Related Liver Transplantation also

[49] It has occasionally been the response of a living donor that had they been aware that a transplant was not a permanent procedure for most recipients, they would have allowed the patient to wait for a cadaveric organ instead: see EUROTOLD Project Report to the European Commission of the European Communities (ed. P. Donnelly and D. Price), *Questioning Attitudes to Living Donor Transplantation*, EUROTOLD, 1997, at 78. Donors should be routinely informed of any novel or experimental features of the transplant itself for the recipient.

[50] The Council of Europe Resolution (78) 29 specifically required that this information be disclosed.

[51] See C. McGhee and M. Fox, 'Bilateral Lung Transplantation from Living Donors' in Spielman, *Organ and Tissue Donation*, at 103.

[52] Cross and Churchill remark generally that 'A physician may feel so strongly about the need for a procedure that he is unable or unwilling to list the alternatives accurately. Strong feelings may take the form of exaggerated statistics, evoking fear in the patient, or enlisting others to urge the patient to accept the procedure': see A. Cross and L. Churchill, 'Ethical and Cultural Dimensions of Informed Consent' (1982) 96 *Annals of Internal Medicine* 110 at 111. See further Dickens, 'Donation and Transplantation', at para. 15.50.

[53] Article 11.

stipulates that 'The consent of the donor should be obtained only after a full explanation of the risks . . . by a third party, that is a "donor advocate" independent of the transplant team.'[54] Such a requirement finds expression in legislation in a handful of jurisdictions only. Polish law states that 'A candidate for a donor must be informed in detail about the intervention, the risk connected with it and any possible typical consequences for his health condition *by a doctor not taking direct part in the transplantation procedure*' (my emphasis).[55] In the United Kingdom, a similar statutory provision exists, but it is applicable to non-genetically related donors only. Although the transplanting surgeon should be a source of information for the donor, particularly as regards the potential benefits anticipated for the recipient, this should not be the only source of information.

Comprehension

Neither laws in general, nor specific transplant legislation, generally require that information disclosed relating to medical procedures actually be understood by donors, as opposed to the individual having the *capacity* to understand the information. This is too demanding in general circumstances. However, a few legislative provisions go further than general laws here. In Sweden, the physician must 'ensure that the person giving his consent has understood the implications of the information communicated to him',[56] and both Norwegian and Lebanese laws stipulate likewise.[57] In the UK, a registered medical practitioner must ensure that the *non-genetically related donor* 'understands the nature of the medical procedure and the risks',[58] and it is anticipated that these provisions will

[54] Recommendation of the Committee of Ministers to Member States on Liver Transplantation from Living Related Donors, 1997, at (iii).

[55] Law of 26 October 1995, Article 9(1)(5). Finnish law has a comparable provision: see Law of 26 April 1985, section 3. In Manitoba, a consent to organ removal is not valid unless a physician who does not have, and has never had, an association with any person benefiting or likely to benefit from the consent certifies in writing that the person giving consent has been advised of and understands the nature and effect of the procedure: see Human Tissue Act 1987, section 9(4).

[56] 1995 Law, section 10.

[57] 1973 Law, section 1 and 1983 Law, section 1 respectively.

[58] Human Organ Transplants (Unrelated Persons) Regulations 1989 (SI 1989 No. 2480) reg. 3(2)(b).

inform judicial determinations as to requirements with respect to *related* donors also.

The goal is the giving of an informed 'consent' not information disclosure *per se*, and this is fundamentally important in respect of procedures where the individual stands to gain no clinical benefit from the procedure, and may also suffer harm. As has been observed,[59] 'the central problems about informed consent are issues of communication rather than the abstract and disembodied issues about proper legal standards of disclosure that have so long dominated the subject literature'.[60] Thus, mandated verification of donor comprehension is wholly warranted here. The means whereby information is communicated will inevitably impact upon the level of donor comprehension. As the Institute of Medical Ethics Report states regarding medical procedures generally, 'It appears that (as one might expect) the level of comprehension is largely a function of the method and effectiveness of the communication rather than of the patients' inherent ability (or lack of it) to understand.'[61] Nevertheless, most laws are generally silent on this subject.[62] Dutch law, however, contains a unique, and very comprehensive, provision[63] which stipulates that the donor must be 'clearly informed orally and in writing and, where appropriate, with the aid of audiovisual means' of the prescribed matters. Such a provision stresses the need for information to be tailored to the needs of each potential donor and properly absorbed and understood. The highly emotionally charged nature of the donation decision, which is recognised as a 'clouding' stressor factor to understanding, clearly suggests a need for information to be available in a permanent form and not on a 'one off' basis.[64] The Institute of Medical Ethics Report

[59] See T. Beauchamp, 'Informed Consent' in R. Veatch (ed.), *Medical Ethics*, Jones and Bartlett, Boston, 1989, 175 at 176. Beauchamp has also observed generally that 'it has become progressively clear that the focus of statutory law, case law and regulatory guidelines has been on disclosure and that this focus is misguided. Problems about the quality and adequacy of consent probably cannot be resolved unless conventional disclosure requirements are abandoned and a shift occurs towards quality of understanding in the subject, patient and representative': ibid.

[60] See also generally S. McLean, *A Patient's Right to Know*, Dartmouth Press, Aldershot, 1989.

[61] A Report of the Institute of Medical Ethics, 'Informed Consent: A Review of the Empirical Evidence', *Institute of Medical Ethics Bulletin*, December 1986 (Supplement No. 3), 1 at 14.

[62] Although in both Bolivia and Kuwait the donor must be given written information regarding potential adverse effects upon his health.

[63] Law of 24 May 1996, section 3(2).

[64] See G. Kent, 'The Role of Psychology in the Teaching of Medical Ethics: The Example of Informed Consent' (1994) 28 *Medical Education* 126.

has remarked that in general 'The optimal combination appears to be simple written information combined with opportunities for dialogue with the doctors.'[65]

Operational matters

Michielsen, amongst others, argues that the obtaining of an informed consent to an organ removal from a living person for transplantation purposes is not possible in the face of a lack of objective information concerning the donor, arising as a consequence of (a) the incompleteness and retrospectivity of much of the published data and (b) conflicting published evidence as to the risks involved in donation.[66] Incontrovertibly, many of the data on short- or medium-term post-operative risks to living (even renal) donors are not only lacking in comprehensiveness but also, being largely centre-based, are often difficult to contrast with other centre data due to variability in the categorisation and labelling of morbidity risks (for example serious/minor, etc.) and the pre-operative health of donors. This may even account, to some degree, for the conflicting nature of some of the published donor health data. Further, albeit inevitably, significantly fewer data exist relating to *long-term* risks to donors from nephrectomy (due partly to the modest LDT experience of many centres).

Addressing the uncertainty point first, there is no legal or ethical prerequisite that *all* relevant information should be certain and complete at the time a particular decision is made. Interestingly, the Colombian transplantation law mandates that the donor be told of the '*impossibility of knowing with certainty* all the risks that the procedure may entail, on account of the possible occurrence of unforeseen situations' (my emphasis).[67] Uncertainty is not a stumbling block to informed consent – it is an inherent feature of non-therapeutic research procedures and experimental therapeutic procedures such as the first kidney or heart transplants. The King's Fund Institute Report considered that 'An uncertain level of risk is insufficient to deny people the opportunity to

[65] Institute of Medical Ethics Report, 'Informed Consent: A Review', at 7.

[66] P. Michielsen, 'Medical Risk and Benefit in Renal Donors: The Use of Living Donation Reconsidered' in W. Land and J. Dossetor (eds.), *Organ Replacement Therapy: Ethics, Justice, Commerce*, Springer-Verlag, Berlin, 1991, at 32.

[67] Decree of 6 June 1989, section 35(c).

donate, as long as this uncertainty is properly communicated to the donor.'[68] In any event there *is* now considerable evidence as to even long-term post-operative risks from nephrectomy. Some studies, with very large cohorts of donors, suggest only modest risk from living kidney donation. Najarian's and Kasiske's meta-analysis data, and long-term single centre data from certain US centres and from Norway, are of particular note here.[69] It is true to say though that there is somewhat less information available as regards the risks of *non-renal* (for example lung lobe) donation, because of the more recent origins of these treatment modalities.

With regard to the variability and conflicting nature of published data, one may consider that this is a feature of most areas of medicine. In any event, a reasonable degree of consensus *would* appear to have emerged from published studies on risks to living *renal* donors – we will never reach the stage where all data are harmonious when the criteria and contraindications for becoming a donor vary between centres and other 'centre effects' are at work. Clinicians are, however, given broad discretion in terms of what *sources* of information about risks they draw, and rely, upon. Walter Land has commented that

> One must, however, bear in mind that the process of providing information about short-term and long-term risks to both the donor and the recipient, something which should be as extensive and detailed as possible, is based upon the individual, and perhaps unconscious, discretion of the informing transplant surgeon/physician and is not clear-cut or sharply governed by legal rules. This may, in fact, be the point at which potential doubts regarding the justification of donor nephrectomy begin.[70]

[68] King's Fund Institute, *A Question of Give and Take*, Research Report 18, King's Fund Institute, London, 1994, at 67.

[69] J. Najarian *et al.*, '20 Years or More of Follow-up of Living Kidney Donors' (1992) 340 *Lancet* 807; B. Kasiske *et al.*, 'Long-term Effects of Reduced Renal Mass in Humans' (1995) 48 *Kidney International* 814; D. Laskow *et al.*, 'Analysis of 22 Years' Experience in Living-Related Transplantation at the University of Alabama in Birmingham' in P. Terasaki and J. Cecka (eds.), *Clinical Transplants 1991*, UCLA Tissue Typing Laboratory, Los Angeles, 1991, at 179; L. Westlie *et al.*, 'Quality of Life in Norwegian Kidney Donors' (1993) 8 *Nephrology Dialysis Transplantation* 1146. See also the introduction to Part II in this volume.

[70] W. Land, 'The Problem of Living Organ Donation' (1989) 2 *Transplant International* 168 at 170. A clinician attempting to convey data on risks accurately may be hindered by a lack of data from his own centre or the unreliability of such data based on a small sample, but, on the other hand, meta-studies or data from other centres with long experience may not truly reflect the actual degree of risk at the centre involved.

This is partly why access to independent assessments of risk, etc., are so important here. The King's Fund Report has sensibly recommended that donors should always be advised on the basis of the 'worst case' scenario. Arguably, concerns linked to subjectivity support the argument for a limited amount of *standardised* information being given to prospective donors,[71] preferably written information, possibly as part of an initial and preliminary disclosure process.[72]

Donor reflex

Psychological perspectives on the validity of decision-making place great emphasis on a deliberative model of decision-making. Basic conditions are the ability to understand the relevant information necessary to reach a decision, to deliberate about the information bearing on the decision and to reach a decision in favour of or against the procedure. Grisso and Vierling have argued that the ability to make an informed decision implies that the individual must be capable of understanding facts and procedures when they are explained to him, *and must possess the ability to delay impulses and refrain from making a decision without reflection.*[73]

In this vein, Fellner and Marshall have commented that

[71] Such standardisation would also help to mitigate the 'framing effects' created by the use of varying terminology to convey risks, etc. See H. Sutherland *et al.*, 'Communicating Probabilistic Information to Cancer Patients: Is there Noise on the Line?' (1991) 32 *Social Science and Medicine* 725, and G. Kent, 'Psychological Aspects of Informed Consent' (1994) 6 *Current Practice in Surgery* 235. The commentary to the Draft Council of Europe Protocol recommends that descriptions of risks should as far as possible be related to other risks encountered in everyday life.

[72] See further D. Price, 'The Voluntarism and Informedness of Living Donors' in Price and Akveld, *Living Organ Donation in the Nineties*, 107.

[73] T. Grisso and L. Vierling, 'Minor's Consent to Treatment: A Developmental Perspective' (1978) 9(3) *Professional Psychology* 412. Janis and Mann assert that a failure to satisfy any of the following creates a defect in the decision-making process: (a) thorough canvassing of the alternatives; (b) surveying the full range of objectives; (c) careful weighing of the risks and benefits flowing from each alternative course; (d) intensive search for new evidence for further evaluation of the alternatives; (e) correct assimilation and taking into account of any new information; (f) re-examination of all alternatives; and (g) planning implementation of the chosen course: see I. Janis and L. Mann, *Decision Making: A Psychological Analysis of Conflict, Choice and Commitment*, The Free Press, New York, 1977, at 11. See also A. Tepper and F. Kaslow, 'Informed Decision-Making Capacity: A Patient's Ability to Participate in Treatment Determinations' (1981) 6 *Law and Psychology Review* 49, and A. Tepper and A. Elwork, 'Competence to Consent to Medical Treatment as a Psycholegal Construct' (1984) 8 *Law and Human Behavior* 205.

> When a person is faced with a decision between two alternatives his behaviour is expected to be oriented toward making an objective and impartial evaluation of the merits of the alternatives. This usually takes the form of information seeking which probably continues until sufficient confidence is acquired that the preference will not be upset and reversed by subsequent information. At this level of confidence the rational person then will make a decision (predecision process). Contrary to this expectation, we found that our donors made an immediate major decision, before even inquiring into the possible consequences for themselves, or seeking reassurance as to the eventual benefits for the recipient.[74]

Their 1970 study of US renal donors revealed that 'decision making is an early event preceding all information-gathering and clarification offered by the renal team'.[75] They asserted that 'The criteria required for an "informed consent" type decision simply do not apply to the potential donor in this situation.'[76] Simmons *et al.*'s survey of living kidney donors at the University of Minnesota supported these findings. The authors found that in the majority of cases the decision to donate was an immediate, instantaneous one, made with no deliberation and usually with no later regret.[77] EUROTOLD's more recent European findings also support these earlier studies. Of respondent donors, 75 per cent engaged in non-deliberative decision-making on their own admission.[78] This phenomenon occurs despite the general lack of 'haste' surrounding living kidney donation; although living liver segment or lung lobe donations are often much more hurried in view of the critical condition of the patient. Clearly there is an issue of the *timing* of disclosure here.

[74] C. Fellner and J. Marshall, 'Twelve Kidney Donors' (1968) 206 *Journal of the American Medical Association* 2703 at 2706. See also J. Marshall and C. Fellner, 'Kidney Donors Revisited' (1977) 134 *American Journal of Psychiatry* 575. The authors interviewed twelve donors nine months after surgery and re-interviewed them after eight to nine years.

[75] C. Fellner and J. Marshall, 'Kidney Donors – The Myth of Informed Consent' (1970) 126 *American Journal of Psychiatry* 1245.

[76] Ibid., at 1251.

[77] R. Simmons *et al.*, *Gift of Life: The Effects of Organ Transplantation on Individual, Family and Societal Dynamics*, Transaction Books, New Brunswick, 1987. Between 62 and 78 per cent of the donors made virtually instantaneous decisions and only 25 per cent could be regarded as complying with a deliberative model of decision-making to any substantial degree: at 241 and 255.

[78] EUROTOLD Project Report, *Questioning Attitudes*, at 73–5.

Fact or fiction?

On the basis of their study, Fellner and Marshall concluded that informed consent was a 'myth',[79] a view endorsed by Hessing.[80] However, although the rational model of decision-making accords, to some degree, with legal and ethical perceptions of the informed consent process it is a counsel of perfection and, if taken too prescriptively and inflexibly, is at odds with the realities of everyday practice. Moreover, the British Institute of Medical Ethics remarked that 'The emphasis on rationality inherent in the informed consent doctrine tends to obscure emotional influences on decision making' and added that 'These studies suggest that doctors' criteria for what constitutes a rational informed consent may be quite different from the criteria used by patients.'[81]

There is nevertheless a very definite tension here. As Meisel and Roth have asserted, 'To the extent that patients decide to undergo procedures, and are only informed of risks just prior to their performance, they may become psychologically committed to the procedure and the disclosure of risks may be unlikely to change their minds.'[82] Indeed, Fellner and Marshall discovered that once a decision to donate had been made in a prospective donor's mind, the individual tended to insulate himself from questioning this decision again or from considering further information which might challenge that initial decision (termed 'cognitive dissonance').[83] No donor in their study who initially agreed to donate later changed his or her mind. Indeed, psychologists have asserted that generally individuals find it more difficult to resist following through with a form of conduct after an initial decision to do it has been made (at least in the individual's mind), even though less favourable aspects of the procedure are *subsequently* brought to the decision-maker's attention – a phenomenon known as 'low-balling'.[84] Unless there is information avail-

[79] Fellner and Marshall, 'Twelve Kidney Donors', at 2707. All their donors described their own decision-making as 'irrational'.

[80] D. Hessing, 'Living Kidney Donors: Some Psychological Aspects of Informed Consent' in Price and Akveld, *Living Organ Donation in the Nineties*, 99 at 104.

[81] Institute of Medical Ethics Report, 'Informed Consent: A Review', at 12.

[82] A. Meisel and L. Roth, 'What we do and do not Know about Informed Consent' (1981) 246 *Journal of the American Medical Association* 2473 at 2475.

[83] C. Fellner and J. Marshall, 'Kidney Donors' in J. Macauley and L. Berkowitz (eds.), *Altruism and Helping Behavior*, Academic Press, New York, 1970, at 279.

[84] R. Cialdini *et al.*, 'Low-Ball Procedure for Producing Compliance: Commitment then Cost' (1978) 36 *Journal of Personality and Social Psychology* 463.

able at that point about drawbacks, sufficient to give him pause, he will move rapidly to a resolution of the matter.[85] LDT surveys support the idea of a donor's will to donate being largely unshakable after an initial 'commitment' has been made. Simmons *et al.* additionally found that a small proportion of donors conformed to a 'postponement model' of *decision-making* (5 per cent of cases) whereby decisions were deferred indefinitely or until the very last minute. Some individuals considered that *no* decision to donate had ever been made at all. Certain donors reported feeling 'locked into' a positive decision and as each small exploratory step was taken withdrawal became more difficult – in one or two cases this generated extreme ambivalence.[86] These findings are consistent with the notion that rates of commitment increase following a series of small acts of compliance ('the foot-in-the-door' principle) which consists of either making a large request first followed by a more minor one or making a small request first and then, later, a larger one.[87] This has been shown to be influential in relation to blood donation and it could also be relevant to nephrectomy in so far as this follows on from an extensive series of tests and counselling, etc. Saks has observed that there is a great deal of opportunity for this process to have effect in the context of living organ donation.[88] Again, early information might prevent (ambivalent) individuals from proceeding too far down the line.

Majeske, Parker and Frader have questioned whether, in the light of the current individualistic, autonomy-orientated approach to decision-making by living donors, an ethic of care or other approach is more suited to this context, where *relationships* are crucially significant.[89] But whilst sensitivity to the context and complexity of decision-making is essential, there is a need to bolster the rationality of decision-making, in order to

[85] Janis and Mann, *Decision Making*, at 224.

[86] Simmons *et al.*, *Gift of Life*, at 260. Fellner and Marshall also found that donors tended to avoid a predecision conflict either by making a split second decision (yes/no) or by pretending not to decide and to go along passively and let the selection process decide for them.

[87] See J. Freedman and S. Fraser, 'Compliance without Pressure: The Foot-in-the-door Technique' (1966) 4 *Journal of Personality and Social Psychology* 195; G. Kent, 'Psychological Aspects of Informed Consent' (1994) 6 *Current Practice in Surgery* 235 at 238; and S. Schwartz, 'Elicitation of Moral Obligation and Self Sacrificing Behavior: An Experimental Study of Volunteering to be a Bone Marrow Donor' (1970) 15 *Journal of Personality and Social Psychology* 283.

[88] M. Saks, 'Social Psychological Contributions to a Legislative Subcommittee on Organ and Tissue Transplants' (1978) *American Psychologist* 680.

[89] Majeske, Parker and Frader, 'In Search of an Ethical Framework', at 95.

avoid decision-making which is less than satisfactory to that individual and which may generate post-decisional regret. Janis and Mann found that the more defects there are in the decision-making process, the more likely the decision-maker is to experience unanticipated setbacks and post-decisional regret.[90] However, we need also to rethink the meaning of 'rationality' in this context. There is no necessary conflict between 'autonomy' and the influence of personal relationships and 'partiality', and there is a danger that another model may itself create a ceding of autonomy in the name of 'interrelationship'. Informed consent is *not* legally or ethically suspect, simply because decision-making is relatively instinctive and instantaneous. Indeed, the speed and instinctiveness of much of the decision-making of donors is in many ways unsurprising. Research illustrates that certain relationships generate very high percentages of highly motivated individuals prepared to donate kidneys, to siblings and children in particular.[91] It has also been argued that decision-making by living donors accords with the model of *moral decision-making* advanced by Schwartz, applicable to interpersonal decisions having implications for the welfare of others, the three key ingredients being: awareness of consequences, ascription of responsibility and moral norms.[92] Donors typically appreciate the potential consequences for patients and immediately ascribe responsibility to themselves for outcomes in the context of existing moral norms. There is, nonetheless, an ethical obligation to ensure that as informed a decision as possible is made. Janis and Mann have argued that when a scanning of the alternatives reveals only one acceptable course of action, possibly from the perspective of personal moral responsibility, the decision-maker is likely to ignore the attendant risks.[93] The above discussion suggests that *some* information about risks and alternatives is properly given at a very early

90 Janis and Mann, *Decision Making*, at 11.

91 J. Shanteau and J. Skowronski, 'The Decision to Donate Organs' in J. Shanteau and R. Jackson Harris (eds.), *Organ Donation and Transplantation: Psychological and Behavioral Factors*, American Psychological Association, Washington D.C., 1991, at 59–67. Borgida and Simmons have hypothesised that the closeness of the relationship between donor and recipient would influence the immediacy of, and degree of deliberation involved in, the decision to donate: see E. Borgida *et al.*, 'The Minnesota Living Donor Studies' in Shanteau and Harris, at 108–21. Simmons *et al.* found that decisions to donate between such relatives were generally perceived to be 'easy' decisions to make (by over 70 per cent): *Gift of Life*, at 156.

92 S. Schwartz, 'Moral Decision Making and Behavior' in Macauley and Berkowitz (eds.), *Altruism and Helping Behavior*, 127.

93 Janis and Mann, *Decision Making*, at 241.

stage in the proceedings before the donor has, in his mind, made an irrevocable or irreversible commitment – something that appears to occur very early in the process.[94]

The President's Commission in the US commented that 'Because the operation of informed consent does and should differ substantially, owing to the varied structure of medical practice, the traditional, monolithic legal model of informed consent may require re-thinking.'[95] It found that the operation of the doctrine even in respect of therapeutic procedures was partly dependent on (health care) context, including whether it was a *surgical procedure* or not. It continued:

> The decision that surgery should be performed is ordinarily viewed in law as a relatively clear-cut event in which the doctor reviews the risks and benefits with the patient and the patient then decides. In actuality the twin processes of disclosure and *decision-making* in elective surgery are often much more complex than such a model assumes, and patients may come to understand many of the critical issues much later in the process than at the point at which the formal decision is made . . . The basic decision to have surgery is often made long before any consent form is signed and before many of the critical issues are discussed.[96]

In the LDT context, it would seem that donors have typically committed themselves to donation by the time the evaluation process is complete or even before that time, certainly well before the formal process of obtaining consent to the organ removal itself takes place. Interestingly, many centres now employ a *two-stage* consent process, especially for liver segment and lung lobe programmes, the first focusing on the evaluation process and the second on the organ removal operation.[97] Arguably, a basic degree of written information should be given even before prospective donors undertake medical screening and testing. This would be supplemented with fuller and more detailed oral information given at a later point

[94] Fellner and Marshall also found that the process of *family* selection and screening was also operative at a very early stage and diminished once the process of medical selection took over. See Fellner and Marshall, 'Kidney Donors – The Myth', at 1248.

[95] President's Commission for the Study of Ethical Problems in Medicine and Biomedical and Behavioral Research, *Making Health Care Decisions: The Ethical and Legal Implications of Informed Consent in the Patient–Practitioner Relationship*, US Government Printing Office, Washington D.C., 1982, Appendix C at 325.

[96] Ibid., at 329.

[97] See P. Singer *et al.*, 'Ethics of Liver Transplantation with Living Donors' (1989) 321 *New England Journal of Medicine* 620 at 621, and L. Shaw *et al.*, 'Ethics of Lung Transplantation with Live Donors' (1991) 338 *Lancet* 678 at 680.

addressed to the specific intended donor and tailored to his or her needs. The President's Commission highlighted the importance of *reinforcement* of information to assist understanding.

Voluntariness of consent

The voluntariness of a decision to donate an organ is crucial to a legitimate LDT. Its absence nullifies the validity of a consent given to such a medical procedure, thereby creating the potential for criminal or civil (tortious/delictual) liability. However, voluntariness is a slippery and nebulous concept generating substantial confusion in both law and philosophy.[98] The English Law Commission recently remarked that 'The problem is to determine what it is that makes some of these choices less "voluntary" than others; and the concept of voluntariness, on examination, proves to be at best ambiguous and at worst little more than metaphorical.'[99] Although voluntariness is a general legal precondition of a valid consent, transplant legislation is itself frequently mute on this issue in relation to LDT. The WHO Guiding Principles, however, dictate that the consent given by a donor should be free of any undue influence or pressure.[100] Some commentators, for instance Michielsen, allege that obtaining a voluntary consent to LDT is never possible due to a lack of certainty, and the fact that its assessment depends wholly upon subjective judgement.[101] While less dogmatic, the King's Fund Institute remarked that 'The most serious ethical concerns about live organ donation relate to the possibility of improper pressure.'[102]

Voluntariness is arguably compromised in three specific LDT contexts. The first is a consent to organ removal given by a related but unpaid donor. Dworkin has stated that 'The relationship between donor and

[98] One leading thesis on the concept of voluntariness in the context of both law and philosophy is Alan Wertheimer's *Coercion*, Princeton University Press, Princeton, New Jersey, 1988.

[99] Law Commission Consultation Paper, *Consent in the Criminal Law*, Consultation Paper No. 139, HMSO, 1995, at para. 6.57.

[100] Principle 3. The Council of Europe Convention on Human Rights and Biomedicine merely states that all consents to medical interventions must be 'free': see Article 5.

[101] Its importance is underscored by the fact that in some centres lack of surety about the ability to guarantee voluntariness of consent has in the past led clinicians either to abandon or to avoid setting up an LDT programme, for example at Munich.

[102] King's Fund, *A Question of Give and Take*, at 68. It called on the Department of Health in Britain to issue guidance for living donors, including appropriate mechanisms for making relatives aware of the possibility of live donation, and to ensure that adequate safeguards exist to protect the potential donor from improper emotional pressure: at 83.

donee may be, for example, that of twins or parent and child: in these family situations the social and psychological pressures upon a person who knows that his failure to give consent will result in the death of the sick person must be very strong indeed. It may often be difficult to decide whether a consent in this situation is truly voluntary.'[103] The second context is where a consent to donation is given by an institutionalised individual such as a prisoner. Annas, Glantz and Katz state: 'The problem in obtaining informed consent from prisoners is that the very fact of their incarceration may prevent them from giving their consent voluntarily.'[104] Finally, there is the situation where consent is given by a paid vendor of an organ, whether the provider is in desperate poverty or otherwise. Broyer states that 'Donor voluntariness is a key ethical concern and is completely cancelled when the real incentive of the donation is monetary gain.'[105]

Where there's a will there's a way

'Voluntariness' is employed in two distinctly different senses, an ambiguity which perpetually dogs this concept. There is a deviation between the narrow meaning which revolves around the ability to *control* one's actions and to exercise a *choice* between alternatives, and the broad meaning covering situations where where one's will is influenced as opposed to wholly absent;[106] *la contrainte physique* as opposed to *la contrainte morale*.[107] The 'highwayman' scenario neatly illustrates the distinction. A person handing over valuable possessions to a robber on pain of otherwise forfeiting his life does so voluntarily in a narrow sense as his action is deliberately 'chosen', but involuntarily in a broad sense as he

103 G. Dworkin, 'The Law Relating to Organ Transplantation in England' (1970) 33 *Modern Law Review* 353 at 359.

104 G. Annas, L. Glantz and B. Katz, *Informed Consent to Human Experimentation*, Bollinger Publishing Company, Cambridge, Mass., 1977, at 103.

105 M. Broyer, 'Aspects of Living Organ Donation with Emphasis on the Fight against Commercialism' in Land and Dossetor, *Organ Replacement Therapy*, 197 at 199. Sells also contends that in such a situation voluntariness is at least compromised, if not entirely negated, by such sale: see R. Sells, 'Voluntarism of Consent in both Related and Unrelated Living Organ Donation' in Land and Dossetor, *Organ Replacement Therapy*, 18 at 21.

106 *Non-volitional* rather than *constrained volitional* actions, in the terminology of Alan Wertheimer: see *Coercion*, at 6–7.

107 George Fletcher has also distinguished moral from normative involuntariness: see G. Fletcher, *Rethinking Criminal Law*, Little Brown, Boston, 1978, at 803, the former being adopted by the Supreme Court of Canada in the context of duress, in *R* v. *Perka* (1984) 13 DLR (4th) 1.

did not act willingly, that is it was a coerced choice.[108] Philips contends that

> A coerced agent is presented with unwanted, unpleasant alternatives, but is free to choose and to act upon the least obnoxious of them. He is a victim of imposed conditions of choice, but still he may choose. His act is an expression of his will in his situation. This is not so in the case of an agent who acts involuntarily in the strict sense. His will is *overborn* [*sic*]. He is incapable of either making a rational choice or of acting on one.[109]

This perspective conflates a person acting voluntarily with a person exercising a choice. However, in the criminal law the term is usually employed in this narrower sense,[110] but even here responsibility may also sometimes be avoided where there has been a 'coerced choice', for example under the defence of duress,[111] although this is a moral evaluation based on the nature of the threats which are deemed sufficient to excuse[112] rather than the psychological impact of the threats on their victim.[113]

Undue influence

The narrow approach is therefore operative in the context of assessing responsibility for actions, whereas in the context of consent and in

108 Albeit for specific purposes, Aristotle subscribed to the narrow concept of voluntariness, viewing all actions as voluntary apart from those where one has no control over one's actions or where one acts in ignorance of relevant features of an action: see Aristotle, *Ethica Nicomachea* 1110, W. Ross (ed.), trans., 1925.

109 M. Philips, 'Are Coerced Agreements Involuntary?' (1984) 3 *Law and Philosophy* 133 at 133. Held maintains on the other hand that 'Coercion is the activity of causing someone to do something against his will, or of bringing about his doing what he does against his will': see V. Held, 'Coercion and Coercive Offers' in J. Pennock and J. Chapman (eds.), *Nomos XIV*, Aldine & Atherton, Chicago, 1972, at 50–1.

110 In some instances they are not even viewed as his actions at all. These are actions carried out as a result of the application of either *external* forces or automatism resulting from, for example, an epileptic seizure: see P. Fitzgerald, 'Voluntary and Involuntary Acts' in A. White (ed.), *The Philosophy of Action*, Oxford University Press, Oxford, 1968, 120.

111 Murphy states: 'What does seem true of duress, therefore, is this: When person A consents to a proposal from B, and when his only or paramount reason for consenting to the proposal is his suffering wrongful treatment from B, then in such a case A has no moral obligation (even prima facie) generated from the act of consent': see J. Murphy, 'Consent, Coercion, and Hard Choices' (1981) 67 *Virginia Law Review* 79 at 81. This defence is often described as a 'concession to human frailty'.

112 In *R* v. *Perka* (1984) 13 DLR (4th) 1, the Supreme Court of Canada described this assessment as being based on 'society's expectations of appropriate and normal resistance to pressure'.

113 These features are also apparent in the law of contractual obligations: see A. Burrows, *The Law of Restitution*, Butterworths, London, 1993, at 162.

everyday discourse the broader *extended* meaning of 'voluntariness' which equates with *free will* is routinely employed.[114] The English Law Commission recently stated that 'Circumstances which reduce or obliterate voluntariness and may invalidate consent include (literal) compulsion (that is physical force), *coercive threats or offers* ('*duress*') and defective beliefs induced by fraud or mistake' (my emphasis).[115] The more expansive meaning is operative in the civil law in relation to both unintentional and intentional torts, as regards the potential liability *of another* where the party concerned agreed to the risk of injury or consented to a harm inflicted. In *Bowater* v. *Rowley Regis Corporation*, in connection with the defence of *volenti*, Scott LJ stated that

> a man cannot be said to be truly 'willing' unless he is in a position to choose freely, and freedom of choice predicates, not only full knowledge of the circumstances on which the exercise of choice is conditional, so that he may be able to choose wisely, but *the absence of any feeling of constraint* so that nothing shall interfere with the freedom of his will [my emphasis].[116]

The issue has also been addressed by the English appellate courts with respect to a consent given to medical treatment, in *Re T (Adult: Refusal of Medical Treatment)*.[117] An adult woman who was thirty-four weeks pregnant was involved in a road accident but refused consent to any blood transfusion being administered to her. She ultimately developed an abscess in her lung requiring surgery and a blood transfusion. The Court of Appeal reversed the decision of the trial court, saying she had refused consent to the transfusion in 'form' but not in 'reality' because the decision had been influenced by her mother who was a fervent Jehovah's Witness (the patient was not herself a member of the sect), so that the refusal should not therefore be binding upon medical staff. Lord Donaldson stated:

> A special problem may arise if at the time the decision is made the patient has been subjected to the influence of some third party. This is by no means to say that the patient is not entitled to receive and indeed invite

[114] Gert states that where a person chooses to act in a situation only because of an unreasonable incentive, he prefers to say that the individual acts voluntarily but not *freely*: see B. Gert, 'Coercion and Freedom' in Pennock and Chapman, *NOMOS XIV*, 30 at 32. But this appears to be more linguistic than substantive.

[115] Law Commission, *Consent in the Criminal Law*, at 260.

[116] [1944] KB 476 at 479.

[117] [1992] 4 All ER 649 (CA).

> advice and assistance from others in reaching a decision, particularly from members of the family. But the doctors have to consider whether the decision is really that of the patient. It is wholly acceptable that the patient should have been persuaded by others of the merits of such a decision and have decided accordingly. It matters not how strong the persuasion was, so long as it did not overbear the independence of the patient's decision.

Lord Justice Staughton commented that 'In order for an apparent consent or refusal of consent to be less than a true consent or refusal, there must be such a degree of external influence as to persuade the patient to depart from her own wishes, to an extent that the law regards it as undue.'[118] The judgments purported to elicit the 'true will' of the patient as a subjective state of mind. Feinberg endorses such an approach, and states: 'For moral purposes we should always use the subjective "willingness" standard, and judge voluntariness by reference to the actual motivation of the person whose choices are at issue. That is the approach that is most respectful of autonomy and individuality.'[119] Feinberg concedes though that 'in human legislatures and courts of law, however, a person's degree of willingness while under coercion is often permanently shrouded in obscurity, and legislatures are forced for practical reasons to formulate rules based on the presumptive preferences of standard persons, thus discouraging subsequent judicial inquiry into the actual preferences of real individuals'.[120] Gardner has observed that 'It may be that in some contexts in which the law refers to consent, it is more appropriate that emphasis should be placed on attentiveness to the individual victim, accepting the indeterminacy that that entails; whilst in other contexts it is more appropriate to set greater store by determinacy, at the expense of being attentive to the individual victim.'[121] It is submitted that LDT is just such a context requiring attentiveness to the individual.[122]

118 At 669C. Lord Justice Butler-Sloss stated that 'The degree of pressure to turn persuasion or appeals to affection into undue influence may be very little': at 667–8.

119 J. Feinberg, *The Moral Limits of the Criminal Law. Vol. II: Harm to Self*, Oxford University Press, Oxford, 1986, at 258.

120 Ibid.

121 S. Gardner, 'Appreciating *Olugboja*' (1996) 16(3) *Legal Studies* 275 at 296.

122 It is noteworthy that the English Court of Criminal Appeal argued that consent in the context of the offence of rape was a state of mind of a person feeling 'reasonably favourable toward the activity occurring': see *Olugboja* [1982] QB 321 (CA). It stated that a 'real consent' ran along a continuum from actual desire to reluctant consent. This is in contrast to the traditional judicial approach which instead focused upon the actions of the defendant, for example threats (that is force, fear or fraud). This decision has been criticised, and the recent Law Commission Consultation Paper reverts to the more traditional approach.

Although admittedly the attempt to treat voluntariness as a black and white issue is artificial when it is in reality a matter of degree, rather than a quality that is wholly present or otherwise in particular cases,[123] nonetheless some threshold level of voluntariness needs to be established for legal purposes. However, it is necessary to consider the *context* within which the decision is being made, and the consequences of any determination, in assessing whether the relevant threshold level of voluntariness has been attained.[124]

Living related donation

Between a rock and a hard place

Simmons *et al.* reported one mother who donated to her son who commented to the interviewer that, as regards the decision to donate, 'I think it is as involuntary as if you saw one of your kids slip off a curb . . . [Y]ou would do what you could to help him.'[125] The lack of choice felt here is a consequence of the *need* of the patient and the *relationship* between the two individuals. But few would doubt the intensity of the pressure experienced by many potential donors. As Caplan has asked rhetorically, 'Does anyone really think parents can say "No" when the option is certain death for their own son or daughter?'[126] However, any supposed unity between the mere existence of dramatically unequal or limited alternatives and a lack of voluntariness of consent is unsustainable. The view that a proper consent cannot be given in such circumstances trades on a confusion between the possession of a limited range of options and an inability to choose properly between the alternatives. Indeed, any other view would be calamitous for patients with serious medical conditions for which there is only a solitary realistic (therapeutic) option (including transplantation).[127]

[123] George Fletcher states that 'The need to force borderline cases into one category or the other often entails a serious philosophical error': see *Rethinking Criminal Law*, at 451.

[124] Feinberg agrees that standards of voluntariness should be formulated according to the context: see Feinberg, *Harm to Self*, at 117–24. The English Law Commission recently accepted that this determination will have to take into account the nature of the act consented to, and offered the view that it would never be proper to obtain consent to injury by a threat: see Law Commission, *Consent in the Criminal Law*, at para. 6.63.

[125] Simmons *et al.*, *Gift of Life*, at 164.

[126] A. Caplan, *Knight-Ridder Newspapers*, 14 December 1989.

[127] Skegg has commented that 'Consent is no less legally effective when it is unwillingly or

Pressure points

Although pressures are an inherent feature of living related donation, contrasts have been drawn between internal and external pressures. Majeske, Parker and Frader have stated that

> Internal pressures, such as feelings of obligation and compulsion, are likely to result from the relationship between the potential recipient and the donor, from the severity of the potential recipient's medical condition, and from feelings of guilt since – without the procedure – the potential recipient will likely die . . . Sources of external pressure include other family members (particularly the potential recipient's spouse or another family member picked to be an intermediary between the potential recipient and donors), researchers and transplant team members, other health care professionals (a family doctor, for example), and the low likelihood of obtaining a suitable cadaveric donor in time.[128]

It has been asserted by various commentators, including many moral philosophers, that external pressures undermine voluntariness whilst internal pressures do not.[129] Nozick, for instance, asserts that there is an important difference between *circumstances* that limit alternatives and specific interpersonal *threats* that coerce – only the latter undermine voluntariness, because the will of another is operating or predominant.[130] Sells uses a contrast between *obligations* and *duties* for the purpose here. He states:

> An *obligation* is an externally applied constriction of an individual's right to choose not to donate. In addition to legal compulsion, I would include in this category blackmail (within families as between unrelated people)

reluctantly given; few patients would consent to major surgery if it were not for the force of surrounding circumstances, and the knowledge that health or even life may be in jeopardy if they do not consent': see Skegg, *Law, Ethics and Medicine*, at 97. Whilst generally entirely cogent, I would take issue with the joinder of 'unwilling' and 'reluctant' consents. The latter may be wholly valid whereas the former may not.

128 Majeske, Parker and Frader, 'In Search of an Ethical Framework', at 94.

129 Staughton LJ in *Re T* spoke of *external* pressures in the context of describing potential undue influence in that situation.

130 R. Nozick, 'Coercion' in S. Morgenbesser, P. Suppes and M. White, *Philosophy, Science and Method (Essays in Honour of Ernest Nagel)*, St Martin's Press, New York, 1969, at 459. Faden and Beauchamp have also asserted that even severe pressures will not undermine the will of another unless someone else is 'in control of' the intentional or situational threat: see R. Faden and T. Beauchamp, *A History and Theory of Informed Consent*, Oxford University Press, Oxford, 1986, at 345.

> . . . [where] (. . . the element of voluntariness of donation must be at least compromised, or in extreme cases, abolished). *Duty*, however, I define here as an internal motivation arising from love of, friendship with, or respect for another individual. A sense of duty can be sufficiently strong in a person to make it difficult to distinguish between duty and obligation. For example: a volunteer donor of a kidney to his ailing brother was asked by a surgeon whether he felt compelled to donate a kidney. The donor replied that he could not conceive of any stronger pressure than the obligation of a close brother to donate a kidney whatever the risks; the benefits to the recipient would be such that the demands imposed on the donor by his love for his brother amounted to compulsion. Does such internal pressure amount to an obligation as defined above? I think not: the brother still has the freedom to choose not to give, and, in my experience, other no less well-motivated relatives have decided not to donate when the hazards are pointed out to them . . . In these cases, the recipient's plight has forced the dilemma onto the relative, the degree of compulsion (duty) experienced by the brother being proportional to the strength of their relationship. The donor is compelled to make the decision one way or the other. He is not compelled to donate. Voluntariness survives.[131]

There is substantial evidence of family pressures affecting the processes of searching for and selecting a donor, and also the decision of a relative as to whether to donate or not. Simmons *et al.* found such overt pressure in 11 per cent of instances.[132] They also found that 'subtle situational pressure' might also exist but would be more difficult to document.[133] In *Re T*, Lord Donaldson commented that

> When considering the effect of outside influences, two aspects can be of crucial importance. First, the strength of will of the patient . . . Secondly, the relationship of the 'persuader' to the patient may be of crucial importance. The influence of parents on their children or of one spouse on

131 Sells, 'Voluntarism of Consent', at 21.

132 Simmons *et al.*, *Gift of Life*, at 158. They discovered family stress in the donor search in approximately 25 per cent of cases (twenty-one out of seventy-nine). However, 57 per cent of donors explicitly stated that their decisions had been made 'voluntarily'.

133 Ibid., at 159. The EUROTOLD Project uncovered only pressure not to donate rather than to donate: see EUROTOLD Project Report, *Questioning Attitudes*, at 76–8. Smith *et al.*'s US study showed that 86 per cent of donors had not been influenced by either family members or friends, and 94 per cent said that they had not been pressured by health professionals: see M. Smith *et al.*, 'Living-Related Kidney Donors: A Multicenter Study of Donor Education, Socioeconomic Adjustment and Rehabilitation' (1986) 8(4) *American Journal of Kidney Diseases* 223.

> the other can be, but is by no means necessarily, much stronger than would be the case in other relationships.[134]

These remarks have particular significance for LDT where one could anticipate substantial overt pressures in certain contexts. Research has shown, for instance, that one member of the family tends to 'orchestrate' the donor search process, and this member may often be the source of such pressure (I ignore, for the present, potential pressure from medical personnel).

Of course, where there *were* specific external threats or pressures precipitating a decision to donate we would not hesitate to question the willingness (voluntariness) of the donor. There would indeed be *undue influence.* There are in fact various explicit legislative provisions relating to the use of such coercive pressures. The law of the Russian Federation even makes it a criminal offence to 'coerce' a living donor to consent to organ donation.[135] In other instances the existence of such pressure casts doubt on the validity of the consent given to donation itself. In Hungary, the 1972 Law states that the consent must be given 'of his own free will and in the absence of any pressure'[136] and in Spain an objection can be raised to a living donation if there is any evidence of outside pressure on the donor. Moreover, the WHO Guiding Principles require a consent to be given in the absence of undue influence or pressure. Nevertheless, the existence of pressure does not undermine consent *per se.* Coercion (undermining voluntariness) is generally regarded as having occurred only when the person targeted by the threats regards them as being irresistible.[137] The law would require the individual's will to have been sufficiently overborne.[138]

Circumstances and threats

But even if external pressures can potentially undermine a consent given by a living related donor, are the commentators quoted above correct to assert that *internal* pressures cannot have the same effect? Caplan's remark

134 He noted that those in pain or who are depressed or very tired may be less able to resist pressure than someone rested and cheerful: see [1992] 4 All ER 649 at 662E–F.

135 1992 Law, section 3.

136 Section 2(2).

137 See, for example, T. Beauchamp and J. Childress, *Principles of Biomedical Ethics*, 4th edn, Oxford University Press, Oxford, 1994, at 164.

138 The pressure might be only to make the individual do what they had previously resolved to do.

implies that the pressures on parents in particular are so compelling as to leave them unable to say 'No'. Crouch and Elliott throw further light on the nature of this contention, stating:

> To be clear about just what these objectors are saying is important. They are not saying that parents can be pressured into donating by other family members or by the healthcare team. They are saying that parents might somehow pressure *themselves*. By virtue of their emotional ties to their child and their sense of moral obligation, parents will feel 'forced' to donate.[139]

Majeske, Parker and Frader state that 'Traditional interpretations of the requirements of voluntariness have focussed on the lack of controlling outside influences rather than on the nature or authenticity of the decision maker's aims', and that 'Such responses clearly seem to jeopardise the possibility of obtaining informed consent because living related donors' decisions do not seem to be autonomous in the sense of being free from coercive or substantially controlling influences.'[140] They contend that the normal perception of autonomy in decision-making fails to take properly into account the context of the relationship inherent and state that 'In living related donation, however, partiality and personal relationships frequently play essential roles because personal relationships importantly influence or even constitute potential donors' personal goals.'[141] But if one views this issue from the proper perspective of subjective willingness, one can observe that again the mere existence of, even overwhelming, pressure does not render every consent involuntary. Paradoxically, the relatives who are the most motivated to donate organs (that is parents of sick children) will feel the *least* choice in the matter. Indeed, empirical studies show that parents who are donating to their children typically display *the least ambivalence of all* donors. It is not normally a difficult or tortuous decision for either the individual or the family, although parents naturally experience anxiety.[142]

139 R. Crouch and C. Elliott, 'Moral Agency and the Family: The Case of Living Related Organ Transplantation' (1999) 8 *Cambridge Quarterly of Healthcare Ethics* 275 at 276.

140 Majeske, Parker and Frader, 'In Search of an Ethical Framework', at 91.

141 Ibid., at 95.

142 Simmons *et al.*, *Gift of Life*, at 189.

Dissonance

Although the great preponderance of living related donors make decisions to donate without any compromise of their will, there is evidence that some donors are not entirely amenable volunteers. Simmons *et al.*'s Minnesota survey revealed that 12 per cent of prospective donors would have been 'relieved' if they were not able to donate and a further 1 per cent would have been 'very relieved'. Whilst this may reflect simple anxiety prior to undergoing invasive surgery, there is also evidence of significant post-transplant regret, generally in around 3–8 per cent of cases.[143] Such data highlight the potential for voluntariness to be compromised in this context, as well as showing potential concerns relating to the donors' post-operative psychological health. Siegler and Lantos have cautioned in this context against 'internal coercion' created by guilt.[144] As regards the internal compulsion felt by parents *per se*, Crouch and Elliott suggest that this may emanate from a tension between public and private faces of morality, that is that parents who might not wish to donate feel ashamed should anyone else be made aware of this.[145] Moreover, Simmons *et al.*'s research showed a quarter of donors agreeing that the decision to donate was partly motivated by the desire to make up for the previous wrongs done to others (so-called 'black sheep' donors).[146]

The fact that parents are the most likely relatives to volunteer to donate partly reflects the normative obligation felt by parents in our society. Simmons *et al.* nonetheless revealed that donors who perceived donation

[143] Simmons *et al.* found that 5 per cent of donors regretted their decision post-transplant. Westlie's study of Norwegian donors revealed that 94 per cent of donors would either definitely or probably have donated again: see Westlie *et al.*, 'Quality of Life', at 1149. Bunzendahl *et al.*'s survey of eighty-one living donors in Hanover found that five of them would not have donated if put in the same situation again: see H. Bunzendahl *et al.*, 'Retrospective Evaluation of Psychosocial Factors in Former Living Related Kidney Donors' in Land and Dossetor, *Organ Replacement Therapy*, 57 at 59. Only one of the seventy-six donors surveyed by the EUROTOLD Project would fail to do the same again if the clock were turned back: see EUROTOLD Project Report, *Questioning Attitudes*, at 78.

[144] M. Siegler and J. Lantos, 'Commentary: Ethical Justification for Living Liver Donation' (1992) 1 *Cambridge Quarterly of Healthcare Ethics* 320 at 323. It is well known that guilt will lead to pressures towards expiation and compliant behaviour: see J. Freedman *et al.*, 'Compliance Without Pressure: The Effect of Guilt' (1967) 7 *Journal of Personality and Social Psychology* 117.

[145] Crouch and Elliott, 'Moral Agency', at 277.

[146] Simmons *et al.*, *Gift of Life*, at 189.

as a family obligation were *less* likely to experience ambivalent feelings in respect of the donation.[147] However, whilst it is not convincing to contend that voluntariness is undermined whenever donation arises wholly from the force of societal expectation, there may nonetheless be tensions in some instances. Spousal relationships in particular have been seriously questioned, because of the strength of the emotional relationship and the possibility that the spouse might feel undue pressure to donate as a result of his or her role. This might be particularly problematic in certain cultural contexts where wives are particularly subservient, and thus also in multi-cultural societies. Moreover, there is a preponderance of women as opposed to men becoming living related organ donors. However, there is abundant and accumulating evidence from certain quarters that, in general, spouses are especially well-motivated donors.[148] In terms of married persons donating to their *blood* relatives though, some donors feel a conflict between the duties accepted towards the recipient and those owed to their own immediate family,[149] although generally with the latter creating a pressure in favour of *non-donation* rather than donation.

Beauchamp and Childress argue that autonomous choices can nonetheless be made even though they may derive from cultural traditions and expectations. Such a heritage socialises the individual and moulds his/her character. It is not external to him/her. Indeed, it has been asserted that strength of will and its being rooted in one's own beliefs and value systems is the primary prerequisite of voluntary action, that is when an individual's decisions are consistent with his/her internal evaluation system – in the same way that it is acknowledged that normal methods of persuasion do not undermine voluntariness. Rather such views are absorbed and integrated into one's own belief system and not *overlaid* upon it. Sadler has previously observed that the inner motivating force for donors is typically to be found in the core of the individual's personality, the self. He states: 'That which motivates us is not logical or reasonable but is a manifestation of an already existing design lying at the core of the self, which impels us to respond in our characteristic styles.'[150] Nevertheless,

[147] Ibid., at 165.

[148] For instance from the Basle centre: see G. Thiel, 'Living Unrelated Kidney Transplantation' in Collins *et al.*, *Procurement, Preservation and Allocation*, at 369.

[149] Simmons *et al.*, *Gift of Life*, at 189–90 and 294.

[150] H. Sadler, 'The Motivation of Living Donors' (1973) 5 *Transplantation Proceedings* 1121 at 1122.

there will be some individuals who experience tension and dissonance between socialising influences/expectations and their own will. These feelings will generate ambivalence, and possible later regret. Moreover, ambivalence pre-transplant has been shown to correlate with enhanced feelings of post-transplant regret.[151] Schneewind has commented that 'Although in most cases the quality of the donor–recipient relationship proved to be mutually satisfying or changed for the better in the post-transplantation phase there are also particular relationship constellations that need special attention in order to prevent negative outcomes.'[152] In a review of seventy-nine cases, Simmons *et al.* found family tension in only five out of twenty-one cases of donation from a parent to a child, contrasted with thirteen out of the nineteen cases of donation by one sibling to another.[153] This is especially important as, from a clinical perspective, a sibling is often the preferred choice of donor.

No man is an island

There is no incompatibility between independent voluntary decision-making and bonds or ties that drive responses. Crouch and Elliott state: 'The picture is not of children and their parents located in a context of intimacy, but of sovereign, independent human agents free of the moral and emotional connections that typically bind family members to each other',[154] and add: 'The moral commitments associated with intimacy, such as loyalty and devotion, are seen as "coercive" because they motivate a person to actions that a completely independent person would not take.'[155] They contend that the orthodox legal and moral frameworks for analysing such situations adopt an inappropriate view of moral agency,[156] by equating freedom with independence. Majeske, Parker and Frader also doubt the ability of the existing framework to deal properly with these cases. But it is the effect on the donor's will rather than the *source* of the pressure which is the principal concern here. Inevitably, voluntariness/

[151] R. Simmons and C. Anderson, 'Related Donors and Recipients: Five to Nine Years Post-Transplant' (1982) 14 *Transplantation Proceedings* 9 at 11.

[152] K. Schneewind, 'Psychological Aspects in Living Organ Donation' in Collins *et al.*, *Procurement, Preservation and Allocation*, 325 at 329.

[153] Simmons *et al.*, 'Family Tension', at 910–11.

[154] Crouch and Elliott, 'Moral Agency', at 276.

[155] Ibid., at 277.

[156] Ibid., at 278.

willingness runs along a spectrum and in most instances is clearly at one or other end, thereby presenting no problems of screening and evaluation. But testing for ambivalence requires a clear set of guidelines and procedures set against clear standards.

Tailoring standards

Feinberg states that

> If our purpose is to determine whether a person had an excuse for harming or endangering others, then varying with the seriousness of the harm involved we will select largely untailored standards. If, on the other hand, our purpose is to decide whether some person's impending dangerous but self-regarding conduct is voluntary enough to exempt him from protective interference, then we are likely to use standards tailored more closely to the special circumstances.[157]

'Voluntariness' must therefore be moulded by circumstances, the interests at stake, and the moral and legal purposes to be served. The tailoring of standards should take account of, *inter alia*, the riskiness and irrevocability of the conduct,[158] both factors supporting a rigorous standard in the LDT setting.

Protocols

If 'willingness' is the touchstone, then this has the potential to impose excessive burdens on medical practitioners procuring consent to medical procedures. Feinberg states: 'But if we impose subsequent liability on A even though A had no reason to know that coercive pressures or fraudulent misrepresentations were shaping B's motives for agreeing, then our treatment of A is unfair to him, even though he did impose a risk on B without B's valid consent.'[159] Indeed, in certain contexts concentration on the existence of objective overt evidence of pressure in order to cast suspicion on a consent is a fairer guide. Gardner identifies surgical treatment and other forms of invasive medicine and dentistry as fields

[157] He noted that it was once said that the circumstances rendering a confession inadmissible by the Supreme Court would not have been sufficient to vitiate a will: see Feinberg, *Harm to Self*, at 121.

[158] Feinberg explicitly recognises the importance of these factors in tailoring standards: ibid.

[159] Ibid., at 175–6.

where determinacy may be particularly desirable.[160] In relation to medical treatment, where the decision accords with the apparently best therapeutic option, there is generally no reason to doubt voluntariness, and the autonomous nature of the decision may normally be assumed and taken at face value, particularly where the decision is *prima facie* a reasonable one. However, living organ donation is not a therapeutic procedure at all and has potentially irreversible and permanent effects. Hewlett argues that in the analogous research context 'Whilst circumstances and people will always influence any decision we make, it is the responsibility of the researcher to ensure that in clinical research, these are not so strong as to be controlling.'[161] This has equal force as regards LDT. Moreover, there are inherent and substantial, and widely appreciated, pressures on all such donors, which at least create a *prima facie* concern on that score. These pressures, even overt threats, will nearly always be hidden from the clinicians procuring the consent. Whilst the law is largely unable to police and ensure voluntariness of decision-making, apart from setting up certain procedural criteria, protocols in place at different transplant centres should seek to provide supplementary measures to ensure that donors really do donate as a result of the exercise of free will. As has been noted above, the King's Fund Institute drew specific attention to the deficiencies in Britain in this regard and prompted the formulation of guidelines, which the British Transplantation Society has recently translated into specific advice.[162] Pressure will undoubtedly at least appear to exist in most instances where there is no mechanism for a potential donor to opt out without losing face. A right to withdraw consent is an inherent feature of all laws, and many jurisdictions have explicit legislation to reinforce this fact.[163] Moreover, transplant protocols routinely and appro-

[160] He states: 'There appears to be a major interest in allowing proponents of them to proceed safely on the basis of a standardised, determinate, formula as to the presence of consent. Under the *Olugboja* approach, a proponent would have to ponder whether a victim's apparent acceptance of the relevant invasion was "real consent" or was instead the product of sufficiently grievous felt pressure (induced, say, by an unassertive nature being overborne by all manner of social pressures) or of a mistake as to something of major moment to the particular victim': see Gardner, 'Appreciating *Olugboja*', at 296.

[161] S. Hewlett, 'Consent to Clinical Research – Adequately Voluntary or Substantially Influenced?' (1996) 22 *Journal of Medical Ethics* 232 at 233.

[162] Working Party of the British Transplantation Society and the Renal Association, *United Kingdom Guidelines for Living Donor Kidney Transplantation*, British Transplantation Society, London, 2000.

[163] Including Algeria, Bolivia, Colombia, France, Hong Kong, Hungary, Kuwait, Mexico, Panama, Poland, Portugal, Romania, the Slovak Republic, Slovenia, Spain and Tunisia.

priately allow for a 'clinical incompatibility excuse' for those relatives who do not wish to donate.

There are normally only a relatively modest number of such donors at each centre, whose work-up spans a significant period of time. Consequently the 'transaction cost' will generally be worth the investment of time and effort required (the 'attentiveness' to the subject). Ironically, in some jurisdictions, such as in the UK, the law mandates a significant investment of effort in determining motivation, but only in respect of genetically unrelated donors where, apart from possible commercial influences, such pressures are less obvious and expected. As regards related donors, it is left entirely up to centres whether to employ a specific process for ascertaining the motivation and strength of commitment/willingness of the individual prospective donor. However, a system involving a third, independent party assessing motivation and willingness would obviate much of the difficulty and ensure against potential prospective legal action. Recent protocols established for non-renal organs using living donors frequently employ third parties here.[164] The recent Recommendation of the Council of Europe on Living Related Liver Transplantation also stipulates that 'A mechanism for independent assessment of the donor should be available as a minimum requirement to ensure that he/she is not under pressure to consent.'[165] Eisendrath *et al.*, on the other hand, view such screening of prospective renal donors as being necessary only where there are indications of anxiety, ambivalence or coercion, rather than routinely.[166]

164 See N. Habid, X. Rogiers and C. Broelsch, 'Living Related Liver Transplantation' in Collins *et al.*, *Procurement, Preservation and Allocation*, at 19, and Shaw *et al.*, 'Ethics of Lung Transplantation', at 680.

165 Recommendation No. R(97) 16 of the Committee of Ministers to Member States on Liver Transplantation from Living Related Donors. In the United Kingdom under HOTA Regulations, this is a legal requirement for genetically unrelated donors only. This procedure might also be used to assess the psychological health of the donor as part of an attempt to avoid post-operative psychological harm. Article 10 of the Council of Europe's Draft Protocol states that 'Before organ and tissue removal, appropriate investigations and interventions shall be carried out to evaluate and reduce the physical and psychological risks to the health of the donor.' In fact, Cramond *et al.* have previously asserted that 'psychiatric screening of potential donors is essential if undesirable psychological sequelae are to be avoided': see W. Cramond *et al.*, 'Psychological Screening of Potential Donors in a Renal Homotransplantation Programme' (1967) 113 *British Journal of Psychiatry* 1213 at 1220.

166 R. Eisendrath *et al.*, 'Psychologic Considerations in the Selection of Kidney Transplant Donors' (1969) 129 *Surgery, Gynecology & Obstetrics* 243 at 244–5.

Soliciting?

Pressure may also be induced by the means by which a potential donor is approached to donate or even informed of the possibility of donation. Laws fail to address such issues, but in any event they are matters dealt with more appropriately in transplant centre protocols. Simmons *et al.* stated that 'When a direct question is formulated, the situation itself becomes structured so that avoidance is difficult and there is pressure to respond' and that 'The parties present at the time of such a request [that is to donate] may also exert situational pressure on the donor. If the recipient himself is present when the issue is raised, refusal or delay of decision-making becomes more difficult.'[167] In their survey they found that there was a higher level of ambivalence amongst the sub-group of 54 per cent of donors who experienced situational pressure than in relation to the donor population as a whole.[168] The King's Fund Report stated that

> simply being told that live donation is an option, and to consider coming forward for the relevant tests, would seem a defensible policy. In this way potential donors would be obliged to consider what they could do for a family member before anyone knows who is or is not medically suitable. Emotional coercion would be avoided, but personal responsibility encouraged . . . Some might argue that such a situation is still unfair: merely by virtue of being presented with the option the individual is immediately placed under an unwarranted moral burden. However, if this were accepted it would be tantamount to denying that we ever have a duty to face up to difficult decisions relating to the welfare of others. Indeed, there is a strong case for systematically informing relevant family members of the option. This is the only way of ensuring that those individuals who would genuinely have no difficulty in choosing to donate are not denied the opportunity through lack of knowledge.[169]

These remarks should elicit broad support.

In summary, whilst it is unrealistic to expect full voluntariness, that is total subjective willingness, in such decision-making, the large majority of donors are extremely willing and well motivated and do not later regret having donated. It is nevertheless incumbent on practitioners and centres practising LDT to create procedures and mechanisms for detecting

[167] Simmons *et al.*, *Gift of Life*, at 160.
[168] Ibid., at 161 (34 per cent as against 9 per cent).
[169] King's Fund, *A Question of Give and Take*, at 67.

ambivalence and allowing opportunities for withdrawal, for counselling and for registering the existence of pressure.[170] The tensions in relation to informed consent are clear, but the legal framework seems up to the task. There seems no reason yet to throw the baby out with the bathwater.

Institutionalisation

Although prisoners rarely donate organs for transplant whilst alive, some of the very first donors were prisoners who agreed to donate in order to reduce their sentences, and the debate is still current and contentious.[171] Opinions have been recently shaken up in the US by one Milton V. Griffin who was on death row in Missouri, and who offered to donate either a kidney or bone marrow in exchange for his life being spared. Indeed, on the very day of his scheduled execution, 25 March 1998, a Missouri House committee debated a bill allowing condemned inmates to donate bone marrow or a kidney in exchange for having their sentence changed to life in prison without parole.[172] Voluntariness is the principal concern surrounding organ donation by persons subject to imprisonment, whether whilst still alive or after death. A handful of jurisdictions explicitly prohibit prisoners from donating organs for transplantation purposes though. In Panama, the statute states that 'Minors, incompetent persons, prisoners, and, in general, any person who is subject to a restriction on his legal rights, shall be excluded from the scope of this Law',[173] and Paraguay has a similar proscription.[174] But should institutionalisation be viewed as fatally impairing the voluntariness of each and every consent?

Generally in law a person may be capable of giving a voluntary consent to medical treatment despite circumstances of detention. In *Freeman* v. *Home Office (No. 2)*[175] a prisoner serving a life sentence who had been administered tranquillisers sued for battery. It was held by the Court of

[170] Schneewind has proposed a 'rational counselling' model for the selection and evaluation of donors: see Schneewind, 'Psychological Aspects in Living Organ Donation', at 329.

[171] Many of the first seventy-five donors used at Denver in the US were prisoners for instance.

[172] See Internet, 18 March 1998, at http://europe.cnn.com/US/9803/16/briefs/death.row.donors.ap/.

[173] Law of 11 July 1983, section 22. The Slovak Republic does not permit organ donation by any person serving a prison sentence: see 1994 Law, section 46(2).

[174] Section 2789 of the Law states that organ removal from 'persons suffering from the disabilities prescribed by law, pregnant women or detainees' is forbidden. It is reported that Guatemala has a comparable provision.

[175] [1984] 1 All ER 1036 (CA).

Appeal that a prisoner is not *ipso facto* incapable of exercising a free choice and consenting to medical treatment. Whether a consent was freely and voluntarily given to a particular medical procedure was a question of *fact* for decision in each particular case, rather than being a matter of law, and incarceration was simply a feature of the circumstances within which such decisions are made. Stephen Brown LJ endorsed the view of the trial judge who stated that 'The right approach, in my judgment, is to say that where, in a prison setting, a doctor has the power to influence a prisoner's situation and prospects a court must be alive to the risk that what may appear, on the face of it, to be real consent, is not in fact so.'[176] A different approach was adopted in the US in *Kaimowitz* v. *Michigan Department of Mental Health.*[177] In that case, which concerned the prospect of psychosurgery being performed upon an institutionalised mental patient, the Michigan court stated:

> Involuntarily confined mental patients live in an inherently coercive institutional environment. Indirect and subtle psychological coercion has a profound effect upon the patient population. Involuntarily confined patients cannot reason as equals with the doctors and administrators over whether they should undergo psycho-surgery. They are not able to voluntarily give informed consent because of the inherent inequality in their position.[178]

Indeed, it would appear that the patient had given consent to the psychosurgery partially out of a desire to show the doctors that he was a co-operative patient. However, this approach creates problems in the context of uncontroversial and clearly beneficial therapeutic treatments. Indeed, Annas, Glantz and Katz argue that the courts ultimately weigh the choices available and reach an overall decision as to the 'acceptable' nature of the procedure itself.[179] In *Kaimowitz* the procedure was extremely invasive, experimental and irreversible.

[176] [1984] 1 All ER 1036 at 1043G.

[177] 42 USLW 2063 (Michigan Circuit Court, 1973).

[178] The court added that 'It is impossible for an involuntarily detained mental patient to be free of ulterior forms of restraint or coercion when his very release from the institution may depend upon his co-operating with the institutional authorities and giving consent to experimental surgery.'

[179] Annas, Glantz and Katz, *Informed Consent to Human Experimentation*, at 151.

The price tag of non-compliance

But if the very fact of incarceration does not remove voluntariness, what about explicit or implicit 'carrots' to donate? In the philosophical literature a distinction has traditionally been drawn between *threats* which may coerce and therefore undermine voluntariness, on the one hand, and *offers* which are non-coercive and do not undermine because they are 'freedom enhancing', on the other. Nozick states that in an offer situation a person would prefer the 'post-proposal' position (because his options are expanded) but in the case of threats, he would prefer still to be in the 'pre-proposal' state.[180] Annas, Glantz and Katz, however, state that the promise of release or reduction of sentence as a reward must always be inherently coercive. One is saying that a failure to participate in the particular activity will result in sustained imprisonment.[181] These views may, as they stand, be rather too dogmatic, although they depend upon what one views as being the *status quo ante*. Beauchamp and Childress cite the actual example of the inmates of Newgate Prison sentenced to death who were given the opportunity of release and freedom if they participated in a research procedure involving smallpox. They all survived and gained release![182] Certainly from the point of view of the inmates this proved to be a highly beneficial, and presumably voluntary, decision!

The sword of Damocles

The distinction between an offer and a threat is not always clear though, and some 'offers' are in substance threats dressed up as offers. This issue is not, however, simply a matter of form. The Law Commission ultimately decided that the *reasonable expectations* of the individual might be a critical factor.[183] Other than in a purely 'one off' case, there will be a perception in instances where there is a prospect of a reduced sentence that the reality is that the sentence will be 'extended' if donation is not forthcoming – so that the donation in effect *becomes part of the sentence.* This would be wholly unacceptable and should be avoided. Moreover, one would have particular reason to be sceptical where the prison population

[180] Nozick, 'Coercion', at 458–64.

[181] Annas, Glantz and Katz, *Informed Consent to Human Experimentation*, at 115.

[182] Beauchamp and Childress, *Principles of Biomedical Ethics*, at 167.

[183] Law Commission, *Consent in the Criminal Law*, at para. 6.71.

was specifically targeted for any particular form of 'altruistic' conduct and it would be preferable to proscribe such conduct on the basis that suspicion as to the motivational forces or pressures at work creates an 'impression' of coercion whatever the reality may be.[184] Of course, probably for this reason, there have frequently been views expressed that, at the very least, prisoners should not be able to become living organ donors to strangers.[185] As Feinberg observes, the opportunities for abuse through coercion are so great in a prison setting that one cannot be sufficiently certain that an 'apparent' consent is indeed without some improper coercive influence.[186] These remarks apply equally to executed prisoners being used as cadaveric donors, despite their supposed 'consent'.

But what of donation by prisoners to close relatives who are in need? One could very easily imagine a prisoner giving a wholly voluntary consent to donate a kidney to a needy son, daughter, parent, spouse or sibling and without any other inducement. In fact, a prisoner serving a thirteen-year term for burglary and heroin possession recently requested to donate his only remaining kidney (he had previously donated his other to her) to his daughter whose own kidney was now failing.[187] Indeed, Akveld and De Charro argue

> It is true, the situation in which the detainee finds himself may make it uncertain whether or not he may come to a free decision, but detaineeship does not mean that someone lacks the possibility to determine his own will freely and independently. Thinking along these lines, we consider it wrong to deprive a detainee from his right to act as a donor, as a matter of course. That would comprise a restriction of self-determination, which does not naturally flow from deprivation of liberty.[188]

Thus, each case should be assessed, rigorously, on its merits. Certain jurisdictions do permit donation by prisoners in defined circumstances.

[184] With regard to the ethics of research using prisoners, the National Commission for the Protection of Human Subjects of Biomedical and Behavioral Research argued that the closed nature of prison environments creates a potential for abuse of authority and therefore invites the exploitation and coercion of prisoners: see *Report and Recommendations: Research Involving Prisoners*, Washington D.C., DHEW Publication No. OS 76–131, 1976.

[185] For instance by Gutmann and Gerok, 'International Legislation', at 320.

[186] Feinberg, *Harm to Self*, at 260.

[187] See D. Josefson, 'Prisoner Wants to Donate his Second Kidney' (1999) 318 *British Medical Journal* 7.

[188] J. Akveld and F. De Charro, 'Living Organ Donation in The Netherlands and in some other Countries' in Land and Dossetor, *Organ Replacement Therapy*, 44 at 47.

Mexico's 1976 Law, which states that the donor must not be deprived of his liberty at the time of the transplant, is qualified[189] so that 'Persons deprived of their liberty may give their consent to the use of their organs and tissues for therapeutic purposes only if the recipient is the spouse, concubine, or relative of the donor.' Bolivia's 1982 Law states that 'persons detained in closed institutions may donate organs and tissues only to immediate blood relatives or relatives by marriage'.[190] There are one or two other similar examples.[191]

Commercial incentives

An offer you can't refuse

Much of the discussion in the literature contrasting threats and offers seeks to avoid the view that offers can undermine voluntariness because, otherwise, the extraordinarily attractive job offer would undermine voluntariness when the intuition is that this is totally unobjectionable. In an offer situation, one can keep what one already has, that is maintain the status quo (which would usually be a very desirable property, for example liberty) without any preconditions. Consequently if an individual changes his/her position in response to the temptation created by an offer, it can be assumed that this was a voluntary choice reflecting the true will of the individual. When the continued exercise of a good is, however, made dependent on the performance of a condition with deleterious effects, there is at least a *prima facie* assumption that the individual did not really want to perform the condition and would not have done so in the absence of the threat. Nozick argues that where a person does something because of threats the will of another is operating or predominant, but that where he does something because of an offer his own will is still

[189] By section 328 of the 1987 General Law on Health.

[190] 1982 Law, section 5.

[191] Colombia's Decree No. 1172 of 6 June 1989 states, in section 32, that 'the donor must, at the time of expressing their wishes, not be deprived of liberty, except where the donation is made for the benefit of consanguineous relatives up to the fourth degree, relatives by marriage up to the second degree, or relatives of the first civil degree'. Section 269 of Burkina Faso's Law No. 23/94 of 19 May 1994 states that 'Persons deprived of their liberty may not consent to the cession of their organs or tissues for therapeutic purposes, unless such removal is for the benefit of members of their family . . .'

operative, he is expressing his own choice and making a voluntary decision.[192]

Whilst there have been attempts to argue that offers can be coercive,[193] this is not the general view. It may be, on the other hand, that an offer to an organ vendor in dire poverty could amount to *exploitation* instead. The English Law Commission recently considered whether their proposed offence of procuring consent by threats ought to include this sort of exploitation. It stated:

> The argument against holding such exploitation to be criminal is based on what is said to be a fundamental distinction between a threat to harm someone's interests and an offer to confer a benefit on them. It is obviously wrong to try to procure their consent by threatening to harm them (at any rate in an unlawful or otherwise 'improper' way); and it may in certain circumstances be wrong to try to procure it by taking advantage of their urgent need for something that one is in a position to provide. But it is not wrong in quite the same sense. The former is not just morally wrong in the abstract: it is a wrong *against the other person*, an infringement of his or her autonomy. The latter may be wrong but it is arguable that it does not wrong *the other person*: it cannot, because that person's position is either unaffected (because he or she declines the offer, in which case no harm is done) or improved (because he or she regards the offer as more attractive than what was hitherto the best available option).[194]

This concept is clearly orientated around the exploiter not the exploitee and is focusing upon the 'exploitive behaviour', for instance, of a commercial broker or middleman. It does not in itself undermine the validity of the seller's consent. It is interesting to note, in relation to genetically unrelated persons, that the UK Parliament has declared it to be a condition for a valid organ donation by such an individual that 'the donor's consent to the removal of the organ in question was not obtained by coercion *or the offer of an inducement*' (my emphasis).[195] This appears to presume that an offer of money in return for the donation of an organ

[192] Nozick, 'Coercion', at 459.

[193] See, for instance, Held, 'Coercion and Coercive Offers' and H. McCloskey, 'Coercion: Its Nature and Significance' (1980) 18 *Southern Journal of Philosophy* 335. See also Feinberg, *Harm to Self*, chapter 24.

[194] Law Commission, *Consent in the Criminal Law*, at para. 6.69.

[195] Per Regulation 3(2)(c), Human Organ Transplants (Unrelated Persons) Regulations 1989 (SI 1989 No. 2480).

is not necessarily coercive in a fashion which undermines consent, but is nevertheless illegitimate (inducement).

Gert has argued that there is a substantive difference between the 'gaining of a good' and the 'avoidance of an evil'[196] and that if the need to accept the job offer is driven by the latter we may properly argue that the person is forced to accept it.[197] It has been suggested that for those below what might be termed the 'moral subsistence level', payments required to raise a person above that level are necessarily coercive, when a similar offer to a person living above that level would not be. The irony of this would be that under such a scheme those people wishing to sell but who are not in compelling need would be able to sell, whereas those who *truly* want to by virtue of their plight would not. Notions of a minimum moral entitlement are especially difficult. In relation to potential, desperately poor, organ sellers, if all coercive circumstances undermined consent regardless of the will of the individual, they would be unable to take dangerous paid jobs and, in the context of paid organ donation, only the already rich would be able to sell organs. Arguably, it is the person's desperate situation of poverty which is the coercive influence and which 'controls' such decision-making, not the offer of money. The view has already been advanced above that circumstances alone do not, without more, undermine the voluntary character of a consent. Rawls, for instance, asserts that poverty does not coerce because it does not undermine freedom. Thus, although some poor donors may unwillingly consent to the donation of a kidney for money, one cannot make any blanket assessment of the voluntariness of decision-making of such a class of donors on the basis of such an offer alone. Although there is certainly a substantial inducement to the potential vendor in the prospect of payment, living donors are also subject to pressures, including related donors. The potential death of a relative must surely create a very great degree of coercion which ought therefore similarly to preclude donation. Ultimately, one can conclude that whilst some organ vendors may be subject to pressures of expectation or detriment which might undermine

[196] Gert, 'Coercion and Freedom', at 36. Feinberg similarly argues that where the acceptance of an offer is necessary to avoid a very great evil the offer is coercive, albeit that the individual was 'pulled' rather than 'pushed', but even he regards this as generally not being sufficient to undermine the voluntary nature of a given consent: see Feinberg, *Harm to Self*, at 248.

[197] This argument has been employed in connection with the use of paid prisoners as research subjects. If such payment is necessary to 'lift' them to a minimally decent standard of living it may be viewed as a 'forced' involvement.

the will of the individual, this is by no means inherent in the situation and could be determined in the same fashion as with any organ *donor*. The view that an offer of great magnitude to a person in desperate need is inherently exploitative is ultimately appealing to the notion of *(in)justice* rather than coercion or voluntariness.

8

Contentious classes of donors

The classes of donors considered here include unrelated persons, minors, mentally incapacitated adults, prisoners and pregnant women. They are all 'contentious' in the sense that they have all been relatively rarely used as living donors (although with fluctuating popularity), and have typically been viewed with a substantial degree of scepticism.[1] Moreover, the donation of organs by such persons is frequently subject to legislative restriction. Caution needs to be exercised though with regard to terminology here. Concepts of, for instance, an 'unrelated person' or a 'minor' are often highly jurisdiction or culture specific.

It is suggested that all of these classes of donors have been subject to unwarrantably dogmatic attitudes, resulting in excessive paternalism and arbitrary limits on permitted action. This disposition is principally driven by perceptions as to the vulnerability of,[2] and the extent of risks to, certain classes of potential donors, and possibly their capacity for altruistic action. In some instances this constitutes an indefensible denial of autonomy. Only with regard to genetically unrelated donors have *clinical* concerns linked to outcomes for recipients been a significant factor.

Living unrelated donors

The language of the discourse

There is no universal definition of an 'unrelated donor'. Donors can be related genetically, emotionally (formally, through marriage or engage-

[1] Sometimes described instead as 'unconventional' donors. High risk donors may also fall into this category. They present problems with regard to risk/benefit assessments.

[2] Restrictions on commercialism in this sphere typically focus on the exploitation or vulnerability of donors, although there are various other rationales for prohibition explored in chapter 9.

ments to be married), or otherwise (for example through friendship) or they can be strangers. Donors have historically appeared in all manner of guises, from volunteer prisoners in the United States to a German transplant surgeon[3] and to priests and nuns in Italy, allegedly with Papal blessing! In general though, distinctions are drawn on the basis of *genetic* ties. However, not only is there a difference between genetically related and other forms of 'related' donor,[4] even definitions of genetically related persons frequently *exclude* certain classes of donor with a genetic connection to the recipient. For instance, the United Kingdom Human Organ Transplants Act 1989 (HOTA) states that, for the purposes of the statute, a person is genetically related only to his natural parents and children, his siblings, aunts and uncles, cousins and nephews and nieces.[5] The definition excludes grandparents and grandchildren, amongst others, although it even includes many relations of the half blood as well as whole blood.[6] Other laws utilise alternative definitions of 'relatedness'. For instance, the Federal Indian Transplantation of Human Organs Act 1994 employs the concept of a 'near relative', which includes spouses as well as closely genetically related individuals. Definitions reflect the purposes of the legislation and the weighing of competing priorities, especially whether the avoidance of commercialisation is accorded precedence over the facilitation of transplantation.[7] Hong Kong legislation incorporates a unique compromise between these matters with regard to spouses. The

[3] Jochen Hoyer, a transplant surgeon from Lübeck, donated a kidney to an anonymous recipient in Munich in 1996 to highlight living donation, which accounts for only a small percentage of all donors there. The Bavarian Health Minister, however, criticised this action in view of the risks of commercialisation connected to the practice: see 'German Transplant Surgeon Donates His Kidney' (1996) 348 *Lancet* 328.

[4] Although providing no explanation of the expression, the Recommendation No. R(79) of the Council of Europe speaks of a 'closely related' donor in Article 8.

[5] In the United Kingdom this was primarily because blood relationships can be reliably, and fairly conclusively, 'proved' through (DNA) testing.

[6] Section 2, HOTA, 1989. Verbatim it states that a person is genetically related only to 'his natural parents and children, his brothers and sisters of the whole or half blood, the brothers and sisters of the whole or half blood of either of his natural parents, and the natural children of his brothers and sisters of the whole or half blood or of the brothers and sisters of the whole or half blood of either of his natural parents'.

[7] It has been remarked that in India it would not be acceptable to reduce spouses 'to the status of a nonrelation': see R. Kishore, 'Organ Transplantation: Legislative Perspectives and the Indian Law' in D. Price and J. Akveld (eds.), *Living Organ Donation in the Nineties: European Medico-Legal Perspectives*, EUROTOLD, 1996, 79 at 82, although the obligations accepted by wives in Indian culture (as well as in countries such as China) may create problems as regards voluntariness: see previous chapter.

statute employs the same general definition as in HOTA but treats analogously as a relative a spouse whose marriage has subsisted for at least three years, where the genuineness of the relationship is transparent.[8]

Clearly, in view of the heterogeneity of classes of unrelated donors it will be impossible to detect a homogeneous attitude towards them even within a single culture. Moreover, some of the reservations about using unrelated donors have more force in respect of donors unrelated by certain criteria than others. Nonetheless, First has recently asserted that living unrelated donors (LUDs) may become 'a major source of organs in the future';[9] certainly the donor pool is extremely large.[10] An important recent development has been the establishment of paired kidney exchange protocols[11] under which individuals not medically suitable to their own sick relatives may be suitable as donors for other patients, who in turn have willing but medically unsuitable relatives. These individuals may be able to be 'paired off' so that both transplants can take place. Although, strictly, such donors are 'unrelated' to their recipients, such a strategy offers hope to many who otherwise might not be able to be transplanted at all, or at least not so expeditiously.[12] Interestingly, in 1998 an Israeli Arab man donated his kidney to a Jewish man whose wife in turn donated her kidney to the Muslim wife.[13]

[8] Hong Kong Human Organ Transplant Bill 1992 and Ordinance No. 16 of 1995. Although the latter Ordinance was enacted in February 1995, it did not come into force until 1 April 1998.

[9] M. First, 'Controversies in Organ Donation: Minority Donation and Living Unrelated Renal Donors' (1997) 29 *Transplantation Proceedings* 67 at 68.

[10] It appears that a living unrelated programme need not hinder the development of a cadaveric programme at a later stage, as this has occurred in Iran: see A. Daar *et al.*, 'Reimbursement, "Rewarded Gifting", Financial Incentives and Commercialism in Living Organ Donation' in G. Collins, J. Dubernard, W. Land and G. Persijn (eds.), *Procurement, Preservation and Allocation of Vascularized Organs*, Kluwer, Dordrecht, 1997, 301 at 310.

[11] For instance, at the University of Chicago. This is a pilot scheme: see 'Ethics of a Paired-Kidney-Exchange Program' (1997) 336 *New England Journal of Medicine* 1752.

[12] Such a scheme was first suggested by Felix Rapaport who envisaged an extremely large kidney donor pool akin to international bone marrow registries: see F. Rapaport, 'The Case for a Living Emotionally Related International Kidney Donor Exchange Registry' (1986) 18 (Supp. 2) *Transplantation Proceedings* 5. Fellner even foresaw the possibility of such a 'pool' producing an identically matched donor for every potential recipient: see C. Fellner, 'Organ Donation: For Whose Sake?' (1973) 79 *Annals of Internal Medicine* 589.

[13] See 'Israeli Kidney Swap Unites Jews and Muslims' (1998) 351 *Lancet* 1641.

Forgotten and unwanted volunteers

There has been what has been described as a 'widespread aversion' to LUDs from the outset,[14] although it has been argued that 'the reasons for the unrelated donor rejection appear to be unscientific, emotional, and prejudicial',[15] and although unrelated donors are the *norm* for blood donation and are commonly used as bone marrow donors. A survey of fifty-four transplant centres worldwide in the late sixties by Sadler and colleagues revealed that half disapproved of using unrelated donors. The replies contained 'Much evidence of distrust and suspicion toward the motivation of such donors and a definite repugnance concerning their use'.[16] In the absence of authoritative and comprehensive guidance from the professional bodies, attitudes and practices have generally devolved to individual centres,[17] and Spital contends that

> Implicit in the paternalistic approach of transplant centres toward living donors is the assumption that the centre knows what is in the donor's best interest. But having the advantage of medical expertise is not sufficient to justify this claim . . . When a centre rejects a competent individual who wants to donate despite the risk, presumably for the donor's own good, the centre is imposing values foreign to that person.[18]

Nonetheless, in the sixties LUDs were a fairly attractive option for end-stage renal patients because of the shortage of dialysis facilities and the poor results from – and the meagre volume of – cadaveric transplantation, and constituted as much as 10 per cent of the total donor pool.[19] Their

[14] A. Spital, 'Unrelated Living Kidney Donors: An Update of Attitudes and Use Among US Transplant Centers' (1994) 57 *Transplantation* 1722 at 1723.

[15] C. Fellner and S. Schwartz, 'Altruism in Disrepute: Medical Versus Public Attitudes Toward the Living Organ Donor' (1971) 284 *New England Journal of Medicine* 582.

[16] H. Sadler *et al.*, 'The Living, Genetically Unrelated, Kidney Donor' (1971) 3 *Seminars in Psychiatry* 86.

[17] Borgida *et al.* contend that 'Until recently, the lack of clear policies governing living unrelated donation has discouraged many transplant centers from tapping this source of kidneys': see E. Borgida *et al.*, 'The Minnesota Living Donor Studies: Implications for Organ Procurement' in J. Shanteau and R. Jackson Harris, *Organ Donation and Transplantation: Psychological and Behavioral Factors*, American Psychological Association, Washington D.C., 1991, 108 at 109.

[18] A. Spital, 'The Ethics of Unconventional Living Organ Donation' (1991) 5 *Clinical Transplantation* 322 at 323–4.

[19] Up to 1966 LUDs provided almost 10 per cent of the 1,488 kidneys reported to the Renal Transplant Registry: see Advisory Committee to the Renal Transplant Registry, 'The Ninth Report of the Human Renal Transplant Registry' (1972) 220 *Journal of the American Medical Association* 253.

use was virtually abandoned in the seventies however with the exception of centres such as the University of Wisconsin at Madison and those in some parts of Asia,[20] because of poor results (no better than cadaver transplantation), the increasing availability of dialysis (in developed transplant nations), and concerns about the donor's motivation and the risks involved.

Negativity remained pervasive in the West into the eighties even in respect of donors with whom the recipient had an emotional bond, for example spouses, fiancé(e)s, established partners, close friends, etc. The First Report of the Conference of European Health Ministers in 1987 asserted that

> Where the future donor is only legally related (spouse) the positions are less clear as one can very easily imagine that the reasons which lead one spouse to donate a kidney to improve the other's living conditions have a real and profound emotional basis. On the other hand, opinions concerning organ removal from unrelated living persons are very divided, although a majority is emerging against this practice.[21]

However, the utilisation of such donors has grown of late. In the US the volume of transplants tripled between 1991 and 1995[22] and in the UK the number has risen from nine in the 1995–6 period to twenty-five in 1997–8.[23] Within Europe generally however, there is substantial diversity between countries and even from centre to centre within the same nation.[24]

Spital's survey of US renal transplant centre attitudes in 1993 revealed an increasingly liberal attitude towards unrelated donation. Of the 127

[20] In Japan between 1964 and 1991, just over 2 per cent of all transplants used unrelated donors: see K. Ota, 'Living Donor Kidney Transplantation in Japan' (1994) 26 *Transplantation Proceedings* 2084.

[21] First Report of the Conference of European Health Ministers (Paris, 16–17 November 1987) *Ethical and Socio-cultural Problems Raised by Organ Transplantation*, Council of Europe, Strasbourg, 1987, at 9. The Report noted that the use of unrelated donors for transplantation would be more likely to be viewed as acceptable where there was a lack of dialysis facilities available: ibid.

[22] See M. Suzuki, J. Cecka and P. Terasaki, 'Unrelated Living Donor Kidney Transplants' (1997) 53 (No. 4) *British Medical Bulletin* 854 at 859. In 1991, this constituted only 1 per cent of all renal transplants but by 1994 this had risen to 4 per cent: see First, 'Controversies in Organ Donation', at 68.

[23] *Unrelated Live Transplant Regulatory Authority Report 1995–8*, ULTRA, 1999, at 5.

[24] In 1995, Norway performed fourteen LUD transplants, Italy eleven, Switzerland eight and there were 11 within the Eurotransplant area, but neither France nor Spain performed any at all.

responding centres 88 per cent stated that they would accept spouses as donors, 63 per cent of them friends and 15 per cent even strangers.[25] By contrast, a similar study in 1984–5 found 60 per cent of US centres *opposed* even to spousal donation.[26] EUROTOLD's 1996 survey of European transplant centres discovered that nearly 60 per cent of centres would accept spouses and 10 per cent friends.[27] However, such increasing openness does not fully reflect itself in the actual use of such donors. Indeed, a 1994 survey in the US revealed that although 90 per cent (154) of responding centres stated that they accepted emotionally related donors,[28] only about one-third of those centres *actively encouraged* spousal donation and only 25 per cent encouraged friends.[29] The public have always displayed less aversion to the use of unrelated kidney donors than clinicians though.[30] A 1987 survey of public attitudes showed that 77 per cent believed it was acceptable for friends to donate a kidney to one another and 70 per cent for strangers,[31] although of course not everyone would do what they say they would do.

[25] See Spital, 'Unrelated Living Kidney Donors: An Update', at 1722. This contrasted with a similar survey conducted in 1987, which found that seventy-five out of ninety-nine responding centres (76 per cent) would have allowed spouses to donate to each other, 48 per cent of centres would have allowed adult friends to donate and 8 per cent would have allowed strangers: see A. Spital, 'Unconventional Living Kidney Donors – Attitudes and Use Among Transplant Centers' (1989) 48 *Transplantation* 243 at 244.

[26] A. Spital, M. Spital and R. Spital, 'The Living Kidney Donor: Alive and Well' (1986) 146 *Archives of Internal Medicine* 1993.

[27] EUROTOLD Project Management Group Report to the European Commission of the European Communities (ed. P. Donnelly and D. Price), *Questioning Attitudes to Living Donor Transplantation*, EUROTOLD, 1997, at 137–41. Eighty-five centres responded to this question. See further D. Price, 'The EUROTOLD Project' (1998) 3(2) *Annals of Transplantation* 34. A British Transplantation Society survey in 1996 found that in the UK twenty-six out of the thirty-one centres with a living donor programme accepted spouses and partners and twelve of them accepted either friends or strangers, or both: see Report of the British Transplantation Society Working Party on Organ Donation, British Transplantation Society, London, 1996.

[28] A. Spital, 'Do US Transplant Centers Encourage Emotionally Related Kidney Donation?' (1996) 61 *Transplantation* 374.

[29] Ibid., at 374–7. Thus, most of these centres merely present it as an option.

[30] See Sadler *et al.*, 'The Living, Genetically Unrelated' at 97. On this, Burley and Stiller state that Fellner and Schwartz reported that 'the decision to bar him [the unrelated donor] appears to have been made somehow by private consensus of the medical teams involved who do not seem to be aware that in doing so they are grossly out of step with public opinion': see J. Burley and C. Stiller, 'Emotionally Related Donors and Renal Transplantation' (1985) 17 *Transplantation Proceedings* 123 at 124.

[31] A. Spital and M. Spital, 'Living Kidney Donation: Attitudes Outside the Transplant Center' (1988) 148 *Archives of Internal Medicine* 1077. An earlier survey found that 11 per cent of the public would 'definitely' and 43 per cent would 'probably' donate a kidney to a needy

Policy matters

International and national policy statements have invariably been either negative or ambivalent regarding unrelated living organ donation. World Health Organisation Guiding Principle 3 states: 'Adult living persons may donate organs, but in general such donors should be genetically related to the recipients. Exceptions may be made in the case of transplantation of bone marrow or other acceptable regenerative tissues.'[32] There is inherent ambiguity here, but the accompanying Commentary states that the intention underpinning it is to discourage donation from genetically unrelated donors.[33] The notion that living unrelated donation should be 'exceptional' is pervasive in other official policy statements.[34] Article 4 of the Council of Europe Resolution (78) 29 states that 'Removal of substances which cannot regenerate must be confined between genetically related persons except in exceptional cases where there are good chances of success.'[35] Whilst the Council of Europe Convention is silent on this matter, the recent Draft Protocol states, more reservedly, that organ removal shall only be carried out for the benefit of a recipient 'with whom the donor has an appropriate relationship'.[36]

Laws display considerable diversity in relation to LUDs. Whilst most legislation is silent on the subject, thereby preserving this as a matter for clinical discretion, the distinction between related and unrelated donors

stranger – only 24 per cent totally ruled out the possibility: see Fellner and Schwartz, 'Altruism in Disrepute', at 583. Sadler's survey of San Francisco residents related that only 46 per cent of respondents would 'definitely not' donate a kidney to a stranger: see Sadler *et al.*, 'The Living, Genetically Unrelated', at 97.

32 World Health Organisation, *Guiding Principles on Human Organ Transplantation*, 1991, WHO.

33 Because of the link between commercial practices and the use of unrelated donors, particularly in South America and parts of Asia.

34 The General Medical Council's 'Guidance for Doctors on Transplantation of Organs From Live Donors' states that 'Unrelated live donor transplants should be considered only under exceptional circumstances' (Guideline 7), GMC, December 1992. Similar guidance has been issued to doctors by the Medical Ethical Committee of the Dutch Transplantation Society: see D. Hessing, 'Living Donors: Some Psychological Aspects of Informed Consent' in Price and Akveld, *Living Organ Donation in the Nineties*, 99 at 102.

35 It is similarly explicit in the Guidelines issued by the Transplantation Society that 'Living unrelated donors (that is not first degree relatives) should be used exceptionally when a satisfactory cadaver or living related donor cannot be found': see Council of the Transplantation Society, *Commercialisation in Transplantation: The Problems and some Guidelines for Practice*, 1985.

36 Article 9, Council of Europe Draft Protocol on Transplantation of Organs and Tissues of Human Origin, 9 March 1999.

frequently appears in the context of the ability of *minors* to donate body materials.[37] However, a significant minority of jurisdictions do totally prohibit organ donation by certain 'unrelated' adult persons. In Slovenia, a person may only donate a kidney or part of a liver to a genetic or familial relative,[38] and in the Russian Federation organ donation is limited to persons with a 'genetic relationship' to the recipient. In Germany, 'the removal of organs which cannot regenerate is only admissible for the purpose of transplanting to relatives of the first or second degree, spouses, fiancés or other persons with whom the donor obviously entertains an especially intimate personal relationship'.[39] In other jurisdictions, donation is prohibited beyond certain *degrees* of relationship.[40] In Portugal, the donor and recipient must be related up to the third degree.[41] In certain jurisdictions, although a particular class of unrelated living donation is not proscribed, it is only permitted to take place in exceptional cases. In France, the recipient must be the father, mother, son, daughter or sibling of the organ donor, but a spouse may also donate in an 'emergency'.[42] Sweden's 1995 Law[43] states that *in special cases* persons not related to, nor particularly close to, the donor, may donate non-regenerative biological materials for transplant purposes.

Some nations, whilst not precluding unrelated donation *per se*, have

[37] For instance, Article 8 of Sweden's Law No. 831 of 8 June 1995 states that a minor who is incapable of giving consent may not donate any body materials unless the donor is 'related' to the recipient. In Michigan also, a minor over fourteen years of age may donate to a parent, child or sibling: see Mich. Comp. Laws Ann. s. 700.407 (West 1980). See also Belgian Law of 13 June 1986, section 7.

[38] Law of the Transplantation of Human Body's Parts for the Sake of Medical Treatment, 1996, Article 8.

[39] Law of 5 November 1997, section 8(1). Italian law restricts LDT to the nuclear family unit (including half-brothers and sisters).

[40] In Honduras, only siblings are permitted by decree to become donors: see H. Fuenzalida-Puelma, 'Organ Transplantation: The Latin American Legislative Response' in World Health Organisation, *Informal Consultation on Organ Transplantation*, WHO, Geneva, May 1990, Appendix. In Venezuela, donation may only be made to first degree blood relatives but the National Executive has a discretion to approve a wider range of donors.

[41] Law of 22 April 1993, section 6(2). In Costa Rica, a person may only donate to a relative up to the fourth degree of consanguinity or up to the third degree of affinity, or to a spouse: see Law of 20 August 1974, section 15. In Argentina, 1993 Law, section 15 prohibits donation beyond the fourth degree of relationship. Less dogmatically, Mexican law states that a donor is '*preferably* a first degree relative of the recipient' (my emphasis), Federal Regulations, 16 August 1976, section 31.

[42] Law of 29 July 1994, Article L. 671–3.

[43] Law of 8 June 1995, section 7. This Law came into force on 1 July 1996 and repeals the earlier 1975 legislation.

prescriptions relating to the degree of (histo)compatibility between donor and recipient, which might impact on the practice of using unrelated, even spousal, donors. In Ecuador and Greece, for instance, the donor and recipient must be 'histocompatible'. However, these laws require only *some* degree of compatibility and would therefore only very occasionally be exclusionary.[44] Nevertheless, such provisions highlight the danger of embedding evolving clinical criteria in a concrete legal form. This problem is offset by the wording of the Cypriot law which stipulates that the recipient must be 'immunologically compatible with the donor *or, according to scientific criteria, should tolerate the biological materials removed*' (my emphasis).[45]

In certain jurisdictions, additional legislative pre-conditions exist for LUDs. In the UK, HOTA, whilst not excluding genetically unrelated individuals, requires that all such potential donors, even those emotionally related to the recipient, be screened by an independent statutory body, ULTRA (Unrelated Live Transplant Regulatory Authority), to ensure the absence of commercial influence and the existence of a proper voluntary and informed consent to donation.[46] Similarly in Poland 'other close relatives' (not direct linear relatives, siblings, spouses or adopted relatives) require the approval of the regional court.[47]

Reservations and rejections

The following objections to the use of unrelated donors have been consistently raised: first, that the results are not good enough to justify the risks; secondly, that accepting such individuals opens the door to commercialism in transplantation; thirdly, that the donor must be either coerced or crazy to do such a thing; and fourthly, that the donor is subjected to risk without the chance of benefit.[48] These condense down

[44] Indeed, if the parties are not incompatible in a specific instance then there *is* (histo)compatibility by definition.

[45] Law of 22 May 1987, section 7.

[46] HOTA section 2, and the Human Organ Transplants (Unrelated Persons) Regulations 1989 (SI 1989 No. 2480).

[47] Law of 26 October 1995, Article 10. In India, non-'near relatives' require the prior approval of the Authorisation Committee and in Hong Kong they require the prior approval of the Board of Regulation.

[48] A. Spital, 'Unrelated Living Donors: Should They be Used?' (1992) 24 *Transplantation Proceedings* 2215. See also Burley and Stiller, 'Emotionally Related Donors', at 123.

into two main concerns: that relating to results and that to issues of altruism.[49]

A break with tradition

With respect to the initial, primarily clinical, concern, recent studies show that, whatever the historical position, very good results are obtainable using genetically unrelated donors. Terasaki *et al.*'s survey of LUD transplants performed across ninety-seven US centres revealed graft survival of 85 per cent at three years from spouses and 81 per cent from living unrelated non-spousal donors, contrasted with over 90 per cent from HLA (Human Leucocyte Antigen) identical siblings, 82 per cent from parents and 70 per cent from cadaveric donors.[50] Similar results have been reported at individual centre level.[51] The authors of a recent US study concluded that 'The use of LURD [living unrelated donor] transplants provides patient and graft survival comparable to LRD [living related] transplants, and superior to CRD [cadaver] transplants, despite inferior HLA matching.'[52] Data from within Europe are less extensive and complete, but comparable. At La Sapienza at the University of Rome, 177 LUDs were performed between December 1983 and January 1998, with actuarial graft survival results at fourteen years superior to cadaver grafts for both emotionally related donors (149) and donors related by law (28).[53] Moreover, results show very good outcomes from spousal

[49] See further D. Price and H. Akveld, 'Living Donor Organ Transplantation in Europe: Re-evaluating its Role' (1998) 5 *European Journal of Health Law* 19.

[50] P. Terasaki *et al.*, 'High Survival Rates of Kidney Transplants from Spousal and Living Unrelated Donors' (1995) 333 *New England Journal of Medicine* 333. See also Suzuki *et al.*, 'Unrelated Living Donor Kidney Transplants', at 854.

[51] Ploeg *et al.* reported on four-year graft survival from 990 kidney transplants performed at the University of Wisconsin. Results of 95 per cent were achieved for HLA identical related donors, 86 for haplo(half-)matched related donors, 85 for living *unrelated* donors (thirty-two spousal, eight friend and six relative by marriage) and 76 for cadaveric donors: see R. Ploeg *et al.*, 'Living Unrelated Kidney Donation: An Under-utilised Resource?' (1993) 25 *Transplantation Proceedings* 1532.

[52] J. Lowell *et al.*, 'Living Unrelated Renal Transplantation Affords Optimal Donor Utilisation' (1996) 28 *Transplantation Proceedings* 63. Graft survival for LUDs (86 per cent of whom were spouses) after five years was 85.9 per cent compared with 70.7 per cent for cadaveric donors. In Asia, 88 per cent graft survival at five years has also been reported from Seoul: see K. Park *et al.*, 'Single-Center Experience of Unrelated Living-Donor Renal Transplantation in the Cyclosporine Era' in P. Terasaki and J. Cecka (eds.), *Clinical Transplants 1992*, UCLA Tissue Typing Laboratory, 1992, at 249.

[53] See D. Alfani *et al.*, 'Issues in Organ Donation: Living Unrelated Kidney Transplantation' (1998) 30 *Transplantation Proceedings* 2255. At Oslo, between 1969 and 1995, 115 LUD

transplants in both directions, despite potential immunisation of the wife by previous pregnancies. These data suggest that there is no good *a priori* reason to exclude genetically unrelated donors on clinical grounds today, nor even necessarily permit LUDs only as a last resort, where no other suitable donors are available. Each case needs to be evaluated on its merits.[54] There is no doubt that much of the recent reluctance to use unrelated donors, and the notion that they should be a *last resort*, has partially stemmed from the perceived need for genetic matching to ensure satisfactory graft survival.[55] This attitude may require revision. In any event, Spital has remarked that at most US centres genetically related donors are clearly preferred, but that 'While the potential benefit from genetic matching likely contributes to this view, it is probably not the only factor.'[56] Thiel argues that the barriers for surgeons and physicians are essentially 'psychological' here rather than clinical.[57]

Altruistic?

Other objections revolve around doubts about the motivations or willingness of such donors. In a 1993–4 US survey, it was revealed that the most frequent reason for rejecting strangers was uncertainty concerning altruistic motivations. Some centres were concerned about ulterior motives, including financial gain, and some about possible psycho-

transplants were performed, with results overall significantly better than with cadaveric donors: see A. Jakobsen, 'Living Donor Practices in Europe' in Price and Akveld, *Living Organ Donation in the Nineties*, 1 at 6. Eurotransplant data show three-year graft survival for living spousal donors comparable, or slightly superior, even to cadaveric transplants with zero mismatches: see G. Thiel, 'Living Unrelated Kidney Transplantation' in Collins *et al.*, *Procurement, Preservation and Allocation*, 367 at 368.

54 There is evidence to suggest that as well as tissue match, age matching may also have a significant bearing on outcomes, especially for spousal donation: see P. Donnelly *et al.*, 'Living Donor Kidney Transplantation in the United Kingdom and Ireland: Does Donor–Recipient Age Difference Matter?' in W. Land and J. Dossetor (eds.), *Organ Replacement Therapy: Ethics, Justice, Commerce*, Springer-Verlag, Berlin, 1991, at 54.

55 In this respect non-related and emotionally (but not genetically) related donors share similar characteristics.

56 This is borne out to some degree by the fact that even wholly mismatched *siblings* have been used from the beginning at some centres: see Burley and Stiller, 'Emotionally Related Donors', at 125.

57 The historical reliance upon the vital importance of tissue compatibility is, if anything, declining, although the importance of especially good tissue matches to outcomes from LUDs (and the importance of avoiding total HLA mismatches) has recently been emphasised on the basis of the results of the Collaborative Transplant Study: see G. Opelz, 'HLA Compatibility and Kidney Grafts from Unrelated Live Donors' (1998) 30 *Transplantation Proceedings* 704.

pathology.[58] In the early seventies, Fellner and Schwartz stated that 'If he is unrelated and not connected to the recipient by any emotional ties, he is suspected of being mentally ill or emotionally unbalanced and almost all transplant centers will exclude him *a priori* from donation.'[59] The 1993–4 survey also revealed reservations about the use of friends, on the basis that the emotional attachment might not be sufficiently strong to ensure an altruistic motive.[60] The Conference of European Health Ministers displayed similar scepticism, stating that 'Although altruism is a noble sentiment, it is unfortunately not a common one. Outside the immediate family circle, it is not very likely that donors will be found acting from sheer altruism. This consideration has led some countries to refuse to accept non-related donors. Most countries will, however, accept them only in exceptional circumstances.'[61] As a consequence of such perceptions the genetic relative has dominated the scene.

The profit motive

Concerns linked to commercialism have lately become more preoccupying in relation to the use of living organ donors. In 1970 the first international policy statement linking commerce with organ procurement was published, in the Statement of the Committee on Morals and Ethics of the Transplantation Society. The linkage with *unrelated* donors soon followed. The World Health Assembly adopted Resolutions (WHA40.13 and WHA42.5) condemning trade in human organs in 1987 and 1989 (Fortieth and Forty-second Assemblies). These became embodied in the WHO Guiding Principles in 1991, the Preamble to which states: 'Rational argument can be made to the effect that shortage has led to the rise of commercial traffic in human organs, particularly from living donors who are unrelated to recipients.' Broyer even argues that 'It is so difficult to be sure that an unrelated living donor is not paid that it is better to refuse such donors a priori.'[62] But genuine marriages, non-marital partnerships

[58] Spital, 'Unrelated Living Kidney Donors: An Update', at 1722.

[59] Fellner and Schwartz, 'Altruism in Disrepute', at 582.

[60] Spital, 'Unrelated Living Kidney Donors: An Update', at 1725.

[61] Third Report of the Conference of European Health Ministers (Paris, 16–17 November 1987), *Organ Transplantation: Legislative Measures in Relation to Organ Transplantation and to European Co-operation*, Council of Europe, Strasbourg, 1987, at 5.

[62] M. Broyer, 'Aspects of Living Organ Donation with Emphasis on the Fight Against Commercialism' in Land and Dossetor, *Organ Replacement Therapy*, 197 at 198.

and friendships are not properly and inevitably connected to profiteering.[63] Yet, jurisdictions that either exclude such classes of donor or make donation by such individuals subject to special scrutiny on this ground establish a presumption of commercial influence even where the parties are emotionally related. Yet even Broyer would make exceptions in the case of parties with a deep emotional bond, such as spouses. Of course, establishing the genuineness of a relationship may be problematic in some contexts and in some circumstances, but where stability exists in the relationship such concerns are generally misconceived. As noted above, in Hong Kong spouses are within the permitted classes of donors without further scrutiny where the marriage has subsisted for at least three years. By contrast, in India all spouses are defined as 'related' and require no further scrutiny, whereas in the UK donation by spouses is *prima facie* illegal and requires independent endorsement. In Germany, recent legislation even explicitly includes fiancés within the class of permissible donors. The response should be proportionate to the risk. In the UK, however, the response was a direct result of a scandal involving purchases of organs from Turkish peasants which threatened to rock public confidence in the transplantation system. In that light the sweeping legislative provisions enacted are understandable in view of the bogus relationships claimed by some parties entering the country for donation/transplantation purposes, although amendment may be appropriate now. In fact, in Britain ULTRA received eighty-five applications up to 1998 relating to kidneys, and one concerning a lung lobe transplant, and found no evidence of commercial influence in any instance.[64] Furthermore, Evans properly observes that, if designed to eradicate the existence of *third party brokers*, 'a formal "genetic relative" restriction would be misplaced. The way to prevent trafficking is to act against those who would actually take commercial advantage of the need for organs, that is, those who would undertake the procurement arrangements on a solely commercial basis.'[65]

[63] There is evidence though that intra-familial financial benefits are received fairly routinely, although not overtly, in certain jurisdictions. In India it is estimated that up to 40 per cent of genetically related donors are subtly coerced or stand to obtain a monetary benefit from donation of a kidney: see K. Reddy, 'A Perspective on Reality' in C. Kjellstrand and J. Dossetor (eds.), *Ethical Problems in Dialysis and Transplantation*, Kluwer, Dordrecht, 1992, 155.

[64] *Unrelated Live Transplant Regulatory Authority Report 1995–8*, at 5.

[65] M. Evans, 'Organ Donations Should Not be Restricted to Relatives' (1989) 15 *Journal of*

Of course, as the WHO Preamble set out above explicitly recognises, it is the very shortage of organ donors itself which creates the *demand* and conditions for commercialisation to flourish. Moreover, Kishore observes that rejecting *unpaid* unrelated donors entirely may even cause demand for unrelated *paid* donation to flourish.[66] Countries with extremely low rates of cadaveric transplantation and pervasive poverty, such as India, are prime locations for such commerce and attract trade from foreign patients unable to obtain organs in their countries of origin. There is, however, substantial evidence of high rates of infection through using unrelated donors in countries such as India. Johny *et al.* from Kuwait state: 'The major concern is the transmission of infection, especially by viral carriers or through blood transfusions.'[67] Such perceptions are widely shared by clinicians across a variety of nations, including Germany. This of course is not a function of unrelated organ donation *per se*, but of lax standards in many centres using such donors for profit and the poor pre-operative health of many of the donors used. Commercial incentives clearly encourage a high 'turnover' and cutting corners wherever possible.[68] But that need not be an argument against using unrelated donors, rather against commercialism generally or just in certain contexts.[69] In any event, these donors are typically strangers without an emotional tie to the recipient. One may permit certain forms of genetically unrelated, but emotionally related, donation without necessarily creating the same potential for commercial influence. In 1986, British Transplantation Society guidelines stated that the donor should be either a spouse, a blood

Medical Ethics 17 at 19. He added that 'the proper response is to attack the exploitation of the act of donation, not the act itself': ibid. Socio-economic factors are a potential influence on donation, as has been noted by the British Medical Association: see *Guidelines on the Transplant of Tissues and Organs*, revised August 1990, at 3. Interestingly, the law in the Russian Federation precludes any transplant where the donor is 'dependent upon the recipient, either because of their functions or in any other manner': see Law of 22 December 1992, section 3. This would preclude spousal and child-to-parent donations in many instances.

66 R. Kishore, 'Organ Donation: Consanguinity or Universality', paper lodged with the EUROTOLD Project, 1996.

67 K. Johny *et al.*, 'Values Gained and Lost in Live Unrelated Renal Transplantation' (1990) 22 *Transplantation Proceedings* 915 at 916.

68 Using limited immunosuppression, discharging from hospital prematurely and providing no follow-up are examples of such phenomena.

69 Cameron and Hoffenberg assert that even paid organ procurement need not take place under unsatisfactory medical conditions: see S. Cameron and R. Hoffenberg, 'The Ethics of Organ Transplantation Reconsidered: Paid Organ Donation and the Use of Executed Prisoners as Donors' (1999) 55 *Kidney International* 724 at 727.

relative of the spouse (in law relative) or a 'friend who has a close and enduring relationship with the recipient'.[70] I return to the question of whether commerce is itself independently legitimate in a later chapter.

Pressure points

With regard to pressures upon and coercion of LUDs, leaving aside commercial influences, it has been remarked that 'it should be apparent that the more distant the donor's relationship to the recipient, the *less* his/her sense of obligation and the more certain he/she is to be a true volunteer' (my emphasis).[71] Indeed, it would seem that it is genetically related donors who are subject to the greatest pressure to donate (and also often *not* to donate).[72] Burley and Stiller comment: 'There is frequently subtle or overt pressure brought to bear on a related donor by the family, the recipient, or the medical team.'[73] Nevertheless, one of the rationales stated to underpin the requirement for an 'appropriate relationship' was 'to prevent undue pressure to donate being brought to bear on people without a strong emotional relationship with the recipient',[74] with the implication being that a strong emotional relationship *minimises* pressure. Of course, pressure may well sometimes be present in donations by emotionally related, but genetically unrelated, persons. This may be an especially potent threat in nations such as India and China where the expectations and financial dependency of wives are very great. However, Thiel and others by contrast have reported very high levels of spousal motivation to donate and there seems no reason to anticipate inordinate pressure in the normal situation where there are no strong cultural influences in play.

This simply highlights the need to assess pressure in each individual case. *A priori* suppositions reflect unwarranted generalisations. Many centres routinely use a psychiatric or psychological (or both) evaluation of

[70] British Transplantation Society, 'Recommendations on the Use of Living Kidney Donors in the United Kingdom' (1986) 293 *British Medical Journal* 257 at 258.

[71] Spital, 'Unrelated Living Donors: Should They be Used?', at 2216.

[72] It would seem that pressure is frequently placed on spouses *not* to donate to a blood relation: see for example, R. Simmons *et al.*, *The Gift of Life: The Effect of Organ Transplantation on Individual, Family, and Societal Dynamics*, Transaction Books, New Brunswick, 1987.

[73] Burley and Stiller, 'Emotionally Related Donors', at 126.

[74] See Commentary to Article 9 of the Council of Europe Draft Protocol on Transplantation of Organs and Tissues of Human Origin, 9 March 1999.

all unrelated donors, thereby reducing the likelihood of a coerced or pressured person becoming an organ donor. In the US 63 per cent of centres employ an even more rigorous psychosocial evaluation of such donors.[75] The US Task Force on Organ Transplantation stated that 'There is no reason to exclude all living unrelated donors, such as spouses and friends, but special care should be taken to ensure that the decision to donate is informed, voluntary, and altruistic.'[76] There is much to commend in this. In Britain, HOTA and the functions of ULTRA attempt to ensure the voluntariness of a (non-related) donor's decision, but the question arises why such an enquiry should be confined only to *unrelated* donors.

Barmy?

Fellner states that 'No doubt there are many such persons [emotionally disturbed individuals], but there are also many sane people who, for reasons of their own that are not crazy reasons, want to donate part of themselves to a stranger in need.'[77] Sadler's early survey of volunteer stranger donations in San Francisco revealed that three of the twenty-two potential donors studied had a character disorder, but that the remaining individuals displayed no signs of psychiatric or personality disorder and were seemingly well-adjusted persons.[78] On the basis of such evidence, Spital asserts that 'The fear that unrelated living donors are generally motivated by psychopathology has been contradicted by several studies; furthermore, this should not even be an issue for genetically unrelated donors who are closely related to the recipient emotionally, where the bonds may be as strong or stronger (for example spouses) than when genetically related donors are involved.'[79] He goes further and states that 'It [such a supposition] fails to recognise that some among us truly

75 Spital, 'Do US Transplant Centers', at 375.

76 Report of the Task Force on Organ Transplantation, *Organ Transplantation: Issues and Recommendations*, US Department of Health and Human Services, Washington D.C., 1986, at 37.

77 C. Fellner, 'Organ Donation: For Whose Sake?' (1973) 79 *Annals of Internal Medicine* 589 at 591. Hamburger *et al.* state: 'Should unrelated donors be accepted? In our view they should not. It is our experience that it is often the mentally abnormal who come to a transplantation center to offer a kidney to a total stranger': see J. Hamburger *et al.*, *Renal Transplantation: Theory and Practice*, Williams and Wilkins, Baltimore, 1972, at 239.

78 Sadler *et al.*, 'The Living, Genetically Unrelated', at 94.

79 Spital, 'Unconventional Living Kidney Donors', at 246.

consider themselves part of a brotherhood of man. These noble people are willing to take risks not only to help their relatives, but also to help their non-blood related "brothers".'[80] This was illustrated most graphically in 1999 when an adult woman, Joyce Roush, donated a kidney to an unknown recipient (who ultimately transpired to be Christopher Bieiek, aged thirteen) at Johns Hopkins University in Baltimore.[81] In addition, at the end of 1999 an Englishman, Ron Johnson, flew to St Louis, Missouri, in order to donate a lobe of lung to Lisa Ostrovsky, a ten-year-old Jewish girl who was predicted to be going to die imminently from cystic fibrosis.[82] Whilst not denying the need to be aware of its potential presence, it appears that psychopathology is assumed in instances where clinicians are themselves unable to understand the motivation behind offers to donate and would be unlikely to make a similar sacrifice themselves.[83]

Evans contends that 'altruism receives its highest expression in the absence of personal relationships . . . The gift of an organ to a complete stranger . . . seems worthy of the highest respect. Any formal restrictions to related donors would rule out altruism of this supreme kind.'[84] Certainly, vis-à-vis potential *cadaveric* donors, this seems to be a compelling remark. On the other hand, it has been observed, by Hessing, that most psychologists, if not all, are convinced that there is no unselfish altruistic behaviour between (living) strangers.[85] This begs the question though whether 'altruistic' and 'selfish' forms of conduct are mutually exclusive, brought out graphically in the policy statement of the Council of the Transplantation Society that 'It must be established by the patient and transplant team alike that the motives of the donor are altruistic and in the best interests of the recipient and not self-serving or for profit.'[86] Fellner, however, observes that

[80] Ibid.

[81] See 'Does Anyone Want My Kidney?', *Guardian*, 12 October 1999.

[82] See S. Weale, 'Body Parts', *Guardian*, 30 November 1999.

[83] Pabst Battin has observed that 'Non-immediate personal altruism is regarded with some suspicion', and that 'More robust acts of altruism (say, donating a kidney) are typically permitted only if they are personal and immediate': see M. Pabst Battin, *Least Worst Death*, Oxford University Press, Oxford, 1994, at 43.

[84] Evans, 'Organ Donations Should Not be Restricted', at 17.

[85] Hessing, 'Living Donors: Some Psychological Aspects of Informed Consent' in Price and Akveld, *Living Organ Donation in the Nineties*, at 101.

[86] The same attitude is manifest in the policy position of the Medical Ethical Committee of the Dutch Transplantation Society which has expressed concerns regarding genetically unrelated donors based on the difficulty in discovering financial and other kinds of pressure to donate.

> we find it morally unacceptable if a person wants to sacrifice one of his kidneys for his own sake, simply out of a deep inner need, out of a desire to give, motivated by what could be called self-interest in its highest form. Ironically, on closer examination of most genetically related live donors, it was precisely this motivation, the need to act in this way because of one's own inner obligation to one's self ('if I did not do it, I could not live with myself') which moved them to volunteer.[87]

Fellner has observed that 'the immediate motivation of most donors is not pity for the other . . . but an inner imperative: the occasion for their action is indeed the call to help the other, but they are doing it *for their own sake*'.[88] Indeed, Thiel observes that 'There is often a direct personal advantage for the donor. Spouses in particular profit directly from the success of the transplantation, in a manner that cannot be compared with the donation between siblings.'[89] Fellner draws attention also to the increased self-esteem usually experienced by such donors after donation. Thus, if altruism is taken to mean the absence of all self-interested motivations, there is a difficulty in so far as it appears that most, if not all, donations are made for partially self-interested motives. Does this mean then that all living donors are acting other than altruistically? Whilst it is submitted that such donations are 'altruistic', such donors undoubtedly have regard to the benefits (for example maintenance of a marriage, etc.) to be obtained from donation. This is only reasonable and strengthens rather than diminishes the motivation and will of such donors.

It is submitted that altruism does not require wholly selfless conduct so that the exclusion of such donors does not inevitably follow. As Nietzsche states:

> The 'disinterested' action is an exceedingly interesting and interested action. Anyone who has really made sacrifices knows that he wanted and got something in return – perhaps something of himself in return for something of himself – that he gave up here in order to have more there, perhaps in order to *be* more or at least to feel that he was 'more'.[90]

It considered that such donations are only permissible in exceptional cases and stated that 'The motives of the donor must be altruistic and directed toward the interest of the recipient; self-serving motives or financial motives on the part of the donor should be excluded completely': see ibid., at 100.

87 Fellner, 'Organ Donation: For Whose Sake?', at 592.

88 Ibid., at 591.

89 Thiel, 'Living Unrelated Kidney Transplantation', at 368.

90 F. Nietzsche, *Beyond Good and Evil*, Random House Inc., New York, 1966, at 148.

Altruistic conduct is supererogatory conduct which, by definition, excludes commercial reward, although that does not itself mean that commercially induced organ sales are therefore inevitably illegitimate. But even assuming for the present that they are, commercial concerns have most intensity in relation to donation by strangers. Where the genuineness of an emotional attachment can be established there is no *prima facie* reason to assume that emotionally related donors are influenced by commercial concerns. In the absence of any psychopathology or undue pressure there is no non-clinical reason to refuse access to donation to such individuals, unless there are grounds for suspecting an illegitimate commercial motivation, even where there is a suspicion that the donation is being done for self-interested reasons.

Relatively speaking

The tenacity of relatedness criteria is reflected in the Draft Council of Europe Protocol on Organ Transplantation, which states: 'Organ removal from a living donor shall only be carried out for the benefit of a recipient with whom the donor has an appropriate relationship as defined by law, or otherwise with the approval of an independent body.' This formulation may signal a more sophisticated and open-minded stance than hitherto, with its provisions more closely tailored to the rationale underpinning the criteria. As the explanatory guidance to the Draft Protocol makes clear, these provisions are designed to protect against organ trafficking and the use of inducements and other pressures. It allows individual jurisdictions to decide what is an 'appropriate relationship' but states that this may include members of the recipient's immediate family and also 'Spouses or long-standing partners, godparents or close personal friends'.[91] The commentary to the Protocol, however, emphasises that the appropriateness of the relationship is a matter to be determined on the basis of national law, guided by cultural and other local factors. The cultural perspective is well illustrated in the remarks expressed by Mani regarding spousal donation in India where arranged marriages remain common. He says: 'It would be too easy for a young man to marry for a kidney. Once married, no Indian woman will refuse to sacrifice anything for her

[91] See Commentary to Article 9 of the Council of Europe Draft Protocol on Transplantation of Organs and Tissues of Human Origin, 9 March 1999.

husband.'[92] The Draft Protocol contains implicit recognition that emotional relationships are ones where there is no reason to 'tar' every scenario with the 'brush of commerciality' and recognises that it may be appropriate to treat genetically and emotionally related donors as being on a par with each other. Of course, overarching legal prohibitions on commercial transactions involving organs will presumably remain in place in all instances anyhow. The Draft Protocol also advises the establishment of a regulatory structure for the scrutiny of cases where there is a real *prima facie* risk of improper (that is commercial) motivations.

Evidence of good results using LUDs supports an open-minded stance at the very least where an emotional bond exists. Where such a bond is transparent, living genetically unrelated kidney donation is entirely appropriate in the absence of a willing relative with potential to produce a better outcome or a cadaver donor with equally promising potential. Even non-renal donation may be acceptable from a living emotionally related donor in certain circumstances, despite the higher risk. In the United Kingdom, a *friend of the family* was accepted as one of the two living lobar lung donors required for a lung transplant into a young girl with cystic fibrosis.[93] In the US also, living unrelated lobar lung donors have been utilised. However, as regards segments of liver it would appear to be the implicit view of the Council of Europe in its Living Related Liver Transplantation Recommendation that such donors be related in all instances. Rigid insistence on certain classes of donor creates other tensions though. In Britain, the need to establish the existence of particular relationships by means of specified tests (for example DNA tests) proved too inflexible and was amended in 1998 so that the 'tester' has a discretion as to which tests to employ in an individual case.[94]

[92] M. Mani, 'The Argument against the Unrelated Live Donor' in Kjellstrand and Dossetor, *Ethical Problems in Dialysis and Transplantation*, 163 at 167. Reddy also suggests that spousal donations are probably coerced in India unless the marriage has subsisted for at least ten years: see Reddy, 'A Perspective on Reality', at 156.

[93] This was the first living lung lobe transplant performed in Britain, in December 1995. The recipient, aged twenty, received one lung lobe from her father and another from a close friend of her mother.

[94] Human Organ Transplants (Establishment of Relationships) Regulations 1998 (which came into force on 8 August 1998 and in Northern Ireland on 21 December 1998) amending the Human Organ Transplants (Establishment of Relationships) Regulations 1989 (SI 1989 No. 2107).

Minors and mentally incapacitated adults

Although the numbers have only ever been small,[95] many of the very first successful organ (kidney) transplants involved the use of (identical twin) minor donors.[96] But as Lantos observes, 'Although children have been used as organ donors since the earliest days of organ transplantation the justification for their use has always been problematic',[97] and this observation applies equally to mentally incapacitated adults.[98] By comparison with organ donation though, both minors and mentally incapacitated adults quite frequently serve as *bone marrow* donors around the world.[99] Today, the vastly improved outcomes and volume of cadaveric transplants have largely, but not entirely, eliminated the necessity for such donors of organs. However, the potential for a highly compatible tissue match (perfect in 25 per cent of siblings and in all identical twins) gives significance to the subject exceeding its importance in purely numerical terms. Such donors are not presently used for solid organ transplants other than kidneys.

Attitudes

By contrast with LUDs, clinician attitudes towards the use of minors as organ donors would appear to be hardening. A 1987 US study found that forty-four out of seventy-four renal centres (59 per cent) would consider using a donor below the age of eighteen (twenty would even consider

[95] In the US, minors (under twenty-one) comprised only 38 out of 5,952 living donor transplants between 1953 and 1974 and (under eighteen) only 31 between 1987 and 1993: see E. Santiago-Delpin, 'Medico-Legal Management of the Juvenile Kidney Donor' (1974) 6 *Transplantation Proceedings* 441, and UNOS data. Their use has been even more limited in Europe: see EUROTOLD Project Report, *Questioning Attitudes*, at 131–3.

[96] By 1965, at least thirty-six twin transplants had been attempted in the United States.

[97] 'Ethically complex' in the words of the Australian Health Ethics Committee of the National Health and Medical Research Council in its publication *Ethical Issues in Donation of Organs or Tissues by Living Donors* (Draft Discussion paper 2), Canberra, 1996, at 11.

[98] Such organ transplants tend to be very isolated incidents. For instance, in 1999 in India a kidney was removed from a 36-year-old deaf and mute individual for transplantation into his brother. The doctors stated that there was no way of making the individual comprehend the procedure, but he co-operated and they believed that a genuine affection existed between them: see D. Sharma, 'Indian Organ Donation goes ahead without Consent' (1999) 353 *Lancet* 1076 and 'Doctors take Kidney from Patient Incapable of Giving Consent' (1999) 318 *British Medical Journal* 753.

[99] Successful bone marrow grafting requires a very compatible tissue match, which can only generally be attained between siblings.

donors below sixteen years), but in a similar study in 1996, only thirty-five (24 per cent of those responding) centres stated that they would consider using a minor donor, and, of these, twenty-one would require the donor to be at least sixteen or seventeen years of age.[100] A 1996 EUROTOLD Project survey of eighty European renal transplant centres found that only five centres employed a lower minimum age than the age of majority – in all instances sixteen years.[101] Although data as regards clinicians' attitudes towards the use of mentally incapacitated adults as donors are even more limited, they are undoubtedly more restrictive still. Legislative and other policy directives are increasingly 'shutting the door' on organ donation from such classes of individuals and establishing a bright line between the (permissible) donation of regenerative tissues (that is bone marrow) and the (impermissible) donation of non-regenerative tissues. It is suggested that this is too dogmatic a posture.

The Law Reform Commission of Canada identified three potential objections to, or rationales for proscribing, the use of minors as organ donors:[102] first, that consent is a prerequisite of all bodily intrusions; second, that a balancing of social worth is inevitably implicated in such a scenario; third, that donor benefit is illusory. These objections can also be applied to mentally incapacitated adults.[103] Such rationales are tied to anxieties concerning the vulnerability of such individuals and their potential to be exploited. From a (Kantian) non-consequentialist perspective the use of such individuals as donors may appear to be their use solely as a means to the ends of others, constituting a lack of respect for them as persons. Moreover, this might be perceived as the sharp end of utilitarianism, obliging such persons to donate body parts when competent adults could not similarly be compelled.[104] Regarding minors, such concerns are themselves frequently underpinned by (arguably dubious)

[100] Spital, 'Unconventional Living Kidney Donors', at 246–7 and A. Spital, 'Should Children Ever Donate Kidneys?' (1997) 64 *Transplantation* 232 at 233.

[101] Individual clinicians' attitudes may not necessarily reflect centre policies though. EUROTOLD questionnaire responses showed that one-third of responding clinicians would have considered a perfectly (HLA) matched fourteen-year-old sibling donor in a case of exceptional need: EUROTOLD Project Report, *Questioning Attitudes*, at 133. See also Price, 'The EUROTOLD Project', at 34.

[102] Law Reform Commission of Canada, *Procurement and Transfer of Human Tissues and Organs*, Working Paper 66, Minister of Supply and Services, Ottawa, 1992, at 48.

[103] See further D. Price, 'Minors as Living Organ Donors: Ethics and Law' (1996) 28 *Transplantation Proceedings* 3607.

[104] We have already seen that adults cannot be compelled to donate body tissue for transplantation: see *McFall* v. *Shimp* 10 Pa. D. & C. 3d 90 (Allegheny County Ct 1978).

perceptions of lack of decision-making autonomy.[105] Even where the minors or adults concerned undoubtedly lack decision-making capacity though, it must still be questioned why they should be excluded *a priori* as potential donors. Could it be that, from an alternative perspective, the very (restrictive) principles designed to protect such individuals could ultimately end up doing them harm? Gutmann and Gerok comment that

> In general, there are two opposing attitudes towards this problem. On the one hand, laws of total prohibition have the advantage of certainty and maximise the overall legal protection of these groups of persons. On the other hand, however, the removal of a body part from a minor can be ethically justified in exceptional cases, while total prohibition can be unjust because its inflexibility fails to take account of the difference between mature and immature minors. In very exceptional cases even tragic injustice could be done by a blanket ban.[106]

One central issue here is the extent to which the minor (or incapacitated adult) is the primary focus of attention, rather than the family unit as a whole. The Health Ethics Committee of the Australian National Health and Medical Research Council (NHMRC) stated that some people

> argue that the good of the family as a whole is more important than the interests of only one member. Other people would argue that more importance should be placed on the interests of individual family members. Reaching a balance between helping others and concern for oneself is typical of family relationships and is not unique to donation, although the seriousness of questions of living donation can make such questions especially difficult.[107]

Various commentators have maintained that a 'familial' or 'relationship-based' focus is more appropriate here than the traditional individualistic approach. Indeed, the best interests test, which predominantly governs organ donation in 'permissive' jurisdictions, has attracted criticism because of its egocentric focus. Crouch and Elliott comment that 'When it comes to moral decisions about the family, the tools of moral philosophy and the law have not always served us well, particularly when the question

105 Spital's 1996 survey revealed that the primary reason for US centres rejecting minors was concern about the possibility of obtaining an informed consent to donate: see Spital, 'Should Children Ever Donate Kidneys?', at 233.

106 T. Gutmann and B. Gerok, 'International Legislation in Living Organ Donation' in Collins *et al.*, *Procurement, Preservation and Allocation*, 317 at 319.

107 NHMRC, *Ethical Issues*, at 12.

involves exposing one family member to risks for the sake of another.'[108] They continue that conventionally 'The picture is not of children and their parents located in a context of intimacy, but of sovereign, independent human agents free of the moral and emotional connections that typically bind family members to each other.'[109]

Legislative and other policy responses

The World Health Organisation Guiding Principles on Organ Transplantation issued in 1991 unequivocally state that 'No organ should be removed from the body of a living minor for the purpose of transplantation' (Principle 4) and that adults should be 'sufficiently informed to be able to understand and weigh the risks, benefits and consequences of consent' (Principle 3), the net effect of which is to declare organ donation by either minors or mentally incapacitated adults impermissible. In like vein, the European Parliament called on the European Commission in 1993 to create a code of practice which *inter alia* declares that organs must not be removed from living minors or from legally incapable adults for transplantation purposes.[110] A less dogmatic posture appears to have been adopted in the recent Council of Europe Convention which stipulates that 'No organ or tissue removal may be carried out on a person who does not have the capacity to consent',[111] whilst leaving open the question whether minors could ever possess sufficient capacity to donate such non-regenerative tissues.[112]

Although legislation in most nations *proscribes* the use of minors as

[108] C. Crouch and C. Elliott, 'Moral Agency and the Family: The Case of Living Related Organ Transplantation' (1999) 8 *Cambridge Quarterly of Healthcare Ethics* 275.

[109] Ibid., at 276.

[110] Resolution on Prohibiting Trade in Transplant Organs, adopted by the European Parliament on 14 September 1993, at para. Q.5(e). Council of Europe Recommendation No. R(79) similarly stipulated, in Article 9, that 'A removal may only be effected from an adult who is capable of giving his/her consent freely.'

[111] Article 20(1). This is included as an exception to Article 6, which states that where a person lacks capacity any medical intervention must be for his/her direct benefit. There is a 'saving' for donation of regenerative tissue though by individuals lacking capacity, in certain defined circumstances.

[112] Council of Europe Resolution (78) 29 is similarly vague as regards whether minors might ever be capable of possessing the necessary capacity to consent to organ donation, although again it would seemingly not permit the donation of non-regenerative tissue by mentally incapacitated adults under any circumstances, as the donor would not have the 'capacity for understanding' required by Article 6(2).

organ donors,[113] a handful of jurisdictions have legislation expressly *permitting* organ donation by minors. In Belgium, a person who has not attained the age of eighteen may donate a nonregenerative organ which 'does not normally have serious effects on the donor' to a brother or sister. In Sweden, parents may authorise organ donation on behalf of their minor children for transplantation to a relative, subject to the agreement of the National Board of Health and Welfare.[114] However, in various jurisdictions, only minors *possessing capacity* may donate organs for transplantation. In Norway, the 1973 Law states that where there are special grounds, minors under eighteen may consent to organ donation subject to the obtaining of the agreement of their parent or guardian and the permission of the Directorate of Health Services.[115] In Britain, whilst the Human Organ Transplants (Unrelated Persons) Regulations 1989 state that *non-genetically related* donors must display understanding of the nature of the procedure and the risks, this again begs the question whether minors *are* ever capable of possessing such understanding. Moreover, they are silent as regards whether minors without capacity may donate organs to genetically *related* persons. The Nuffield Council Report on Human Tissue opined that

> For non-therapeutic removal, the law is complicated and unclear. The important legal principles would seem to be that any child under 18 would be deemed incompetent to consent, as a matter of public policy, to anything other than a trivial intervention, for example, perhaps, the taking of a blood sample; the consent of the person with parental responsibility must therefore be obtained; such consent could then only validly be given if the removal of tissue were not against the child's interests, that is, if it

[113] I.e. Algeria, all the states and territories of Australia apart from the Australian Capital Territory, Belarus, Bolivia, Burkina Faso, the Canadian provinces of Manitoba and Ontario, Colombia, Costa Rica, Finland, France, Germany, Greece, Iceland, India (under Federal Law), Lebanon, Mexico, the Netherlands, Panama, Poland, Portugal, the Russian Federation, the Slovak Republic, Slovenia, South Africa, Spain, Sri Lanka, Tunisia and Zimbabwe. In Syria, minors may only donate to siblings (although the law actually states that donation is only permitted for twin 'brothers', presumably this extends to siblings generally).

[114] Law of 8 June 1995, section 8. Luxembourg has a similar law under which organ donation is permitted by a minor to a sibling if his/her legal representative and a committee of three experts appointed by the Minister of Health have given their authorisation.

[115] Law of 9 February 1973, section 1. In Denmark, donations may occur on special grounds where parental consent has been obtained as well as the consent of the minor: see Law of 13 June 1990, section 13(2). The law in Turkey would appear to provide for such donations in similar terms: see Law of 29 May 1979, section 6.

posed no more than negligible risk and minimal burden, and the tissue could not equally well be taken from an adult.[116]

This would imply that living *organ* donation by a minor would be illegal in the United Kingdom without, and maybe even despite,[117] valid parental consent.[118] Whether this opinion accords with the 'judicial verdict' in the case law will be considered below. In the United States the legal position is determined by state law and is also generally governed by case law rather than by legislative provision.[119] There are various instances of state courts previously approving living kidney donations by minors, creating precedents which may well hold good today. These are evaluated below.

There is therefore no legal consensus as regards allowing minors to act as organ donors. By contrast though, a clear consensus *has* crystallised *against* the removal of non-regenerative tissues from mentally incapacitated adults. Many jurisdictions expressly prohibit mentally incapacitated adults from becoming living organ 'donors'.[120] In certain other jurisdictions, mentally *disordered* persons may not donate,[121] but whether this is to be viewed as being synonymous with an absence of decision-making capacity is not clear.[122] The situation is once again much less clear in the United Kingdom and the United States in the absence of explicit legislation. Whilst the 1989 Regulations mentioned above forbid a

116 Nuffield Council on Bioethics Working Party, *Human Tissue: Ethical and Legal Issues*, Nuffield Council on Bioethics, London, 1995, at 56.

117 The BMA have stated: 'There is considerable legal doubt about a parent's right to give consent on behalf of the child, but even if this exists that cannot extend to procedures which are not in the child's best interests': see British Medical Association, *Guidelines on the Transplant of Tissues and Organs*, BMA, London, August 1990, at 3. However, this simply shifts the question to whether or not such a procedure *is* in the child's best interests.

118 Although it might permit bone marrow donation for instance. The BMA has expressed a similar view, maintaining that 'There are probably no circumstances in which a child can be considered suitable as a donor for nonregenerative tissue': ibid.

119 Although there are relevant statutory provisions in both Alabama (bone marrow) and Michigan (organs).

120 I.e. in Algeria, Bolivia, Burkina Faso, Colombia, Cuba, Cyprus, Germany, Mexico, the Netherlands, Panama, Poland, Portugal, Romania, the Russian Federation, the Slovak Republic, Spain, Sri Lanka, Syria and Tunisia. In Greece, adults who have been declared incompetent in a court of law or who are in the care of a guardian may not donate organs. In Turkey, legally incompetent individuals may not become organ donors either.

121 For instance, persons of unsound mind may not donate organs in Sri Lanka, nor may mentally ill individuals in South Africa, nor mentally disordered or defective persons in Zimbabwe.

122 This will depend upon the jurisdiction, but in nations such as the United States and Britain mentally disordered/ill individuals are not, by that fact alone, incapable of giving consent to medical procedures: see for instance *Re C* (1994) 15 BMLR 77.

mentally incapacitated adult to donate an organ to a genetically unrelated person in the UK, due to their inability to understand the procedure and its risks, the position with regard to the donation of organs to genetically *related* persons is uncertain. The Nuffield Council Report recognised this uncertainty but opined that in the light of the 1989 Regulations '*It may well be* that a court would apply this principle equally in the case of the proposed removal of an organ from an incompetent person for transplantation into someone who was genetically *related*' (my emphasis).[123] This, however, remains to be seen and there are judicial remarks suggesting this may be rather too dogmatic. Again US law is state, and case law, based.

Donation by competent minors

Laws declaring competence to be presumed in relation to health care decisions at an age lower than majority are unlikely to apply to living *donors*, as opposed to organ *recipients*. For instance, in the UK, section 8(1) of the Family Law Reform Act 1969 states that 'The consent of a minor who has attained the age of 16 years to any surgical, medical or dental treatment . . . shall be as effective as it would be if he were of full age' and it has been held not to extend to the donation of organs or blood since, 'so far as the donor is concerned, these do not constitute either treatment or diagnosis'.[124] Thus, in relation to organ donation, competence is *presumed* only upon reaching majority.[125]

Jurisdictions with absolute prohibitions on donation by minors in effect equate presumed capacity with the attainment of majority – typically eighteen years of age. However, such a stance is at odds with that relating to 'therapeutic' medical procedures performed upon minors. In that context, the developmental stage achieved by the minor and the capacity for understanding typically assume greater importance than age *per se*. In the UK the House of Lords in *Gillick* v. *West Norfolk and Wisbech*

[123] Nuffield Council, *Human Tissue*, at para. 7.10. It noted that the English Law Commission considered that it would be unlawful to carry out non-therapeutic *research* upon such individuals.

[124] Per Lord Donaldson in *Re W (A Minor) (Medical Treatment: Court's Jurisdiction)* [1992] 3 WLR 758 at 767C.

[125] See further D. Price and A. Garwood-Gowers, 'Transplantation from Minors: Are Children other People's Medicine?' (1995) 1(1) *Contemporary Issues in Law* 1 at 6–7.

Area Health Authority[126] held that minors who have the capacity to understand the nature and implications of the decision concerned (dubbed 'Gillick competence') are able to afford a valid consent to medical treatment for themselves.[127] In the United States, although historically minors have typically been unable to consent to their own medical treatment, an exception evolved for emancipated minors in most states, and the 'mature minor' rule has now also taken strong root in the health care context.[128] Where laws do permit competent minors to make health care decisions for themselves the question arises as to whether this approach is also appropriate in the context of organ donation. In the UK it was stated *obiter* in *Re W* that such principles *were* equally applicable to organ and blood donation. Indeed, there seems no reason why such a functional approach should not extend to such a procedure despite its being, strictly speaking, 'non-therapeutic'. It would seemingly apply to non-therapeutic *research* procedures.[129] A Report of the Council on Ethical and Judicial Affairs of the American Medical Association (AMA Report) recommends that 'If a child is capable of making his or her own medical treatment decisions, he or she should be considered capable of deciding whether to be an organ or tissue donor.'[130] The alternative perspective (for example of the Nuffield Council) is that policy should intervene here, in view of the non-therapeutic character of the procedure.[131]

126 [1985] 3 All ER 402.

127 In the words of Lord Scarman, a minor is able to give a consent to medical treatment when he/she 'achieves a significant understanding and intelligence to enable him or her to understand fully what is proposed': see [1985] 3 All ER 402 at 423J. Lord Fraser stated similar views and principles: see 3 All ER 409D–E.

128 One of the seminal authorities on this subject is *Belcher* v. *Charleston Area Medical Center*, 422 S.E. 2d 827 (Sup. Ct W. Va. 1993). Further, it was applied to a transplant *recipient*, Benny Agrelo, in a Florida trial court decision: see D. Dickenson and D. Jones, 'True Wishes: The Philosophy and Developmental Psychology of Children's Informed Consent' (1996) 4(2) *Philosophy, Psychiatry and Psychology* 287 at 301.

129 This is the view expressed by M. Brazier in *Medicine, Patients and the Law*, 2nd edn, Penguin, London, 1992, at 421, and by J. Mason and A. McCall Smith in the third edition of their treatise *Law and Medical Ethics*, Butterworths, London, 1991, at 373.

130 Council on Ethical and Judicial Affairs of the American Medical Association, *The Use of Minors as Organ and Tissue Donors*, Report 56, January 1994, at 240–1.

131 The attitude explicit in the views of the Nuffield Council and the BMA: see text at notes 116–18.

Capacity determinations in action

Despite the acceptance of the *principle* of informed consent to organ donation by a minor in *Re W*, Lord Donaldson regarded it as a 'highly improbable conclusion' that a minor would be regarded as being sufficiently competent to be able to consent to 'so serious a procedure' as donation of a kidney,[132] although he saw no difficulty in a minor's being found competent to donate *blood*. Lord Donaldson was implicitly applying a higher standard of competency in this, 'so serious' a context.[133] The AMA Report seemingly concurs with this approach, and states that 'it is reasonable to match the capabilities of a minor with the level of difficulty involved in a particular decision . . . [D]onations which pose a serious risk to the minor require a higher level of maturity in decision-making'.[134] Lord Donaldson's scepticism as regards potential achievement of 'actual' capacity for organ donation would appear to be overly emphatic though, despite the substantial risks and a complicated assessment of benefits. An Alabama court had previously held that a seventeen-year-old was able to give an informed consent to the donation of a kidney to his sixteen-year-old sister.[135] It was seemingly also the case that the Massachusetts courts found the minor donors (some aged only fourteen) to possess capacity to donate a kidney in the *Harrison* cases discussed below.[136] Moreover, the Canadian Model Law accepts the potential for such capacity, and this has been enacted by, for instance, the province of Prince Edward Island.[137] As long ago as 1977, the Australian Law Reform Commission stated that 'There are some of those who insist that some children below the age of majority are capable of understanding the nature and quality of the issues

132 [1992] 3 WLR 758 at 767F (CA).

133 See L. Roth, A. Meisel and C. Lidz, 'Tests of Competency to Consent to Treatment' (1977) 134 *American Journal of Psychiatry* 279, for a discussion of standards of competency linked to varying risk/benefit ratios.

134 AMA, *The Use of Minors as Organ and Tissue Donors*, at 232.

135 See G. Smitherman, 'The Legal Dilemma of Minor Sibling Kidney Donation' (1982) 19(3) *Alabama Journal of Medical Sciences* 309. In addition, in *Rappeport* v. *Stott* Civil No. 1 74–57 (Mass. 28 Aug., 1974), the Massachusetts Supreme Judicial Court decided that a seventeen-year-old was capable of giving consent to donation of bone marrow.

136 Although in one of the cases, the 'minors' were nineteen years of age: see pp. 348–9 below.

137 Human Tissue Donation Act 1992, section 6 states that a person who is over sixteen years of age and who understands the nature and consequences of transplanting tissue (which includes organs and other non-regenerative tissues) from his or her body during his or her life may consent to the removal of the tissue specified in the consent for the purpose of implanting such tissue into another person.

involved in tissue donation. This seems undeniable, but the difficulty from the point of view of legislation lies in fixing an age'[138] – I shall return to this point below.

Magical transformation

Studies of intellectual development have suggested that from seven to eight years of age, a child is capable of certain logical reasoning processes applied to concrete objects or events in the immediate present, although not to hypothetical situations. From eleven to fifteen years, the ability to reason hypothetically also develops, a process which is an intrinsic aspect of the organ donation decision-making process.[139] Weithorn and Campbell have conducted extensive research into the decision-making competence of minors.[140] Their findings were that the fourteen-year-olds in the study displayed levels of competence and ability to make a judgement equivalent to those of the adults.[141] However, there is no uniformity here,[142] and in any event the above findings have been properly criticised for being too closely tied to a Piagetian age-based approach.[143] Further, such studies have tended overly to emphasise the cognitive aspects at the expense of emotional elements or relationships.[144] Studies nevertheless

138 Australian Law Reform Commission Report, *Human Tissue Transplants*, ALRC, Canberra, 1977.

139 Piaget asserts that formal operational thought starts at about age eleven and is well developed by age fourteen: see J. Piaget, *Logic and Psychology*, Basic Books, New York 1957, and J. Piaget, *The Child's Construction of Reality*, Routledge, London, 1958.

140 L. Weithorn and S. Campbell, 'The Competency of Children and Adolescents to Make Informed Treatment Decisions' (1982) 53 *Child Development* 1589.

141 Nicholson summarises the above research findings by stating that they support two developmental turning points, at ages seven and fourteen, and that at age fourteen such decisions should generally be respected: see R. Nicholson (ed.), *Medical Research with Children: Ethics, Law, and Practice*, Oxford University Press, Oxford, 1986, at 151.

142 If anything, recent research suggests that minors acquire such capacity even *earlier* than previously thought. Ondrusek *et al.* recently concluded on the basis of empirical study that the age of nine was a particularly important one from the point of view of understanding and consent to clinical research: see N. Ondrusek *et al.*, 'Empirical Examination of the Ability of Children to Consent to Clinical Research' (1998) 24 *Journal of Medical Ethics* 158.

143 Dickenson and Jones, 'True Wishes', at 294.

144 It is appreciated that competence may also be influenced by experience and the social context of the individual, for example the network of relationships and cultural influences impacting on the minor, and not just inherent attributes: see P. Alderson, 'In the Genes or in the Stars? Children's Competence to Consent' (1992) 18 *Journal of Medical Ethics* 119. See also P. Alderson, *Children's Consent to Surgery*, Open University Press, Buckingham, 1993. Where the suffering of a close relative is very close and visible, this may also serve to heighten capacity.

tend to support the *potentiality* of older minors being able to comprehend complex decisions such as organ donation.[145]

Giesen has, however, asserted that

> Where the procedure is not for the benefit of the child but for that of society the question to be addressed is no longer one of appreciation and intelligence. Acts of self-sacrifice, such as those entered into by research subjects, are predicated upon the ability of the individual to make a free choice as to the values by which he lives. It is submitted that the altruistic decision to balance risks to oneself against gains for society requires a considerable level of maturity and a capacity to determine and order one's value priorities which should be presumed in fully competent adults only.[146]

This view may be taken to be suggesting that altruistic decisions are different to other, therapeutic, decisions and require a greater life, partially adult, experience.[147] But is there any reason to doubt whether a seventeen-year-old identical twin sister lacks capacity to donate a kidney to her sick twin or is unduly vulnerable due to her limited life experience?[148] It has also been suggested that minors are unable to give *voluntary* consent to organ donation because of family pressures. Campbell has noted how vulnerable and dependent children are, in view of their reliance upon their parents for continued love and protection.[149] However, some similar

[145] See also L. Kohlberg, 'Moral Stages and Moralisation: The Cognitive-Developmental Approach' in T. Lickona (ed.), *Moral Development and Behavior: Theory, Research and Social Issues*, 1976.

[146] D. Giesen, 'Civil Liability of Physicians for New Methods of Treatment and Experimentation: A Comparative Examination' [1995] 3 *Medical Law Review* 22 at 42.

[147] There are, however, shades of the same approach in a therapeutic context in the English High Court decision in *Re L (Medical Treatment: Gillick Competency)* [1998] 2 FLR 810, in which the court failed to respect the wishes of a fourteen-year-old girl with a life-threatening condition who refused a blood transfusion because of her deeply felt religious (Jehovah's Witness) convictions, viewing her as lacking competency, and saying 'there was a distinction between a view of this kind and the constructive formulation of an opinion which occurred with adult experience; this had not occurred in this child's case'.

[148] In Ireland a thirteen-year-old identical twin successfully donated a kidney to her sick sibling and publicly declared her later affirmation of her decision to donate: see S. Doyle, 'A Very Courageous Act' and L. Doyle, 'I Still Have My Sister' (1985) *Support* (Irish Kidney Association) 5.

[149] See A. Campbell, 'Infants, Children, and Informed Consent' (1974) (3) *British Medical Journal* 334. There are also very extensive expectations of offspring in some cultures. This factor was prominent in the thinking behind the exclusion of living minors donating organs in the 1994 Federal Transplant Law in India.

pressures apply to all living related donors, whether adult or minor, yet we usually do not doubt the ability of adults to consent freely. Moreover, although there may be a greater dependency by minors upon their parents than is inherent in other familial relationships, the vulnerability of the minor varies with age and circumstances, for example maturity and independence (the minor may even be married with his/her own children!).[150] As with the life experience issue, this is an important factor but again provides no rationale for any blanket posture as opposed to a determination in each individual instance.

It may, on the other hand, be that Lord Donaldson's view reflects the stance exhibited in the Nuffield Report, namely a policy assertion rather than an empirical assessment of individual capacity. In other words, it may be an approach based not upon capacity at all, but instead upon other considerations. But, if so, what is their underpinning rationale?

Implications

Where a minor possesses the maturity to weigh the pertinent issues and is able to make his/her own decision, he/she should not be denied the possibility of altruistic behaviour. Chronological age *per se* is too crude a measure of either decision-making capacity for organ donation or the ability to protect one's own interests.[151] A totally flexible standard (along the lines of *Gillick*) determining competence ought to be applied, or alternatively a flexible standard operative only once a threshold age has been attained, but *below* the typical age of majority. The latter approach is adopted in the Canadian Uniform Human Tissue Donation Act 1990 (age sixteen for non-regenerative tissues), which has been enacted in various provinces, and is employed also in the US state of Michigan (at fourteen).[152] It is submitted that the latter strategy is the preferred one,

[150] Indeed, in two instances in Minnesota where the court authorised kidney donation from minors they were totally independent, living and working away from home. The AMA Report noted that studies show older adolescents generally able to demonstrate independence of thought: *The Use of Minors as Organ and Tissue Donors*, at 231. The Human Organ Transplant Ordinance in Hong Kong dictates a general minimum age of eighteen for organ donation but modifies this to sixteen where the donor is married: see section 594.

[151] It might also incidentally preclude minors from engaging in other non-therapeutic activities such as certain research ventures.

[152] Minors fourteen years old and over may donate a kidney to a family member with court approval: Michigan Statute 700.407, Act 642, 1978.

providing flexibility but with a threshold to protect against actual, or perceived, abuse[153] and with an upper ceiling to permissible risk taking.

The AMA Report implies that parental consent should be obtained for any organ donation, even where the minor possesses decision-making capacity.[154] Indeed, it appeared to be the combination of the informed consent of *both* the minor and the parents, as well as anticipated benefit to the minor, which was the critical factor in the *Harrison* cases discussed below.[155] Indeed, certain jurisdictions which specifically permit organ donation by competent minors have legislation which requires the consent of the person exercising parental authority, for example in Denmark.[156] In one or two instances the approval of an external agency is also required, for example in Sweden[157] from the National Board of Health and Welfare. Norway has similar provisions. Lord Donaldson in *Re W* considered that as a matter of English law the consent of a competent minor would be sufficient to authorise such a procedure, although, as a matter of *ethics*, he thought that supporting parental consent would also have to be sought.[158] It is submitted that parental consent is a desirable but not a *necessary* ingredient of living donation by competent minors, although capacity and other preconditions may require verification in a judicial forum.[159] In *Re W*, Lord Donaldson also insisted that, at least theoretically, a parent could even give consent to the removal where the competent minor had *declined* to do so, although he again thought that from an *ethical* perspective doctors should not proceed

153 A threshold of this kind would, despite criticisms, be consistent with the developmental research relating to decision-making set out earlier. Such a view is also consistent with the attitude we take towards using minors as babysitters: see G. Koren *et al.*, 'Maturity of Children to Consent to Medical Research: The Babysitter Test' (1993) 19 *Journal of Medical Ethics* 142. An alternative to a cut-off would be a rebuttable presumption that minors under a certain age lack the capacity to consent to donate. Starkman advocates a 'presumption of undue influence': see B. Starkman, 'Inter Vivos Transplantation: The Child and Dependent Adult as Donors' (1985) 17 (Supp. 4) *Transplantation Proceedings* 40 at 44.

154 The NHMRC Report also recommends that parental consent be obtained in every instance: at 12.

155 Consent of parents is generally also required under guidelines governing non-therapeutic research upon minors, for example Department of Health and Royal College of Physicians guidelines in the UK.

156 Law of 13 June 1990, section 13(2).

157 Law of 8 June 1995, section 8.

158 Crouch and Elliott implicitly appear to support organ donation by competent minors without more: see 'Moral Agency', at 278–82.

159 Of course, the parents would sometimes provide the consent for the minor *recipient's* transplantation.

without the agreement of the minor. But it is submitted that on this latter issue the refusal of consent from a competent minor should constitute a veto to organ donation in every case. Principles cannot simply be 'imported' uncritically from the therapeutic context here.[160] If this was the case (competent) minors would indeed be more vulnerable to exploitation and utilitarianism than adults. We shall see further on that legislation frequently accords minors a decisive right of veto even where they lack competency.

Mentally incapacitated donors

There is an understandable reluctance to permit physically invasive non-therapeutic procedures to be carried out upon individuals incapable of giving informed, voluntary consent. Non-maleficence and beneficence are the principal ethical tenets applicable to decision-making by persons lacking capacity. In law, this generally equates with what is in the best interests of that person, which in turn ordinarily involves a search for prospective *benefit* to him/her. The Council of Europe Convention states that generally 'an intervention may only be carried out on a person who does not have the capacity to consent, for his or her direct benefit'.[161] Labels such as 'therapeutic' or 'non-therapeutic' should not be decisive though.[162] In most jurisdictions even certain 'non-therapeutic' procedures might be in a mentally incapacitated person's best interests anyhow.[163]

Pretty thin soup?

In a significant number of instances American courts have determined that organ (kidney) donation by a minor or mentally incapacitated adult

160 See further B. Dickens, 'Donation and Transplantation of Organs and Tissues' in I. Kennedy and A. Grubb, *Principles of Medical Law*, Oxford University Press, Oxford, 1998, at para. 15.56.

161 Article 6; although an exception is laid down in relation to the removal of regenerative tissues for transplantation purposes.

162 Dworkin notes that in various US cases the procedures were dubbed, dubiously, 'therapeutic', as they were necessary for continued good health and well-being and conferred benefits on the donors: see G. Dworkin, 'Law and Medical Experimentation: Of Embryos, Children and Others with Limited Legal Capacity' (1987) 13 *Monash University Law Review* 189 at 199–200. But this would not appear to have been especially material to the decisions.

163 This was the attitude adopted by the House of Lords in both *Re F* [1990] 2 AC 1 (HL) and *Re B* [1987] 2 All ER 206 (HL) in a contraceptive sterilisation context. By contrast, the Supreme Court of Canada in *Re Eve* (1986) 31 DLR (4th) 1 did confer decisive effect upon such a 'non-therapeutic' categorisation in the same setting.

was to the benefit of that individual and therefore legitimate by virtue of being in his/her best interests.[164] Minors were permitted to donate kidneys to siblings in *Hart* v. *Brown*,[165] *Little* v. *Little*,[166] *Masden* v. *Harrison*,[167] *Hushey* v. *Harrison*[168] and *Foster* v. *Harrison*[169] amongst other decisions.[170] In some instances the minors were of an extremely tender age, for example the seven-year-old identical twins in *Hart*.[171] In *Strunk* v. *Strunk*[172] Jerry Strunk, an adult with very serious learning difficulties, was permitted by a Kentucky court to donate a kidney to his adult sibling brother, Tommy, who had renal failure.

In certain other instances donation was refused by the US courts though. For example, in *In Re Richardson*[173] Samuel J stated with respect to the possible donation by Roy, a seventeen-year-old with a mental age of three or four, to Beverly, his 32-year-old sister,

> Counsel for plaintiff argues the transplant could be in Roy's best interest because, if it is successful, Beverly could take care of Roy after the deaths of both Mr and Mrs Richardson. Such an event is not only highly speculative but, in view of all of the facts, highly unlikely. We find that surgical intrusion and loss of a kidney clearly would be against Roy's best interest.[174]

Roy's estimated lifespan was only up to twenty-five years of age however. In *Guardianship of Pescinski*, the Supreme Court of Wisconsin considered that 'There is absolutely no evidence here that any interests of the ward will be served by the transplant.'[175] There was no evidence of any substantial emotional bond between the brother and sister in that case

[164] Even where the *substituted judgement* test was employed, the courts explicitly required that a benefit accrue to the donor, in order to satisfy that test, for example in *Hart* v. *Brown* 289 A. 2d 386 (Conn. 1972) and *Strunk* v. *Strunk* 445 S.W. 2d 145 (Ky. 1969).

[165] 289 A. 2d 386 (1972).

[166] 576 S.W. 2d 493 (Tex. Civ. Ct 1979). The donor in this case was a fourteen-year-old girl with Down's syndrome who donated a kidney to her brother.

[167] No. 68651 Eq., Mass. Sup. Jud. Ct, 12 June 1957.

[168] No. 68666 Eq., Mass. Sup. Jud. Ct, 30 August 1957.

[169] No. 68674 Eq., Mass. Sup. Jud. Ct, 20 November 1957.

[170] In Minnesota between 1967 and 1973 the courts approved fourteen cases of donation by minors: see Santiago-Delpin, 'Medico-Legal Management', at 441.

[171] It was unclear whether in the *Harrison* cases the minors were regarded as possessing capacity to consent (they were aged nineteen, fourteen and fourteen respectively), but even if they were, it is uncertain whether this played any part in the judicial decision-making.

[172] 445 S.W. 2d 145 (Ky. 1969).

[173] 284 So. 2d 185 (La. App. 1973).

[174] Ibid., at 187.

[175] 226 N.W. 2d 180 at 181 (Sup. Ct Wis. 1975).

and, furthermore, the potential donor, a 39-year-old suffering from catatonic schizophrenia, lacked an awareness of his circumstances (his state was described as a 'flight from reality') and showed general indifference even whilst he was in contact with his environment. However, by contrast with the above cases where donation was permitted, no clear prospective benefit to the donor was predicted in these latter cases. In *Curran* v. *Bosze*, Justice Calvo stated: 'In *Strunk*, the donor lived in a State institution. The recipient was a brother who served as the only connection with the outside world. In both *Hart* and *Little*, there was evidence that the sibling relationship between the donor and recipient was close. In each of these cases, both parents had given their consent.'[176] In the three *Harrison* cases in Massachusetts the Court also found that there was clear prospective benefit likely to accrue to the (twin) minor donors.[177]

No English court has yet been required to determine whether organ donation from a minor or an adult lacking competence to consent is permissible,[178] but with regard to donations to *related* individuals, certain *obiter* remarks in *Re W* suggest that a parent could give consent to kidney donation on behalf of a minor.[179] In *Re F* members of both the Court of Appeal and the House of Lords also contemplated (in various *obiter dicta*) the possibility of a mentally incapacitated *adult* lawfully donating an organ for transplantation.[180] Moreover, the English High Court recently allowed the removal of bone marrow from a 26-year-old severely mentally and physically disabled woman for transplantation into her 25-year-old sister who was otherwise very likely to die imminently from leukaemia, on the basis of the benefit to, and the best interests of, the donor.[181] The position of both incapacitated minors and adults in relation to the donation of *organs* to relatives remains a matter of speculation however.

[176] *Curran* v. *Bosze* 566 N.E. 2d 1319 (Ill. 1990).

[177] See W. Curran, 'A Problem of Consent: Kidney Transplantation in Minors' (1959) 34 *New York University Law Review* 891 at 892–3. However, due to the age and maturity of some of these donors, Crouch and Elliott remark that 'What the court effectively did was to justify an adult's decision to donate a kidney to his brother using a decision-making framework more appropriate for a much younger child': see 'Moral Agency', at 279.

[178] As noted above, the 1989 HOTA Regulations do not permit an individual lacking understanding to donate to a *non-genetically related* person.

[179] By Lord Donaldson in *Re W (A Minor) (Medical Treatment; Court's Jurisdiction)* [1992] 3 WLR 758 at 767F (CA).

[180] Neill LJ in the Court of Appeal at [1990] 2 AC 1 at 33B and Lord Bridge in the House of Lords at [1990] 2 AC 1 at 51.

[181] *Re Y* (1996) 35 BMLR 111. See also R. Clark, 'Bone Marrow Donation by Mentally Incapable Adults' (1998) 352 *Lancet* 1847.

In *Re Y*, Connell J specifically stated that it was doubtful that that case would constitute any useful precedent in cases where the surgery involved was more intrusive and the risks greater.[182]

Cheating?

David Daube argues that on no account should children be donors and that there should be 'no cheating by maintaining, for example, that the child would suffer a trauma if he were not allowed to give his twin a kidney'.[183] The *application* of the best interests standard in this context has given rise to substantial criticisms which centre around two concerns. First, any benefit is psychological whilst the harm is physical. Kennedy and Grubb have remarked 'if the legal test is "best interests" of the incompetent donor, then they [the decided cases] appear to identify a doubtful notion of benefit, i.e. the psychological and emotional benefits derived from altruism'.[184] However, a narrow approach here may ultimately damage rather than protect those very same individuals' interests. Why should psychological benefits be ignored even if, in view of the non-therapeutic character of the procedure, benefit is essentially incidental to its main purpose? In *Re Y*, Connell J quoted from the judgment of Justice Calvo in *Curran* v. *Bosze* who said, in this context, that 'the psychological benefit is not simply one of personal, individual altruism in an abstract theoretical sense, although that may be a factor. The psychological benefit is grounded firmly in the fact that the donor and recipient are known to each other as family.'[185] A more holistic view needs to be taken.[186] Indeed,

182 *Re Y* (1996) 35 BMLR 111 at 116–17. Courts both at home and abroad have repeatedly endorsed bone marrow donation from mentally incapacitated minor and adult siblings, for example in the Quebec case of *Cayoutte et Mathieu* [1987] RJQ 2230 (Sup. Ct).

183 D. Daube, 'Transplantation: Acceptability of Procedures and the Required Legal Sanctions' in G. Wolstenholme (ed.), *Ethics in Medical Progress*, CIBA Foundation Symposium, 1966, 188 at 198.

184 I. Kennedy and A. Grubb, *Medical Law: Text with Materials*, 1994, 2nd edn, Butterworths, London, at 1086. Crouch and Elliott maintain that the courts merely broadened the best interests test to the extent necessary to authorise a procedure they had already decided should take place: see 'Moral Agency', at 280.

185 35 BMLR 111 at 115.

186 Lawton has commented that 'If . . . we are equally concerned with psychic life, as we are with good 'physical' health, then we must give people a chance to achieve this sort of benefit': see R. Lawton (1978) 8 *Proceedings of the Dialysis and Transplantation Forum* at 30. Indeed, we frequently weigh physical harms against psychological benefits in a one-party scenario, for instance in considering gender reassignment surgery for transsexuals or cosmetic surgery.

Butler-Sloss LJ recently stated in the Court of Appeal that (whatever the historical judicial attitude may have been) 'Best interests are *not limited* to best *medical* interests' (my emphasis).[187] That it is a psychological rather than a physical gain should make us cautious, but it is no more dubious because it is less observable, tangible and quantifiable.

The other focus of denunciation is the evidence typically relied upon to satisfy the best interests test.[188] It has been claimed that the courts that permitted these transplants performed incredible feats of mental gymnastics to reach such an end, including finding benefits where none existed. Certainly some of the psychiatric evidence in the early US cases was rather dubious and contrived,[189] and Baron *et al.* have observed that the medical witnesses were 'consciously providing the court with the necessary words to satisfy the psychological benefit finding requirement'.[190] Moreover, it is an especially speculative assessment where a minor is very young or a mentally incapacitated adult lacks substantial awareness and communication capabilities.[191] To assert that organ donation could *never* amount to a net benefit to a child is too emphatic though, at least in the family context. Adolescents are clearly able to experience substantial benefit from donation, including enhanced self-esteem.[192] Where relationships involving younger children are still to form, one should be very much more cautious however. It is clear that in some of the decided cases[193] the

[187] *Re MB* (1997) 38 BMLR 175 at 188.

[188] In passing it should be said that although these courts tended to speak of the 'avoidance of (emotional) harm' as opposed to the achievement of a 'benefit', nothing hangs on this as they are simply different sides of the same coin in this context.

[189] Dickenson and Jones, however, note that all predictions as to what will be in an individual's best interests are inherently speculative to some degree: see 'True Wishes', at 295. See also R. Mnookin, 'Child-Custody Adjudication: Judicial Functions in the Face of Indeterminacy' (1975) 39 *Law and Contemporary Problems* 226.

[190] C. Baron, M. Botsford and G. Cole, 'Live Organ and Tissue Transplants from Minor Donors in Massachusetts' (1975) 55 *Boston University Law Review* 159. Curran has alleged that the (psychiatric) testimony amounted to no more than the 'cloaking of common sense with legal jargon': see Curran, 'A Problem of Consent', at 894.

[191] Such benefit may be somewhat less speculative, at least with regard to the prediction of a major feeling of loss and guilt in the event of the sibling's death, where identical twins are involved. Evidence of extraordinarily strong bonding between such twins is quite extensive: see *inter alia* M. Lewis, 'Kidney Donation by a 7-Year-Old Identical Twin Child' (1974) 13 *Journal of the American Academy of Psychiatry* 221, and N. Hollenberg, 'Altruism and Coercion: Should Children Serve as Kidney Donors?' (1977) 296 *New England Journal of Medicine* 390.

[192] See D. Bernstein and R. Simmons, 'The Adolescent Kidney Donor: The Right to Give' (1974) 131 *American Journal of Psychiatry* 138.

[193] Lantos's remarks that it is 'usually impossible to determine when or whether donation is in a

minors were too young to have developed an appreciation of the impact and significance of their act of 'donating' so that psychological benefits would not be immediately forthcoming, although they *might* be so once the child has grown older and matured. Crouch and Elliott rightly point out that in cases of mental incapacity not stemming from age such development cannot be expected, and therefore direct psychological benefits are irrelevant.[194] But one might then instead look for emotional and psychological benefit through continued familial interaction rather than altruism *per se*, which is what the courts did in both *Strunk* and *Re Y*,[195] albeit in slightly strained fashion.

Thus, the objection that such benefits are 'illusory' is borne out neither by the empirical evidence nor by intuition, although where the minor is very young the existence of strong and stable 'bonding' should generally be sought. The AMA Report endorses the possibility of kidney donation by minors not capable of making their own medical treatment decisions, subject to a psychological or psychiatric evaluation of the donor, but states that there should be 'clear and convincing' evidence of 'clear benefit' to the prospective donor. A higher standard than the normal civil standard of proof is justified here, especially in view of the prospective nature of any benefits accruing and their less tangible quality, and because organ removal is contrary to the donor's *medical* interests. These conditions are equally pertinent to mentally incapacitated adults. Both the AMA Report and the Australian NHMRC sensibly recommend that the recipient should be a close family member,[196] thus ensuring that the expected benefits are real, and that it is not simply an action designed to promote society's interests in general. This is already a legislative requirement in some jurisdictions. In Sweden, for instance, donation by a minor must be to a 'relative' and in Belgium and Michigan such donation must be to a sibling, parent or child.

child's interests' should be taken to be addressed towards younger children only: see J. Lantos, 'Children as Organ Donors: An Argument for Involuntary Altruism' in G. Burgio and J. Lantos (eds.), *Primum Non Nocere Today*, Elsevier Science BV, Amsterdam, 1994, 67 at 67.

194 Crouch and Elliott, 'Moral Agency', at 282. They emphasise that 'other regarding' interests may not exist in such cases.

195 In this case the judge noted that the benefits of the continued relationship (with her mother) were themselves in the individual's best interests in view of the fact that it was a 'particularly close family': see *Re Y* (1996) 35 BMLR 111 at 116.

196 Although the AMA Report envisages a very exceptional case where a sufficiently close emotional bond with a non-family member might suffice.

Nevertheless, although best interests is the dominating principle even in the context of non-therapeutic procedures, it is not the only conceivable approach. The best interests standard needs to be evaluated alongside other alternatives. The implication of some of the criticism is that the test permits too much. To others though, it permits too little.

Alternative approaches

Leaps of imagination?

Lip-service was paid in some of the US cases considered above to the concept of substituted judgement as the basis for decision-making with regard to both mentally incapacitated adults (for example in *Strunk* v. *Strunk*) and minors (for example in *Hart* v. *Brown*). However, the true foundation of the decision in the cases was not what the incompetent person *would* have decided had they been competent,[197] but rather whether the procedure would have effected a net benefit to them. In *Little* v. *Little*, the court stated: 'It is clear in transplant cases that courts, whether they use the term "substituted judgment" or not, will consider the benefits to the donor as a basis for permitting an incompetent to donate an organ.'[198] In other words, the best interests test was applied in all but name.

Fost has nevertheless argued that we can decide such cases based on an extrapolation of knowledge we have regarding adults, and may reasonably conclude that the minor would be likely to consent in such circumstances.[199] Dwyer and Vig criticise the application of the substituted judgement test here though, and state that 'It is not even clear what it would mean to decide as the young child would if the child were competent.'[200] Lantos rightly regards the danger as being that it in fact

[197] In *Superintendent of Belchertown State School* v. *Saikewicz* 370 N.E. 2d 417 (Mass. 1977), it was stated that in cases where substituted judgement is applicable, the court 'dons the mantle of the incompetent and substitutes itself as nearly as possible for the individual in the decision-making process'.

[198] *Little* v. *Little* 576 S.W. 2d 493 at 498 (Tex. Civ. Ct 1979).

[199] N. Fost, 'Children as Renal Donors' (1977) 277 *New England Journal of Medicine* 363.

[200] J. Dwyer and E. Vig, 'Rethinking Transplantation Between Siblings' (1995) 25 *Hastings Center Report* 7 at 7. Sheldon argues that in any event Fost fails to show a connection between his two contentions: see M. Sheldon, 'Children as Organ Donors' in B. Spielman (ed.), *Organ and Tissue Donation: Ethical, Legal and Policy Issues*, Southern Illinois University Press, Carbondale, 1997, 111 at 116–17.

becomes a decision about what the minor *should* do rather than what he/she *would* do.[201] The AMA Report states: 'Because of the fictional quality of substituted judgment, attempts to predict a specific child's adult values in the name of the child's autonomy need to be checked by other standards so that proxy decision-makers do not have inappropriately far-reaching control over children.'[202] Moreover, many mentally incapacitated adults (Jerry Strunk for instance) have no pre-formed values or life plans upon which to base a substituted judgement. Such an approach might operate as a cloak for the real process of justification, although existing (and possibly past) views and attitudes should always be taken into consideration as part of a broad assessment of the individual's best interests.[203] But what about where the person *was* formerly competent? Even in such a situation, one should require compelling evidence of a person's wishes in this regard formed whilst competent, in view of the potential physical harms associated with such procedures. Substituted judgement is nonetheless in principle broadly appropriate in respect of formerly competent individuals here.[204]

In English law, an alternative '*not against the interests* of the minor' (my emphasis) standard has occasionally been employed in the context of certain non-therapeutic procedures performed on minors, for example blood testing for paternity purposes.[205] It has also been advocated in relation to non-therapeutic research and bone marrow donation.[206] The Nuffield Council suggested that the removal of tissue from a minor might be lawful if it was consented to by someone with parental responsibility, posed no more than a negligible risk and minimal burden, and was 'not against the interests of' the child. It additionally asserted that the

201 Lantos, 'An Argument for Involuntary Altruism', at 71.

202 AMA, *The Use of Minors as Organ and Tissue Donors*, at 236.

203 This would be consistent with the newly formulated best interests test advanced by the English Law Commission: see *Mental Incapacity*, Law Commission Report No. 231, HMSO, 1994, at 44–6.

204 Tomlinson argues that we should base decisions in respect of minors upon reasonable presumptions about a child's goals relative to the potential risks and benefits of the procedures: see T. Tomlinson, 'Infants and Others who cannot Consent to Donation' (1993) 60(1) *Mount Sinai Journal of Medicine* 41. However, he says it would be a 'paradoxical' canon of loyalty if we could only act on presumptions about his/her self-interested values and not on the moral values that make people who they are.

205 See *S* v. *S*, *W* v. *Official Solicitor* [1970] 3 All ER 107 (HL) and *Re H (A Minor) (Blood Tests: Parental Rights)* [1996] 4 All ER 28 (CA).

206 See L. Delany, 'Altruism by Proxy: Volunteering Children for Bone Marrow Donation' (1996) 312 *British Medical Journal* 240.

lawfulness of the removal of tissue from mentally incapacitated adults 'would depend on whether the law would countenance the dilution of the concept of best interests, by adopting the test of "not against the interests" as in the case of a child', but noted that, unlike minors, there is no person, analogous to a parent, who has the power to make decisions on such a person's behalf and to be responsible for this decision.[207] Assuming this test amounts to ascertaining that there is 'no net loss' to the minor, it also requires factoring in non-medical benefits, such as psychological gains.[208] However, the test, which is often applied in the context of non-therapeutic research procedures, is typically presented on the basis that the harm does not exceed a certain threshold,[209] in other words, that any physical harm is *de minimis*.[210] But in any event, even if such an approach were applicable here, it would exclude organ, although not necessarily tissue, donation. As Fost has stated, 'the combined organic and psychosocial risks of renal donation could not be fairly called minimal or trivial'.[211] This alternative approach essentially appeals instead to notions of parental rights which are required to protect parenthood (rather than arising from duties owed to the child).

The mantra of best interests

The best interests test is of course designed to *safeguard* the interests of the minor or mentally incapacitated adult. Lantos argues that 'Proposals to abandon, or even to modify the best interests standard may stimulate fears of a free-floating utilitarianism, wherein vulnerable and incompetent citizens will be routinely exploited and see their interests sacrificed for the

207 Nuffield Council, *Human Tissue*, at 60.

208 Indeed, in *S* v. *S* the court drew attention to the potential psychological and financial gains to be obtained from the paternity testing, and this seemingly also influenced the outcome in the case.

209 Choudry notes that most legal instruments and codes allow non-therapeutic research on children where it is not against the interests of the child. He states: 'This goal is met by limiting the risks inherent in the procedure in contrast to the balancing of risks and benefits seen in therapeutic research: see S. Choudry, 'Review of Legal Instruments and Codes on Medical Experimentation with Children' (1994) 3 *Cambridge Quarterly of Healthcare Ethics* 560 at 566.

210 For instance under the Medical Research Council Code in Britain, *The Ethical Conduct of Research on Children*, Medical Research Council, 1991. Such codes usually prescribe that the harm be no more than 'negligible'.

211 Fost, 'Children as Renal Donors', at 364.

benefit of others.'[212] A simple risk/benefit approach here would place the interests of the minor/mentally incapacitated adult donor in jeopardy in the face of the recipient's need. Dwyer and Vig observe that 'the logic of the standard approach rules out an argument that tries to justify a risk to one person in terms of a benefit to another person',[213] but they ask

> Is our choice really limited to two extremes: to a kind of crude utilitarianism where the benefits to A compensate for the harms and risks to B, or to a kind of crude egoism where every decision must aim to benefit the individual person? Instead of choosing between these two extremes, we can try to take into account the ethical import of relationships.[214]

An inappropriate picture of human agency?

Various commentators have remarked upon the *egocentric* character and individualistic focus of the best interests test here. Crouch and Elliott contend that the way the courts have constructed the notion of best interests of minors paints an 'inappropriate picture of human agency'.[215] Lantos alleges that 'The attempt to protect children from exploitation may reinforce a philosophy which sees all acts as based on self-interest and all self-interested acts as morally obligatory for children and denigrates the notion that children are capable of functioning within a human community in which motivations other than self-interest are relevant or possible.'[216] He advocates 'forced/involuntary altruism' by minors, by which parents would be able to consent to their children donating body tissues, even organs, where they themselves would have so donated had this been appropriate and had they been permitted to do so. He says parents should be free to *teach* their children altruism, that is they learn the importance of altruism by acting altruistically. Whilst Lantos objects to the conceptualisation of the nature of the act generated by the prevailing approach, Dwyer and Vig also argue that parents should be permitted to consent to some forms of donation on behalf of their children, where this is 'expected' as a function of the complex relationship between certain

[212] Lantos, 'An Argument for Involuntary Altruism', at 71.
[213] Dwyer and Vig, 'Rethinking Transplantation', at 8.
[214] Ibid., at 9. They contend that the test often in fact fails to protect minors anyhow.
[215] Crouch and Elliott, 'Moral Agency', at 278.
[216] Lantos, 'An Argument for Involuntary Altruism', at 71–2.

parties, for example parents, children, siblings.[217] Regarding siblings, they imply that in a typical family setting, kidney donation would be permissible. All these commentators support broad scope for parental discretion in decision-making here.[218]

There are difficulties with both these proposals though. The primary weakness with the first resides at the heart of the concept of 'forced altruism'. Can altruism accompany an act forced upon another? This proposal seems to be founded upon a notion of independent parental rights which outstrip those presently recognised by contemporary legal systems and most ethical perspectives. Moreover, the limits to this approach are not clear. How far would parents be able to go in 'teaching' the virtues of altruism? The same dangers as under a wholly utilitarian analysis surface again. Dwyer and Vig's slightly more convincing proposal founders on the idea of 'expected' conduct based on the nature of the requisite relationship. They state that their proposal does not create any kind of general duty of altruism, but this would appear to be the effect of the proposal, although the parameters[219] to such 'expectations' are more apparent.

These commentators seem to regard the supposedly 'selfish' focus of the best interests test as the *antithesis* of altruism, but this is a false perception. Parents and spouses, in particular, typically experience considerable feelings of obligation to and responsibility (expectation) for their children/partners, but it is coercive to require donation based purely on the *class* or type of relationship. We should instead adopt individualised case-by-case assessments, not generalised norms of behaviour, which is what the best interests test at least attempts to do (albeit that there is a lack of principled guidance as to its application). The approaches above not only appear to eschew the importance of benefit to the minor, they appear to *increase* the vulnerability of minors and would require conduct

[217] Lantos and Dwyer and Vig all argue that their reformulated approaches do no more than rationalise our existing practices.

[218] Page comments that 'To say that parents lose their normal rights if they seriously harm or endanger their children is one thing. It is quite another to hold that these rights are lost whenever parents fail to act in the interest of their children, or that they can be set aside on the basis of general benefit to the child': see E. Page, 'Parental Rights' in B. Almond and D. Hill, *Applied Philosophy*, Routledge, London, 1991, 73 at 76.

[219] Limits would be created by the nature of the relationship and the expected forms of conduct, the degree of attendant risk and the anticipated benefit.

not incumbent on adults.[220] In *Prince* v. *Commonwealth*[221] the US Supreme Court properly cautioned that 'Parents may be free to become martyrs themselves. But it does not follow that they are free, in identical circumstances, to make martyrs of their children before they reach the age of full and legal discretion when they can make that choice for themselves.'[222] Paul Ramsey contends that it is a 'canon of loyalty' owed to the individual that risks may only be imposed upon unconsenting minors (and other incompetents) when it is for their benefit.[223] This is equally cogent in the organ donation context and accords with our intuitional sense of the proper approach in such cases. It avoids the perception that such procedures *use*, in Kantian terms, such individuals purely as a means to the ends of others.[224]

Familial perspectives

Another critique comes from Ross, who asserts that the current principles of autonomy and beneficence are inadequate in this context because (a) parents should be permitted to protect family interests collectively up to a point, even at the expense of individual interests, and (b) assessing benefit is a speculative process[225] and depends entirely upon how one 'measures the various factors'.[226] Ross states that 'the moral justification of the child's participation must be based on the intimate family relationship which permits activities that would be unacceptable in the public

[220] The fact that Lantos would require that the parents be willing to do the same would not seem, as Sheldon notes, to be any safeguard as it would in any event be difficult to ascertain in a particular case.

[221] 321 US 158 at 170 (1944).

[222] The decision of the Massachusetts Supreme Judicial Court in *Nathan* v. *Farinelli* Eq. No. 74–87 (Mass. 3 July 1974) was rightly criticised by Baron *et al.* on the basis that to delegate the decision about donation to the parents was no guarantee that the minor's interests would be properly safeguarded: see Baron *et al.*, 'Live Organ and Tissue Transplants', at 167.

[223] P. Ramsey, *The Patient as a Person*, Yale University Press, New Haven, 1970.

[224] Article 2 of the Council of Europe Convention states that 'The interests and welfare of the human being shall prevail over the sole interest of society or science.'

[225] In fact it was because the prospective benefit to the minor donor was too speculative that the court in *Nathan* v. *Farinelli* decided simply to review the decision of the parents.

[226] L. Ross, 'Moral Grounding for the Participation of Children as Organ Donors' (1993) 21 *Journal of Law and Medical Ethics* 251. Ross comments that 'The state tolerates, permits, and even sanctions parental authority which goes beyond promoting a particular child's best interests to advance the family's interests': ibid. at 252. See also L. Ross, *Children, Families, and Health Care Decision-Making*, Clarendon Press, Oxford, 1998.

domain',[227] and would permit parents to consent to low and moderate risk procedures in the interests of the family; although procedures carrying a significant risk, such as kidney donation, would additionally require the consent of a competent minor. To a degree, Ross's approach accords with our normal intuitions about the discretionary elements of family decision-making. Although appeals to parental rights divorced from the direct interests of the children to which specific decisions relate run counter to contemporary jurisprudential trends, it is a reasonable perspective when the minor is being asked (not being competent to decide for him- or herself) only to take minimal or negligible risks; indeed this may reflect the 'not against the interests' approach. However, Ross's proposal would rule out the possibility of renal donation by minors without capacity even where there is an anticipated benefit to the donor, and for that reason is a conservative one. Ross argues that donating body materials benefits the child by benefiting the family as an autonomous unit in itself, and maintains that 'An intrafamilial donation enhances the child's well-being by the benefit accrued to the family as a whole, even if his individual welfare is diminished by the transient discomfort.'[228] This *derivative* approach would appear to be a more convincing line of argument, one which is entirely compatible with traditional notions of best interests. Indeed, it would be entirely artificial to assess the interests of the minor in isolation from the effect of the decision on the family unit because of the minor's interest in, and benefit from, the proper functioning of the family as a whole.

The AMA Report considers that a minor's wishes are relevant to the decision as to whether a benefit is likely to accrue psychologically to the minor.[229] This is consistent with the views expressed by Lord Donaldson and Lord Justice Nolan in *Re W*.[230] On such an approach, lack of assent would not constitute an absolute bar to the procedure taking place. However, the Nuffield Council would preclude donation where such persons 'object, or appear to object, to the procedures'[231] and there are various transplant laws which specifically proscribe it. For example, under

[227] Ross, 'Moral Grounding', at 251.

[228] Ibid., at 253.

[229] *The Use of Minors as Organ and Tissue Donors*, at 242.

[230] [1992] 3 WLR 758 at 770 and 781. The Council of Europe Convention states generally that 'The opinion of the minor shall be taken into consideration as an increasingly determining factor in proportion to his or her age and degree of maturity': Article 6(2).

[231] Nuffield Council, *Human Tissue*, at 13.19.

Swedish law it is expressly stated that 'Removal may not be carried out against the donor's wishes.'[232] It is submitted that a refusal of assent even by an incapacitated individual should constitute an absolute bar to proceeding and not merely a factor to be taken into consideration.[233]

It is necessary to guard against not only actual abuses but also any *appearance* of exploitation of incapable, vulnerable persons. The Law Reform Commission of Canada perceived this in law as being the distinction between equity and a strict application of rules. It stated:

> Advocates of the former approach have confidence in the ability of human beings to discern what is right or best in particular idiosyncratic circumstances. Thus, some analysts regard transplant cases decided on psychological-benefit theories as 'judgements . . . characterised by humanity and compassion rather than blind adherence to one principle or test'. Others disparage psychological-benefit theories as a speculative and unreliable standard dependent on situation ethics and palm-tree justice. In their view, general principles or rules need to be applied uniformly to avoid the evils of bias and subjectivity. They hold that consistency is the hallmark of both principled morality and the rule of law and must be observed even if it results in uncompassionate or unfair outcomes in some cases.[234]

Whilst the likelihood of benefit in individual cases would persuade the act utilitarian to permit donation in specific instances, the deontologist (and maybe even the rule utilitarian) would seemingly prefer to have clear rules prohibiting donation because of the possibility of exploitation and maybe even the appearance of individuals being used disrespectfully and solely as the means to the ends of others. However, a stringent set of preconditions and safeguards should be capable of ensuring that the very exceptional instance of kidney donation by a minor or mentally incapacitated adult was transparently *not* a case of exploitation (or balancing of social worth). A ban could itself cause harm as a consequence, not least to the very individuals one is seeking to protect, as Guttmann and Gerok observed at the outset.

232 Law of 8 June 1995, section 8. In France, minors may donate bone marrow to a sibling but not if the minor refuses: see Law of 29 July 1994, Article L. 671–5.

233 The relevance of the child's assent is increasingly being recognised in codes and protocols governing non-therapeutic research procedures, although again here there is no universal consensus. The Council for International Organisations of Medical Sciences (CIOMS) considers that the child's unwillingness should be balanced against the possible benefit to the child, whilst the Medical Research Council in Britain considers such a refusal should be a veto.

234 *Procurement and Transfer*, at 50.

Parameters and safeguards

The AMA Report states that 'If the safeguards in the remainder of the recommendations are followed, minors should be permitted to serve as a source when the risks are *low* (for example blood or skin donation), *moderate* (for example bone marrow donation) or *serious* (for example kidney donation, which involves more extensive anaesthesia and major invasive surgery).'[235] The recommendation of the Nuffield Council on Bioethics that only procedures of 'negligible risk and minimal burden' should be permitted upon minors and mentally incapacitated adults is on this view restrictive. Despite the 'serious' character of kidney donation, the probability of psychological/emotional benefit and the modest risks suggest a less stringent ceiling. The AMA's Report, however, considered that minors should not generally be donors in relation to 'very serious' risk procedures such as partial liver or lung donation.[236] It took the view that such very serious procedures were still at the developmental stage and the risks and benefits were as yet unclear. The Council of Europe Recommendation on Living Related Liver Transplantation concurred with this view vis-à-vis segmental liver transplants. Such limits would presumably apply equally to adults lacking decision-making capacity.

There should be some likelihood that the transplant will provide a substantial benefit to the recipient. The AMA Report requires a 'reasonable probability of success', and additionally that 'Ideally the minor should be the only possible source.'[237] In Sweden, legislation stipulates that donation by a minor is only feasible where 'it is not possible to obtain medically compatible biological material from another person'.[238] In *In Re Richardson* the court required that the risks be minimal, the circumstances urgent and reasonable alternatives lacking. However, in many of the early American cases the procedure was life-preserving – a cadaver organ transplant was not a realistic prospect and dialysis was not available. These days, it would be rare that a minor would be the only possible donor source. The AMA Report added that 'all other available sources of organs, both donor pools and competent adult family members, must be

235 AMA, *The Use of Minors as Organ and Tissue Donors*, at 240.

236 Although this might be permissible, for instance from a minor to his/her child.

237 *The Use of Minors as Organ and Tissue Donors*, at 238.

238 Such a 'criterion of necessity' is embedded in most contemporary research protocols, that is the information could not be generated from other sources, namely adult volunteers. This is a condition in the guidelines of the British Paediatric Association for instance.

medically inappropriate or significantly inferior'.[239] Such a scenario was indeed the position in cases such as *Hart* v. *Brown*, in which the Connecticut court even declared that it would be cruel and unusual punishment to subject a minor *patient* to the additional harms associated with donation from an alternative source, where a strict and extensive immunological regime would have had to have been imposed.

Procedural aspects

The AMA Report considers that those procedures which pose a 'serious risk' should receive court authorisation in all cases. It asserts that the rationale for court involvement in cases where the minor possesses capacity to consent to donation is to confirm that the minor is competent to make the decision and that the decision is a voluntary decision made without undue family pressure or coercion.[240] Regarding minors, Lord Donaldson suggested in *Re W* that in all cases a doctor would need to seek the opinion of other doctors as well as being 'well advised to apply to the court for guidance'.[241] With respect to mentally incapacitated adults the *obiter* remarks of members of both the Court of Appeal (Neill LJ) and the House of Lords (Lord Bridge) in *Re F* were also to the effect that in England and Wales court involvement was desirable in any such case.[242]

Dwyer and Vig argue that it is the very fact that the parents *do have* a conflict of interest that makes their place in decision-making so vital, that is to balance the needs of the family. This contrasts with the views of certain commentators who point to the dangers of the best interests of the (mentally incapacitated) individual becoming intertwined with the self-interest of the dominant party, possibly the parents. The AMA Report remarked:

> In their desire to save a seriously ill child, parents may temporarily subordinate the welfare of another child who is a potential source. Additionally, inappropriate factors could influence parental decision-

[239] The paper issued by the National Health and Medical Research Council of Australia, Discussion Paper No. 2, *Ethical Issues in Organ Donation*, stated that donation should be the 'last resort in treatment for the recipient'.

[240] AMA, *The Use of Minors as Organ and Tissue Donors*, at 233.

[241] Ibid. Lord Justice Nolan made similar remarks at [1992] 3 WLR 758 at 782C, stating that court involvement would be essential in any case 'in which a child of any age consented to donate an organ'.

[242] [1990] 2 AC 1 at 33B and 52E–F.

> making if the potential source were particularly disfavored in the family or the potential recipient particularly favored. In general, parents faced with difficult choices may weigh the costs and benefits of all alternatives and choose the course of action which brings the most good to the family as a whole. Parents do make utilitarian decisions that benefit the family to the detriment of one child. However, for potentially harmful medical procedures, such as the retrieval of an organ for transplantation, society's concern about the physical well-being of children may outweigh the desirability of parental utilitarian balancing.[243]

It is submitted that the final decision here should be for either a court or a tribunal in this very special context.[244]

Thus, whilst such organ donations would always be rare and exceptional there would appear to be no need or justification for closing entirely a door which at most is only slightly ajar anyhow, subject to the above prerequisites. The desire for certainty should be subservient when benefit can be achieved without risk of undue harm. The AMA Report's view that 'Minors need not be prohibited from acting as sources of organs, but their participation should be limited', seems cogent.[245] The Australian Law Reform Commission previously adopted a parallel posture.[246]

Prisoners

The issue here is the voluntariness of a consent given in circumstances of detention, which was surveyed in the previous chapter.

Pregnant women

Paraguay has a proscription[247] in statute which states that it is prohibited to remove organs or tissues for transplantation purposes from 'persons

243 *The Use of Minors as Organ and Tissue Donors*, at 234–5.

244 The Law Commission Report on *Mental Incapacity* recommended that court authorisation should be sought in every instance where a mentally incapacitated adult was implicated: at para. 6.5.

245 *The Use of Minors as Organ and Tissue Donors*, at 240–1.

246 I.e. allowing for donation of non-regenerative tissues by minors in exceptional instances: see ALRC Report, *Human Tissue Transplants*, at para. 112.

247 Section 2789 of the Law states that organ removal from 'persons suffering from the disabilities prescribed by law, pregnant women or detainees is forbidden'. It is reported that Guatemala has a comparable provision.

suffering from the disabilities prescribed by law, pregnant women or detainees'.[248] In most jurisdictions though the matter is left to clinical judgement as regards women who are pregnant.

[248] One or two other jurisdictions have restrictions on pregnant women becoming organ donors, for example Bolivia, Colombia and Mexico. These laws are for the protection of unborn children.

PART III

General issues

9

Commerce

'Every one lives by selling something'
Robert Louis Stevenson, Across the Plains, *IX. 'Beggers', iii*

Elements of commercial influence pervade certain aspects of organ transplantation in every society, from the payment of individuals (including clinicians) and institutions involved in the process of retrieval, storage, processing, testing or transportation of organs to the limitation of access to transplantation services and facilities to those with the means to pay. In general these influences have generated little public controversy, indeed they are a common feature of the delivery of health care services generally, and therefore part of a broader debate. However, and by contrast, the spectre and practice of payments being made to organ providers has generated enormous public debate and furore in almost every domestic environment, as well on the international stage. Daar remarks that 'Few questions in biomedical ethics are as challenging at present as the question of paid organ donation for transplantation, raising as it does difficult issues related to the body, the soul, property rights, autonomy, limitations of freedom, cultural/ethical pluralism and professional versus societal perceptions.'[1]

Necessity knows no law

Of course what fuels commercial incentives given to organ providers is the actual or perceived insufficiency of organs for transplantation. The World Health Organisation stated in the Preamble to its Guiding Principles that

[1] A. Daar, 'Paid Organ Donation: The Grey Basket Concept' (1998) 24 *Journal of Medical Ethics* 365.

> A feature of organ transplantation since its commencement has been the shortage of available organs. Supply has never satisfied demand, and this has led to the continuous development in many countries of procedures and systems to increase supply. Rational argument can be made to the effect that shortage has led to the rise of commercial traffic in human organs, particularly from living donors who are unrelated to recipients.[2]

Markets have predictably tended to evolve in, generally Third World, nations where poverty is endemic and where the supply is consequently highly elastic and plentiful.[3] In India, where despite the high incidence of end-stage renal failure there are no public dialysis facilities and no national cadaveric organ transplantation programme, the domestic dilemma is starkly 'To Buy or Let Die?'.[4] As a consequence, some centres were prepared to accept paid donors since outcomes using living unrelated donors dramatically improved in the eighties, with the advent of more effective immunosuppressant agents. Daar notes that the international outcry regarding commerce merely had the effect in countries such as India of driving commercialisation underground.[5]

Such trading is by no means always conducted covertly though. Adverts offering to buy or sell organs have been published all around the world, although in the Indian and South American press especially. They come in all guises, as a couple of examples will suffice to show. A piece in the *Guardian* in 1984, entitled 'Debtors Sell their Kidneys to Pay Loans', described how people in Japan were offering to sell kidneys to avoid being subjected to violence from loan sharks.[6] This was followed by another in 1988 stating that a penniless Italian awaiting trial for murder had offered to donate a kidney in exchange for a defence lawyer![7] Even more starkly, an online auction of a human kidney in the US via the Internet on 26 August 1999 started bidding at $25,000. The bidding on this and another

[2] WHO, *Guiding Principles on Organ Transplantation*, 1991.

[3] Broyer states: 'It is possible to understand the mechanisms of this market, which are mainly the pressure applied by uremic patients who are able to pay on the one hand, and the vital needs of poverty-stricken people on the other hand': see M. Broyer, 'Aspects of Living Organ Donation with Emphasis on the Fight Against Commercialism' in W. Land and J. Dossetor (eds.), *Organ Replacement Therapy: Ethics, Justice, Commerce*, Springer-Verlag, Berlin, 1991, 197 at 198. One Indian slum, Villivakkam, was nicknamed 'Kidney-vakkam' after more than 20 per cent of residents had sold a kidney.

[4] K. Reddy, 'Should Paid Organ Donation be Banned in India? To Buy or Let Die!' (1993) 6(3) *National Medical Journal of India* 137 at 137.

[5] Daar, 'The Grey Basket Concept', at 302.

[6] *Guardian*, 23 November 1984.

[7] *Guardian*, 11 January 1988.

identical auction ran up to $4 million before the advertisement was 'pulled'.[8]

Organ tourism

Patients will travel where they can to receive necessary treatment unavailable in their country of residence,[9] so the shortage of organs in certain regions additionally promotes trade elsewhere. There was an explosion of such activity in India in the eighties, with 80 per cent of the renal organs procured there being transplanted into rich foreign patients, primarily from the Middle East, who then returned to their native countries for after-care.[10] The traffic is also intercontinental. It is reported that an increasing volume of German patients are undergoing paid transplants in Indian, Pakistani, Iraqi and Philippine centres.[11] Moreover, in May 1997 a report appeared in the *Sunday Times* of a Turkish company, Trans Transplantsyon, offering to fly individuals with kidney failure to India or Russia to undergo a kidney transplant at a local centre for a reported fee of £22,000,[12] despite commercialism in organ procurement being illegal in the UK, Russia, Turkey, and virtually all other parts of the world.[13] Obviously, such transplants generate substantial and much needed foreign revenue for many poorer

[8] 'Online Bidders' Stake in Kidney' *The Times*, 4 September 1999. The seller identified as 'hchero' from Sunrise, Florida, advertised a 'fully functional kidney for sale' on the eBay auction site and stated a preparedness to give either kidney. The second sale was pulled before any bids were received. It is not known if these were genuine attempts to sell or not. See also http://www.floridastuff.com/kidney.

[9] This may not necessitate the purchase of organs, where individuals can gain access to waiting lists in other nations/regions. For instance, Italians have received transplants in various nations, but notably in France, Belgium and Austria.

[10] These nationals came from Kuwait, Dubai, Bahrain, United Arab Emirates, Oman, Saudi Arabia, as well as Malaysia and Singapore. Due to the same shortages, residents of Taiwan, Hong Kong, Korea and Singapore have regularly visited mainland China, and Japanese patients visited the Philippines on a similar quest.

[11] 'German Doctors Protest Against "Organ Tourism"' (1996) 313 *British Medical Journal* 1282.

[12] It was reported that the company, which had been operating on the Continent for six years and had organised 400 successful transplants, was due shortly to open an office in London: see 'Kidney Patients Offered Transplant Flights to India' *The Sunday Times*, 11 May 1997. Colabawalla reports on similar adverts appearing in the German press: see B. Colabawalla, 'Commerce and Trade in Human Organs', Paper to Second International Conference on Organ Transplantation, Kuwait, 15 March 1990, at 557.

[13] Indeed, a Dr Yusuf Sozen was reportedly awaiting trial in Turkey on charges of paying £5,000 for a kidney to be transplanted to a visiting Israeli.

nations.[14] However, such traffic is not, geographically speaking, all one way. A storm broke out in the mid-eighties in Britain after it was discovered that a Turkish peasant had had a kidney removed at a private London hospital in return for a fee of around £3,000, which led to the striking off of a Harley Street nephrologist from the medical register, and indirectly to the passing of the Human Organ Transplants Act 1989 which outlawed such payments.[15] Even in regions where no overt payment for organs is made, financial incentives may influence organ distribution patterns. In 1985, it was reported that American and European surgeons were soliciting wealthy or influential foreign patients able to pay the extremely high charges, guaranteeing rapid and preferential (queue-jumping) transplantation in renowned centres.[16] Transborder trading invites a variety of thorny questions, which raise broader issues relating to organ allocation in general and are considered in chapter 10.[17]

Grease[18]

Apart from the organ trading that currently exists, largely with regard to *living* providers, the general debate on the desirability of commercial incentives has intensified lately, especially in North America. Proposals range from 'rewarded gifting' to 'futures' markets to full-blown organ trading markets. These are generally targeted at solving *domestic* organ transplantation shortages and typically focus upon *cadaveric* rather than living 'vendors'.[19] Guttmann and Guttmann claim that 'The growing

[14] Whilst conversely the cheaper cost of the procedure in these nations is itself an attractive feature to many non-residents.

[15] See further D. Price and R. Mackay, 'The Trade in Human Organs' (1991) *New Law Journal* 1272 (Part I) and 1307 (Part II).

[16] See S. Porter, 'Organ Transplants: Questions and Controversy' (1984) 80(1) *The New Ethics* 33 at 37. In 1984, 300 kidneys from the United States were transplanted into non-residents.

[17] The Bellagio Task Force reported that Belgian and Austrian hospitals do not send available organs abroad for transplantation in all instances, but require patients to come to their hospitals, in part because they want to receive their fees: see D. Rothman *et al.*, 'The Bellagio Task Force Report on Transplantation: Bodily Integrity, and the International Traffic in Organs' (1997) 29 *Transplantation Proceedings* 2739 at 2741.

[18] Kevorkian's description of the role money plays in the organ transplant process: see J. Kevorkian, 'A Controlled Auction Market is a Practical Solution to the Shortage of Transplantable Organs' (1992) 11 *Law and Medicine* 47 at 54.

[19] George Smith II states that 'Included among the various approaches to resolving the critical shortage of human organs for transplantation are post mortem harvesting, escheatage, prospective contingent sales, and standard death benefit payments – with the latter being perhaps the most attractive in the United States': see G. Smith, 'Market and Non-Market

numbers waiting for cadaveric donations and the high costs of technology such as dialysis . . . will force the issue of commercialisation into the national political arena in the future.'[20]

At one extreme is the scheme put forward by Dr Jack Kevorkian for a national or international 'controlled auction market' for transplantable organs under the supervision of a specially created commission independent of government.[21] The price of such organs would be fixed by the market, with organs going to the highest bidder. The anticipated advantage would be to drive prices up, without cost to the state, increasing the prospects of those patients waiting to be transplanted and producing surplus cash to support transplants for indigent persons free of charge. Kevorkian acclaims the value of the market here with regard to both organ *distribution* and procurement, describing these two facets of the scheme as 'complementary and synergistic'.[22] By contrast, most advocates of commerce confine their attention to the organ procurement side.

Market-based systems are often contrasted with systems of indirect or modest *reward*, frequently dubbed 'rewarded gifting' with regard to living providers. With regard to cadaveric sources, Peters has proposed payment of a 'death benefit' to families of organ donors paid through organ procurement organisations, which 'would be neither coercive nor result in loss of altruistic values'.[23] Payments would be fixed and universal and would thus prevent the opportunity cost for organs spiralling out of control. The payment of funeral expenses or final medical expenses related to deceased donors has already been actively proposed. Indeed, the state of Pennsylvania passed Act No. 102 of 1994 creating an 'Organ Donation Awareness Trust Fund' and authorising the Department of Health to use 10 per cent of the fund to help pay for hospital and other medical, and funeral, expenses that donor families incur in connection with the donation process. No payment may exceed $300 and it may only be paid directly to the hospital or the funeral

Mechanisms for Procuring Human and Cadaveric Organs; When the Price is Right' (1993) 1 *Medical Law International* 17 at 17.

20 A. Guttmann and R. Guttmann, 'Sale of Kidneys for Transplantation: Attitudes of the Health-Care Profession and the Public' (1992) 24 *Transplantation Proceedings* 2108 at 2108.

21 His system would apply to living donors, prisoners on death row and any other individuals facing imminent and unavoidable death, for example patients opting for physician-assisted death.

22 Of course, the wealthy recipients would then be removed from the cadaveric waiting list.

23 T. Peters, 'Life or Death: The Issue of Payment in Cadaveric Organ Donation' (1991) 265 *Journal of the American Medical Association* 1302. These are often termed 'spot markets'.

home and not to the family.[24] The law has not yet come into force,[25] but was carefully crafted to avoid proscriptions on organ sales under federal law, by avoiding direct payments to families.

Investing in the futures

There have been three major proposals advanced by individuals for commercialisation of cadaveric organ procurement practices through forms of *futures* markets. All of these schemes are trumpeted as promoting the autonomy of the organ source, avoiding unpleasant discussions with relatives at a time of grief, and removing the need to use living donors. Moreover, the House of Delegates of the American Medical Association recently adopted the recommendations of a Report of the Council on Ethical and Judicial Affairs of the AMA (AMA Report) that strongly endorsed a futures market concept, arguing that it might obviate some of the ethical difficulties generally attendant upon commercial schemes, and called for implementation of a pilot scheme.[26]

The first proposal was advanced by Richard Schwindt and Aidan Vining in 1986, under which an organ bearer might enter into a lifetime contract and would receive compensation *at the time he contracted with an organ purchaser* for agreeing to donate his organs upon his death.[27] The state would be the sole entity entitled to purchase organs in this way and the buyer would acquire the right to harvest the bearer's organs if the bearer died under circumstances in which the organs were transplantable.

[24] 20 Pa. Cons. Stat. Ann., s. 8622(b)(1) (West Supp. 1995). A remarkably prescient piece previously stated that although a purely private market was still unpalatable in the US, 'allowing the government to pay the organ donor's final medical bills or funeral expenses, with the government acting as the sole purchaser of organs as part of its larger commitment to organ transplantation, should be a politically palatable alternative': see 'Developments in the Law – Medical Technology and the Law: Organ Transplantation' (1990) 103(7) *Harvard Law Review* 1614 at 1630.

[25] An advisory committee was required to develop a pilot programme but it was only on 9 June 1999 that the Committee proposed a plan to the health department. At the time of writing, Republican Governor Tom Ridge was expected to approve the plan, although it has attracted a great deal of publicity and adverse comment. My thanks to Professor Robert Rains of the Dickinson School of Law, Penn. State University, for providing details of this proposal.

[26] Council on Ethical and Judicial Affairs of the American Medical Association, 'Financial Incentives for Organ Procurement: Ethical Aspects of Future Contracts for Cadaveric Donors' (1995) 155 *Archives of Internal Medicine* 581.

[27] They are both professional economists from Simon Fraser University: see R. Schwindt and A. Vining, 'Proposal for a Future Delivery Market for Transplant Organs' (1986) 11 *Journal of Health Politics, Law and Policy* 483.

Relatives would have no right to sell the deceased's organs after death. The second proposal emanated from Henry Hansmann in 1989.[28] Under this proposal, organ bearers would also receive immediate payment for entering into a yearly renewable futures contract. The buyers would primarily be the large health insurance companies, and the 'payment' would be in the form of a reduction in health insurance premiums.[29] The ultimate organ recipient would be obligated to pay the organ buyer or its assignee the latter's stated price upon accepting the organ for transplantation. If the person died without entering into such a contract, the relatives would again have no right to sell the deceased's organs. The third proposal came from Lloyd Cohen in 1989,[30] under which compensation (estimated at approximately $5,000 for each solid organ retrieved) would be paid *at the time of the bearer's death and after organ harvesting* to the organ bearer's estate or other assignee. Gregory Crespi has supported the latter scheme, although he believes that Cohen has radically underestimated the probable payment needed, but he advocates an alternative choice by which a (significantly lower) payment would be made to the organ-bearer's estate *whether or not any organs are harvested.*[31]

Contrasting the above schemes, an important difference relates to the time of payment to the organ bearer. Is it at the time of the agreement or at the time of harvesting? If the former, the payments would have to be more modest as many of the organs concerned would ultimately prove to be unusable for transplantation. Moreover, lifetime binding contracts might generate unconscionable restrictions upon the organ provider's lifestyle and activities, although these might be avoidable under a series of renewable contracts.[32] On the other hand, where relatives stand to benefit, in Banks's words, 'Ethical considerations arise in posthumous organ sales

[28] He gained a PhD in economics and then worked at the Yale University Law School: see H. Hansmann, 'The Economics and Ethics of Markets for Human Organs' (1989) 14 *Journal of Health Politics, Law and Policy* 57.

[29] Estimated at around $10 per annum.

[30] He came from the Chicago-Kent Law School and similarly holds an economics PhD. See Lloyd Cohen, 'Increasing the Supply of Transplant Organs: The Virtues of a Futures Market' (1989) 58 *George Washington Law Review* 1, 'The Ethical Virtues of a Futures Market in Cadaveric Organs' in Land and Dossetor, *Organ Replacement Therapy*, at 302, and 'A Futures Market in Cadaveric Organs: Would it Work?' (1993) 25 *Transplantation Proceedings* 60.

[31] G. Crespi, 'Overcoming the Legal Obstacles to the Creation of a Futures Market in Bodily Organs' (1994) 55(1) *Ohio State Law Journal* 1.

[32] As Banks recognises: see G. Banks, 'Legal and Ethical Safeguards: Protection of Society's Most Vulnerable Participants in a Commercialised Organ Transplantation System' (1995) 21(1) *American Journal of Law and Medicine* 45.

where the transferor's death is caused or motivated by persons who may benefit from the sale or where the organ provider commits suicide in order to benefit surviving family members.'[33] The AMA Report considered that the most promising form of financial incentive would be a modest payment for cadaveric donation at the time that the organs were retrieved, and that any ethically permissible futures market would have to prohibit payment of financial incentives to the estates of organ providers who had committed suicide. The other distinctive feature of such schemes is the nature of the purchaser(s) and the associated potential for regulation and price control. Many commentators advocate a *monopsony* here. The AMA Report envisaged a state agency purchasing all organs. In the United Kingdom the National Health Service could fulfil this role.

Barnett, Blair and Kaserman focus their attention instead on the current lack of incentives for physicians, other clinicians and procurement officers to solicit cadaveric organs for transplantation from relatives, as opposed to incentives to donors. They argue that a market system would provide a profit incentive for Organ Procurement Organisations (OPOs) actively to seek out and solicit organs through contractual arrangements. Organs would be purchased at market rates and sold on to transplant centres.[34] It has, however, been argued that in the US the current system already offers financial incentives to hospitals and OPOs through 'reimbursement' of costs, especially where multi-organ donors are concerned.[35] Reimbursement of procurement institutions varies markedly elsewhere.[36]

[33] Ibid., at 77.

[34] See A. Barnett, R. Blair and D. Kaserman, 'Improving Organ Donation: Compensation Versus Markets' (1992) 29 *Inquiry* 372 and A. Barnett and D. Kaserman, 'Shortage of Organs for Transplantation: Exploring the Alternatives' (1993) 9(2) *Issues in Law and Medicine* 117.

[35] In fact, the Health Care Financing Commission has attributed the generally successful procurement efforts in the US to the 'flexibility of the reimbursement system': see R. Evans, 'Organ Procurement Expenditures and the Role of Financial Incentives' (1993) 269 *Journal of the American Medical Association* 3113 at 3117. Evidence of substantial variation in the 'organ acquisition fee' between hospitals has however led to calls for such costs to form part of a Diagnosis Related Group (DRG) to standardise payments, although this could of course itself contain 'built in' incentives. It would inevitably drive up the overall costs of transplantation though.

[36] In the UK, procurement hospitals receive £1,000 for each retrieval, whereas in Spain considerably more substantial reimbursements are made.

Official responses

Daar states that there was 'little to indicate that in the 1960s, when transplantation was practically confined to the USA and Europe . . . there was any trafficking or commerce in organs'.[37] Nevertheless, in 1970 the Transplantation Society issued a blanket condemnation of sales of organs by living or cadaveric donors which was accepted by all members of the Society and by the profession as a whole, and was reiterated in a slightly revised and expanded content in September 1985.[38] There has been a very broad and lasting consensus against such practices within the transplant profession and the medical profession as a whole. Outside the professional sphere, condemnation of organ trading occurred in Europe as early as 1978. Council of Europe Resolution (78) 29 stated succinctly that 'No substance may be offered for profit.'[39] More recently, the Council of Europe Convention on Human Rights and Biomedicine has stipulated that 'The human body and its parts shall not, as such, give rise to financial gain.'[40] Moreover, in 1985, 1987 and 1994, the World Medical Association resolved that 'The purchase and sale of human organs for transplantation is condemned.'[41] In 1991, the World Health Organisation (WHO) Guiding Principles on Organ Transplantation declared that 'The human body and its parts cannot be the subject of commercial transactions.

[37] A. Daar, T. Gutmann and W. Land, 'Reimbursement, "Rewarded Gifting", Financial Incentives and Commercialism in Living Organ Donation' in G. Collins, J. Dubernard, W. Land and G. Persijn (eds.), *Procurement, Preservation and Allocation of Vascularized Organs*, Kluwer, Dordrecht, 1997, 301 at 302.

[38] Council of the Transplantation Society, 'Guidelines for the Distribution and the Use of Organs from Cadaver Sources and from Living Unrelated Donors', 1985. These are still accepted by all members of the Society today. See A. Daar, 'Nonrelated Donors and Commercialism: A Historical Perspective' (1992) 24 *Transplantation Proceedings* 2087. Such condemnation is reflected also in the policy statements of all the major domestic and international professional transplant organisations which typically prohibit doctors from engaging in transplantations implicating such practices.

[39] Resolution (78) 29 on Harmonisation of Legislations of Member States to Removal, Grafting and Transplantation of Human Substances, adopted by the Committee of Ministers of the Council of Europe on 11 May 1978, Article 9. The final text of the Third Conference of European Health Ministers held in Paris on 16–17 November 1987 similarly stated that 'A human organ must not be offered for profit by any organ exchange organisation, organ banking centre or by any other organisation or individuals whatever.'

[40] Article 12.

[41] In 1985 the 37th World Medical Assembly endorsed the World Medical Association's 'Statement on Live Organ Trade' calling on governments of all countries to take effective steps to prevent commercial use of human organs. This was further endorsed by the 39th World Medical Assembly in 1987.

Accordingly, giving or receiving payment (including any other compensation or reward) for organs should be prohibited.'[42] WHO proclaimed that trade was 'Inconsistent with the most basic human values and contravenes the Universal Declaration of Human Rights and the spirit of the WHO constitution',[43] and called upon Member States 'To take appropriate measures to prevent the purchase and sale of human organs for transplantation'.[44]

Legislative provisions

Legislative proscriptions of commercial organ procurement practices can be found even in the sixties,[45] and by the nineties a substantial majority of jurisdictions had such provisions;[46] only a handful of transplanting nations still have none.[47] Occasionally, the proscription is even embedded in the country's Constitution. In Brazil, for instance, the Constitution of the Federal Republic dated 5 October 1988 states that transplantation must not be the subject of any commercial transaction. These statutory provisions were not infrequently a direct and immediate response to adverse publicity surrounding proposed commercial brokering arrangements for organs. In September 1983, one Dr H. Barry Jacobs gained instant notoriety when he established the 'International Kidney Exchange, Ltd' which was intended to broker the sale and purchase of kidneys from indigent immigrants to willing American recipients. The company never in fact came into operation because the Commonwealth of Virginia immediately passed legislation prohibiting the sale of body parts.[48] More-

[42] Guiding Principle 5. Principle 6 adds that 'Advertising the need for the availability of organs, with a view to offering or seeking payment, should be prohibited.'

[43] Resolution WHA40.13.

[44] Resolution WHA42.5.

[45] Italy enacted statutory provisions in 1969 and six states in the US had (pre-UAGA) statutes with similar prohibitions: Delaware (Law of 1 Aug. 1968 ch. 429, 56 Del. Laws 1773 (1967) repealed 1970), Hawaii, Maryland, Massachusetts (Act of 12 June 1967, ch. 353, 1967 Mass. Acts 202, repealed 1971), Nevada and New York (Law of 22 Apr. 1964, ch. 702, 1964 N.Y. Laws 1827, repealed 1971). See Note, 'The Sale of Human Body Parts' (1974) 72 *Michigan Law Review* 1182.

[46] A WHO survey between 1987 and 1991 revealed this to be the case: see WHO, *Human Organ Transplantation: A Report on Developments under the Auspices of the WHO* (1987–1991), WHO, Geneva, 1991, by contrast with a similar survey conducted twenty years or so previously, when only a minority of jurisdictions had similar legislation: see WHO, *Use of Human Tissues and Organs for Therapeutic Purposes*, WHO, Geneva, 1969.

[47] For example, Denmark, Norway and Sweden.

[48] Va. Code Ann. tit. 32.1, ch. 8, Art. 2 (Michie 1993).

over, the US Government was moved to pass federal legislation, the National Organ Transplants Act (NOTA), banning interstate commerce in organs, in 1984.[49] In the UK, Count Reiner Rene Adelmann zu Adelmannsfelden, a self-styled 'specialist in legal loopholes', announced a similar intention, targeting individuals declared bankrupt or who had sizeable debt problems.[50] Such proposals drew a less immediate but identical response from the UK Government in the shape of the Human Organ Transplants Act 1989 (HOTA).

Most of the statutory regimes apply to both living and cadaveric organ providers, although Austria's 1982 Law states only that 'Organs or parts of organs of deceased persons may not be the subject of transactions carried out with a view to profit', and some laws apply merely to living providers, for example in Lebanon. Of course it should be appreciated that, regardless of legislation, general laws may prohibit commercial arrangements involving human body parts for use for transplantation. For instance, Bernat argues that, despite the limited ambit of the Austrian statute, payments to *living* organ providers would also be at least unenforceable, if not illegal.[51] Generally, where there is legislation though, donors and recipients, as well as third parties such as brokers, are potentially guilty of offences relating to such buying and selling.[52] The WHO Guiding Principle 8 states that 'It should be prohibited for any person or facility involved in organ transplantation procedures to receive any payment that exceeds a justifiable fee for the services rendered.' Whether *clinicians* are potential subjects of such offences will depend upon the statutory wording though. Under HOTA, clinicians could not properly be said to 'supply' or 'offer to supply' organs where they are merely involved in the organ removal or organ transplant procedures in their normal professional capacity, although they may become accomplices to the offences of others where they possess the requisite knowledge.[53] The situation is similar in Belgium, where the offence relates to

49 The 1968 Uniform Anatomical Gift Act is itself silent on this subject although it is frequently suggested that proper inferences of rejection of such practices should be drawn.

50 'Karl's Kidney: For Sale', *40 Minutes*, BBC, April 1990. He was allegedly operating out of Germany which did not expressly forbid the practice by law either, and it is reported that fifty to sixty individuals in Britain responded by offering to sell their kidneys to the Count.

51 E. Bernat, 'Marketing of Human Organs?' (1995) 14 *Medicine and Law* 181 at 186–7.

52 By contrast, legislation prohibiting commercial arrangements often exempts the 'contracting' parties themselves from liability: for instance under the Surrogacy Arrangements Act 1985.

53 See, for instance, Law of Kuwait 1987, section 7. This Law prohibits clinicians being involved in any transplant where they are aware that procedures for buying and selling are implicated.

the 'providing' of the organ for profit. Such laws though are often reinforced by persuasive disciplinary sanctions which may have an even more potent impact upon practitioners.[54]

Profit and loss accounts

Certain jurisdictions outlaw *any* financial payments whatever in the context of organ procurement. For instance, Algeria's law states: 'The removal and transplantation of human organs and tissues may not form the subject-matter of any financial transaction.'[55] Greek law similarly states that 'any financial exchange between the donor, the recipient, their families or any other person is prohibited'.[56] Arguably, such provisions are so broad that they would even outlaw compensation for lost earnings and expenses associated with the removal. Very commonly though, contemporary laws explicitly endorse payments to donors to reimburse these losses. A Federal Order recently passed in Switzerland, for instance, prohibits payment for organs for transplantation, but states that this does not include 'the reimbursement of the direct costs incurred for the donor'.[57] Under HOTA, although payment for an organ, or the offer to supply an organ, is forbidden, it is stated that 'payment' does not include any payment for defraying or reimbursing 'any expenses or loss of earnings incurred by a person so far as reasonably and directly attributable to his supplying an organ from his body'.[58] This should also extend to any

Moreover, under the Hong Kong Ordinance, it is explicitly made an offence for a doctor to remove or transplant an organ where he either knew or ought to have known that a payment was or was to be made for the supply of an organ: 1995 Ordinance, section 4(5)–(7). See A. Liu, 'Human Organ Transplant Ordinance: Facilitating Adult Live Donor Transplant?' forthcoming in *Current Legal Issues*, paper given at Law and Medicine Colloquium, University of London, July 1999.

[54] In 1996, the Israeli Government banned a leading transplant surgeon who had allegedly knowingly participated in transplants involving the selling of kidneys by Palestinians for transplantation into wealthy Israelis and foreigners, although there was no law, only health ministry regulations, in force at that time prohibiting these practices: see 'Israel Investigates Organ Sales' (1996) 313 *British Medical Journal* 1167.

[55] Law of 16 February 1985, Section 161.

[56] Law of 2 August 1983, section 2. Section 4 of the Cypriot Law of 1987 similarly states that 'commercial agreements or transactions' are prohibited and section 13 of the Law of 20 August 1974 in Costa Rica outlaws 'any remuneration or compensation for organs'. Sections 3 and 4 of the Law of 29 May 1979 in Turkey prohibit 'The removal or purchase or sale of any organ or tissue for profit or any other kind of remuneration'.

[57] Federal Order of 22 March 1996, Section 17.

[58] Also excluded are the costs of removing, transporting or preserving the organ. Belgian law stipulates that, despite the ban on profit, provision shall be made for living donors to be

medical expenses associated with the donor work-up or organ removal. Panama's explicit and comprehensive legislation entitles the donor to payment of 'hospital medical charges, laboratory charges, and similar expenses incurred by him, as well as compensation for loss of earnings during his absence from work by reason of examinations and other necessary procedures'.[59] Even where there is no such explicit provision, there is still a strong presumption that such 'losses' are outside the scope of prohibitions on commercial arrangements and that there was no intention to prohibit such payments. Indeed, whilst proscribing trafficking in organs, most public policy statements permit *recompense* for donor losses incurred with regard to the donation. For instance, whilst the WHO Guiding Principles stridently condemn commercial trading in organs, the Commentary to Guiding Principle 5 states that 'This Principle is designed to prohibit traffic in human organs for payment . . . The principle does not prohibit payment of reasonable expenses incurred in donation, recovery, preservation and supply of organs for transplantation.' The Explanatory Memorandum to the Council of Europe Convention similarly comments that the proscription in Article 21 does not prohibit the receiving of equitable remuneration for expenses incurred or lost earnings.[60] Whether a legitimate distinction can properly be drawn between these two types of 'payment' will be debated below.

An inconvenience allowance

Some laws not imposing a blanket ban on financial transfers *might* even allow some leeway for financial arrangements beyond the mere recovery of actually incurred losses, such as sums reflecting the hardship, inconvenience, pain and suffering and labour of the donor. Certain statutory provisions succinctly forbid the 'buying and selling' of organs, for instance

compensated at public expense or by the relevant social security agency, and that this shall 'cover both the costs and loss of income directly resulting from the provision of an organ': Law of 13 June 1986, section 4(2).

59 Law of 11 July 1983, section 4. Under Spain's Law of 27 October 1979 and the Crown Decree of 22 February 1980, 'costs incurred as a result of the donation' are recoverable: 1980 Decree, section 5.

60 Council of Europe Resolution (78) 29 was even more explicit, stating that 'loss of earnings and any expenses caused by the removal or preceding examination' are reimbursable. The Guidelines issued by the Council of the Transplantation Society in 1985 set out a comparable reservation, stating: 'However, reimbursement for loss of work earnings and any other expenses related to their donation is acceptable.'

in Russia[61] and Iraq.[62] Under German law it is forbidden to 'trade' in organs[63] and Belgian law condemns the provision of organs or tissues 'for profit'.[64] NOTA declares that it 'shall be unlawful for any person to knowingly acquire, receive or otherwise transfer any human organ *for valuable consideration* for use in human transplantation if the transfer affects interstate commerce' (my emphasis), and various US states have enacted prohibitions in similar terms.[65] However, not only does the terminology employed vary greatly, but expressions such as 'sale', 'purchase', 'valuable consideration', 'gain', 'profit', etc., are all inherently uncertain and beg questions regarding their ambit which can only be resolved by reference to the gravamen or 'mischief' at which the provision is aimed. What might usually be described as a 'profit' or 'gain' would be that financial amount which exceeds the costs of production, that is only the amount in excess of the 'labour' costs would constitute payment for, or the sale of, the organ itself, which might suggest that, literally, such provisions would allow some 'hardship/inconvenience' payment. Whether such payments *should* be permitted will be debated below, but it is suggested that it is extremely likely that such ambiguous provisions will be interpreted to proscribe such 'allowances' for the reasons set out below.

In certain jurisdictions commercial practices have continued despite legislative prohibition. This would appear to be the case in many parts of South America, in Asia and in the Russian Federation for instance.[66] In other regions, legislative prohibitions clearly seem to have inhibited and stifled commercial practices in respect of organ procurement, for example in the United Kingdom and the United States.

[61] Law of 22 December 1992, Section 1.

[62] Decree of 27 August 1986, Section 3.

[63] Act of 5 November 1997, Section 17.

[64] Law of 13 June 1986. The phrase is used in Council of Europe Resolution (78) 29 at Article 9. The Council of Europe Convention in similar vein forbids arrangements resulting in 'financial gain', in Article 21.

[65] In Michigan, for instance, it is an offence to 'knowingly acquire, receive, or otherwise transfer a human organ or part of a human organ for valuable consideration for any purpose', and there are similar laws in California, Maryland, New York and Texas. In Virginia, it is an offence to 'sell, offer to sell, to buy, to offer to buy, or to procure through purchase any natural body part for any reason'.

[66] In India, where commercial arrangements have been most pervasive, federal legislation was enacted in 1994 forbidding commercial procurement arrangements, but is still to be adopted in all the provinces and territories. The effect of this law therefore remains to be seen.

A shudder of revulsion

Bernard Levin considers that such commercial practices speak to a deep human instinct. He states:

> The shudder knows better, it speaks for interests far deeper than any surgeon's knife can cut, and far older than any furniture ever sold. And it says no. No to such transactions; no to the abandonment of reverence in the presence of the human body live or dead; no to the arguments of those who so irrationally call themselves rationalists; no to the belief that we own our own bodies as we own our clothes that cover them; no to those who ask us to believe that they have never felt the shudder, and would ignore it if they had.[67]

Such sentiments have been echoed in official fora. Introducing the Human Organ Transplants Bill on behalf of the United Kingdom Government, Roger Freeman stated in the House of Commons that 'The idea is utterly repugnant. It is entirely unacceptable in a civilised society.'[68] Whether such a reaction should act as a moral guide is a distinct question though. Many contend that we should require more than our feelings of repugnance to proscribe an activity with life-saving potential. The International Forum on Transplant Ethics has commented: 'The weakness of the familiar arguments suggests that they are attempts to justify the deep feelings of repugnance which are the real driving force of prohibition, and feelings of repugnance among the rich and healthy, no matter how strongly felt, cannot justify removing the only hope for the destitute and dying.'[69] In *R* v. *Brown*, Lord Mustill asserted in the House of Lords that more than mere feelings of disgust would be required to justify criminalising conduct which was otherwise legal.[70]

This popular gut reaction nevertheless undoubtedly prevails despite the fact that payment for blood and plasma has occurred, and still is occurring, in many jurisdictions. Sweden has always relied entirely upon a paid blood acquisition system and historically the United States had a predominantly paid blood donor regime; even today plasma is collected

67 *The Times*, 13 February 1989.

68 Second Reading Committee, Parliamentary Debates: Official Report, House of Commons, 16 May 1989, at 9, col. 1.

69 J. Radcliffe-Richards *et al.*, 'The Case for Allowing Kidney Sales' (1998) 351 *Lancet* 1950 at 1951.

70 [1993] 2 All ER 75 at 116H.

on a commercial basis. Germany has a mixed blood collection system.[71] Clinical research volunteers are routinely and substantially remunerated in most jurisdictions, and funeral costs are usually covered in the case of a body that is made available for medical research.[72] Payments for the retrieval of reproductive tissue are also common.[73] These payments raise issues as to whether there is a legitimate distinction between payments for non-regenerative and regenerative body parts, and between the sale of a body *part* and payment for *services*.[74]

Surveys in North America suggest that public opinion may be at odds with public policy and professional views here though. Based on case scenarios creating a possible commercial option in two situations, a survey by Guttmann and Guttmann in Canada revealed that a significantly lower proportion of physicians than the public would accept the commercial option.[75] This is reinforced by the findings of surveys of the US public by the Ad Hoc Donations Committee established by UNOS,[76] by the National Kidney Foundation[77] and in Richmond, Virginia.[78] Thus,

[71] The Bellagio Task Force noted that bone, dura mater and fascia lata are bought and sold routinely today: see Rothman *et al.*, 'The Bellagio Task Force Report', at 2741.

[72] B. Cohen and J. D'Amaro, 'Contemporary Ethical Considerations Related to Organ Transplantation' (1996) 28 *Transplantation Proceedings* 144.

[73] In the US, the majority of egg donors are paid. It was reported that in New York in 1997, egg donors were being paid up to $2,500. Sperm donors are given on average $50 in the US and £15 in the UK.

[74] A distinction that has also arisen in the context of surrogate motherhood.

[75] Based on the two scenarios, the percentage of the public which would have accepted the two options was 74 and 69 per cent respectively contrasted with 43 and 21 per cent respectively for respondents from the transplant community: see A. Guttmann and R. Guttmann, 'Attitudes of Healthcare Professionals and the Public Towards the Sale of Kidneys for Transplantation' (1993) 19 *Journal of Medical Ethics* 148, and 'Sale of Kidneys for Transplantation', at 2108.

[76] In the UNOS survey, 52 per cent of respondents said that some sort of financial or non-financial compensation should be offered in an effort to increase donations: see D. Kittur, 'Incentives for Organ Donation?' (1991) 338 *Lancet* 1441 at 1442.

[77] In the NKF study, 65 per cent of persons aged between eighteen and twenty-four years favoured some form of financial incentives: see R. Evans, 'Organ Procurement Expenditures and the Role of Financial Incentives' (1993) 269 *Journal of the American Medical Association* 3113 at 3117.

[78] This latter survey found that in 1994 and 1995, 35 per cent of respondents strongly agreed or agreed that a contribution to the donor's funeral expenses should be made, rising to 40 per cent in 1996. With respect to cash payments to the donor's estate, 32 per cent agreed or strongly agreed with this, dropping to 26 per cent in 1995 and 20 per cent in 1996: see T. Cosse, T. Weisenberger and G. Taylor, 'Public Feelings about Financial Incentives for Donation and Concern about Incurring Expenses due to Donation in one US City' (1997) 29 *Transplantation Proceedings* 3263.

even if there is a widespread 'gut reaction', views may be less homogeneous than assertions such as those above would suggest.

If I were a rich man . . .

The impact of such practices on organ distribution and allocation is a repeatedly occurring anxiety.[79] Radcliffe-Richards has remarked: 'I'm only guessing about the causes of repugnance, but it's the idea that people should get care, because they are rich.'[80] There is a severable connection between organ procurement and distribution arrangements though. Blumstein states: 'The original banning of market transactions in transplantable organs stemmed from an understandable yet ultimately unsophisticated linkage of demand and supply issues. A market in transplantable organs can function on the supply side, yet, if desired on ethical grounds, society can leave the demand side to a nonmarket form of distribution.'[81] Indeed, most of the 'proposers' make no assumptions about, or amendments to, the existing means of allocating organs, partly because they typically assume that organ allocation problems would not arise, as sufficient organs would be generated to enable an organ to be transplanted into everybody who required one.

Obviously though, the effect of some particular schemes would be to give a preferential entitlement to organ buyers over others.[82] Even

[79] WHO Guiding Principle 9 states that 'In the light of the principles of distributive justice and equity, donated organs should be made available to patients on the basis of medical need and not on the basis of financial or other considerations.' See chapter 10 for further discussion.

[80] General Discussion, 'The Intra- and Intercultural Commerce in Human Organs and Tissues' in Land and Dossetor, *Organ Replacement Therapy*, at 231. The practice of charging for tissues or organs is controversial especially where they were donated by members of the public free of charge. In Queensland and New South Wales, an outcry developed over reports that recipients of transplanted corneal tissue were being charged (A$425 and A$754 respectively) for it. A leading transplant opthalmologist described this as a 'breach of faith with those people who have willingly donated living tissue so that others can see': see P. Harrigan, 'Australian Transplant Payment Criticised' (1995) 346 *Lancet* 628.

[81] J. Blumstein, 'The Case for Commerce in Organ Transplantation' (1992) 24 *Transplantation Proceedings* 2190 at 2194. Harvey has set out a scheme detaching these elements. He states: 'Suppose an organisation which sees itself as a charity collects freely donated money which is then used to pay individuals for blood donations, bone-marrow donations, and kidney donations. The blood, bone marrow and organs are then given, without charge, to suitable recipients selected by a non-related medical association': see J. Harvey, 'Paying Organ Donors' (1990) 16 *Journal of Medical Ethics* 117 at 117.

[82] Crespi has argued though that such 'trading' would lead to a more efficient allocation system by virtue of the inevitable shift to a national distribution system based upon medical criteria. He has spoken in disparaging terms about the conventional 'rule of capture' strategy

Kevorkian's auction scheme which would include a 'top slicing' of fees from the rich to be used to subsidise and fund transplantation for indigent patients,[83] would create a 'two-tier' system. Whether lesser quality organs would be the lot of the poorer members of society is difficult to say in the abstract. Others have proposed analogous voucher schemes for poor patients and suchlike or the creation of a 'donor trust'.[84] Whether any allocation 'distortion' would occur depends therefore largely on whether such financial incentives do indeed increase the supply of organs. If not, then patients on the transplant waiting list without the ability to pay will be waiting longer than before for an organ. But how, it might be asked, are others harmed if only *additional* organs are made available on the basis of ability to pay? And even if enhanced procurement *did* produce the concomitant effect that the rich were the primary beneficiaries, is this unethical? Blumstein states that to object

> One must take the position that it is better to deprive the wealthy person of a transplant, which by hypothesis would not be otherwise available, in order to preserve some sense of egalitarian justice. This is a difficult outcome to impose in the name of fairness since the economically disadvantaged person is not benefited in any tangible way by prohibiting wealthier persons from using their resources to pay for a transplantable organ.[85]

Utility and uncharted seas

Whilst libertarian arguments based upon respect for persons typically *bolster* the case for allowing one to sell organs, such proposals are generally stimulated by the need to increase rates of organ procurement for transplantation. Cohen remarks that 'As against the saving of innocent lives, poetic statements about the dignity of human life being degraded by commercialism would stand revealed as the empty moral pieties of armchair philosophers incapable of a reasonable balancing of human needs.'[86] There are certainly grounds for believing that financial incentives

employed in most states including the US: see Crespi, 'Overcoming the Legal Obstacles', at 19–20.

[83] Under a national health system where treatment was free at the point of delivery, such payments would be made directly into the national health transplantation budget to cover the costs.

[84] Such as R. Sells, 'Towards an Affordable Ethic' (1992) 24 *Transplantation Proceedings* 2095.

[85] Blumstein, 'The Case for Commerce', at 2194.

[86] Cohen, 'A Futures Market in Cadaveric Organs', at 60.

to *living* providers would be likely to increase procurement as unrelated vendors (that is strangers) would generally not be potential organ *donors*. As Harvey states, 'It is doubtful that there is a great number of willing, non-related potential organ-donors who will give without payment.'[87] As regards cadaveric sources of supply, Crespi contends that

> In practice, however, one would expect that virtually all persons who would currently donate their organs would either continue to do so or would sell their organs under a regime permitting sales. In addition, there certainly must be at least some persons who are currently unwilling to donate their organs, but could be induced to supply them by sufficiently strong market incentives.[88]

Despite the simplistic and unsupported nature of these assertions, and the enormous difficulties in predicting the impact of such schemes, there are at least *prima facie* grounds for believing that such increases would be forthcoming. But would such schemes be ethical?[89]

The pros and cons of buying and selling organs: the comfy never-never land called altruism

The principal supporting argument in favour of allowing (and regulating) commerce in organ procurement is the fundamental libertarian perspective that individuals have the right to supply parts of their body for therapeutic purposes if they wish where this does not cause harm to others. Moreover, as Childress points out, 'The libertarian argument, if it succeeds, holds whatever the consequences, including a decrease in the number of available organs, while the utilitarian argument holds only if the good consequences can be realised and outweigh the bad consequences.'[90] Many advocates of the market see reinforcement of the importance of the autonomy of the donor as being its primary virtue. Lori

87 Harvey, 'Paying Organ Donors', at 119.

88 Crespi, 'Overcoming the Legal Obstacles', at 21.

89 There is an issue as to where the burden of persuasion lies here. Radcliffe-Richards argues that in view of the anti-libertarian, autonomy-restricting impact of a prohibition, it must be presumed *unjustified*: see J. Radcliffe-Richards, 'From Him that Hath Not' in Land and Dossetor, *Organ Replacement Therapy*, 190 at 193–4. Blumstein would similarly place the onus on the prohibitionists, because a fundamental aspect of US health policy in recent years has generally been the role of markets and competition: see Blumstein, 'The Case for Commerce', at 2193–4.

90 J. Childress, 'The Body as Property: Some Philosophical Reflections' (1992) 24 *Transplantation Proceedings* 2143 at 2144.

Andrews, for instance, contends that 'such an approach gives people more clear control over what is done to their bodies. In our market-based society, our laws are often more protective of property than persons.'[91] Whilst it must be conceded that rights of ownership and alienability of property do not necessarily confer co-existent rights of saleability (market alienability), it is necessary to establish rights of property over body parts in order to assert a right to sell them. As Erin and Harris state, 'Any system of commerce in human body parts presupposes that we hold property rights in those parts and products.'[92] The Law Reform Commission of Canada Working Party commented that competing philosophies of the relationship between one's body and one's 'self' 'colour our views on the good or ills of bodily property and bodily commerce'.[93] Engelhardt, for instance, views the body as being a *quintessential* example of property, which includes the right to trade commercially.[94]

Costing an arm and a leg

Harris observes that until recently human tissue rarely possessed sufficient value or utility to provoke disputed property claims, but that this is now changing.[95] Paradoxically, it is precisely because of the fact that property rights are inferentially connected to rights to buy and sell that many shun them in this context. The Law Reform Commission of Canada observed that 'It is tempting for those who want to forestall a commercial market in organs to contend that bodies are not property.'[96] Indeed, commenting on the Nuffield Working Party (of which she was a member) Report, Professor Onora O'Neill illustrates such concern about this linkage, when stating that

[91] L. Andrews, 'The Body as Property: Some Philosophical Reflections – A Response to J. F. Childress' (1992) 24 *Transplantation Proceedings* 2149 at 2150–1. See also L. Andrews, 'My Body, My Property' (1986) 16 *Hastings Center Report* 28.

[92] C. Erin and J. Harris, 'A Monopsonistic Market: Or How to Buy and Sell Human Organs, Tissues and Cells Ethically' in I. Robinson (ed.), *Life and Death under High Technology Medicine*, Manchester University Press, Manchester, 1994, 134 at 134.

[93] Law Reform Commission of Canada, *Procurement and Transfer of Human Tissues and Organs*, Working Paper 66, Minister of Supply and Services, Ottawa, 1992, at 55.

[94] Engelhardt relies upon Hegel and Locke in particular and regards the body as being separate from the 'personhood' of the individual.

[95] J. Harris, 'Who Owns My Body?' (1996) 16(1) *Oxford Journal of Legal Studies* 55 at 75. However, he notes that hair for wigs has been bought and sold for many years without controversy.

[96] Law Reform Commission of Canada, *Procurement and Transfer*, at 56.

> A property rights approach to the use of human tissue leads to various problems. It flies in the face of the common law tradition: the courts have consistently refused to view living tissue as property; even cadavers may at most be 'lawfully possessed' rather than owned; only certain long-dead, or at least very dead, tissue (mummies, relics, some pathological specimens) has been treated by the courts as an object of commerce. Moreover, there are quite serious concerns both about the adequacy of ordinary commercial consent procedures to protect the more vulnerable should a market in human body parts be permitted, and about the broader unintended consequences of such a market (for example would commercial incentives put pressure on safety standards?).[97]

A similar observation might also be targeted at the decision of the California Supreme Court in the *Moore* case, about which Freeman observes that 'Implicit in the Court's reasoning is the assumption that ownership is absolute or it is not ownership.'[98] In fact, ironically, rather than rejecting property claims outright, the Nuffield Report endorsed the notion of *users* possessing property rights in such parts or tissues, although not the *source*.

A spectacular *non sequitur*

The above remarks, however, seem more pertinent as objections to *commercialisation* than they are to property rights in human body parts or tissues *per se*.[99] These sources improperly conflate the severable notions of property rights and commercialism. Margaret Radin, for instance, regards body parts as 'market inalienable', that is transferable but without sale.[100] (Resnik terms them 'incomplete commodities'.[101]) Radin contends that in order to be a person one needs to have some control over resources in the

[97] O. O'Neill, 'Medical and Scientific Uses of Human Tissue' (1996) 22 *Journal of Medical Ethics* 5 at 5.

[98] M. Freeman, 'Biotechnology, Patients and Profits: How is the Law to Respond?' in Robinson, *Life and Death under High Technology Medicine*, 118 at 122.

[99] Indeed, the Nuffield Working Party seems to have been primarily concerned about the promotion of biotechnological research rather than with the broader aspects of property rights in body parts generally: see Nuffield Council on Bioethics Working Party, *Human Tissue: Ethical and Legal Issues*, Nuffield Council on Bioethics, London, 1995, at 9.13.

[100] M. Radin, 'Market-Inalienability' (1987) 100(8) *Harvard Law Review* 1849.

[101] D. Resnik, 'The Commodification of Human Reproductive Materials' (1998) 24 *Journal of Medical Ethics* 388.

external environment to achieve proper self-development, that is identity and personhood.[102] Indeed, Childress asks rhetorically,

> If the response is that we do not 'own' our bodies and thus cannot sell their parts, it is incumbent on the respondent then to show how people can 'give' or 'donate' what they do not 'own'. Indeed, as I noted, all the modes of transfer of human organs from one person to another presuppose some notion of property and property rights. Or at least they presuppose some cluster of rights associated with property.[103]

This last perspective is persuasive, although a little less easy to apply in some jurisdictions to parts taken from cadavers than to those from living persons, especially in so far as they cannot seemingly form part of the deceased's estate. But how could 'futures' contracts be legally sound if a person does not have proprietary rights in the items which he/she is purporting to sell for valuable consideration? There is surely no reason why an individual cannot own property which will be 'created' only in the future through severance, even an item which originally was part of that person's own identity. Trading in future commodities is entirely plausible in respect of body parts and there seems no reason to stick slavishly to notions of *scintilla temporis*.

Thus, although we can find that property rights exist in body parts severed for transplantation and that such rights are transferable by gift, the question remains whether commercial sales should be permitted. Before examining some of the arguments for and against allowing this, we should note that the perceived advantage of promoting autonomy through commercial transactions in organs is inapplicable to schemes whereby *relatives* of dead persons are permitted to benefit from the giving of permission for organ removal. Pellegrino contends that Peters's proposed scheme of this type is illegitimate as the family does not have proprietary rights over the relative's dead body and that the payment of a death benefit improperly legitimates family interests over the deceased's.[104] In other words, property-based notions are being used negatively here, to *oppose* the rights of others to control the use of the parts of the cadaver.

102 See N. Duxbury, 'Law, Markets and Valuation' (1995) 61 *Brooklyn Law Review* 657 at 665.

103 Childress, 'The Body as Property', at 2144.

104 E. Pellegrino, 'Families' Self-Interest and the Cadaver's Organs' (1991) 265 *Journal of the American Medical Association* 1305 at 1306.

Con?

The arguments against commerce in this sphere are a mixture of deontological and consequentialist (partly 'slippery slope' based) objections. Some of these are targeted at the impact on donors themselves, others at the effects on recipients or on society generally. Certain criticisms, for instance those based on harmful effects and exploitation of the 'seller', are principally targeted at *living* rather than cadaver sources. The Bellagio Task Force asserted that there has yet been no general or convincing rationale offered for a prohibitory stance upon commerce. The main arguments put forward against commercialism in organ procurement are:

1) That we *do not* have a right to do just as we please with our body parts;
2) That the donor's health, or even his life, is compromised by such selling;
3) That commerce in organ procurement militates against the obtaining of a proper voluntary and informed consent;
4) That organ selling constitutes exploitation of the 'vendor';
5) That it will lead to a commodification of the human body;
6) That there will be a consequential reduction in altruism;
7) That it is against the interests of recipients because they frequently experience poor graft survival and poor post-operative medical care and follow-up, and complications are common as is the incidence of communicable diseases contracted through such arrangements;
8) That it will ultimately lead to the growth of nefarious practices such as organ 'stealing' or killing for organs, because of the value now given to the organ;
9) That such markets reduce the incentives to national governments to establish national cadaveric transplant programmes or provide for end-stage organ failure sufferers generally.

The autonomy paradox

The first criticism, that we have no right to do just anything with our body (parts), does not carry us very far. One can concede the point and still ask why we should not be able to sell certain parts if we so wish. The sometimes related argument that we would end up allowing people to kill themselves incrementally is simply fallacious. We allow individuals to *donate* certain organs, but not knowingly to kill themselves in the process. Daar refers to the paradox here that whilst medical professionals generally abhor commerce they also endorse autonomy, yet selling is simply an extension of autonomy.[105]

Harm to the vendor

It has been pointedly noted by Cohen regarding cadaveric sources that such 'vendors are neither rich, nor poor, merely dead'![106] But what of living organ sellers? Radcliffe-Richards has commented: 'Perhaps, then, the idea is to protect not other people, but the would-be vendors themselves . . . This idea is certainly more in keeping with the tone of the popular outcry, which does, after all, express indignation on behalf of the exploited victims of the rich.'[107] However, we *do* generally allow people to do things with their bodies where this will not cause harm to others, at least unless serious harm may attach to the individual him/herself and assuming that the individual is capable of making autonomous decisions; and this includes organ *donors*. It would be unwarrantably paternalistic in general to preclude persons from acting in ways which may be harmful to them but which would not cause harm to others. Caplan has noted ironically that 'when the proposal was made to buy and sell kidneys what had historically been deemed "minimal risks" suddenly escalated into intolerable dangers when profit became an obvious motive!'.[108] But the fact of sale cannot affect the severity of the risk of harm in itself. It should be recognised that living organ providers under any commercialised system are often already disadvantaged in terms of health because of the undoubted link between poverty and ill-health. As regards giving solid organs, there are no problems analogous to the long-term professional blood donor phenomenon though. Where no serious harm will generally result which would typically forbid organ *donation*, the issue then is

[105] Daar, 'The Grey Basket Concept', at 366.
[106] Cohen, 'The Ethical Virtues of a Futures Market', at 305.
[107] Radcliffe-Richards, 'From Him that Hath Not', at 190.
[108] A. Caplan, 'Blood, Sweat, Tears and Profits: The Ethics of the Sale and Use of Patient Derived Materials in Biomedicine' (1985) 33 *Clinical Research* 448 at 450.

whether the person *should* be allowed to sell parts of their body. This is not solved by simple rhetoric.

Hard choices

The above remarks are all premised on the ability of individuals to make autonomous decisions and give a valid consent to removal. It is frequently stated that the respect for autonomy which forms the central plank of such proposals is misplaced, and that there can be no real autonomy in practice. If this were so, then paternalistic arguments would carry great weight and libertarians would also concede the need to intervene to prevent harm.

It has been suggested by some commentators that an informed consent by organ vendors is not possible because of the typical level of education and knowledge and the pre-existing misinformation already in their possession. In various countries where commercial practices currently exist, such as India, this objection is cogent, but nevertheless may not justify banning the practice altogether. Proper regulation could ensure enhanced levels of understanding, and even if some potential vendors would remain lacking in sufficient knowledge and comprehension to provide an informed consent, this would not justify banning *all* persons from selling their organs, only certain individuals. These remarks apply *a fortiori* in nations with higher basic levels of education and capacity for comprehension across the board. In the absence of such knowledge and understanding even *organ donation* ought to be precluded in many instances. It is also frequently asserted that commerce in organ procurement undermines the *voluntariness* of consent given by organ sellers. However, any sweeping assumptions here have already been rejected in an earlier chapter with regard to both living *donors* and *sellers*. It must be questioned why, if the rich may take excessive risks purely for pleasure or danger, the poor should be perceived to be acting irrationally when they propose to take risks to ensure their own, and probably their family's, survival.

Dubious exploits

Even though payments do not in themselves always coerce or undermine the voluntariness of consent of organ vendors, it is consistently argued that it is a form of *exploitation*. However, rarely is the precise gist of this exploitation articulated, that is why, if organ donation is non-exploitative, is payment for the same act exploitative?

Gillon has said:

> Exploitation is an emotive and ambiguous term meaning the use of someone to achieve the exploiter's own ends. The morally undesirable form of exploitation is the use of people for our own ends in ways that are detrimental to those people and/or that fail to respect their autonomy and thus, in Kantian terminology, use them merely as means and not also as ends in themselves.[109]

But in our situation, the autonomous consent surely precludes the (instrumental) use of such persons as means only to the ends of others. As regards reducing such individuals' net welfare or acting in ways detrimental to them, Radcliffe-Richards claims, 'To forbid the trade is to take away what seems to be the best option open to someone whose position is already so appalling that this *is* his best option. It is to make the worst off worse off still.'[110] Harris also points out the danger of wrongly assuming that if we prevent the poor from being exploited this is the same as helping or caring for the poor.[111] An analogy has been made with a decision to bulldoze slums in which the poor are living because it is believed that persons should not have to suffer such living conditions, that is to harm them to prevent them being exploited![112] As Reddy observes, 'the main agent of exploitation is the poverty itself'.[113]

Zohar contends that, unlike coercion, exploitation is a 'relational evil', and that the evil lies in the *taking advantage* of another's (valid) consent

[109] R. Gillon, 'Commerce and Medical Ethics' (1997) 23 *Journal of Medical Ethics* 67 at 67. He consequently concludes that although *blood* donors might be exploited, there is no reason to believe that this must necessarily occur where there is proper regulation. Tomlinson asserts a congruous view to Gillon. He states: 'Inducements are exploitative only when they cause us to act in ways that are per se irrational or immoral; that is, when they reduce rather than increase our net welfare, or they degrade us as a person': T. Tomlinson, 'Inducements for Donation: Benign Incentives or Risky Business?' (1992) 24 *Transplantation Proceedings* 2204 at 2205.

[110] Radcliffe-Richards, 'From Him that Hath Not', at 190.

[111] J. Harris, *Wonderwoman and Superman: The Ethics of Biotechnology*, Oxford University Press, Oxford, 1992, at 131. Harris discusses Robert Goodin's contention that the duty not to exploit others emanates from our imperative to protect the vulnerable, but doubts whether a desperately ill organ purchaser could be properly dubbed an 'exploiter' nonetheless, being equally vulnerable: ibid., at 121–7.

[112] See Radcliffe-Richards, 'From Him that Hath Not', at 192.

[113] Reddy, 'To Buy or Let Die!', 137 at 139.

given under adverse circumstances so that the one taking advantage can get away with paying substantially less than he would have to with respect to someone with a greater range of options.[114] We are here witnessing a subtle shift towards the conduct of the 'exploiter' and away from the effect on the organ vendor. Thus, maybe instead it is not the fact of payment that exploits such (vulnerable) individuals, but the *size* of the payment, that is not 'wrongful use' but 'unfair exchange'.[115] What if they were all offered £1 million for each kidney donated? Would we say they were exploited then? Moreover, the question arises as to 'Whom is being exploited?' The Turkish peasant visiting London with the sick daughter requiring money to fund life-saving medical treatment? As Erin and Harris state, 'if prices are set too low the vendor could be said to be exploited; equally, if prices are set too high the purchaser could be said to be exploited'.[116] In the Indian context, Reddy has commented:

> In this country you get a poor man who goes down into the drains, in the sewage, wearing nothing but a simple loincloth. What he is doing is far more hazardous to himself than donating a kidney for money . . . Nobody ever says you're exploiting this poor man because he has to work and he's willing to do it. So I think we have to be very clear in our minds who it is who's being exploited. After all, the person who is buying the kidney is not doing it because he wants to have steak and kidney for lunch! He's doing it to save his life. And the poor guy who's giving it, whatever his reasons may be, is doing it for a beneficial purpose, for himself or for his family. What's wrong with that?[117]

Perhaps then it is only the involvement of profiteering middlemen (including possibly sometimes medical professionals and institutions) that is ethically objectionable. Thus, a system of regulation might be *more* appropriate, dictating fair and proper levels of payment, including the exclusion of avaricious brokers. The notion of exploitation relies upon an *a priori*, but ill-defined, notion of fairness or justice, which does not dictate a banning of the practices implicated here. Manga[118] contends that 'that the poor are relatively greater sellers of organs will be seen as "a

[114] N. Zohar, 'Toward Justice in the Organ Trade' (1993) 27 *Israel Law Review* 541 at 555.
[115] As Harris distinguishes the two distinct senses of the term.
[116] Erin and Harris, 'A Monopsonistic Market', at 139.
[117] Quoted in T. Stark, *A Knife to the Heart*, Macmillan, London, 1996, at 145.
[118] Citing from the Report of the Massachusetts Task Force on Organ Transplantation, 1985, at 17.

highly visible and symbolic exploitation, and one that has the potential to undermine society's belief in the integrity of the entire transplantation enterprise"'.[119] But whether symbolism can outweigh tangible benefits in this context is doubtful. If this perception were to impact upon levels of procurement though, this *would* be a relevant concern.

A preliminary audit at this juncture would conclude that there are no morally wrongful harms to vendors inherent in a system of trading in organs, on account of the feasibility of an autonomous consent being given to the sale, and that the libertarian viewpoint should prevail. Deontological considerations do not suggest the need for a ban, rather for regulation. But are there harms to others or alternative justifications for limiting liberty here? Bernat asserts that 'If deontological observations show us that profit oriented living donations are basically not as bad as we would intuitively assume, consequentialist observations lead us to a quite opposite conclusion.'[120] Childress similarly states that 'The various available arguments do not convince me that the act of selling an organ is intrinsically immoral. However, there may be extrinsic reasons for prohibiting, or at least not encouraging, as a matter of social practice what is not intrinsically immoral.'[121] Although financial incentives are not wrong *per se*, what of consequentialist concerns? For instance, Richard Titmuss identified three potential negative effects of a paid blood donation system, namely discouragement of altruistic conduct, reduced safety and the exploitation of the weakest socio-economic groups.[122]

Sacra

It is frequently said that organ selling results in a *commodification* of human body parts. The US Task Force summarily concluded that 'Society's moral values militate against regarding the body as a commodity.'[123] In one sense this is both a truism and a platitude. If an organ is sold it is an object of commerce and therefore a commodity. But why is

119 P. Manga, 'A Commercial Market for Organs? Why Not' (1987) 1(4) *Bioethics* 321 at 327.

120 Bernat, 'Marketing of Human Organs?', at 188.

121 Childress, 'The Body as Property', at 2144.

122 R. Titmuss, *The Gift Relationship: From Human Blood to Social Policy*, Allen & Unwin, London, 1971.

123 United States Task Force on Organ Transplantation, *Organ Transplantation: Issues and Recommendations*, Department of Health and Human Services, Washington D.C., 1984, at 1623.

this an argument against such sales? Freeman remarks that 'Ultimately, where the commodification objection fails is in identifying what the objection is.'[124] Kant argued though that a person should not cut off one of his own fingers, not even for 1,000 thalers, as if human beings may be bought and sold they have a market value, meaning they can be treated as mere objects, which would violate human dignity and worth.[125] Keown similarly argues that paid blood donation devalues the human body by depersonalising and commodifying it, promoting an instrumental view of human beings.[126] On the other hand, Radcliffe-Richards considers that allowing people the freedom to decide what to do with their bodies is quite the *opposite* of treating people as commodities and instrumentally as mere objects. Brecher also alleges that such sales commoditise human beings but argues that it is the purchaser rather than the seller who is always in the wrong in such transactions.[127] His objection is that it institutionalises a set of unacceptable *values*. Wilkinson and Garrard argue though that this objection is simply too broad and sweeping and does not wholly ring true anyhow – why should a dying organ buyer be viewed as being at fault?[128]

These arguments based on commoditisation implicitly appeal to the importance of community and social solidarity and of altruism in donation. This may be either because of their inherent value, or because of the impact that their loss would have on the willingness of society to continue to donate organs voluntarily. The latter issue is an empirical rather than an ethical matter and is considered further on.

Altruism: overrated?

It is often maintained that financial incentives reduce or even eliminate altruistic motives for donation. Sells, for instance, contends that 'The warm satisfaction that accompanies cadaveric donation must necessarily

124 Freeman, 'Biotechnology, Patients and Profits', at 129. Manga describes it as an 'emotionally charged assertion and not a reasoned argument': see 'A Commercial Market', at 325.

125 I. Kant, *Lectures on Ethics* (trans. L. Infield), Harper and Row, New York, 1963, at 124.

126 J. Keown, 'The Gift of Blood in Europe: An Ethical Defence of EC Directive 89/381' (1997) 23 *Journal of Medical Ethics* 96 at 99.

127 B. Brecher, 'The Kidney Trade: Or, the Customer is Always Wrong' (1990) 16 *Journal of Medical Ethics* 120 at 122.

128 S. Wilkinson and E. Garrard, 'Bodily Integrity and the Sale of Human Organs' (1996) 22 *Journal of Medical Ethics* 334 at 336.

be threatened and probably extinguished by sale.'[129] Gillon cautions though that 'There is a danger in being too ready to offer blanket condemnation of commerce in health care in lofty favour of altruism and social solidarity that health care may suffer.'[130] Thus, even conceding for a minute that all organ *donations* are altruistic and not influenced by self-interested motives, this still does not answer the question why only altruistic motivations are appropriate here. Wilkinson and Garrard observe that 'Organ donation is (often) supererogatory; so payment would seem to make it merely non-supererogatory, rather than impermissible.'[131] They nonetheless consider that where sale is involved there is nothing to outweigh the harm implicated by the necessary invasion of bodily integrity, but that where donation is involved the *pure altruism* of giving, together with the potentially beneficial consequences of donating, is sufficient to tip the scales in favour of allowing it. But this seems to leave them in the same bind as at the beginning. What is it about sale that is so detrimental that it ought not to be permitted where it achieves significant benefit to others? Radcliffe-Richards observes that it may be *best* if a kidney is offered out of love by a relative, but that does not in itself imply that what is less than best must be wrong,[132] and that it would seem bizarre to prefer that neither side should benefit rather than that both should. However, if changes in values and attitudes have a knock-on effect on levels of organ procurement and the clinical make-up of the donor pool this may be different.

Indirect altruism

Dossetor argues in favour of permitting a system of *rewarded gifting* based upon 'indirect altruism' where the 'good of the altruistic intent outweighs possible harm to society', in certain cultural and societal contexts.[133] He describes this as

> when I, person A, want to perform a particular act of altruism toward my family member, person B, but can only do so by obtaining money . . . from

[129] R. Sells, 'The Case Against Buying Organs and a Futures Market in Transplants' (1992) 24 *Transplantation Proceedings* 2198 at 2199.

[130] Gillon, 'Commerce and Medical Ethics', at 68.

[131] Wilkinson and Garrard, 'Bodily Integrity', at 338.

[132] See Radcliffe-Richards, 'From Him that Hath Not', at 194.

[133] J. Dossetor, 'Rewarded Gifting: Is it Ever Ethically Acceptable?' (1992) 24 *Transplantation Proceedings* 2092 at 2094.

> a third party, person C. My action toward C is commercial and contractual, not altruistic. But the money I get from my commercial contract with C enables me to act altruistically toward my family member B, which was my original intention.[134]

In the developing world he considers that the process of giving should be vetted by an institutional committee of socially committed persons and health care professionals to prevent selling purely for personal gain. However, whilst many would endorse this form of sacrifice for the benefit of others, by the term 'altruistic giving' we generally intend to refer to an attitude *accompanying the donation*. It is difficult to see how the use of the monies received could itself affect the essence of the arrangement itself where the use may not even be apparent except retrospectively. In any event, almost all sales would qualify for the tag, in so far as the motivation is invariably to improve one's family's standard of living. What this argument does tend to highlight though is the fact there is no bright line between (altruistic) donors and vendors. There seems to be no reason why altruistic and financial motivations should not co-exist here as elsewhere, as for instance in the case of the Turkish peasant. Indeed, some suggest that a market for organs may even *enhance* altruism by allowing one to 'give' without payment when *one could instead be paid*.

A kind (of) payment

The term 'rewarded gifting' is derived from the expression 'gifting with reward'[135] but has now generally been replaced by 'donation with incentives'. However, its precise ambit is somewhat vague. Its practice originated in India where, for instance in Madras, donors were offered a sum of money (£1,000) and additionally given free health insurance for three years for the giving of a kidney.[136] The concept ostensibly seeks to endorse the notion of the donation of an organ as a gift whilst at the same time being partially motivated by monetary factors, that is a form of 'indirect altruism'. However, confusion arises from the fact that some (albeit modest by Western standards) direct financial payment was made in these instances. Indeed, Colabawalla has gone so far as to

134 Ibid., at 2093.

135 It is credited to Dr C. Patel in 1987.

136 See A. Daar, 'Rewarded Gifting' (1992) 24 *Transplantation Proceedings* 2207.

describe the concept as a 'terminological subterfuge' meant to obfuscate the issue.[137]

It appears though that the concept is intended to describe a whole protocol where only a modest financial gain may be made,[138] which can be contrasted with so-called 'rampant commercialism', described in the following terms by Sells (in the Indian context):

> The hallmarks of this 'rampant commercialism' were that middlemen were involved taking a large proportion of the fee, surgeons were alleged to be making a lot of money out of the trade, and in those centres where such procedures were performed 'underground' there was no proper medical screening of the donor. Informed consent rules were being ignored, no independent review of the procedures was conducted: the postoperative care of the donor was substandard, and often resulted in serious morbidity.[139]

It seems then that the concept is designed to avoid the excesses and effects of a full-blown market system rather than commerce *per se*, including middlemen and even profit-making by clinicians. Bear in mind also that the proposal was tailored for a system lacking public dialysis facilities or a national cadaver transplant programme, and where end-stage organ failure typically invites death.

Further confusion stems from the alternative meaning given to the expression, that is rewards in kind as opposed to money. Examples mentioned by the Nuffield Council Working Party Report are the offer of lifetime medical treatment in exchange for kidney donation and of free IVF treatment in return for the donation of ova.[140] These might also include, in addition to free health insurance, payments towards funeral or medical expenses. However, although these are often viewed as less objectionable than direct cash payments, it is submitted that there is no intrinsic difference between money and payments in kind. The Nuffield Council Report recommended that 'rewarded gifting arrangements should be viewed as commercial transactions in that they offer inducements for permitting removal of human tissue'.[141] Moreover, inter-

[137] B. Colabawalla, 'Commerce and Trade in Human Organs' in C. Kjellstrand and J. Dossetor (eds.), *Ethical Problems in Dialysis and Transplantation*, Kluwer, Dordrecht, 1992, 555 at 557.

[138] Although of course £1,000 was a substantial sum in India at that time.

[139] R. Sells, 'Transplants' in R. Gillon (ed.), *Principles of Health Care Ethics*, John Wiley, Chichester, 1994, 1003 at 1014.

[140] Nuffield Council, *Human Tissue*, at para. 13.25.

[141] Ibid. It went on to recommend that 'removal of human tissue should be neither encouraged nor recompensed by rewarded gifting': ibid.

national policy statements, from, for example, WHO, generally appear broad enough to embrace both, as does most legislation. In Britain, HOTA extends to both money and 'money's worth', and the expressions 'valuable consideration' and 'gain' in federal and state legislation in the United States and elsewhere also seem expansive enough to encompass both.

Now the above critique is not intended to deny the ethical acceptability of any of these schemes in certain circumstances, merely to deny the non-commerce rationale often proffered for them. Commerce is still commerce even if there are selfless motives underlying its pursuit.

A lack of direction

The above discussion also begs the question of the materiality of the *directness* of incentives, an issue which arises most commonly in the context of discussion of incentives for potential cadaver sources. Prottas has argued that

> Indirection is called for, and most of the more sensible proponents of payment seek to separate in some way the incentive and the act to be 'incentivised'. One approach has been to seek less explicitly monetary incentives, such as offering to pay for funeral costs or to allow tax deductions. Other approaches have leaned on insurance models in which the government makes a promise to pay a death indemnity if organ donation occurs. There is, in fact, a general unwillingness to offer an explicit exchange of money for organs at the time that a family can actually dispose of the organs.[142]

I will argue below that one's attitude to less direct and more modest rewards should be conditioned by the supposed gravamen of any commercial exchange occurring at all, assuming one exists. However, there is no difference in nature between a reduction in a bill and giving a lump sum in order to pay the original bill, by virtue of its 'indirectness' alone.

Harms to recipients: iatrogenic disease

The ability to purchase organs, often outside one's country of origin, may encourage patients to undertake a transplantation at an earlier juncture

142 J. Prottas, 'Buying Human Organs – Evidence that Money Doesn't Change Everything' (1992) 53 *Transplantation* 1371 at 1372.

than would otherwise have occurred and, possibly, subject to greater risks. Roscam Abbing has stated that 'The not-for-profit principle is not only a moral notion. There are serious health risks involved when economic considerations enter the field . . . The not-for-profit idea also contributes towards protecting the health of the recipient. It is a daily reality that one tends to become lenient on safety requirements when trade is involved.'[143] Indeed, there have been various studies, the foremost example being that of Richard Titmuss, showing that trading in blood has lowered the quality of blood obtained and contributed to high rates of infection from diseases such as hepatitis. However, the AMA Report commented that

> In fact, although debate on this issue continues, it is not clear that paid donation damages blood supply. Early differences in the quality of blood derived from paid vs unpaid donors were due mainly to the populations being recruited as paid donors – often prisoners or inhabitants of socio-economically depressed areas – and the lack of adequate laboratory screening techniques for hepatitis and other diseases. In recent years, routine donor and laboratory screening tests have largely eradicated any quality differences between blood plasma from paid vs unpaid donors.[144]

Moreover, hepatitis rates have historically been higher in Japan, which has a voluntary blood donation system, than in Sweden, where a market system prevails, and in France higher health and safety standards have been noted in relation to paid rather than unpaid blood donation.[145] There are also differences between blood and organ procurement here. Barnett *et al.* observe that 'It is highly unlikely that paying for organs will lead to a greater supply of dead people with infectious diseases', for instance.[146] However, in nations where paid *living* organ donation is rife, the pool of vendors is constituted primarily by individuals with poor levels of nutrition and health, and exposure to a variety of infectious agents. Indeed, such concerns are borne out by studies of recipients

[143] H. Roscam Abbing, 'Organ Trading: Responsibilities of the EU Countries' in Y. Englert (ed.), *Organ and Tissue Transplantation in the European Union: Management of Difficulties and Health Risks Linked to Donors*, Martinus Nijhoff, Dordrecht, 1995, 99 at 99–100.

[144] AMA, 'Financial Incentives', at 585.

[145] See A. Fagot-Largeault, 'Does Non-Commercialisation of the Human Body Increase Graft Security?' in Englert, *Organ and Tissue Transplantation in the EU*, 9.

[146] Barnett, Blair and Kaserman, 'Improving Organ Donation', at 376. They noted as regards the living that even if the overall quality were to drop, if payment resulted in a much greater volume of organs, the 'trade-off' would still be worth it and the overall quality would be at least as good.

returning to their countries of origin having travelled abroad to obtain a transplant for payment.[147] There is evidence of a higher than tolerable transmission of hepatitis and HIV from donors on the Indian sub-continent for example, in addition to substantial surgical and medical complications. Daar from Oman reported encountering an 'unacceptable level of human immunodeficiency infections in transplants performed in this way in Bombay'.[148] Abouna *et al.* studied fifty-nine Kuwaitis who travelled to India and the Philippines for transplant. Six had died, thirteen had lost their grafts through complications, and fourteen had sustained serious surgical complications and various other infections.[149] Similar perceptions are shared by Al Khader *et al.* from Saudi Arabia.[150]

Certainly the standards and conditions of medical care which many organ vendors and their recipients experience in such countries are a good deal less than optimal. But this is partly a function of the health care systems in those countries as a whole, and not just of when organs are bought and sold. A properly regulated commercial system, with proper screening and selection of donors, need not necessarily be associated with poor clinical conditions in every instance. Moreover, the AMA Report noted that there are today various standard tests, which are relatively quick and inexpensive, applied to all organ sources to screen for infections and communicable diseases. Cameron and Hoffenberg state that

> The fact that paid organ donation usually takes place under unsatisfactory medical circumstances has no bearing on the argument. If one accepts the practice, then well-organised programs in which the donor is properly apprised of risk, fully assessed and followed up, with results available for

147 German doctors have complained about the post-operative condition of patients returning to Germany following renal transplantation in India: see H. Karcher, 'German Doctors Protest Against "Organ Tourism"' (1996) 313 *British Medical Journal* 1282.

148 A. Daar, 'Nonrelated Donors and Commercialism: A Historical Perspective' (1992) 24 *Transplantation Proceedings* 2087 at 2087. Similar experiences with patients from Oman and Dubai are reported in P. Morris, *Kidney Transplantation*, 3rd edn, W. B. Saunders, Philadelphia, 1988, at 72.

149 G. Abouna *et al.*, 'Commercialisation in Human Organs: A Middle Eastern Perspective' (1990) 22 *Transplantation Proceedings* 918. See also K. Johny *et al.*, 'Values Gained and Values Lost in Live Unrelated Renal Transplantation' (1990) 22 *Transplantation Proceedings* 915.

150 Al Khader *et al.* found that 95 per cent of patients returning to Saudi Arabia from Bombay required in-patient admission to counter infection, to treat rejection or to adjust immunosuppression: see Al Khader *et al.*, XI International Congress of the Transplantation Society, Helsinki, August 1986, Abstract No. S11.4.

public audit, can and have been organised, for example, in India. It is the marginalisation of paid organ donation that leads to its performance in less than ideal circumstances.[151]

Harms to society

Slippery slopes and camels' noses

Abouna states: 'Another possible negative impact on society is potential criminal consequences which the sale of organs for profit is likely to bring, just as drug trafficking has brought with it.'[152] There have been numerous reports of criminal acts, for example child kidnapping and non-consensual removal of organs, around the world, allegedly associated with commercialism in transplantation. In the eighties such reports appeared in the press in South America, emanating initially from Honduras in 1987 (and spreading in the same year to Guatemala, Cuba and the Dominican Republic), and were repeated in the Soviet press.[153] A particularly widespread allegation related to the practices alleged to have occurred at the state-run mental institution in Lujan in Argentina, involving the murder of patients and the sale of their organs and blood.[154] In 1995, French television broadcast a programme showing the non-consensual removal of kidneys from Indians suffering from leprosy which were sold on a worldwide basis.[155] It was also reported only in 1999 that in Egypt twenty-

151 J. Cameron and R. Hoffenberg, 'The Ethics of Organ Transplantation Reconsidered: Paid Organ Donation and the Use of Executed Prisoners as Donors' (1999) 55 *Kidney International* 724 at 727.

152 G. Abouna, 'Negative Impact of Trading in Human Organs on the Development of Transplantation in the Middle East' (1993) 25 *Transplantation Proceedings* 2310 at 2312. This danger is also explicitly referred to in the Preamble to the WHO Guiding Principles on Organ Transplantation.

153 In 1994, June Weinstock, an environmental writer from Alaska, was brutally attacked and left severely disabled in Guatemala after reports of children being snatched for transplantation purposes had been circulating there.

154 'Argentina Uncovers Patients Killed for Organs' (1992) 304 *British Medical Journal* 1073. Some patients who had allegedly escaped from the institution were said to have been found with eyes missing.

155 J. Dausset and F. Rapaport, 'Criminal Hazards of Human Organ Traffic' (1996) 28 *Transplantation Proceedings* 42. There have also been reports on French television that corneas obtained on the black market have been brought into France, causing donation rates to fall in both France and Colombia.

five children at an institution had been sold to private hospitals and killed for their body parts.[156] Such stories spread like wildfire.

An urban legend?

It must be noted, however, that these are invariably unconfirmed reports, whose authenticity remains a matter of great doubt. On 23 July 1987, the European Parliament announced that it was aware of no transplant network operating in Europe using kidneys provided by Latin American infants. The Special Rapporteur of the United Nations Report on the Sale of Children, Child Prostitution and Child Pornography in 1993 contained the results of a questionnaire survey of all national governments and selected non-governmental organisations in 1991 and reported that not one response declared an awareness of any sale of a child's organs having occurred in their jurisdiction.[157] Kreis states: 'In fact, since 1987, when this story appeared for the first time, no tangible proof has been established, no arrests have been made related to crimes of the type propagated by this rumour, and that in spite of the apparent extent of this criminal activity.'[158] He has highlighted the organisation and the extent of the infrastructure and personnel web necessary to support such a trade, and is extremely sceptical about such criminal activities as a consequence. Recent research by Véronique Campion-Vincent, a French social scientist specialising in the study of urban myths, concluded that media reports of children being murdered to supply organs for transplants were merely rumour. After a lengthy study she concluded that there was no evidence that children in the developing world were being dismembered for the benefit of recipients in the West.[159] Nevertheless, these stories not only play on people's fears but

[156] See 'Organs of Orphans "Sold to Wealthy" ', *The Times*, 18 March 1999 and 'Egypt Denies Child Organs for Sale', *The Times*, 19 March 1999. On 12 July 1998, the BBC's Ceefax service carried a report on page 143 that doctors had removed organs from children abandoned during the unrest in Albania in 1997, and had passed them to Mafia gangs for export.

[157] 'Rights of the Child: Sale of Children', January 1993, at para. 111.

[158] H. Kreis, 'Worldwide Organ Trafficking: Fact or Fiction?' in Englert, *Organ and Tissue Transplantation in the EU*, 67 at 71. He is scathing about the role of the media here, attributing deaths from want of donated organs to unconfirmed rumours spread by such means.

[159] See discussion in A. Dorozynski, 'Organ Thieving is Urban Myth' (1996) 312 *British Medical Journal* 1442.

are also plausible. As one Cairo doctor is reported to have said, 'In a society where children's arms and legs are broken by their own parents to make them better street beggars, such stories cannot be quickly dismissed.'[160] Regrettably, therefore, true or not, such stories have a deleterious effect on ordinary transplantation procurement efforts and the image of legitimate transplantation generally.

However, these practices are not inevitably intertwined with commerce in organ procurement *per se*, and should be kept conceptually distinct in the absence of cogent evidence of their potential interconnectedness in any specific environment. A conflation with much more nefarious practices is sometimes simply, and wrongly, assumed. Moreover, to ban commerce in organ procurement may not be the panacea for such activities even if they do exist. Prohibition often drives practices underground rather than eradicating them. Kidnapping of children and forcible organ removal are of course already illegal in every jurisdiction. This may suggest a need for greater *regulation* of organ trading rather than simple prohibition.

The easy option?

Some commentators contend that commercialisation of living organ procurement creates disincentives to governments to establish national cadaver transplant programmes and will thus retard their implementation. Abouna alleges that this has actually occurred in Kuwait 'when it was much easier to write a cheque for their citizens to go and buy a kidney abroad'.[161] This objection should not be underestimated. Ultimately, the growth of proper cadaveric programmes is the backbone of adequate domestic transplantation endeavours. However, there may be a period when the latter is an unrealistic option from a financial perspective, and consequently funding 'one-offs' even over the normal rate is inevitably viewed as a cost-efficient short-term strategy.

[160] 'Egypt Denies Child Organs for Sale', *The Times*, 19 March 1999.

[161] G. Abouna, 'The Negative Impact of Paid Organ Donation' in Land and Dossetor, *Organ Replacement Therapy*, 164 at 168. See also E. Kazim *et al.*, 'Buying a Kidney: The Easy Way Out?' (1992) 24 *Transplantation Proceedings* at 2113.

Weighing the options

A pound of flesh?

Accepting the premiss that incentives will generate an increased volume of organs for transplantation, an attempt is made here to evaluate the ethical acceptability of different forms of commercial incentives.

Most contemporary laws and policy directives permit the recovery of expenses and other (pecuniary) losses sustained through donation. These are references to *actual* losses and are seemingly intended to remove *disincentives* to donation, by contrast with making a profit or gain, which is perceived to be a positive *incentive* to donation. Whether the former should even be viewed as a form of commerce at all is itself debatable. Manga states:

> Whether an essentially cost-reimbursement approach to paying donors should still be referred to as 'commercialisation' is an interesting question. Since there is no monetary gain – dare one say, profit – to the donor or his/her family, it could reasonably be argued that it is unnecessary and inappropriate to label such reimbursements as commercialisation. Opponents may counter-argue that even a cost-reimbursement scheme is objectionable if it induces persons to donate organs who otherwise would not have done so. To such purists any (financial) inducement sullies what should be truly a charitable act. This is an argument over definition and involves people's subjective judgements and perceptions of what is or is not an act of charity or giving.[162]

It would seem unlikely though that merely restoring the individual to the economic situation they would have been in anyhow had they not donated could be any real 'incentive'. The individual concerned would have already formed an 'initial predisposition' to donate, which would have been acted upon if there was no financial impediment to so doing, an impediment that has simply been removed.

Of course most living donors would not be dissuaded anyhow, but would almost always be relatives of the patient, either genetically or emotionally, and would tend to view economic losses as merely an incidental part of a larger sacrifice relating to the benefits expected to result from the eventual transplantation. Nevertheless, there should be an

[162] Manga, 'A Commercial Market', at 325.

enforceable legal right to such reimbursement of expenses.[163] We should not expect a physical *and* financial sacrifice here. In so far as living organ donation for transplantation purposes is an act furthering the public/health interests of the state, and produces financial savings able to be used for other health imperatives, it seems entirely reasonable that a person should be compensated for losses actually incurred with respect to such donation, from central funds.[164]

Thus, recovery of actual losses, rather than being conceived of as objectionable, should be a moral and legal imperative. Of course, if organ donation was an *evil* in itself, then it might even be proper to propagate financial disincentives to donation but, far from it, it is universally viewed as a good.

Schmerzensgeld

Some commentators, however, appear to view such reimbursement as a form of *incentive* to donation *per se*. It is even sometimes discussed in the same breath as straightforward profit-making. Indeed, the Law Reform Commission of Canada Working Party Report stated that

> It is not clear, for example, how a meaningful line can be drawn between direct payments and indirect incentives. There might appear to be a principled difference between offering cash as an incentive to donate and reimbursing out-of-pocket expenses. But in practice the difference may vanish. Direct payment may be thought objectionable because it constitutes an undue incentive. Reimbursement of expenses, in contrast, may be thought unobjectionable because it functions to remove disincentives rather than to create incentives. Yet, social reality indicates that what counts as an incentive depends as much upon the situation of the potential recipient as it does upon the amount and spirit of the offering. The sum of

[163] See A. Garwood-Gowers, 'To Pay or not to Pay; That is the Question – The Economic Rights of the Living Donor' in D. Price and J. Akveld (eds.), *Living Organ Donation in the Nineties: European Medico-Legal Perspectives*, EUROTOLD, 1996, 179. As argued in an earlier chapter, donors should be automatically informed of such reimbursement entitlements. Indeed, the new Dutch law requires this.

[164] The EUROTOLD research revealed that in Europe only 37 per cent of centres reported any financial help being available to donors from either governmental or centre sources: (P. Donnelly and D. Price (eds.)) *Questioning Attitudes to Living Donor Transplantation*, EUROTOLD, 1997, at 102. Smith *et al.* in the US and Westlie in Norway found that 23.2 per cent and 16.2 per cent of donors respectively reported experiencing some degree of financial hardship from donation.

> $250 for participating in a drug research protocol does not have the same economic value for a salaried professional as for a poor student. To the former it does not approach adequate compensation; to the latter it might tend towards undue incentive. Some analysts thus regard such distinctions as illusory or fictitious.[165]

It would seem though that the Working Party was alluding to a notion rather different from recovery of *actual pecuniary losses* here, and was considering compensation for time, inconvenience and maybe pain and suffering. Lack of recompense for the latter may also be viewed as a *disincentive* to donate, at least for a living unrelated donor,[166] but different issues are implicated.

It is true that research volunteers in the West are generally paid for their participation over and above their actual pecuniary losses,[167] as are sperm (and often egg) donors.[168] Moreover, although commercial surrogacy arrangements are unlawful in Britain, up to now surrogates have nevertheless been paid a sum of as much as £10,000–15,000, dubbed as 'expenses', clearly exceeding their actual expenditures.[169] It might therefore seem reasonable in the light of such practices to provide living organ donors with some form of payment for effort and inconvenience, and it is in fact reported that such payment (*Schmerzensgeld*) is currently being made to renal donors in Munich. Indeed, the Nuffield Working Party Report, whilst viewing rewards in kind as a form of commercial transaction, recommended allowing donors to be recompensed for their 'reasonable expenses *and inconvenience incurred*

[165] Law Reform Commission of Canada, *Procurement and Transfer*, at 60. Tomlinson, in like vein, states: 'A $1,000 benefit would mean a lot more to a mother on welfare than it would to Donald Trump. Thus, monetary incentives will tend to induce disproportionately more donations from the poor': see Tomlinson, 'Benign Incentives', at 2205.

[166] Even unpaid blood donors typically get a cup of tea and a biscuit!

[167] It has been necessary to do so because the voluntary unpaid approach to non-therapeutic medical research has failed to produce enough volunteer research subjects: see D. Evans, 'Procuring Gametes for Research and Therapy' (1995) 21 *Journal of Medical Ethics* 261.

[168] Section 12(e) of the Human Fertilisation and Embryology Act 1990 states that money or benefits should not be given to the suppliers of gametes unless authorised by the Authority. This was seemingly intended to be the exception rather than the rule in gamete procurement: see D. Dickenson, 'Procuring Gametes for Research and Therapy: The Argument for Unisex Altruism – A Response to Donald Evans' (1997) 23 *Journal of Medical Ethics* 93 at 93.

[169] This has been criticised in a Government review of surrogacy arrangements in Britain, the Brazier review: *Surrogacy: Review for Health Ministers of Current Arrangements for Payments and Regulation*, Cmnd 4068, Department of Health, 1998.

[but this] should not act as an inducement' (my emphasis).[170] This statement implies that modest payments for 'inconvenience' are permissible whilst other payments are not, and takes the view that payments for inconvenience will not act as an 'inducement' to donate.[171]

Carrot or stick?

Any types of compensation and subsidy apart from the recouping of actual financial losses are, however, problematic. Nonetheless, whether such payments *should be permitted* depends upon perceptions as to where the evils of commercialisation lie. If the degradation from the perceived *commodification* of the human body through organ trading is the principal evil to be avoided, then the debate seems to revolve around whether payments are to be perceived as *for* body parts or simply for services connected therewith. Modest payments might be perceived merely to reflect the effort and labour involved, in the same way that charges for transplants themselves will typically be acceptable, assuming that they are not so inflated that they appear to include an additional sum *for the organ itself*.[172] An analogous debate surrounds whether surrogacy arrangements involve payment for the woman's services or for the baby. A dichotomy could be made between services and goods, with altruism being viewed as wholly attaching to the organ itself. However, many view this as 'convenient' and disingenuous. It is 'paid work' even if the reimbursement is extremely modest. Admittedly, money might have been earned instead in other labours during the same period, but the operative term here is 'might', that is they are not 'actual losses'. In fact to call such amounts 'expenses' at all is euphemistic – they are payments, albeit modest ones, and it is likely that laws prohibiting 'sale' or financial gain' will be interpreted in this vein.

If, on the other hand, the objection is to the harmful *incentive effects*, then the debate is somewhat different. Whilst there is a desire in many quarters to avoid any form of 'incentives' to donation, this is what such

[170] Nuffield Council, *Human Tissue*, at para. 13.24.

[171] In fact the HOTA Regulations as they apply to genetically unrelated donors require ULTRA to be satisfied that there has been no 'inducement' to donate: see HOTA (Unrelated Persons) Regulations 1989 (SI 1989 No. 2480).

[172] For this reason, the WHO's Guiding Principle 8 states that 'It should be prohibited for any person or facility involved in organ transplantation procedures to receive any payment that exceeds a justifiable fee for the services rendered.'

commercial arrangements are typically striving for and designed to do. However, one cannot generalise about the incentive effects of certain fixed financial sums or rewards, as this depends upon the situation of the potential offeree.[173] If payment is viewed as being deleterious in either deontological or consequentialist terms then, if regulation cannot prevent these ill effects, there is a reason for banning the practice. The General Medical Council in Great Britain stated that 'Where human organs are bought and sold, transplantation will be governed by money rather than by the medical interests of the donors and recipients, with the vulnerable and the poor inevitably exposed to exploitation.'[174] Practices around the world to date appear to bear the Council out. Standards of safety and quality have routinely been compromised in some areas for the sake of profit, whether personal or institutional. However, there seems no doubting that the lesser nature of any financial incentives *mitigates* the potential harmful 'fallout' of such (commercial) arrangements. Reddy's clinic in Madras seems to have superior results and less harmful side-effects than more extreme commercial arrangements in other parts of India for instance. Daar has stated that

> in rampant commercialism the enterprise is predicated on profit for the doctors, the hospital, and the middlemen. The patient is a mere tool for profit-making. As a result, objective medical criteria are less important, standards are likely to fall, and complications, such as human immmuno-deficiency virus (HIV) infection, are likely to be acquired. This was shown to be true between 1984 and 1988 in Bombay. With rewarded gifting, on the other hand, the patient's interests are paramount.[175]

Obviously if large sums are offered the supply of 'vendors' might be very large indeed but such potentially large gains also attract the biggest potential dangers. Where large gains are in prospect 'fat cat' middlemen become involved so that vendors are even more likely to be exploited through receiving an insufficiently large share of the spoils for their sacrifice. Profiteering by medical professionals is a further issue, and the WHO Guiding Principles attempt *inter alia* to restrict entrepreneurial

[173] The (Brazier) surrogacy review in Britain came to the unavoidable conclusion that the more lucrative the practice the more women will be induced to offer themselves as surrogates: see 'Surrogate Mothers should be paid Expenses Only' (1998) 317 *British Medical Journal* 1104.

[174] GMC, 'Transplantation of Organs from Live Donors' (Guidance for Doctors), November 1992 (1993) 44(2) *International Digest of Health Legislation* 370.

[175] A. Daar, 'Rewarded Gifting' (1992) 24 *Transplantation Proceedings* 2207 at 2209.

practice in organ recovery and implantation. Moreover, it has been remarked that 'Allowing health care professionals to profit from organ procurement would exacerbate the popular mistrust of physicians, currently one of the principal obstacles to organ donation.'[176] If additional gains to medical professionals are removed however, then the effects of profits to donors on medical and clinical factors impinging on the organ removal and transplant process are less clear. If improper screening, selection and matching occur in some regions, then maybe these should be addressed directly instead.

We are, however, in the grips of a paradox. If the rewards are small, they will only be worth it to the very poor, and then the rewards would be so small that some would say that they are being exploited! Moreover, as Prottas observes, an indirect incentive 'weakens the probable efficacy of the incentive represented by payment. The more indirect and obscure the connection between reward and behavior, the less effective a motivator rewards are.'[177]

Tensions created by a commercial system

The Nuffield Council Working Party Report in the UK asserted: 'Our conclusion is that there are strong reasons against organising the procurement of human tissue along commercial lines.'[178] Society should not endorse such a scheme involving living donors where other options remain which are preferable in ethical terms. However, some societies around the world have few other viable options to pursue in the short term, and Reddy is right to assert that there is an *immediate* moral imperative to help the suffering. Maybe some modest reimbursement scheme is justifiable there? One can distinguish here between the effects of markets for organs from living sources and those from cadaveric sources. As regards organs taken from living donors, payment would tend to occur in a different sphere from *donation* and the degree of interaction would probably be limited. Unlike blood and certain tissues, organs are not generally donated into a 'pool' and allocated to strangers. Donation is

[176] 'Medical Technology and the Law', at 1629.

[177] Prottas, 'Evidence that Money', at 1372.

[178] Nuffield Council, *Human Tissue*, at para. 13.24. It recommended that bodies such as NHS trusts and independent hospitals should operate on a non-commercial basis when removing donated human tissue.

motivated by the relationship between the parties which would not be significantly influenced by the prospect of payment. Instead, a market of paid unrelated strangers, 'vendors', would emerge. By contrast, with regard to cadaveric donors, some overlap would occur with respect to the same pool of potential 'suppliers' of organs, and the effects are less predictable.

The Bellagio Task Force felt that the abuses of commercial arrangements associated with organ sales from living donors justified a ban relating thereto. It concluded that

> existing social and political inequities are such that commercialisation would put powerless and deprived people at still graver risk. The physical well-being of disadvantaged populations, especially in developing countries, is already placed in jeopardy by a variety of causes, including the hazards of inadequate nutrition, substandard housing, unclean water, and parasitic infection. In these circumstances, adding organ sale to this roster would be to subject an already vulnerable group to yet another threat to its physical health and bodily integrity. Because persons selling their organs would be drawn exclusively from the economically deprived, regulation cannot prevent fundamental abuses. Transparency and fairness cannot be assured.[179]

It based its objection primarily on the abuses which currently occur in connection with commercial practices around the globe and the likely ineffectiveness of regulatory safeguards. The Task Force, however, went on to recommend that pilot programmes to reward families of cadaveric donors should proceed. It stated: 'payments for cadaveric organs do not promote the same abuses; although the poor would still feel greater pressure to seek these benefits, families from all social classes might be prepared to accept them'.[180] Daar, Gutmann and Land have also noted that it is easier to regulate a cadaveric than a living donor system.[181] Indeed, it would be easier to regulate such practices in developed nations generally. A system of regulation should be able to prevent the harmful effects to society and to recipients, and also should ensure that vendors were adequately informed and able to give an entirely voluntary consent.

[179] Rothman *et al.*, 'The Bellagio Task Force Report', at 2741.
[180] Ibid., at 2742.
[181] Daar, Gutmann and Land, 'Reimbursement, "Rewarded Gifting"', at 304.

Compatibility

In this section we are primarily exploring the impact of a commercial system on *cadaveric* organ practices. One supposedly advantageous effect of a system of 'futures' is that decision-making is placed squarely in the hands of the decedent. Indeed, where a positive wish to 'sell' has been expressed by the deceased in a 'strong' (express or presumed) consent regime, where only the views of the decedent 'count', this is an entirely congruous development. It would be clear, for instance, in Austria that relatives had no right to receive compensation for transplanted organs. However, this would not be the effect elsewhere. As Bernat states, 'If a legal system has adopted a modified opting in system, the question whether relatives can sell the organs of the deceased cannot be answered as clearly.'[182] The AMA Report considered that such futures contracts would remove the need to intrude into relatives' grief – the need for family permission would no longer arise, and if only a modest payment were made to a person's family or estate after death, 'voluntariness of decisions to donate would not be threatened'.[183] It emphasised the degree of thwarting of deceaseds' wishes which currently pervades the US system because of the reliance upon relatives' permission[184] and additionally alluded to the substantial survey evidence that families will adhere to a deceased's wishes if known.

Problems arise in countries where the practice is to allow relatives to decide the fate of the deceased's organs, whatever the terms of the relevant statutory provisions. Although, if donor cards were binding legal contracts, there would be a great deal less compunction about approaching relatives for permission to donate,[185] Sells envisages problems and tensions in jurisdictions such as the UK. He contends:

> My first criticism of a future delivery market is that a contract between the dead person and the insurance company in life, which legally requires donation after death, takes no account of the injurious effects on families caused by removal of that protective veto. It is unlikely that the emotional objections of a close relative would be reduced by the knowledge that the dead loved one had received money for his organs during life, since in my

[182] Bernat, 'Marketing of Human Organs?', at 183.
[183] AMA, 'Financial Incentives', at 586.
[184] A remark equally apposite vis-à-vis the UK.
[185] See 'Medical Technology and the Law', at 1627.

> experience most objections (in the United Kingdom) originate from distaste for interference with the body after death, and not monetary consideration.[186]

Moreover, under such a commercial futures system, those individuals who had not entered into such a contract whilst alive would presumably have to be assumed *not* to have wanted to donate their organs, yet relatives would have no power to donate them. This might well reduce the number of organs available for transplant.

Spot markets

George Smith has questioned why, since reasonable payments are permissible to those involved in harvesting the organs for transplantation (for example surgeons, hospital staff, etc.), reasonable payments to the family of the donor are not allowed.[187] Sells, on the other hand, argues that it is difficult to defend this sort of scheme whereby we would encourage the incursion of greed into people suffering from grief.[188] It might also create conflicts with regard to decisions as to whether to terminate life-sustaining treatment measures. The AMA Report rejected the idea of relatives having the right to sell the deceased's organs, on the basis that this seems implicitly to recognise proprietary rights of the family over the deceased. Prottas states that 'If families of potential organ donors refuse to consider the bodies of their relatives as saleable commodities, then the economics of supply and demand are irrelevant.'[189] He points to the fact that surveys show 78 per cent of the American public to be against the notion of families being paid to donate relatives' organs. He states: 'It takes little imagination to anticipate the reaction of a mother offered money to allow the removal of her dead daughter's heart.'[190]

186 R. Sells, 'The Case Against Buying Organs and a Futures Market in Transplants' (1992) 24 *Transplantation Proceedings* 2198 at 2200. He also notes that there is no evidence that relatives are less likely to object if a deceased relative entered into a futures contract whilst alive.

187 Smith, 'Market and Non-Market Mechanisms', at 25.

188 Sells, 'The Case Against Buying Organs', at 2199.

189 Prottas, 'Evidence that Money', at 1371.

190 Ibid., at 1372.

Flushed with success?

Cohen focuses upon the current lack of incentives to donate and comments that prospective donors are 'currently unwilling to donate because they are being asked to assume those costs without being offered a sufficient compensating benefit'. He says that he might not want to clean public toilets, but that he would do so if the financial inducement were sufficient.[191] Some question whether a scheme such as that proposed by Cohen would create sufficient incentive though, in so far as only the deceased's survivors, rather than the deceased himself, could benefit from the agreement. It has been suggested though that whilst limited financial benefits after death 'would not induce those strongly opposed to organ donation, [they] might persuade many who are undecided'.[192] Indeed, many argue that most individuals do not object to organ donation after death, they merely do not register their wishes at present, and they need very little in terms of persuasion to get them to agree to give and are also not vulnerable to harm in the same way that living donors may be. Indeed, Cohen considers such a system will be effective in inducing organ donation and will 'allow economic incentives to work as a blast of water through a clogged pipe, flushing out any reluctance to participate in the transplantation process'.[193] The view is also held that being dead at the point of organ removal, individuals have very little reason to refuse to donate as they are not susceptible to harm at that time.

Fox summarises such views as follows:

> In this economically deterministic framework of thought, rooted in a *homo economicus* conception of the human person, the 'bottom-line' problem with a gifting system is defined as a lack of material rewards to provide incentives for organ donation. The receipt of sufficiently beneficial financial compensation, it is contended, will overcome whatever psychological, social, cultural, ethical, religious, or aesthetic deterrents to donating or procuring organs currently exist.[194]

191 Cohen, 'A Futures Market in Cadaveric Organs', at 61.

192 'Medical Technology and the Law', at 1628.

193 Cohen, 'The Ethical Virtues of a Futures Market', at 309. Crespi, in similar vein, states: 'I expect that most potential organ bearers will regard the prospect of sufficiently substantial contingent payments being made to their estates to be an adequate incentive to enter into organ futures contracts': 'Overcoming the Legal Obstacles', at 37.

194 R. Fox, 'Regulated Commercialism of Vital Organ Donation: A Necessity? Con' (1993) 25 *Transplantation Proceedings* 55 at 56.

However, he is sceptical, stating that not only might such incentives not be sufficient to increase the number of transplantable organs that are donated, but they might even prove counterproductive. He argues that to apply simple economic theory in this context 'trivialises some of the deeper, more covert reasons why people feel reluctance about donating their organs'.[195] Thomas Murray also counsels against excessive reliance upon economic models here, saying that 'It presumes that the only measure of human flourishing is the maximisation of wealth measurable by the economist's own instruments. And it presumes that the only source of value is money.'[196] He says that the narrowly economic view of people is 'deformed, shrunken, and defective' and fails to appreciate why people value relationships and upon what they are based. He adds: 'Perhaps the simplest way to put it is to say that markets are principally about goods and money; gifts are about human relationships.'[197] Indeed, research by Prottas showed that hostility to payment amongst the public was strongest amongst the 80 per cent of the population presently most willing to donate, which lends some credence to the above assertions. He suggests that, 'based on the best data available about attitudes, it is far more likely that many of those who presently give when asked would refuse to sell'[198] and observes that the worries that people have about either being declared dead prematurely or being given inadequate or insufficient medical care prior to death leading to an avoidable death or delayed time of death may be exacerbated under a commercial system, resulting in an increased 'declining' rate.

The perceived likelihood of commercialism *reducing supply* was one of the primary reasons why Titmuss rejected commercial influences in blood procurement policies in favour of a wholly voluntary system. Keown, continuing this line of argument, states that 'It seems reasonable to conclude that a significant number of donors who presently donate for altruistic reasons and reasons of social solidarity would cease to donate if payment were introduced.'[199] Indeed, in the United States, when the sale of blood was permitted, albeit at very low prices, the overall blood supply

195 Ibid.

196 T. Murray, 'Organ Vendors, Families, and the Gift of Life' in S. Youngner, R. Fox and L. O'Connell (eds.), *Organ Transplantation: Meanings and Realities*, University of Wisconsin Press, Madison, 1996, 101 at 114.

197 Ibid., at 120.

198 Prottas, 'Evidence that Money', at 1372.

199 Keown, 'The Gift of Blood', at 97.

dropped sharply because of the decrease in voluntary donations which, for whatever reason it occurred, was larger than the increase occasioned by paid donation.[200] Some contend that the introduction of market relations may reduce people's capacity for altruistic conduct in the long term. Advocates of commercialisation, on the other hand, argue that there is nothing to prevent unpaid altruistic donation despite the alternative of sale, and that giving rather than selling where the latter alternative exists may be viewed as an even *more* praiseworthy act. Cohen states that 'Charitable donation of organs not only remains possible, it becomes a more noble act when sale is permitted.'[201] But Guttmann argues that

> Such payment revalues the act and primarily treats consent and secondarily the organs to be transplanted in the future as commodities, parts to be traded. My belief is that ordinary people view themselves as whole persons; one's exterior phenotype including one's behavior as well as one's private mind, not as an aggregation of organs and tissues to be bartered in a meat market.[202]

He alludes to the revised *value* that organ donation possesses under such a revised system and suggests that this may produce a negative impact overall. In the debates in the British Parliament preceding the passing of the Human Organ Transplants Bill 1989, the Minister introducing the Bill expressed concerns that commercialisation would 'have a catastrophic effect upon our voluntary system of donation, whether the donor came from the United Kingdom or abroad'.[203] However, in some jurisdictions where there are shortages of certain human tissues, payments have been made to ensure an adequate supply.[204] One cannot be certain if or when such an expedient might be forced upon a particular society. Indeed, Cameron and Hoffenberg stridently assert that 'the blunt fact is that altruism alone has failed to supply enough organs to meet the demand'.[205]

200 Crespi, 'Overcoming the Legal Obstacles', at 20 n. 100.

201 L. Cohen, 'A Market Proposal for Increasing the Supply of Cadaveric Organs' (1991) 5 *Clinical Transplantation* 467 at 470.

202 R. Guttmann, 'Regulated Commercialism in Transplantation: The Factitious Focus' (1993) 25 *Transplantation Proceedings* 58 at 58.

203 Mr Roger Freeman, Second Reading Committee on the Human Organ Transplants Bill, Parliamentary Debates: Official Report, House of Commons, 16 May 1989, at 9, col. 1.

204 Payments to gamete donors in the UK and to blood donors in India are two examples of expedients to ensure an adequate supply. Caplan notes that many European nations which prohibit payment to plasma donors have been forced to import plasma from countries such as the United States where donors are paid, because of their own shortages.

205 'The Ethics of Organ Transplantation Reconsidered', at 726.

All in all, one can be by no means sure of the potential impact on procurement rates of a commercialised system, even for cadaveric organs. However, where commercial incentives were available, the costs of transplantation overall would certainly expand materially. Moreover, there is much in Sells's view that the primary difficulties surrounding futures markets seem to be practical rather than philosophical. The fixing of the price of an organ is an immediate problem. The AMA Report prefers 'modest' payments at the time the organs are retrieved. It recommends that 'In instituting a system of future contracts, it would be best to start with the lowest incentive that can reasonably be expected to encourage donation', that is modest enough not to create undue pressure or coercion to sell.[206] This is broadly in line with Cohen's proposal. Cohen estimated that a probable cost of $5,000 per organ would be a sufficient incentive, but some have argued that this is wildly optimistic. Even such modest payments as this under a futures market would require changes to the law almost everywhere, including under the Human Organ Transplants Act in Britain. Crespi states that arguments that the 'facially restrictive language of NOTA can reasonably be reinterpreted to allow at least a futures market – if not a cash market – in bodily organs to operate are unconvincing'.[207] Indeed, the Pennsylvania scheme is unconvincing in terms of an evasion of NOTA, if this applies to *intra-state* commerce. As Crespi states, 'The term "valuable consideration", however, is one of the broadest in all the law, and is universally understood to cover non-cash compensation, deferred compensation, and payment of compensation as directed to third parties.'[208] Indeed, he alleges that as it currently stands, NOTA constitutes facilitation of an unconstitutional taking of property without compensation.[209] Moreover, the ramifications of an organ possessing an intrinsic value in financial terms need to be thought through, especially as they all implicate substantial transaction costs. Sir Roy Calne foresees previous organ donations between spouses forming part of a financial divorce settlement for instance, and the Bellagio Task Force invited us to imagine a revamped social welfare system in which organs were assets that could be sold before a person was eligible for public relief. These concerns are potent, counselling against societies of any hue hurrying into such a reform, even as a pilot scheme.

206 AMA, 'Financial Incentives', at 587.

207 Crespi, 'Overcoming the Legal Obstacles', at 17.

208 Ibid., at 57.

209 Ibid., at 65.

10

Recipients

Transplantation has been the arena for many innovative and pioneering therapies,[1] ranging from the first human-to-human and animal-to-human (Baby Fae) heart transplants and five-year-old Laura Davies's[2] seven-organ entire digestive system transplant to the first temporary (the 'bridging' heart inserted into Haskell Carp[3]) and 'permanent' (inserted into Barney Clark) artificial heart transplants. These procedures all generated considerable controversy and the charge that these patients were no more than 'human guinea pigs' undergoing treatment for the benefit only of society. This section is intended primarily to identify standards of treatment selection/recommendation and information disclosure relating to transplantation procedures, and the extent to which these vary depending upon the novelty and experimental nature of the procedure. The issue of whether innovative transplant procedures should be subject to the panoply of regulation usually associated with research procedures will also be briefly touched upon. Standards of treatment implementation themselves are governed by the general principles of negligence/malpractice law and raise few peculiarly specific (conceptual) issues in this context, although safety and quality issues relating to the transplanted organ will be fleetingly canvassed in view of the unique feature of body materials being transferred from one human corpus to another.

[1] Furrow *et al.* have stated that 'Organ transplantation often involves therapeutic innovation': B. Furrow, S. Johnson, T. Jost and R. Schwartz, *Health Law: Cases, Materials and Problems*, West Publishing Co., St Paul, 1987, at 130.

[2] She received a new bowel and liver, plus a stomach, pancreas, two kidneys and a small intestine. She died two months later from cancer-like growths on the new organs facilitated by the immunosuppressant FK-506 administered to her to prevent rejection.

[3] Which precipitated the litigation in *Karp* v. *Cooley* 493 F. 2d 408 (5th Cir. 1974) considered further on.

Terminology matters

Inconsistency of terminological usage has often served to obfuscate clear analysis here, stemming principally from the conflation of 'research' on the one hand and 'experimentation' on the other. Dickens once stated that 'Therapeutic innovation in seeking to aid a patient may be acknowledged. The fact of novelty alone, however, does not make the procedure experimental',[4] and in *Brook* v. *St John's Hickey Memorial Hospital* the Supreme Court of Indiana protested, in the context of a medical malpractice suit, that 'Too often have courts confused judgemental decisions and experimentation. Therapeutic innovation has long been recognised as permissible to avoid serious consequences.'[5] However, despite the apparently synonymous treatment of the two concepts in these contexts, it is submitted that a novel treatment is by its nature 'experimental', although not necessarily also research. Mason and McCall Smith properly contend that 'Research and experimentation are commonly used as interchangeable terms – we, however, believe that there is a distinction to be made. Research implies a predetermined protocol with a clearly defined end-point. Experimentation, by contrast, involves a more speculative, ad hoc, approach to an individual subject.'[6]

The rationale underpinning this distinction is founded on the *intention* of the clinician.[7] The (systematic) design of a research protocol is intended to facilitate the objective of the procedure, to contribute to generalised knowledge.[8] The Royal College of Physicians (RCP) Report states that 'when a clinician departs in a significant way from standard or accepted

[4] B. Dickens, 'What is a Medical Experiment?' (1975) 113 *Canadian Medical Association Journal* 635 at 635. He even considered the first kidney transplant not to have been experimental in view of the lack of existing orthodox therapy available: ibid. at 637.

[5] 380 N.E. 2d 72 at 76 (Sup. Ct Ind. 1978).

[6] J. Mason and A. McCall Smith, *Law and Medical Ethics*, 4th edn, Butterworths, London, 1994, at 350.

[7] Kennedy and Grubb suggest that innovative therapy should be regarded either as research, with all that flows from that, or as therapy, and declare that 'To the extent that the intention is to acquire knowledge and not solely to care for the patient it is our view that innovative therapy should be subject to the same regime of control that attends research properly so-called': I. Kennedy and A. Grubb, *Medical Law: Text with Materials*, 2nd edn, Butterworths, London, 1994, at 1032.

[8] Federal regulations applicable to US institutional review boards define research as 'A systematic investigation designed to develop or contribute to generalizable knowledge': see Department of Health and Human Services Rules and Regulations, 45 CFR 46, revised 8 March 1983, Washington D.C.

practice *entirely for the benefit of a particular individual patient*, and with consent, the innovation need not constitute research, though it may be described as an experiment in the sense that it is novel and unvalidated' (my emphasis).[9] The Belmont Report in the US expressed almost identical views.[10] In most transplantation contexts, because the singular intention is to benefit the patient, it is a 'therapy', and consequently not research *per se*.[11] Indeed, in Canada the court in *Zimmer* v. *Ringrose* recognised innovative procedures as (experimental) *therapies*, rather than research. An Institute of Medical Ethics (IME) Report noted that much innovative therapy is surgical in nature.[12] This is partly why transplantation is such a fertile sphere for innovation, that is surgical evolution and the use of original donor sources and procedures. But, in addition, refinements and alterations in (immunosuppressive) drugs regimes are often just as dramatic in this sphere, for example Starzl's dramatic kidney transplant success rates published in 1962 achieved using Imuran (a standard anti-rejection drug) in combination with Prednisone.

Scientifically worthy

Chadwick, however, asserts that in determining that a procedure is therapeutic it is necessary not only to establish an aim of providing some benefit to the patient but also to find some evidence (normally provided by animal studies), that is good reason, for the belief that the procedure

[9] Royal College of Physicians, *Research Involving Patients*, Royal College of Physicians, London, 1990, at 5. The Report additionally stated that 'The distinction between therapy and research derives from *intent*. In medical practice the intention is to benefit the *individual* patient not to gain knowledge of general benefit, though such knowledge may incidentally emerge from the clinical experience gained. In *medical research* the primary intention is to advance knowledge so that *patients in general* may benefit; the individual patient may or may not benefit directly': ibid.

[10] The Belmont Report in the US stated that 'For the most part, the term "practice" refers to interventions that are designed solely to enhance the well-being of an individual patient or client and that have a reasonable expectation of success . . . By contrast, the term "research" designates an activity designed to test a hypothesis, permit conclusions to be drawn, and thereby to develop or contribute to generalizable knowledge': National Commission for the Protection of Human Subjects of Biomedical and Behavioral Research, *The Belmont Report: Ethical Principles and Guidelines for the Protection of Human Subjects of Research*, Department of Health, Education and Welfare, Washington D.C., 1978.

[11] Ibid. Jones states that innovative therapy 'may not constitute research, although it may be described as experimental in the sense that it is novel and unvalidated': M. Jones, *Medical Negligence*, Sweet and Maxwell, London, 1996, para. 3–044 at n. 94.

[12] Institute of Medical Ethics Working Party Report, *Medical Research with Children*, Edinburgh, 1986, at 36–7.

might be beneficial.[13] Annas alleges that many early transplantation procedures were in reality purely *non-therapeutic* and intended only for the benefit of society. For instance, with regard to Dr Leonard Bailey's attempt to transplant a baboon's heart into Baby Fae, he says that a successful outcome was 'never a realistic or reasonable expectation'[14] despite the fact that the surgeon himself asserted that he had been engaged solely in therapy. Whilst the likelihood of success in many of these procedures was very low and they almost routinely failed, there is no obvious reason to doubt the genuineness of these intentions. That there was some minimally supportive scientific evidence would appear to be confirmed by the modest extension of life in one or two isolated instances. Although only two of the first sixty-six recipients of a human heart survived for longer than six months, one very early recipient, Philip Blaiberg, survived for approximately eighteen months, and one of the first animal organ recipients survived for nine months.[15] Of course, quality of life was another thing.

Gaze and Dawson have observed that

> The physician's motives . . . may not always be separable. Motives, however, are not necessarily clear, or easily identified or distinguished from one another, especially where no established treatment exists. For example, while the doctor wishes to heal the patient, if the new treatment works, it will inevitably benefit others as well as the patient, and the doctor must be aware of this. If the test turns on subjective motivation, there is the problem of proving or establishing what was in a person's mind at some time in the past.[16]

[13] R. Chadwick, 'Corpses, Recycling and Therapeutic Purposes' in R. Lee and D. Morgan (eds.), *Death Rites: Law and Ethics at the End of Life*, Routledge, London, 1994, at 56–7.

[14] G. Annas, 'Death and the Magic Machine' (1987) 9 *Western New England Law Review* 89 at 98 n. 27. He added that Barney Clark 'came to realise shortly before his death that he had become involved in pure non-therapeutic experimentation for others': at 99–100.

[15] Of course, many of these procedures are now standard therapies. Even by 1986, Medicare had stated that cardiac transplantation had, despite a long moratorium, become a 'medically reasonable and necessary service' for adults: see D. Lamb, *Organ Transplants and Ethics*, Routledge, London, 1990, at 14. There may have been less supporting evidence in favour of the first artificial heart transplants. Dr Michael DeBakey expressed the view that there was insufficient data accumulated prior to the fitting of Barney Clark's artificial replacement heart to justify its attempted use: *Horizon*, BBC 2, 18 February 1999.

[16] B. Gaze and K. Dawson, 'Distinguishing Medical Practice and Research: The Special Case of IVT' (1989) 3(4) *Bioethics* 301 at 307. They argue that the better approach is to have regard to the nature of the procedure in the light of current biomedical knowledge: ibid., at 308.

There may also be strong personal or institutional incentives at play. But as Stauch, Wheat and Tingle comment regarding innovative procedures,

> Significantly, from the doctor's point of view, the desire in such cases is *solely* to benefit the individual patient being treated in this way. Of course, he may *foresee* the likelihood of gaining new knowledge in this process, but this merely equates to a wide intention on his part to have it (contrast therapeutic research where it is part of his desire) [my emphasis].[17]

As they then observe, in such (former) scenarios there is no conflict between the doctor *qua* doctor and *qua* scientist: he acts as the former alone – the patient is not being used as a means to any further end. Thus, there is no substitute for an assessment of the clinician's subjective motivation in determining the appropriate legal and ethical framework of analysis, albeit that in the absence of some scientific basis it must be open to third parties to doubt the genuineness of such intentions at all (that is the objective evidence creates a kind of 'evidential threshold'). This is without prejudice to the fact that certain procedures *ought* to be brought under the procedural and substantive umbrella of 'research' in certain instances (elaborated upon further below) and that it may indeed have been the case that some of these procedures should not have been undertaken at the time that they were. These matters should, however, be subjected to interrogation on the basis of standards applicable to therapy rather than research. Schneiderman and Jecker usefully categorise therapeutic procedures into three types: beneficial treatments or *therapies* (interventions which have been shown to benefit patients); *innovative interventions* (for which there may be promising but insufficient supporting evidence, which therefore should be regarded as *experimental treatments* worthy of further investigation); and *futile* procedures.[18] In reality the dividing line between the latter two categories may not always be that bright.

[17] M. Stauch, K. Wheat and J. Tingle, *Sourcebook on Medical Law*, Cavendish, London, 1998, at 527. Howard Brody states: 'The doctor who juggles the doses of his patient's antihypertensive medications to see if he can get better control of blood pressure without excessive side-effects is experimenting, in that he doesn't know beforehand what dose will be best; but he is experimenting within the context of medical practice, as the patient's benefit is the main goal, and any new knowledge gained would be purely coincidental': see H. Brody, *Ethical Decisions in Medicine*, 2nd edn, Little Brown, Boston, 1981, at 190.

[18] L. Schneiderman and N. Jecker, 'Is the Treatment Beneficial, Experimental, or Futile?' (1996) 5 *Cambridge Quarterly of Healthcare Ethics* 248.

Therapy vs experiment

What is it that turns an innovative therapy into a standard form of therapy?[19] The metamorphosis will inevitably often be blurred and gradual.[20] A point of transition was nearly achieved as regards kidney transplantation at a meeting of twenty-five of the world's leading doctors and researchers in 1963 in Washington D.C. The delegates refused to endorse such transplantation as an 'acceptable' therapy even though many notable successes had already occurred, because on average less than 10 per cent of transplant patients survived for three months after the operation. Nearly all the speakers agreed though that they were on the verge of success but, in the words of Tony Stark, this was 'just out of reach'.[21] Yet, by 1969 Sir Peter Medawar was able to remark that kidney transplants had been 'almost completely received into the ordinary repertoire of surgical practice'.[22] Indeed, very many years after the performance of numerous heart transplants, they were still experimental and not yet standard.

Legal issues

In this section we shall examine the legal obligations attaching to treatment selection and information disclosure as they affect both standard and experimental transplant therapies, and the extent to which the latter generate obligations over and above the norm. First though, there are one or two remarks concerning the criminal law and the issue of consent to such procedures and standards of treatment generally.

In jurisdictions with a general Criminal Code there is often a specific

[19] McCullagh asserts that therapy constitutes the 'indefinite repetition of procedures that are judged to be successful': see P. McCullagh, *The Foetus as Transplant Donor: Scientific, Social and Ethical Perspectives*, John Wiley, Chichester, 1987, at 7.

[20] The degree of repetition is not itself conclusive. In *Hepworth* v. *Kerr* [1995] 6 Medical Law Reports 139, the English court considered that the hypotensive anaesthetic technique employed was 'experimental' despite the fact that the clinician had used it on 1,500 previous occasions and it was described as 'his lifetime's work', as it was wholly outside the scope of accepted procedures at that time. See also the Canadian *Ringrose* cases below.

[21] T. Stark, *A Knife to the Heart*, Macmillan, London, 1996, at 48. In fact the Supreme Court of New York in *Colton* v. *New York Hospital* 414 N.Y.S. 2d 866 (1979) stated that even in 1972 a kidney transplant was 'concededly an experimental operation, having the obvious risks of tissue rejection, shock, and possibly death': at 869.

[22] P. Medawar, 'The Future of Transplantation, Biology and Medicine' (1969) 1 *Transplantation Proceedings* 666 at 667.

provision catering directly for the legitimacy of medical or surgical procedures either within the Code itself or in separate legislative provisions. For example, section 61 of the New Zealand Criminal Code states that 'Everyone is protected from criminal responsibility for performing with reasonable care and skill any surgical operation upon any person for his benefit, if the performance of the operation was reasonable, having regard to the patient's state at the time and to all the circumstances of the case.'[23] Whilst this clarifies the situation in various civil law jurisdictions, the position is cloudier in terms of principles, as opposed to practical effect, in many common law jurisdictions. Under the common law, transplant surgery *prima facie* constitutes a battery or other offence against the person, despite Skegg's compelling assertion that 'The ordinary and natural meaning of bodily harm scarcely includes medical procedures which benefit the bodily health of the person on whom they are performed. Benefit is, after all, the converse of harm.'[24] Nonetheless, such transplantation procedures would easily be justified in general by reference to the 'public interest' and would therefore be lawful in any event. In England in *Attorney-General's Reference (No. 6 of 1980)*, Lord Lane spoke of 'reasonable surgical interference' as being an exception justified by the public interest.[25]

Negligence in treatment

Disease/infection transmission

Occasionally, an organ transplantee has received diseased or malignant tissue from a particular donor source presenting a particular risk to him or her. This might give rise to fault liability in the tort of negligence/delict or for breach of contract, or alternatively to strict liability (without fault)

23 Section 45 of the Canadian Criminal Code similarly states that 'A person performing a surgical treatment for the benefit of the patient is protected from criminal liability if it is performed with reasonable skill and care and it is reasonable to perform the operation.'

24 P. Skegg, *Law, Ethics and Medicine*, Clarendon Press, Oxford, 1988, at 31.

25 [1981] QB 715 at 719E. The Law Commission Consultation Paper, *Consent in the Criminal Law*, Law Com. 139, HMSO, 1995, recommended that a person should not be guilty of an offence where any injury is caused during the course of proper medical treatment or care administered with the consent of that person: see para. 8.50. In the unlikely event though that a patient was to die during the performance of a procedure unable to be justified as being in the public interest, liability for manslaughter (constructive manslaughter in the UK) might arise.

under products liability or for breach of a contractual term. In England in *Sumners* v. *Mid-Downs Health Authority*, a cancerous kidney had been transplanted into a patient who developed cancer from the kidney. The kidney was eventually removed and the patient received a second transplant and survived. The action for negligence in failing to detect the cancer was rejected by the High Court, but the hospital admitted liability for failing to inform the patient and to remove the kidney immediately, as soon as it was appreciated that the donor had cancer.[26] However, in *Ravenis* v. *Detroit General Hospital*[27] two patients received a cornea from the same donor and both lost an eye due to infection. The US court found the hospital liable in malpractice for failure to test and select the donor properly. Similarly, in France, a surgeon was held liable for transplanting a cornea into a recipient from a person who had died of rabies.[28] Recently, in Scotland,[29] there have also been reports of corneas being transplanted into three patients from donors who died of Creutzfeldt–Jakob disease (CJD), although no litigation has apparently resulted,[30] and an enquiry was launched in England in December 1999 after it was discovered that a transplant patient had been given a liver from a man who had died of meningitis (although the patient developed no symptoms or signs of the disease).[31]

Strict liability may arise out of the law of products liability or through principles of commercial law. As regards the former, products liability regimes are operative across most of Europe and are the subject of the 1985 European Products Liability Directive. In the UK the Consumer

[26] *Sumners* v. *Mid-Downs Health Authority* (1996) (unreported) LEXIS transcript, ENGGEN Library. See also (1996) 298 *British Medical Journal* 1544.

[27] 234 N.W. 2d 411 (1975).

[28] Cited by D. Giesen in *International Medical Malpractice Law*, Martinus Nijhoff, Dordrecht, 1988, at 251.

[29] 'Health Alert after Eyes of CJD Victim are Transplanted', *The Times*, 1 December 1997. The post-mortem results in this case had not been passed on to the UKTSSA. There were also reports that instruments used to remove the eyes from the donor may have contaminated (up to six) more recipients: see 'More May Have Been Infected in CJD Case', *The Times*, 8 December 1997. The Nuffield Council Report also referred to an incident in the US where a bone graft recipient developed AIDS from an implant from a donor who subsequently tested positive for the HIV virus, despite having previously tested negative: see Nuffield Council on Bioethics, *Human Tissue: Ethical and Legal Issues*, Nuffield Council on Bioethics, London, 1995, at para. 12.32.

[30] Organs and tissues are not routinely screened for CJD due to its rarity. Moreover, although corneas can be kept for up to two months, such testing would not be feasible for hearts or livers as they must both be transplanted within six hours.

[31] R. Jenkins, 'Donor in Liver Transplant had Meningitis', *The Times*, 24 December 1999.

Protection Act 1987 creates strict liability in respect of 'defective products', begging the question whether transplanted organs or tissues could constitute 'products' for the purposes of the legislation. The Nuffield Council Working Party Report took the view that 'Contaminated blood supplied to patients, or a defective organ used for transplantation, are likely to be regarded as "defective products" regardless of the information which is given to patients.'[32] This was also the recommended view of the Royal Commission on Civil Liability and Compensation for Personal Injury (the Pearson Report).[33] In the US, blood has also been held to be 'goods' in some instances.[34] Indeed, if drugs are covered, why not body parts and fluids which have been subjected at minimum to screening and preservation techniques, and in many instances much more?[35] In the context of private medical treatment (where the supplier acts 'in the course of business') the issue also arises as to whether terms applicable to sales of goods apply to transplanted organs, such as terms of merchantable quality and fitness for purpose (in Britain under the Sale of Goods Act 1979). However, it is most likely that the organs themselves would be viewed as an ancillary aspect of the treatment and thus the contract would be viewed as one for 'services' rather than a contract for the sale of 'goods'. In *Perlmutter* v. *Beth David Hospital*[36] in the United States, even though blood was given, the court viewed the transaction as a supply of services.[37] It is submitted though that one should concur with the view of Davies that 'In principle, blood or body products should be "goods" within the meaning of the 1979 Act whenever they are dealt with commercially.'[38] In any event, in Britain the same terms would be implied by statute into a contract for the supply of services where goods are

[32] Nuffield Council, *Human Tissue*, at para. 12.57. It stated that human tissue used for medicinal purposes would 'possess the essential characteristics attributable to an industrial or other process': ibid. at para. 12.58. Matthews agrees with this view: see P. Matthews, 'The Man of Property' [1995] 3 *Medical Law Review* 251 at 270.

[33] Cmnd 7054–1, 1978.

[34] In *Carter* v. *Inter-Faith Hospital of Queens* 304 N.Y.S. 2d 97 (1969).

[35] There have been many instances of disease transmission from infected blood and other products in recent years, including 1,000+ mothers contaminated with hepatitis C in Ireland through contaminated anti-D immunoglobulin in the mid 1970s.

[36] 123 N.E. 2d 792 (1954).

[37] The US courts have been inconsistent on this point. By contrast with *Perlmutter* see *Belle Bonfils Memorial Blood Bank* v. *Hansen* 579 P. 2d 1158 (1978) and *Carter* v. *Inter-Faith Hospital of Queens* 304 N.Y.S. 2d 97 (1969).

[38] I. Davies, 'Live Donation of Human Body Parts: A Case for Negotiability' (1991) 59(2) *Medico-Legal Journal* 100 at 105.

supplied therewith.[39] There is an important need for quality control procedures in this sphere, for the protection not only of the recipient but of society generally. This remark has most relevance in the context of xenotransplants where the nature and extent of risk is largely unknown, although *animal* organs, and even the animals themselves, are undoubtedly 'products' or 'goods' in law.

Organs and tissues are routinely screened for various diseases and bacteria and also for tumours. Malignant tumours are typically regarded as a contraindication to transplantation except for low-grade skin tumours and tumours of the central nervous system (which have low metastatic rates). But should donors with known tumours be used at all? In the United States such donors constitute 15 per cent of the entire donor pool, and in view of the low risk of transmission to the recipient, continue to be used, even though patients are known to have died as a consequence,[40] just as donors with hepatitis C are used around the world. Of course, with an adequate supply of donors, the need to run such a risk would be eliminated. Whilst it may not be negligent to use such a donor source *per se*, the emphasis will shift to the issue of informed consent, discussed more fully below, and the need to inform the recipient specifically of the enhanced risk posed by such a donor source.

Treatment selection

Therapy simpliciter

Standard legal malpractice rules are applicable here, which will often include the relevance of adherence to a practice accepted as proper by a *responsible* body of medical opinion, where applicable.[41] This is generally unproblematic, although where the donor presents an enhanced risk (due, for example, to infection) there must be a proper weighing of the benefits and risks in the light of the alternative strategies. The difficulties attach to experimental therapies which, by their nature, are *deviations* from gen-

[39] Supply of Goods and Services Act 1982. See A. Bell, 'The Doctor and the Supply of Goods and Services Act 1982' (1984) 4 *Legal Studies* 175.

[40] See P. Healey and C. Davis, 'Transmission of Tumours by Transplantation' (1998) 352 *Lancet* 2 and 'Transplant Risk in Tumour Death', *The Times*, 2 July 1998.

[41] In the UK this is especially so, where *Bolam* v. *Friern Hospital Management Committee* [1957] 1 WLR 582 and *Bolitho* v. *City & Hackney Health Authority* [1997] 4 All ER 771 are the central authorities on this issue.

erally accepted practices – although that does not necessarily mean that it will constitute negligence to employ them.

Novel and experimental treatments

Jones states: 'The practitioner who departs from the accepted methods of treatment will normally have to provide some justification for doing so if, as a consequence, the patient suffers injury.'[42] Giesen uncontentiously asserts that 'treating a patient with new procedures must be regarded as malpractice where approved methods may be expected to produce the same degree of success with less risk'.[43] The law has to balance the need for progress in medicine against the obligation to avoid reckless and potentially dangerous and untried techniques. Such a departure is not necessarily negligent though, even where the outcome is poor.[44] The clinician will have to convince the court that he acted as a reasonable doctor would do.[45] The better view is that the degree of departure from normal practice enhances the precautions necessary to satisfy the standard of care but that the standard does not itself change.[46] Courts will scrutinise the existing scientific basis for the belief in the potential efficacy of the treatment proposed. It might constitute negligence, for instance, to offer a xenotransplant before scientific research, on animals in particular, had reached a certain stage.[47] Indeed, there is much to be said for the view that

[42] Jones, *Medical Negligence*, at para. 3–040.

[43] D. Giesen, 'Civil Liability of Physicians for New Methods of Treatment and Experimentation: A Comparative Examination' [1995] 3 *Medical Law Review* 22 at 29.

[44] Courts in Britain are particularly mindful of the need not to thwart medical progress. In the Court of Appeal in *Wilsher* v. *Essex Area Health Authority* [1986] 3 All ER 801, Lord Justice Mustill stated that 'if the decision to embark on the treatment at all was justifiable and was taken with the informed consent of the patient, the court should . . . be particularly careful not to impute negligence simply because something has gone wrong': at 812.

[45] See *Hunter* v. *Hanley* [1955] *Scots Law Times* 213, where Lord Clyde stated that 'In the realms of diagnosis and treatment there is ample scope for genuine difference of opinion and one man is not negligent merely because his conclusion differs from that of other medical men . . . The true test for establishing negligence in diagnosis or treatment on the part of the doctor is whether he has been proved to be guilty of such failure as no doctor of ordinary skill would be guilty if acting with ordinary care': at 217.

[46] Jones, *Medical Negligence*, at 115 n. 91. Giesen alternatively argues that the degree of care varies with the extent of such departure, citing the remarks of Cawsey J in *Poole* v. *Morgan* that 'where the risks involved in the treatment are great, or the treatment is a new one, the standard of care increases' [1987] 3 WWR 217 at 254: see Giesen, 'Civil Liability of Physicians', at 30.

[47] The British Department of Health Advisory Committee Report on Xenotransplantation is a reflection upon this crucial issue of 'timing': see A Report by the Advisory Group on the

there was an insufficient base of research on animals to justify moving to the first mechanical heart devices. In *Karp* v. *Cooley*, the court took an unduly lax and lenient approach, relying heavily on a fairly vaguely worded and signed consent form and not rigorously examining the limited animal research pre-dating the transplant in the absence of any peer review of the protocol. In dismissing the claim, the Fifth Circuit Court of Appeals applied standard 'malpractice evidentiary standards' and did not give proper weight to the 'experimental' nature of the procedure.[48] In the first heart transplant cases the risks were very high and many of the potential hazards as yet unknown but, in view of the absence of life-prolonging alternatives, it was apparently tacitly conceded to be permissible to offer the therapy. This will probably be the justification employed in the forthcoming round of clinical trials of xenotransplants in Britain. Jones states: 'Where the patient's condition is very serious and the standard treatment is ineffective, a doctor will be justified in taking greater risks in an attempt to provide some effective treatment.'[49] However, whilst broadly acceptable, it is necessary also to factor into the assessment the possible 'costs' in terms of suffering and diminished quality of life potentially imposed by the novel therapy.[50] There should be a 'bottom line' even where the patient is prepared to consent to it.[51]

Information disclosure

In a small minority of jurisdictions, statute dictates a certain level of information disclosure to transplant *recipients*,[52] although the generality of the provisions is such that it is unlikely they go beyond the existing

Ethics of Xenotransplantation, *Animal Tissue into Humans*, Department of Health, HMSO, 1996.

48 *Karp* v. *Cooley* 493 F. 2d 408 (5th Cir. 1974). It also rejected the claim on the basis that even if the patient had been given sufficient information to give a properly informed consent, he would have agreed to the procedure anyhow.

49 Jones, *Medical Negligence*, at para. 3–041.

50 Transplantation is rarely a permanent cure and in any event always has side-effects attaching to the immunosuppression regime, etc. See generally L. McChesney and S. Braithwaite, 'Expectations and Outcomes in Organ Transplantation' (1999) 8 *Cambridge Quarterly of Healthcare Ethics* 299.

51 It is this that forms the basis of Annas's criticisms of the Federal Circuit Court of Appeals' decision in *Karp* v. *Cooley*: see Annas, 'Death and the Magic Machine', at 94–5.

52 They sometimes merely restate the self-evident necessity to obtain the recipient's consent, for example Law of 30 June 1989 in Vietnam.

requirements of their general laws. In the Russian Federation, statutory provisions require that the recipient be informed of 'the possible complications that the envisaged intervention may present for his health' and there are similar provisions elsewhere.[53] The provision in Article 5 of the Council of Europe Draft Protocol requires information to be communicated as to the nature and purpose of the procedure and its risks and consequences, as well as the alternatives, essentially the same requirement as in relation to patients generally set out in the Convention.[54] The 1993 Law in Portugal contains one of the more extensive legislative stipulations in mandating that the recipient must be informed 'in an honest, appropriate, and comprehensible manner of the possible risks, the consequences of donation and treatment, and any untoward effects, as well as the precautions to be observed subsequently'.[55] Most jurisdictions rely on their general laws though. It is submitted that essential information regarding 'consequences' should also embrace potential complications and implications connected to the donor source. Many potential recipients have qualms about accepting an organ from a living related person (whose health might be jeopardised thereby), *a fortiori* where the organ source is animal rather than human. Thus, Bolivian law is particularly laudable in so far as it requires that the head of the transplantation team must inform the recipient of the *origin* of the organ or tissue to be transplanted (for example whether a living or cadaveric source), and also of the results of tissue compatibility testing.[56] As regards xenotransplantation, the Advisory Group Report on the Ethics of Xenotransplantation, whilst broadly accepting the applicability of the

[53] Law of 22 December 1992, section 6. In Panama, the physician must inform the recipient of the risks involved in the procedure and the possible consequences thereof: Law of 11 July 1983, section 6. In Greece, he must be given details of the consequences of the transplantation: Law of 2 August 1983, sections 5–6. In Argentina, the recipient must be informed of the likely risks and benefits: Law of 24 March 1993, section 13. Indian federal law requires that the recipient be informed of the possible effects, complications and hazards of the transplantation procedure: Act No. 42 of 1994, section 12.

[54] Although the Draft Protocol also specifically requires information about *alternatives* to be given to organ *recipients*: see Draft Protocol to the Convention on Human Rights and Biomedicine, on Transplantation of Organs and Tissues of Human Origin, Council of Europe, 9 March 1999, Article 5.

[55] Law of 22 April 1993, section 7. In Spain, in addition to this information, he/she must also be informed of the results of histocompatibility and other immunological studies carried out on the donor and the recipient: see Law of 27 October 1979, section 6. Hong Kong law requires the recipient of an organ from a genetically *unrelated* individual to *understand* information about the procedure and its associated risks: see Ordinance No. 16 of 1995, section 5(4).

[56] Law of 15 March 1982, section 9.

existing legal framework surrounding consent in Britain, considered that (extremely extensive) specific information should always be given regarding, *inter alia*, the source of the tissue; the breeding, genetic modification and raising of animals; the degree of suffering to which the animals would be exposed; the nature of the tissue to be transplanted, for example whether it might affect personality; and the potential psychological and social effects that xenotransplantation could have. The Report states that the latter should even specifically incorporate information that 'people might react in a hostile or uncertain way to a xenotransplant recipient'.[57]

Therapy simpliciter

In terms of transplantation as a therapy *simpliciter*, an action for battery under common law (or delict in civil law jurisdictions) would lie where the patient 'did not know in broad terms the nature of the procedure',[58] and a failure to inform an organ transplant recipient sufficiently of the alternative treatments and the risks and consequences implicated by the transplant could lead to a civil action for negligence (or again an action in delict in civil law jurisdictions), as with any other form of treatment. There is an issue as to whether, where a patient does not know the source or origin of the organ, or where the organ presents an above-average risk to the recipient due, for example, to latent infection, the patient could be said to know the 'nature' of the procedure.[59] Arguably though, he/she would know, but might be unaware of some of the 'implications', that is risks, relating to the transplant, and might be unaware of the alternatives available. These matters would then devolve to a potential action in negligence/malpractice rather than battery. Where a donor source is utilised which presents risks greater than the norm to recipients, or even to others, it should nevertheless be mandatory for this information to be given to such recipients.[60] In relation to xenotransplants, the Advisory

[57] *Animal Tissue into Humans*, at 114.

[58] Per Bristow J in *Chatterton* v. *Gerson* [1981] 1 All ER 257 at 265.

[59] It has been suggested by some commentators that it should be mandatory, for instance, for a recipient to be told whether the donor was heart-beating or non-heart-beating: see J. Alvarez-Rodriguez *et al.*, 'Posttransplant Long-Term Outcome of Kidneys Obtained from Asystolic Donors Maintained under Extracorporeal Cardiopulmonary Bypass' (1995) 27 *Transplantation Proceedings* 2903, discussion at 2904.

[60] Even the risks of hepatitis C which would generally not become significant until many years after the transplant. See M. Panico, M. Soloman and L. Burrows, 'Issues of Informed Consent

Group Report states that recipients should always receive information regarding risks of infection, what is known and what is *not* known, monitoring arrangements and the implications for the patient's close contacts, especially partners.[61]

As regards the requirements of information disclosure the position is governed by the principles applicable to consent to health care decisions in general. In the United States these vary between the states, which either adopt a reasonable doctor standard, which frequently gives great sway to bodies of professional medical opinion, or a reasonable patient standard, which requires disclosure of the information that a 'prudent patient' would regard as being material to the decision whether or not to undergo the procedure. In Britain the former principles, laid down by the House of Lords in *Sidaway* v. *Board of Governors of the Royal Bethlem Hospital*,[62] are generally applicable, giving more weight to accepted practice. McK Norrie has stated:

> These principles are to be applied to transplant operations, so that the recipient is to be given at least such information as fulfils the standard of disclosure of risks required by the relevant legal system. So, whatever the precise determination of that standard, the recipient of the donation must be given information concerning the risks of the operation itself and its consequences (e.g. the possibility of tissue rejection), the chances of its success, possible alternative modes of treatment, the consequences of failure, and, indeed, the consequences of success (e.g. the need, particularly with heart transplants, to receive various anti-rejection drugs for the rest of the patient's life).[63]

In jurisdictions such as Australia, Canada and many of the civil law jurisdictions[64] which employ a 'patient-oriented' standard, all the above

and Access to Extended Donor Pool Kidneys' (1997) 29 *Transplantation Proceedings* 3667. In various situations, a plaintiff would fail on the grounds of causation in any event.

61 Indeed, under Colombian law, a recipient must be informed, *inter alia*, of the impossibility of knowing with certainty all of the risks entailed by the procedure: see Decree of 6 June 1989, section 35.

62 [1985] 1 All ER 643; which in turn relied heavily upon *Bolam* v. *Friern HMC* [1957] 1 WLR 582.

63 K. McK Norrie, 'Human Tissue Transplants: Legal Liability in Different Jurisdictions' (1985) 34 *International and Comparative Law Quarterly* 442 at 451. Overcast *et al.* note that the most significant items of information for recipients relate to the inherent risks and possible complications, and the likelihood of the procedure succeeding: see T. Overcast *et al.*, 'Malpractice Issues in Heart Transplantation' (1984) 10(4) *Journal of Law and Medicine* 363 at 379–80.

64 In civil law jurisdictions and Australia a *subjective* patient standard in fact generally prevails.

information would likely have to be disclosed. In those jurisdictions endorsing the *reasonable doctor* standard, where accepted practice has much force, such disclosure requirements may be more limited, although in the transplantation context one would expect the obligations to be greater than in relation to most medical procedures. In *Sidaway*, Lord Bridge (supported by Lord Keith) stated that if there was a 'substantial risk of grave adverse consequences' then disclosure of risks would be necessitated despite the existence of the views of a body of responsible medical opinion to the contrary. More recently, the Court of Appeal in *Pearce* v. *United Bristol Healthcare NHS Trust* even went so far as to say that 'in law if there is a significant risk which would affect the judgment of a reasonable patient, then in the normal course it is the responsibility of a doctor to inform the patient'.[65] However, Lord Woolf used the same example of the 10 per cent risk of a stroke used by Lord Bridge in *Sidaway* as an example of a 'significant risk', suggesting there may be less of a change of emphasis than implied.[66] Nevertheless, this would seemingly apply anyhow to all organ transplant therapies which by their nature carry very significant risks, where rejection and the risks of infection may lead to death, and where inevitable long-term changes to lifestyle are implicated,[67] especially with heart, lung and liver transplants. This should include information relating to post-operative treatment complications connected to the long-term use of immunosuppressant drugs (for example loss of libido, physical changes, risks of infection, etc.). Information regarding likelihood of success should relate to the centre itself where there is adequate data on past recipients to draw upon, otherwise any centre data in existence should be coupled with multi-centre study data wherever possible.[68] As mentioned above, information should also be conveyed as regards any above-average risks presented by the nature of the donor source.

An example of the application of general principles in the transplant

[65] (1999) 48 BMLR 118 at 124.

[66] Lord Woolf stated *obiter* that a greater duty of disclosure would apply where the patient asked questions, but this is a moot point in English law in the light of the Court of Appeal's decision in *Blyth* v. *Bloomsbury Health Authority* [1993] 4 Medical Law Reports 151.

[67] Due partially to the absence of maintenance procedures analogous to kidney dialysis. Liver transplantation is also among the most complicated from a technical, surgical perspective.

[68] Overcast *et al.*, 'Malpractice Issues', at 384–5. These commentators question whether disclosure should extend to financially related matters, for example insurance complications, effects on employment, etc., and suggest a limited duty.

context in Britain is the High Court litigation in *Poynter* v. *Hillingdon Health Authority*.[69] In 1987, a child aged one year, Matthew Poynter, had a heart transplant at the Harefield Hospital. He sustained massive irreversible brain damage which resulted from a period of time, after the anaesthetic was administered and the surgery was commenced, during which his heart stopped and his brain was starved of oxygen. The allegation was that the hospital clinician was negligent in failing to inform his parents of the risk of serious brain damage attaching to the procedure. The trial judge, applying *Sidaway*, concluded that whilst there was a body of medical opinion, at the time of Matthew's operation, that would have informed the parents of such a risk (approximately 1 per cent) of brain damage, there were many other clinicians who would not have done so, and that it was not negligent in this case to adhere to a practice supported by such a responsible body of medical opinion. Thus, there was no breach of duty on the facts. The court referred to the 'exception' approved by Lord Bridge in *Sidaway* but considered that it did not apply to the instant case (that is there was no substantial risk of grave adverse consequences).[70] However, the decision can be justified on the basis that the very modest risks were not specific to transplantation and were generic to operative procedures generally under anaesthetic, which are widely understood, and which were referred to by Lord Templeman in *Sidaway* as 'general' rather than 'special' risks, to which a lesser duty of disclosure applied.

Inherently risky

Stricter requirements of information disclosure may be mandated by both law and ethics in respect of experimental therapeutic procedures contrasted with therapy *simpliciter*. Both Jones and McK Norrie argue that this is because of the higher degree of risk implicated by such procedures.[71] Giesen states that

> The informational requirements of actual and reasonable patients and even, it is submitted, the level of disclosure to be expected of a reasonable doctor will increase with the degree of novelty of the method intended to be applied. The doctor must accordingly explain to the patient why he

[69] (1997) 37 BMLR 192 (QBD).

[70] Ibid., at 205–6.

[71] McK Norrie, 'Human Tissue Transplants', at 451. Giesen also concurs with this view: see 'Civil Liability of Physicians', at 35.

> intends to treat the patient's condition with new methods or drugs and what the possible consequences of failure to apply this treatment would be. The patient must be informed, not only of the risks known to accompany the procedure, but also of the fact that there may be unknown risks, or at least that the doctor has reason to believe that unknown risks could materialise.[72]

But would such a cause of action for non-disclosure at common law sound in battery or negligence? Giesen states that it is unacceptable to 'place the burden of this experimentation upon the patient by confining his right of recovery in relation to consent to the tort of negligence',[73] but it would appear that this was at least partially borne out of its supposed association with research. Whilst this might be a warranted perspective applied to research, it is arguably less persuasive with regard to innovative therapeutic procedures. More likely is the judicial approach presaged by Jones, who remarks that 'If the court placed the emphasis on the therapeutic nature of the procedure, the fact that it was also experimental . . . might be regarded as collateral to the therapy to which consent "in broad terms" had been obtained.'[74] There is a paucity of judicial guidance here though, at least in Britain. The likelihood of negligence rather than battery being the proper cause of action for non-disclosure in this context is supported by the Canadian and US courts. In *Zimmer* v. *Ringrose*, the plaintiff was subjected to a *novel and experimental* method of sterilisation but had not been informed of the fact that the procedure had not yet been accepted by the medical profession and that the procedure carried a 30 per cent failure rate. At first instance MacDonald J applied *Halushka*, which concerned non-therapeutic research procedures, and held the defendants liable for battery. On appeal, however, the Alberta Court of Appeal reversed, holding that *Halushka* was not directly relevant because it concerned non-therapeutic procedures; whereas the proposed sterilisation method was directed to a therapeutic end.[75] Nonetheless, the defendants were held liable in negligence for failing to discuss alternative methods with the plaintiff and to weigh the competing risks – a reasonable

[72] He has elsewhere expressed the view that patients should be informed of *all* the risks presented by experimental transplantation procedures: see Giesen, *International Medical Malpractice Law*, at 608–9.

[73] Giesen, 'Civil Liability of Physicians', at 33.

[74] Jones, *Medical Negligence*, at para. 6–127.

[75] 124 DLR (3d) 215 (Alta.).

patient standard was employed for the purpose.[76] On almost identical facts the trial judge similarly distinguished *Halushka* on the same basis, in *Cryderman* v. *Ringrose*.[77] The court applied a negligence analysis[78] to a procedure described as 'experimental'. The British Columbia Court of Appeal also upheld the liability of the defendants in negligence in *Coughlin* v. *Kuntz*[79] for failing to disclose to the plaintiff that the proposed procedure was novel, unique to the defendant, and under investigation by a professional body, etc. There are no actual cases in the transplantation sphere itself though.

Even if negligence or malpractice, as opposed to battery, is the most likely cause of action for non-disclosure in this context, a stringent duty of disclosure should apply. In *Zimmer* v. *Ringrose* it was held, applying the prudent patient standard, that the physician should have informed the patient that the procedure had not been approved by the medical profession, as a prudent person would have been influenced by this factor in reaching a decision. In *Cryderman* the court stated that 'When an experimental procedure is employed the common law requires a high degree of care and also disclosure to the patient of the fact that the treatment is new and risky.'[80] In *Fiorentino* v. *Wenger* also, a New York court held that disclosure of risks was required by virtue of the procedure being 'experimental'.[81] The 'exception' in *Sidaway* is also more likely to apply, even if standard principles are applicable, because by definition novel and experimental procedures are associated with uncertain and high risks. Alternatively, it may be the case that the general approach in *Sidaway* is not applicable in this context anyhow. Giesen argues that approved practice should be irrelevant here. An alternative view is that, in relation to innovative techniques, whilst professional opinion should not be dominant, it must surely be very relevant. Nonetheless, in view of their novelty, and despite prevailing professional opinion, it is submitted that typically a 'reasonable doctor' would tell a patient of the risks attaching to the procedure and the alternatives, *a fortiori* a 'prudent patient' would

[76] Although the action failed on the basis of causation; it was found that the plaintiff would have accepted the treatment in any event.

[77] [1977] 3 WWR 109; aff'd [1978] 3 WWR 481, 89 DLR (3d) 32 (Alta. CA).

[78] Although it was pleaded in this way and the court did not actually decide that the action could not have been successfully pleaded in battery instead.

[79] [1990] 2 WWR 737 (BCCA).

[80] 89 DLR (3d) 32 at 41.

[81] 272 N.Y.S. 2d 557 (1966).

wish to be so informed. Indeed, in *R* v. *Mental Health Commission ex parte X*[82] the High Court stated that the applicant mental patient should 'realise that the use on him was a novel one and the full implications with use on young men had not been studied, since trials had only been involved with animals and older men'.[83] More recently, in the High Court Ebworth J stated in *Newbury* v. *Bath District Health Authority*: 'There might be circumstances in which a patient would be entitled to be told that a proposed operation was not in the mainstream of treatment. That would obviously be so if the treatment involved a method which was either entirely new, or relatively untried.'[84]

Causation is a major stumbling block here where liability for non-disclosure revolves around negligence. In the *Poynter* case the judge (even employing a subjective patient standard) found that the parents would still have consented to the transplant even had the risk of brain damage been disclosed to them, despite the fact that they vehemently denied this at trial.[85] A breach of duty based on non-disclosure in *Zimmer* v. *Ringrose* also foundered on the issue of causation.

Experimentation and research revisited

Lind notes that 'Physicians have been granted the right to innovate if the innovation is performed in the best interest of an individual patient, without calling the therapy research' and also observes that 'Innovative medical therapies lie on a spectrum bounded at one end by very radical procedures such as transplanting animal organs into human recipients, and at the other by deviations from standard practice that are so minimal

[82] (1988) 9 BMLR 77 (QBD).

[83] Indeed, Teff notes that a higher degree of disclosure has been required in relation to experimental procedures from the very earliest days, emanating from *Slater* v. *Baker* in the eighteenth century: see H. Teff, 'The Law and Ethics of Medical Experimentation' (1987) (Nov./Dec.) *Professional Negligence* 182.

[84] (1999) 47 BMLR 138 at 150 (QBD). Where a doctor misrepresented the scale or nature of the risks involved this might give rise to an action for battery where this related to the nature of the procedure, or alternatively for negligence. It has been alleged, for instance, that Christiaan Barnard misled the first heart transplantee into believing that the procedure had an 80 per cent chance of success when in fact these were merely the odds of surviving the operation: see Annas, 'Death and the Magic Machine', at 92–4.

[85] Indeed, the parents' own personal views were wholly opposed to transplantation. They viewed it as unnatural and wrong on spiritual grounds (the heart having deep spiritual significance). Mrs Poynter gave evidence that information about such a risk would have been sufficient to 'tip the balance' in favour of refusal: 37 BMLR 192 at 206–8.

as to pass unnoticed by many (typified by minor alterations in the dose or timing of licensed drugs used for standard indications).'[86] Indeed, the Royal College of Physicians (RCP) and other bodies have been keen to avoid subjecting all new strategies and procedures employed for primarily therapeutic purposes to the scrutiny typically associated with research procedures.[87] Stifling clinical discretion would inevitably slow medical progress. In the United States (and Canada) proactive peer review and approval of the Institutional Research Board (IRB) (Research Ethics Board in Canada) is normally required for all research procedures. In Britain the RCP recommends that all such procedures receive the prior approval of a local Research Ethics Committee. These procedures are *prospective* in contrast to the *retrospective* processes which have generally been applicable to therapeutic innovations, that is litigation, disciplinary processes, clinical audit, complaints procedures, etc. However, this may be an insufficient protection for vulnerable patients undergoing serious and invasive procedures with potentially devastating consequences. As Gaze and Dawson note, 'Approaches which focus on subjective motive are useful primarily for assigning responsibility ex post facto, and do not provide a useful basis for designing a scheme to minimise the risk occurring.'[88]

It has been noted that 'there has been a tendency for surgeons to rely on series of operations without objective assessment of their value'.[89] Indeed, in Britain, unlike experimental procedures using drugs or medical devices, there is no licensing procedure governing the introduction of new therapies or surgical techniques.[90] New drugs and medical devices, on the other hand, typically require approval from the FDA in the US and a (product) licence from the Medicines Control Agency and a licence from the Secretary of State for Health in Britain.[91] There is a great deal to be said

[86] S. Lind, 'Innovative Medical Therapies: Between Practice and Research' (1988) 36 *Clinical Research* 546 at 546.

[87] Dossetor notes the 'considerable ethical tension' generated by the simultaneous wish to preserve clinical discretion to innovate in patients' interests, whilst also protecting patients from the risks of uncontrolled therapeutic exploitation: see J. Dossetor, 'Innovative Treatment versus Clinical Research: An Ethics Issue in Transplantation' (1990) 22 *Transplantation Proceedings* 966 at 966.

[88] Gaze and Dawson, 'Distinguishing Medical Practice and Research', at 307–8.

[89] J. Hyde *et al.*, 'Removing Bias in Surgical Trials' (1997) 314 *British Medical Journal* 914 at 914.

[90] Although in Britain the British Academy of Royal Medical Colleges has recently set up a voluntary safety and efficacy register of new interventional procedures, SERNIP.

[91] 'Transplants or tissues or cells of human origin' are specifically excluded from the scope of the Medical Devices Regulations (SI 1994 No. 3017), reg. 3(f).

for subjecting new therapies to research procedures and protocols. In their absence, there is also the probability that outcomes risk being inadequate in terms of the ability to draw generalisable conclusions from the experience. In many instances prior clinical trials as part of a research protocol would seem to be the proper mode of introduction of the therapy itself. Arguably, xenotransplantation has been applied as a therapeutic methodology in humans in the past when a properly designed controlled trial should have preceded this. In Britain, such a protocol will undoubtedly be formulated to govern the new era of xenotransplantation.[92]

To require a full research protocol to accompany every adaptation of transplantation therapies and procedures is too stringent and unnecessary though, even if that is the 'ideal'. Nonetheless, it is submitted that novel forms of treatment with substantial repercussions for patients (not simply minor modifications of existing treatments) should undergo some form of prospective evaluation. Indeed, in the United States 'drastic departures from standard practice' *do* usually receive the approval of an IRB and in New Zealand all untried or unorthodox procedures require prior review and approval. This seems compelling and could be applied to local research ethics committees in Britain and similar agencies elsewhere. McNeill states:

> While I accept that as an ideal, I would not restrict ethics review to properly conducted research trials. I believe that all experiments which are conducted on human beings, for the purpose of obtaining new knowledge or for testing innovative procedures, should be included in the review process . . . I would include for review, experimentation in medical research and the use of innovative medical procedures such as innovations in surgery . . . My reason for arguing that experimentation rather than research is the appropriate term is that the emphasis of review should be on the protection of the subjects of experiments. The distinguishing feature of experimentation is that something new is being tried. Experiments necessarily carry with them unknown consequences. Once the consequences are known, they are no longer experiments . . . The major concern of volunteers for experimentation is not whether the study is scientifically well grounded. Rather, it is whether there is inconvenience, or economic loss, or a risk of physical or psychological harm.[93]

92 In the UK, patient trials must be approved by the UK Xenotransplantation Interim Regulatory Authority.

93 See P. McNeill, *The Ethics and Politics of Human Experimentation*, Cambridge University Press, Cambridge, 1993, at 12–13.

Minors

The issue aired here is whether transplantation as a therapy is properly consented to by parents on behalf of their children or by children themselves. Laura Davies's parents' consent to a multi-organ transplant for their five-year-old daughter raised a degree of disquiet globally, although in this instance the sheer scale and extent of the surgery, coupled with the novelty of the procedure, was the primary concern.

It is clear that a minor may refuse consent to a transplant procedure in many countries provided that he/she is able to understand the nature of the decision, the anticipated benefits of transplantation and the implications of refusal, that is where the minor is competent. In Florida, Benny Agrelo, aged fifteen years, refused a (third) liver transplant. He determined to take no further anti-rejection medication. The Florida courts respected this decision in view of the undoubted capacity of Benny to make this decision for himself, and he died the following year. However, capacity will be judged against the procedure intended. The Nuffield Council Working Party Report stated that any consent to the transplantation of an animal organ requires a higher level of maturity than normal, and the report recommended that parental consent be obtained before any such procedure is carried out upon a minor.[94]

However, in Britain, at least where the parents are in favour of the procedure, the courts will sometimes be prepared to authorise it even where the child herself objects and is not found to lack capacity, where the patient's life would be jeopardised by the refusal of treatment. In a recent case, a fifteen-year-old girl, M, who suffered sudden heart failure, and who would not survive without a heart transplant, refused to consent to it primarily because, as she put it, 'I would feel different with someone else's heart, that's a good enough reason not to have a heart transplant, even if it saved my life.' She apparently understood that she would die without the transplant but persisted in her refusal, saying that although she did not want to die she did not want to take drugs for the rest of her life either. The High Court ordered the transplant to take place. Mr Justice Johnson stated that all the risks implicated had to be weighed against the *certainty* of death. He found that the transplant was in her best interests. The

[94] Nuffield Council on Bioethics, *Animal-to-Human Transplants: The Ethics of Xenotransplantation*, Nuffield Council on Bioethics, London, March 1996, para. 7.24.

parents wished the operation to take place.[95] The judge was heavily influenced by the suddenness of the crisis and the lack of time in which the minor was able to absorb her situation and come to terms with the implications of treatment. The child was interviewed on behalf of the Official Solicitor who formed the opinion that she lacked capacity, but the judge made no such finding.

Where the minor lacks capacity to consent, the decision would typically be made by the parents, subject to the overriding of that decision by the courts on the basis that the decision is not in the best interests of the child. In *Re T (A Minor) (Wardship: Medical Treatment)*,[96] a child who was born with a life-threatening liver defect required a liver transplant, without which, according to the medical experts, he would not live beyond two and a half years. He was seventeen months old at the date of trial. Although the medical experts assessed the liver transplant as having a good chance of success, the parents refused to give consent to the operation primarily because of their assessment of the child's likely quality of life after the transplant, based partially on the experience of the child after an earlier (different) surgical procedure which had been unsuccessful. In the High Court it was decided that the transplant operation was in his best interests and that the decision of the mother to refuse to consent was not the decision of a reasonable parent. It was held on appeal, reversing the decision of the High Court, that the paramount consideration was not whether the decision was that of a reasonable parent but what the welfare of the child dictated. However, it was held that in the instant case the welfare of the child was intertwined with the predicament and attitude of the mother, who would be expected to care for him through the surgery and for many years after. Her views were therefore extremely relevant, and for the trial judge to ignore them was an error of law.[97] In the light of this, the court held that it was not in the best interests of the child for consent to the transplant to have been given.

This case has a parallel in the decision of the Saskatchewan Provincial Court in *Re Minister of Social Services and P et al.*,[98] where the court

[95] *Re M (Child: Refusal of Medical Treatment)* [1999] 2 FCR 577 (Fam. Div.). See also 'Teenage Girl's Life or Death Dilemma', *Daily Telegraph*, 16 July 1999.

[96] [1997] 1 All ER 906 (CA).

[97] The mother would have been expected to return to the jurisdiction, probably without the father, and would therefore have had to have borne the burden of caring unaided.

[98] 69 DLR (3d) 134 (1990).

deferred to the wishes of the parents of an infant approximately one year old who had an incurable liver disease, who refused to consent to a liver transplant when the child was likely to die within twelve months without it. The court found that the parents had properly considered wider issues than the purely medical ones, including the reduced quality of life thereafter caused by the perpetual drugs regime required, etc. A heavy burden was seemingly imposed upon the state to justify overriding the 'thoughtful and carefully considered decision' of the parents. A great deal of deference to parental views can be seen in these decisions, partially because the quality of aftercare itself bears on the likely success and quality of life of the transplantee.

These cases are extremely significant ones. There was no other potentially life-saving therapy available in either instance. It was therefore a balancing of quality- and quantity-of-life factors, with the views of the parents bearing heavily on the former. In so far as the parents are very likely to be the only proposed carers for the child post-transplant, the decisions display substantial deference to parental discretion and could be widely replicated. It might be thought that the decisions are very specifically linked to transplantation procedures in so far as organ recipients at present have to undertake a lifetime commitment to a toxic immunosuppressant drugs regime and are continually prone to infection because of this. Nonetheless, they are fairly surprising decisions in so far as the procedure has a good success rate and there are limited long-term (surgical) implications. Moreover, the intensive 'care' of the parents is limited in time (assuming no complications). In fact one can think of very many operations with similar, if not more substantial, long-term repercussions: in particular, the care of those with serious learning difficulties who require surgery to correct or alleviate physical anomalies. Further, the patient's quality of life, assuming no significant complications such as rejection were to develop, would be likely to be transparently more rewarding and satisfying than in very many other instances. They are therefore decisions with very great resonance.

Allocation issues

Resource issues relating to transplantation occur at the macro-level, in terms of the percentage of the available health care budget allocated to transplantation in general or to a specific transplant procedure,[99] and also at the micro-level in terms of which *patients* are allocated the relevant resources, that is organs or tissues. Resources for all therapies are of course finite, but (human) organ transplantation[100] is unique in so far as it involves an 'intrinsic scarcity';[101] even if unlimited monies were made available this would not necessarily ensure an adequate supply of organs to meet the relevant demand. However, if sufficient monies were available at the macro-level to fund all necessary transplant procedures *and* sufficient organs were available to meet the demand fully, no micro-issues of selective allocation between patients would arise (only of their most effective distribution). Regrettably, this is a contingency rarely witnessed over the history of transplantation.

Rationing and allocation decision-making occurs at different levels and involves diverse groups of decision-makers. Of course, what funding priority transplantation receives and the degree of funding of a specific transplant procedure are principally political matters usually decided at a national or regional level. Distribution decisions as they affect individual patients occur at four distinct stages. First, there is the question of which organs are available for allocation. This is essentially a question of the size of the organ pool, which in turn is partially a function of the organ procurement system in force. Secondly, there is the matter of who is eligible to receive a transplant if an organ is available. Thirdly, a person must be accepted on to a relevant waiting list for the organ(s) concerned, that is accepted as a (transplant) candidate. Finally, his/her 'claim' for a particular organ needs to be weighed against the claims of others with similar conditions.[102]

There has been much debate about whether these are matters for determination by clinicians or by society as a whole. Some have argued

[99] Of course, on an even broader plane, there is the issue of what priority health care funding receives as compared with competitors such as defence, education, welfare, etc.

[100] Of course, this is by virtue of the donation system for human organs. Where there is an abundant potential supply constrained only by cost considerations the situation is different, for example implicating artificial or animal organs. There will be very substantial development costs associated with such therapeutic modalities.

[101] Moody remarks that 'Organ transplantation involves an intrinsic scarcity: the desired object cannot simply be produced in greater quantity by spending more money so the scarcity is unavoidable': see H. Moody, 'Allocation, Yes; Age-based Rationing, No' in R. Binstock and S. Post (eds.) *Too Old for Health Care?*, Johns Hopkins University Press, Baltimore, 1991, at 193.

[102] This analysis borrows from A. Caplan, 'Equity in the Selection of Recipients for Cardiac Transplants' (1987) 75(1) *Circulation* 10.

that medical professionals should have either sole or ultimate control over the process, as indeed they have had historically. Veatch challenges this view, claiming that allocation is a moral not a technical matter and observing that such decisions are not properly made wholly on the basis of either factual or clinical information, even if such information is involved in the decision.[103] Notions of property and responsibility infiltrate the debate here. The United States Task Force on Organ Transplantation considered that

> Organs are donated on behalf of all potential recipients; this implies that the organ is to be used for the good of the community, and ultimately the community must decide what serves the public interest. Although the gift is presently made to a person, agency, or institution, surgeons and organ procurement agencies should view themselves as stewards or trustees of this resource. The physicians who select the recipient of a donated organ are making decisions about how a scarce public resource should be used. Such a decision should be determined by criteria based on need, effectiveness, and fairness that are publicly stated and publicly defended.[104]

On the other hand, Land has noted that 'The history of development and establishment of post mortem organ procurement over the past two decades has been dominated by the profession-driven assumption that transplant surgeons and physicians (or institutions involved in organ procurement) are supposed to obtain (lawful) ownership of transplantable organs',[105] leading to the idea of 'locally owned' organs for disposal according to the discretion of the centre concerned. Of course, whatever criteria are employed, clinicians will, through assessments of diagnosis and need, be centrally involved in the destination of organs in any event.

Allocation issues are unavoidably intertwined with organ procurement practices. As the US Task Force put it, 'Continued public support for organ transplantation depends on public confidence that organs are

[103] R. Veatch, 'Who Empowers Medical Doctors to Make Allocative Decisions for Dialysis and Organ Transplantation?' in W. Land and J. Dossetor (eds.), *Organ Replacement Therapy: Ethics, Justice, Commerce*, Springer-Verlag, Berlin, 1991, 331. He views organs as belonging to society which is then obliged to determine how they should be distributed within the society.

[104] Report of the Task Force on Organ Transplantation, *Organ Transplantation: Issues and Recommendations*, US Department of Health and Human Services, Washington D.C., 1986, at 86.

[105] W. Land, 'The Dilemma of Organ Allocation: The Combination of a Therapeutic Modality for an Ill Individual with the Distribution of a Scarce Valuable Public (Healing) Good' in G. Collins, J. Dubernard, W. Land and G. Persijn (eds.), *Procurement, Preservation and Allocation of Vascularized Organs*, Kluwer, Dordrecht, 1997, 359 at 360.

distributed equitably to those who need them.'[106] In France and Germany organ procurement levels have fallen recently partly on account of perceived inequities in this regard. In the United States, although blacks have a higher rate of end-stage renal failure, they also have historically donated at a lower rate than whites, partially it would seem because of perceived injustices in allocation.[107] There are also occasional cases arising involving celebrities or very wealthy individuals which, fairly or not, are perceived by many to fail the so-called 'smell test': for instance, Pennsylvania Governor Robert Casey received a heart and liver transplant within twenty-four hours and the baseball great, Mickey Mantle, received a liver transplant in June 1995 only days after being placed on the waiting list. In the UK in 1999, controversy surrounded a 73-year-old US billionaire who was given a heart transplant at the Harefield Hospital because there was allegedly nobody on the national waiting list who was a suitable match.[108] Even when the allegations lack substance, the stigma lingers, hence the need for the involvement of society in setting criteria and for total transparency in their formulation and application.

Macro-issues: the green screen

Whether all forms of transplantation are paid for by the state depends upon the particular health care system under consideration, but in every case only 'proven' therapies will generally be made widely available. But is there an obligation upon the state to provide without charge all proven transplant modalities? As Dossetor has remarked, 'In the developing world, ability to pay is the main allocative factor for renal transplants.'[109] Whilst all the costs of renal replacement therapies are met by the state in the United States through the Medicare/Medicaid scheme, heart, liver, lung and heart/lung transplants are not so universally funded. Patients will not normally be referred for transplant evaluation at all, or if they are, will not be accepted by the transplant programme, unless they have such insurance or other means of payment. Such transplants are nevertheless

[106] Task Force, *Organ Transplantation*, at 85.

[107] Which may be justified, because the prevailing US system relies heavily on HLA tissue matching which disadvantages blacks as a consequence, due to their less distinct antigen composition.

[108] L. Rogers, 'US Billionaire Jumps Queue for NHS Heart', *Sunday Times*, 28 February 1999.

[109] J. Dossetor, 'Principles Used in Organ Allocation' in Land and Dossetor, *Organ Replacement Therapy*, 393 at 394.

extremely expensive and benefit a relatively small number of individuals. These factors probably explain the low priority accorded to such (liver and thoracic) transplants by the voters in Oregon under their health care funding referendum. Thus, whilst donors would probably prefer that donated organs be distributed according to medical need rather than ability to pay, as Moskop states, 'it does not follow that the state has a moral or legal obligation to them to make their organs available to all in need'.[110] A thought regarding developing nations without even adequate primary care shows the obvious correctness of this view.[111] It does not, however, mean that individuals *with* the means to pay should be denied such therapy where it is available.[112] Of course, where a therapy is limited by the ability to pay there is a danger that the poor will decline to donate on the ground that they are not themselves potential beneficiaries under the scheme, but it nevertheless is appropriate in some instances but not others for the state to provide reimbursement for certain transplant procedures, and in other contexts for the state to fund no transplantation whatever.

As mentioned above, such decisions would be essentially political decisions, and on account of this, no legal recourse would generally lie for a failure to allot sufficient resources. In Britain, public law actions for judicial review would generally be brought on the basis of the duties imposed upon the Secretary of State for Health and relevant health authorities by the National Health Service Act 1977. Section 1 creates a duty on the Secretary of State to 'continue the promotion of a comprehensive health service in England and Wales', whilst section 3(1) states that he also has a duty to provide, 'to such extent as he considers necessary to meet all reasonable requirements', certain forms of health care, for

110 J. Moskop, 'Ability to Pay and Access to Transplantation' in Land and Dossetor, *Organ Replacement Therapy*, 433 at 435.

111 Laura Davies's second, and regrettably ill-fated, transplant at Pittsburgh was estimated to have cost £1 million, paid primarily from public donations and by a public benefactor, King Fahd of Saudi Arabia. However, in the US context, the US Task Force rejected ability to pay as a criterion for a liver or heart transplant and recommended that the government fund such therapies, based on the commitment of society to meet basic health needs and the fact that organs are donated for the good of the public as a whole: see Task Force, *Organ Transplantation*, at 102.

112 An interesting case arose with respect to a prisoner, James Earl Ray, Martin Luther King's killer, who developed cirrhosis of the liver caused by a chronic hepatitis C infection he acquired in prison. He requested that the state pay $250,000 for a life-saving liver transplant. He alleged that an incarcerated person was unable to raise insurance money in the same way as a free person was able to do, as insurance is usually an employment-related privilege.

example medical, dental, nursing and ambulance services. An action was brought in *R* v. *Secretary of State for Social Services ex parte Hincks* on the basis of both sections 1 and 3 with regard to the failure to allocate funds to an anticipated new hospital orthopaedic wing. The Court of Appeal held that there was no absolute duty created under either section and that the availability of resources was a relevant consideration to take into account. Lord Denning MR went so far as to state that 'it cannot be supposed that the Secretary of State has to provide all the kidney machines which are asked for, or for all the new developments such as heart transplants in every case where people would benefit from them'.[113] For such an action to succeed in the absence of any procedural impropriety, it would have been necessary to establish that the failure to allocate such resources constituted *Wednesbury*[114] unreasonableness, that is an omission that no reasonable person in that position could have made. The grounds for challenge are generally unlawfulness, irrationality, a failure to take into account relevant considerations or the inclusion of irrelevant factors in decision-making.[115]

Thus, even if sufficient donor organs existed this does not in itself place a legal obligation on the state to fund all such transplants. However, it has been suggested by Kennedy and Grubb that in an extreme case where no services at all were provided an action for judicial review might succeed.[116] This view is borne out by the decision of the Court of Appeal in a recent case involving a health authority's refusal to fund gender reassignment surgery for male-to-female transsexuals.[117] The Court held that such a blanket ban was bad in law as rational consideration had not been given to the fact that it was a recognised medical condition requiring surgery in some instances to avoid extreme mental distress. Relevant considerations had not been taken into account whereas irrelevant considerations had. However, one should bear in mind the limitations of such an action. No damages could be awarded (only an order of *certiorari*) nor could the authority be required to allocate funding to such surgery. Moreover, had funding been refused

113 (1980) 1 BMLR 93 at 95 (CA).

114 Following the name of the relevant case, *Associated Provincial Picture Houses Ltd* v. *Wednesbury Corporation* [1948] 1 KB 223.

115 See *Council of Civil Service Unions* v. *Minister for the Civil Service* [1985] AC 374 (HL).

116 Kennedy and Grubb, *Medical Law*, at 429.

117 *R* v. *West Lancashire Health Authority ex parte A* (1998) LEXIS Transcript. The Authority had decided that psychotherapy was the appropriate therapy for such a condition instead.

following an individual assessment of need no proper legal challenge could have been successfully mounted as the authority would not then have 'fettered its discretion'.

Thus, where resource implications are attached to medical decision-making, it is necessary to preserve medical discretion to the appropriate degree and to avoid arbitrariness in the allocation of a particular therapy.[118] Whilst a blanket ban on a specific therapy might not be permissible under a national health scheme such as in the United Kingdom, a decision to refuse a transplant to an individual patient linked to issues of cost may be sustainable in a case where the benefits of the therapy are at least arguable, if not dubious. For instance, a failure to stump up £1 million for a second (highly experimental) transplant for Laura Davies would have been unimpeachable. This is borne out by the decision of the Court of Appeal in England in *R* v. *Cambridgeshire Health Authority ex parte B*[119] where the health authority refused to fund further chemotherapy treatment and a potential further bone marrow transplant for Jaymee Bowen, an eleven-year-old with leukaemia. The court rejected the action for judicial review, emphasising the broad discretion accorded to health authorities in the allocation of funds. This 'hands off' approach was endorsed by the Court of Appeal in the earlier case of *R* v. *Secretary of State for Social Services ex parte Walker* where Sir John Donaldson MR stated that 'It is not for this court, or indeed any court, to substitute its own judgment for the judgment of those who are responsible for the allocation of resources.'[120]

Where a resource is finite, there will often be an attempt to limit access to a therapy according to particular (non-economic) criteria. In 1997 Wiltshire Health Authority issued guidance to doctors that priority for treatment for kidney failure should be given to those whose lives could be prolonged and who could regain an independent lifestyle, bearing in mind that it only had sufficient funds to pay for the treatment of forty-two new

[118] This is reinforced by the recent decision of the High Court in *R* v. *Secretary of State for Health ex parte Pfizer Ltd* [1999] Lloyd's Law Reports (Medical) 289 (QBD), where overly rigid guidance to general practitioners concerning the prescribing of the drug Sildenafil (Viagra) was struck down on both domestic and European law grounds.

[119] [1995] 2 All ER 129 (CA). Montgomery argues that this case was based primarily upon clinical considerations, that is the child's best interests: see J. Montgomery, *Health Care Law*, Oxford University Press, Oxford, 1997, at 65. However, resource factors clearly also played a sizeable role.

[120] (1987) 3 BMLR 32 (CA).

cases per year.[121] In Britain access to transplantation, notably cardiac transplantation, has also previously been subject to age limits. An age range of fifteen to fifty was initially established at some centres, with the upper limit transparently guided by the need to ration the therapy by limiting the number of potentially eligible patients by reference to clinical effectiveness. In the US there is a common age limit around sixty-five years of age. But are such limits ethically or legally defensible? In *R* v. *Sheffield Health Authority ex parte Seale*,[122] the health authority imposed an age ceiling of thirty-five upon *in vitro* fertilisation (IVF) services. The applicant was thirty-seven and was refused access to such services. Her action for judicial review failed. The health authority's decision was held not to be irrational and therefore not *Wednesbury* unreasonable. The policy was based on reliable advice that the efficacy of IVF decreased with age. If based on the same rationale, a restriction on transplantation to individuals above a certain age might also be upheld, based similarly on declining efficacy. Graft and patient transplant survival rates published by UNOS for the years up to 1996 highlight the fact that survival rates for recipients of heart transplants were optimal between eleven and thirty-four years of age, and that kidney transplants were less efficacious for recipients above forty-nine years of age.[123] But a word of caution is required. No 'blanket ban' could be justified purely on the basis of age on *clinical grounds* in either instance – this would have been 'irrational'. It is the resource allocation rationale underpinning it which bolsters its acceptability, subject of course to the patient being able to establish that he or she is an exceptional case in any specific instance, so as to avoid an authority fettering its discretion. Thus, justifiable restrictions, even those based on certain classes of individual, might be upheld if based on adequate justificatory criteria.

Eligibility

Not only may eligibility turn upon allocation policies imposed by public institutions or individuals acting in a public capacity, but limitations may seemingly attach to the 'donation' itself.

[121] 'Doctors Told How to Ration Kidney Care', *The Times*, 31 May 1997. The approach adopted was seemingly analogous to the application of Quality-Adjusted Life Years (QALYs) here.

[122] (1994) 25 BMLR 1.

[123] See UNOS, OPTN Annual Report 1998, UNOS, at http://www.unos.org/data/anrpt98/ar98_data_03.htm.

Designated donation

Questions arise here as to the legitimacy of organ donation restricted to a specific individual recipient or to a specific *class* of recipient. Certain legal regimes appear specifically to contemplate the former. The 1987 version of the Uniform Anatomical Gift Act in the United States stipulates that amongst eligible 'donees' of a gift are, *inter alia*, 'a designated individual for transplantation or therapy needed by that individual'.[124] Moreover, UNOS has recently itself accepted the possibility of relatives of the deceased donating to specific individuals. Designated donation is moreover the norm for *living* organ donation. Almost all organs are donated to specific known individuals, usually members of the same family by law or by blood. This appears to be accepted and to generate no controversy whatever. Of course, such organs would not otherwise be offered to any other person and so do not 'deplete' the existing donor pool, indeed they decrease the number of recipients waiting for a cadaveric organ. Kluge observes that it is the fact that the living individual is donating to a member of their family that is the principal 'ethically distinguishing' and justificatory feature. He states: 'family ties, then, are uniquely privileging and identifying, and designated organ donation occurring within the immediate family context does not violate the equality-and-justice condition'.[125] One might even extend such a rationale to close emotional 'relatives'. If this is so for living organ donation there does not seem any reason why the same should not apply also in respect of cadaveric donation.[126] Indeed, in 1994, a gift was accepted from relatives of a woman who had died in a motor vehicle accident in Tennessee for the benefit only of her father, who was on the waiting list for a heart transplant in Michigan.

However, where the donation is a 'class-directed' donation we may have reason to think differently. In 1990, in Florida, the family of a member of the Ku Klux Klan who was shot and killed agreed to organ

[124] Section 6. The Human Tissue Act 1961 is entirely mute on the question of the 'donee'.

[125] E. Kluge, 'Designated Organ Donation: Private Choice in Social Context' (1989) 19 *Hastings Center Report* 10 at 12.

[126] One of the reasons given for rejecting payment to living *unrelated* donors is that, in the words of the US Task Force, 'payments to living unrelated donors also violate equitable access, because [they give] a recipient who can afford to buy an organ a chance to have a transplant that is denied to someone who cannot pay': see Task Force, *Organ Transplantation*, at 98.

donation but only for the benefit of a white recipient. More recently in Britain an Asian man who was dying was prepared to donate his organs after death, but only to a Muslim. His 'gift' was declined.[127] However, at about the same time a hospital in Sheffield acceded to the wish of a family that the deceased's organs be given only to a 'white' recipient. The British Government immediately declared its abhorrence of such restrictions and set up a panel to consider the issue and report to the Government. The Report of the Panel – 'An Investigation into Conditional Organ Donation' – was issued in February 2000. It condemned the practice of conditional donation and recommended that organs must not be accepted if the donor or family wished to attach conditions about the recipient. It additionally recommended that such guidance be formalised by the Department of Health and should apply to all such conditions, not merely those of a racist nature. It did not, however, consider it necessary to recommend any changes to the law.[128] Whilst UNOS accepts the general relevance of autonomy as a guiding allocative principle, it has stated that 'we believe this kind of autonomy should not be permitted when the recipient is defined by sociological category such as race or gender or religion'.[129] Fox also states that 'I would thus argue that directed donation to recipients personally known to the donor is morally justifiable. Other categories of directed donation are morally problematic, however.'[130] The principle of justice would appear to be infringed in such cases. As Kluge states, according to Rawls, if the otherwise free and unconstrained choice of an individual infringes on equality and justice, it will not be a legitimate exercise of autonomy and must be rejected. He notes that an organ is a *social good* and states that 'Organ donation is not an act that is complete in itself. It is a social act. Directly or indirectly it involves all of society.'[131] In fact, most state statutes appear to have no provision for a gift to be

[127] See 'Surgeons Ignored Donor Conditions', *The Times*, 9 July 1999. This article reports that in the sixties, organs arrived in England from Northern Ireland stating 'Only to be used by a Catholic' or 'Only to be used by a Protestant'. Apparently these 'directions' were ignored.

[128] The Report of the Panel, An Investigation into Conditional Organ Donation, February 2000, at www.doh.gov.uk/organdonation/report.htm.

[129] UNOS Ethical Committee, 'General Principles for Allocating Human Organs and Tissues' (1992) 24 *Transplantation Proceedings* 2227 at 2234.

[130] See M. Fox, 'Directed Organ Donation: Donor Autonomy and Community Values' in B. Spielman (ed.), *Organ and Tissue Donation: Ethical, Legal and Policy Issues*, Southern Illinois University Press, Carbondale, 1997, 43 at 49.

[131] Kluge, 'Designated Organ Donation', at 11.

made to a *class* of donor.[132] Thus, such class-directed donations should be rejected. Indeed, where the distinguishing basis is race or sex in particular, it is very likely that any such allocation would infringe primary legislation in Britain and elsewhere prohibiting discrimination in the provision of goods or services.[133] Contrary to other commentators it would also seem to undermine the gift in its entirety.[134]

Access to waiting lists

This leads us directly into a discussion as to *who is* eligible to receive an available organ for transplantation. The US Task Force stated that 'There is general agreement that the waiting list of transplantation candidates should be determined primarily by medical criteria.'[135] Especially thorny issues arise though, as to whether non-residents should be entitled to receive domestically procured organs and as to eligibility where the patient's condition is a product of his/her prior (supposedly) 'blameworthy' conduct.

Non-residents

Within Europe, the waiting lists of some countries have been disproportionately swelled by foreign nationals, most notably Italian patients on waiting lists for kidneys in Austria, Belgium and France, something which generated substantial disquiet in France in particular.[136] The effect will often be to reduce the likelihood of a resident being transplanted at all, or at least to extend the wait for an organ. Transplants of foreign patients have occurred across the board. In the United Kingdom in 1985 an enquiry took place into allegations that a Greek patient came to London and was transplanted with a kidney from an NHS patient at a private hospital, despite the general allocation principle that NHS kidneys should first go to NHS patients. In the US wealthy foreigners have consistently received organ transplants at major American transplant

[132] See, for example, section 8612, Pennsylvania Act 102, Chapter 86, 1994.

[133] See A. MacLean, 'Organ Donation, Racism and the Race Relations Act' (1999) 149 *New Law Journal* 1250.

[134] Ibid., at 1252.

[135] Task Force, *Organ Transplantation*, at 87.

[136] It also shows that looking at the impact of transplants performed upon waiting list sizes in isolation can be misleading.

centres charging very high fees. The US Task Force forcefully asserted that 'If money is the real reason for assigning priority to non-immigrant aliens, then some transplant institutions are selling organs that have been donated to them without charge',[137] and as a result of its recommendations federal law has limited the number of non-resident citizens permitted to receive US organs to 10 per cent of a transplant programme's patients. Today, UNOS audits any programme that performs more than 5 per cent of transplants on non-residents, and the export outside the US of any organ is authorised by UNOS only on a case-by-case basis, that is where the organ cannot be utilised by any American citizen.

The US Task Force nevertheless rejected a blanket ban or 'Americans first' policy in view of the fact that sickness has no national boundaries[138] – hence the compromise measure currently in force. But many feel that a person typically donates 'to his/her country' and not more widely. Indeed, some support the 'local donor' model on the ground that one generally donates on a more local, for example state or county, rather than a nationwide, basis. A 'national perspective' also generates problems for agencies such as Eurotransplant which procure and distribute organs on a supra-national basis. For example, some Belgian nationals give organs to non-Belgian nationals within the Eurotransplant area. Eurotransplant recently introduced its own 'non-resident' policy for kidney patients from outside the Eurotransplant region.[139] The potential effect on public willingness to donate means that such issues need to be taken seriously. Customary usage may often evidence acceptance and willingness but caution is advisable. On the other hand, refusing treatment to non-nationals may be potentially problematic, especially within the European Union, where there is a duty to ensure the free movement of labour, goods and services within the Member States. It has been held that to refuse dialysis facilities to another EC national is unlawful, where he/she had been receiving it regularly beforehand in another Member State, and

137 Task Force, *Organ Transplantation*, at 93. Similar motives have been imputed to Austrian hospitals permitting foreigners to obtain transplants there.

138 Caplan entirely rejects allocation of medical care on the basis of race, nationality or ethnicity: see Caplan, 'Equity in the Selection', at 15.

139 The policy was specifically introduced to safeguard and guarantee the legitimate confidence of the people within Eurotransplant. See B. Haase-Kromwijk, F. du Pre and B. Cohen, 'Organ Transplantation and European Community Law: The Case of Non-Residents' (1997) 2(3) *Journal of Health Services Research Policy* 168. The view in this article was that this policy did not infringe European competition law because an objective necessity argument could be mounted.

where he/she has travelled to that other state to work.[140] The situation where the person has travelled to another Member State solely for the purpose of accessing treatment and facilities there is less clear. However, where such treatment *is* made available, there are seemingly increasing obligations on the state in which they are domiciled to fund such treatment.[141]

Prior fault

It has been increasingly suggested that a person could be legitimately denied access to a particular therapy such as transplantation on the basis of prior culpable conduct causing or contributing to his condition. It has occasionally been explicitly contended that alcoholics should be denied liver transplants occasioned by the development of cirrhosis of the liver on this basis. Although such a criterion has never explicitly been adopted for access to transplantation, some allege that it operates covertly. The argument surfaced in Britain in 1997 in the context of a fatal accidents inquiry in Scotland concerning a girl aged fifteen years (Michelle Paul) who was refused a liver transplant at Edinburgh Royal Infirmary after having taken an ecstasy tablet. The family alleged that this was a decision based on 'moral' not 'medical' grounds, but at the inquiry it was accepted that medical utility considerations alone were operative in the decision.[142] Whatever the truth, it is essential to screen out moral judgements here. As Gillon states, 'despite the attractiveness of certain "prior fault" arguments, their Achilles heel is that . . . there is an important countervailing moral tradition in medicine. It is that patients should be given treatment in relation to their medical need, and that scarce resources should not be prioritised on the basis of a patient's blameworthiness.'[143] Thus, alcoholics should not be *a priori* excluded from liver transplants but, notwithstand-

[140] See *Re Dialysis Treatment* [1984] 3 CMLR 242.

[141] See *Decker* v. *Caisse de Maladie des Employés Privés* (Case C-120/95); *Kohll* v. *Union des Caisses de Maladie* (Case C-158/96) (1999) 48 BMLR 32 (Court of Justice of the European Communities).

[142] There was evidence that she was not placed on the waiting list because of irreversible brain damage. Her GP also gave evidence that because of the family's history of drug abuse, her post-operative care would have been compromised. See *The Times*, 24 January 1997 and 25 January 1997. See also C. Dyer, 'Doctors Accused of Refusing Transplant on Moral Grounds' (1997) 314 *British Medical Journal* 1370.

[143] R. Gillon, 'On Giving Preference to Prior Volunteers when Allocating Organs for Transplantation' (1995) 21 *Journal of Medical Ethics* 195 at 196.

ing, may ultimately be denied a transplant because genuine allocative factors may tend to prioritise other waiting patients over them.

Free riders

A similar kind of argument is that, as the Law Reform Commission of Canada put it, 'theories of justice and social contract might suggest that one must be willing to give to be entitled to receive',[144] although it ultimately doubted if this principle was a just one in the context of organ allocation. Nevertheless, proposals are frequently put forward based on such a principle. Jarvis's 'modest' *join the club* proposal would make eligibility to receive an organ transplant contingent on that person having registered a willingness to be an organ donor.[145] He argues that the current system encourages the 'free rider' and that his scheme would produce an increase in the number of potential registered donors.[146] However, these proposals are subject to the same riposte as above, that it is the person's medical need that generates the imperative to provide care, not that individual's extraneous behaviour, even selfish, inconsiderate or immoral behaviour in refusing to volunteer their own organs.

Nonetheless, this strategy finds legislative expression in the presumed consent scheme under the Human Organ Transplants Act 1987 in Singapore which applies to the entire population of Singapore apart from Muslims, who are taken presumptively to *object* to organ donation based on their religion and who must 'opt in' instead under a different legal regime.[147] The Law then goes on to state that a person who has not registered an objection to organ removal under the 1987 Act shall have priority in allocation over other individuals. However, Dickens rightly notes that

[144] Law Reform Commission of Canada, *Procurement and Transfer of Human Tissues and Organs*, Working Paper 66, Minister of Supply and Services, Ottawa, 1992, at 51.

[145] R. Jarvis, 'Join the Club: A Modest Proposal to Increase Availability of Donor Organs' (1995) 21 *Journal of Medical Ethics* 199.

[146] S. Eaton, 'The Subtle Politics of Organ Donation: A Proposal' (1998) 24 *Journal of Medical Ethics* 166. She offers a slight modification to this scheme whereby such willingness would 'count' only where there were two equally eligible recipients, and advocates a combined presumed consent and preference system based on the *contingent interdependence* between potential donors and recipients which is recognised and enforced by a presumed consent system (although the symbolic nature of such a scheme was said to be its most important attribute).

[147] The Medical Therapy Act 1972. Muslims comprise approximately 16 per cent of the population.

> In prioritizing the entitlement to receive kidney transplantation of passive non-Muslims over passive Muslims, and requiring the latter to declare and register their willingness to donate their kidneys in order to enjoy the same priority as non-objecting non-Muslims, the legislation is liable to scrutiny under international human rights conventions that prohibit discrimination on grounds of race, religion and ethnic origins.[148]

If such a scheme were to operate under certain other national legal systems it would also be legally suspect domestically. Not only would 'religion' be a suspect classification under the Fourteenth Amendment in terms of equal treatment, but this would probably lead to a successful action for judicial review in Britain based upon irrationality. This is bolstered by the fact that UK law now incorporates the European Convention on Human Rights which includes Article 14 on Prohibition on Discrimination which states that 'The enjoyment of the rights and freedoms set forth in this Convention shall be secured without discrimination on any ground such as sex, race, colour, language, religion, political or other opinion, national or social origin, association with a national minority, property, birth, or other status.' Whilst this is parasitic on the applicability of some other article of the Convention, refusal of transplantation might well call in aid Article 2 on the Right to Life.[149]

Thus, many criteria used to deny access to transplantation would be invalid as supported by irrational considerations and subject to judicial review. This might apply to age-based conditions for instance, *a fortiori* illegal conditions, such as those attaching to race, sex and disability where statutory provisions prohibit discrimination on those bases in the provision of goods and services.[150] There are similar provisions elsewhere, often more extensive ones. A blanket policy of excluding persons with learning disabilities, for instance, might constitute disability discrimination in the United States, and give rise to liability under section 504 of the Rehabilitation Act, the Americans with Disabilities Act 1990, or both.

[148] Although he says that this may not be so if it is perceived that the duty publicly to record one's unwillingness to donate is itself viewed as an oppressive burden: see B. Dickens, 'Legal and Judicial Aspects of Post Mortem Organ Donation' in Collins *et al.*, *Procurement, Preservation and Allocation*, 343 at 351.

[149] See J. Wadham and H. Mountfield, *Blackstone's Guide to the Human Rights Act 1998*, Blackstone Press, London, 1999, at 110–13.

[150] Under the Race Relations Act 1976, the Sex Discrimination Act 1975 and the Disability Discrimination Act 1995 in Britain.

Micro-allocation decisions

The final, and most difficult issue to resolve is, once an organ has become available, who should receive it? It is rare for transplant legislation to contain provisions relating to allocation, but the more recent statutes passed in the Netherlands and Germany both have some provisions of this kind. The former stipulates in section 18(3) that

> In designating the recipient, account is to be taken of no other factors than the blood compatibility and histocompatibility of the donor and the recipient of the organ, the medical urgency for the recipient and other circumstances associated with the state of the organ, and also, if these factors are not decisive, the length of time the recipient must wait.[151]

The primary focus upon medical criteria for allocation was endorsed by the World Health Organisation Guiding Principles which state that 'In the light of the principles of distributive justice and equity, donated organs should be made available to patients on the basis of medical need and not on the basis of financial or other considerations.'[152] The Council of Europe Draft Protocol on Organ Transplantation states, in Article 3, that 'Each Party shall guarantee that a system exists to provide equitable access to transplantation services for patients which ensures that organs and tissue are allocated in conformity with transparent and duly justified rules taking particular account of medical criteria.'[153] The Commentary adds that

> Scarce organs and tissues should be allocated so as to maximise the benefit of transplantation . . . For example, medical criteria such as tissue matching which affect the likelihood of success of the transplant will be arguably the most important criteria but other factors such as time on the waiting list may have to be included if allocation is seen to be fair.[154]

One can see already the heavy reliance placed upon medical criteria, principally revolving around the notion of *utility*. The King's Fund Institute noted a shift towards utilitarianism in organ allocation during the eighties and nineties in Anglo-American debates.[155] Indeed the US

[151] Law of 24 May 1996.

[152] WHO, Guiding Principles on Organ Transplantation, 1991, Principle 9.

[153] Draft Protocol, 9 March 1999.

[154] Ibid.

[155] King's Fund Institute, *A Question of Give and Take*, Research Report 18, King's Fund Institute, London, 1994, at 75.

Task Force similarly spoke of the imperative of *equitable access* and the need for allocation to be both fair and ethical, and stated: 'We believe the most ethical means of organ distribution is to use medical criteria . . . which are designed to use organs to maximise graft and patient survival and quality of life.'[156] It added that the prevailing ethos is to allocate organs to the recipient who will live the longest with the highest quality of life.[157] In fact the UNOS Ethical Committee commented that the principle of utility (interpreted as net medical benefit) is so obvious to many in the transplant community that many assume that well-grounded prediction of good medical outcome is the *only* reasonable principle upon which an ethical allocation could be based.[158] However, there has always been a tension in allocation between the utilitarian approach focusing on maximising potential benefits (outcomes) and an approach based on medical need (that is the sickest) which is more essentially deontological in orientation.[159] In some instances, as the US Task Force noted, 'Urgency of need may conflict with the probability of success.'[160]

In certain instances, allocation criteria are 'centre-based' rather than 'patient-based'. For instance, quite apart from the historical bias in the local use of organs which is discussed further below, the Eurotransplant allocation criteria for livers are, except where there is a 'highly urgent' recipient registered elsewhere, governed by centre criteria rather than patient criteria. Mason and McCall Smith rightly point out that ultimately such organs still need to be distributed as between individuals, but this nevertheless fundamentally alters the nature of the allocation process.[161] The primary goal of such criteria was to reduce the proportion of unused livers, which is clearly a valid goal in itself, supported by both utility and justice considerations, and it is debated more fully below. However, as Land notes, a centre-based policy tends to feed the notion that individual centres own the relevant organs and therefore can create their own individual allocation policies.

156 Task Force, *Organ Transplantation*, at 87.

157 Ibid.

158 UNOS, 'General Principles for Allocating', at 2228.

159 The notion of a 'Quality-Adjusted Life Year' (QALY) which has infiltrated resource allocation decision-making in Britain favours outcome measures and is for that reason regarded by some as discriminatory in not valuing each person equally and not giving as much weight to saving life as the length of preserved quality of life.

160 Task Force, *Organ Transplantation*, at 88.

161 J. Mason and A. McCall Smith, *Law and Medical Ethics*, 5th edn, Butterworths, London, 1999, at 301.

Measures for allocation

Currently, allocation models vary depending upon the type of organ. Where utility is the primary factor, there is a tendency towards heavy reliance upon tissue matching, as the commentary to the Council of Europe's Draft Protocol (above) recognises, which will tend to favour a national, or even broader, procurement and distribution area to maximise the chances of favourable tissue matching. Indeed, the US Task Force recommended a national organ-sharing system in the mid-eighties to replace the existing regime, and also that organ sharing be mandatory for perfectly matched or no-mismatched donor–recipient pairings. Currently within UNOS, a complicated points system, including factors such as HLA matching and waiting time, calculates the priority listing of different potential kidney recipients where there are no (prioritised) zero mismatched potential recipients. Within Eurotransplant also, all recipients without any HLA mismatches are prioritised and prioritisation then occurs according to the number and types of mismatch, although since 1996 points have also been awarded on the basis of waiting time, centre balance and distance between hospital and transplant centre.[162] Methods of allocation are influenced by the maximum acceptable preservation times for various organs (that is four hours for hearts, lungs and heart/lungs, eight to ten hours for pancreases and livers, and thirty-six hours for kidneys), as limited preservation times affect viability and restrict the time available for adequate HLA matching to be performed. Thus, at present such matching is routinely performed only for kidney transplants, although in any event the influence of HLA matching on outcomes is much less well established for hepatic and thoracic than for renal organs. For thoracic and hepatic transplants, organ size is an extremely important factor.

With regard to renal organs the conflict between medical urgency and medical benefit surfaces less acutely and frequently because of the alternative of dialysis for most patients, preventing loss of life. However, it is much more critical for hepatic and thoracic organs. As Steinbrook has

[162] In the UK, the UKTSSA also introduced a new kidney allocation scheme in 1998 under which zero mismatched kidneys are offered to the national pool if there is no zero mismatched local recipient, after which 'favourable' matches are allocated nationally but with one of the pair used locally. All other kidneys are for use by the retrieving unit or by the local waiting list alliance.

said in the context of liver allocation, 'The choices are difficult – for example, whether to assign the highest priority to the sickest patients or those likely to survive the longest or have best quality of life.'[163] With regard to both hearts and livers, primary weight is routinely given to medical urgency. This is especially appropriate in many instances because the individual with the less urgent condition will have a later chance to be transplanted anyhow (which is itself an independent justice factor[164]), whereas the patient in immediate need may even die without being transplanted on this one occasion. However, this will cause problems where the individual's prognosis is poor even with a transplant. Organs are frequently given to patients with an unstable condition who may often not survive the operation. In the United States there are small groups of patients with *acute* liver failure who are prioritised over those with chronic liver disease on account of the fact that they have better prospects for survival than those who have been on the waiting list longer but have a worse overall prognosis. However, the UNOS liver allocation criteria do not disadvantage patients who require a repeat (re)transplantation and whose need is great, despite the rapidly accumulating evidence that results from retransplants are significantly poorer than with first grafts.

Some would accord exclusive priority to maximum possible benefit. Khauli, for instance, states that 'Allowing equitable principles to diminish overall success rates is a betrayal of society as well as the commitment obligation owed to the deceased donor.'[165] Indeed, Kluge is right to point out that the principle of equality of persons ('equitable access') does not require that everyone be *treated equally*. We must not discriminate between persons but may discriminate between their competing claims, for example medical need. In other words, we may adopt *condition-specific* but not *person-specific* criteria. In this sense, justice and utility are not so obviously at odds. However, it is proper that attention should be devoted not just to the aggregate of medical good but to the *way* in which the medical good is distributed between individuals within the community.

[163] R. Steinbrook, 'Allocating Livers – Devising a Fair System' (1997) 336 *New England Journal of Medicine* 436 at 436.

[164] This is why highly sensitised patients are prioritised in most regions, as the likelihood of receiving a transplant subsequently is smaller than in general because of the reduced probability of achieving an appropriate match.

[165] R. Khauli, 'Issues and Controversies Surrounding Organ Donation and Transplantation: The Need for Laws that Ensure Equity and Optimal Utility of a Scarce Resource' (1993) 27 *Suffolk University Law Review* 1225 at 1233.

Indeed, there is a consensus that the allocation of organs be equitable and fair. It is UNOS's view that the principles of utility and justice should be accorded equal weight in relation to allocation decisions in this context.[166] However, even the seemingly simple notion of net medical utility is in fact deceptive. As the King's Fund noted, even using objective criteria, 'organ allocation in such circumstances becomes a way of uncritically perpetuating prior inequalities'.[167]

Poets, playboys and prostitutes

There is often difficulty in identifying whether certain measures *are* outcome measures at all, or merely moral factors 'dressed up'. This debate surfaces with respect to whether alcoholics should receive a liver transplant, which can be seen in terms of the individual having forfeited the right to be transplanted due to 'blameworthiness' or in terms of the likely success of such a transplant being compromised, especially where the patient may resort to or continue similar drinking behaviour in the future. In Britain, certain doctors require potential transplantees who are alcoholics to sign an agreement that they will fight their habit, including attending counselling sessions.[168] Further, centres typically factor post-operative care and patient compliance with treatment regimens, etc., into their decision-making.[169] Clearly this is legitimate in view of predictions of potential benefit from a transplant. However, there is a thin dividing line between this and illegitimate favouritism to individuals from certain class and socio-economic backgrounds. Indeed, in the US, supposedly non-compliant patients are disproportionately black or Hispanic, although it appears that it is the underlying economic circumstances

[166] The US Task Force considered that such factors should only be applied as a 'tie breaker' in parallel cases (although urgency of need would already have been factored into this initial weighting): see Task Force, *Organ Transplantation*, at 89. Sanfilippo has rightly noted that no system could maximise all the relevant criteria though, not even utility and justice: see F. Sanfilippo, 'Organ Allocation: Current Problems and Future Issues' (1993) 25 *Transplantation Proceedings* 2467 at 2467.

[167] King's Fund, *A Question of Give and Take*, at 78.

[168] 'Drinks Pledge for Patients', *The Times*, 21 July 1998. UNOS previously had a policy that all alcoholics had to prove six months' abstinence prior to any transplant. See also C. Cohen and M. Benjamin, 'Alcoholics and Liver Transplantation' (1991) 265 *Journal of the American Medical Association* 1299.

[169] This can be seen in the decision of the Court of Appeal in *Re T* [1997] 1 All ER 906 (CA) in relation to the proposed liver transplant.

which almost entirely produce these effects.[170] Even the emphasis on tissue typing can produce disproportionate effects on a racial basis. It appears that it disadvantages blacks who have less distinct histocompatibility identities. One needs to be especially vigilant to ensure therefore that such (indirectly discriminatory) measures, for example histocompatibility, do truly correlate with improved outcomes and that this is true for all sub-populations.[171] As of 31 July 1999 in the US more than one-third of the 44,691 patients on the kidney transplant waiting list were black.[172]

Moreover, with regard to medical benefit, Veatch has asserted that 'Medical facts alone cannot tell us which of these patients will benefit the most from dialysis or transplantation';[173] in other words, even if we focus solely upon medical outcomes there are problems in evaluating these separately from the *value* of the individual's existence. Nevertheless, there is now virtually universal antipathy towards the adoption of assessments of *social worth* in this context. The infamous antics of the Seattle Artificial Kidney Center which employed such assessments relating to renal dialysis became a target for widespread condemnation despite the superficially attractive notion that some members of society are seemingly more deserving than others – would one really wish a scarce organ to go to a convicted child killer? Indeed, this Seattle 'God squad' rejected potential transplantees on the grounds of former prostitution and a 'playboy' disposition! In any event, quite apart from the lack of merit in the criteria, as Mason and McCall Smith state: 'In our view, allocation tests which attempt to distinguish between, for example, the philanthropic millionaire and the contestant for an international prize in applied mathematics serve no useful purpose in that they are hopelessly subjective.'[174] Yet it is extremely easy to make such assessments without even appreciating it. For instance, if a patient with a severe degree of learning disability were to require a transplant, such an individual might not receive a high priority in terms of allocation of available organs because of an implicit quality of life or value of life assessment. Yet an explicit adoption of such criteria

[170] See King's Fund, *A Question of Give and Take*, at 71.

[171] In the US as of 1996, although the results of kidney transplants were generally poorer for black patients and diminishing still further, the results for Asian patients were better than for any other racial group: see OPTN Report, 1998, Graft and Patient Survival statistics, at website http://www.unos.org/Data/anrpt98/ar98_data_03.htm.

[172] OPTN Report, 1998, Waiting List.

[173] Veatch, 'Who Empowers Medical Doctors?', at 333.

[174] Mason and McCall Smith, *Law and Medical Ethics*, at 302.

would attract a legal challenge on the basis of irrationality or suspect classification and might infringe disability discrimination legislation such as the Disability Discrimination Act 1995 in the UK and the Americans with Disabilities Act in the US.

Age is an interesting issue. If net medical benefit is accorded high, or entire, priority, elderly patients are inherently disadvantaged, albeit indirectly. Is it appropriate to have regard to a patient's age? Langford contends that 'discrimination in terms of age (whether we agree with it or not), while being unfortunate, is not outrageous *in the same way* that discrimination in terms of colour would be, since discrimination in terms of age has a kind of equality built into it, namely that it can be applied to all persons in an equal way'.[175] However, it is well known that physiological rather than chronological age is the best measure of outcome, and this was emphasised by the US Task Force.[176] Thus, whilst the indirect effects of a policy based on longevity and quality of life may be acceptable, direct discrimination on the grounds of age clearly is not. As the UNOS Ethical Committee stated, 'Considerations of justice therefore require that patients be assessed individually rather than by group membership',[177] and allocation must take place on the basis of medical criteria and not on the basis of race, ethnic group or the sex of donors or recipients. Presumably, one might add age *per se* to that list. In Britain, overt discrimination in allocation on the basis of race or sex or disability would be illegal and able to be challenged in a public law suit. Indeed, in the case of *R* v. *Ethical Committee of St Mary's Hospital (Manchester) ex parte Harriott*[178] Schienmann J stated that the courts would not endorse any overtly discriminatory policy such as 'anyone who was a Jew or coloured' being excluded. Age might be encompassed by the phrase 'any other status' in Article 14 of the European Convention of Human Rights incorporated into English law by the Human Rights Act 1998.[179]

Ultimately, whilst utility would be a highly influential justificatory force if judicial determination of an allocation or allocation policy were necessitated, nonetheless justice and discrimination considerations would undoubtedly play a part also. On the other side of the coin, if an organ

175 M. Langford, 'Who Should get the Kidney Machine?' (1992) 18 *Journal of Medical Ethics* 12 at 14.

176 Task Force, *Organ Transplantation*, at 90.

177 UNOS, 'General Principles for Allocating', at 2228.

178 [1988] 1 FLR 512 at 519.

179 Shortly to come into force.

were not used to achieve an appropriate level of medical benefit, a potential recipient might be able to maintain an action in negligence if sufficient proximity could be shown to establish a duty of care, even though no discrimination was involved. This might prove extremely difficult, however, unless an organ was 'earmarked' for a particular patient and was either damaged or used inappropriately elsewhere, so that a duty of care might arise.

Alternatives

Annas has previously identified four possible approaches to rationing scarce resources: the market, the selection committee, the lottery and the 'customary' approaches. The latter is an approach based entirely upon clinical judgement, and the lottery approach was rightly dubbed by Annas as a 'mindless method'.[180] The selection committee and the market ideas were discussed above. Annas himself endorses a scheme whereby a 'first-come, first-served' approach is adopted but with the potential for 'queue jumping' where there is an immediate prospect of death and any other candidates are likely to survive sufficiently long to receive another organ.[181] But although this achieves parity between individuals it will result in many organs being transplanted into individuals who have little or no prospect of benefiting from them. Whilst justice must supplement utility it also includes utility. Donors likely harbour a legitimate expectation that donated organs will be allocated so as to achieve as large a benefit as possible.

Incentives: the dibbers[182]

The UNOS allocation system has historically allocated livers first locally, then regionally and then nationally. Hearts are allocated on a similar basis. Within Eurotransplant, hearts are allocated locally unless there is a recipient elsewhere who is rated at a higher degree of urgency (there are three bands of urgency), as also are livers (on the centre basis mentioned

180 G. Annas, 'The Prostitute, the Playboy and the Poet: Rationing Schemes for Organ Transplantation' (1985) 75(2) *American Journal of Public Health* 187 at 188.

181 Ibid.

182 As A. Monaco described the traditional physician discretion here: see 'Comment: A Transplant Surgeon's Views on Social Factors in Organ Transplantation' (1989) 21 *Transplantation Proceedings* 3403 at 3403.

above) and kidneys.[183] Approximately 50 per cent of hearts are used locally. One can see the bias accorded to local allocation in most of these schemes. Arguably this provides an incentive to maximise procurement efforts at these centres. However, the trend is moving towards larger and larger allocation pools. The new UKTSSA kidney allocation criteria will seemingly tend to reduce the percentage of kidneys used locally, and the US Department of Health and Human Services has recently introduced regulations whereby uniform national criteria will have to be drawn up containing a universal set of criteria for assessing a patient's medical status and eligibility for a place on the waiting list. The effect will be that more organs will have to be distributed nationally, which will create the probability that smaller transplant centres will struggle to survive and that some patients will have problems of access.[184] Moreover, it will remove incentives to local procurement efforts. Yet, this is the price of ensuring that what organs are procured are used in the transparently fairest and maximally beneficial fashion.

There is a general libertarian-based view that not just centres but patients should have a right to refuse an organ. This is their right of *autonomy*. Indeed, where the donor was a high-risk donor in terms of infectivity, for example a carrier of the hepatitis C virus, or where the organ source was an animal, this would seem intuitively to be correct, and should not prejudice the prospect of that person receiving an organ from an alternative source in the future. The same view was taken by the Advisory Committee to the Department of Health and the Nuffield Council on Bioethics in Britain, in relation to xenotransplants.[185]

[183] See J. De Meester, B. Haase-Kromwicjk, G. Persijn and B. Cohen, 'Organization of Donation and Organ Allocation' in J. Chapman, M. Deierhoi and C. Wight (eds.), *Organ and Tissue Donation for Transplantation*, Arnold, London, 1997, 226 at 233.

[184] Indeed, some insurance firms will only pay for transplants performed in their own state: see 'Discontent as US Organ Transplantation Waiting Lists Overhauled' (1998) 351 *Lancet* 1041.

[185] Advisory Group on the Ethics of Xenotransplantation, *Animal Tissue into Humans*; Nuffield Council, *Animal-to-Human Transplants*.

Conclusion

We are experiencing an unprecedented degree of biological interdependence between citizens, both directly through therapeutic organ, tissue and fluid transfer, and indirectly through the fruits of research and commercial development of tissues and cells, and need an integrated, coherent, and global conception of appropriate and proper transplantation practice to convey into the new millennium. An adequate ethical framework for organ donation must detail the provisions necessary to *respect* and *protect* donors and their families and *encourage* donation and *increase* the number of transplantable organs. Moreover, it should include provisions necessary to respect and protect potential organ recipients and involved health care professionals. It has been observed that these tend to pull in different directions. The needs of suffering patients create an urgent need for an accommodation of these varying interests however. Although uncorroborated, it has been stated that around the world someone receives an organ transplant every twenty-seven minutes and someone else dies whilst waiting for one every two hours and twenty-four minutes. Whatever the accuracy of these estimates there is no doubting the scale of the need and the required urgency of response.[1]

It is suggested that greater regard for the autonomy of the participants would yield ethical goods both in increasing protection and respect for involved individuals and in reducing suffering and mortality through organ failure. A communitarian approach to organ retrieval from cadavers based upon routine salvaging is founded upon the notion that members of the community should be willing to provide others with objects of life-

[1] There were 4,327 reported deaths on the United States UNOS waiting list for organs in 1997: see 1998 SR & OPTN Report at http://www.unos.org/Newsroom.critdata. As of 31 July 1999, 64,000 patients were on the UNOS waiting list for an organ transplant: ibid., and there were 6,704 waiting in the UK: see *Transplant Statistics*, UKTSSA, 1999.

saving value when no cost to themselves is implicated. However, any such 'conscription' policy cannot properly be described as a 'consent' policy, or at least only in *societal* as opposed to individual terms. Under such a regime, organs merely become public resources. However, such an approach 'conflicts so deeply with liberal individualistic values that it has not received serious consideration'.[2] Indeed, all societies at the very least permit individuals to 'opt out' of organ removal if they so wish even where the system endorses the legal presumption favouring life. Yet, as Veatch notes, if the preservation of life was the only consideration, then we should not logically permit any opting out at all. However, many of the above perceptions flow from the primacy accorded to autonomy in most contemporary Western societies. Where other ethical orderings apply, perceptions may differ. For instance, Steinberg states that 'Judaism restricts the notion of autonomy to actions that are morally indifferent. Where conflicting values arise, each individual is bound to act in accordance with a high standard of normal moral conduct.'[3] On this theological basis it is easier to see society (that is the sick within it) claiming *a priori* rights over the human body for instance. The LRC of Canada expressed the view that 'One need not adopt an absolutist approach against the routine taking of organs, but just regard the organised giving of organs as *preferable* to the routine use of organs by hospitals' (my emphasis).[4] On this view, routine taking is not inherently wrong under any system but should not be entertained until all reasonable attempts have been made to make the system based on giving 'work'. Much, of course, also depends upon the extent of the 'need' at the relevant point in time.

Some commentators contend that many legal regimes *do* in fact adopt a policy of routine salvaging, whatever the official line. Veatch asserts (without implying moral censure of the actual policy) that 'Many people mistakenly confuse presumed consent with policies authorising organ procurement without any consent. Thus people mistakenly say that many European countries have presumed consent laws when in fact none do . . . What they have is laws authorising procurement without consent, a policy

[2] T. Beauchamp and J. Childress, *Principles of Biomedical Ethics*, 4th edn, Oxford University Press, Oxford, 1994, at 82.

[3] A. Steinberg, 'Medical Ethics: Secular and Jewish Approaches' in F. Rosner (ed.), *Medicine and Jewish Law*, Aronson, Northvale, N.Y., 1990, 19–39.

[4] Law Reform Commission of Canada, *Procurement and Transfer of Human Tissues and Organs*, Working Paper 66, Minister of Supply and Services, Ottawa, 1992, at 43.

that is consistently rejected by a more autonomy-loving, individualistic American society.'[5] He adds that 'there is no basis for presuming the consent of those who have not opted out'.[6] Like Erin and Harris, who regard presumed consent as a 'fiction',[7] he suggests that we should merely be honest and admit that we believe it is right to take organs from the dead to benefit the living even in the absence of consent. By contrast, Beauchamp and Childress state that whilst *express* consent is the paradigmatic consent, 'Presumed consent is still another variety, although if consent is presumed on the basis of what we know about a particular person, it closely resembles implied consent.'[8] The classic dictionary definition of 'consent' alludes to an 'agreement' with another or a 'consensus'. However, in law it operates as an 'authorisation' for the procedure to take place and should therefore generally be entirely unequivocal. It is difficult to see how there can be a 'meeting of minds' when one may not even have considered the subject prior to death. Further, there is 'distance' in reality between what people declare themselves willing to do and what they actually do as regards organ donation and it is this that requires addressing. Finally, in the face of data showing that a small but significant percentage of individuals do not wish to donate organs, it may 'presume' too much. Implied consent is a willingness gleaned from an individual's conduct. Can it really be said that carrying on one's ordinary everyday business without registering an objection to organ donation shows a willingness for this to take place?

The above observation highlights the weaknesses in presumed consent laws as an appeal to autonomous giving. It does not imply that express consent laws are more reflective and faithful to donor *autonomy* than presumed consent laws, and moreover the latter will probably produce more organs for transplant. Nevertheless, the end of term report as regards all organ donation policies is, from an autonomy perspective, 'could do better'. Although we cannot respect the autonomy of the now-

[5] R. Veatch, 'Consent for Perfusion and other Dilemmas with Organ Procurement from Non-Heart-Beating Cadavers' in R. Arnold, S. Youngner, R. Schapiro and C. Mason Spicer, *Procuring Organs by Transplant: The Debate over Non-Heart-Beating Cadaver Protocols*, Johns Hopkins University Press, Baltimore, 1995, 195 at 202. He adds that these societies do not claim to base their laws on presumptions of consent, but this appears to be generally untrue.

[6] Ibid.

[7] C. Erin and J. Harris, 'Presumed Consent or Contracting Out' (1999) 25 *Journal of Medical Ethics* 365.

[8] Beauchamp and Childress, *Principles of Biomedical Ethics*, at 128.

dead person, we can respect the autonomy of the once-living person now represented by the cadaver. There is a need for more direct and better evidence of the pre-deceased's wishes in all systems. Whilst in express consent systems the primary mechanism of donation is the wish of the deceased, in reality in most instances the relatives make a decision whether to consent to donation or not. This is acceptable only to the extent that the relative has information regarding the deceased's explicit wishes, or at least knowledge of his/her general intentions and views in this regard (excluding one's minor offspring where decision-making authority is conceded across the board). In fact, relatives are accorded independent rights of decision-making in most systems and, as a consequence, procurement is thwarted if contact cannot be made with them, as well as where a direct refusal to consent exists. Whilst deference to a relative's fervent wish to avoid organ removal may be acceptable where the deceased expressed no wish and there is no other direct evidence of his/her wishes, the relatives' personal or property-based rights in the corpse confer no right of authorisation of use of the cadaver. It is this fact that prompts Veatch's reference to the 'Dangerous Notion of Property Rights'.[9] Not only are relatives permitted to veto an express wish of the deceased to donate in Anglo-American practice, but as Veatch observes, 'There may be a more serious moral problem. There is evidence that some advocates of postmortem required familial request laws have chosen this device precisely because they believe it will lead to obtaining some organs from persons who would not, themselves, be willing to donate.'[10] He notes that Gallup polls in the US consistently show that people are more prepared to donate the organs of relatives than their own.

To avoid the prospect of removal occurring contrary to the real wishes of the deceased organ provider, better mechanisms for recording objections need to be in place than currently exist in many nations, including Britain and the United States, otherwise the family will have to be routinely consulted at times of acute stress and grief. Beauchamp and Childress themselves allude to the stringent conditions required for an ethically acceptable 'presumed consent' policy to become operative, including knowledge, understanding and an adequate means of recording

[9] R. Veatch, 'The Newly Dead: Mortal Remains or Organ Bank?' in *Death, Dying and Biological Revolution*, Yale University Press, New Haven, 1976, 249 at 256.

[10] R. Veatch, 'The Newly Dead: Mortal Remains or Organ Bank?' in *Death, Dying and Biological Revolution*, rev. edn, Yale University Press, New Haven, 1989, 197 at 216.

objections. In most presumed consent systems registries exist, and indeed seemingly *must* exist, in order to house objections. To this extent they are not only more productive in terms of organ procurement but are likely to operate in a fashion which is *more* faithful to the wishes of the deceased. Nevertheless, this is a second-best system. The ideal is to promote ways of soliciting the positive wishes of the pre-deceased individual so that they are 'available' in a much higher percentage of instances. A mechanism should exist for recording positive wishes, negative wishes or a desire to delegate the decision to a proxy, for example a relative. Opportunities must be increased for the ascertainment of such views, and if a sufficient proportion of the population cannot be persuaded to express their wishes one way or another, it may be necessary to create a situation where individuals are required to make a decision on the matter, that is mandatory choice.[11] Relatives would still be permitted to *object* but only where the deceased's wishes were unknown or the matter had been explicitly delegated to them. As Michielsen has stated, 'From the emotional point of view, there is a fundamental difference between having to take the responsibility for permitting organ removal and not making use of the right to oppose removal.'[12] Legislative endorsement of such a revised scheme should be accompanied by statutory legitimation of post-mortem organ preservation measures (such as cooling and perfusion) along the lines of Bolivian law which stipulates that 'in order to preserve vital organs or tissues in an appropriate condition for transplantation, the vegetative functions of the donor may be maintained after brain death has been confirmed'.[13]

The autonomy of the *living* donor with regard to organ removal is even more obviously a central feature of proper respect for the person. Communitarian claims to organs are far weaker as regards the still living. Even so, whilst there are no duties in law to give organs or tissues to needy individuals, it is often maintained that there are *moral* duties in certain instances to do so. Certain ethical theories appear to place obligations upon some individuals emanating from their relationship with others, and the alleged responsibilities arising therefrom, for example an *ethic of*

[11] See A. Spital, 'Mandated Choice for Organ Donation: Time to Give it a Try' (1996) 125(1) *Annals of Internal Medicine* 66.

[12] P. Michielsen, 'Organ Shortage – What to Do?' (1992) 24 *Transplantation Proceedings* 2391 at 2392.

[13] Law of 15 March 1982.

care philosophy. Such 'relationship-based' theories have been described as a 'family of moral reflections' which share some premisses with communitarian ethics.[14] However, Judge LJ recently opined in the Court of Appeal in *St George's NHS Trust* v. *S* that

> If it has not already done so, medical science will no doubt one day advance to the stage when a very minor procedure undergone by an adult would save the life of his or her child, or perhaps the life of a complete stranger. The refusal would be rightly described as unreasonable, the benefit to another human life would be beyond value, and the motives of the doctors admirable. If however the adult were compelled to agree, or rendered helpless to resist, the principle of autonomy would be extinguished.[15]

The centrality of autonomous decision-making by living organ donors places great weight upon the informed, voluntary consent of donors, a weight it is frequently alleged it is unable to bear. Majeske, Parker and Frader state that

> The traditional model of informed consent is based on an impartialist understanding of the requirements of autonomy that de-emphasises personal relationships so that each decision maker is conceived as being free to pursue autonomous goals. In living related donation, however, partiality and personal relationships frequently play essential roles because personal relationships importantly influence or even constitute potential donors' personal goals.[16]

This contextual feature of living organ donation results not only in inherent coercive pressures to donate (or not to donate), but also in typically reflexive rather than considered decision-making. However, the above observers implicitly recognise that the supposed coercive pressures *per se* need not necessarily undermine the willingness to donate and the voluntariness of consent. Indeed, they may even *heighten* the motivation to donate which may in turn account for the immediacy of decision-making by many donors. Moreover, the very supposed 'pressure' which compromises the voluntariness of consent for some commentators is the very same context which creates the potential benefits for that person and

[14] Beauchamp and Childress, *Principles of Biomedical Ethics*, at 85.

[15] [1998] 3 All ER 673 at 688f.

[16] R. Majeske, L. Parker and J. Frader, 'In Search of an Ethical Framework for Consideration of Decisions regarding Live Donation' in B. Spielman (ed.), *Organ and Tissue Donation: Ethical, Legal and Policy Issues*, Southern Illinois University Press, Carbondale, 1997, 89 at 95.

may significantly preserve or enhance his or her life. What is required is procedures and mechanisms for detecting ambivalence and tension in specific problem cases, where counselling may assist and occasionally a potential donor may take the opportunity to 'opt out' of donation without loss of face. Moreover, there should be early information transmission. It should be taken on board that the *psychological* commitment of donors generally occurs much earlier than the stage of obtaining formal consent, often without deliberate reflection and without adequate knowledge of risks and consequences, a position from which they will often find it hard to resile. An independent party should verify the existence of a voluntary and informed consent with regard to both related and unrelated donors. There is no necessity for any alternative framework or model of decision-making, merely an open-textured supportive application of existing requirements. This highlights the need for a degree of discretion and 'leeway' to be conceded by clinicians to individuals able to provide an informed, voluntary consent, including even mature minors in certain instances. Indeed, it has been observed that an ethic of care model creates the potential for its own form of tyranny in which the relationship itself implies a *duty* to donate.[17]

However, ethical and legal anxieties perennially accompany living organ donation in view of the lack of intended therapeutic benefit for the donor attaching to the procedure and the inherent risks to him or her relating to it. This moves us on to the issue of the proper risk/benefit ratio in this context, which innocently conceals a plethora of ethical facets. It raises the stark contrast between utilitarian and deontological perspectives in the context of weighing benefits to one party against the risks or harms to another, a thread which runs through transplantation procedures as a whole. The conventional utilitarian has primary regard to the overall or net sum of benefit, viewing individuals as interchangeable units, whereas the deontologist bases his approach upon the rights and duties of individuals which would embrace a minimum level of respect and protection for each person. But whilst we would tend towards the latter as regards living (donor) individuals the conventional perception of non-maleficence and the duty to avoid harm to persons would suggest the need to reject an offer to donate organs entirely, at least whilst the donor is still living. However, an 'absolutist' perspective which would prohibit

[17] Majeske, Parker and Frader, 'In Search of an Ethical Framework', at 95–100.

all such procedures is incompatible with contemporary notions of the ambit of legitimate individual autonomy.

In promoting a 'proportionist' approach which focuses on 'whether the benefits are so certain and of a kind that the benefits manifestly outweigh the risks of harm', Caplan states: 'In order to assess the proportionality of risk to benefit, it is necessary to know the nature of the biological relationship that exists between the prospective donor and recipient.'[18] But the question arises as to *whether* and *how* such an appreciation feeds into the process. How are they action guides? Surely, what this implies is that those with a certain relationship with the recipient will anticipate a benefit from the donation and in addition will view the risks as acceptable in that light – as within what Charles Fried terms the person's 'risk budget'.[19] However, this is simply a part of the informed consent given by that person to donation. Although Caplan includes both genetic and emotional relationships in his calculus, such a strategy ties legitimate donation to defined classes of relationship, when altruism is a diverse phenomenon within society. Where the capability of giving an informed, voluntary consent exists, there is no need, where the clinical circumstances are favourable, to exclude *a priori* any specific classes of donor based upon relationship. The dangers inherent in such an approach can be observed in the growing phenomenon of paired kidney exchange between living donors, which is an extremely promising technique for supplementing organ supply and should be cautiously developed.[20] It is analogous to the pools of unrelated bone marrow donors which exist around the world and, subject to (coercive) dangers associated with non-contemporaneous removal, has no inherent major ethical drawbacks despite the absence of any emotional or genetic bond between the donors and their donees. It may also be entirely appropriate to accept, in exceptional cases, donations by complete 'unpaired' strangers.[21] But if autonomy is the thread running through living organ donation, it is not so obvious where the line should be drawn in terms of permissible donation.

18 A. Caplan, 'Am I My Brother's Keeper?' (1993) 27 *Suffolk University Law Review* 1195 at 1201.

19 See C. Fried, *An Anatomy of Values*, Harvard University Press, Cambridge, Mass., 1970, at 155–82.

20 See K. Park, 'Exchange Donor Program in Kidney Transplantation' (1999) 67 *Transplantation* 336.

21 An English man recently donated a part of a lung to a ten-year-old Israeli girl with cystic fibrosis, whom he had never met, and who would otherwise have died: see 'Body Parts', *Guardian*, 30 November 1999.

Various observers have criticised the egocentric nature of the best interests test in the context of proposed organ donations by minors. Crouch and Elliott, for instance, reject the best interests approach vis-à-vis 'donors' lacking capacity, regarding it as a 'formal and abstract framework' when decision-making takes place in reality in intimate and particular associations ('intimate collectivities').[22] They state:

> What is morally important and problematic about organ transplantation is precisely that it may *not* be in the best interests of the donor . . . justification must rest on other grounds that take account of the fact that such transplantations are done not to advance the interests of the child donor as an individual, but for the sake of another family member, and for the sake of the family as a whole.[23]

This is problematic, however, if it requires a 'sacrifice' for the family, that is donation without any potential reciprocal benefit thereafter. Moreover, these commentators view the best interests test as inappropriate even when it takes into account 'other-regarding interests'. Feinberg divides 'self-interested acts' into 'self-regarding' and 'other-regarding'. He states that

> A selfish person is one who pays insufficient attention to the interests of other people, and thus comes to pursue his own self-regarding interests at the expense of, or in disregard of, the interests of others . . . That is quite another thing than pursuing one's own interest in *promoting* the interests of others. The loving parent or spouse and the public-spirited zealot can make no distinction between their own interests and that of their children, or spouse, or party. Far from indicating their selfishness, that identity of interests shows how unselfish they probably are.[24]

Thus, where there is such an 'identity of interests' he views such actions as not being 'selfish' in the true sense at all, but 'other-regarding'. Crouch and Elliott, however, doubt that in many of the decided cases the incapacitated 'donors' were sufficiently mature or mentally developed to have formed such 'other-regarding' interests in their relatives. Whilst accepting this view to some degree, they also go on to state that there is a

[22] R. Crouch and C. Elliott, 'Moral Agency and the Family: The Case of Living Related Organ Transplantation' (1999) 8 *Cambridge Quarterly of Healthcare Ethics* 275 at 285.

[23] Ibid.

[24] J. Feinberg, *The Moral Limits of the Criminal Law. Vol. I: Harm to Others*, Oxford University Press, Oxford, 1984, at 73.

need for a recognition that the interests of family members are 'inextricably intertwined'.[25] But surely to explore the family context in depth and to examine the family networks as they affect the minor (as part of a best interests evaluation) is to do just that, and it is also to be sensitive to the need to avoid exploiting the vulnerable individual. Russell Scott has argued, however, that the use of the best interests test in this context 'would take advantage of a judicial proceeding designed to protect the most vulnerable in our society in order to exploit them in a way that adults cannot be exploited'.[26] The intention here is not to deny the disputatious character of one or two of the existing authorities, merely to deny the *intrinsic nature* of arbitrary and exploitative decision-making. The argument that such decision-making is egoistic in focus rather than 'altruistic' begs broader questions about the essential character of 'altruism' itself, which is an especially thorny issue in the field of organ transplantation as a whole. Whilst this is a determination based upon self-interest, it is surely no less an altruistic deed for all that.

Some commentators have advocated the broader use of the 'substituted judgement' model of decision-making for incapacitated individuals, that is immature minors, adults with severe learning difficulties or mental disorders, or individuals in a permanently insentient state. Robertson recognises the legitimacy of the best interests approach in many cases, observing that it maintains respect for persons, but states that

> We should treat incompetents as they would choose to be treated in a given situation. Where the wishes or preferences of the incompetent are known, we are obligated to act in accordance with them. Where his wishes or intentions have not been articulated and cannot be known, the existence of net benefits serves as a convenient surrogate for determining what he would have chosen, because it is reasonable to assume that an incompetent would want that which benefits him. The benefit rule should thus be subservient to the obligation to do what the incompetent person wants: if there is a conflict between the self-interest and inferred desire of an incompetent, the incompetent's putative choice should prevail.[27]

Thus, on the above view, the proper enquiry is as to the true wishes of the incapacitated individual, although in some instances this equates to

[25] Crouch and Elliott, 'Moral Agency', at 284.

[26] R. Scott, *The Body as Property*, Viking Press, New York, 1981, at 121.

[27] J. Robertson, 'Organ Donations by Incompetents and the Substituted Judgment Doctrine' (1976) 76 *Columbia Law Review* 48 at 56–7.

ascertaining net benefit to the individual. However, Childress alludes to the 'troubling example' of an 'appeal to substituted judgment in circumstances where it does not plausibly apply'.[28] He states: 'However, for patients who have never been autonomous or for previously autonomous patients whose prior preferences and values cannot be reliably traced, it is more defensible to rely on a best-interests standard, based on nonmaleficence and beneficence, rather than on a substituted judgment standard, based on autonomy.'[29] In the latter situations he dubs substituted judgement an 'illegitimate fiction'. Whilst we should accept the general import of Robertson's argument, to impute too easily (altruistic) wishes to donate organs would be 'illegitimate'. Robertson notes that substituted judgement is frequently applied by courts as to the disposition of an incompetent's estate based on an objective view of what a reasonable individual would have done in those circumstances, and may even include altruistic gestures, but there is no physical 'cost' attached to such a decision. Moreover, many such individuals will be unable to experience the sustaining of a relationship facilitated by the donation of an organ for transplant. Without cogent evidence of previously formed wishes or preferences there is a danger of vulnerable people's autonomy being infringed, not furthered, by the imputation of altruistic desires or wishes to, for example, minors or mentally incapacitated adults. Nevertheless, where such evidence does exist, there is good reason to respect such views and wishes of, for example, moribund individuals destined to die imminently. This might even extend to procedures such as elective ventilation where prior awareness of such a procedure existed.

However, it is argued by some that many individuals lacking capacity, principally those in a permanently insentient state, have no interests and therefore cannot be harmed. They consequently possess no right not to be harmed and there is no necessity to find a justification for organ removal or other associated procedures over and above the use of the organs themselves for others. Such arguments are frequently founded on notions of *personhood* and are sometimes also used to challenge the continuing appropriateness of the dead donor rule in the organ donation context. However, as Brody states, 'This argument succeeds only if one is willing to change deontological constraints ("thou shall not kill living human

[28] J. Childress, 'The Place of Autonomy in Bioethics' (1990) 20 *Hastings Center Report* 12 at 15.
[29] Ibid.

organisms") into teleological rules ("killing human organisms is wrong when their interests or social interests are harmed"). The implications of this are very disturbing.'[30] He is addressing the use of anencephalics as organ donors and is right to be perturbed at any such potential conceptual shift, which threatens to make the applicability of protections traditionally conferred depend on the passing of a threshold standard, decided from some removed and objective standpoint. The notion of 'symbolic' harm has arisen in this context, which appears to rely upon the fact that the individual cannot 'experience' any harm and will not recover to regain any surviving interests. But such individuals *do* possess surviving interests even apart from the avoidance of pain and suffering. Insentient beings, even those – such as anencephalics – that have never experienced a sentient existence, are owed duties of respectful treatment and non-instrumental use. This is a minimum entitlement of any living individual.

The above perceptions of 'interest-less' but living beings often depend upon a mind/body dualism which is not supported by mainstream religious, secular or legal thought. Keown notes that 'The law has hitherto rejected the notion of "biological units" which are "inhabited" by a non-bodily person and has, on the contrary, taken the traditional, common-sense view that human life *is* personal life, that living human beings are persons and that persons are, applying standard biological criteria, either alive or dead.'[31] This applies not only to views as to appropriate treatment of the living but also to majority views as to the meaning of death. There is a touch of irony in the fact that many who castigate brain death do so because of its 'technologising' and mystifying of death, yet there is no more mechanically supported 'existence' than brain death. In most instances, the patient's condition would not have warranted further life-sustaining measures. Yet, without the application of such supportive interventions, total bodily shutdown in all dimensions would transparently occur at a significantly earlier stage. In this sense, such a death is not 'rushed' but 'protracted'. Moreover, as Schone-Seifert notes

[30] See B. Brody, 'How Much of the Brain must Die?' in S. Youngner *et al.* (eds.), *The Definition of Death: Contemporary Controversies*, Johns Hopkins University Press, Baltimore, 1999, 71 at 80.

[31] J. Keown, 'Restoring Moral and Intellectual Shape to the Law after *Bland*' (1997) 113 *Law Quarterly Review* 481 at 493. He argues that our mental acts are as much a part of our biological processes as physical acts and are not separate from our bodies: ibid.

> A core objection is the claim that brain death supports a reductionist view of human beings, even if one grants the concomitant loss of mental functions . . . However, supporters of brain death actually hold a holistic view because they conceive of human life as requiring both the mind and body components and leave open whether death requires the loss of one or both.[32]

There is no tension between non-heart-beating donation and brain death; *irreversible* cardiorespiratory cessation is a function of brain death. The concept of death, however, involves a philosophical choice in a specific cultural milieu. Thus, a pluralistic stance is wholly right. Translation into a standard of death supported by law requires consideration of other public policy factors and flexibility in terms of criteria and tests to ascertain the satisfaction of the standard in individual cases.

There are various divergent notions as to what constitutes 'altruism'. On one view, any conduct which results in benefits being obtained by another individual who is in need is altruistic, regardless of the giver's motives.[33] From an alternative perspective, a behaviour is altruistic only when the actor acts empathetically with the person in distress, that is he or she must experience some vicarious or empathic pleasure, or relief of distress, as a consequence of the giving behaviour.[34] Yet another perspective considers a behaviour altruistic when it is carried out for the benefit of another but without anticipation of rewards from external sources.[35] Generally altruism is contrasted with egoism. However, the latter two accounts of altruism would seemingly insist upon 'selfless' conduct, and would for instance exclude donations carried out solely to boost the person's own self-esteem. However, as Audi notes, ethics does not generally require that an action which is morally permissible meet such motivational constraints,[36] and it is primarily concerned with *actions* rather than motives.[37] A view of altruism which requires the sole motivation to be empathy with the plight of the victim or to be based on a

[32] B. Schone-Seifert, 'Defining Death in Germany' in Youngner *et al.*, *The Definition of Death*, at 267.

[33] This is implicitly the view of Darley and Latane: see J. Macauley and L. Berkowitz (eds.), *Altruism and Helping Behavior*, Academic Press, London, 1970, at 2.

[34] See, for example, the views of Aronfreed, ibid.

[35] See, for example, the views of Macauley and Berkowitz, ibid.

[36] Indeed, he notes that we do not have full and direct control of our motives for acting.

[37] R. Audi, 'The Morality and Utility of Organ Transplantation' (1996) 8(2) *Utilitas* 141 at 146.

total lack of self-interest is too limited. As Daar concludes in this context, 'altruism has been overrated'.[38] Whilst so, Harvey observes a conventional reluctance in the transplant sphere to 'elicit an act, morally acceptable – even laudable – in itself, if the motive is self-interest and not altruism'.[39]

Despite these ambiguities, systems of organ donation around the world have been dominated by an 'altruistic model' kept apart from the world of commercial markets. Nevertheless, Banks has asserted that in the US 'It is only a matter of time before this country will be forced to decide on the type of commercial system which should be adopted in order to meet the demand of transplantable human organs.'[40] It is too dismissive to simply sideline at least consideration of commercial schemes relating to organ procurement in the light of the current shortage of transplantable materials. Britain recently experienced a crisis in its 'altruistic' blood supply system[41] and one cannot be confident that a similar scenario will not extend to the organ transplant field in the future. In any event, some have described the existing altruistic organ donation system as a conspicuous failure. It has hopefully been shown that many of the arguments against such commercial practices hold little water and that intuitionism has dominated public policy responses thus far. Further, even if there is either some intrinsically wrong feature or potentially adverse consequence connected to commerce it is essential that this be specifically isolated when considering the possibility of adequate regulation and the necessity for a global strategy/response. The possibility of organ purchasing in one region clearly facilitates the evasion of sanctions in others[42] and suggests the need for a worldwide response to combat trade. If the concern is the potential harm to organ *vendors* one needs to rely on a global human-

[38] A. Daar, 'Reimbursement, "Rewarded Gifting", Financial Incentives and Commercialism in Living Organ Donation' in G. Collins *et al* (eds.), *Procurement, Preservation and Allocation of Vascularized Organs*, Kluwer, Dordrecht, 1997, 301 at 305.

[39] J. Harvey, 'Paying Organ Donors' (1990) 16 *Journal of Medical Ethics* 117 at 119.

[40] G. Banks, 'Legal and Ethical Safeguards: Protection of Society's most Vulnerable Participants in a Commercialised Organ Transplantation System' (1995) 21(1) *American Journal of Law and Medicine* 45 at 110.

[41] See A. Ferriman, 'Decline in Altruism threatens Blood Supplies' (1998) 317 *British Medical Journal* 1405.

[42] The territorial effects of different laws vary. Some statutes such as HOTA criminalise the prohibited conduct where it takes place in the UK wherever the ultimate transplantation takes place. In terms of the general effects of laws, there is a distinction between the common and civil law jurisdictions.

rights-based justification for intervention at a supranational level. On the other hand, if the evil to be countered is harm to potential recipients then this is a legitimate concern of any individual nation state for its citizens who might go elsewhere and receive sub-standard or hazardous treatment. However, one cannot blame the patients for their mobility in search of treatment. Indeed, if developed transplant nations take insufficient steps to increase the organ supply in their countries, they themselves encourage this very trade. The lessons of history relating to anatomical dissection warn as to the potential abuses where an adequate supply of a needed product is not delivered through legitimate channels, and also as to how the value of scarce bodily parts can escalate rapidly under such fertile conditions. There are distinctions though between payment to living organ providers and payment for the supply of organs from a cadaver. The latter practice has been advocated for developed transplant nations as a means of primarily satisfying the domestic need for organs without altering the current allocation mechanisms. Potential harms to organ providers and to recipients are therefore all but removed and it may be that the objections to, for instance, 'futures' markets are pragmatic as opposed to moral.

The issue of rewarded gifting raises the question whether there can be one model of ethical conduct in one culture or nation and a different model in another. Reddy states that 'The different socio-economic circumstances between the developed worlds suggest that we should consider whether the benefits of legalised, regulated paid organ donation might benefit both kidney donors as well as recipients so that this procedure might be ethically acceptable in our part of the world though it is unacceptable in others.'[43] Colabawalla and others have argued that this constitutes a 'second class ethics' to which countries such as India should not subscribe. However, the social, economic, cultural and religious context within each jurisdiction sets a different framework for the debate and causes us to weigh the competing factors differently. If one were to attempt to develop a universal system of ethics for organ transplantation one would have to proceed at a level of generality so that it would form no guide to action anyhow in many instances.[44]

[43] K. Reddy, 'Should Paid Organ Donation be Banned in India? To Buy or Let Die!' (1993) 6(3) *National Medical Journal of India* 137 at 137.

[44] Engelhardt asserts that 'Universality in secular morality is always purchased at the price of moral content. Content in secular morality is always purchased at the price of universality':

Intuitionism is an influential feature in many spheres of organ transplantation. Gut reactions are rife, generating feelings of repugnance towards buying organs for transplant from the poor and taking organs from brain-dead, but still breathing, ventilated donors, for instance. However, the extent to which emotions and intuition are a proper guide to ethical judgement is still largely moot and controversial in ethical discourse.[45] Intuitionism is especially problematic when intuitions differ. Whilst some commentators argue that our intuitions are merely a 'throw-back' to our primitive past, and that the singular contribution of bioethics has been the tempering of our instincts through rational reflection, many are loath to be so dismissive. Callahan adopts a *via media* and regards emotions and reason as being 'mutually correcting resources in moral reflection', which finds a parallel in Rawls's notion of 'reflective equilibrium'.[46] It is suggested that this latter view is persuasive and that our instincts should cause us to strive harder for supporting justifications for all our actions. However, they operate as amber rather than red lights to progress.

The notion has been held by many that living organ donation is a 'necessary evil' to be tolerated until the end of its (anticipated) limited lifespan. Council of Europe Recommendation No. R(79) stated that 'The use of organs from living donors should be restricted and, where possible, gradually eliminated.' However, this 'natural phasing out' perspective is not borne out by experience. Not only will developing transplant nations typically continue to initiate programmes on the back of living donation, but new types of living organ donation will continue to emerge, with liver segment and lung lobe donation being the current therapies that are quickly establishing themselves. Moreover, in the face of regular cadaveric donor 'crises', living donation offers an 'elastic' mechanism for responding quickly and effectively to shortfalls in supply. In the United Kingdom, for instance, a decreased volume of cadaveric organ procurement has precipitated a modest (in terms of overall

see H. Engelhardt, 'Is there a Universal System of Ethics or are Ethics Culture-Specific?' in W. Land and J. Dossetor (eds.), *Organ Replacement Therapy: Ethics, Justice, Commerce*, Springer-Verlag, Berlin, 1991, 147 at 153.

45 See D. Egonsson, *Dimensions of Dignity*, Kluwer, Dordrecht, 1998, at 23–9. He notes the differences of opinion as to whether one should distinguish between 'considered' feelings and 'spontaneous' feelings.

46 S. Callahan, 'The Role of Emotion in Ethical Decision-making' (1988) 18 *Hastings Center Report* 9.

volume but nonetheless sharp) rise in the number of living donor kidney transplants performed. Yet, even the recent Draft Protocol of the Council of Europe, in its attached guidance, states that 'living donation must remain an exceptional procedure', albeit without elaborating on what is meant thereby. Living donation may indeed fade out in time, but at present superior results and the shortage of cadaveric organs, both individually and collectively, support the continued permissibility of kidney donation and, as results improve and skills are refined, may come to do so across the board for organ segment donation also.

Procedures for avoiding conflicts of interest need careful thought and formulation. They are especially acute where decisions are made to withdraw treatment so as no longer to prolong life, where organ retrieval is in prospect. Where such safeguards are rigorously observed, there can be no reservations to controlled non-heart-beating donor protocols where brain death can be reliably evidenced. In Britain, as regards foetal tissue transplants, the Polkinghorne Committee, rather opaquely,[47] found itself 'unable to share' the 'moral taint' perspective where the decision to abort and the decision relating to the subsequent use of tissue are kept distinct. It appreciated that the moral and legal domains of abortion may not be coterminous but seemingly recognised the generally accepted moral justification for performing abortions, at least where the mother's health interests are directly jeopardised.[48] The more widely accepted concern is that the prospect of using the foetal tissue for transplantation might influence the woman's decision whether to abort and might possibly increase the volume of abortions occurring in the future. Robertson describes this as a 'statistical' and probably remote possibility.[49] However, both of these phenomena may depend upon the motivation for pregnancy initially, and for the abortion. In the US it is a federal crime to have an abortion and to designate a potential recipient of the foetal tissue or to sell foetal tissue.[50] Robertson states that 'With these restrictions, it is difficult

[47] See J. Keown, 'The Polkinghorne Report on Fetal Research: Nice Recommendations, Shame about the Reasoning' (1993) 19 *Journal of Medical Ethics* 114 at 117.

[48] *Review of the Guidance on the Research Use of Fetuses and Fetal Material*, Cmd 762, HMSO, 1989, at para. 2.6. There is much difficulty here in the light of the lack of consensus surrounding the morality of abortion and the range of circumstances in which an abortion may occur.

[49] See J. Robertson, 'Fetal Tissue Transplants' (1988) 66 *George Washington Law Review* 443 at 453.

[50] National Institutes of Health Revitalisation Act of 1993, Pub. L. No. 103–43, section 111; 107 Stat. 109 (codified at 42 USC section 289 g–I and II (supp. 4)).

to imagine that a woman would have an abortion solely to donate tissue anonymously to someone who might benefit from it.'[51] In effect then, foetal tissue transplantation is viewed as permissible wherever it is simply a by-product of an already occurring therapeutic abortion.

Hopefully, existing or future strategies will obviate the need for allocation decisions regarding organs, but this seems endemic, and if fairness is not transparent through the application of policies thrashed out at a national level and involving non-medical sections of the community there is a future prospect of a further dwindling supply and ensuing morbidity and mortality. These policies must be very flexible and adaptable but there is also a need for broad *principles* of allocation, often drawn from human rights documents, to be embedded in transplant legislation. Having been 'donated', organs become public property unless allocated to a specific identified individual, when autonomy should prevail.

[51] J. Robertson, 'Abortion to Obtain Fetal Tissue for Transplant' (1993) 27 *Suffolk University Law Review* 1359 at 1360 n. 5, although he objects that it is not appropriate to restrict designated donation in view of the reproductive freedom accorded to women by the law in the United States.

Index